A VERY THIN LINE

OTHER BOOKS BY THEODORE DRAPER

A VERY THIN LINE

The Iran-Contra Affairs

THEODORE DRAPER

HILL and WANG

A division of Farrar, Straus & Giroux

New York

The author is grateful to the following for permission to reprint from previously published
material: *Fortune*, for "Adnan Khashoggi's Soaring U.S. Dreams," by Ford Worthy, copyright
© 1985 by Time Inc. All rights reserved. *Time*, for "Khashoggi's High-Flying Realm," by
Richard Stengel, copyright © 1987 by Time Warner Inc. Reprinted by permission

Library of Congress Cataloging-in-Publication Data
Draper, Theodore.
A very thin line: the Iran-contra affairs / Theodore Draper.
p.   cm.
Includes bibliographical references and index.
1. Iran-Contra Affair, 1985–1990.   I. Title.
E876.D73   1991   973.927—dc20   90-21751   CIP

For Priscilla, who is in every page of this book

Contents

Contents

Introduction

The reader may learn a good deal about the nature of this work by learning how I went about it.

When I first undertook it, I thought that it would take me about three months. I had written a number of articles on the subject for *The New York Review of Books* and expected to fill them out for a small book. At that time, I had worked from the transcript of the congressional hearings in 1987—later published in twelve volumes, many of them with well over 1,000 pages. It is one thing to listen to hours and days of testimony and another to be able to study the words carefully on the printed page. I thought I would contribute something by making such a study and that little more would come out in the near future.

To my horror, I soon learned otherwise. Not long after signing my book contract, I found that twenty-seven volumes of depositions or private hearings, some of them with over 1,500 pages, were being published. These depositions were made by some who had testified publicly but also by many more who had not. Oddly, those who made depositions were assured that they were confidential and would not be made public, and thus they spoke more freely than they might otherwise have done. In many cases, the depositions are easily as important as the public hearings and the full story cannot be understood without them.

But that was not all. President Reagan appointed a "Special Review Board" (called the Tower Board after the name of its chairman, Senator John Tower), which published a report, and the congressional committees followed with a much more voluminous report of almost 700 pages.

The worst was still ahead. Next came three volumes of documents with 1,324, 1,646, and 1,781 pages, respectively. More hundreds of pages of documents appear in the separate volumes of public and private testimony. When I had caught my breath and settled down with this small library, I was faced with still more thousands of pages of testimony and documents produced at the trial of Lieutenant Colonel Oliver L. North in February–March 1989 and again at the trial of Admiral John M. Poindexter in March 1990. And about 2,500 pages of North's personal notebooks were released later in 1990.

This avalanche of material—in all, well over 50,000 pages—forced me to reconsider whether I wanted to do the book at all. It was clear that there was no point in mainly republishing my old articles and that I had to do justice to all the new sources or give up the project. In the end, I decided it was worth the trouble and made up my mind to do as complete and definitive a study as possible, however much time it might take.

One reason that led me to make this decision was the early realization that these affairs were still a largely unknown story. Unavoidably, most of the public's knowledge came from the congressional hearings, especially as they unfolded on television. At best, they told only part of the story, even if someone had listened to every word. For another thing, ordinary journalism could not cope with the immense amount of material now at our disposal. Daily stories in the newspapers or sound bites on television could not conceivably cope with this vast outpouring. Matters essential to the understanding of these events were buried in thousands of pages of testimony and documents that could be made to give up their secrets only by forgetting about time and trouble.

As a result, I made another decision. I decided—to use an old phrase—to let the facts speak as much as possible for themselves. Indeed, I believe that they do speak for themselves. My primary aim, therefore, has been to reconstruct the events as fully and authentically as possible. This reconstruction seemed to me to be necessary before anything further could be said.

But putting the "facts" together is notoriously problematic. The only safeguard is to tell the interested reader where everything comes from and, if necessary, where it can be checked. For this reason, I have taken particular care to give my sources, so that nothing need be taken on faith. If the reader should find that there are surprising, even bizarre, aspects of this story, it is not my doing. I myself was not prepared for what I found in the record as a whole. Again and again, I said to myself: "So that is how it happened!"

My policy has been to make sure that the reader knows what is going on. Where there is more than one version, I have given more than one version. Only then have I tried to sort out what can safely be said on the basis of all the versions. More than that, I have used a good deal of the documentary material to carry the story forward, so that the reader may get a more intimate sense of what the material is before I say anything about it.

The question arises: which type of source material is most trustworthy or should get priority? In a general way, the sources can be divided into documents and testimony. The documents, such as messages sent at the time or the contemporary notebooks kept by Oliver North, were set down without thought of publication or dependence on memory. The testimony, such as at the congressional hearings and in the private depositions, came much later and inevitably contains elements of self-justification and fallible memory.

There is no doubt in my mind that the documentary sources should come first. Nevertheless, they can be relied on only so far in telling the story. They do not always tell the whole story or explain what the circumstances were. The later testimony and remembrances are, therefore, indispensable, even if they must be treated with care and checked against everything else we know.

Why should one go to such trouble in the effort to reconstruct these affairs? At least two reasons occur to me.

Rarely, if ever, have we been given such an opportunity to learn just how our government really works. Dozens of officials, including the highest, testified publicly or privately for hours and even days under oath about what they knew and did. They could not merely say what they might have chosen to say under different circumstances. They were questioned closely, often by skilled lawyers who had the benefit of thousands of documents to prepare them for what to look for and how to check answers. Nothing comparable on this scale has ever opened the government to such scrutiny. Each administration, of course, has its own ways but a good deal is common to all of them and reveals patterns of behavior that do not change easily.

The other reason is that, in my view, these were no ordinary affairs. In retrospect, it will be seen that they threatened the constitutional foundations of the country. This is not a story and a warning for our days alone. If the story of the Iran-contra affairs is not fully known and understood, a similar usurpation of power by a small, strategically placed group within the government may well recur before we are prepared to recognize what is happening. For this reason, I have felt that we cannot know too much about this case history of the thin line that separates the legitimate from the illegitimate exercise of power in our government.

I have not tried to deal with the legal aspects of the Iran-contra affairs, except to use the testimony at the North and Poindexter trials. The litigation following the affairs is a large and complex subject in itself and may go on long after this book has been published. The legal issues in these trials do not change anything about the affairs themselves.

Finally, this book was made possible by the immense material on which it is based. For this material I am indebted to all those who worked on it and saw it through to publication. This work is a distillation of their efforts, though I am, of course, solely responsible for what I have done with their massive labors.

T.D.

I think everyone knew we were walking a very thin line.
—ROBERT W. OWEN

I had not been clear in my own mind where I may have crossed the line.
—LIEUTENANT COLONEL ROBERT EARL

It was a fine line . . .
—VICE PRESIDENT GEORGE BUSH

A VERY THIN LINE

1

Contexts

The Iran-contra affairs were covert operations managed by a member of the National Security Council staff. Each of these terms—Iran-contra affairs, covert operations, the National Security Council and its so-called staff—needs some explanation, because they are not what they may seem.

Owing to common usage, we have been saddled with at least two misnomers. There was not one Iran-contra affair, as if the Iran and contra operations were two parts of one whole. They were not. They were, in fact, quite different operations and dealt with very different problems and countries. That both were managed by the same few officials and sometimes intersected at particular points did not make them one and the same affair. Moreover, putting the Iran affair first reverses the order of precedence in the chain of events. The affair of the contras—otherwise known as "Freedom Fighters," actually the armed opposition to the Sandinista regime in Nicaragua—came first and had its own independent origin. The term "contras" originated with the Sandinistas, who denounced their enemies as "*contrarrevolucionarios*," and the shorter form was generally adopted.

The other misnomer, the "National Security Council staff," takes us into the institutional context of both affairs. Before we get to the Iran-contra stories themselves, it is well to see how this NSC staff, as it is called, fitted into the structure of the American government and thereby enabled the two affairs to take the course they did.

Institutionally, the beginning goes back to the National Security Act of July 26, 1947, during the Truman administration. This legislation gave birth to both the National Security Council (NSC) and the Central Intelligence Agency (CIA). The NSC was set up with four statutory members—the president, vice president, secretary of state, and secretary of defense—and two advisory members, the director of the CIA and the chairman of the Joint Chiefs of Staff. Presidents could also add temporary members at their pleasure. The NSC's main task was to "advise the President on all matters relating to national security."

In theory, the NSC is more than a creature of the president. It was created by an act of Congress and can be changed or abolished by an act of Congress. Its members have a responsibility to advise the president, though he is not obliged to take their advice. Yet the NSC would have no reason to exist if the president never chose to listen to its advice, or if it were prevented from advising him, or if it were cut off from information needed in order to give him its best advice.

This setup was originally thought of as a way of providing the chief cabinet members with a regular forum in which they could influence or at least advise the president before he made important decisions. It has not always worked out that way. Truman himself did not encourage the NSC to fulfill this function; he rarely attended its meetings until the outbreak of the Korean War in 1950. Reagan later virtually excluded the secretaries of state and defense from knowing, let alone advising him, about the Iran affair.

A major change came during the Eisenhower administration. The NSC had originally been given a small staff, headed by an executive secretary. In 1953, President Eisenhower reorganized the setup and made the staff, now headed by a special assistant to the president for national security affairs, into something different. The staff was largely divorced from the NSC as a whole and turned into a virtual adjunct of the presidency. This shift was accomplished by incorporating it into the Executive Office of the President (EOP), first created in 1939 on the eve of World War II. The EOP was originally intended to do no more than provide the presidency with a more efficient administrative office, a largely housekeeping service. But like so much in the postwar period, it gradually took on so many new political, economic, public relations, and other functions, foreign and domestic, each with its own staff and organization, that the presidency was transformed into another swollen bureaucracy. By President Reagan's time, the staff numbered over 1,600 and, as one study put it, "constitutes a bureaucracy probably as compartmentalized in structure and Byzantine in its workings as any in the federal government."[1]

In this way, the staff became the president's, not the NSC's. The assistant to the president for national security affairs—the "special" was dropped and the title was popularly known as the national security adviser—was given the task of managing the staff and, in effect, becoming the president's personal foreign-policy coordinator and adviser as well as serving as executive secretary of the NSC. As time went by, he spent far more time directing his staff than calling the members of the NSC together and preparing their infrequent meetings. If a president so preferred, he could now dispense with advice from the NSC and get it from his national security adviser, one or two cabinet officers, or anyone else, as he pleased. The term "NSC staff" has become so familiar that it is difficult to do without it, but it is a misnomer. The NSC should more accurately refer to the council of cabinet members and other high officials, and the NSC staff to the national security adviser in his capacity as the president's special assistant. It would be far more accurate to refer to the "NSA staff"—the national security adviser's staff—than the NSC staff—the National Security Council's staff. Yet the correspondence of the NSC staff members was sent on letterheads which read "National Security Council," not "National Security Council staff" or "national security adviser."[2]

The confusion inherent in this setup led then Vice President George Bush to stress the difference between the NSC and the NSC staff. To absolve himself as a member of the NSC, Bush strongly objected that the press had reported the Iran-contra affairs as "NSC operations." He insisted that "they weren't. Oliver North wasn't a member of the NSC. He was an NSC staffer, working under [National Security Adviser] Poindexter." The NSC, Bush maintained, "was created to advise the president," whereas the NSC staff "took on a covert operation it wasn't designed to conduct." At no time, Bush protested, had the NSC itself, of which he was a member, ever considered "all phases of the operation."[3]

The NSC and the NSC staff, according to Bush, were two separate entities; whatever Oliver North did should be blamed on the NSC staff, not the NSC. It thus remains a mystery why the staff was called an NSC staff if it was not under the control of the NSC as a whole and owed its allegiance only to the president and the national security adviser. There was something Topsy-like about the development of the national security adviser's function which made it more and more an appendage of the presidency and not of the NSC after which it was named.

One of the most troublesome aspects of the NSC staff—we will follow the common usage in the hope that its true relationship to the NSC and the president will be kept in mind—is its operational role. The original function of the NSC and, therefore, its staff was largely limited to advising the president on issues relating to national security. Existing departments were there to carry out recommendations and decisions. In effect, the president did not at first have the means to bypass the rest of the government if he wished to put a policy into effect. This limitation on the president's power still largely prevailed in the Eisenhower period.

The operational breakthrough came in the Kennedy era. It was the Kennedy administration, according to McGeorge Bundy, then national security adviser, that "deliberately rubbed out the distinction between planning and operation."[4] After the Bay of Pigs fiasco, Kennedy lost confidence in the traditional departments, including the CIA, and, like Roosevelt before him, adopted a more personal style of directing and executing policy, by himself or with close associates.

When the NSC staff went operational, the president now had the means of executing certain kinds of policy without recourse to the traditional operational departments, such as State and Defense. The more the executive office of the president grew, the more it duplicated the rest of the government, sometimes cooperating with the others, sometimes competing with them, and sometimes ignoring them.

In the administration of President Lyndon Johnson, the NSC staff numbered thirty-five, few of them from the military, most on temporary duty from the State Department. It had a budget of $628,000 and occupied an office in the basement of the White House. Under President Richard M. Nixon, his national security adviser, Henry Kissinger, hired 155 staff members, managed a budget of $2,900,000, and moved out of the basement.[5] By 1983–85, in the Reagan administration, National Security Adviser Robert C. McFarlane had a staff of about forty-five "professional officers," with two hundred more in support.[6] Under his successor, John M. Poindexter, the staff was organized into twelve directorates or divisions, such as an African Office, a European Office, a Latin American Office, all duplicating those of the State Department.[7] It was large and varied enough to carry out the president's wishes covertly—covertly, that is to say, from the rest of the government.

2

Originally, the Central Intelligence Agency was also limited in its functions. The 1947 National Security Act had put the CIA under the direction of the National Security Council, not the president alone. The president appointed its director with the advice and consent of the Senate—an indication that Congress could not be ignored in its makeup. Traditionally, the CIA director testified about its activities to congressional committees, thereby giving Congress some check on them. The CIA was first given the function of coordinating the intelligence activities of the various departments and agencies and correlating and evaluating the intelligence gathered by them. No provision was made for covert activities. In December 1947, however, the NSC gave the CIA authority to conduct covert psychological operations. In June 1948, the CIA added a separate covert-action unit, then called the Office of Special Projects. In a major reorganization of the agency in 1952, the separation of the covert unit was given up and its activities were made part of one of the divisions, known as directorates, of the CIA. By that year, clandestine activities consumed 60 percent of the agency's personnel and 74 percent of its budget.[8]

In 1955, an NSC directive spelled out the range of the CIA's covert operations. They were designed to make the CIA into a virtual Cold War machine against Communism—to "create and exploit troublesome problems for international Communism," "reduce international Communist control over any areas of the world," and "develop underground resistance and facilitate covert and guerrilla operations."

Two points in this directive were especially notable. Covert operations were required to be "planned and conducted in a manner consistent with United States foreign and military policies and with overt activities." If this rule had been followed, the contradiction between covert negotiations and U.S. overt policies would have been avoided and acute embarrassment prevented during the Iran affair. The principle of "plausible deniability" of covert operations was also set forth—"so planned and executed that any U.S. Government responsibility for them is not evident to unauthorized persons and that if uncovered the U.S. Government can plausibly disclaim any responsibility for them." The phrase "unauthorized persons" was ambiguous, but it was not yet understood to include the entire U.S. government, including Congress, to which the CIA director was required to report. In both the Iran and contra affairs, "plausible deniability" was made to apply to everyone but the small inner group in charge of the operations.[9]

The Truman administration had started something that was basically responsible for these innovations, yet Truman himself did not realize where they were going to lead. In 1963, eleven years after he had left office, Truman confessed: "I never had any thought that when I set up the CIA that it would be injected into peacetime cloak-and-dagger operations." He no longer liked what he had wrought: "For some time I have been disturbed by the way CIA has been diverted from its original assignment. It has become an operational and at times a policy-making arm of the government." After seeing what had resulted, he wanted no more of it: "I, therefore, would like to see the CIA be restored to its original assignment as the intelligence arm of the President, and whatever else it can properly perform in that special field—and its operational duties be terminated or properly used elsewhere." Finally, he reflected: "We have grown up as a nation, respected for our ability to maintain a free and open society. There is something about the way the CIA has been functioning that is casting a shadow over our historic position and I feel that we need to correct it."[10] To a correspondent, he wrote: "The CIA was set up by me for the sole purpose of getting all the available information to the President. It was not intended to operate as an international agency engaged in strange activities."[11]

In these years, the CIA conducted its activities without much supervision. Until the mid-1950s, no NSC body existed to review them. A group known as the 5412 Committee was formed in 1955 for that purpose but it seldom met. It was succeeded in 1959 by a "Special Group" to authorize covert operations, which met weekly with little effect. In this period Congress knew little beyond what it was told by the CIA and chose to know little more. The prevailing attitude was candidly confessed by Senator Leverett Saltonstall, the ranking Republican on the Armed Services Committee and its Defense Subcommittee:

> It is not a question of reluctance on the part of CIA officials to speak to us. Instead, it is a question of our reluctance, if you will, to seek information and knowledge on subjects which I personally, not as a Member of Congress and as a citizen, would rather not have, unless I believed it to be my responsibility to have it because it might involve the lives of American citizens.

Senator Mike Mansfield, the Democratic majority leader, thought that this attitude was just right. "I see," he immediately responded. "The Senator is to be commended."[12]

This general abdication of responsibility coincided with the era of Allen W. Dulles as head of the CIA. Yet not much was changed even after the departure of Dulles in 1961 as a result of the Bay of Pigs fiasco. A National Security Decision Memorandum in February 1970 did little more than change the name of the NSC's Special Group to the 40 Committee. Its decisions were not necessarily referred to the president, who was supposed to be protected by virtue of his ignorance. He was told of a proposed covert action only if there was disagreement in the committee or if a member thought that it was important or sensitive enough to inform him.

This insulation of the president enabled subordinates to make decisions and take actions in his name without necessarily informing him or seeking his approval. In effect, covert activities were peculiarly a presidential responsibility and at the same time a danger from which he needed to be shielded.

3

The main victim of the emergence of the national security adviser as the president's preferred alter ego was the secretary of state.

There has been no rule about how presidents should use national security advisers. The position is so loosely defined and personally attached to the president that every president has made it over in his own image. The NSC executive secretaries and national security advisers under Truman and Eisenhower were so unobtrusive that their names have virtually vanished from memory.* Not until the Kennedy administration did the post take off. It was then held by McGeorge Bundy, who with his deputy, Walt W. Rostow, according to Arthur M. Schlesinger, Jr.,

---

* It was Sidney W. Souers under Truman and Robert Cutler under Eisenhower.

gave the White House "an infusion of energy on foreign affairs with which the State Department would never in the next three years . . . quite catch up." At first, Kennedy wanted the State Department to be the "central point" in all aspects of foreign affairs. But he was soon "disappointed" in its makeup and performance, as if he had had nothing to do with them. He thereupon came to depend on Bundy and his staff or on Theodore Sorensen, his special counsel. The secretary of state, Dean Rusk, and Kennedy's entourage were said to be so different that they hardly spoke the same language. To Kennedy himself, Rusk's views allegedly "remained a mystery."[13] Sorensen says that Rusk "deferred almost too amiably to White House initiatives and interference." If Kennedy had lived to have a second term, Bundy would have been a "logical candidate for Secretary of State."[14]

In his autobiography, Rusk did not hide his scorn for Sorensen and Schlesinger. Rusk admits that he was slow to make up his mind on major issues and waited until everyone else had spoken up before he ventured to give a cautious opinion. Rusk expresses respect for Bundy, but his son, Richard Rusk, who inserts personal reminiscences in the book, tells "a mischievous White House tale, apparently spread by McGeorge Bundy." It had Kennedy and Rusk alone in the Oval Office with the president asking Rusk for his views. "There are still too many people here, Mr. President," allegedly replied Rusk, whose obsession with confidentiality was legendary in Kennedy's entourage. Rusk mildly notes that Sorensen once rewrote an official message to the Soviet Union "with flowery language that read like an inaugural address but was totally unacceptable for a diplomatic note." One of Rusk's few wrathful remarks is aimed at Schlesinger, who had described Rusk as having sat at meetings like an old Buddha, seldom saying anything. "He was right," Rusk explains, "because when forty and fifty people were in the room, especially people like Schlesinger, I kept my mouth shut; I always wondered how secure our conversations were in Schlesinger's presence." Schlesinger, Rusk adds, was "a fifth wheel in decision making." It is clear that some of those much closer to Kennedy than Rusk enjoyed tearing down the secretary of state and building up the national security adviser.[15]

Kennedy was not the first president to make foreign policy in the White House rather than in the State Department. The pattern had been set by Franklin D. Roosevelt, who had made his secretary of state, Cordell Hull, virtually a figurehead. But Roosevelt had not built up a substitute or shadow foreign-policy agency; he had preferred to work through other officials, at first Under Secretary of State Sumner Welles, and then through other members of his cabinet or his personal emissary Harry Hopkins. Roosevelt and the proliferation of quasi foreign-affairs agencies during World War II were largely responsible for starting the State Department on its downward path, but it was still only the beginning of the road. Presidents who wanted to be their own foreign secretaries followed his example by choosing weak secretaries of state and depending on others to carry out their wishes.

The president who gave this system a pathological twist was Richard Nixon. We know just how pathological it was because his national security adviser, Henry Kissinger, has told us all about it. Nixon hardly knew Kissinger when he took him on; his choice as secretary of state, William Rogers, was one of Nixon's closest friends and a former law partner. When Nixon chose Rogers, he knew him to be unfamiliar with foreign affairs. Kissinger relates that Nixon immediately told him to build up a "national security apparatus" in the White House. The only region that Nixon entrusted to Rogers was the Middle East—for one reason because Nixon believed at the time that any active policy there was doomed to failure. The "back channel" that Nixon and Kissinger set up with Soviet Ambassador Anatoly Dobrynin cut the State Department out of Soviet-American relations, by far the most important field of foreign affairs. According to Kissinger, Nixon repeatedly lied to Rogers, especially about Kissinger's trips to China in 1971 and to Moscow in 1972.

Kissinger's explanation of why Nixon humiliated his old friend clearly suggests that the motive was morbid. In the past, it seems, Rogers had been the "psychologically dominant partner" in the relationship. Now Nixon "wanted to reverse roles and establish a relationship in which both hierarchically and substantially he, Nixon, called the tune for once." Kissinger was only too willing to collaborate in the diseased machination, of which he was the chief beneficiary. "I do not mean to suggest that I resisted Nixon's conduct toward his senior Cabinet officer," Kissinger confesses. "From the first my presence made it technically possible and after a time I undoubtedly encouraged it."

One precedent set by Nixon and Kissinger came back to haunt Reagan's secretary of state, George P. Shultz. Kissinger used the U.S. ambassador in Pakistan to prepare for his China trip without either of them informing Secretary of State Rogers. Shultz was similarly bypassed in the Iran-contra affairs, though he protested against the use of Kissinger's precedent as a justification for treating him the same way with the argument that Kissinger had been unique: "They broke the mold when they made him." Unfortunately, they did not break the mold of what he did, which was far more important in the long run than what he was.

In retrospect, Kissinger knew that there was something wrong with his theatrical China coup. In his memoirs, he virtuously explained what the role of the secretary of state should properly be—a role on which he insisted when he became secretary of state:

> The State Department should be the visible focus of our foreign policy; if the President has no confidence in his Secretary of State he should replace him, not substitute the security adviser for him. If he does not trust the State Department, the President should

enforce compliance with his directives, not circumvent it with the NSC machinery. Yet, while these postulates are beyond argument as a matter of theory, they are not easy to carry out. To achieve the essential coherence of policy there is need for a strong Secretary of State who is at the same time quite prepared to carry out Presidential wishes not only formally but in all nuances.[16]

According to this reasoning, it was Secretary of State Rogers's fault for having been too weak to carry out the presidential wishes. But Nixon had deliberately chosen a weak secretary of state and then had made him all the weaker by treating him with open contempt and by cutting him out of his own constitutional responsibilities. As for the conspiratorial secrecy which enveloped Kissinger's first trip to China in 1971, it was not anything the Chinese had wanted or demanded. They were, he admitted, "extremely suspicious of our desire for secrecy." It was contrived wholly for American consumption, to confront the American public with an accomplished fact.

Kissinger liked to think of himself as the great conceptualizer, one of his favorite terms; he was also a great operator to whom more and more power flowed through his personal rigging of the diplomatic market and his chairmanship of innumerable governmental committees, including one on covert action. Of all those who prepared the way for Reagan's operational NSC staff, Kissinger was the most responsible.

Nixon had fancied himself to be a great expert in foreign affairs; Jimmy Carter had no such illusions. But Carter also wanted to be seen as his own master in foreign affairs. He therefore chose a secretary of state, Cyrus Vance, who would not be too obtrusive. Carter's national security adviser, Zbigniew Brzezinski, was admittedly determined to be the president's prime agent in foreign policy. Brzezinski quickly contrived to freeze out the CIA in the daily intelligence briefing of the president, which he insisted on giving every morning with no one else present. He saw himself as Carter's mentor and in the first few months of his tenure gave the president lessons in "conceptual or strategic issues." Brzezinski's NSC staff controlled "the policy-making output of both State and the Defense Department," as well as the activities of the CIA.

Brzezinski had clearly learned from Kissinger's example. Brzezinski and Vance increasingly disagreed on major issues, with Vance unable or unwilling to assert himself. Vance's "reluctance to speak up publicly, to provide a broad conceptual explanation for what our Administration was trying to do, and Carter's lack of preparation for doing it himself, pushed me to the forefront," Brzezinski later explained, adding in parenthesis, echoing Kissinger: "I will not claim I resisted strongly." Finally Vance could stand no more and resigned over the ill-fated mission to rescue the hostages from the Tehran embassy in 1980. Another secretary of state had spent almost four miserable, humiliating years in office, at least as the national security adviser later described them.[17]

Reagan's first secretary of state, Alexander M. Haig, Jr., was another casualty. Having been Kissinger's deputy on the NSC staff, Haig well knew about the rivalry and threat to the secretary of state from that quarter. When he took office, he says, the president told him that he would be *"the* spokesman" in foreign affairs and "I won't have a repeat of the Kissinger-Rogers situation." Reagan also assured him that the new national security adviser, Richard V. Allen, "would act exclusively as a staff coordinator." Haig did not have much trouble with Allen, primarily because Allen did not have the power to trouble him. They were both deprived of regular direct access to the president, the factor that Haig later thought had brought both of them down.

After Allen's inglorious departure as national security adviser in January 1982, a real rival and threat confronted Haig in the person of Allen's successor, William P. Clark, an intimate friend of the president, whose deputy was Robert C. McFarlane. As Haig tells the story, he began to be bypassed by Clark during the Lebanon crisis of that year. Soon Haig was worried by a situation "in which a presidential assistant [Clark], especially one of limited experience and limited understanding of the volatile nature of an international conflict [at that time the Falklands crisis], should assume powers of the Presidency." Clark would draft a message to Israel for the president to sign without showing it to Haig. Clark thereby restored the position of national security adviser to the eminence that it had had under Kennedy, Johnson, Nixon, and Carter. Yet in the end Haig himself came to denigrate the constitutional position of the secretary of state by offering the view that "it does not really matter whether the secretary of state or the national security adviser, or some other official carries out the president's foreign policy and speaks for the administration on these questions."[18]

The expansion of presidential ambitions in foreign policy has coincided with the expansion of the country's global power. This dual expansion has made foreign affairs the main test of presidential greatness. Presidents have deliberately appointed weak secretaries of state, or rid themselves of those who did not bend to their will, in order to free themselves from traditional or constitutional restraints. The last strong secretaries of state were Truman's George C. Marshall and Dean Acheson, and Eisenhower's John Foster Dulles. It is unthinkable that any president would have treated them the way Rusk, Rogers, Vance, and Haig were treated, or that Marshall, Acheson, and Dulles would have submitted to such treatment.

Thus the way President Reagan used his national security advisers to carry out a covert operation to which his secretary of state objected was not new. It had been made possible by the emergence of national security advisers as rivals and substitutes for secretaries of state. But the Iran-contra affairs were uniquely different in another way—the substitution of the NSC staff for the CIA.

4

Until the Bay of Pigs debacle in 1961, the CIA did very much as it pleased in the conduct of covert activities, its special monopoly. Unlike President Reagan twenty-five years later, President Kennedy accepted full responsibility for the failure, as President Eisenhower had done when a CIA reconnaissance plane had been shot down over the Soviet Union the year before. Kennedy finally ended Allen Dulles's long career as CIA director without doing much to change the way the CIA did business covertly.

Kennedy's successors, Lyndon B. Johnson and Richard M. Nixon, finally brought on a revolt in Congress, which had long failed to bear its share of constitutional responsibility for foreign policy in general and war-making powers in particular. The Vietnam War and the CIA's embroilments in Chile and elsewhere, among other things, led Congress to make a major effort to change the rules which had previously governed its relations with the executive branch.

The first substantial change came in the form of a War Powers Resolution. It required the president to submit a report to Congress within forty-eight hours after any involvement of U.S. armed forces in hostilities or in "situations where imminent involvement in hostilities is clearly indicated by the circumstances." It also required the president to terminate such involvement within sixty days after submitting his report, if Congress had not approved of his action.

The War Powers Resolution was far from being a foolproof congressional check on the president. It did not cover covert wars or paramilitary activities, such as the CIA later conducted in Nicaragua. It was restricted to "United States Armed Forces" and left room for the use of "unofficial" or surrogate forces, such as the Nicaraguan contras subsequently represented. It made Congress irrelevant if the armed action was completed in less than sixty days, as in the case of Grenada in October 1983 and Panama in December 1989.

In any event, Nixon saw fit to veto the resolution, whereupon it was passed over his veto in November 1973. Nevertheless, Nixon announced that he was not going to abide by the resolution on the ground that he considered it to be unconstitutional, thereby arrogating to himself the power given to the Supreme Court to decide on constitutionality. His Republican successors, Ronald Reagan and George Bush, have followed Nixon's example and have refused to recognize the War Powers Resolution as binding on them.

In 1974, Congress was more successful in dealing with covert operations without getting presidential defiance. The Hughes-Ryan Amendment to the Foreign Assistance Act required the president to "find" that each covert activity is "important to the national security of the United States." In addition, a time limit was set on the president's report to Congress of such operations—"in a timely fashion."

Another important measure was added in 1980. An Intelligence Oversight Act sought to stiffen the reporting requirement by obligating the president to provide the congressional intelligence committees with prior notice of any "significant anticipated intelligence activity," including covert operations. In return, the number of congressional committees— in effect, only their chairmen and vice chairmen—to which the president was supposed to report was reduced from eight to two.

Thus came into existence two main requirements which were to haunt the Reagan administration during the Iran-contra affairs. The first was the need for presidential Findings, understood to be written documents describing the need and nature of the covert operations and bearing the president's signature. The second was the obligation to report to the appropriate congressional committees "in a timely fashion." This term was not defined but was understood to mean a matter of days or at most weeks, not months or years or whenever the president should be pleased to do so.

The Reagan administration itself codified the entire intelligence system on December 4, 1981, in its Executive Order 12333. The National Security Council was described as "the highest Executive Branch entity that provides review of, guidance for and direction to the conduct of all national foreign intelligence, counterintelligence, and special activities, and attendant policies and programs." This characterization seemed to give sweeping authority to the entire Council, not merely to the president. The requirements of the Hughes-Ryan Amendment were extended from the CIA to the entire "intelligence community." Covert activities were renamed "special activities" and made the direct responsibility of the CIA and its director.

The role of the NSC's staff in the Iran-contra affairs raised the question whether the staff was part of the "intelligence community" and thus came under the Hughes-Ryan legislation and other reporting requirements. The argument was based on the terms "intelligence community" and "entity of the intelligence community" in the Intelligence Oversight Act of 1980. This act had explicitly named a number of agencies, beginning with the CIA, without specifying the NSC staff. It had, however, contained an omnibus clause that extended the act to "such other components of the departments and agencies, to the extent determined by the president, as may be engaged in intelligence activities." The claim that the NSC's staff was not part of the intelligence community was based on its omission from the list of recognized intelligence agencies. The question was whether any "other components of the departments and agencies" which in fact engaged in intelligence and special activities thereby made themselves part of the intelligence community whether they were on the list or not. In one interpretation, the issue turned on who or what was on the list; in another interpretation, the answer depended on what an agency or entity actually did, not on what it was supposed to do. This issue came up in the Iran-contra affairs, but it is enough to note that the intelligence community as defined in the Intelligence Oversight Act of 1980 was not limited to those "entities" specifically named.

What emerges from all this is that the CIA had long gone its own way with little effective supervision. Congress did not make a real effort to oversee covert activities in general and the CIA in particular until 1974 and even then had limited means of knowing what was going on. The congressional committees, to which the CIA was supposed to report, in fact knew only as much as the CIA chose to tell them or what they read in the newspapers. At the climax of the Iran-contra affairs, a deceptive report to the congressional committees prepared for the CIA's director, William J. Casey, was one of the main breaking points and led to the exposure of the Iran-contra affairs.

All the legislation, from the basic National Security Act of 1947 to Executive Order 12333 of 1981, had given the CIA sole charge of intelligence and covert activities, without even mentioning the NSC staff in these fields. It was still taken for granted that the role of the national security adviser and his staff was purely advisory, not operational. But there was a loophole in the 1981 Executive Order which escaped much attention at the time. It gave the CIA the exclusive conduct of "special activities" (an official alias for covert activities), "unless the President determines that another agency is more likely to achieve a particular objective."[19] This exception seemed to apply more to a unit of the armed forces than to the NSC staff, which did not seem to have the background or personnel to conduct complex and dangerous covert activities.

No one had reckoned with a lieutenant colonel of the Marine Corps under the command of an admiral of the U.S. Navy.

5

The contra affair introduced the Reagan administration to covert operations. The debut took place as the result of an upheaval in Nicaragua.

On July 17, 1979, toward the end of the Carter administration, the forty-two-year-old Somoza dictatorship collapsed. It was overthrown by a broad revolutionary coalition known as the Sandinista National Liberation Front, which took its name from a Nicaraguan revolutionary leader, Augusto César Sandino. Beginning in 1926, he had waged a guerrilla struggle against the U.S. occupation of Nicaragua until he was tracked down and killed in 1934 by the local National Guard, commanded by its U.S.-trained and -appointed commander, General Anastasio So-

moza, the patriarch of the dynasty. That the later opposition to another Somoza should have adopted Sandino as its inspiration was a
portent.

The Carter administration decided to treat the new regime with a show
of goodwill. Nicaragua quickly received $39 million in emergency food
aid from the United States in 1979 and another $60 million in emergency
economic assistance in 1980. At the same time, President Carter signed
a Finding in 1979 to support the democratic elements in Nicaragua in
what promised to be a bitter struggle with extremists. When the moderates
and extremists in the Sandinista movement began to fall apart, the latter
increasingly seized the upper hand. The two moderate members—Violeta
Barrios de Chamorro and Alfonso Robelo—found it necessary to resign
from the five-member governing council. The extremist leader, Daniel
Ortega, emerged as the "Nicaraguan Castro." The triumphant Sandinistas
gave support to the leftist guerrilla movement in neighboring El Salvador,
to which arms began to flow from Nicaragua. In March 1980, a Sandinista
delegation went to Moscow and signed economic, technical, scientific,
and cultural agreements with the Soviet Union. Cuban "advisers" moved
into Nicaragua.

By the time President Reagan was inaugurated in January 1981, U.S.
policy had made a full turn. The Republican election platform had
virtually called for the overthrow of the Sandinista regime—"we will
support the efforts of the Nicaraguan people to establish a free and independent government." The Reagan administration did not waste any
time making good on this pledge. In February 1981, a final $15 million
payment of a $75 million aid package to Nicaragua, previously allotted,
was suspended.

The CIA had first proposed a program of covert action against the
Sandinista regime in March 1981, at which time President Reagan had
authorized a CIA covert program for Central America in general. Reagan
signed National Security Decision Directive 17 to provide covert support
for the anti-Sandinistas on November 17. A Finding of December 1
covered up this decision by stating that the U.S. aim was merely to
interdict the flow of arms from Nicaragua to El Salvador.

Another split in the Sandinista ranks, led by Edén Pastora, gave the
CIA an unexpected opportunity. Pastora, whose *nom de guerre* was "Com-
andante Zero," had been one of the most popular and respected Sandinista leaders. He had broken with the new regime in protest against its
increasingly dictatorial and "Marxist-Leninist" direction. In April 1982,
he organized a Sandinista Revolutionary Front (FRS) and declared war
on the regime in Managua. The CIA decided to support his group, for
lack of any alternative, even though it was based in Costa Rica to the
south of Nicaragua—for one reason because it was the only genuinely
democratic state in Central America—instead of in Honduras to the
north, the administration's main public reason for intervening in Nica-

ragua. Pastora not only was in the wrong place from the CIA's point of view but was just as resistant to control by the United States as he had been by his former comrades-in-arms.

Meanwhile, another anti-Sandinista force was taking shape in Honduras, made up largely of former members of Somoza's National Guard. It was headed by Enrique Bermúdez, formerly a colonel in the National Guard and Somoza's military attaché in Washington. In August 1980, Bermúdez succeeded in bringing together a small group of former National Guard officers and anti-Sandinista civilians to form the Fuerza Democrática Nicaragüense (Nicaraguan Democratic Force, usually known by the initials FDN). The makeup of this force was such that it was repeatedly accused of seeking to restore the Somocistas to power without Somoza, who was in any case assassinated in Paraguay in September 1980. Pastora refused to work with Bermúdez on the ground that he was politically tainted. Forced to choose between them, the CIA chose Bermúdez.

The first attempt to train an anti-Sandinista armed force in Honduras was made by the Argentine military.[20] This effort was supported by the CIA, which was not yet prepared to do the job itself and which faced conflicting views within the administration as to whether it should be done at all. This phase did not last much beyond the Argentine invasion of the British-held Falkland Islands on April 2, 1982. The Argentines did not take kindly to U.S. support of Great Britain in the ensuing war and cut down their investment in the contras, which they had considered to be a favor to the United States.[21]

In the course of 1982, the CIA assumed responsibility for the contra operation. After a discussion with Director Casey, *Newsweek* of November 8, 1982, entitled its cover story "America's Secret War: Nicaragua." Without saying as much, it conveyed the impression that the United States was engaged in a covert military operation to overthrow the Sandinistas in Nicaragua or, as the story put it, "to undermine the Sandinista government." One of the repercussions of this article was a forceful editorial denunciation in *The Boston Globe*. Among its readers was Representative Edward P. Boland of Massachusetts, chairman of the House Select Committee on Intelligence. Casey denied the story to the committee but boasted that the numbers of the contra force had grown from 500 to 4,000. One of Casey's problems was that he did not give the impression of a man who could automatically be trusted.[22]

6

Boland was outraged. He was not the only one. His committee had gone along with the program to interdict the flow of Nicaraguan arms to El Salvador. It was infuriated by the news that U.S. policy had gone beyond interdiction into something far more serious. The episode was an early example of how Congress knew only as much about the contra affair as it read in the press and of how Casey, despite a reputation for shrewdness, could bring on his own troubles.

The opposition in Congress to a policy of seeking to overthrow the Nicaraguan regime was so strong that a determined effort was made to cut off funds for that purpose. On December 8, 1982, the House of Representatives passed the first so-called Boland Amendment, named after its chief sponsor, Representative Edward P. Boland, a Democrat. Boland I, as it came to be known, was attached to the Defense Appropriations Act for fiscal year 1983. It prohibited the CIA and the Department of Defense from using any funds "for the purpose of overthrowing the Government of Nicaragua or provoking a military exchange between Nicaragua and Honduras." It passed by a vote of 411–0. The loophole in Boland I was that the CIA could still support the contras if it claimed that the purpose was something other than the overthrow of the Nicaraguan government. Since it had been attached to the Defense Appropriations Act, the amendment was in effect for only one year and had to be passed annually to do much good.

President Reagan did not challenge the constitutionality of Boland I and signed it on December 21. "We are complying with the law, the Boland Amendment, which is the law . . . But what I might personally wish or what our government might wish still would not justify us violating the law of the land," he said on April 14, 1983.[23] To a joint session of Congress later that month, he declared: "But let us be clear as to the American attitude toward the Government of Nicaragua. We do not seek its overthrow." The president explained that he merely wished to prevent Nicaraguan arms from flowing into the territory of its neighbors.[24]

This seeming moderation did not last long. In the summer of 1983, secret plans sought to enable the CIA to stockpile weapons for the contras in the event that Congress should cut off all support to them. The CIA asked the Department of Defense to provide it with $28 million worth of equipment, from medical supplies to aircraft, which the CIA could pass on to the contras without violating any congressionally imposed aid ceiling, inasmuch as the CIA would not have paid for it. The scheme was clearly unconstitutional, since it meant that money appropriated by Congress for the armed services for their needs was to be used by the CIA for other, unauthorized purposes. This maneuver was ruled out by the general counsel of the Department of Defense on the ground that it violated the Economy Act, which required the department to be reimbursed for any interagency transfers—a provision which came up again later in one of the most embarrassing episodes of the Iran affair. Despite the legal objection, the CIA still obtained three surplus Cessna aircraft without paying for them and other equipment at cost.[25]

In response to congressional pressure, the Reagan administration agreed to issue a new Finding that was intended to get around congressional objections. This Finding of September 19, 1983, gave the purpose of American policy as that of providing "support, equipment and training assistance to Nicaraguan paramilitary resistance groups" in order to induce the Sandinistas and Cubans "to cease their support for insurgencies in the region" and negotiate peace treaties with their neighbors. To mollify Congress, paramilitary assistance by U.S. citizens was apparently barred and limited to third-country nationals. The CIA was ostensibly forbidden to engage in such paramilitary operations. This stratagem was the beginning of trying to accomplish through so-called third countries what the Reagan administration was prohibited by law from doing on its own. For the next three years, the problem before the administration was how to violate congressional constraints without seeming to violate them or without getting caught at it.

Congress had its own problems. A dispute soon broke out between the Democratic House and the Republican Senate over the amount of contra assistance. The House wanted to cut off all aid, the Senate to continue it. The result in December 1983 was a compromise putting a "cap" of $24 million on the next year's contra funding—not enough to take the contras through the next fiscal year.

This compromise merely postponed the showdown for a few months and gave the administration hope that it could do better by soon going back to Congress for supplemental assistance to the contras. In a divided Congress, it was believed that the contending sides could be influenced by future events and political pressures. As a result, no decision needed to be accepted as final; administration strategy was always to hold on and wait for a more favorable turn of Central American events and U.S. public opinion. The problem for the administration was that it could not merely wait for Congress to change its collective mind. Money and equipment were almost always in short supply, with the result that the administration, while constantly hoping for a congressional change of mind the next time around, was yet determined to keep the contras in the field with or without it.

7

CIA Director Casey was soon in even greater trouble. Again, Nicaragua was the reason.

On January 7, 1984, the CIA, with the approval of President Reagan, began to place magnetic mines in three Nicaraguan harbors. More mines were placed on February 29. The mining was no secret and attracted little immediate attention because the contras—at the instigation of the CIA—first claimed credit for it. But on April 6, *The Wall Street Journal* revealed that the CIA and not the contras had been responsible for the action, which had resulted in damage to several ships, including a Soviet oil tanker. The mines had been American, the ship placing them American, and the command American.

This operation had been discussed at a meeting of the top-level National Security Planning Group in December 1983. As one of those present, Donald P. Gregg, a CIA official for about thirty years before he became Vice President Bush's national security adviser, later testified, the purpose of the mining had been to sink a Soviet ship or any ship bringing military supplies to the Sandinista regime or to block a channel through which military supplies would have to pass.[26]

The reaction in Congress was wrathful. It was especially furious in the Senate Select Committee on Intelligence, of which a Republican, Barry Goldwater of Arizona, was chairman, and a Democrat, Daniel Patrick Moynihan of New York, was vice chairman. By law they were supposed to be informed *in advance* of any important covert operation. This action was important enough for the International Court of Justice later to rule that it was a violation of international law. The news was especially embarrassing to Senator Goldwater, who had not been informed about the president's approval. The news story was doubly galling because it said that the House Select Intelligence Committee had been told about the action, apparently on January 31.

On April 9, Senator Goldwater shot off a "Dear Bill" letter to Casey. It is worth giving in full to show how tense relations between the administration and one of its leading supporters had become:

> All this past weekend, I've been trying to figure out how I can most easily tell you my feelings about the discovery of the President having approved mining some of the harbors of Central America.
>
> It gets down to one, little, simple phrase: I am pissed off!
>
> I understand you had briefed the House on this matter. I've heard that. Now, during the important debate we had all last week and the week before, on whether we would increase funds for the Nicaragua program, we were doing all right, until a Member of the Committee charged that the President had approved the mining. I strongly denied that because I had never heard of it. I found out the next day that the CIA had, with the written approval of the President, engaged in such a mining, and the approval came in February.
>
> Bill, this is no way to run a railroad and I find myself in a hell of a quandary. I am forced to apologize to Members of the Intelligence Committee because I did not know the facts on this. At the same time, my counterpart in the House did know.
>
> The President has asked us to back his foreign policy. Bill, how can we back his foreign policy when we don't know what the hell he is doing? Lebanon, yes, we all knew that he sent troops over

there. But mine the harbors of Nicaragua? This is an act violating international law. It is an act of war. For the life of me, I don't see how we are going to explain it.

My simple guess is that the House is going to defeat this supplemental [aid of $21 million to the contras] and we will not be in any position to put up much of an argument after we were not given the information we were entitled to receive; particularly, if my memory serves me correctly, when you briefed us on Central America just a couple of weeks ago. And the order was signed before that.

I don't like this. I don't like it one bit from the President or from you. I don't think we need a lot of lengthy explanations. The deed has been done and, in the future, if anything like this happens, I'm going to raise one hell of a fuss about it in public.[27]

In reply, Casey maintained that he had briefed Goldwater's committee on March 8 and 13. The national security adviser, Robert C. McFarlane, also claimed that the congressmen had been told about the mining. These disclaimers so enraged Senator Moynihan that he took the unusual—almost unprecedented—step on April 15 of resigning from the committee in protest. Moynihan pointed out that Casey's March briefings had not been "full," "current," or "prior" as required by the Intelligence Oversight Act of 1980. On March 8 and 13, it seems, Casey had artfully slipped in a reference to the action, in "a single sentence in a two-hour Committee meeting and a singularly obscure sentence at that." It was apparently so brief and obscure that committee members had missed its significance and had not followed it up.* Casey was a notorious mumbler and could not pronounce "Nicaragua"; it usually came out as "Nicawawa."

The key question was one of timing. Moynihan pointed out: "If this action was important enough for the President to have approved it in February, it was important enough for the Committee to have been informed in February." Moynihan later added: "All references by Mr. Casey and his associates were made to committee hearings or individual briefings which had taken place after the event. Two or three months after the event, to be exact." McFarlane soon told Moynihan that "either what he had been told was disingenuous or outright wrong." Moynihan believes that "Mr. Casey lied to him, as to so many others."

After mulling over Goldwater's letter for two weeks and Moynihan's resignation for ten days, Casey decided to apologize to both Goldwater and the committee as a whole, whereupon Moynihan withdrew his res-

---

* The sentence read: "Magnetic mines have been placed in the Pacific harbor of Corinto and the Atlantic harbor of El Bluff as well as the oil terminal of Puerto Sandino." But the contras had claimed to have laid the mines. Casey's sentence did not implicate the CIA and seemed to apply to the contras.

ignation. Yet the senators felt that they had to do something to prevent another such breach of trust, as they understood it. The statute in question referred to significant anticipated activities. But what was "significant"? Moynihan offered a definition—it was anything that the president signed. Thereupon an agreement, known as the "Casey Accords," was reached between the Senate Intelligence Committee and the CIA, with the approval of the president, and signed on June 6, 1984. Casey promised to provide the committee with any presidential Findings concerning covert action as well as with notification prior to implementation, even if the activity did not require separate higher authority or presidential approval. The CIA was also obligated to keep the committee fully informed on the progress and status of each covert operation and to give the committee a comprehensive annual briefing on all such activities.[28]

In retrospect, Senator Moynihan considered the behavior of the CIA and especially its director in the Nicaraguan mining episode to be "the outset of this challenge to American constitutional government," the "first acts of deception that gradually mutated into a policy of deceit." He saw the Iran-contra affairs two years later as the culmination of this insidious process. "In the history of the American Republic," he said, "I do not believe there has ever been so massive a hemorrhaging of trust and integrity. The very processes of American Government were put in harm's way by a conspiracy of faithless or witless men: sometimes both."[29]

The mining episode set off a congressional outburst that deprived the administration of its most important ally in Congress, Senator Goldwater. He was not so much opposed to the administration's contra policy in general as infuriated by the treatment of his committee in this instance. If Casey had not been so careless or devious in his handling of Goldwater's committee, the mining incident might well have had much less serious repercussions on the administration's Nicaraguan policy.

Thus a crisis of trust had already arisen between Congress and the executive branch by early 1984. Casey had shown that he was capable of conceiving of an outlaw operation, getting President Reagan's approval for it, and carrying it out surreptitiously—for a while. He had also shown himself to be vulnerable as soon as the story came out publicly. The operation was an indication of the political risks Reagan and Casey were willing to run in behalf of the contras. They might have learned from this experience that a covert activity that could not survive public and congressional knowledge was not likely to be worth the trouble. The result of the mining episode was most humiliating for Casey and seemingly forced him to agree to congressional conditions far more onerous than the ones that had previously bound him. If Casey had thought that he had stayed within the letter and spirit of the law, he would not have demeaned himself by apologizing for his behavior and agreeing to such conditions. Another president might have saved Casey the indignity by assuming responsibility himself for an action that he had approved. Instead, President Reagan let Casey take all the heat, as if the president had been an innocent bystander.

The congressional Iran-contra investigation brought out an aspect of the mining operation that had hitherto been hidden. Normally and legally, covert activities such as the mining were the sole responsibility of the CIA. In this case, however, a new element entered into the operation. It was the NSC staff in the person of Lieutenant Colonel Oliver L. North, the chief "action officer" for Central American affairs. He was privy to the mining and reported regularly about it to National Security Adviser McFarlane.

A message from North to McFarlane of March 2, 1984, before the congressional furor, brought the latter up to date on the operation. North reported that four magnetic mines had been emplaced in the harbor at Corinto, Nicaragua, on the night of February 29. Prior arrangements had been made for one of the contra groups to take credit for the operation. "Our intention," North wrote, "is to severely disrupt the flow of shipping essential to Nicaraguan trade during the peak period." The immediate objective was to destroy a tanker as the most effective way of "accomplishing our overall goal of applying stringent economic pressure," though "we could probably find a way to overtly stop the tanker from loading/ departing." North recommended that McFarlane should "approve this operation and brief the President." McFarlane and Reagan approved. This message showed that the operation was not exclusively in the hands of the CIA and that the NSC staff was closely implicated in it.[30]

The Nicaraguan government sued the United States in the International Court of Justice in The Hague for damages incurred in the mining incident. The verdict went against the United States, which took the position that it did not recognize the jurisdiction of the court in this matter and refused to pay the award. By 1990, according to Nicaraguan estimates, the amount had risen, with interest, to as much as $17 million and had disturbed relations with the post-Sandinista government headed by President Violeta Barrios de Chamorro.

8

By the end of 1984, as a result of the mining muddle and other misgivings, the majority in Congress was fed up with funding the contras. The administration had been put on notice the year before that the appropriation of $24 million was to be the last, even though it was expected to run out by the summer of that year.

The result of congressional disillusionment was another Boland Amendment, signed by the president on October 12, 1984, more drastic than the previous one. Known as Boland II, it prohibited any military or paramilitary support for the Nicaraguan contras for the period of October 3, 1984, to December 19, 1985, in these terms:

> No appropriations or funds made available pursuant to this joint resolution to the Central Intelligence Agency, the Department of Defense, or any other agency or entity of the United States involved in intelligence activities may be obligated or expended for the purpose or which would have the effect of supporting, directly or indirectly, military or paramilitary operations in Nicaragua by any nation, group, organization, movement or individual.

On the surface, this language would seem to be broad enough to prohibit any covert activity in behalf of the contras. If there was any doubt about the scope of the amendment, it should have been resolved by the debate before its passage in which Representative Boland, again the chief sponsor, had taken part. He had stated flatly that "the compromise provision clearly ends U.S. support for the war in Nicaragua." There then ensued the following exchange between Boland and Representative Robert L. Livingston of Louisiana:

> *Livingston:* Does this prohibition prevent any expenditure of funds, direct or indirect, for arms or weapons or use of force in Nicaragua by the United States?
>
> *Boland:* If it is directed against the government of Nicaragua, the answer would be in the affirmative, yes.
>
> *Livingston:* Are there no exceptions to the prohibition?
>
> *Boland:* There are no exceptions to the prohibition.[31]

Later in the same session, Representative Thomas S. Foley of Washington asked Boland whether the amendment would not restrict the authority of U.S. agencies other than intelligence agencies in distributing humanitarian aid to the contras. Boland answered, "Yes."

Opponents of the amendment had no difficulty grasping the scope of the amendment. Representative Dick Cheney of Wyoming went so far as to characterize it as a "killer amendment," designed to force the contras "to lay down their arms."

Lee H. Hamilton, chairman of the House Intelligence Committee, later explained the rationale behind the Boland Amendment:

> We drafted the Boland Amendment broadly for precisely the reason that we wanted to cover the National Security Council. And we briefed in the Committee and the intent of the Committee was to cover the National Security Council because it was involved in

intelligence activities. So members of that staff could not do their work without using intelligence.

The language says any other agency or entity of the United States involved in intelligence activities. If it were to cover the President, I think it would have to be precise and to include the President by term, by designation. I did not personally read the Boland Amendment as applying to the President except in the manner I have suggested to you. I did read it as applying to other entities of the United States Government that might be involved in intelligence activities and I certainly considered the National Security Council involved in intelligence activities.[32]

In any case, Hamilton pointed out, neither McFarlane nor Poindexter had ever claimed executive privilege to deny the committee the information it sought.[33]

Constitutionally, the question was not whether the amendment was good or bad. Once it was passed by the Senate and House of Representatives and signed by the president, it was the law of the land. Inasmuch as the CIA had been in charge of aid to the contras, the law was obviously aimed primarily at it. The law did not name the president, a point later made as a way of evading it, because he clearly could not act alone and would have had to act through governmental agencies specified directly or indirectly in the amendment.

But there were two troublesome issues that later arose about the Boland Amendment. One was—as in the case of the Hughes-Ryan Amendment—whether the NSC staff was an intelligence agency or entity covered by the Boland Amendment. In previous lists of intelligence agencies or the intelligence community, the NSC staff had not been included. The answer to this objection was that the Boland Amendment had gone beyond the specific enumeration of intelligence agencies, except for the obvious mention of the CIA and the Department of Defense, by including a general clause covering "any other agency or entity of the United States involved in intelligence activities." The other problem with the amendment was that attaching it to an appropriations bill gave it a life span of only one year. The issue would have to be debated and a similar amendment passed year after year, so long as the contras held out hope of overthrowing the Sandinista regime. As a result, the administration could think it possible to resort to stopgaps in the expectation that the next year's amendment might be defeated. The one-year span of the amendment was an invitation to seek ways of evading it until the next appropriations bill came around.

By the time Boland II was passed, however, the Reagan administration had committed itself to the care and feeding—or, as the president put it to National Security Adviser McFarlane, holding together the "body and soul"—of the contras at all costs. The problem for the administration was how to get around the amendment for the next twelve months.

For the present, only the status of the NSC staff need occupy us. One rationale for excluding it from coverage by the Boland Amendment rested on a distinction between a collecting intelligence agency and a coordinating one. The CIA was admittedly the first and thus came under the Boland Amendment; the NSC staff was supposedly not and therefore did not come under it. The implication was that the CIA was an operational agency, the NSC staff was not; the latter was merely an extension of the president's person and, in that sense, a recipient, not a collector, of intelligence information.

In practice, what counted most was what the NSC staff did, not what it was theoretically supposed to do or not do. The staff, especially Oliver North, was so freewheeling that the distinction between gathering or collecting and coordinating intelligence hardly mattered. NSC staff members routinely tried to get as much intelligence as possible in the course of their activities, especially when they could not get it from the CIA or other intelligence agencies. NSC staff members had been operational at least since President Lyndon Johnson had sent his national security adviser, McGeorge Bundy, to South Vietnam in 1964 and President Nixon had sent Henry Kissinger to China in 1971, but the staff was never so fully operational as it was during the Reagan administration. Yet hours of argument were expended during the Iran-contra hearings on the plea that the NSC staff was not an intelligence or an operational agency or entity and that it was just as immune as the president himself from congressional interference in the conduct of his office.

Thus the main factors and issues in the Iran-contra affairs—covert operations, NSC staff, Findings, the Boland Amendment—were in place, waiting to be fought over.

2

Body and Soul

In the beginning, U.S. support for the contras was virtually unconcealed. On May 4, 1983, President Reagan went so far as to say publicly that he was willing "to accept the idea of overt aid to the anti-Sandinista guerrillas in Nicaragua."[1] At about the same time, he committed himself to the principle that Congress had a role to play in Nicaragua as in any other aspect of foreign policy. In an address before a joint session of Congress, he said: "The Congress shares both the power and the responsibility for our foreign policy."[2]

Congress had shared the power and responsibility for foreign policy in passing the Boland Amendment, which was one of the ways Congress had to share such power and responsibility. Yet by the time of Boland I for 1983 and even more Boland II for 1984, the Reagan administration had committed itself to backing the contras at all costs. This policy could not be carried out without defying Congress. Open defiance was politically unfeasible. The only other way was to do it covertly.

Two methods were hit on. The amendments had prohibited the use of any funds available to the CIA, Department of Defense, or "any other agency or entity . . . involved in intelligence activities." This language seemed to leave two openings through which the administration might evade the barriers of the law.

One was to work through the NSC staff instead of the CIA, on the theory that the staff was not a proscribed intelligence agency or entity. The other was to use "private" or "third-country" funds, on the assumption that only U.S. official funds had been prohibited. The two methods were linked, because the national security adviser or members of his staff and other high officials were directly or indirectly active in getting private or third-country funds to the contras.

By this time Robert C. McFarlane was the national security adviser and Oliver L. North was a key member of his staff. Neither of their careers would seem to have been the best preparation for preeminent roles in both the contra and Iran affairs.

2

McFarlane's background was primarily military, though politics ran in the family; his father had been a Democratic congressman from Texas. After graduating from the Naval Academy at Annapolis in 1959, he had been commissioned in the U.S. Marine Corps and had served outstandingly in the Vietnam War, in which he had led the first U.S. combat unit. After some study in Switzerland and a White House fellowship, McFarlane's career shifted to a different track. Through acquaintance with another politicized military officer, General Alexander Haig, he was taken on as military assistant to then National Security Adviser Henry Kissinger, whose deputy was Haig. McFarlane retired from the Marines as a lieutenant colonel and spent two years on the staff of the Senate Armed Services Committee. When Haig became President Reagan's first secretary of state, he took McFarlane along as counselor of the department. In January 1982, as Haig was nearing the end of his short-lived secretaryship, McFarlane returned to the NSC staff as deputy—Haig's old job—to William P. Clark. In October 1983, McFarlane replaced Clark as national security adviser.[3]

McFarlane's record as deputy to Clark was marred by a tragic fiasco, for which he has been partially blamed. In September 1983, McFarlane was sent to Beirut as special Middle East envoy. He found himself between the Christian-dominated government headed by Amin Gemayel and an assortment of armed Moslem groups united only in their enmity to Gemayel. Meanwhile, a force of U.S. Marines had been sent to Beirut to support Gemayel's shaky government. On September 19, as Moslem forces attacked Gemayel's so-called Lebanese army, McFarlane is said to have ordered U.S. naval vessels offshore to come to its rescue by firing its heavy guns against the attackers, thus plunging the United States into the midst of the Lebanese civil war. Four days later, apparently in retaliation, a Moslem suicide mission in the form of a truck filled with dynamite drove into the Marine headquarters, killing 241 marines. McFarlane was blamed for the ill-advised naval bombardment that may have been linked to the suicide mission.[4] A member of the NSC staff has also accused McFarlane of staging "a premature grab for power" during the Lebanese crisis.[5] Whatever may have been McFarlane's poor judgment in Lebanon, he happened to be the man on the spot carrying out an official policy that was ill conceived and ill executed.

Early in his career as national security adviser, McFarlane infuriated Senator Daniel Patrick Moynihan. In April 1984, just as Moynihan was boiling over in reaction to the CIA's minings of the Nicaraguan harbor,

McFarlane chose to give an address at the Naval Academy in which he contended that the congressional oversight committees had been fully informed of the minings. It was McFarlane's statement that led Moynihan to resign temporarily from the Senate Select Committee on Intelligence.[6]

Yet McFarlane survived to meet far more serious challenges in the Iran and contra affairs. He had risen in the first three years of the Reagan administration from the comparative obscurity of a minor staff position to the critical post of national security adviser. That he was a serious, intelligent ex-marine and had been in a position to observe the political folkways of Washington for over a decade could in no way explain his sudden eminence in the presidential bureaucracy.

The most convincing explanation of the choice of McFarlane for national security adviser has come from Michael K. Deaver, then a member of the "White House troika." It included the White House counsel, Edwin Meese III, the chief of staff, James A. Baker III, and the deputy chief of staff, Deaver. Baker was supposed to replace Clark as national security adviser and Deaver to succeed Baker as chief of staff. A press release had been prepared to announce the changes when Reagan at the last minute confided them to Clark and Meese. They objected heatedly, on the ground that the moves would not sit well with the far right. Reagan was talked out of the plan, leaving Baker and Deaver in place and a vacancy in Clark's post.[7]

The decision for McFarlane to replace Clark thus was made more in order to avoid appointing Baker than for any other reason. McFarlane was both lucky to have a president who put him into office so cavalierly and unlucky to have a president who was equally cavalier about how his wishes were carried out. As the Lebanese naval shelling and the Nicaraguan harbor mining incidents showed, McFarlane was willing to take chances and assert himself on behalf of administration policy.

On the one hand, McFarlane saw himself as more than "an honest broker of advice coming to the President from outside the White House." He also thought of himself as "an independent adviser and policy manager for the president on national security affairs" and occasionally as "a policy initiator, placing issues on the agenda when the departments are unwilling and unable to do so." As he wrote in 1984, the national security adviser must even be "a policy arbitrator, drawing heavily upon his personal knowledge of the president's values."[8] This conception of the national security adviser's role was reminiscent of Henry Kissinger's and Zbigniew Brzezinski's in the Nixon and Carter administrations.

On the other hand, however, he did not have the personality or prestige to live up to this ambitious role. He did not have the self-confidence to stand up against a policy he privately believed was misguided or worse. In the rabidly anti-Communist atmosphere of the Reagan administration, McFarlane suppressed his doubts and conformed. When McFarlane was asked why he had not told the president that his NSC staff was not the

right instrument to use against the Nicaraguan regime, as McFarlane
professed to believe it was not, he replied:

> Succinctly put, where I went wrong was not having the guts to
> stand up and tell the President that. To tell you the truth, probably
> the reason I didn't is because if I had done that, Bill Casey, Jeane
> Kirkpatrick and Cap Weinberger [Secretary of Defense] would have
> said I was some kind of commie.[9]

McFarlane, like other national security advisers, was mercilessly overworked. The contra affair was only one of his responsibilities, and not
the major one. He came in to the office very early, held a staff meeting
every morning at 7:30, and had so much to do that he left the paperwork
for the evening, from 6 to 10 p.m., after everyone else had left.[10] The
strain of overwork and of not being equal to the contending chieftains
in the executive departments told on him and led him to take the easy
path of doing whatever he thought the president wanted him to do. For
someone like McFarlane, Reagan was not an easy president to serve,
because Reagan disliked matters of detail and was satisfied to make his
wishes known without giving his subordinates a clear idea of how to carry
them out.

3

McFarlane's chief "action officer," North, had a somewhat similar background but lacked the variety of McFarlane's political experience.

Oliver Laurence North, born in 1943, was raised in a small town in
New York State south of Albany. His father owned a textile mill; his
mother, a schoolteacher and a devout Catholic, instilled a deep religious
streak in him. He first attended a small teachers college but soon obtained
an appointment to the U.S. Naval Academy, following McFarlane by
several years. While at the Academy, North was injured in an auto
accident when the driver of the car struck a truck; his right knee required
two operations before he could return to school. After graduating in 1968,
he was sent to Vietnam, where he spent about a year as a platoon and
company commander in the 3rd Marine Division, coming out with a
Bronze Star, a Silver Star, two Purple Hearts, a Navy Commendation
Medal—and the memory of a war that he and others like him thought
should have been won at all costs. He spent the next three years, until
1973, as an instructor at the Quantico Naval Base, after which came a
one-year tour of duty at a training facility in Japan.

Whether as a result of delayed military strain or a personal crisis, in
early 1975 North suffered something resembling a psychological or emotional breakdown and spent twenty-two days in the Bethesda Naval Hos-

pital. After recovering, he was assigned for about three years to a desk job in the Manpower Division at Marine Headquarters in Washington. Now Major North, he went in 1978 as operations officer to Camp Lejeune, North Carolina, where he spent the next two years. In 1980, he was selected to attend the Naval War College in Newport, Rhode Island, for a year.

Thus far, North had been a fairly typical marine officer, moving from one military post to another. Yet North soon found himself in a post for which he was almost totally unprepared and which he said he did not want. "My Marine Corps career was untracked in 1981," he related, "when I was detailed to the National Security Council [staff]. I was uneasy at the beginning, but I came to believe that it was important work, and as years passed and responsibilities grew, I got further from that which I loved—the Marine Corps and Marines."[11] He came to the staff under Richard Allen on August 4, 1981, but, unlike McFarlane, never resigned from the Marine Corps so long as he was on the staff. It was supposed to be a temporary assignment; it lasted for about six years and came to an end that was not of his making.

It did not take North long to realize that he had left the Marines far behind. At his trial in 1989, a question-and-answer went:

Keker [Counsel]: Did you think by—at any time on November 21, 1986, that you had gotten a long way from the Marine Corps?

North: As soon as I entered into the covert operations field, Mr. Keker, I knew I was a long way from the Marine Corps.[12]

North first worked for Major General Robert L. Schweitzer, who directed the Defense Group on the staff. North's duties as a beginner were largely menial. Whatever North had to do, however, he struck Schweitzer as "hard-working, dedicated, very loyal to the president, and he understood what the president wanted to do."[13] From the outset, these qualities impressed his superiors and enabled North to get more and more important assignments, though he had had no experience or training to prepare him for them. He threw himself into every new responsibility as if his life or the country's safety depended on it.

North's first task under Allen was to work on a controversial sale of AWACS to Saudi Arabia. He apparently acquitted himself well, though his role was minor. When Allen was replaced by Clark, North was put on counterterrorism, which had become a major preoccupation of the government, on "crisis management," which amounted to planning while waiting for a crisis, and on contingency planning for such eventualities as a nuclear disaster. None of these promised to attract much immediate attention. North owed his first big chance to his fellow marine, Deputy National Security Adviser McFarlane, who was in a position to be his first mentor and patron. In 1982, McFarlane directed a Crisis Pre-Planning Group to deal with the crisis in Lebanon and appointed North its secretary.[14] In 1983, North was delegated to work on the U.S. intervention in Grenada and soon afterward was promoted to lieutenant colonel. At this time, North also began to take an increasing interest in Central America, a major concern of the Reagan administration. In the fall of 1983, he went down to Central America as the NSC staff's liaison with the Kissinger Commission, a twelve-member board appointed to give the administration a more popular policy on Central America. It visited six countries in six days and made its members instant experts.

Nevertheless, North would have been just another marine lieutenant colonel if he had gone back to the Marines in 1984 as had been planned. He had received a special assignment from the Marines to the NSC staff in 1981 for a three-year period. In the spring of 1984, the Marine Corps called North back to the 2nd Marine Division at Camp Lejeune, North Carolina, a step which entailed a promotion to infantry battalion commander. By this time, McFarlane considered North too valuable to lose. According to General Paul X. Kelly, commandant of the Marine Corps, McFarlane asked him to give North an extension of one year. Kelly argued against it on the ground that it would damage North's career by keeping him out of the mainstream of the Marine Corps. McFarlane and Kelly compromised on six months. North was sufficiently known in like-minded circles for CIA Director Casey and UN Ambassador Jeane Kirkpatrick to intervene on his behalf.*[15]

In October 1984, North was again reprieved. He was ordered to attend the Naval War College in Newport, Rhode Island, but he protested that it would create undue hardship for his family because it was too far away and he wanted to stay in closer proximity to Washington. McFarlane again asked for an extension, against Kelly's better judgment. "We left it," General Kelly recalled, "at a sort of impasse whereby he could stay as long as he was doing those relevant things but we wanted him back just as soon as we could conceivably get him back so we did not do damage to his career." This time North was given an extension of one year.[16]

In this period, a mutual friend brought North together with retired Air Force Major General Richard V. Secord, who had first met North in 1981, to discuss North's future. Secord urged him to go to the Naval War College "if he wanted to progress to senior ranks" in the Marine Corps. But North, according to Secord, now considered his work on the NSC staff to be of "transcending importance."[17]

---

* Meese said that Casey called him about May 13, 1984, requesting him to prevent North from returning to the Marine Corps "because there were critical problems with respect to Central America." It seems that Meese thought North had been reassigned "in deference to Colonel North's career because the transfer back to the Marine Corps would have given him the opportunity to command a battalion at Camp Lejeune." Instead, North stayed on the NSC staff (Meese, NT, pp. 5741–42).

In this way, someone who was cut out to be a marine commander was transformed into a covert operator. At his trial, North looked back at his initiation and said: "I didn't know the first thing about covert operations when I started in this."[18] North also explained that one reason he went to Casey so often for advice was that "he was the expert on covert operations and I certainly was not."[19] That someone like North should have been chosen to take charge of two of the most tangled covert operations in U.S. history was fortuitous. The tasks ordinarily should have gone to someone in the CIA who presumably had been trained for them or who at least had the full backing of the Agency. But the Boland Amendment put Casey in the position of hiding behind someone in another agency and yet controlling the operation from behind the scenes. North, a novice, was expected to do for the CIA what the CIA could no longer openly do alone. In other circumstances, Oliver North would have served out his three years on the NSC staff and gone back to lead an infantry battalion in the Marine Corps.

4

Sometime in 1984, according to McFarlane, President Reagan told him to make sure to keep the contras together "body and soul." This statement, McFarlane said, was made in the presence of Vice President George Bush and Chief of Staff James Baker.*[20] The phrase "body and soul" seemed to express the lengths to which Reagan was willing to go on behalf of the contras. But just what the phrase meant was later put in doubt by McFarlane himself. He claimed that he had explained to North that Reagan's instruction meant no more than that North should try to turn the contras into a "credible political organization" in order to impress Congress that it was "a political movement of real substance interested in negotiation."[21] The difficulty with McFarlane's alleged interpretation is that stressing the strictly political side of the contras' cause in the United States was likely to be far from enough to keep them together "body and soul."

McFarlane also testified that his discussions with Congress had convinced him that the NSC staff was covered by the Boland Amendment.[22] If so, there was no part of the U.S. government in a position to violate the amendment; the CIA, which had previously kept the contras together body and soul, recognized that it could no longer do so, and the NSC staff could not, if McFarlane is to be believed, take the CIA's place.

North confirmed that McFarlane had told him of the president's instructions to keep "the body and soul of the contras together."[23] But

---

* It is not hard to believe that Reagan said some such words to McFarlane, since on March 1, 1985, Reagan publicly called the con ras "the moral equivalent of the Founding Fathers" (*Weekly Compilation of Presidential Documents*, March 11, 1985, p. 245).

North also testified that in his opinion Boland did not apply to the NSC staff and that he had never heard McFarlane say that it did apply.[24] To make matters even more perplexing, McFarlane admitted that President Reagan did not agree with him about Boland. Referring to "things proscribed by the Congress," McFarlane said that the president "had a far more liberal interpretation of that than I did."[25] Nevertheless, Reagan and McFarlane protected themselves by telling subordinates to "obey the law," even in reference to Boland.[26]

This was not the only contradiction. McFarlane also said that he had made a special point of stressing to his staff "not to solicit, encourage, coerce or otherwise broker financial contributions to the contras."[27] But again North testified that he could not remember receiving any such instructions from McFarlane.[28]

These apparent disagreements between McFarlane and North were never resolved. Yet they concerned the two methods the administration had hit on by which to get around the Boland Amendment—the substitution of the NSC staff for the CIA, and the use of private or third-country funds to support the contras. North himself let on what the difficulties of his position were. "My understanding was," he said, "that, first of all, we were to work to comply with Boland and that we were to work to keep alive the Nicaraguan Resistance."[29] If that was his understanding, it was contradictory. If "we," including himself, were told to work to comply with Boland, there was no point in maintaining that "we" did not need to comply with Boland.

Complying with Boland and keeping the contras together "body and soul" were not compatible. If McFarlane really meant to confine North to impressing Congress that the contras were a credible political organization, they were hardly likely to succeed in keeping them together body and soul. Congress was just then in no mood to be impressed, and there was no telling how long it would take to transform the contras into a credible political organization. If McFarlane's version of how compliance with the Boland Amendment would limit what North could do for the contras can be trusted, North may have had good reason not to take McFarlane's admonitions seriously.

McFarlane had further trouble explaining himself. He gave this reason why the president had been forced to turn to the NSC staff for the Nicaraguan covert operation:

> Congressional restrictions made it impractical for either the Defense Department or the Central Intelligence Agency to function even as a liaison with the Contras. The State Department has always been disinclined to be associated with a covert action.
>
> But the President had made clear that he wanted a job done. The net result was that the job fell to the National Security Council staff. I think it is fair to say that this occurrence was not an example

of an NSC staff eagerly grabbing power from other departments and agencies. In the case of the Contra operations, it was the NSC that was the agency of last resort.[30]

The trouble with this explanation is that there would have been no need to resort to the NSC staff for a covert operation unless there had been an intention to get around the Boland Amendment. The job the president wanted done for the contras could only be done covertly if it were to escape the attention of Congress.

Yet McFarlane may not have known all that North did for the contras for the same reason that President Reagan later claimed that he did not know. McFarlane was twice asked why North had kept information from him and answered that he had to believe that North had done it "to protect me."[31] Protecting a superior who wanted something done without being caught at it was an old Washington custom.

5

By 1984, North was the NSC staff's "point of contact" with the contras in recognition of his service as the staff's representative with the so-called Kissinger Commission the year before.[32] In the spring of 1984, McFarlane instructed North "to go make contact with the Resistance." North went down to Central America to be introduced to the contra leadership by Dewey R. (Duane) Clarridge, then the flamboyant head of the CIA's Latin American Division.[33]

North's larger role in the Nicaraguan operation was stage-managed by the CIA's Casey. We know what Casey had in mind for North from the testimony of Vincent Cannistraro, a senior official in the CIA until he transferred to the NSC staff in December 1984.

In a meeting in Casey's office in early 1984 before the passage of the second Boland Amendment, Casey, Clarridge, Joseph Fernandez, the head of the CIA's Latin American Task Force, Cannistraro, and a contra leader met to discuss future strategy. Cannistraro explained the motive:

> Mr. Casey had wanted to meet with the senior official of the contras in order to explain to him that there was a lot of Congressional sentiment running against continuation of the paramilitary program, that he, Bill Casey, wanted to assure the Freedom Fighters that the United States Government would find a way to continue its support to the Freedom Fighters after the 30th of September, 1984, if the Boland Amendment became part of the operational restrictions against the involvement of CIA.

Casey pointed out that North, as a member of the NSC staff, would not be subject to the Boland restrictions and therefore would be "a principal point of reference." Casey told the group that "he had discussed this with the President of the United States and that it was agreed with the President that this was how it should be handled."[34] Casey added that "the President was committed to sustaining the contras and that the President agreed that Colonel North would be the principal point of reference following the passage of the Boland Amendment."[35]

In the late spring of 1984, Clarridge, Cannistraro, and North met with Adolfo Calero, one of the three civilian leaders of the FDN, to make known to Calero that North had been designated "as the authorized spokesman of the White House to deal with the contras."[36] A few weeks later, the four met in North's office to convey the message that North was going to be the only one to deal with the contras after October 1, 1984.[37] As North put it, he was told in the late summer of 1984, before Boland was passed: "Okay, you have got it all." He understood that it meant he was to replace the CIA.[38]

North boasted that, after the withdrawal of the CIA from active support of the contras, "I was given the job of holding them together in body and soul," and that after Boland II was passed in October of that year "I was the only person left talking to them . . . The U.S. contact with the Nicaraguan Resistance was me, and I turned to others to help carry out that activity."[39]

Foremost among the "others" to whom North turned was retired Air Force Major General Richard V. Secord. He was the model of a modern American major general—blunt, stocky, can-do, a seasoned veteran. By 1984, Secord had spent twenty-eight of his fifty-two years in the U.S. Air Force. He had served tours of duty in Vietnam, Laos, and elsewhere. He had commanded the Air Force Mission to Iran from 1975 to 1978, getting out six months before the fall of the Shah. He had headed the U.S. Air Force International Programs office in the Pentagon from 1978 to 1981, after which he was appointed deputy assistant secretary of defense in charge of the Middle East, Africa, and Southern Asia. Secord had never worked in Latin America, but that was no deterrent for one of his varied experience.[40]

Secord's official career came to an abrupt end in 1983, when he retired from the air force in compromising circumstances. He was linked with the former CIA agent Edwin P. Wilson, who was convicted of selling arms to the Libyan regime of Muammar al-Qaddafi. Secord's suspected ties with Wilson were investigated for about three years, after which he was officially cleared of having broken the law. Nevertheless, enough doubt about him remained so that he was denied a security clearance and could never get it back. Secord retired in a falling-out with the Defense Department, because, he said, senior officials had refused to provide him with counsel and he had incurred legal expenses that had put him in debt.[41]

Secord first met North in 1981 in connection with the sale of AWACS to Saudi Arabia. Secord had been senior representative of the Pentagon to the Interagency Group that dealt with the sale. North was attached to the group for the NSC staff and given such tasks as scheduling meetings.[42] In their second encounter three years later, Secord was a frustrated, rejected old warrior and North a rising young star. In 1984, according to North, Casey suggested to him that he should set up "outside entities" to support the contras, ostensibly to "comply" with the Boland Amendment by getting around it. Casey recommended Secord as someone who could be useful in this connection.[43]

Meanwhile, Secord had found employment that was just the kind of thing that Casey had had in mind. While chief of the Air Force Mission in Iran, Secord had made the acquaintance of Albert Hakim, an Iranian businessman. Hakim had spent his first twenty years in Iran, had then come to California for one year in high school and three years at a technical college, after which he had returned to Iran. There Hakim had prospered, mainly by selling U.S.-made electronic equipment to the Iranian government, particularly its air force. In 1978, just in time to get out before the Shah's collapse, Hakim had returned to the United States, where he continued to do the same sort of business on an increasingly large scale. He became an American citizen and looked around for U.S. government deals.

At this point, Hakim and Secord joined forces. When Secord retired in 1983, Hakim offered to take him in as a partner in his Stanford Technology Trading Group International on the West Coast. Hakim operated with seven or eight different companies, the most important of which figured prominently in the contra and Iran affairs.[44] He had an agent in Geneva, Switzerland, set up Energy Resources International for arms purchases for the contras, mainly from Defex, a Portuguese arms dealer. Lake Resources, Inc., was incorporated in Panama with a bank account at the Crédit Suisse bank in Geneva. A third, Hyde Park Square Corporation, also shared in the Hakim-Secord financial manipulations. The Geneva agent, Willard Zucker, testified that millions of dollars went into these accounts and that the profits went to Hakim and Secord.[45]

As North told the story, Casey had suggested Secord to North "as a person who had a background in covert operations" and "who got things done, and who had been poorly treated." In the summer of 1984, North approached Secord and asked him to become "actively engaged" in behalf of the contras. Secord took some time to think it over and then agreed.[46] Hakim came in as Secord's partner. Secord took charge of technical operations and Hakim of finances. They agreed to split all profits equally.

To get Secord started, North introduced him to Adolfo Calero, whose background made him an ideal go-between. A Nicaraguan by birth, he had been educated in the United States at a boarding school in New Orleans and at Notre Dame University. Returning to Nicaragua, he had spent twenty-five years as the manager of a Coca-Cola bottling plant in Managua. He was one of those who had first opposed the Somoza regime and then its Sandinista successors. Forced out of Nicaragua in 1983, he joined the FDN, the exiles' main armed opposition, and became the CIA's favorite leader in it. Calero's former business had been dependent on a U.S. company, and now his movement was dependent on the U.S. government.

At a subsequent meeting with Calero, Secord brought with him Rafael Quintero, known as "Chi-Chi," a Cuban exile who had previously been a CIA intelligence officer for Central America. Quintero had left Cuba for the United States in 1959 soon after Castro had come to power. Quintero had been picked up by the CIA and trained to go back to Cuba to prepare for the ill-fated Bay of Pigs invasion in 1961. He had been taken prisoner and had escaped, after which he had worked for the CIA for about ten years, then had spent some years working for other U.S. agencies.[47]

Secord, who knew little about the region, had taken Quintero on as his adviser and agent. Quintero specialized in the transportation of weapons to the contras, for which he was paid $4,000 per month plus a bonus of $5,000 for each air shipment and $10,000 for each boat shipment. He received $228,378 for 1985 and 1986, on which he did not pay taxes.[48]

Secord had been put in touch with Quintero by another former CIA official, Thomas Clines, for whom Quintero had worked in the CIA.[49] Secord and Clines had first met in 1968, when they had served together in the "secret war" in Laos.[50] Both Clines and Quintero had been linked with the CIA renegade Edwin Wilson. Clines had paid a $10,000 criminal fine and a $100,000 civil fine for the overbilling of the U.S. government by a transport company with which he had been associated. Secord recruited Clines as an expert in the procurement of weapons.

At a meeting with Secord and Quintero, Calero chiefly complained that the contras were paying too much for their arms and needed to find some way to bring down the cost. Secord went off with a list of needed arms and took it to a Canadian arms dealer, Transworld Armament, to see whether he could do better. He could—and eventually the first arms deal was struck in November 1984 between Calero for the contras and the Secord-Hakim combination. One transaction with the Canadian arms dealer involved a small shipload of munitions from the Far East, another a planeload of approximately 90,000 pounds from Europe.[51]

When the Canadian arms dealer failed to deliver his arms on time, Secord brought Clines in to replace him as his procurement agent. Clines obtained his arms mainly from Defex, later encountered in an episode of the Iran affair. After Clines obtained the arms, Quintero took charge of their arrival in Central America, delivering them to the contras and dealing with local authorities.[52] By the summer of 1985, Secord was made the contras' sole purchasing agent, a function previously entrusted to Adolfo Calero's brother, Mario. After rumors spread that Mario was mishandling the money, North and Secord decided to replace him with Secord.[53] Subsequently, Mario Calero complained that "they were getting ripped off by Secord."[54] Secord, Hakim, and Clines charged on an average a 20 percent markup, the profits divided among the three of them.[55]

In the end, Secord sold about $11 million worth of arms and other equipment to the contras. North said that he never knew what Secord was getting out of it.[56] Secord and Hakim were happy to combine patriotism and profit. They felt that they were serving their country by doing the work that the CIA had previously done, at the request of someone in a commanding, official position like North's, at the same time lining their pockets as businessmen were supposed to do. It seemed possible to serve both God and mammon.

Secord's most difficult and ambitious service for the contras was an airlift operation to make parachute drops to resupply contra forces in the field. Begun in November 1985, this operation caused Secord to bring in Richard B. Gadd. Gadd was another specialist in covert operations with over twenty years in the armed services. As a lieutenant colonel in the air force, he had first met Secord in connection with the abortive attempt to rescue the American hostages in Iran in 1980.[57] Retired since 1982, Gadd had set up a number of shadowy companies through which he claimed to have assisted the U.S. government in covert and other activities. Secord and Hakim leased space in Gadd's office complex and also made use of his staff. In January 1985, Secord asked Gadd to arrange charter flights for the delivery of munitions from Portugal to Guatemala. Gadd used Southern Air Transport, based in Miami, which had been a CIA "proprietary" during the Vietnam War. Later, Gadd was Secord's chief aide in the dangerous and ultimately exposed operation to drop supplies from the air to contra forces in Nicaragua.[58]

In effect, Secord organized a shadow CIA type of covert operation with the help of former CIA agents and retired military officers like himself. As North later explained, Secord's operation was like the CIA's previous operation by another name.

What General Secord did was to set up a series of organizations that would do what the CIA had done before, set up a company to do air supply. Set up a company to obtain weapons. These were the kind of—set up a company to deliver this stuff. That is essentially what the CIA had been doing before. Boland would prohibit the CIA from doing it, would prohibit the U.S. Government, the Pentagon, the CIA from doing it so you had to go outside and he basically created a mirror image outside the government of what the CIA had done.[59]

Thus the NSC staff, through North, could not take the place of the CIA without reproducing a miniature CIA. It had the advantage of being made up of private citizens who did not have to testify before congressional committees and get payments that could be traced to the U.S. government. So long as North was the only point of contact with the government, the system—or as it sometimes called itself, the "Enterprise"— was much less vulnerable to exposure.

To carry out his new assignment, North was given a special setup within the NSC staff. He was made deputy director for political-military affairs, a vague title that set him apart from the traditional divisions of the staff.* North did not fit into the normal table of organization; his position was created for him alone, insulated from the rest of the staff. He dealt directly with the national security adviser, who was the only one above him. For some time, it was virtually a one-man operation; only later was he given two aides, Lieutenant Colonel Robert Earl, also a marine and a classmate of North's at the Naval Academy, and Lieutenant Commander Craig P. Coy, originally of the Coast Guard—both on temporary assignment from their services. North, Earl, and Coy formed a separate, wholly military enclave above which was, first, a former marine, McFarlane, later an admiral, Poindexter. In effect, North's mission to replace the CIA's operation in Nicaragua was implemented by setting him up on his own, free from the usual bureaucratic restraints of a staff position. So long as his immediate superior, McFarlane or Poindexter, was complaisant about his activities, North could go about organizing a miniature CIA that owed its existence and allegiance to him personally. In this respect, it was only nominally an NSC staff operation or at least a very unusual one for the NSC staff.

6

North occupied an anomalous position on the NSC staff. He was a military man on a normally political staff. He was now in a position to be both the political representative to the contras and the commander in chief of the military system he had set up. This dual role was irresistible to one of his activist temperament and professional training. Later North claimed that he had merely provided the contras with "broader strategic military advice," not the planning of "any specific tactical operation."[60] Even such military advice was not in keeping with the function of an

---

* There was another Political-Military Affairs Directorate headed by Howard Teicher in the NSC staff, but it was wholly separate from North's operation.

NSC staff member, but what North said he did and what the contemporary documents produced by him say he did were not the same.

One early example of North's role is recorded in a memorandum from North to McFarlane, dated November 7, 1984. It reports that Calero was then worried about the delivery to the Sandinistas of Soviet HIND-D helicopters. Calero complained that he had not been warned of the delivery by the CIA and advised that he was making plans to "take out" the machines. For this operation, he turned to North to provide him with all possible information on their location. North promised to try to do so.

North called Robert Vickers, the national intelligence officer for Latin America, and General Paul F. Gorman, head of the U.S. Army's Southern Command. Gorman recalled that he had briefed North on the helicopters but had not known that the information was supposed to go to Calero's FDN and that he had not briefed him for that purpose.[61] North was able to tell Calero where the HINDs had been moved. North continued his efforts to get more information to Calero about the HINDs and Nicaraguan antiaircraft defenses. Calero reported to North on plans made to attack the HINDs.[62]

McFarlane was later asked whether North had violated the Boland Amendment by asking Vickers and Gorman for information on the location of the helicopters. McFarlane replied: "Well, on its face I would think if that information in turn were provided to the Contras, that it would."[63]

The Soviet helicopters came up in another memorandum to McFarlane, dated December 4, 1984. North reported that, at the request of Secretary of the Navy John Lehman, he had met with David Walker, a British subject who headed two companies "which provide professional security services to foreign governments." Walker had suggested to North that "he would be interested in establishing an arrangement with the FDN for certain special operations expertise aimed particularly at destroying HIND helicopters." North agreed with Walker that it would be easier to destroy the helicopters on the ground than from the air. North advised McFarlane: "Unless otherwise directed, Walker will be introduced to Calero and efforts will be made to defray the cost of Walker's operations from other than Calero's limited assets."[64]

When North was questioned about Walker, who continued to be active in behalf of the contras into the next year, North testified:

Representative Thomas S. Foley: David Walker is an international arms and security specialist [who] is a British subject, is that right?

North: That's my understanding, yes, sir.

Foley: Did you authorize or have any discussions with him regarding activities inside Nicaragua?

North: I did.

Foley: Did you authorize him to perform military actions in Nicaragua?

North: I did.

Foley: What were those actions?

North: David Walker was involved, his organization, as I understand it, in support of the Nicaraguan Resistance with internal operations in Managua and elsewhere in an effort to improve the perception that the Nicaraguan Resistance could operate anywhere that it so desired. . . .

Foley: We are talking about military actions, attacks on military aircraft of the Sandinista Government?

North: Yes, sir.

Foley: Did you directly authorize that?

North: I didn't directly authorize anything. I encouraged Mr. Walker to be in touch with the people who could benefit from that—the expertise that he had.[65]

Whether directing or encouraging, North was clearly the Calero-Walker go-between without whom the arrangement would not have gone through. The intention was to make everyone believe that the contras were capable of operating anywhere in Nicaragua, even in the capital, by hiring some British mercenaries to do the work for them.

In the end, Walker was not much good. Only one raid by his men seems to have come off—the explosion of an arms depot in Managua, the capital of Nicaragua, on March 6, 1985.[66] North once referred to Walker's operation as that of "my British friend."[67] The planned attack on the Sandinistas' helicopters was aborted because Walker finally considered it to be too dangerous. Later, Walker's men again disappointed. This fiasco was described by Colonel Robert C. Dutton, whom Secord had later hired.

Dutton was another air force officer, with twenty-six and a half years in the service, almost twenty of them in "special operations." He had served in Vietnam and in the abortive operation headed by Secord to rescue the American embassy hostages in Tehran in 1980.[68] Dutton told a tale about one of Walker's more striking disappointments.

North and Secord, according to Dutton, had drawn up a plan to hire a British crew from Walker, consisting of two pilots and a loadmaster, to fly a mission inside Nicaragua. Walker's men were taken on, Dutton said, because "we did not want to have to expose Americans to those kinds of flight." Unfortunately, Dutton himself went on a flight with one of the pilots and discovered that he had not flown enough in the required type of plane and that the other did not have sufficient experience. The British group also had some trouble in the country from which the flight was to take off and were asked to leave. As a result, the plan was never carried out, though Walker was apparently paid for his trouble.[69]

Even more indicative of North's intervention was another early project that could not be carried out. In a memorandum to McFarlane, dated February 6, 1985, North sent word that a Nicaraguan merchant ship, the *Monimbo*, was unloading cargo at Teichung, Taiwan, and was expected to stop over at Shikama, Japan, for engine repairs. It was apparently suspected of carrying arms via North Korea to the Sandinistas in Nicaragua. To prevent this delivery, North presented three options:

The shipment could be seized and the weapons delivered to the FDN;

the ship could be sunk; or

the shipment and the [deleted] parties involved therein could be made public as a means of preventing the delivery.

North noted that, despite the sensitive cargo, there was apparently no armed security detail aboard the ship. Calero, he went on, was willing to finance an operation to seize the ship on the high seas but unfortunately did not have a sufficient number of trained maritime "special operations personnel" to do the job. North thought that it would be best to seize the ship as it cleared the East China Sea en route to the Nicaraguan port of Corinto, which had been mined the year before. North evidently had in mind a U.S. covert operation or one for which Calero could find the means. His concluding words were:

If time does not permit a special operation to be launched, Calero can quickly be provided with the maritime assets required to sink the vessel before it can reach port at Corinto. He is in contact with maritime operations experts and purveyors of material necessary to conduct such an operation.

Significantly, North asked McFarlane to "authorize Calero to be provided with the information on *Monimbo* and approached on the matter of seizing or sinking the ship." It was evidently up to McFarlane to decide what Calero was going to do. This memorandum also contained a handwritten note signed by the deputy national security adviser, Poindexter: "We need to take action to make sure ship does not arrive in Nicaragua."[70] It appears that the action was never carried out, because another government refused to be drawn into it.[71]

When McFarlane was later asked about this message, he first replied evasively that he *may* have seen it at the time and did not authorize this action. From the documentary evidence, there can be no doubt that it was brought to his attention. He also said that he did not "fault him [North] for it," that North was an "energetic" person who tried to accomplish his mission by trying to be "imaginative and to think up things that hopefully will be both prudent, feasible, successful, wise, but that many times they don't."[72]

If McFarlane was able to be so untroubled about this incident at the congressional hearings, long after the event, one can understand why North thought that his superiors tolerated or encouraged him to be "imaginative" and "aggressive." McFarlane, after all, also claimed that he had told his staff that it was covered by the Boland Amendment, which could not, however imaginatively, have permitted planning by North to sink a Nicaraguan ship. At this time, North had taken over the contra cause only a few months earlier and Boland II was less than four months old. North was clearly learning on the job by doing what was expected of him.

For North, another difficulty with the Boland Amendment was that he could not give intelligence advice to the contras from his own resources. North admitted that he had obtained the intelligence information from the CIA and the Department of Defense. Yet they were expressly forbidden to pass such information on to the contras. "That is why we did it that way," North explained. He also justified this side of his activity by protesting that the higher-ups knew about it. He named Vice Admiral Arthur Moreau of the Joint Chiefs of Staff office, the CIA's deputy director of operations, the chief of the Central American Task Force, two CIA station chiefs in Central America, and CIA Director Casey.[73] North often seemed to think that he could clear himself by pleading that his superiors knew what he was doing. Others might draw the conclusion that if there was any wrongdoing all of them were culpable.

"I never did sit down in the battlefield, and sit and plan a specific tactical operation with them," North insisted, referring to the contras.[74] He did practically everything else.

7

While North was engaging Secord and company, he recruited a more personal addition to his unofficial entourage. More than any one else, Robert W. Owen, otherwise known as "TC" or "The Courier," exemplified North's methods.

Owen was not yet thirty when he began his political career working for Republican Senator Dan Quayle of Indiana, later vice president. One day in 1983, an Indiana constituent who owned land in Costa Rica, John Hull, came in with a small delegation to talk about the threat from the Sandinistas. Owen was delegated to listen to their story and was so impressed by it that he made appointments for them to repeat it in the Senate and House of Representatives, the Department of Defense, and the NSC staff. At the latter he met North for the first time.[75] In August 1984, Owen, now working in Dallas as a "volunteer for Reagan" during the presidential campaign, again met North, who was there to make a speech for a conservative organization. Owen had picked him up at the airport and had taken part in informal conversations with North, Calero, and former General John K. Singlaub, an early fund-raiser for the contras.[76]

Meanwhile, Owen left the Quayle office and took a job with the public relations firm of Gray & Co. in Washington, a step which again led him to North. Sometime in 1984, Owen said, the firm was approached by Calero's FLN to represent the contras.[77] Owen was asked to look into the proposal and went to see North to get to know more about it. North told him that the contras were running out of money and had been advised to look for "representation" in Washington to get more. The Gray-contra deal never went through, but Owen was now determined to make the contras his cause. He met with Calero and offered to leave Gray & Co. to work for the contras full-time. Calero took him on and agreed to pay him $2,500 a month plus expenses. Owen wrote to North about his new job and offered to help him in every possible way. A week later, North asked Owen to go down to Honduras and deliver photographs and maps obtained from the CIA showing the gun emplacements around the airport in Managua, Nicaragua, to Calero. On his return trip, Owen brought North a list of needed munitions from Calero.[78]

Owen was now "working with" North, as Owen put it in a letter to North of July 2, 1984. It was addressed to "Dear Ollie" and signed "Rob." This letter showed how their relationship had progressed and what role Owen was to play. "Your commitment to this country," it said at the outset, "to truth and justice, and to man's freedom is an example that so many people can and should learn from." It went on to tell North about "the toys we talked about"—"toys" meant "arms," Owen later explained. Owen warned North that a certain journalist, who was working on a story dealing with the CIA's role in covert actions, could not be trusted. Someone who had "access to the contacts for the toys" wanted to meet North—"obviously off-the-record with no promises, just feelers." A contra leader in Florida had given him figures on immediate needs for two weeks ($100,000), one month's cost for food for 10,000 contras ($150,000), and "firecracker [another term for arms] costs" ($1,500,000). "To close on a positive note," the letter said, "may I just say it is a pleasure and an honor working with you."[79] Owen was an instant hero-worshipper.

From then on, Owen became North's "eyes and ears" in the contra affair. One of Owen's lengthy reports to North was addressed to "The Hammer," another to "Steelhammer," from "TC," as Owen was pleased to call himself.[80] Another of Owen's nicknames for North was "BG" or "Blood and Guts."[81]

Owen met with contra leaders in Washington and elsewhere, traveled to Costa Rica to reconnoiter the ground for a secret airfield, and acted as if he were North's personal investigator or emissary. In November 1984, North again gave him maps and photographs, obtained from the CIA, for delivery to the contras for a military operation to destroy Sandinista equipment. Owen flew to Honduras and gave the maps, with North's opinion of the operation's probable success, to Calero.[82]

In February 1985, North sent Calero a letter via Owen in which he informed the contra leader that a sum in excess of $20 million would be deposited in "the usual account," referring to a Swiss bank account. He advised Calero to use $9 to $10 million "for nothing but logistics." He also urged him "to make use of it for my British friend [Walker] and his services for special operations. I can produce him at the end of this month." In conclusion, North warned:

> Please do *not* in any way make *anyone* aware of the deposit. Too much is becoming known by too many people. We need to make sure that this new financing does *not* become known. The Congress must believe that there continues to be an urgent need for funding.[83]

Conspiring with Calero to deceive Congress was evidently not regarded by North as a serious transgression, because he repeatedly admitted "misleading" Congress.[84] On the way back from delivering this letter, Owen brought to North from Calero a list of arms and munitions needed by the contras. Owen agreed that Calero had sent the list so that North "could fulfill those ammunition needs." According to Owen, "Colonel North was in essence at times the quartermaster of the effort, and when various equipment was needed, it would usually be discussed with him or asked how he could supply the assistance."[85]

One of the richest stories to come out was how North put Owen on a government payroll. In 1984, when Owen went to work for North as his "secret agent"—Owen said that he would not "quibble" at the term[86]—Owen was paid by Calero. This arrangement lasted only until North could find another source of funds for Owen. At North's suggestion, Owen formed a tax-deductible, tax-exempt, nonprofit organization entitled Institution for Democracy, Education and Assistance, Inc. (IDEA). The money to fund it came from Calero. It had no employees; Owen was its only unpaid "volunteer." It had no office; Owen worked out of his home. IDEA was Owen. For most of 1985, little or nothing came of it.[87]

North still had to find a way to pay for Owen's services. The opportunity came when Congress in July 1985 voted $27 million in humanitarian aid to the contras with the stipulation that it could not be administered by the CIA or the Department of Defense. As a result, a new organization, the Nicaraguan Humanitarian Assistance Office (NHAO), was set up in the State Department to administer the aid. A former ambassador, Robert W. Duemling, was put in charge of the NHAO. Now North had something to work on to get Owen a piece of the $27 million.

Duemling was a thirty-year veteran foreign service officer on the verge of retirement, with almost no experience in the work to which he was assigned. Duemling prepared for his job by going to see North on September 11, 1985. Duemling explained that "I was told that nobody in Washington knew more about the contras than Oliver North." They talked about the state of the contras, what they needed, and how the NHAO could fit into whole picture.[88] What Duemling did not know was that North already had in mind putting Owen on the NHAO's payroll.[89] North told Owen that "it was time to make me [Owen] a little bit more legitimate than I had been in the past."[90]

One week later, on September 18, 1985, at North's suggestion, Owen came to see Duemling for a job. According to Duemling's notes at the time, Owen told him that he had his own consulting company on Central America; knew the three contra leaders, Adolfo Calero, Arturo Cruz, and Alfonso Robelo; knew "Ollie North very closely"; had no connection with the CIA or the Department of Defense; and was a "believer in the cause," a "true believer." For various reasons, Duemling answered noncommittally.[91]

On September 24, 1985, North came to see Duemling on behalf of Owen. Duemling's notes read: "North wants me to use Rob Owen. He is 'can-do' and knows the scene." North merely told Duemling that he was a good friend of Owen and did not let on what their actual relationship was. Duemling was still disposed to hold off hiring Owen; he later said that he merely looked on "the North-Owen relationship as being part of this whole crowd of Republicans who are helping the contras and so forth."[92]

The campaign for Owen soon took another turn. On October 3, 1985, the contra triumvirate—Calero, Cruz, and Robelo—sent Duemling a letter, composed by Owen, formally requesting the NHAO to give IDEA a "monthly donation" of $4,850 to pay for "the full time services of Mr. Owen" for the purpose of working "on behalf of the UNO [United Nicaraguan Opposition]." It was to be a most peculiar arrangement; the NHAO was expected to subsidize Owen indirectly through his IDEA, which was a virtually nonexistent organization dedicated wholly to the support of its one unpaid official, Robert W. Owen.[93]

An embarrassing incident soon gave North another reason for pressing the case for Owen. On October 10, 1985, an NHAO flight from New Orleans was permitted by Mario Calero, without authorization, to bring along a commercial television crew. The plane landed on the military side of a Honduran airport without proper clearance for the television crew. The Honduran military had not been forewarned, and the presence of the television crew was regarded as a violation of a highly sensitive arrangement. The Honduran government protested to Washington and suspended NHAO flights for several months.[94]

On October 17, 1985, Duemling attended a meeting of the Restricted Interagency Group (RIG), a top-level body on Central American policy, in which the dominant figures were Assistant Secretary Elliott Abrams for the State Department, North for the NSC staff, and Alan Fiers, the Central American Task Force chief, for the CIA. At this meeting, North went all out for Owen. Duemling testified:

> North very vehemently and vigorously advanced the view that if we had Rob Owen on board working for NHAO, that this kind of episode [the television crew in Honduras] would have been avoided.
>
> He argued that NHAO needed some kind of an expediter in the field to work to get things moving. North had been saying regularly—this meeting, after all, is mid-October. North had been saying for the better part of a month or six weeks that we weren't getting the assistance moving fast enough.
>
> I don't recall whether in this meeting, but I do note from my earlier notes of my office call, he invoked the name of Bob Mc-Farlane and Jeane Kirkpatrick. And there was quite a lot of talk about heat from the White House. . . .
>
> So there was a lot of heat and pressure about why isn't it moving. And so North also played that theme, and basically he said, you know, you've simply got to have Owen to handle this.

As Duemling put it, he was "essentially isolated." He continued to protest that there was no need for a middleman between the NHAO and the UNO, and that the NHAO could deal directly with the UNO without a middleman. Finally Abrams, the RIG chairman, turned to him and said: "Well, Bob, I suppose you probably ought to hire Owen." Duemling knew that he was beaten. "All right," he said, "I will hire Owen, but I will hire Owen only under some specific conditions." At this, North relaxed. "Ollie North typically," Duemling related, "which is the way Ollie behaves, then of course when he's got what he wants he then becomes sweetness and light and very congenial."[95]

On November 6, 1985, Duemling informed Owen that the NHAO was granting IDEA the sum of $50,675 for the period of October 28, 1985, to April 12, 1986. The grant to IDEA specified that it had to employ Owen on a full-time basis but make all of his time available to the UNO as the latter directed, not to the NHAO. He was forbidden to perform any service relating to weapons in any form.[96]

Owen casually violated the terms of this grant. For the next six months, he worked for North at the expense of the NHAO. He handled requests for weapons and any other chores that North gave him. Duemling later testified that "those activities were a direct violation of his contract to us," but that Owen had never mentioned those activities in his reports to the NHAO.[97] No one ever checked on Owen's reports.

All that the NHAO obtained from Owen, despite its favors to him, was his contempt. "I don't think Congress could have put together a worse package," he testified. "On one hand, it's like giving someone the keys to a Cadillac and then saying don't drive it, in that there was plenty of opportunity with the way it was going to be managed for misuse of funds."[98]

Owen was not the only one to share in the NHAO's largesse. Mario Calero was put in charge of collecting supplies at an NHAO warehouse in New Orleans. The contract for flying the NHAO supplies to Central America was given to Air Mach, one of Richard Gadd's companies—the same Gadd who was working closely with Secord. Gadd had obtained the contract as a result of a request by North via Owen to Mario Calero.[99]

Unfortunately, Air Mach had no planes of its own, though Duemling did not know this at the time; Gadd merely hired planes that the NHAO itself could have hired. When Duemling was dissatisfied with Gadd's performance, Duemling was told that "somehow the U.S. government owed Gadd something" and that Gadd had apparently done something for which he had not been "adequately compensated." Gadd held on for a few more months, then went with Secord.[100]

In the end, these machinations increasingly disillusioned Owen, and his reports to North took on a tone of desperation. Of the men around Calero, he wrote on March 17, 1986: "Unfortunately, they are not first rate people; in fact they are liars and greed and power motivated." Of the NHAO, which was still paying him, he declared: "NHAO was the worst possible vehicle which could have been devised to pay the bills. Because there is no verification it is impossible to ensure the integrity of the operation." Owen said that he had "probably never been more discouraged" and told why:

> UNO is a name only. There is more and more fluff being added, but there is no substance. I care and believe in the boys and girls, men and women who are fighting, bleeding and dying. But the reality as I see it is there are few of the so called leaders of the movement who really care about the boys in the field. THIS WAR IS BECOMING A BUSINESS TO MANY OF THEM; THERE IS STILL A BELIEF THE MARINES ARE GOING TO HAVE TO INVADE, SO LETS GET SET SO WE WILL AUTOMAT-ICALLY BE THE ONES PUT INTO POWER.[101]

This attitude did not endear Owen to Calero and those around him. In the same message, Owen told North: "Mario told me in Miami why

Adolfo and company are upset with me and freezing me out. I am looked on as the responsible party for a number of the problems they are having. They look at me as the one carrying the water for you. They are also saying I am intimately tied to Seacords [sic]." Owen mourned: "I am burned beyond belief." Meanwhile, Owen learned that his name had come to the attention of Congress in connection with North's increasingly publicized activities. In his last available message to North of April 7, 1986, Owen worried: "No question, I am a hot property, as even people on the hill are asking questions about me. I want to see this through, but not at the cost of jeopardizing it, as I am the only one out on a limb without a genuine safety net or fall back position."[102]

After the NHAO, Owen went to work for the Institute on Terrorism and Subnational Conflict, formed by Neil C. Livingstone. North got Owen the job by getting a donor to give money to this institute.[103]

In retrospect, Owen said: "I think everyone knew we were walking a very thin line."[104]

3

Big Money

Holding the contras together "body and soul" required propaganda and money.

The inspiration for the propaganda came from a speech by President Reagan to the British Parliament on June 8, 1982. He called for a "campaign for democracy" to "fashion the infrastructure of democracy" and assist "democratic development" throughout the world.[1] This call to ideological arms was not followed by much action until CIA Director Casey prodded National Security Adviser Clark on December 21, 1982, for "more effective governmental instrumentalities to deal with public diplomacy and informational challenges."[2]

"Public diplomacy" was a new and peculiar term. This "diplomacy" was not at all diplomatic in the usual sense; it was meant to be closer to ideological indoctrination and popular propaganda than to the official conduct of relations between nations as commonly understood.

Action soon followed. National Security Decision Directive 77 in January 1983 provided for strengthening "the organization, planning and coordination of the various aspects of public diplomacy." A cabinet committee, called the Special Planning Group, was formed to provide overall guidance. Four other committees were created for special purposes—an International Political Committee, an International Information Committee, an International Broadcasting Committee, and a Committee on Public Affairs. This maze of committees showed that an extraordinary effort was put into this program, which soon came to be known as "Project Democracy."[3]

Its main support came from Casey and Clark. To help it along, Casey assigned Walter Raymond, Jr., who was the senior director of intelligence. Raymond was an old hand—on active duty with the Army, or some other part of the government, for some thirty years—and considered himself to be "sort of a foreign affairs expert." He left the CIA for the NSC staff, where he was made head of the Intelligence Directorate and also put in charge of the Public Diplomacy project. He headed a Central American Public Diplomacy Task Force, out of which came a new agency in July 1983—the Office of Public Diplomacy for Latin America and the Caribbean (LPD).

The pioneers of "public diplomacy" recognized that in its scale and character it was a new American phenomenon. Raymond called it "a new discipline."[4] Another insider, W. Scott Thompson of the CIA, told Casey that "we are creating a 'new art form.' "[5] Despite the term "diplomacy," which suggested foreign affairs, Raymond pointed out that "obviously there was a domestic dimension to it." The domestic dimension was actually most important in the LPD.

The director chosen for the LPD was Otto J. Reich, who had come in with the first Reagan administration in 1981 as assistant administrator of the Agency for International Development (AID). He was Cuban-born, a former Democrat who had worked for the 1972 Democratic presidential nominee, George McGovern, and had gone over to the Republicans through the "neoconservative" wing of the party.[6] His main preparation for the job had been five years with the Washington office of the Council of the Americas, a Rockefeller-sponsored organization of businesses with Latin American interests. He was, as he admitted, a political appointee, whose chief qualification was his ideological sympathies.[7] The LPD was attached to the State Department, which had recently acquired a new secretary, George Shultz, whose interest in Latin America was notoriously minimal.

One of the ways in which Reich did his "diplomatic" business was not intended to come out publicly. Though Reich built up a staff of about twenty, he decided to contract out part of the work. One of his first acts at LPD was to enter into a contract with Francis D. (Frank) Gomez, another former Democrat who prospered during the Reagan years.[8] Gomez knew his way around Washington; he had been employed by the U.S. Information Agency (USIA) for almost twenty years before leaving in 1984, just as Reich was looking for help. Like so many others, Gomez had decided to cash in on his experience in government and go into business for himself as a consultant. Reich first hired him as a contractor in February 1984 at the modest sum of $9,500 for five months and renewed the contract on the same basis in July of that year. It was only a beginning.

While Reich was hiring Gomez, Gomez made a deal with Richard R. Miller, then in his mid-thirties, another former government employee turned consultant. Miller had served in 1980 as the Reagan presidential campaign's director of broadcast services under the campaign director, William Casey.[9] From 1981 to 1983, Miller had worked as director of public affairs for the Agency for International Development, after which he had decided to form his own business, International Business Communications (IBC). He, too, obtained a consultant's contract, this time with AID, his former employer. Miller and Gomez had known each other in government service and soon decided to join forces, first as Francis D. Gomez International Business Communications, later without Gomez's name.[10] Gomez, who spoke Spanish fluently and had lived in Central America, provided the expertise; Miller managed the operation.

The IBC first obtained a State Department contract of $90,000 on behalf of Reich's LPD, which ran for a year through September 30, 1985. Another contract rose to $278,725 for a single year, October 1, 1985, to September 30, 1986. In order to avoid competitive bidding, IBC was classified as the "sole source" for this type of work. The entire arrangement was made a contractual secret: "The services and the contractual arrangement with IBC are not to be publicly disclosed because of their character, ingredients, and components."[11] All in all, the IBC was paid $356,471.66 from the U.S. Treasury.[12]

The 1985–86 contract listed nineteen services to be performed by the IBC, all of them of a public relations and propagandistic character. One was: "Compose and edit letters to the editor of major newspapers and magazines in response to articles on Central America." Another read: "Provide S/LPD with op-ed pieces and feature articles for distribution to selected newspapers and magazines."[13] Since the IBC or LPD did not sign or acknowledge its role in these letters to the editor or op-ed pieces, they ostensibly came from unofficial sources.

Some of the articles fed to unsuspecting newspapers and magazines were proudly reported to the higher-ups by Johnathan Miller (no relation to Richard Miller), one of Reich's two deputies. Miller was a typical product of the period. At the age of twenty-seven, he had moved to Washington in 1979 to work in the vice presidential campaign of George Bush. After the election, he was taken on as an administrative assistant of Representative William F. Goodling of Pennsylvania, a Republican. After a few months of that, he went on to AID, where he met Otto Reich and Richard Miller, who were also there at the time. After something over a year at AID, he went to Botswana in southern Africa as Peace Corps director, but was called back in December 1983 by Reich to work at the LPD, though he had had no previous training or experience in Latin America or the Caribbean.[14]

Miller boasted to Pat Buchanan, the White House director of communications, of the success of what he called "Reich white propaganda operation." By "white propaganda," he meant that it was not based on deception and disinformation, which was called "black propaganda." Examples of white propaganda were two op-ed pieces for *The Washington Post* and *The New York Times*, signed by contra leaders, which Gomez had prepared and which Miller proudly reported to Buchanan.

Washington in the early 1980s was full of such bright, ambitious, aggressive young men and women on the make with newly minted conservative convictions. Many had enlisted in the Republican presidential campaign of 1979–80 as the first step toward higher things in the government, especially in those politicized agencies that were thirsting for true believers. They often moved from agency to agency, gaining experience in the ways of the Washington world and making acquaintances that would prove useful to them in the future. Johnathan Miller himself referred to "itinerant government employees that move around from point to point like I do."[15] He stayed in the LPD until August 1985, went to the NSC staff until May 1986, and finished up as deputy assistant to the president for management, when he resigned in May 1987 as a result of Robert Owen's testimony that he had cashed traveler's checks for Oliver North. If these "itinerant employees" were self-important, interested in making more money, or at loose ends, they could always go into business for themselves as consultants or contractors. A working knowledge of the Washington bureaucracy—of what was done where by whom—was itself enough for a lucrative career.

The other Miller—Richard R.—was a prime example of the entrepreneurial-political type that became increasingly prominent in the evolution of the Iran and contra affairs. Through his IBC, he became entangled in fund-raising for the contras. This story takes us back to how the contras were supposed to be held together "body and soul."

2

One of the means to get around the Boland Amendment was to raise funds for the contras through private and third-country sources instead of through congressional appropriations to the CIA.

Oddly, in view of his later actions, President Reagan had dealt with the subject in a press conference on May 4, 1983. When asked about cutting off covert aid to the contras, he had argued against it in these terms:

> Well, except that then the only help that you can give is through other governments, and I don't think that's an effective thing to do. And how do you know that the other governments would want to, themselves, then, participate in helping the people that need the help? In other words, we'd be asking some other government to do what our own Congress has said that we can't do.[16]

If this fundamental constitutional principle had prevailed, the Reagan administration would never have tried to get or have permitted private sources or other governments to do what Congress had forbidden. Casey, however, was not inhibited by such scruples. On March 27, 1984, he advised McFarlane that the funds for the "Nicaraguan project" were going to run out by mid-May. He anticipated that it would be difficult to get supplemental congressional appropriations to carry the project for the rest of the year. He therefore proposed, as one alternative, to resort to a private American citizen to establish a foundation to receive nongovernmental funds that could be made available to Calero's FDN, his favorite contra group.[17] On July 16, Casey met with McFarlane and again urged him to "look at the possibility of private funds being used, but that the agency would have to stay out of it."[18]

This strategy raised a question of how far it was unethical, if not illegal, for public officials to go to evade a law. Private citizens were entitled to raise funds for the contras on their own. But this case was different. It entailed the deliberate conspiring or at least conniving of high officials to use private funds for the express purpose of defying a law. In any case, these private funds were not to be raised altogether privately; official cooperation was indispensable; Casey hinted that some other agency might not have to stay out of it, even if his did.

The private American citizen who best succeeded in putting Casey's plan into effect was Carl R. (Spitz) Channell. He was another of those who had considered themselves to be liberals. His conversion to conservatism, as he described it, was seemingly fortuitous. In 1976, at the age of thirty-one, he had happened to see an advertisement of the newly formed National Conservative Political Action Committee (NCPAC), devoted to working for the election of right-wing conservative candidates, about its training program on how to conduct political campaigns. He decided to enroll without knowing what the NCPAC stood for but was quickly won over to its program. After this schooling, he was sent to work for a Republican congressional candidate in Iowa, admittedly without knowing what the latter's political views were or whether they were similar to his own. Three years later, he was made national finance chairman of the NCPAC and raised about $2 million for it in two years. Here it was that Channell made his great discovery—that "there was so much money ready for conservative organizations in the United States that we needed ways to spend that money."[19]

Channell was now all set to do what so many others were doing—to start up his own one-man consulting company, Channell Corporation, to give advice on fund-raising. This venture did not work out, but Channell soon hit on his real métier. In 1984, he organized the American Conservative Trust (ACT), a federal political action committee, which meant that it was not tax-exempt. This venture was soon followed by a nonprofit, tax-exempt National Endowment for the Preservation of Liberty (NEPL), supposedly dedicated to educating the general public. Also in 1984, he formed one more lobbying group, Sentinel. In 1986, he set up another political action committee, the Anti-Terrorist American Committee.[20]

The idea of a tax-exempt foundation, such as the NEPL, to collect funds for the contras was apparently not original with Channell. North testified that others in the Reagan administration had had the same idea in 1984, that "steps were even taken to set up" such a foundation, and that "a former Secretary of the Treasury was contacted, not by me but by others in the White House, to actually set it up, to incorporate it, to do the appropriate paperwork." But Channell seems to have been the first and only one to put it across. Once he had set it up, he was able to tell North that he already had such an organization, complete with a much-prized "donor list."[21] At his trial, North saw nothing incompatible about using a tax-exempt foundation devoted to humanitarian assistance for the purpose of buying military equipment for the contras, as this exchange showed:

> *Question:* Did you think that raising money for military goods was a charitable purpose?
>
> *North:* Well, in helping the Nicaraguan Resistance, yes, I did. In fact, I proposed something similar to that, I think, back in 1984.[22]

Nothing much happened to advance Channell's fortunes during 1984. Then he once again stumbled on good fortune. In January 1985, his ACT spent most of its money on a full-page political advertisement congratulating President Reagan on his inauguration. This act brought him to the attention of Edie Fraser, of the public relations firm of Miner and Fraser Public Affairs, Inc.[23] One of its clients was the Nicaraguan Refugee Fund, which was holding a money-raising dinner on April 15. To make the dinner a spectacular success, the sponsors decided, an appearance by President Reagan was necessary. Edie Fraser went to see Oliver North to get his support, and North agreed to help. One of her remarks to North later bore strange fruit—that the Sultan of Brunei had given generously to UNICEF and might do so again for the Nicaraguan refugee children. She followed up with a letter to North in which she gave him information about the Sultan, who, she ventured, "might kick in a million dollars" for Central American refugees.[24] She invited a number of philanthropic and conservative groups to get together and cooperate in the cause. Channell came to the meeting, enthusiastically offered to assist, and in this way opened the way for him to go on to bigger things.[25] The invitation made it appear that the dinner was being held to honor President and Mrs. Reagan at $250 per person and $2,500 per table.[26] One of those who paid for a table was the Sultan of Brunei; its cost was much less than the million dollars Edie Fraser had hoped for, but the Sultan was not forgotten, and his millions were saved for another time.[27]

Channell soon brought exciting news to Fraser—he had major contributors who would give a significant amount of money if they could meet the president. Fraser improved on this by writing to North: "*Ollie Very imp[ortant]. Two people want to give major contrib[ution]s i.e. 300,000 and up if they might have one 'quiet' moment with the President.*"[28] Word came on March 26 that the president was willing to deliver the keynote address at the dinner.[29] Success was assured. The dinner itself took in $200,000, of which, after consultants' fees and expenses, $3,000 went to the cause.[30] Channell says that he raised $40,000 to $50,000 for the Nicaraguan Refugee Fund.[31]

The dinner was Channell's turning point. He realized that it was his big chance to show what he could do but that he could not do it alone. To help, he now called on Daniel L. Conrad, then forty-two years old, a professional fund-raising expert based in San Francisco, where he had formed a Public Management Institute and taught the seminar on fund-raising which Channell had once attended. Conrad came to Washington and spent about a month and a half giving advice on how to make the dinner a success, for which Channell paid him $10,000 to $15,000, the Nicaraguan Refugee Fund $10,000, and Miner and Fraser $1,500.[32] After the dinner, Conrad stayed on in Washington to become Channell's second-in-command. Conrad was paid $15,000 a month as executive director of all of Channell's organizations.[33]

Conrad testified that North closely followed the contributions. Channell would tell Conrad what contributors were expected to give; Conrad would tell North what was expected of each one and ask North for a statement of contra needs amounting to the same figure. Contributors of $100,000 or more were given a special award, made up of an American flag in a large mahogany presentation box, with a letter of appreciation from North. Conrad showed North the checks or stock certificates before depositing them as North directed in the account of the Miller-Gomez IBC on Grand Cayman Island, from which the money went to the Secord-Hakim Lake Resources account in Switzerland. Conrad was paid $70,000 in 1985 and $112,000 in 1986 through his Public Management Institute in addition to $40,000 in 1985 and $70,000 in 1986 paid directly to him by Channell's NEPL.[34]

Conrad and Channell had very different attitudes toward their enterprise. Conrad was more the pure fund-raiser; his interest in the Nicaraguan cause was minimal. Channell saw himself as a political fund-raiser par excellence and made the contras his cause. The catalyst in his career was his discovery that there was big money to be had in exploiting the anti-Sandinista cause. Until then he had thought little of Nicaragua or Central America. "I really hadn't focused on the essential characteristics of Nicaragua as a burgeoning communist state," he said. "This experience, talking to people who were from there coming up to see us, preparing for the dinner, reading the literature that was sent over so we could talk to people about it really opened my eyes considerably, considerably." He was surprised to find that his conservative contributors were intensely interested in the anti-Sandinista cause and had been giving money to it for some time.[35] They were far more militant than he had expected. "All of my contributors are very action-oriented. In fact, they have been characterized quite accurately I think in the newspaper as warriors. They are somewhat ill at ease at a time of peace, I gather. They are very activist, very activist-oriented."[36]

Channell had now spent almost a decade mastering the art of money-raising but, as he recognized, he still had much to learn about politics. After the dinner had taught him how to cash in on a cause, he later related, "I realized that maybe there was a political dimension to this Nicaraguan issue which I hadn't thought of or it's very possible that I began to see the political dimension that was there that I hadn't seen before."[37] Always the quick learner, he decided to go to the source to make up for his political inadequacy—to the White House. He decided to call Edward Rollins, the political director who had helped manage President Reagan's reelection campaign in 1984, whom Channell had previously met. He could not get to Rollins but reached Rollins's aide, John Roberts, whom he promptly invited to lunch. Channell says that he did not hide his political naïveté: "I really was ignorant about so much of this [the congressional debate on Nicaragua]. I didn't even know how the coalitions on Capitol Hill broke down. I wasn't even sure what the President was doing."[38]

Roberts knew just what Channell needed. Roberts said, "If you want to know where to go you should go to see IBC, those fellows Rich Miller and Frank Gomez. They are the White House—outside the White House on this issue. . . . Those are the people. That is where the expertise sits and if you want to help and if you want to know how to help and want to know about Nicaragua, they are the people who can help you."[39]

Channell was still so diffident that he asked Roberts to call Miller for him, because he felt that "we were unknown. I was unknown." Channell soon met Miller and was highly impressed by him: "I was coming at this from a neophyte position—I was very impressed with what they knew, who they knew. They knew an awful lot of people whose names I never heard of but they said this person is this and this person handles this and they knew a great deal about the politics of Latin America in detail."[40]

Channell quickly decided to tie on to Miller and Gomez. They first agreed on a contract for part of a month at $5,000 plus expenses, and then Channell's tax-exempt National Endowment for the Preservation of Liberty signed on for a longer term with the Miller-Gomez IBC at a monthly retainer of $15,000. With the latter's help, Channell succeeded in arranging for a briefing on Nicaragua at the White House for thirty-five of his past and prospective donors on June 27, 1985.

There Channell was introduced to Oliver North by Richard Miller and discovered what North could do for him.[41] The main performance at the briefing was a slide show on Nicaragua by North. Channell de-

scribed its effect—the people in the room "were all excited to death."
Toward the end, which showed a contra buried with a wooden cross,
North "suddenly became so powerfully emotive it was just like his whole
spirit exploded. He became tremendously emotional and became compelling in his language and in his presentation just about at the end and
about the need to save Latin America, to save freedom, that these people
were sacrificing for America and for freedom all over the world, and we
have a major responsibility to see that the President's policies are successful there." When North finished, "everybody was just riveted to
him."[42]

At this, Channell decided that North was just the man he needed.
North even agreed to give one of Channell's main contributors, Mrs.
Barbara Newington, who could not attend on June 27, a personal briefing
of twenty minutes in his office two or three days later.[43] To get to know
North better, Channell characteristically invited him to a dinner, together
with Miller and Gomez, on July 9. Channell presented North with a
problem—his contributors were worried about where the money went
and suspected that the contra leadership could not be trusted. North's
solution was simple—"just to work it through Rich [Miller] and Frank
[Gomez]." Channell took his advice and proceeded to transfer all the
money received from contributions to the Miller-Gomez IBC.[44]

North's briefings became an essential part of Channell's money-raising
technique. In 1985, North gave his slide show to two large and four small
groups. He gave a number of others in 1986. The donors soon knew
what to expect. After North's briefings on the needs of the contras, Channell met with them, generally at the Hay-Adams Hotel in Washington,
without North, and asked them to make contributions to his NEPL,
because they were tax-deductible. If the contributions were large, Channell would call North "and say you won't believe what we have received
from X person."[45]

As Channell's calls increased, North had reason to believe.

3

Some of Channell's main contributors afford an intimate glimpse into
his methods.

One was Barbara Newington, a rich, elderly widow of Greenwich,
Connecticut. Her late husband and Larry P. McDonald had been the
founders of another tax-exempt organization, Western Goals. McDonald,
a Democratic congressman from Georgia and chairman of the extremist
John Birch Society, had died in the crash of Korean Air Lines Flight
007, shot down by a Soviet plane in September 1983.[46] Mrs. Newington
supported Western Goals after McDonald's death and needed someone
to run it. Since Mrs. Newington contributed to other conservative or-

ganizations, including Channell's American Conservative Trust, Channell invited her to come to New York in February 1985 and asked her to make a contribution to enable him to pay for newspaper advertisements and television commercials on Nicaragua. One thing led to another, and soon she was making checks out, as he directed, to his various organizations—the American Conservative Trust State Election Fund, Sentinel, the Anti-Terrorist American Committee, and the National Endowment for the Preservation of Liberty. Of these organizations, she said, "It was never clear until he asked me to make a check out to so-and-so. I never particularly knew which organization was which." Toward the end of 1985, Channell offered to relieve her of a burden by taking over Western Goals.[47]

Channell soon arranged for Adolfo Calero to meet with Mrs. Newington in New York and to assure her of his support for her favorite cause. "My trip to New York was an inspiration," wrote Calero. "The Larry McDonald task force is already forming. I am grateful to Spitz Channell for the opportunity to get to know you. Your support and patriotic contribution touches all of us."[48] Mrs. Newington later explained that Calero and McDonald had been friends and that the Larry McDonald Task Force was a contra military unit for which she had made a contribution to Channell's NEPL.[49]

In June 1985, Channell invited her to come to Washington for what she thought was to be a meeting with President Reagan and a briefing by Oliver North. In his briefing, she said, North told her that the contras "needed equipment and food and weapons and everything to keep them going." Afterward, Channell and Miller had dinner with her at the Hay-Adams Hotel, where Channell used North's exhortation to solicit a contribution from her.[50] Later that evening, David C. Fischer joined them to tell her what to expect when she met with the president.

Fischer was another product of the times. After law school, he had served his political apprenticeship working in Ronald Reagan's campaigns. In 1980, he had come to the White House as President Reagan's Special Assistant. The job enabled him to have a daily working relationship with the new president, making sure that he went through the schedule of events as planned and knew who was coming to see him. Fischer also accompanied him on his travels. Fischer left the White House in April 1985 and started up his own consulting business, David C. Fischer and Associates—the only associate was his wife—in January 1986.

Fischer came to Channell through Richard Miller, who had come up through the same route. Channell and Miller had often talked about how wonderful it would be if President Reagan would endorse Channell's programs and meet with his contributors. In late 1985, Miller came to Channell with the answer to the latter's prayer. Miller offered Fischer to Channell as just the kind of consultant that he needed—"an ex-private aide to the President . . . he will be able to help us facilitate those meetings, none are guaranteed, of course, but he knows the people, he knows how to write the request, he knows the people in the White House . . . worth his weight in gold."[51] After some hesitation about getting tied up with Channell, Fischer agreed. Instead of contracting with Channell directly, Fischer made a deal with Miller's IBC, but Channell agreed to pay IBC for Fischer's services. The negotiations did not go smoothly. Fischer at first asked for $50,000 for every meeting that he arranged with President Reagan. The figure finally came down to $20,000 a month.[52]

A similar type of Washington insider came with Fischer. He was Martin L. Artiano, not long out of law school when he had met Fischer in 1976, while both of them were working in Ronald Reagan's first, unsuccessful, presidential campaign. They had come together again in Reagan's successful 1980 campaign, during which Artiano met Richard Miller. Fischer and Artiano teamed up to work for Channell through Miller, splitting the $20,000 a month equally. Artiano soon complained that he was not getting enough and ended with about $200,000 between December 1985 and the end of 1986.[53]

This was how the game was played in Washington—work in a presidential campaign, get rewarded with a more or less desirable political job, learn the ropes in government, and finally make the experience pay off in private business.

Fischer was the main link to the Reagan administration. To get a meeting with the president for a selected group of Channell's contributors in January 1986, Fischer sent a memorandum on Channell's work for the president to Chief of Staff Donald Regan. "No private group of Americans have better supported the President's Central American program as well as other issues critical to Ronald Reagan," he wrote. "Once these men and women realize the President recognizes and appreciates their contribution towards his programs their continued enthusiastic support will be guaranteed."[54] The proposed meeting caused some anxiety that the president's presence on behalf of Channell's organizations might violate the spirit of provisions against lobbying Congress. The matter was submitted to Fred F. Fielding, the president's counsel, who decided that there was no legal objection to such a meeting but that care should be taken to avoid any suggestion of White House control of those organizations. In any case, lobbying Congress was one of Channell's main objectives and he had a lobbyist, Dan Kuykendall, on his payroll.[55]

Fischer's coup was a briefing on January 30, 1986, for about twenty of Channell's contributors. It was a full-dress affair, for which North carefully prepared National Security Adviser Poindexter, whose role was to bring in the president. Regan was expected to make some introductory remarks, followed by an hour of North, with the added participation of Buchanan and Elliott Abrams, the assistant secretary of state for inter-American affairs. The climax was a "drop-by" on the part of President

Reagan. "The meeting," North explained, "is an opportunity to express Administration support for the efforts of ACT [American Conservative Trust] as we gear up for a Congressional vote during March."[56] It was only one of many such examples of North's preoccupation with domestic politics and the manipulation of public opinion to influence Congress.

The president arrived while Abrams was speaking. Everyone rose and applauded. Channell recalled:

> He [Reagan] smiled at everybody and came in and stood at the head of this long table and looked right at one of my contributors, Mr. Fred Sackler, from San Juan Capistrano, California, who was sitting beside him to his right, and he said Fred, the first thing I want to do is thank you so much for all the television you're providing in support of the Freedom Fighters.[57]

The president spoke about a bill to give the contras $100 million he was planning to send to Congress. The next incident was unexpected:

> No one moved except one person, that was Mr. Tom Clagett, who raised his hand. He was halfway down the table. And the President looked at him and said yes, what can I do, and Tom pointed across the room to this picture of President Theodore Roosevelt and also there's on the left side a picture of President Franklin Roosevelt and his finger went between the two pictures so you weren't sure exactly who he was referring to and he said to the President, Mr. President, why don't you act like those people and get something done. The President looked at him, I'm sure the President couldn't read his name tag, and said right to him, Tom, I'm doing the best I can and it's very tough.[58]

Ellen Garwood spoke up to criticize the State Department, which she thought was too liberal. Reagan listened and said that he would like to shake hands and take pictures with everyone present. He spent about twenty minutes with the twenty-five people there and talked to several of them. One woman from Atlanta dropped her glasses when she was about to have her picture taken with him. He took off his glasses and said, "Well, I'm just as vain as you are." No doubt everyone was delighted and felt their money well spent.

In early June 1986, Reagan telephoned Channell. The latter remembered how the conversation went:

> Spitz, how are you? And I didn't tell him the truth because I was a nervous wreck. I told him that I was fine, and he said he had gotten the proposal that I had sent him the previous weekend . . . I wrote the President a letter the previous week suggesting ten dif-

ferent ways that he might get this Freedom Fighter bill for $100 million unstuck, that was stuck in the Congressional process. And I listed ten different ideas to set it moving again.

And he said that he had a staff meeting that morning regarding my ideas and that some of them were being implemented right away. He then . . . thanked me for sponsoring all the television that we had sponsored, told me that our support was necessary to continue.

Then he said to me, you know, I just do not understand Tip O'Neill [Democratic Speaker of the House of Representatives, Thomas P. O'Neill, Jr.]. I cannot understand him. I don't know what's wrong with him, why he doesn't see the need to be supporting the Freedom Fighters.

He went on like this for a minute, and I said to him, Mr. President, I need to tell you something. Every night Tip O'Neill drops by his bed and prays to the same God that you do and prays for the strength that's necessary the next day to defeat everything you believe in. And that's the way he is. And you must fight him as an enemy and must defeat him. . . .

There was this long pause, and he ended by saying, Spitz, I just don't understand Tip O'Neill.[59]

Mrs. Newington had already met the president in person. Her reception was typical of these experiences. She was brought to the White House by Channell. Buchanan ushered her alone into the Oval Office. "It was very brief," she said. "There were photographers around. We just stood shaking hands and exchanging thank-you's." She told the president that "I thought he had brought God back into the White House." He replied: "I've been talking to him a lot lately and I intend to take him to the summit [with the new Soviet leader, Gorbachev] with me."

She went back to the hotel with Channell, and North appeared after dinner. He came to bring her a gift from the president that she had missed by leaving the Oval Office too quickly—a glass plaque with the words etched in the president's handwriting: "There is no limits [sic] to what a man can do or where he can go if he does not care who gets the credit." North also reminded her of the needs of the contras—"food and equipment and weapons." He had even brought a map of Central America with him and had pointed out to her what was going on in Nicaragua, though she was always hazy about the details of his military briefings.[60]

North continued to pay special attention to Mrs. Newington. On January 24, 1986, he sent her a letter addressed to "Dear Barbara." In it he virtually appealed in behalf of Channell's tax-exempt organization. "During 1985," it began, "the hope [of] freedom and democracy in Nicaragua was kept alive with the help of the National Endowment for the Preservation of Liberty and fine Americans such as you." It concluded, as if to forewarn her that she was expected to give some more: "In the weeks ahead, we will commence a renewed effort to make our assistance to the Democratic Resistance forces even more effective. Once again your support will be essential."[61]

Mrs. Newington met President Reagan again on February 28, 1986. It was for her another of those unforgettable encounters. Channell took her over to the White House, where she met North, who was planning to take her in to see the president. But they waited so long that North had to leave and, when the time came, she went in alone. "It was a very brief meeting, and we exchanged thank-you's again," she recalled. "And he handed me a jar of jelly beans and said to give this to my daughter, and I handed him a book and said I had something for him to give him some strength. It was a little spiritual book of some kind. And that was it."[62]

All this attention to Mrs. Newington paid off. Between October 1985 and March 1986, her contributions to Channell's NEPL amounted to approximately $1.5 million in stocks and $500,000 in cash or checks.[63] Some of her checks were originally made out to the non-tax-exempt American Conservative Trust, but Channell later, at her request, sent her acknowledgments for the money as if they had been gifts to the NEPL, so that she could take the deductions.[64] North later testified that he had directed Channell to give Mrs. Newington's check to Miller. "Yes," North agreed, "I suppose directed is a proper word there." The arrangement North had with Miller was that the latter put money such as Mrs. Newington's "in an overseas bank account on another account number, and then it would be vectored to various directions as needed by the Resistance." Some of this money, North said, went to Calero and Secord.[65]

One more of Channell's important contributors was another rich widow, Ellen C. Garwood of Austin, Texas. Her late husband was an associate justice of the Supreme Court of Texas; her father was Will Clayton, under secretary of state for economic affairs in the Truman administration. She had first met Channell in 1980 and North in 1984. Like Mrs. Newington, she had been brought to Washington to see North and President Reagan. North had once given her a private briefing lasting about twenty minutes.

On another occasion, Channell had shown her in North's presence a price list of weapons needed by the contras, the total amount of which had come to about a million and a half dollars. She recalled that after North had left the room, Channell had said: "This is the list of things needed, and can you do something about it? Can you help provide for this and some of the other needs Colonel North has described?" She had replied: "It is a tremendous amount of money. I don't know whether I can afford to do it, whether I am able to or not. I will have to consult my banker back in Austin."[66] Eventually, Mrs. Garwood sent a total of $2.5 million to Channell's NEPL.[67]

Mrs. Garwood was asked whether North had been responsible for her faith in Channell. She replied:

Well, certainly the fact that he brought me to Colonel North, and what he asked me for later was related to what Colonel North had said, although Colonel North didn't ask me, and this seemed to be a guarantee that this was the executive department of the Government that was asking for this help, and that it was essential and that it was going to the right place.

The fact that Mr. Channell took me to see Colonel North, who was part of the National Security Council, and who was part of the administration, of the executive department of the administration, was a kind of reliable gesture on his part, I would think.[68]

Mrs. Garwood subsequently thought that she should perhaps have said that the executive branch of the government "was presenting a case that would make people later on want to give. Because they didn't ask exactly." Asked by Representative Peter W. Rodino, Jr., of New Jersey whether she had "really recognized that this was a request coming from the principals at the White House," she had replied: "Oh, yes, it was the executive department of the White House."[69]

A third contributor, William B. O'Boyle of New York, an oil and gas investor, told a straightforward story of money for weapons. He was hooked by a telephone call from NEPL asking whether he was interested in coming to the White House for a briefing on the political and military situation in Nicaragua. He came and, with about a dozen others, was brought to North for a briefing. North, according to O'Boyle, told them about an airport in a Central American country which was ostensibly commercial but was in fact a disguised military airport. If O'Boyle can be believed, North told them that "one of the uses which the airport was intended [for] was to recover the Russian Backfire bombers after they made a nuclear attack on the United States."* Fired up by North's presentation, O'Boyle told one of Channell's assistants that he was willing to make a large contribution, but only for weapons and other military equipment for the contras.

After the usual dinner at the Hay-Adams Hotel, Channell made his approach. As O'Boyle recalled it, Channell told him "that there was a

---

* O'Boyle later explained the reasoning behind this reference to a Soviet nuclear attack: "Apparently the Backfire bombers, after a nuclear attack on the United States, can't make it all the way back to Russia. Rather than lose them, they can recover them in Nicaragua. That was one of the purposes of building that air base" (O'Boyle, 100-3, p. 138). North, according to O'Boyle, apparently expected the United States to be interested in preventing the Soviet bombers from landing in Nicaragua after the devastation of a nuclear attack, as if the Soviets ran no danger of a similarly devastating nuclear attack on themselves and as if Nicaragua might not suffer from such an attack on the United States. O'Boyle also said that he had understood that the plan was one made by the U.S. government (ibid., pp. 166–67).

small group of people in the United States that the President relied on to make that kind of contribution, that this was a cause that was very dear to the President's heart, and he thought that perhaps I might be interested in joining this group of people." At some point, Channell also confided to him that "if one were to give approximately $300,000 or more, the President would actually meet with the contributor and thank him personally, spend 15 or so minutes with him on an off-the-record kind of meeting; and thank him for the contribution he was making to the national security."

Channell offered another meeting with North at breakfast the next morning. He introduced O'Boyle to North as "someone who was willing to provide money for weapons." North took out a small notebook and read out how much various weapons cost—$20,000 for a Blowpipe missile, but only to be purchased in packs of ten, Stinger missiles, and the Maule light aircraft. North also impressed on O'Boyle that he was giving him secret information which he was not to tell anyone else.* O'Boyle ended by giving $130,000 to Channell's NEPL to pay for two of the Maule aircraft. While North listened and said nothing, according to O'Boyle, Channell repeated the offer of an audience with the president for "around $300,000."[70] O'Boyle subsequently informed Channell that he was not going to make any further contributions, but after another private briefing by North and an assurance by Channell that he would ask for no more, O'Boyle sent another $30,000. When asked how he could have thought that contributions for the purchase of weapons were tax-deductible, O'Boyle said: "I felt that since this was a covert foreign policy operation that had the blessings of the administration, that it was all right."[71]

The blessings of the administration were also the key to another contribution but in a different way. Joseph Coors, of the beer company, was an old friend of CIA Director Casey and the financial backer of numerous conservative organizations. He did not need any blandishments from Channell to contribute to the contras' cause. On June 18, 1985, Coors came directly to Casey to say that he wanted to give money to the Nicaraguan Freedom Fighters and to ask how to do it. Casey responded that he couldn't do anything like that for Coors but that he knew someone who could. "Just point blank," Coors recalled, "he said Ollie North is the guy to see." Coors went to see North immediately and had no difficulty getting advice from him. North told him to buy a Maule aircraft for the

---

* O'Boyle testified that the secret information concerned plans made in the event that Congress did or did not approve money for the contras. If Congress did not, the plan called for the contras to seize part of Nicaragua, establish a provisional government, after which the U.S. Navy would blockade Nicaragua, prevent supplies from coming in to the Sandinistas from Cuba, and thus bring about the fall of the Sandinista regime. If Congress did approve the money, the same thing would come about "on a slower time scale" (O'Boyle, 100-3, pp. 181–82).

contras, showed him a brochure of the Maule company, and pointed out the model that he wanted Coors to buy for $65,000.

For once, North was incautious. In his cooperation with Channell, North deliberately restricted himself to the ideological motivation of the prospective contributor and absented himself when it came time for Channell to ask for the contribution. It was the technique that Senator Warren Rudman of New Hampshire later described as "the old one-two punch."[72] This time, however, there was no Channell to come between North and the contributor, and there was no need to give Coors any ideological motivation. Instead, North handed Coors a piece of paper on which was written: "Lake Resources Inc., Account No. 386430-22-1, Credit Suisse Bank, Eaux Vives Branch." Whereupon, in August 1985, Coors made a payment of $65,000 to the Lake Resources account.[73]

This incident was the closest North seems to have come personally to getting a contribution for the contras. The Lake Resources account was not controlled by the contras. It had been set up by Secord and Hakim and was technically controlled by Hakim, but the two did what North told them to do.

Another contributor, Nelson Bunker Hunt of Dallas, Texas, met five to seven times with President Reagan in a group and once with the president alone for about ten minutes. He gave $475,000 to Channell, half contribution and half loan.[74] At one dinner in Dallas, North told Hunt about the planes, ammunition, clothing, food, medical supplies, and everything else the contras needed and put a price on each item. According to Channell, the conversation went this way:

> Bunker said to him what are you going to do? Do you mind getting in trouble for this? And Ollie said no, I don't care if I have to go to jail for this and I don't care if I have to lie to Congress about this and Bunker just sort of—he didn't laugh but he just sort of chortled a little and that was it.[*][75]

All in all, Channell's NEPL took in $10,385,929 in contributions in 1985–86. His other organizations accounted for $1,685,535, for a total of $12,071,464.[76] With this much money at his disposal, Channell could afford to spend on a very large scale. He paid $1,700,000 to Miller and Gomez, and more than $650,000 to Fischer and Artiano. The contras received only $2,700,000, or little more than 20 percent.[77] This sum was considered to be enough to sustain the contras for about two months.

* Channell told the same story in grand-jury testimony on June 10, 1987, in somewhat different words: "At one point Bunker said to him, Ollie, if this policy goes down the drain are you prepared to go to prison for it? Ollie said, Oh, yes. He might have said hell, yes. I don't remember exactly which one. But yes was included. Then he also said if you needed to lie before Congress are you willing to do that and he said oh, yes too" (NT, p. 3637).

4

The collection of private funds for the contras was a highly orchestrated operation. It was an intricate intermingling of Channell's activities, the assistance of his consultants and other associates, and the cooperation of officials in the government.

Of these, the cooperation of Reagan and North was critical. Channell was after the big money from a few major contributors. Three of them gave about three-quarters of all that he collected in 1986.[78] All of them had to be convinced that Channell was doing the work of the Reagan administration, with its knowledge and approval. Nothing was more likely to be convincing than to have Channell arrange for them to be addressed and thanked by the president himself or to have a private briefing by North, who was to them the voice of the White House. For such services Channell was willing to pay more than $650,000 to Fischer and Artiano.[79]

If Channell's contributors had any doubts at all, they could be reassured by official letters, which Channell and Miller contrived to get for them. At a very early stage of his collaboration, North sent Channell a "Dear Spitz" letter on August 15, 1985, which was virtually a seal of approval for Channell's NEPL. It began: "Throughout the struggle for freedom and democracy in Nicaragua, there are those who have carried this great burden with dedication and a true sense of patriotism. You and the people involved in the National Endowment for the Preservation of Liberty are at the center of the struggle." The latter ended as if the NEPL were the decisive factor in the struggle: "The programs you have undertaken are crucial. Without the means you provide, those who seek a democratic outcome in Nicaragua will fail."[80]

North also sent personal letters of thanks to Channell's contributors. One began: "During 1985, the hope of freedom and democracy in Nicaragua was kept alive with the help of the National Endowment for the Preservation of Liberty and fine Americans such as you. Because you cared, the spark of liberty still glows in the darkness of Nicaragua."[81] A form letter was signed by North beginning: "In supporting the President's policy on Nicaragua, the National Endowment for the Preservation of Liberty does all Americans a great service."[82] These letters were sent out in batches—at least three on December 17, 1985, and thirty on January 24, 1986.[83] North seems to have handwritten the text of the December 17, 1985, letter before having it typed.[84]

One contributor even thought that North determined what the NEPL was going to do with his money:

Enclosed is the contribution which I mentioned to you on the telephone ten days ago. I am a couple of days late sending it but I hope it will do some good.

Please have Ollie contact me to let me know what he is going to do with it, if that is possible.[85]

The president could also be enlisted to do his part for a particularly big contributor. His letter to Mrs. Newington was more nuanced and referred to the NEPL only by implication. It began: "I want to take this opportunity to express to you my deep appreciation for the selfless, patriotic support you have provided so unflinchingly to this Administration and to our policies."[86] Since Mrs. Newington's selfless, patriotic support had come unflinchingly through the NEPL, the two could not have been separable in her mind.

Richard Miller claimed credit for having asked North to draft thank-you letters, or Miller himself drafted the president's and North's letters.[87] Channell sent North's letter of August 15, 1985, "all over the country, hundreds and hundreds and hundreds of copies" to show people "that we were trying to help the President and that help was being noticed, and we were getting a response from the White House."[88]

The one to whom Channell owed by far the most was Oliver North. If anyone was selfless, patriotic, and unflinching in his support of the administration and its policies, it was North.

North once referred to the president's meetings with Channell's contributors as if they were part of his personal enterprise and implied that the president was well aware of its purpose. "I have no idea what Don Regan does or does not know re my private U.S. operation," he informed Poindexter, "but the President obviously knows why he had been meeting with several select people to thank them for their 'support for Democracy' in CentAM [Central America]."[89]

One case shows how North's wishes were carried out. In June 1985, North telephoned Richard Miller to say that he wanted $30,000 for the Nicaraguan resistance. To get it, he gave Miller the number of an account and told Miller to put the money in it. Miller spoke to Channell, who gave him the telephone number of John W. Ramsey, Jr.[90] Ramsey described Miller's call this way: "He seemed rather embarrassed, indicated he needed $30,000 right away, and said he couldn't tell me what it was for, but he would sometime. I said, 'Well, I'll let you have 5.' And he said, you know, 'Could you make it 10?' I said, 'All right.' " Ramsey never found out what the money was going for.[91] Channell suggested that a letter of thanks should be sent to Ramsey; Miller got in touch with North, who told Miller to send Ramsey a telegram in North's name.[92]

In this way the system devised by North for the disbursement of Channell's money went through Miller at North's direction. As Miller put it, "he [North] directed me to direct the expenditures."[93] The Miller IBC put the money in the Swiss account of the Secord-Hakim Lake Resources or a Miller-controlled account.[94] Miller also set up a company, first known as I.C., Inc., subsequently changed to Intel Cooperation, Inc., in the Cayman Islands, where the transfer of funds could not be traced.[95] Miller described how the system worked: "I would notify Col. North that I had it [money from the NEPL to the IBC], and I would send it to I.C., Inc., and deposit it and wait for some instructions [from North] as to where to transfer it."[96]

Whenever Miller received money from Channell, he informed North, who told him what to do with it.[97] Miller and Gomez did not perform their financial services without cutting themselves in. They set up World Affairs Counselors, Inc., in the Cayman Islands to funnel off for themselves 10 percent of all receipts from Channell's organizations, without informing Channell. According to Miller, they told North what they were doing, and he indicated "that he believed that 10 percent was reasonable" because other people providing assistance to the contras were taking 20 to 30 percent. Miller and Gomez netted "somewhere around $250,000 to $300,000," if not more, from the 10 percent.[98]

North did not use this money for the contras alone. He acted as if he were the Maecenas of like-minded conservative organizations. He instructed Miller to send $75,000 to the Institute on Terrorism and Subnational Conflict, and $5,000 to the Latin American Strategic Studies Institute, and others of the same kind.[99] North also wanted Miller and Gomez to use the Institute for North-South Issues (INSI), which they had set up in 1984, as a conduit for contra contributions. The INSI received two contributions, one of $100,000 from the Heritage Foundation, as a grant to produce a mythical "study on foundation information services in the Caribbean and Latin America." INSI took a 20 percent "overhead charge," because Miller and Gomez considered the operation so risky. Miller checked with North, who agreed to 20 percent for the INSI. Miller sent $80,000 of the Heritage Foundation's "grant" to his Intel Cooperation (IC), disbursed as North had directed, and kept $20,000 for his INSI. The latter also received a second contribution of $60,000, which it immediately transferred to the Lake Resources account in Switzerland. After this, Miller decided the risk was too great and told North that he did not want any more of it.[100]

In this way North was able to circumvent the Boland Amendment by helping to raise millions of dollars of private money. Most of it went to the money-raisers, who rewarded themselves generously for their trouble. North seems to have permitted the money to flow freely to everyone but himself.

4

Third Countries

Private American contributions to keep the contras going did more for the money-raisers than for the contras. The foreign or third-country method paid off with far less effort and brought far more money.

The basic idea first came to McFarlane. In the spring of 1983, he learned that Israel might be willing to provide security assistance and agricultural training to other countries. In a note to North, he wondered whether, since U.S. appropriations for Israel increased every year, Israel might not be willing to sign over the increase for use in Central America.[1]

This line of thought took on greater concreteness the following year, as the contras' funding by the United States was expected to run out in the spring of 1984. McFarlane again thought of Israel as the way out of the Boland dilemma. The idea of "farming out the whole Contra support operation" to Israel was even considered, not only for funding but to give the operation "some direction." In February or March 1984, McFarlane met with David Kimche, his Israeli counterpart, and proposed a deal. Israel, McFarlane knew, was interested in getting the United States to help it qualify for agricultural contracts or water resource development in the Caribbean. Would Israel also be interested in instructing the contras in basic tactics, maneuvers, and the like?[2]

Casey was of a similar mind. On March 27, 1984, Casey informed McFarlane that he fully agreed with him about exploring "funding alternatives" with Israel "and perhaps others." But Casey wanted to keep the CIA out of it and advised McFarlane: "I believe your thought of putting one of your staff in touch with the appropriate Israeli official should be promptly pursued since funds run out in mid-May." Casey also suggested that "one of the alternatives would be acquiring from the Israelis additional ordnance which had been captured by them."[3] It was an early indication that the NSC staff could be pressed into service in an operational role to do what the CIA would have done if it had not been restrained by the Boland Amendment.

McFarlane took Casey's advice and instructed Howard J. Teicher, then a junior member of the Near East and South Asia Directorate of the NSC staff, to get a message to the Israeli Foreign Ministry that "the U.S. government would appreciate help for the contras and that this was to be kept as discreet as possible." By "help," McFarlane meant material and financial assistance.[4] The Israelis declined the proposal, with the result that McFarlane told Teicher to explain to them that the matter was important to the United States, that we were very conscious of "the vulnerability it would create" for Israel, that help to the contras should be carried out bilaterally if Israel should change its mind, and that McFarlane was "a little disappointed" but would not press Israel or raise the matter again.[5]

This was the first overture to Israel on behalf of the contras. It suggested that the United States looked to Israel to cope with the problem of Nicaragua, as it later looked to Israel in the Iran affair.

At this stage, however, Casey and McFarlane encountered some resistance from Secretary of State George P. Shultz. The latter had previously accepted the possibility of third-country support. In a message to President Reagan of September 6, 1983, Shultz had noted that the contras might continue to be funded, if necessary, by "alternative benefactors."[6] But on April 18, 1984, Shultz told McFarlane that he was opposed to approaching Israel for contra support, that he could not agree on using another country as an intermediary or conduit for aid to the contras, and that he questioned its legality. Shultz soon learned that his latest convictions had not impressed McFarlane. U.S. Ambassador Samuel Lewis sent word from Israel that Teicher had already approached an official of the Israeli Foreign Ministry for a contribution to the contras and had said that the U.S. government was willing to serve as a conduit for it. Shultz was offended, because he had not been informed that such an approach was going to be made and had expressed opposition to it. At the beginning of May, Shultz told McFarlane that he objected to the whole thing. McFarlane, according to Shultz, disingenuously replied that Teicher had gone to Israel without instructions and "on his own hook." Teicher promptly informed Lewis that he was there "under instructions." McFarlane later admitted that he had told Teicher to go.[7]

The incident revealed how far outside the normal channels of government the national security adviser was willing to go. Though the approach to Israel clearly came within the sphere of foreign affairs and the U.S. ambassador was expected to know what was going on in Israel, the secretary of state had not been consulted and had to learn about it from his ambassador, who had received the information from Israeli sources, not from Teicher. One part of the U.S. government had to find out from a foreign government what another part of the U.S. government was doing. In effect, McFarlane behaved as if he were authorized to conduct his own foreign policy in this area.

It was not the last time that a senior cabinet member would have to find out from another country what the NSC staff was doing.

In 1984, there were also some confused moves by the CIA to get assistance for the contras from South Africa. It seems that in January a South African official had given Director Casey reason to believe that South Africa was prepared to provide equipment and training for the contras. By April, however, it was clear that both sides had had second thoughts. The South African offer was never clearly defined, and the more the CIA learned about it, the more problematic it became, for one thing because the South Africans wanted to be paid by the United States for whatever they were expected to do. The CIA backed out altogether after the eruption of the Nicaraguan mining "furor," as a CIA message put it, because it did not wish to add a South African entanglement to the existing imbroglio.[8] Despite his qualms, Secretary of State Shultz was reported in a CIA cable to have approved of the "initiative."[9] In effect, the incident was the second unsuccessful effort to get third-country assistance for the contras.[10]

Both Casey and McFarlane were clearly groping for ways to get "alternative benefactors" for the Nicaraguan contras. They did not have to grope for long.

2

Shultz was another embattled secretary of state.

On May 25, 1983, Shultz had sent President Reagan a memorandum entitled "Managing Our Central American Strategy." It complained that "the present management situation is a mess and would not work even if the problems were simple." Shultz reminded the president that they had agreed that "you will look to me to carry out your policies." Shultz had taken this position:

> If those policies change, you will tell me. If I am not carrying them out effectively, you will hold me accountable. But we will set up a structure so that I can be your sole delegate with regard to carrying out your policies.

Shultz proposed appointing an assistant secretary of state "who will report to me and through me to you." He also wanted a "negotiator," a position that was only temporarily filled. Finally, he called for an Interagency Committee (IC), made up of representatives from the interested departments and agencies, as "a tool of management and not a decision-making body." In short, he wanted the line of authority to go from the president to the secretary of state to the assistant secretary to the Interagency Committee.[11]

Shultz did not get his wish. The president sent him a reply that evaded the main question—whether the secretary of state was his "sole delegate" to carry out his policies. Instead Reagan refused to change the existing system, which made the policy process function primarily through the Interagency Committee and the National Security Council, in both of which the State Department was only one of several members. If the IC agreed, the issue did not need to go any higher, and even if it disagreed, the issue would go to a Senior Interagency Group (SIG) and from there, if necessary, to the National Security Council and finally to the president himself.

The language of the president's decision left no doubt that the secretary of state, though a "lead Cabinet officer," was merely one among several, without any special prerogative in Central American affairs:

> Success in Central America will require the cooperative effort of several Departments and agencies. No single agency can do it alone nor should it. Still, it is sensible to look to you, as I do, as the lead Cabinet officer, charged with moving aggressively to develop the options in coordination with Cap [Secretary of Defense Weinberger], Bill Casey and others and coming to me for decisions. I believe in Cabinet government. It works when the Cabinet officers work together. I look to you and Bill Clark [then national security adviser] to assure that that happens.[12]

This system made the secretary of state a cog in the machine, not the driver. In theory, the secretary of state, secretary of defense, director of the CIA, and national security adviser were expected to cooperate and coordinate. In practice, the national security adviser was put in the most strategic position to serve the policies and interests of the president. At the time, National Security Adviser Clark was particularly close to the president and benefited most from the decision.

When Clark was replaced by McFarlane, who did not have the same intimate relationship with the president but who as Clark's former deputy knew all about the president's decision, the system did not change. Despite McFarlane's lesser prestige and authority, he carried on as if he could send a subordinate to Israel on a sensitive mission without the knowledge or approval of the secretary of state. When Shultz protested, the line drawn by the president between their respective spheres was so unclear in practice that McFarlane was constrained to dissemble rather than to assert his own right to make an independent overture to Israel.

This confusion of roles could only have been straightened out by a more alert and forceful president or a more spirited and assertive secretary of state. Instead, President Reagan was not one to inquire too closely into actions of those right under him, unless they were brought to him directly as the result of a falling-out among his top advisers. Shultz had put himself in a false position by demanding that he should be the president's "sole delegate" and by being forced to accept an inferior role. At this point, he was confronted with the choice of protesting, up to the point of resignation, or abjectly accepting the implied humiliation. When Shultz decided to go along with the president's decision, he let himself in for more such unpleasant indignities and pathetic complaints. The end of this road for Shultz came at the climax of the Iran-contra affairs, when he was forced to admit publicly that he did not speak for the administration. In fact, he had put himself on a slippery slope of increased embarrassment from the moment his proposal of May 25, 1983, had been turned against him.

A year later, Shultz again found himself on the losing end. By their failure, the efforts of Casey and McFarlane to find a third-country substitute for the United States to take care of the contras raised more questions than they answered. The very legality of such approaches was still questionable. To face the issue, a meeting of the National Security Planning Group (NSPG) was called on June 25, 1984.

This meeting is of special interest not only because of its intrinsic importance but because we have unusually full minutes of it, covering almost fourteen single-spaced pages. The highest level of the administration's officialdom was present—President Reagan, Vice President Bush, Secretary of State George P. Shultz, Secretary of Defense Caspar W. Weinberger, CIA Director William J. Casey, UN Ambassador Jeane J. Kirkpatrick, Chairman of the Joint Chiefs of Staff General John W. Vessey, Jr., White House Counselor Edwin Meese III, National Security Adviser Robert C. McFarlane, and Deputy National Security Adviser John M. Poindexter. The minutes were taken by Constantine C. Menges, a member of the NSC staff. They provide a unique insight into the thinking of the top leadership at this juncture.

The meeting was called to discuss what to do about the Nicaraguan contras. They had run out of money by May 1984, and no additional funds were expected from Congress. After general remarks by McFarlane, Shultz, Casey, Weinberger, and Vessey, President Reagan stated the purpose of the meeting:

> It all hangs on support for the anti-Sandinistas. How can we get that support in the Congress? We have to be more active. With respect to your differences on negotiating, our participation is important from that standpoint, to get support from Congress.[13]

Weinberger and Shultz briefly disagreed on a detail of the U.S. negotiating position. Again Reagan broke in:

> If we are just talking about negotiations with Nicaragua, that is so farfetched to imagine that a Communist government like that

would make any reasonable deal with us, but if it is to get Congress to support the anti-Sandinistas, then that can be helpful.

The main object of the meeting came down to where to get money for the contras if Congress refused to appropriate it. Kirkpatrick urged that it should come from somewhere else:

> If we don't find the money to support the contras, it will be perceived in the region and the world as our having abandoned them . . . If we can't get the money for the anti-Sandinistas, then we should make the maximum effort to find the money elsewhere.

"Elsewhere" implied getting money from other, or "third," countries. Secretary Shultz's response showed what had been implied and revealed his own misgivings:

> I would like to get money for the Contras, also, but another lawyer, Jim Baker [then Chief of Staff], said that if we go out and try to get money from third countries, it is an impeachable offense. *

Thereupon an argument broke out over Baker's view as Shultz had stated it. Casey insisted that Baker had said getting money from third countries without notifying the congressional oversight committees might be a problem, but that he had dropped his objection as soon as he had been informed that a previous Finding of September 19, 1983, had provided for "the participation and cooperation of third countries."†

Shultz was not convinced: "Jim Baker's argument is that the U.S.

---

* In his deposition before the Senate Select Committee, June 22, 1987, Baker was confused about the June 25, 1984, meeting, which he thought had taken place in the fall of 1984. Though Baker is not listed as a participant in the earlier NSPG meeting, he claimed to recall a similar discussion at the later meeting. When he was asked what his view had been, he replied: "My view was that we should take a very close look at that question and I so stated in the meeting. And it was my view that we could not do indirectly what we could not do directly. My recollection is that a similar reservation was expressed by Secretary Shultz, that the meeting generally concluded with a decision to take a hard look at the legality of third-country solicitations." This statement suggests that Baker had serious doubts about their legality.

When Baker was asked whether he recalled making the "impeachable offense" statement, he said: "No, I don't recall using that language or having a specific opinion such as that" and repeated that he had felt that "we should take a very close look at the question of legality and feeling that we could not do indirectly what we couldn't do directly." Shultz had also told his executive assistant, Charles Hill, that Baker had used the phrase about "impeachable offense" (B-2, pp. 677–80). McFarlane recalled hearing Baker use the same words (McFarlane, NT, p. 3943).

† This Finding, of which we now have three different versions, illustrates the absurdity of the classification system. Two versions appear in A-1, pp. 776–78 and 252–54. The deletions are so great that little more than a single sentence appears in each version, but there are a few words more in the second than in the first. The third version appears in Defense Exhibit 58 of the North trial, where it is nearly complete. Two words censored in the third version appear in the second. The 1983 Finding merely recommended "cooperation with other countries" and "support of and work with other foreign governments and organizations to carry out this program." It clearly fell short of authorizing getting money from third countries.

Government may raise and spend funds only through an appropriation of Congress." Weinberger supported Casey by arguing that the United States would not be spending its own money. Shultz fell back with a request for an opinion from the attorney general "on whether we can help the Contras obtain money from third sources."

Reagan spoke up for a third time, on the question of holding U.S. troop exercises in Honduras:

> Even the appearance of movement of U.S. troops into Honduras for exercises, the movement of small units, would likely help the morale of Honduras.

And the president spoke up for the fourth time, fifth time, sixth time, seventh time, and eighth time on the advisability of negotiations with the Nicaraguans and the Contadora nations. The significance of this number is less in what he said than in the many times he chose to say it, suggesting a very active engagement in this policymaking.

Toward the end, Vice President Bush put in a few words:

> How can anyone object to the U.S. encouraging third parties to provide help to the anti-Sandinistas under the Finding? The only problem that might come up is if the United States were to promise these third parties something in return so that some people could interpret this as some kind of an exchange.

That there was still some doubt about the advisability of such help from third parties was made clear by McFarlane toward the close:

> I propose that there be no authority for anyone to seek third party support for the anti-Sandinistas until we have the information we need, and I certainly hope none of this discussion will be made public in any way.

President Reagan had the last word in his ninth and most prophetic pronouncement:

> If such a story goes out, we'll all be hanging by our thumbs in front of the White House until we find out who did it.

This peculiar statement has seemed in need of interpretation. Reagan later said it meant "if we ever get our hands on the people who are doing the leaking of this various secret information that—that we'd be hanging by our thumbs in front of the White House until we found out."[14] In effect, the "story" of seeking third-country monetary support for the contras by the United States was so explosive that it had to be prevented from getting out at all costs, even if the president and all those present at this meeting had to hang by their thumbs in front of the White House until they found out who was leaking it. McFarlane gave a more specific reason why a leak could not be tolerated—because it "would lead Congress to react."[15] The point would seem to be that third-country support in place of congressional appropriation needed unusual secrecy because it was constitutionally or politically dubious or even indefensible.

This NSPG meeting was critically important. It dealt with one of the most questionable and secretive aspects of Reagan's new Nicaraguan policy—the decision to bypass congressional appropriations and to resort to implied solicitation of funds from other countries. The president's final words, however they are to be interpreted, showed how dangerous he knew it to be. Shultz, by citing Baker, had even called up the specter of impeachment.

Baker recalled a similar discussion in the fall of 1984, in which he had taken the position that "we could not do indirectly what we could not do directly."[16] Bush had blurred this essential constitutional issue. If the Reagan administration wheedled money out of other countries to do what it could not do with congressionally appropriated funds, it put a fundamental constitutional principle at risk. Third-country funding of the contras was subversive of the very core of the constitutional separation of powers. To deprive Congress of its "power over the purse" was to deprive it of effective legislative power.* By finding a substitute source of money, the administration in effect found a substitute for Congress. Bush's intervention was also the first time on record that the problem of a "quid pro quo" was raised in the contra affair.

The issue of legality was confronted the very next day, June 26, 1984, at a meeting attended by Casey, Attorney General William French Smith, CIA General Counsel Stanley Sporkin, and other departmental lawyers. In the end, Smith offered the opinion that there was no legal reason why the United States could not discuss contra funding with other countries so long as certain conditions were met. Other countries had to use their own funds to support the contras and could not use any U.S. appropriated funds or expect the United States to repay them in the future. Casey gave an assurance that the CIA would inform the congressional oversight committees in the event that it decided to seek contra funds from other countries.[17]

This was not the only legal opinion sought and obtained by the CIA on the subject. In August 1984, as a result of the pending Boland Amendment, Casey asked for another opinion from CIA General Counsel Spor-

---

* In No. 58 of *The Federalist,* James Madison wrote: "This power over the purse may in fact be regarded as the most compleat and effective weapon with which any constitution can arm the immediate representatives of the people, for obtaining a redress of every grievance, and for carrying into effect every just and salutary measure."

kin on third-country funding. A study done in Sporkin's office found that the Agency could legally request third countries to carry on the Nicaraguan program of the United States so long as it was at their own expense and without U.S. repayment. The more difficult question, however, was whether CIA personnel could be used to solicit contributions. The answer was that CIA personnel could not be used for this purpose, "because such efforts would have the effect of indirectly supporting paramilitary operations."[18]

After the passage of Boland II, Sporkin and other officials met to go over some of the same ground. Sporkin's opinion was now based on a subtle distinction, in order to give the CIA as much leeway as possible. It was all right to communicate with third countries about any plans or intentions they might have to aid the contras, on the ground that such inquiries came within the sphere of traditional intelligence-collecting activity. But the United States could not give other countries any "inducements" to support the contras. Sporkin recognized that the difference might be questioned "pragmatically" and suggested that all conversations with third-country representatives should be fully documented to show that no inducements had been offered.[19]

From all this one gathers that soliciting funds for the contras from other countries was something new in American policy. There was no precedent for such action, and the legal opinions were based on the language of the Boland Amendment rather than on any larger constitutional framework. The only question was what the CIA was permitted to do. Despite all the legal activity, according to Shultz, the State Department never received a legal opinion on the matter from the attorney general. "The subject seemed to die down," Shultz said.[20]

CIA Deputy Director McMahon, to whom Sporkin's legal opinion was addressed, was refreshingly realistic about why other countries might be willing to come to the aid of the United States with support of the contras. He recognized that the Boland Amendment made it illegal for the CIA to support the contras, "because the Agency under our ground rules can never ask someone to undertake an action that it can't legally do itself." A surrogate would have to have the same authorization "of what we want the surrogate to do." But, he was asked, would not another country expect something from the United States in the future? McMahon replied: "They obviously will do something to curry our favor, but it may not be anything specific at the time. They just want to stay in good terms, much as they would vote favorably for us at the U.N., knowing that that kind of incurs a debt of unspecificity in the future."[21]

For McMahon, it was not so much a question of an immediate quid pro quo as of a "debt of unspecificity," a nice distinction that had not occurred to the lawyers who had been giving their legal opinions about barring "inducements" to get third-country support. Whether the lawyers chose to take it into account or not, that kind of unspecific debt was not likely to have escaped the notice of the next third country that was solicited to come to the aid of the contras.

In the end, it was decided that it was not a good idea, as McFarlane put it, to campaign for the contras in an election year. This left only foreign countries as possible sources of money for the contras.[22]

3

The odd thing about all the legal discussions and opinions was that they had already been overtaken by events.

While McFarlane was participating in these discussions, he had already successfully arranged for a substantial contribution from Saudi Arabia. As he told the story, he was accustomed to meet with the Saudi ambassador, Prince Bandar bin Sultan, at intervals of about every three months. Before talking to Prince Bandar about the contras, McFarlane had discussed the advisability of doing so with the Interdepartmental Group on legislative strategy, whose chairman was Chief of Staff Baker, but not with the president himself.[23] In June 1984, McFarlane told Prince Bandar that the administration was almost certainly going to lose the vote in Congress on support for the contras and that it would represent "a substantial loss for the president."[24] Two or three days later, Prince Bandar informed McFarlane that the Saudis, ostensibly from private funds, were willing to contribute $1 million a month for the rest of the year to enable the contras to survive. This money actually came to $8 million and extended into early 1985.[25] When McFarlane told President Reagan about the contribution, the president "made clear to me that no one should [know about it] and let's keep it that way."[26]

McFarlane stressed that he had not solicited the money; he had merely said that "this impending loss would represent a significant setback for the president, and if anyone with any gumption could manage without being led or asked, then a contribution would have been welcome." McFarlane later explained: "And I think it became pretty obvious to the ambassador that his country, to gain a considerable amount of favor and, frankly, they thought it was the right thing to do, they would provide the support when the Congress cut it off."[27]

Saudi Arabia, 12,000 miles away, had no national interest in Nicaragua, with which it did not even have diplomatic relations. It was clearly intimated that money for the contras would "gain a considerable amount of favor" with President Reagan. The transaction was so unprecedented that neither McFarlane nor the ambassador knew how to proceed. McFarlane went back to his office, informed his deputy, Poindexter, and then instructed North to find out from the contra leaders in what bank account to put the money.

The entire business was handled with extraordinary furtiveness. North obtained the number of Adolfo Calero's account in the Miami branch of a bank on Grand Cayman Island. McFarlane handed the Saudi ambassador a 3 by 5 index card with the number on it. Calero did the rest. *

A day or two later, at their usual meeting at nine-thirty in the morning, McFarlane informed President Reagan of his success by handing him a note card to the effect that Saudi Arabia had "chosen to volunteer $1 million per month through the end of the year for Contras' subsistence." McFarlane used the method of the note card because he did not wish others present to know of the transaction. After the meeting, McFarlane was told to come back to get the card, on which was expressed "the President's satisfaction and pleasure that this had occurred."

McFarlane soon told Vice President Bush of the Saudis' largesse. At a regular weekly breakfast on Wednesdays with Shultz and Weinberger, McFarlane also informed them that the contras had been provided for through the end of the year but did not tell them who had done the providing.[28] In effect, McFarlane could claim that he had not solicited Saudi funding for the contras, in much the same way that North claimed not to have solicited private donors. By not soliciting, they seemed to mean that they had done everything but actually ask for money. No heed was paid to Baker's dictum that the government could not do indirectly what it could not do directly.

By February 1985, the first $8 million of Saudi money was running out. Just when the contras seemed to be set for another financial crisis, the Saudis again came to the rescue.

In that month, King Fahd ibn Abdul-Aziz paid a visit to Washington. In preparation for it, McFarlane again reminded Prince Bandar that the United States was still faced with the problem of funding the contras. King Fahd was given an unusual reception by President Reagan. They met once in the Oval Office, which was customary, but now a second meeting took place in the family residence of the White House, which, as McFarlane explained, "represents a special level of cachet and singling out for special treatment of a foreign visitor." At the end of the second session, Fahd was also treated to a one-on-one or private session with the president, "which is also an added measure of respect and standing."[29]

When Reagan soon afterward debriefed Shultz and McFarlane about his private meeting with King Fahd, he made no mention of anything to do with additional contra funding. A day or two later, however, McFarlane was told by Prince Bandar that the Saudis were going to give the contras $2 million a month for another year, for which McFarlane thanked him.[30] McFarlane sent Reagan a note about the new contri-

---

* McFarlane later recalled that the Saudi ambassador had asked him where to send the money; McFarlane asked North to find out where the contras did their banking so he could tell the ambassador; North got the information—a bank in Miami—and McFarlane passed it on to the ambassador (McFarlane, NT, p. 3950).

bution, thinking that it was going to be news, but soon learned that
Reagan, for good reason, already knew about it.[31]

Just what had happened between President Reagan and King Fahd was
not known until Reagan himself told about the scene five years later:

> And nothing was said about the contra or contra aid until he
> stood up to leave. And as he was leaving the Oval Office and I was
> escorting him to the door, he told me of the contribution that he
> had been making to the contras. There had been no discussion of
> that in our meeting until that. He told me that, and his last words
> were—was that he was going to double it.

In effect, the contras were going to get $2 million a month from the
Saudis. The president merely replied: "I think that's fine."[32]

When he later discussed foreign contributions to the contras, Reagan
candidly said that "I wanted them [others] to be involved [in helping the
contras], but I didn't want to be on record as doing it." Like North, he
stopped short of actually soliciting: "Yes, I remember that I said that our
fellow democracies ought to be as interested in heading off this com-
munization of a country as we are. And I did not suggest actually soliciting, but that it would be worthwhile to mention to those democracies
what we were doing, and we believed it was something that democracy
should be interested in."[33] It did not seem to occur to him that Saudi
Arabia was as far from democracy as a country could be. "No solicitation"
apparently meant not asking for money outright but rather intimating
that it would be much appreciated.

Some officials knew about the Saudi money, some did not. The chairman of the Joint Chiefs of Staff, Admiral William J. Crowe, Jr., and
Secretary of Defense Weinberger knew; Secretary of State Shultz and
CIA Director Casey did not. McFarlane did not tell Shultz the good
news until June 1986, after the money had run out.[34] McFarlane never
told Casey about it, though Casey undoubtedly had his own sources for
the information, because Casey once complained to McFarlane that
North was talking too much and had told a CIA official where the money
was coming from, an accusation that North hotly denied.[35] No one in
Congress was told.[36] In any case, the total of both Saudi contributions
has been put at about $32 million.[37]

McFarlane was asked whether he had been "uncomfortable that you
might be creating some implicit quid pro quo." He replied: "Yes. You
always have to consider what is it that you may invite by way of reciprocal
gesture or concession, what obligation do you incur for having had some
contribution of this kind. Yes."[38] Yet the Saudis at the time did not ask
for anything in return; such debts, as McMahon put it, were "unspecific."

A peculiar coincidence soon took place at a meeting between Mc-
Farlane and four Republican congressmen, including Representative

Henry J. Hyde of Illinois. On March 4, 1985, they came together to discuss aid for the contras, in the course of which, as McFarlane reported, Hyde "felt that we should expand private sector and third country assistance, such as Taiwan and Saudi Arabia, in the effort to support the resistance. I explained why these are just not tenable alternatives—for the freedom fighters or for us."*[39] Oddly, Hyde had hit on the very two countries that made contributions to the contras. Nevertheless, McFarlane felt obliged to deny that support from them was "tenable," though one had already provided such support and the other was going to do so.

By April 1985, in any case, North again served notice to McFarlane that the contras needed more money. He reported that Calero's FDN had received a total of $8 million from July 1984 through February 1985, and $16.5 million from February 22, 1985, to April 9, 1985, for a grand total of $24.5 million. Of this sum, $17,145,594 had been spent for arms, munitions, combat operations, and support activities. This funding had enabled the contras' manpower to increase from 9,500 in June 1984 to over 16,000 in April 1985.

Nevertheless, he warned that the remaining $7 million was insufficient to make any more progress. He called for efforts to get an additional $15–$20 million from the "current donors," understood to be Saudi Arabia, by June 1985.[40] McFarlane thought that this was going too far and turned down the proposal. He testified that he considered another approach to the Saudis to be both illegal and unbefitting, the latter because we should not "rely on somebody else to sustain a policy, we couldn't"—considerations that applied just as well to the Saudis' magnanimity earlier.[41]

McFarlane, if one can believe his later professions, tended to do things, or tolerate others' doing them, even though he knew better. North had no such qualms; he never seems to have cared where the money was coming from. Casey also had misgivings at this time similar to Shultz's and McFarlane's. He and McMahon met with McFarlane in March 1985, soon after the Saudis' second contribution, on the strategy adopted by the administration to ask Congress for an additional $14 million for nonlethal aid to the contras. Casey expressed some concern about "relying on third countries to supply either arms or funds for arms." McMahon feared that reliance on them virtually let Congress "off the hook" and would even give congressional opponents of contra aid a motive "to ferret out those countries providing arms or dollars to the contras and will then seek to cut off any aid or arms sales we have with those countries."[42] The third-country quick fix was by no means without risks and drawbacks, even to its promoters. Yet so long as President Reagan knew about it and was even a party to getting the money, no one put up much opposition to it or had anything better to propose.

---

* The other three were Robert Stump, Arizona; Robert Livingston, Louisiana; and Bill McCollum, Florida.

Thus the contras were expected to need more money by at least the end of 1985. Only the Saudi money, McFarlane admitted, had enabled them to survive in the field thus far.[43] If the Reagan administration had not relied on somebody else to pay, it would have risked a collapse of its Nicaraguan policy by 1984.

Meanwhile, North was worried that Congress might find out about the Saudis' prodigality. He informed Calero: "Next week, a sum of $20 million will be deposited in the usual account." It was enough, he estimated, "to bridge the gap" until Congress was expected to renew funding for the contras.[44] He then conspiratorily instructed Calero:

Request you advise me soonest regarding the deposit and destroy this letter. . . . Please do *not* in any way make *anyone* aware of the deposit. Too much is becoming known by too many people. We need to make sure that this new financing does *not* become known. The Congress must believe that there continues to be an urgent need for funding.[45]

There was, in fact, no urgent need at this time. The urgent need, according to North, was to conceal from Congress that there was no urgent need. North alone was privileged to decide what Congress should or should not know.

In fact, Saudi Arabia was not the only foreign country to come to the aid of the contras. In the summer of 1985, North came to see Dr. Gaston J. Sigur, then an NSC consultant for East Asian and Pacific Affairs and later the assistant secretary of state for the same region. North told Sigur that he and McFarlane wanted him to get in touch with the Taiwanese ambassador to get help in Central America, because, according to North, the contras were in "a desperate situation." The ambassador indicated that a previous approach had already been made and thought that his government was willing to help financially, but "they want to provide the money through the U.S. government," not directly to the contras. McFarlane replied: "That can't be done. Can't do that."

Sigur subsequently arranged a meeting for North with the Taiwanese defense attaché in Washington. To influence Taiwan to part with the money, North gave him the curious assurance that Adolfo Calero was willing to make a commitment to recognize the Taiwanese regime after the contras had succeeded in taking power in Nicaragua.[46]

Sigur was next informed that Taiwan was prepared to offer $1 million to the contras. North told Sigur to inform the ambassador that someone would come to his office and tell him how to make the contribution. North then gave his usual courier, Robert Owen, an envelope, which contained the number of the secret Secord-Hakim bank account in Switzerland, to deliver to the ambassador.[47] Later this procedure was repeated, and Taiwan chipped in with another million.[48]

Even the relatively small sum of $2 million was worth North's repeated importunity, as if the United States had been reduced to accepting any handout to the contras. Sigur was later asked whether he had had any qualms about asking a third country to donate to the contras. Sigur replied that he had asked North whether "you are sure everything you are going to do here is legal." North had answered, "Oh, yes," that he had checked it out with lawyers. Did Sigur ever think of consulting the State Department on what was clearly a foreign affair in Latin America not remotely in his area of responsibility? Sigur explained:

> I never thought about it one way or the other. I thought this was a request from McFarlane. He was my boss and I did what he asked me to do. It was as simple as that. My assumption was that this was agreed upon policy. . . . I had no reason to doubt Ollie at all. . . . Everybody knew, at least I thought, that on matters involving this area Ollie spoke for McFarlane. There was never any question about that.[49]

Sigur was thus made an accessory to North's fund-raising activities by simply doing what he was told to do. In effect, North had at his disposal a far-flung network in the government by virtue of his own position on the NSC staff and his assumed authorization from McFarlane, who in turn was assumed to have been authorized by the president.

Sigur was one of the few who ever asked Oliver North whether what he was doing was legal. North always answered with a confident "yes," thus cutting short further questions. If Sigur had known how North knew it was legal, he might have had some qualms.

The president had a counsel; the State Department had a legal adviser; the Department of Defense had a counsel; the CIA had a general counsel; the NSC staff had a counsel. But none of these was asked to pass judgment on the issue. Instead, the task was somehow taken on by an obscure young lawyer at the equally obscure Intelligence Oversight Board (IOB), a body that had been set up in 1976 by President Gerald Ford as a pacifying gesture after previous intelligence misconduct.

The IOB's counsel was Bretton G. Sciaroni, thirty-two years old when he was hired in 1984. He had passed his bar examinations on his fifth try, had never practiced law, had been employed in a legal capacity for the first time by the IOB, and had never before written a legal opinion on a legislative act. One of the lighter moments in his testimony at the congressional hearings came when he was asked why he had been chosen to give an opinion on the case. Sciaroni replied:

> Frankly, sir, that's—that thought has crossed my mind, as well. You have a White House counsel's office, you have an NSC general counsel, and if they were too busy, they had a Department of Justice

to get an opinion from. I don't know why my opinion was the only one.

Sciaroni did not work very hard to find out what the issue was all about. He limited his investigation to about twenty-five minutes of conversation with the NSC staff counsel, Commander Paul B. Thompson, spent no more than five minutes with North, and went over some papers that Thompson gave him, none of them the incriminating ones, in North's office. He was not shown documents which he later admitted would have "jumped out at me" and "would have been relevant to my query." In fact, according to Sciaroni, Thompson had assured him orally that no effort had been made to get third countries to enable the contras to purchase arms. All Sciaroni had asked North was whether the newspaper reports of his activities in behalf of the contras were true, and North had merely denied everything—which satisfied Sciaroni.

Sciaroni's opinion predictably said that the NSC staff was not covered by the Boland Amendment, though North himself was covered, because he was paid by funds from the Department of Defense. Sciaroni later admitted that he had been misled and that his legal opinion had been partially based on "incorrect facts." North blithely confessed that he had denied having engaged in fund-raising and having given military advice "because, after all, we viewed this to be a covert operation and he [Sciaroni] had absolutely no need to know the details of what I was doing."[50] Yet North apparently used Sciaroni's opinion to fend off questions about the legality of his actions.

4

Another fund-raiser who did not wait for a decision on the the legality of third-country contributions was retired Major General John K. Singlaub. He was a filibustering type, who had injected himself into the contra affair without anyone's leave and who operated without official status but not without the blessing and cooperation of some officials, especially North.

Singlaub had spent over thirty-five years in the army, with service in World War II, the Korean War, the Vietnam War, and afterward. His career had come to an abrupt halt in 1978, when he had publicly denounced President Jimmy Carter in congressional hearings for Carter's intention to withdraw troops from Korea. Though Carter later changed his mind—or had it changed for him by congressional pressure—and withdrew the withdrawal, Singlaub thought it the better part of wisdom to put in for voluntary retirement in May of that year.

This climax to a long military career showed that Singlaub did not play by the rules. He was particularly obsessed by the Communist threat and took it upon himself to put the world on guard against it. In 1981, he formed the U.S. chapter of the World Anti-Communist League, founded in 1954 by the first president of South Korea, Syngman Rhee. Singlaub was also an unpaid military consultant to the GeoMiliTech Consultants Corporation, which handled an arms shipment to the contras.

Singlaub says that his introduction to Central American politics in the early 1980s took the form of recruiting former U.S. military personnel to train the army of El Salvador. By 1984, he was briefing U.S. officials on similar antiguerrilla operations. One of those briefed was North, whom he had first encountered at one of his briefings three years earlier. Singlaub testified that he saw North whenever he came to Washington, eight to ten times a year. When Singlaub's activities were reported in the press in the summer of 1985, however, North is said to have asked Singlaub to cut down the number of his meetings in North's office.[51]

Singlaub did not need an invitation to get into the increasingly difficult Nicaraguan struggle. In January 1984, he approached Adolfo Calero on his own and offered to help by raising funds and recruiting military advisers, as he had done in El Salvador. He informed North of his intentions and went ahead to implement them.[52] North's notebook shows that Singlaub was constantly in touch with him, at least until Singlaub attracted too much public attention to himself and made North nervous about seeing him in his office.

Singlaub became a one-man collection agency. He was responsible for several shipments of medicines to the contras in 1984.[53] Toward the end of 1984, he met with the ambassadors of Taiwan and South Korea, both of whom he had long known. Despite his military background, he was a high-pressure salesman, who presented himself on behalf of the contras as a private citizen who did not have to abide by the restrictions of the Boland Amendment. Unlike U.S. officials, he could openly solicit funds for guns, bullets, missiles, and anything else the contras might need. The ambassadors expressed sympathy for his cause but were apprehensive that Congress might be irritated if their collusion leaked out. Singlaub decided that he could do better by going to both countries and meeting with high officials on the spot.

Before setting off in January 1985, Singlaub says, he went to see North about his trip. North encouraged him to go and asked him to report upon his return. They also discussed using foreign nationals to conduct operations inside Nicaragua, and North particularly mentioned the British mercenary David Walker, of whom Singlaub approved.

In Taiwan and South Korea, Singlaub met with high officials who knew him from his service as chief of staff during the Korean War. He again stressed that the United States was encountering great difficulties in helping the contras and that he hoped "they would come to the aid of a country that had been friendly with them for many, many years at this difficult time." He asked for $10 million in all, half from each one. It was understood that they were primarily being asked to help the United States and to help the contras only to please the United States. To ease their anxiety about the effect on Congress, Singlaub assured them that he could arrange to conceal their contributions. One of Singlaub's proposals to Taiwan was ingenious. Since Taiwan bought a large quantity of expensive materials from private dealers in the United States, Singlaub suggested that he should get the vendors to give a commission on their sales to the contras. [54]

The Taiwanese wanted to know about Singlaub's relationship with the U.S. government. Singlaub told them that his role was unofficial but that he could get someone in the Reagan administration to send a "signal" that he was not operating entirely on his own and without the administration's knowledge as an "unguided missile." When he returned to Washington, he reported to North, who told him that such a signal would be arranged. Though Singlaub was not told of it, the signal came from North through the meeting set up for him by Sigur with the Taiwanese defense attaché. [55]

Singlaub next planned to pay a personal visit to the FDN's camp in Honduras. Like Sigur and others, he first asked North about the legality of supplying arms for the contras. North, Singlaub says, assured him that he had obtained the rules governing these activities from lawyers in the Justice Department—that all was legal so long as solicitation, banking, and movement of supplies were done outside the United States.

In March 1985, on his visit to the FDN camp, Singlaub met with the military commander, Enrique Bermúdez, and drew up a list of desired arms and ammunition, which he brought back to North, who approved after making some modifications. Singlaub next met in Washington with an arms dealer who was able to get weapons produced in the Soviet bloc, especially AK-47 rifles and SAM-7 air defense missiles. By this time, however, Singlaub found himself in competition with Secord as the contras' supplier. Singlaub related that he could get SAM-7s for half the price at which Secord had previously sold them to the contras but that North and Calero had decided in favor of Secord on the ground that the latter could also provide trainers in the use of the weapons.

Singlaub's arms arrived in Honduras in July 1985, thanks to the cooperation of a Honduran official in charge of the port. They were Soviet-bloc weapons acquired from Eastern Europe, a paradoxical circumstance in view of the contras' belief that they were fighting a Communist regime in Nicaragua. [56] Singlaub paid the supplier $4.8 million and received $5.3 million from the contras; after various expenses, he claimed to have had $200,000 left over, with which he allegedly bought "humanitarian" aid. [57] It was his first and last delivery; though Singlaub was Calero's favorite, North and Secord decided to cut him out of the arms business with the contras. Singlaub complained to Calero that Secord was making a profit; Secord told Calero that Singlaub's prices were so low that he could not deliver.[58] Singlaub himself seems to have raised a relatively modest amount for them—$279,612 in 1985 and $259,173 in 1986.[59]

Singlaub was not finished and brought unwelcome attention to himself at a later stage. Meanwhile, he was another of North's contacts and collaborators. Singlaub says that he made it a rule to keep North informed of his activities and to get his approval for them. North in turn would inform McFarlane of his dealings with Singlaub. On December 4, 1984, for example, a memorandum from North to McFarlane told of Singlaub's role in soliciting funds from Taiwan. If it wanted to help, North wrote, "Singlaub can arrange a meeting [of a Taiwanese official] with Calero."[60] In another message to McFarlane, North reported that both Taiwan and South Korea had indicated that they wanted to help "in a big way" as a result of Singlaub's recent trip. North added that, "with your [Mc-Farlane's] permission," he would ask Singlaub to urge them "to proceed with their offer. Singlaub would then put Calero in direct contact with each of these officers. No White House/NSC solicitation would be made. Nor should Singlaub indicate any U.S. Gov. endorsement whatsoever."[61]

Singlaub was a self-appointed free lance who was useful up to a point. He felt it incumbent upon himself to report to North and to get his approval. Casey was more circumspect. He received Singlaub but would say: "Jack, I will throw you out of my office" if Singlaub wanted to talk about raising money for the contras.[62] Singlaub was so indiscreet that even North finally decided to avoid him.[63]

5

The least successful effort to get money for the contras was as ludicrous as it was incredible. There are three basic versions—by McFarlane, by an FBI report, and by Richard Miller.

In May 1984, McFarlane said that he had learned that "a foreign national" was offering to contribute to the support of the contras. Instead of telling the unnamed intermediary to go directly to the contras, McFarlane said that he had advised him where to send the contribution in the United States. McFarlane estimated that this benefactor may have given as much as $5 million of his own money.[64] Yet McFarlane's memory had played tricks on him and, judging from other sources, the story was quite different.

An FBI investigation in July 1985 disclosed that the first approach on behalf of this "foreign national" had been made to North in 1984; North had probably been delegated by McFarlane to take care of the matter. The mysterious stranger was said to be Prince Ebrohim bin Aboul-Aziz bin Saud al-Masoudi, now better known in the Iran-contra investigation as Ibrahim al-Masoudi. His representative, one Kevin Kattke, went to see North with the information that Masoudi, an alleged prince of Jedda, in Saudi Arabia, wanted to make a large monetary contribution to the contras and wished to see North for that purpose. North later told Miller that Kattke had tried to get into the CIA and had been rejected as un-reliable because he "tended to talk about people whom he had no real connection with." At this time, however, North advised Kattke that he could not meet with the alleged prince directly and told him that Richard Miller, of the Channell entourage, would get in touch with him. The FBI report strangely adds: "Information regarding the prince's expressed interest in donating to the Nicaraguan freedom fighters was discussed by North personally with President Ronald Reagan and National Security Adviser Robert Mac Farlane [sic] as recently as June, 1985."

The FBI Criminal Investigative Division had been called in by the William Penn Bank of Philadelphia because a check in the amount of $250,000 from the alleged prince had been refused clearance by the Saudis' French bank. Since North and Miller were still hoping to get a large contribution from him for the contras, they had intervened to postpone the FBI's interview with the so-called prince in order to give him time to make the contribution. The FBI report states: "North spe-cifically requested that attempts by the FBI to interview the prince be held in abeyance until after the week of 7/22/85, due to the critical timing of the prince's possible but remote large donation to the Nicaraguan Freedom Fighters."[65]

Miller's story is the most circumstantial. He says that he began working with Masoudi in the summer of 1985 on an oil contract which Masoudi claimed to have received from the Saudi royal family. In return for Miller's assistance in selling the oil in the United States—Masoudi es-timated the oil to be worth $60–$70 million—Masoudi offered to donate $14 million to the contras, with another $1 million going to Miller for his trouble. As a sidelight, North and Miller privately referred to Masoudi as "Jewel," because he wore a ring set with seventeen one-carat diamonds.

As his notebooks show, North closely monitored Miller's dealings with Masoudi. The latter was so successful for a time that he convinced North and Miller that he might be able to rescue the hostages in Lebanon. For this purpose, Masoudi and Miller, accompanied by two Drug Enforce-ment Administration agents, made a trip abroad at a cost of thousands of dollars. Miller had even borrowed money in order to pay for Masoudi's registration fee for the oil contract—an unexplained service for someone with a multimillion-dollar oil contract. Miller went to the Merrill Lynch brokerage firm to get information for the alleged Masoudi about how to market the alleged oil contract. When the oil contract proved to be evanescent, Masoudi—never short of temptations—held out a gold contract.

Miller began to suspect that something was wrong when the FBI was called in to investigate the check that had bounced at the William Penn

Bank. Miller, according to the FBI report, came to Masoudi's defense and told North that this embarrassment to Masoudi had been caused by religious differences which had led him to be out of favor with the Saudi government. When Miller had tried to intervene with the bank in favor of Masoudi, the FBI had grilled Miller as if he were an accessory to the crime, much to Miller's mortification. Both the CIA and the FBI took the trouble to try to figure out who Masoudi really was; the FBI thought that he was probably a fraud, the CIA that he was not.

Miller spent a weekend in the library at the University of Maryland doing research on the Saudi royal family in an effort to find out whether his Masoudi belonged to it. North, according to Miller, finally sent someone, who Miller thought was Secord, all the way to Jedda to check on the real Prince Masoudi, who was found and who proved that Miller had been deceived.

The jewel of North and Miller was, in short, an impostor. One version is that he was an Iranian, Mousalreza Ebrahim Zadeh, not at all a Saudi prince.[66] By the end of 1985, the false Masoudi had skipped out of the United States and had forfeited a bond of $100,000, which North ordered Miller to make good. When last heard of, the phony prince was languishing in jail in Geneva, Switzerland.

The impostor was an expensive fiasco. In the end, he cost the contras $367,000, in addition to a 10 percent charge by Miller for his services. The money came from the funds raised by Channell for the contras, all of it authorized by North.[67]

The strange case of the false Saudi prince was probably the most bizarre episode in the Iran-contra affairs, which were not lacking in bizarre episodes. Both North and Miller seem to have been taken in for a considerable period; they had hoped to get a huge contribution even after they knew that Masoudi's checks were as fictitious as he himself was and that he had attracted the attention of the FBI. By the middle of 1985, there was reason to question how good a judge North was of dubious Middle Eastern characters.

6

All in all, the third countries made contributions to the contras for a total of $34 million, all but $2 million of it from Saudi Arabia. It was enough, together with other private contributions, to enable the contras to survive and grow well into 1985.

This money went either into the Secord-Hakim bank account in Geneva, Switzerland, or to Adolfo Calero as the chief recipient for the FDN. Calero testified that $19 million was spent on arms purchases and some of the rest on nonmilitary items. Another $3 million was converted into traveler's checks that Calero used at his discretion and of which we will hear more.[68] Enough money was floating around to feed all sorts of rumors of payoffs, profiteering, and corruption.

North also had free-floating money at his command. According to North, Casey suggested to him at the end of 1984 that he should set up an "operational account," such as the CIA employed, from which he could support contra leaders when they came to the United States. Eventually this money, which came from Calero and Secord, was used for whatever purposes North thought best. It finally amounted to approximately $300,000, including about $100,000 in traveler's checks and $200,000 in cash. The traveler's checks were blank on both sides, so that they could be used as cash, and anyone could cash them. North said that he had paid more than forty people with this fund and reimbursed others to the amount of tens of thousands of dollars. He claimed to have reimbursed himself with checks which he then considered his own in a peculiar bookkeeping system, using his own money and the checks interchangeably.* He once cashed a $50 traveler's check at a Giant Food store. When Fawn Hall went out of Washington for a weekend and had no cash with her, he gave her three $20 traveler's checks to help her out. None of this free and easy method of personal financing could be checked, because North said that he had destroyed the ledger in which he had kept these accounts.[69]

Until 1985, the third-country money was by far the largest component. Though deposited in the Secord-Hakim bank account, it was controlled by North, who admittedly gave Secord his orders. At North's trial, Judge Gesell questioned North about the relationship between the two.

> *Judge Gesell:* Who gave him [Secord] his orders, is what I am talking about?
>
> *North:* Well, I suppose I did, Your Honor.
>
> *Gesell:* So it was run out of the White House, right?
>
> *North:* Yes, sir.
>
> *Gesell:* Right.[70]

The contras were the ultimate beneficiaries, but they were not masters in their own financial house, primarily because Calero was content to take orders from wherever the money came from. Essentially, nothing

---

* On one occasion, North cashed two $500 traveler's checks to pay for a Pan Am flight and a stay at the Hotel Intercontinental in London. When he returned, he received reimbursements for the same expenditures. North gave this explanation: "I'm sure I did it on many other trips where I used traveler's checks that were properly mine because I had reimbursed myself for earlier expenses. I used the traveler's checks for the trip because it was my money and then I sought reimbursement as one properly does at the NSC or any government agency" (North, NT, p. 7179). It seems that North considered the traveler's checks to be his own money because he reimbursed himself with them for previous expenditures.

much had changed since the passage of Boland II in October 1984. Control of the contras had shifted from the CIA to the NSC staff and virtually to North as the officer responsible for Central America. Mc-Farlane and Poindexter after him were busy with many other things, and North was never too busy to attend, almost day-by-day, to the needs of the contras.

The intention of the Boland Amendment had been to get the United States out of the business of supporting the contras. It was circumvented because it had tried to accomplish this purpose by prohibiting the use of U.S. funds, the usual way for Congress to make its wishes known. By using other funds, North and his network thought that they were getting around the law without directly defying it and without getting the United States out of the business of supporting the contras.

It was, as Owen said, a very thin line.

5

Arms and the Man

While money was coming in from third-country and private sources, North did not neglect the military side of his service to the contra forces. Their main body was the FDN, located in Honduras on the northern border of Nicaragua.

In July 1985, North and Secord went to Miami for a high-level meeting with the FDN's chief leaders, including Adolfo Calero and Enrique Bermúdez. They discussed the critical need for an airlift of supplies to the FDN and the importance of establishing a southern front in Costa Rica in order to prevent the Sandinistas from concentrating against the northern front. When the meeting was over, North asked Secord to take charge of establishing the new airlift operation. Secord agreed, against the better judgment of his associates, Thomas Clines and Rafael Quintero, whom he had brought along to the meeting.[1]

Quintero managed to set up a main base in El Salvador, north of Nicaragua, then in the midst of its own civil war against homegrown guerrillas. But this base was not enough, Secord explained, because it was necessary to fly out over the Pacific or the Atlantic for a very long round trip of nine hours or more. The solution, he decided, was an emergency landing field in Costa Rica.[2] It was this decision that more than any other put the entire operation at risk.

The decision was essentially North's. As previously noted, North testified later that "I never did sit down in the battlefield, and sit and plan a specific tactical operation with them."[3] It was true that North never did sit down in the battlefield to plan a specific tactical operation; he sat down with them in Miami to plan the same thing. Oddly, while North denied ever planning a tactical operation for the contras, he admitted organizing "a resupply operation" for the contras and asking Secord to run it.[4] He also admitted that he had "coordinated" activities in connection with this operation and had even sent messages in which he had advised how and when to make airdrops.[5]

To construct and operate the airfield, North and Secord called on Richard Gadd and Robert Dutton. At a meeting in late September 1985, Gadd testified, North had asked him to build an airfield in Costa Rica near the Nicaraguan border.[6] For this job, Gadd was paid through Secord.[7] Like Owen, Gadd also succeeded in getting a contract from the ostensibly humanitarian NHAO.[8] Dutton took over the direction of nineteen pilots and flight crew as well as maintenance personnel.[9]

Dutton understood that the operation was commanded by Secord and North and went to either of them for instructions:

If we were working operational problems, equipment that was required, strategy on how to conduct operations, General Secord was the number one man. If we had policy problems, relations with the host country that was helping us, then Col. North usually would take care of that.

Now, it wasn't that clear a distinction. They went back and forth. I mean, if General Secord was gone and I had an operational problem or something I wanted to discuss, I would never hesitate to talk to Col. North about it.[10]

Dutton said that North had assured him that they were working for the president of the United States, not merely a privately run outfit.[11] Dutton did not think it was necessary to discuss the legality of the operation with North, because "Colonel North was operating out of the NSC and, as far as I understood, he was working for the President and I had no need to question the legality of what we were doing." North once told him that "you will never get a medal for this but someday the President will shake your hand and thank you."[12] When North was in Washington, Dutton used to communicate with him at least every other day, and Dutton used to send almost daily reports of his missions to North.[13]

By the end of May 1986, a new southern front began to receive drops of matériel from Dutton's crews. North took an active part in these operations by receiving messages from CIA Chief of Station Joe Fernandez, in Costa Rica, and passing them on to Dutton. One message of June 16, 1986, from Dutton to "Max Gomez," the alias of Felix Rodriguez, to "Ralph," the alias of Rafael Quintero, reads:

Bob [Dutton] to Max to Ralph: Goode [North] advises Joe unable to determine exact location of troops. Therefore, tomorrow fly in support of northern forces. We will fly the southern missions when we get the number 1 C-7 operating or use number 2 later in the week.[14]

These operations required the assistance of U.S. officials in the area, such as Fernandez and the "MilGroup Commander" in Costa Rica—the latter being the head of the U.S. military group that worked with the local military forces. The air resupply to the drop zones demanded long flights of six and seven hours, after which it was necessary for the planes to get back to the main airport for refueling. As Dutton explained:

> In order to make the flight down, get to the drop zone with any kind of a load that would have done the people any good, we had to make arrangements to have some refueling stop somewhere for the aircraft to return back home.
>
> So we made arrangements with the neighboring country where Joe was the Chief of Station, and he and the MilGroup Commander in that country made arrangements for, after the airdrop, for us to land at their international airport and refuel. They arranged for our flight plan to return to our main operating base.[15]

Fernandez also made possible the airdrops:

> We would make arrangements with Joe to contact the force that we were to drop to, we would get instructions back that they would have three bonfires. In some cases they would even give us a pattern that they were going to be laid out in.[16]

Rafael Quintero, another of Secord's band, worked closely with Fernandez. Quintero testified that every time he went to Costa Rica he made contact with Fernandez first: "It was his territory." Quintero said that Fernandez gave him the "coordinates" for the airdrops, and Quintero then passed them on to the pilots. Quintero described how one cargo of weapons came through. It had arrived by ship at San José, Guatemala, and was moved in twenty trucks to the border of Honduras, protected by Guatemalan army units and five helicopters for air cover. There Honduran army units took over the convoy to Tegucigalpa, where the matériel was stored before being flown to the contras in the field.[17]

Quintero also testified about his relations with Colonel James J. Steele, the U.S. MilGroup commander in El Salvador. North, according to Quintero, had told him in April 1986 who was to be responsible for making decisions about drops of weapons and ammunition—Steele in El Salvador and Fernandez in Costa Rica.[18] Quintero said that he had been ordered to "clear with him [Steele] every step of the operation." Quintero revealed that he had had a building to house matériel put up at Ilopango with the permission of Steele and the Honduran commander of the base.[19] Dutton had also known of Steele's helpfulness. "Use him," Dutton told an associate. "He is a friend."[20] Dutton said that Steele had acted as a liaison between Dutton's people and the U.S. embassy in El

Salvador, that Steele "was sort of a watchdog for me to make sure that things stayed very professional."[21] Steele and Fernandez were the only two officials who were given KL-43 encryption devices which enabled them to keep in direct touch with the Secord-Dutton operation.[22] Steele, as Dutton pointed out, would not have acted on his own without his superiors knowing about it: "In dealing with Colonel Jim Steele, who was the commander of the military group in the Central American country where we were operating out of, to me it was obvious that Colonel Steele could not be caused to either react or to back away unless his chain of command understood what he was doing and what we were doing."[23]

Secord's unofficial operation could not have functioned without official cooperation by CIA and military personnel on the spot. They knew that North stood behind Secord and assumed that North must have acted in accordance with his own chain of command, which went directly up to Poindexter and from him to President Reagan.

North's next move was to get the cooperation of the newly appointed U.S. ambassador to Costa Rica, Lewis A. Tambs. He was a former history professor at Arizona State University who had worked on the NSC staff in 1982, after which he was appointed ambassador to Colombia in 1983 and to Costa Rica in July 1985. Before leaving for his new post, he testified, he came to see North, who asked him "to go down and open up the Southern Front."*[24] Tambs said that he took it to be administration policy and complied.

Tambs was asked how it came about that a member of the NSC staff had the authority to give a mission, such as opening a military front, to a U.S. ambassador. Tambs explained: "Mr. North was working for the National Security Council [sic], and obviously my assumption was that any instruction he gave me came from obviously his superiors." Tambs was also asked whether he did not consider that such a mission came into conflict with the Boland Amendment. "They have a saying in the Foreign Service," Tambs replied. "When you take the king's shilling you do the king's bidding."[25]

Tambs also assumed that North spoke for the highest authority in the executive branch. He had such confidence in North that he had not checked with anyone higher in the NSC staff or with his own superiors in the State Department.

The CIA chief of station in Costa Rica was José (Joe) Fernandez, also known as "Tomás Castillo," a veteran of almost twenty years' service in

---

* Tambs told the Tower Board: "Before I went [to Costa Rica] Ollie said when you get down there you should open the southern front." When asked what this mission meant to him, Ambassador Tambs responded that "the idea was that we would encourage them to fight" (TR, C-12). North testified that he had not specifically instructed Tambs but "I certainly did encourage him in every way possible to support an open, active Southern Front, both politically and militarily" (North, 100-7, Part II, pp. 176–77).

the Agency.[26] According to Quintero, he provided map coordinates to the pilots using the airstrip.[27] When Fernandez was asked whether he was surprised that an ambassador was given the assignment to establish a southern front by an NSC staff officer, he replied laconically: "No."[28] Tambs testified that he was told by Fernandez that North wanted the ambassador to approach the Costa Rican government to get its approval for the emergency airfield on Costa Rican territory. Tambs understood that the airfield was going to be constructed "by private hands for use by private facilities" for refueling and for emergency purposes on behalf of the contras.[29]

2

In this way, a U.S. ambassador undertook to open a military front and to become the diplomatic intermediary for a "private" pro-contra military installation in a neutral country. When he was again asked whether these activities did not conflict with the Boland Amendment, Tambs answered that he had never read the amendment and that, anyway, "I have difficulty reading a contract for a refrigerator."[30]

The agreement with Costa Rica later became a subject of some controversy. In August 1985, Costa Rican President Luis Alberto Monge met at Tambs's request with four U.S. officials. Frank McNeil, the U.S. ambassador to Costa Rica from 1981 to 1983, says that Monge told him the following story: The four U.S. officials, armed with maps, informed Monge of a Nicaraguan plan to invade Costa Rica. The threat was not unbelievable, because Nicaraguan forces had been making short incursions into Costa Rican territory, though whether they were intended to prepare the way for a full-scale invasion was doubtful. In any case, it is said that the U.S. officials asked Monge's permission to lengthen a rudimentary airstrip in the Santa Elena peninsula at the northwestern corner of Costa Rica, allegedly for use by the U.S. Southern Command in Panama in the event of a Nicaraguan invasion. Monge was reluctant, but a second visit by the U.S. officials, who insisted on the urgency and certainty of the Nicaraguan threat, led him to give his approval, which he later regretted.[31] In this case, Monge was asked to approve the lengthening of an airstrip that did not yet exist and for a reason that was a cover story for contra operations against Nicaragua.

At the trial of Oliver North in 1989, a different reason was given for Monge's approval:

In August 1985, Costa Rican President Monge indicated to U.S. officials that he would be willing to provide assistance to the Resistance if the United States government would help fund a certain operation in Costa Rica. The U.S. officials concluded that the operation could be funded if President Monge would take certain specified actions to assist the Resistance.

In the fall of 1985, Benjamín Piza, a senior Costa Rican official, agreed to permit the Resistance to construct an airstrip in Santa Elena in northern Costa Rica. Payments were made to Colonel Montero, an official of the Costa Rican Civil Guard, for the official's service in guarding the Santa Elena airstrip. [32]

In a later interview, Monge denied that there had been a quid pro quo and stated that he had had no idea what the "certain operation" was. Monge acknowledged that he had met with the four U.S. officials, but could not recall any discussion about an airfield. He declared, however, that he had eventually authorized the "expansion" of the airstrip after Minister of Security Benjamín Piza Escalante had negotiated the details. [33]

These versions agree that the United States did obtain some sort of Costa Rican approval for the airstrip. As for the agreement itself, it seems to have been carefully drawn up to keep Costa Rica as much as possible out of the Nicaraguan morass. It provided, according to Tambs, for the airfield to be used only for the storage of supplies or provisions, and for any plane landing there to have already completed its mission, so that it would be empty and merely require to be refueled. [34]

While approval by Monge as president was necessary, North's main Costa Rican connection was Security Minister Piza. As North reported to Poindexter, Piza frequently intervened with Monge to make the airstrip and the southern front possible and apparently did not ask much for his favors. Piza was bent on making a trip to Washington, and "all he wanted was a photograph with the President," North recalled. [35] North got his airstrip and Piza his photograph.

North sent his "courier," Owen, to Costa Rica to reconnoiter the land. Owen met with Tambs, who suggested that Owen and Fernandez should look at a site for the emergency airfield. They made a survey by helicopter, and Owen took photographs, which he brought back to North. According to Owen, the two of them discussed "what kind of cover operation could be established, so that we would not draw too much attention." The best way, they decided, was to have some Americans buy or rent the property, set up a Panamanian company, and camouflage the deal as an agricultural testing center or some such thing. [36]

North also sent William Charles Haskell, who used the name Robert Olmstead, to acquire the land. Haskell, then in the tax preparation business, had met North in Vietnam when both were platoon commanders. The land was owned by one Joseph Hamilton, who granted the use of the land but not its ownership to the government of Costa Rica, in order to explain why Costa Rican forces were providing security and keeping people away from it. Haskell became the nominal owner of the land in the name of the Santa Elena Development Corporation, of which Haskell, William C. Copp [Secord], and William C. Goode [North] were directors.[37] The property was turned over to a dummy company, the Udall Research Corporation, registered in Panama in the name of Richard V. Secord.[38] He claimed to own it, together with its "assets," valued at over $1 million.[39] Secord had invested none of his own money in the Udall front; the money had all come from private contributions to the contras.[40] According to Quintero, the airstrip cost between $200,000 and $250,000.[41]

The Santa Elena land was so rough and isolated, according to Fernandez, that it was almost impossible to get any kind of grader or bulldozer into it.[42] An airstrip rather than an airfield was all that could be constructed on it. Nevertheless, some former U.S. military engineering personnel were hired to supervise the construction of a 6,000-foot-long dirt strip, with one wooden building to store barrels of fuel and other supplies.[43]

When the Santa Elena airstrip was first conceived, North was not yet embroiled in the Iran affair. Yet even after the Iran affair claimed much of his time by the end of November 1985, he was still very much at the center of the airdrop and airstrip operations. To Secord, he relayed reports sent him by Quintero and Fernandez about the airdrops, and North even presented his own "alternative plan" for improving the airdrop operation.[44] This did not surprise the others, because, as Fernandez put it, North had "coordinated" the entire operation.[45] From Dutton, who was in charge of it, North received the most detailed reports, even to the timing of flights.[46] When asked why he had been sending regular, almost daily, reports to North, Dutton answered that "as I think in any special operation, you report to your bosses."[47] Dutton explained that "Colonel North was operating out of the NSC [sic] and, as far as I understood, he was working for the President and I had no need to question the legality of what we were doing. I just took it as an assumption that it was legal."[48]

For all the effort put into the airdrops, they missed more often than not. Fernandez described how difficult they were:

Drops, several drops that were made, parts of the drops were never found. If there were eight bundles, maybe they recovered five, possibly six. The only way that pilots could identify the drop zone was if the people on the ground lit bonfires. There was no—they had no ability to navigate right to the place where they were supposed to, so the way it would work is the communication center in [deleted] would tell them the airdrop is due between 2:00 and 2:30 a.m., please light your bonfires 15 minutes before and keep them burning for 15 minutes afterwards of the period when the drop is expected.

Then the plane, if it got to the area at all, would circle, an ever-widening circle, to try to spot the bonfires on the ground. Obviously, if it is raining, this is a jungle, a rain forest or tropical jungle, you don't always find wood that will burn, you don't have kerosene or gasoline because of where they are located, so it was simply by chance that they could keep the fires burning for an hour, and then they would have to be big enough.[49]

The airdrops were hard enough; the Santa Elena airstrip was still more hazardous politically. For one thing, the Costa Rican government was not happy with it. In May 1986, an election brought in a new president, Oscar Arias Sánchez, who quickly revoked Costa Rican permission for use of the airstrip.[50] This might have been the end of the Santa Elena story if the U.S. operators had obeyed Arias's decision. By ignoring it, they gave the story a costly ending.

3

Tambs's troubles were not over. His ambassadorial career was soon tarnished by an incident that resulted from the peculiar combination of official, semiofficial, and unofficial agents mixed up in the contra affair.

In March 1986, retired General Singlaub, the contras' self-appointed savior, decided to take on a mission that went far beyond his usual money-raising activity. He took it upon himself to go down to Costa Rica for the purpose of reaching an agreement with Edén Pastora, long the most independent and recalcitrant of the contra leaders. Pastora was opposed to both the Sandinistas in Nicaragua, with whom he had broken on democratic grounds, and the anti-Sandinista forces in Honduras, represented by Adolfo Calero, whom he considered to be hopelessly reactionary. Pastora had been trying to organize an anti-Sandinista front in Costa Rica, on the southern border of Nicaragua. Pastora's shaky but unsubmissive position had long frustrated the coordination of an effective Costa Rican "southern front" with the Honduran-based "northern front." By the end of 1985, Pastora's leadership of his own forces was challenged by his field commanders, who began to leave him, with the excuse that he could not get enough support for their troops.[51]

Just when Pastora needed help desperately, Singlaub undertook to come to his rescue. Apparently unaware that Pastora was now persona non grata in Washington, Singlaub decided to heal the breach between Pastora and the Honduras-based chieftains all by himself. The latter had recently been cajoled into temporarily hushing up their own rivalries and had formed a United Nicaraguan Opposition (UNO), into which Singlaub wanted to bring Pastora. Before taking on this one-man diplomatic mission, Singlaub sought to find out whether it was officially approved or at least not disapproved. He said that he had met with Assistant Secretary Abrams, who, according to Singlaub, expressed some doubts that "that could be done" but "posed no objection" to his plan.[52] Abrams, however, said that he saw Singlaub after, not before, his mission to Pastora in Costa Rica, but Abrams admittedly thought that "what Singlaub was doing seemed like a good idea."[53]

In any event, Singlaub's overture to Pastora came in the midst of an administration split on the issue of Pastora. "Basically," Abrams testified, "Colonel North and the CIA hated Pastora with great passion. They had concluded, on the basis of their dealings with him, that he was not only untrustworthy, but conceivably disloyal. And they wanted to have literally nothing to do with him." Singlaub and Abrams disagreed; they thought, according to Abrams, that this view was "extremely shortsighted."[54] For this reason, Singlaub did not clear his initiative with North and instead sought out Abrams. Singlaub also had the backing of the archconservative Republican Senator Jesse Helms, who had requested Singlaub to "assess the situation of Edén Pastora and his troops." In fact, Tambs regarded Singlaub as an "envoy" of Helms.[55] At the same time, the CIA had already made Pastora persona non grata and had ordered its personnel to have nothing to do with him.[56]

On March 23, 1986, Singlaub flew down to Costa Rica to negotiate a new deal with Pastora. When Singlaub met with Ambassador Tambs and described his mission, Tambs did not express any objection, according to Singlaub, who took it to mean that he was free to go ahead.[57]

On March 24, Singlaub visited Pastora's camp and found only 230 men. Singlaub and Pastora reached an agreement two days later and Tambs sent it off to Alan Fiers, the head of the CIA's Central American Task Force, Abrams of the State Department, and North in the White House. It took the form of a written statement, signed by Singlaub and Pastora, which began with these words:

The United States will provide:

1. Boots
2. Food
3. Ammunition
4. Medicine
5. Maps
6. Encrypted Communications Systems
7. Military needs for Pastora's troops including new men who join his arms.

These provisions were based on commitments by Pastora to move his force inside Nicaragua, act "in a cooperative and good faith manner with the other elements of the Nicaraguan resistance," and cooperate with "advisers" sent to train his men. Pastora allegedly agreed to travel to Europe, South America, and other Central American countries "to explain the true nature of the Marxist-Leninist Sandinista government."[58]

Tambs sent the agreement to Washington with only a reservation about whether "Pastora will comply." He noted that Pastora had agreed to get all supplies, equipment, and training through the Honduran-based UNO, not directly from the United States.[59]

Singlaub said that Tambs had been "very pleased" with and surprised by his ability to get the agreement. Singlaub next conferred with the UNO's Calero, who, he said, "was not enthusiastic" but agreed to give Pastora's group 100 uniforms, 100 pairs of boots, and 15,000 rounds of ammunition from UNO stocks.[60]

Tambs's trouble with the Singlaub-Pastora agreement started in his own embassy. Fernandez, the CIA's chief of station in San José, had already tried to dissuade Singlaub from attempting to win over Pastora. After Fernandez learned of the agreement, he says that he was "extremely upset," that the part committing the United States to provide ammunition and equipment struck him as "just incredible," and that he expressed his "righteous indignation" to Tambs. The ambassador, according to Fernandez, "apologized" and blamed Fernandez's deputy, who told Fernandez: "What the hell am I going to do when the ambassador tells me, he dictates the message to me?"[61]

When Tambs's report of the agreement reached Washington, the reaction was explosive. The main objection was that Singlaub had negotiated with Pastora without official warrant and had apparently committed the United States to the terms of the agreement. Alan Fiers, the CIA chief of the Central American Task Force, said: "I went bonkers."[62] Abrams cabled Tambs furiously on March 29: "I fail to understand how you and the CIA representative could associate yourselves with an agreement which purports to commit the United States to provide military material [deleted] and advisers in exchange for a series of undertakings on Pastora's part."[63] Abrams found himself in the embarrassed position of being called in by Deputy Secretary of State John C. Whitehead, to be told of "deep concern" about Tambs's role in the whole affair and asked to explain it. The impression in Washington was that Singlaub had committed the U.S. government to provide support for Pastora, and that Tambs's "association with this initiative gives this document an unwarranted stamp of official approval." Abrams peremptorily demanded answers from Tambs.[64]

In reply, Tambs pleaded that he had merely reported the Singlaub-Pastora agreement to Washington without having associated himself with it in any way. Singlaub, he said, had told him that the reference to the "United States" in the agreement had referred to Singlaub and his supporters, not the United States government. The entire arrangement, according to Tambs, had been nothing more than one between private individuals.[65]

Despite Tambs's explanation, the State Department's legal adviser took the matter more seriously. He insisted that "it is impossible to rule out the possibility that your [Tambs's] disclaimers of USG[overnment] involvement notwithstanding, Pastora might attempt to use the Singlaub agreement to pressure or embarrass the USG." Tambs was ordered to inform Pastora that Singlaub was not authorized to negotiate on behalf of the United States, which did not consider itself bound by the agreement, but Tambs could not reach Pastora with the message.[66]

In the end, the whole affair was a total fiasco. Everyone who touched it was burned. Singlaub was forced to withdraw from his agreement with Pastora and never delivered anything that he had promised. Pastora, Singlaub learned, had gone back to his troops and had waited for supplies that never arrived. Singlaub later thought that "we had reneged—'we,' meaning collectively the people of the United States," as if he had actually committed the United States and not himself alone to make good the agreement.[67]

The most equivocal role was played by Assistant Secretary of State Abrams, whose explanations left much to be explained, as was usually the case with him. Abrams was actually in sympathy with Singlaub's effort to support Pastora and continued for some time to keep a semblance of the agreement alive. Abrams was far more upset with Tambs for having sent the incriminating cable of March 27, 1986, than with Singlaub's original deal with Pastora. Abrams subsequently met with Singlaub, at a time when Abrams admittedly "didn't think that he [Singlaub] had done anything wrong," and gave Singlaub to understand that he could go ahead with sending a "token" allotment of UNO equipment to Pastora.[68] Pastora was even promised in May that "we would try to give him resources" out of the $100 million fund which the administration was trying to get Congress to appropriate for the contras.[69] It is clear that Pastora, who met with Abrams in Washington in May, was still being wooed and had every reason to believe that his agreement with Singlaub was viable.

On May 7, however, Singlaub met with Calero in Miami and learned that Calero's "counselors" had advised him against giving anything to Pastora. Singlaub hurried to Washington to "turn this around," as Richard H. Melton, the director of the Office of Central American Affairs under Abrams, who conferred frequently with Singlaub, put it.[70] As late as May 12, Melton asked Abrams "whether to notify Adolfo Calero of your approval to transfer to Pastora limited amounts of equipment from UNO stocks."[71] By May 15, Singlaub was told that "we were engaged in a damage-limiting operation with Pastora," which turned out to be "a brief conciliatory statement noting that we hoped Pastora would not abandon the fight against the Sandinistas."[72]

In effect, Pastora was the victim of a bureaucratic conflict within the administration. Abrams, who wished to make use of Pastora, was opposed by North and Fiers.[73] Abrams lost this battle at the expense of Pastora, who soon decided to give up the struggle; he turned himself over to the Costa Rican authorities and went to jail. Tambs, whom Abrams blamed the most for the mix-up, remained at his post until January 1987.

The fate of the Singlaub-Pastora agreement was in itself a tempest in a teapot. It was mainly significant for the way the use of unofficial agents, such as Singlaub, could result in damaging confusion and cross-purposes. Once the CIA was forced to give up the complete direction and support of the contras, the makeshift arrangements left room for free-lance volunteers like Singlaub, who was too useful to get rid of and too erratic to adopt openly.

It was all very confusing—Singlaub, with Helms's backing, both hard-line conservatives, wanted to prop up Pastora, who represented a left-wing tendency, with the help of Calero, who regarded Pastora as a dangerous rival, and with the tacit indulgence of Abrams, against the bitter opposition of North and Fiers. No wonder Fiers thought, when he learned of the Singlaub-Pastora agreement: "What is this? This is contrary to everything we are doing"—which was to make every effort to destroy Pastora's influence militarily and discredit him politically.[74]

The airstrip fiasco, Tambs's tribulations, and Singlaub's misadventure showed North at his most slipshod. North was central to the planning and execution, but he was doing too many things at once, and his methods were hit-and-miss. The only one who could have kept a tight rein on him was Poindexter, his only superior, but Poindexter repeatedly fell back on the excuse that he was doing too many other, more important things.

4

Until the trial of Oliver North in 1989, it was unclear how the cooperation of Central American governments had been obtained. They were not likely to do what the United States wanted without getting something in return. At that trial, new evidence was introduced in the peculiar form of "admitted facts." In order to get around the government's opposition to the presentation of classified documents, Judge Gerhard A. Gesell succeeded in getting the government to agree to a compromise—a digest of "admitted facts," or as the jury was told: "You are instructed that the United States has admitted for purposes of this trial the following facts to be true."[75] These "admitted facts" consisted of 107 summarized documents, covering 42 pages, over half of them dealing with the official relations between the United States and the four most implicated Central American countries—Costa Rica, Guatemala, El Salvador, and Honduras.

As North later explained, the cooperation and connivance of high

Central American officials were indispensable for the care and feeding of the contras.

> It would be impossible to do these things without the permission of the highest levels of their governments. I mean, it would be a disaster if you tried to do it without their help. And so as it became necessary to do these things, whether it was the delivery of weapons into the country or even the delivery of humanitarian support, we had to have the agreement of the top officials in those countries. And in some cases I even had to meet the Presidents of those countries so that those people would agree to the kinds of support and the kinds of measures that we were taking. And they would determine how often and how frequently or where or when certain things could take place.[76]

Costa Rican cooperation was vital so long as the United States was engaged in opening a "southern front" along the Costa Rican border with Nicaragua. The collusion of the Costa Rican regime of President Monge had also been necessary for the construction of the Secord operation's airstrip near the Nicaraguan border. The airstrip was given up after Monge was replaced by Oscar Arias Sánchez in May 1986, but a post-Pastora "southern front" was supplied by the airdrops reorganized under Dutton's leadership.

Guatemala was important because it permitted the transportation of matériel through its territory and supplied many of the "end-user certificates" necessary to get weapons to the contras.[77] U.S. sales of weapons to other countries required written statements attesting to the identity of the "end user" of the weapons in order to prevent them from being resold or otherwise given to countries or groups ineligible to receive or use U.S. weapons. Guatemala was a major source of falsified end-user certificates that enabled the contras to obtain U.S. weapons and ammunition.

At his trial, North explained how the system worked:

> I would go down, or others using the name of myself or others, would say, please, give us some end-user certificates to go buy ammunition in Europe or ammunition and equipment in other places that we can deliver to the Resistance. And these military officials, senior officials in their government, were doing it for us.[78]

El Salvador was important for the same reasons, but especially for the use of the Ilopango airfield. Secord told how Quintero had managed to get the use of the airfield:

> Mr. Quintero went there and negotiated with the local military and with an old friend of his who was working there too—and got

an agreement, in principle, about this timeframe—that is the fall of 1985—for the basing of a small airlift operation at that location.[79]

But Honduras was by far the most important, because the main contra force was based there. Wherever the weapons and supplies came from, they had to be brought there to be distributed to the FDN or UNO. According to one "admitted fact," in mid-November 1984, a CIA officer had reported that "Guatemala had provided aircraft and agreed to facilitate Resistance shipments of munitions and other materiel. Honduras had permitted the Resistance to operate from within its borders, had repaired Resistance aircraft at cost, had allowed government aircraft to bring in aircraft parts, had permitted the Resistance to borrow ammunition when Resistance stocks were too low, and had provided the Resistance with false end-user certificates."[80] On February 2, 1985, the CIA reported that "Honduran military officers were assisting the Resistance in transporting materiel (including ammunition) bought on the international arms market through Guatemala to Resistance camps in Honduras."[81]

These Central American countries knew that they were taking risks on behalf of the contras, that they were responding to U.S. pressure, and that they had been given a rare opportunity to make the United States pay for what it wanted from them. Without a quid pro quo, the Hondurans and others would have missed the opportunity of their lives to get something in return for their help.

That there was a price for Central American complicity with the contras was recognized at a meeting on February 7, 1985, of a Crisis Pre-Planning Group (CPPG), made up of representatives from the NSC staff, Department of State, Department of Defense, CIA, Joint Chiefs of Staff, and the ubiquitous Lieutenant Colonel North. According to an "admitted fact," this group agreed that

> a Presidential letter should be sent to President [Roberto] Suazo of Honduras and to provide several enticements in exchange for its continued support of the Nicaraguan Resistance. These enticements included expedited delivery of military supplies ordered by Honduras, a phased release of withheld economic assistance funds (ESF) and other support. The CPPG was in agreement that transmission of the letter should be closely followed by the visit of an emissary who would verbally brief the "conditions" attached to the expedited military deliveries, economic assistance, and other support. The CPPG did not wish to include this detail of the quid pro quo arrangement in written correspondence.[82]

The letter to Suazo was sent by President Reagan later that month through Ambassador John Negroponte.[83] The term "quid pro quo," which was later indignantly denied, appears in this document.* North had previously written to McFarlane on January 15, 1985, on the occasion of the latter's trip to Central America: "Guatemala's leaders remain supportive of the broad objectives of U.S. policy in the region but the extent of cooperation will be contingent upon a quid pro quo system."[84]

In early March 1985, Secretary of Defense Weinberger informed National Security Adviser McFarlane that the Department of Defense "had commenced expedited procurement and delivery of military and other items to Honduras."[85]

On March 16, 1985, Vice President Bush met with Suazo in the Honduran capital. The "admitted facts" state that

> Bush told Suazo that President Reagan had directed expedited delivery of U.S. military items to Honduras. Vice President Bush also informed Suazo that President Reagan had directed that currently withheld economic assistance for Honduras should be released; that the United States would provide from its own military stocks critical security assistance items that had been ordered by Honduran armed forces; and that several security programs underway for Honduran security forces would be enhanced.[86]

When nothing else worked, President Reagan was called on to intervene personally to expedite the "stuff" in Honduras. On April 23, 1985, McFarlane informed him that the Honduran military had "stopped a shipment of ammunition from an Asian country en route to the Resistance after it had arrived in Honduras." This shipment was made up of surface-to-air missiles that had come all the way across the Pacific to Guatemala. North had arranged for the purchase of these missiles from Communist China in late November 1984 at a luncheon with the Chinese military attaché in Washington.[87] The Guatemalan Army had provided helicopters and an armed escort to trek the missiles all across Guatemala so that they would not fall into the hands of Guatemala guerrillas. When the missiles arrived in Honduras, they were seized by the Honduran military, which lacked such weapons.[88]

As a last resort, McFarlane asked Reagan to call Suazo to get the Honduran military to release the missiles. Reagan obediently put in a telephone call to Suazo, who agreed to turn the ammunition over to the contras, in return for which he "raised the subject of U.S. government aid for his country." Reagan noted that Suazo was coming to Washington

---

* Former ambassador Negroponte, who had attended the meeting between Bush and Suazo, said that while Bush "may well have alluded to" the expedited aid to Honduras, "there was no discussion of a quid pro quo." Former Assistant Secretary of State Langhorne A. Motley, who was also present, tried to make a delicate semantic distinction: "You don't have to be clairvoyant to understand you do things to expedite stuff . . . It shows good faith and the guy knows what you are interested in. That's a step back from a quid pro quo" (*Washington Post*, April 12, 1989).

and expected to get "about $15 million in aid."[89] Negroponte soon reported that Suazo had promptly carried out Reagan's request to release the ammunition. In May 1985, "President Reagan personally approved increased U.S. special support to Honduras and Guatemala for joint programs with those countries."*[90] McFarlane soon recommended giving $75 million in economic assistance to Honduras.[91]

This incident shows that Reagan was kept currently informed of the problems associated with the contras and, when needed, stepped in to help out. A telephone call from a U.S. president to a Honduran president about a holdup of ammunition for the contras was not an ordinary or a customary practice to be expected from the White House. Whatever one may think of its propriety, it reveals how intimately Reagan was kept abreast of and how willingly he participated in the contra program.

In Costa Rica, Colonel Montero of the Costa Rican Civil Guard was hired as the general construction boss and to provide protection for the Santa Elena airstrip. Quintero disclosed that Montero was paid $190,720 plus a personal retainer of $30,000, and another retainer for an unstated purpose.[92] The Hondurans were particularly unhappy, because they did not have some of the sophisticated weaponry that the United States was providing to the contras. In March 1986, an agreement was reached to give Honduras ground-to-air missiles worth approximately $20 million. This additional payment, according to an "admitted fact," was known to President Reagan, Vice President Bush, and others.[93] Again in May 1986, President José Azcona, Suazo's successor, "indicated to President Reagan that Honduras's continued support for the Resistance depended upon significant increases in U.S. government military aid to the Honduran armed forces and the Resistance."[94]

An even more unusual offer apparently came from Panama:

> In late August 1986, North reported to Admiral Poindexter that a representative of Panamanian leader Manuel Noriega had asked to meet with him. Noriega's representative proposed that, in exchange for a promise from the USG[overnment] to help clean up Noriega's image and a commitment to lift the USG ban on military sales to the Panamanian defense forces, Noriega would assassinate the Sandinista leadership for the U.S. government. North had told Noriega's representative that U.S. law forbade such actions. The representative responded that Noriega had numerous assets in place in Nicaragua and could accomplish many essential things, just as Noriega had helped the USG the previous year in blowing up a Sandinista arsenal.[95]

---

* At his confirmation hearings as U.S. ambassador to Mexico in 1989, Negroponte disclosed that he had heard about President Reagan's telephone call to Suazo from Suazo (p. 57).

North's report is said to have brought this reaction:

Admiral Poindexter responded that if Noriega had assets inside Nicaragua, he could be helpful. The USG could not be involved in assassination, but Panamanian assistance with sabotage would be another story. Admiral Poindexter recommended that North speak with Noriega again.[96]

Two more "admitted facts" carry the story so far as it is known:

101. In mid-September 1986, LtCol North notified Admiral Poindexter that Noriega wanted to meet with him in London within a few days. North had discussed the matter with Assistant Secretary of State Abrams, who had raised it with Secretary of State Shultz. Shultz thought that the meeting should proceed. Admiral Poindexter approved.

106. In late September 1986, LtCol North reported to Admiral Poindexter on his London meeting with Noriega. Noriega would try to take immediate actions against the Sandinistas and offered a list of priorities including an oil refinery, an airport, and the Puerto Sandino off-load facility.

North gave Casey credit for having provided the names of Central Americans who could be counted on to cooperate in support of the contras: "Each one, El Salvador, Honduras, Costa Rica [he later added Guatemala] were people that Director Casey told me to work with. And he told me to work with them because they were totally reliable people, that they had worked with the CIA before, that they were people who we could trust in Central America." North added that a maintenance facility had been built in El Salvador with the help of a "very senior Salvadoran official" with whom Casey had told him to work, and North had passed on the word to Secord.[97]

These services and payoffs were part of an extensive system of bribery and blackmail. They were indispensable to the contra operation, which was dependent on the goodwill and cooperation of ostensibly neutral Central American countries. The shift of control from the CIA to the NSC staff did not change all that much; the same methods and the same personnel worked for North as they had been accustomed to work in the past, so long as military, CIA, and diplomatic representatives believed that the policy was coming from the very top of the U.S. government.

5

Throughout these hectic misadventures, a threat of exposure hung over North. The threat was inherent in the nature of covert operations. Such operations do best when they are relatively short and determinate. If they try to do too much for too long, they run an increasing risk of exposure. This is especially true of operations that are primarily made covert to hide them from the American people and not from those against whom the operation is aimed. In the contra affair, the covert nature of the operation was dictated by domestic considerations, not by a need to conceal it from the Sandinistas, who knew only too well that the United States was behind the contras. The contra operation was neither short nor determinate.

The risk of exposure was particularly acute for North. So many people had been playing so many parts for so long in the contra affair—the contra leaders, Secord's little army, the Channell-Miller money-raisers, the rich donors who could have seen no reason to hide their patriotic largesse (at the taxpayers' expense), North's own colleagues, some of whom were not sympathetic to his antics—that the wonder was how long it took for the story to break out of its covert shell.

On May 31, 1985, National Security Adviser McFarlane received a warning message from a press secretary, Karna Small. She advised him that Robert Parry of the Associated Press—"who can be *tough*, but has awfully good sources"—was working on "a big piece" about private, outside funding for the Nicaraguan contras. Parry wanted to know from McFarlane whether it was true that President Reagan at the end of 1983 or the beginning of 1984 had instructed McFarlane orally to arrange for such non-U.S. government funding. McFarlane refused to see him but advised her that "the guidance was firmly to the contrary."[98]

North was alarmed. On June 3, 1985, he wrote a memorandum to Poindexter, McFarlane's deputy, about rumors for the past several weeks that stories were being prepared connecting the NSC staff with private funding and other support for the contras. He named two reporters, Alfonso Chardy of *The Miami Herald* and Parry. North told Poindexter that he had requested Adolfo Calero to tell Chardy "if he printed any derogatory comments about the FDN or its funding sources that Chardi [sic] would never again be allowed to visit FDN bases or travel with their units." North said that Chardy had promised Calero to drop the story but that Parry's efforts were "more disturbing," because he "is an avowed liberal with very close connections in the Democratic party."[99]

Chardy was the first reporter to mention North by name. In *The Miami Herald* of June 24, 1985, Chardy cited government employees, legislative aides, and a former rebel leader as his sources. This report, entitled "U.S.

Found to Skirt Ban on Aid to Contras," was largely based on an interview with Edgar Chamorro, a disaffected former contra leader. He told of North's visit to a contra base in Honduras in the spring of 1984 during which North assured the contras that the Reagan administration would never abandon them. After North's visit, Chamorro said, Calero called Chamorro from Washington "with orders from the CIA" to place advertisements in several U.S. newspapers appealing for aid for Nicaraguan refugees. Most of the money for the contras at that time, however, was said to be coming from Singlaub's activities. The story said that Singlaub, never loath to show that he was acting in coordination with administration officials, said that he kept "administration contacts" advised of his efforts.

It took about two weeks for the major national newspapers to pick up the story. When they did, they were almost talked out of mentioning North's name.

North's notebook shows that he was warned on August 6, 1985, that Steven Roberts of *The New York Times* was asking questions about him. Roberts claimed to have confirmation from the Senate Armed Services Committee that North was raising private money for the contras in violation of the law.[100] North evidently learned only on August 7 about the previous article by Alfonso Chardy in *The Miami Herald* of June 24. The *Times*'s article appeared on August 8, 1985, signed by Joel Brinkley, but only insiders could have known the identity of the chief character in the following account:

> The operation has been run by a military officer who is a member of the National Security Council [sic]. Officials said the officer, who has extensive experience in intelligence work, meets frequently with rebel leaders in Washington and on trips to Central America and briefs President Reagan. He also gives frequent speeches and lectures on the subject of Nicaragua and, when asked, advises people on how they might donate money to the rebel cause.

Apart from some exaggeration, the military officer was inescapably Lieutenant Colonel Oliver North. The article went on to suggest that one of its sources was critical of North's operation. It cited a senior White House official who said that "there is a lot of frustration within the White House because they do not believe that N.S.C. is the logical place to manage the program. The staff is too small." Another senior administration official called the anonymous officer "a worker bee" and said that "you know our policy is to support them," meaning the contras, "and that's his job."

This article attracted attention in the State Department. One official called North to say that it was "very bad," and Assistant Secretary of State Elliott Abrams noted that North's name had been "protected."[101]

The first story in *The Washington Post*, by Joanne Omang on August

9, 1985, came a bit closer to North but still failed to mention him by name:

> Various current and former government and rebel officials confirmed that a Marine officer on the NSC staff has played a key role in formation and implementation of U.S. policy in Central America over the last three years.

Curiously, this article cited the *New York Times* story of the previous day as confirmation. The *Post* later revealed that it had withheld North's name at the request of White House spokesman Larry Speakes, who had called North the night before.[102]

North's name finally appeared in a follow-up page-one story, again by Joanne Omang, in the *Post* on August 11, 1985:

> In a city of largely invisible staff workers, Marine Corps Lt. Col. Oliver L. North of the National Security Council staff has emerged as an influential and occasionally controversial character in the implementation of the Reagan administration's foreign policy.

The article featured an interview with North's superior, McFarlane, who had worked out a public relations line with North two days earlier.[103] McFarlane gave assurances that "we would not provide any support" involving money or matériel to the contras. "It was a matter of handholding," McFarlane declared virtuously, and North had been put in charge of holding hands. "He's not like a rogue elephant," McFarlane declared, but rather "like a son of mine." The article also cited Representative Vin Weber, Republican of Minnesota, a leader of the House Conservative Opportunity Society, as saying of North: "He's pretty highly regarded as one of the better guys on the inside, pretty hard-line."

The publication of this article displeased other hard-liners. The *Post*'s managing editor, Leonard Downie, was harassed for days by early-morning telephone calls until he informed North and the phone calls stopped.[104]

The *Times* mentioned North's name for the first time on August 17, 1985, and explained that it was doing so because *The Washington Post* had done so six days earlier. The *Times* explained that North had been meant in its story of August 8, 1985, and that it had been asked by the White House to withhold his name. In addition, the *Times*'s story by Joel Brinkley indicated that someone in the White House had been talking rather freely about North:

> Last week, the White House acknowledged that Colonel North, who is a deputy director for political-military affairs on the National Security Council, had been helping several rebel groups plan some

operations and raise private funds. A senior Administration official also said Colonel North, a Marine, had provided "tactical influence" on rebel military policy.[105]

In this way, North opened himself up to journalistic scrutiny. The stories in both the *Times* and the *Post* gave readers reason to believe that their sources were within the administration. Some who were able to watch North closely apparently did not admire his methods and behavior.

We know of one such adverse reaction from Constantine C. Menges, himself an anti-Communist "hard-liner," so hard that North was too soft for him. Menges had served on Ronald Reagan's Foreign-Policy Advisory Committee during the presidential campaign of 1980, after which he had been taken on in 1981 by Director Casey as the CIA's national intelligence officer for Latin America. After two years in the CIA, he went on to two more years in the same field on the NSC staff. As he tells the story, he was so thoroughly displeased with what he considered to be the vacillating policies of McFarlane, Poindexter, and North that he was eased out of the Latin American assignment in July 1985. He was made a special assistant to the president for national security affairs, a title with little influence, which only lent itself to more frustration. He resigned in July 1986, convinced that he was one of the few real Reagan loyalists in the government, always prevented from saving the republic by less able and less devoted bureaucrats.

No love was lost between Menges and North. Yet Menges's work on the NSC staff made it possible for him to observe North closely. Whatever Menges's own prejudices, we can get some sense from him of the hostility to North that existed in the latter's immediate working environment.

On July 15, 1985, just as North was attracting attention from the press, Menges had recalled a conversation with Elliott Abrams, the new assistant secretary of state for inter-American affairs. Menges decided to give Abrams some advice about North:

> I want to tell you my opinion about Ollie's work. He's a dedicated, hardworking man, and he's been given more and more power by McFarlane and Poindexter. Unfortunately, Ollie doesn't know what he doesn't know about international politics. He also wants to control and run everything he gets involved with, and he thinks he can do almost everything by himself. It took me almost a year to understand that Ollie has a habit of giving his colleagues misleading information, even about important matters, not just the self-important boasting and name dropping some of us at the NSC [sic] have come to know well. His style is to preempt people, to "make things happen" his way. I urge you, never take *any* important action based solely on what Ollie tells you. If he says he has an intelligence report about some coming danger that has to be stopped, check it

out with CIA. If he claims to have intercepts, get your own copies. I'd advise you to work closely with people like Fred Iklé at Defense, the national intelligence officer for Latin America at CIA, and the regional NSC staff—especially Jacqueline Tillman, who has good political judgment—as well as Ollie.*[106]

Abrams, according to Menges, merely said: "Oh." Jacqueline Tillman did not have to be convinced about North's transgressions. She was a protégée and former assistant of Jeane Kirkpatrick, the U.S. representative to the United Nations. Tillman was made deputy director for Latin America on the NSC staff in February 1984 but worked on Central American affairs only until December of that year, after which she devoted herself to South America. Asked why she had made the change, she explained that "Ollie had a very proprietary attitude about Central America" and had tried "to take over that account for himself." She says that she tried to get across to North that a "collaborative effort" was needed, but that she could not change his behavior.[107] On one occasion, Menges says, she told him: "I've worked here at the NSC for some weeks now with Ollie North, and I've concluded that not only is he a liar, but he's delusional, power hungry, and a danger to the president and the country. He should not be working on the NSC staff."[108]

Vincent Cannistraro, who had worked for both the CIA and the NSC staff, recalled that Alan Fiers, head of the CIA's Latin American Division, had told him in late 1984 that "I don't know what he [North] is doing but it is probably illegal and he is going to jail." Two years later, Cannistraro heard similar rumblings. In the summer of 1986, others on the NSC staff made comments "about Ollie stepping over the line." Raymond Burghardt and Jacqueline Tillman were said to have been concerned "about Ollie's advocacy of the contras, that this had become an all-consuming passion." In 1986, Cannistraro said, he was also worried that North had "crossed the line" between advocacy and objectivity. And Rodney McDaniel, the staff's executive secretary, had told Cannistraro of similar misgivings—that "the press speculation that had come out at that time period [1986] was hurting the NSC, was hurting the national security adviser, Admiral Poindexter, that Ollie had become an advocate of them [contras] and he, Rod McDaniel, would like to see Ollie removed from that portfolio."[109]

Cannistraro revealed why he had distrusted what North had told him:

> With Colonel North you could never be certain that what he was telling you was true or was fantasy or was being told you deliberately to mislead you so my normal modus operandi when receiving in-

---

* It may be noted that Menges could not resist implying in his title that he was "inside the National Security Council," not the National Security Council staff.

formation from Colonel North as I'm sure it was for most other people who knew him for some time was to take everything with about four grains of salt and try to sort it out from there.[110]

One of the least critical appraisals of North came from Ronald Sable, an Air Force colonel assigned to the NSC staff as senior director of legislative affairs.

> Oliver North was someone if you wanted something done, you could guarantee it was going to get done. You might not be certain of the way it was going to get done.
> As I said to Ollie one morning: If we wanted to get on the other side of the wall, you would be there before anyone else, but you might not check to see if there was a door.*

Whatever the warrant for these views, they were made by staff members on a level comparable to North's and in the same Latin American field. Some "White House officials" cited in the press may have had similar grievances, though no such impassioned denunciations appeared in print. McFarlane and Poindexter either were oblivious to the disruption caused by North in their staff or preferred to give North his head.

6

The newspaper articles in August 1985 were unwelcome but not immediately threatening. In Congress, however, they set off a minor commotion that was both unwelcome and potentially threatening.

In swift succession, letters inquiring about the revelations in the press came from Representative Michael Barnes, chairman of the Subcommittee on Western Hemisphere Affairs of the House Committee on Foreign Affairs, and from Representative Lee Hamilton, chairman of the House Permanent Select Committee on Intelligence. These letters were notable for what they admittedly did not know as well as for what they wanted to know. They admitted that these congressional committees had known little or nothing about what the NSC staff had been doing in Nicaragua. All these committees knew was what they had read in the newspapers. Congress had passed Boland Amendments, but it was totally ignorant of how or whether they were being carried out.

This state of affairs was apparent from the first sentence of Representative Barnes's letter of August 16, 1985, to McFarlane: "I am writing in response to recent press reports detailing the activities of certain National Security Council staff members in providing advice and fundraising

---

* Sable, PT, p. 1945. Sable also said that North "occasionally misled me" (p. 1945).

support to Nicaraguan rebel leaders." It went on to say these reports raised serious questions whether the Boland Amendment was being violated in letter and spirit by direct U.S. support of the contras.[111]

The letter from Representative Hamilton of August 20, 1985, based itself similarly on "recent press reports" and asked for information on NSC staff support of the contras as well as its legal justification, if any.[112]

McFarlane described how he had managed to get around Barnes's request for "all information, including memoranda and any other documents, pertaining to any contact between Lt. Col. North and Nicaraguan rebel leaders." McFarlane asked Barnes to come to his office, where a stack of documents was piled on a table. McFarlane invited Barnes to read them but, to make sure that he could not get very far with them, gave Barnes only about ten minutes of his time. McFarlane was asked whether "it was part of your thinking that if a busy Congressman came down to your office and saw a substantial stack of documents, and you were having a short meeting, it was very unlikely that he would ask to read through the documents from one end to the other?" McFarlane replied: "I think that is true, yes."[113]

McFarlane first chose to answer Hamilton in writing on September 5, 1985. McFarlane put up a perfectly innocent, totally unrepentant front. He said that he had thoroughly examined the facts and anything which could remotely bear upon the charges in the press. From that review, he assured Hamilton, "I can state with deep personal conviction that at no time did I or any member of the National Security Council staff violate the letter or spirit of the law," particularly the Boland Amendment. McFarlane then listed what his staff had *not* done:

> We did not solicit funds or other support for military or paramilitary activities either from Americans or third parties. We did not offer tactical advice for the conduct of their military activities or their organization.

All they had done, McFarlane asserted, was to influence the contras to emphasize "a political rather than a military solution" to the Nicaraguan problem. The legal justification for his staff's activities had been merely to gain information on which to base policy decisions.[114]

McFarlane replied to Representative Barnes on September 12, 1985, in a similar vein. He, more specifically, gave assurances that his staff's activities were fully in conformity with the Boland Amendment and that Lieutenant Colonel North in particular had been in contact with the contras only for the purpose of helping to shape U.S. policy. He flatly denied that these contacts had been used "to provide tactical influence" or to plan military operations.[115]

McFarlane met with members of Hamilton's committee on September 10, 1985, and offered to answer specific questions about North and the

NSC staff. These questions, submitted two days later, were based on the newspaper articles and were far more detailed than before. On October 7, 1985, they were answered in writing by McFarlane, who no longer contented himself with general protestations of innocence. One question brought the specific assurance, which gives the tenor of the exchange: "There is no official or unofficial relationship with any member of the NSC staff regarding fund raising for the Nicaraguan democratic opposition."[116]

Other questions were received from Senators David Durenberger and Patrick Leahy of the Senate Select Committee on Intelligence on October 1, 1985, and answered in like fashion on October 7, 1985.[117]

The congressional inquiries served to involve Congress, for the first time, in oversight of the contra affair and to put McFarlane on record as North's guarantor and protector. Congressional oversight, however, amounted to nothing more than asking McFarlane questions based on newspaper reports and getting answers that everything in them was nothing more than lies or fantasies. So long as McFarlane denied everything, nothing short of public hearings could have saved the committees from pursuing dead ends. Without public hearings, McFarlane's replies successfully fended off further intervention by Congress for another year. On October 24, 1985, *The New York Times* reported that both committees were frustrated and unable to carry through the "vigorous inquiries" which they had promised.[118]

McFarlane's replies to the committees went through a curious process. When Barnes's first letter of August 16, 1985, was received, McFarlane was in Santa Barbara with President Reagan. He says that he told Reagan about the congressional inquiries but received no guidance from him.[119] Barnes's letter went to Poindexter, who immediately commented: "Barnes is really a trouble maker. We have good answers to all of this."[120] Thereupon Poindexter sent the letter to North for "action."[121] By "action" Poindexter meant that North was assigned to prepare the first draft of the response. Poindexter explained under questioning:

> *Liman* [counsel]: And when you suggested that he prepare the first draft of the response, was it your intention that Colonel North be able to answer that letter with finessing a description of his activities?
>
> *Poindexter*: That is exactly right.
>
> *Liman*: That is why you designated him as the action officer?
>
> *Poindexter*: That is right, because my objective here again would have been to withhold information.[122]

North also wanted to withhold information. "I didn't want to show Congress a single word on this whole thing," he declared. North explained his approach as "what I wanted to do in terms of answering these questions, was to simply not answer them at all."[123] North says that he told McFarlane to "simply say we're not going to respond to this. That the activities of the NSC, the National Security Council and the National Security Council staff is part of the office of the President, is not a matter for congressional intrusion."[124] But, according to North, McFarlane insisted that he take a "stab" at concocting a reply. In the end, McFarlane himself wrote the final draft, using only two paragraphs from North's original version.[125] In his congressional testimony McFarlane gave the impression that North had been responsible for the replies.[126]

North made his first offer to leave the NSC staff as a result of the embarrassment caused by the attention paid to him in the press and Congress. "I am sincerely sorry," he wrote to McFarlane, "that this very difficult time has occurred and wish to reiterate my offer to move on if this is becoming a liability for you or the President."[127] North stayed.

McFarlane explained why he had not been too much upset by the fabricated replies. For four or five years, he said, he had been "reading things which I knew to be not compatible with the realities of things."[128] With some reluctance, he admitted that he knew from his own experience that he had deceived the committees by telling them that "none of us has solicited funds"; he himself had done a good deal of implicit soliciting of third-country contributions to the contras.[129] Unlike North, however, McFarlane was later contrite. "What weighs most heavily on my mind," he said, "is that, when Congress inquired about administration support for the contras in 1985, my own response was categorical. I was not sufficiently probing or self-critical. This has been and remains for me a matter of remorse—even anguish—for me, and for many reasons."[130]

This incident showed how limited were the resources to carry out the oversight mission given to the congressional committees. As Representative Lee Hamilton pointed out, his committee was charged with authorizing the activities of the intelligence community and overseeing their implementation. The intelligence committees, however, did not have the authority to block covert actions so long as the committees were duly notified. Even more critically, the committees could get intelligence information only by asking the executive branch for it.[131] If the executive branch chose to conceal or misrepresent, there was little the committees could do about it.

The handling of the congressional inquiries in 1985 haunted McFarlane, Poindexter, and North. It provided the later cases against them with the most damaging charges—the deception and obstruction of Congress. Yet Congress had been helplessly deceived and obstructed at a time when there still existed a possibility of cutting short the covert defiance of the law.

6

Middlemen

We must now turn to the Iran affair and see how it developed.

In the beginning, it had nothing to do with the contra affair. At first they did not have much more in common than that both were covert operations and the responsibility of the same people. Only later did they get mixed up with each other.

In the case of the contras, the trouble had come from the Boland Amendment. In the case of Iran, it came from Operation Staunch. By the spring of 1983, the Reagan administration was so determined to punish the Khomeini regime in Iran that it had launched an international campaign to prevent the sale of arms to Iran. A steady stream of protests went out from Washington to countries known or suspected to have made such sales, including South Korea, Italy, Portugal, China, and Israel. The United States, with the State Department in the lead, was clearly trying to show that it meant business in its effort to prevent the Iran infection from spreading.

Iran was accused of supporting international terrorism and placed on a list of countries subject to strict export controls, especially of arms. The watchwords were: No deals with terrorists, no bargaining for hostages, no compromise with blackmail. As late as June 30, 1985, President Reagan had expressed the policy as: "The United States gives terrorists no rewards. We make no concessions. We make no deals."[1]

By this time, seven American hostages had been taken in Lebanon by presumably pro-Iranian Shiite groups. Three seized in 1984 were: Jeremy Levin, Beirut chief for the Cable News Network (later released); William A. Buckley, the CIA's chief of station in Beirut; and the Reverend Benjamin Weir, a Presbyterian minister. Four more were taken in 1985: Father Lawrence Martin Jenco, director of Catholic Relief Services in Beirut; Terry Anderson, chief Middle East correspondent for the Associated Press; David P. Jacobsen, director of the American University

Hospital in Beirut; and Thomas P. Sutherland, acting dean of agriculture at the American University in Beirut.

These hostages severely tested the administration's policy of no concessions, no deals, and no arms to Iran. The fate of Buckley was naturally a matter of particular concern to CIA Director Casey. If, as was believed, the hostages' captors were linked to or even controlled by Iran, their freedom was more likely to come through dealings with Iran than through efforts in Lebanon, from which the United States had been eliminated. The problem for the administration was that it had the choice of changing its policy to get back the hostages or resigning itself to their captivity in order to keep faith with its policy.

2

Instead of dealing directly with this dilemma, the Reagan administration, after a false start within its own ranks, stumbled into a new Iran policy.

The question first arose whether the United States should adopt a different attitude toward Iran for long-range geopolitical or geostrategical reasons. The hostages-for-arms predicament came later.

The outlines of a more activist line originated in the NSC staff. On January 13, 1984, just as the official anti-Iran policy was hardening, Geoffrey Kemp, senior director for Near East and South Asian Affairs, sent a provocative memorandum to National Security Adviser McFarlane. Kemp suggested that the administration should reevaluate its attitude toward Iran on the ground that the Ayatollah Khomeini was not long for this world and, therefore, something should be done to influence a successor regime. He proposed a program of covert activities to help Iranian exiles, with whom he regularly communicated, overthrow the Khomeini regime and perhaps install a pro-Western government.[2]

Kemp's proposal took half a year to be acted on. McFarlane waited until August 31, 1984, to request a formal interagency analysis of how the United States could influence a post-Khomeini Iran.[3] When this study was completed in October 1984, it did not hold out a prospect of much change in U.S. policy. It argued that Khomeini's death was probably a precondition for any hope of improved U.S.-Iran relations. It touched on the resumption of arms shipments to Iran but made that dependent on the restoration of formal relations with Iran. "The study," it is said, "conveyed an impression of relative American powerlessness that would continue indefinitely."[4]

This sense of impotence continued for some time. The CIA agreed that covert operations were not likely to be useful. A State Department document at the end of 1984 reaffirmed existing policies so long as the situation in Iran remained the same. It also discouraged arms transfers to Iran as a means of changing the situation.[5]

Thus far, the impetus for a new Iran policy seemed to arise from a vague hope of influencing a post-Khomeini regime in Iran to be more friendly to the West rather than from freeing the hostages. Such efforts as were made to think through the problem did not get very far, and the policy vacuum was filled by Operation Staunch, which did not leave much room for maneuvering. By the end of 1984, it seemed that the administration had cut off its line of retreat from its adamant Iran policy. Something else was needed to break through the impasse.

3

Something else came from the most unlikely sources. They were two foreign middlemen who made themselves central characters in the whole story.

One was Adnan Khashoggi, who has had a biography in English, and two novels, one in English and one in French, said to have been based on his life.[6] If only a small portion of the stories that have been published about him are true, he belongs in a novel.

Khashoggi was born in Saudi Arabia in 1935. He was the eldest son of a Saudi physician, Dr. Mohamed Khaled Khashoggi, said to have been the first Saudi doctor with a Western medical degree. This distinction enabled him to become the personal physician of King Abdul-Aziz, the first ruler of modern Saudi Arabia, and of the royal court. His son Adnan attended Victoria College in Alexandria, Egypt, where all instruction was in English. He came to the United States for the first time at the age of eighteen to study at California State University in Chico, where there were other Saudi students. In Khashoggi folklore, it was the scene of his first business triumph. As he has told the story, his father had sent him money to buy an automobile. Instead, he used the money to set up a trucking business, buying American Kenworth trucks and selling them to customers in Saudi Arabia, where they were still rare. After only three semesters at Chico State, he transferred to Stanford University, which he left after a single semester to devote himself to his trucking enterprise. At the age of twenty, he boasted to a French journalist, he had made his first $3 million.[7]

Returning to Saudi Arabia, Khashoggi started his business career in earnest. He formed his first company, Al-Nasr [Victory] Trading and Industrial Corp., which specialized in doing business with the regime of King Saud, the successor of Abdul-Aziz. Khashoggi, still in his twenties, had found his métier as middleman; he served both the regime and himself as agent for foreign corporations—Rolls-Royce, Marconi, Chrysler, and others. In 1964, King Faisal came to the throne and soon aligned Saudi Arabia politically with the United States. One result was a great Saudi

arms buildup, in which U.S. weapons makers were the favored beneficiaries.

Khashoggi, with his ties to the royal family and his command of
American English, was ideally placed to make his fortune as the Saudis'
favorite middleman. Just as oil was beginning to bring in more money
than the Saudis knew what to do with, the word spread that Khashoggi
was the key to arms deals with the Saudi government. For enabling
Lockheed to sell its Hercules transports to the Saudi Defense Ministry,
Khashoggi was paid $106 million in commissions. He is said to have
received more than $100 million from the Raytheon Co. for an integrated
defense system outside the port city of Jedda. Sometimes Khashoggi's
methods misfired. Northrop Corporation confessed to a U.S. Senate
investigation that it had given Khashoggi $450,000 in bribes for two Saudi
generals in order to sell fifty of its F-5 fighter planes to the Saudi Air
Force at a total cost of $140 million. Khashoggi claimed that he had kept
the money "to show the Americans that Saudi generals are not for sale."[8]

In 1967, Adnan, then thirty-two, and his brothers, Adel and Essam,
expanded their commercial horizons by forming the Triad Holding Co.,
named after the three of them, incorporated in Liechtenstein but operating out of Geneva. The Triad empire came to include a Triad Natural
Resources Corp., a Triad Leisure Holding Corp., and a Triad Capital
Management Holding Corp. In 1981, Khashoggi boasted that he controlled about fifty companies, in Asia, Europe, the United States, South
America, and the Middle East, with interests in industrial production,
banks, insurance companies, tourism, agriculture, transport, and regional
development.[9]

By now, Khashoggi's exploits were legendary. He had left his roots in
Saudi Arabia far behind, and one British expert in these matters called
him the "Modern Multinational Man—placeless and rootless."[10] Known
as "the richest man in the world," he gravitated to the very rich, the very
powerful, and the very glamorous. His name was linked with King Juan
Carlos of Spain, Imelda and Ferdinand Marcos of the Philippines, President Gaafar Nimeiri of the Sudan, President Mobuto Sese Seko of Zaire,
"Baby Doc" Duvalier of Haiti, the Sultan of Brunei, and the like. His
private life, some of it lurid, was the stuff of innumerable articles in the
European press. Khashoggi was a glutton for publicity.

If Khashoggi was not the richest man in the world, he lived as if he
were. He maintained a dozen homes—or at least residences—in New
York, Cannes, Paris, Rome, Monte Carlo, Beirut, Riyadh, Jedda, the
Canary Islands, and Marbella, Spain.[11] In the United States, one of his
companies had properties in Utah, Florida, Texas, and Tennessee.[12] His
private airplane was lovingly described in *Time* magazine:

> High above the clouds, at 35,000 ft., Adnan Khashoggi's DC-8
> is cruising noiselessly toward his estate in Marbella, Spain. His

guests, sipping 1961 Château Margaux from crystal goblets with triangular silver bases, lounge on the jet's cream-colored chamois-and-silk banquettes. His masseur, his valet, his barber and his chiropractor—they accompany him everywhere—are relaxing as well because "A.K.," as he is known to his employees, is fast asleep on the $200,000 Russian sable spread covering his 10-ft.-wide bed in one of the plane's three bedrooms.

In the plane's fully equipped kitchen, Khashoggi's chef is preparing hors d'oeuvres. They will be served on white triangular china, embossed in gold with the letters AK designed along with the crystal and flatware, at a cost of $750,000. The plane, which Khashoggi bought in 1982 for $31 million and had reconfigured for an additional $9 million, has the streamlined feel of a flying 21st century Las Vegas disco . . . [13]

Time also noted Khashoggi's other possessions: "His 282-ft. yacht Nabila (complete with helicopter) makes Queen Elizabeth's Britannia look like a package-tour ship. His fleet includes three commercial-size jets, twelve stretch Mercedes limousines, a total of 100 vehicles and a stable of Arabian horses." Of Khashoggi's fiftieth birthday in 1985, Fortune magazine reported:

Adnan Khashoggi, the Saudi Arabian businessman who made a fortune brokering military hardware sales to his government in the 1960s and early 1970s, celebrated his 50th birthday in late July with a medieval bash at his sumptuous estate in Marbella on Spain's Costa del Sol. Armor-clad knights on horses welcomed the 500 guests and strolling minstrels serenaded them. At the appointed moment, an actor costumed as Henry VIII appeared, extolling Khashoggi's contributions to "the brotherhood of man." The king was so awed by his subject that he renounced his throne, fulfilling a headline in newspapers printed up for the party: "Henry the Eighth Abdicates to Adnan the First."*[14]

In addition to all this, Khashoggi yearned for something more. According to an American who worked for him, Khashoggi "didn't like being referred to as an arms dealer. He would become very upset about that." He and his brother "wanted to be referred to as brokers and mer-

---

* Kessler's biography, Khashoggi: The Rise and Fall of the World's Richest Man, lists some of the 400 guests: Count Jaime de Mora y Aragón, Countess Gunila von Bismarck, Prince and Princess Von Thurn und Taxis, Princess Bridgett of Sweden, Princess Fabiola of Belgium, Archduchess Helene and Archduke Ferdinand von Habsburg, Prince Hubertus von Hohenlohe, Prince Heinrich Hanau, U.S. Ambassador Maxwell M. Rabb, Brooke Shields, Sean Connery, Shirley Bassey (pp. 13, 21). Kessler has an elaborate description of the affair.

chants and business statesmen. He was always interested in being referred to as a merchant statesman."[15] In this guise, he entered the Iran affair.

4

According to Khashoggi, he met with National Security Adviser Mc-Farlane for the first time in the White House in 1983. He tried to persuade him that the way to bring peace to the Middle East was through a tax on oil, the money to go to the development of the region.[16] McFarlane said that he had routinely sent Khashoggi's messages to his staff, where they would be "filed and forgotten."[17]

Khashoggi was not one to be easily discouraged. In April 1984, he made contact with Geoffrey Kemp of the NSC staff and again met with McFarlane. He evidently wanted to arrange a meeting between an American official and a Middle Eastern representative.[18]

Official Washington soon heard that Iranian agents were trying to buy TOW missiles.[19] The information came from Theodore G. Shackley, a former high CIA official and a man who had a past to live down.

From 1976 to 1979, Shackley had been the CIA's associate director of operations, the division in charge of covert activities. Caught up in the scandal surrounding former CIA official Edwin Wilson, Shackley had retired from the CIA in August 1979 and now headed a "risk management" firm, Research Associates, Inc. Its only client was a U.S. oil trading and refining company for which he allegedly monitored developments in oil-producing countries throughout the world and also designed security systems and training.

According to Shackley, this employment caused him to take a more than ordinary interest in the Iran-Iraq war. To follow it, he had enlisted the aid of an Iranian named Razmara who had been a "colleague" of General Manucher Hashemi, the former head of the counterespionage Department VIII of SAVAK, the Shah's notorious secret police. Through Razmara, Shackley obtained and passed on Hashemi's views on the war. Hashemi, according to Shackley, monitored developments in Iran and wanted "to see Iran become a non-communist nation with an orderly and just form of government when Ayatollah Khomeini passes from the scene and his revolution becomes a spent force."[20]

In October 1984, Shackley and Razmara met with Hashemi in California, where the latter had gone to visit his daughter and grandchildren. They "got along very well," and Hashemi offered to introduce them to "interesting people" from Iran with whom he frequently met. In late October, Hashemi called to invite them to meet with just such people.[21] According to George Cave, Shackley led Hashemi to believe that "he was functioning on behalf of the NSC."[22] Cave was the CIA's expert on

Iran until February 1980, when his status was changed to consultant; he was the only one in the Agency who spoke Farsi fluently.

On November 20, 1984, in the fashionable Vier Jahreszeiten Hotel in Hamburg, West Germany, Shackley and Razmara met with Hashemi, who produced three others—Manucher Ghorbanifar, introduced as president of the Bylex Trading Company in Paris; Dr. Shahabadi, head of the Iranian purchasing office in Hamburg; and Hassan Karoubi, known in the later investigation of the Iran affair as the "First Iranian." Ghorbanifar, Shackley reported, had been another SAVAK agent and was now an international deal maker. Shackley described Ghorbanifar as "a 'wheeler dealer' and [one who] could play both ends against the middle for a profit in a business deal." Hashemi introduced Ghorbanifar as one whose contacts in Iran were "fantastic."

This occasion was Ghorbanifar's first known appearance in the Iran affair.

In his report of the meeting to the CIA, Shackley gave this account of Ghorbanifar's approach:

> Ghorbanifar said his business was successful but he was also an Iranian nationalist. Due to the latter factor, he was vitally concerned with developments in Iran. He feared that Iran would become a Soviet satellite within the near term—three to five years—if he and people like General Hashemi did not do something to stem the tide. He rhetorically asked what can we do, for despite our ability to work with the "moderates" in Iran, we can't get a meaningful dialogue with Washington. According to Ghorbanifar, it is President Reagan who has the destiny of the Iranian people in his hand. When at this juncture Ghorbanifar was asked if he had tried to open a dialogue with the Americans, he said, "We know the CIA in Frankfurt. They want to treat us like kleenex—use us for their purpose and then throw us out the window. We can't work with them as they are unreasonable and unprofessional. In fact, if you check on me with them, they will tell you I am unreasonable and undisciplined."[23]

At one point, Ghorbanifar "asked if there was some way maybe he should work toward establishing his bona fides with the Americans when he was discussing this," by which he meant the possible sale of missiles to Iran. Shackley said: "What do you have in mind?" Ghorbanifar replied that Iran had some "equipment" that Americans might want in return for which "Tehran would want TOW missiles." The "equipment" was Soviet arms that Iran had captured from Iraq. Ghorbanifar also suggested that it might be possible to pay a cash ransom for four American hostages in Lebanon, including the CIA's Buckley, who he said, after making telephone calls, were still alive. Ghorbanifar offered himself as the middleman to disguise the "ransom deal" and demanded a response to it by December 7.

Shackley had no official status that could enable him to meet Ghorbanifar's demands but knew enough to demur at the request for TOW missiles. When Ghorbanifar brought them up, Shackley says that he advised him that "they ought to find a simpler way to establish his bona fides" and that Ghorbanifar ought to "forget it, find something simpler."[24]

At this meeting in Hamburg in November 1984, there emerged for the first time the main themes that served Ghorbanifar and beguiled the Americans in contact with him for the next two years—the Soviet threat to Iran, the lure of alleged Iranian "moderates," the sale of U.S. missiles to Iran, and the ransom of U.S. hostages.

Ghorbanifar's overture was not the first of its kind. According to the chief of the CIA's Near East Division in the Operations Directorate, the CIA had been receiving thirty to forty requests every year from Iranians and Iranian exiles "to provide us with very fancy intelligence, very important internal political insights, if we in return can arrange for the sale of a dozen Bell helicopter gunships or 1,000 TOW missiles or something else that is on the contraband list."[25] What made Ghorbanifar different was his persistence, his guile, and the emergence of a new set of Americans to bedazzle with his wiles.

5

Manucher Ghorbanifar was well known to the CIA. He had first come to its attention in 1980 through a European intelligence service. As he later explained to Charles E. Allen, the CIA's national intelligence officer, he had cooperated with the Agency from 1980 to 1982 but had cut himself off because the Agency had merely wanted to use him as "another source," a somewhat softer version of the complaint that he had made earlier to Shackley. At that time, Ghorbanifar said, he had suffered as a result of his break with the CIA, which had sent out word that he could not be trusted. In retaliation, he had made sure that some of his Iranian contacts had also broken off their relationship with the CIA or had fed the Agency false information.[26]

The CIA, it seems, had decided by 1983 or earlier to have nothing more to do with him on the ground that he was untrustworthy. Ghorbanifar, however, came back to haunt the CIA. In March 1984, after Ghorbanifar had allegedly fabricated information concerning an assassination plot against U.S. presidential candidates, he was given and failed a polygraph test. In June 1984, he was examined again in relation to information he claimed to have about the whereabouts of the U.S. hostages in Lebanon—with the same result.[27] In July 1984, the CIA issued a "burn notice" to other government agencies to stay away from him.

This "burn notice" contains as much information about Ghorbanifar as the CIA was able to gather. He was described as a man of "medium height, overweight, dark eyes, thinning dark hair, round face, well dressed." His manner was "personable, convincing, fast talker, difficult to keep to subject at hand." He had allegedly been a former Iranian army officer and claimed to have worked for SAVAK. He was now in the import-export business, had formerly served as managing director of the Star Line Shipping Co., and was a "self-proclaimed wheeler-dealer since his early 20's." He had operated under various aliases—Ja'far Souzani, Manuel Pereira, Nikolaos Kralis—and carried Portuguese, Greek, and Iranian passports made out to different names.

Politically, according to this account, Ghorbanifar had been an informant for Iranian intelligence prior to the Iranian revolution of 1979. He claimed to have access to many senior-ranking officers in the Iranian armed forces as well as "to Iranian underworld characters of various illicit hues." For about a year after the revolution, he was still able to travel freely between Iran and Europe in connection with his import-export business, but then was implicated in an abortive anti-Khomeini coup in July 1980, and his trips had been curtailed. He claimed to have a "group" in Iran for which he kept in touch with other exile leaders.

This CIA profile summed up his record skeptically: "He had a history of predicting events after they happened and was seen as a rumormonger of occasional usefulness. In addition, the information collected by him consistently lacked sourcing and detail notwithstanding his exclusive interest in acquiring money."[28]

Another CIA report noted that the Star Line Shipping Co., of which he had been managing director, had become a "joint Iranian/Israeli venture" in late 1980. This document was somewhat more favorable to Ghorbanifar: "There well may be something to what he is saying—but exactly what, and why he is telling us needs to be determined."*[29]

When Ghorbanifar met with Shackley at the end of 1984, he was well aware of his reputation with the CIA and took care to protect himself in advance by warning Shackley that he was persona non grata with the Agency. Ghorbanifar had given up hope of getting back into the good graces of the CIA; his problem was how to establish his "bona fides" with another part of the U.S. government. He was apparently counting on Shackley to give him access to other high American officials who might treat him differently.

In this he was quickly disappointed. When Shackley returned to the United States, he sent a memorandum about his meeting in Hamburg to Vernon Walters, the State Department's ambassador at large and a former deputy director of the CIA. Walters passed it on to other officials

---

* Cave said that Ghorbanifar had been the Iranian director of the Star Line Shipping Co., "which was a joint Iranian-Israeli concern with heavy intelligence overtones" (B-3, p. 575).

in the State Department, including Robert B. Oakley, the head of its office of Counterterrorism and Emergency Planning, and Richard W. Murphy, assistant secretary of state for Near Eastern Affairs. Oakley and Murphy dismissed the hostage ransom proposal as a "scam." On December 11, 1984, Shackley was informed that the State Department was not interested in pursuing Ghorbanifar's proposal, replying with, in effect, a "thank you but we will work this problem out via other channels."[30]

Thus, until the end of 1984, Ghorbanifar was still an untouchable for both U.S. policy and intelligence. But he was a hard man to put down and soon sought other ways to make the Americans warm up to him.

6

A chance encounter between Adnan Khashoggi and Manucher Ghorbanifar effectively set the Iran affair in motion.

As Khashoggi told the story to the French writer Michel Clerc, the meeting took place in Hamburg in April 1985. Khashoggi happened to be told by his American associate Roy M. Furmark about a sale of Persian rugs that had belonged to the deposed Shah of Iran. At the sale, Furmark introduced him to the mysterious Ghorbanifar. The three went off to a restaurant, where they talked about the latest news from the Middle East. Ghorbanifar held forth on the factional struggle in Iran. He told them about three factions struggling for power in Iran. One was liberal and wanted an opening to the West; another was extremist and fanatically wanted to spread the Islamic revolution by means of terror; a third was centrist and was mainly interested in trade but devoted to the Islamic faith. All three factions agreed that the war with Iraq had lasted too long. "A gesture by the United States would be enough to end it," Ghorbanifar assured them.

Ghorbanifar spoke as if he were an unofficial Iranian emissary. Khashoggi was apparently fascinated. If the Americans were to be convinced, he saw himself as the man to do it. "The two of us, acting behind the scenes," Ghorbanifar said, "have all that is needed to get the necessary negotiations started." Khashoggi thought to himself: he would handle the Americans and Ghorbanifar would advise him on Iranian politics. Khashoggi had been rebuffed by the Americans before; this was his best chance to impress them with his statesmanship.[31]

There are at least three other versions of the first Khashoggi-Ghorbanifar meeting. Furmark testified that he had introduced Khashoggi to Ghorbanifar in Hamburg about June 12, 1985, at a meeting about a troubled barter arrangement between Iran and the German Mannesmann Co. Furmark does not explain why Khashoggi and Ghorbanifar were there or what they could do about the problem.[32] Kessler's biography repeats Furmark's story.[33]

In an interview with Thomas L. Friedman in *The New York Times*, the Israeli Yaacov Nimrodi said that Khashoggi had introduced Ghorbanifar to King Fahd of Saudi Arabia at the end of 1984.[34] This incident would have antedated the versions of both Khashoggi and Furmark and seems farfetched.

Samuel Segev, an Israeli journalist, says that Khashoggi met Ghorbanifar in the fall of 1984, repeats Khashoggi's story that the occasion was buying Persian rugs in Hamburg, but has them going to lunch "at the invitation of a sometime business partner, an Iranian carpet dealer." Segev seems to have conflated two or three different versions. He attributes his account to what Khashoggi and Ghorbanifar later related to Israeli participants.[35]

At this point, Israel was drawn into Khashoggi's grand design. As usual, versions differ on the details, but they agree on the main issue.

In his interview with Michel Clerc, Khashoggi said that he had decided to check on Ghorbanifar, having just met him. Khashoggi first applied to his friends in the Egyptian intelligence service, who knew nothing about Ghorbanifar. His next thought was to get in touch with Israel through Prime Minister Shimon Peres, whom he called "my old friend." This time Khashoggi was more successful; the Israelis vouched for Ghorbanifar. In the summer of 1985, in Hamburg, another meeting took place, attended by Khashoggi, three Israelis, and Ghorbanifar, accompanied by Hassan Karoubi as the Iranian representative.[36]

The three Israelis present at this meeting were Yaacov Nimrodi, Adolph (Al) Schwimmer, and David Kimche.

Nimrodi, in his early sixties, was an Iraqi-born Israeli who had spent a quarter of a century in Iran, among other things as Israeli military attaché and representative of Israeli and European arms manufacturers.[37] His commissions from arms sales had made him a millionaire and one of the richest men in Israel. According to Israeli journalists, he had lost millions of dollars in Iran as a result of the Shah's downfall, and continued to lobby on behalf of Western contacts with Khomeini's Iran in the hope of regaining his wealth there, "but the line that separated Nimrodi's own interests from those of the State of Israel was often blurred."[38]

Schwimmer, in his late sixties, was a U.S.-born Israeli citizen who had founded the Israel Aircraft Industries and had long had dealings with pre-Khomeini Iran. The new Begin regime had succeeded in getting Schwimmer, who was close to the former Prime Minister Shimon Peres, to leave the Israel Aircraft Industries in 1977, whereupon he had gone into the arms-dealing business for himself, or in partnership with Nimrodi.[39]

Kimche, British-born of Eastern European parentage, was an Israeli success story. After some journalistic experience, he had shifted to the Mossad, the Israeli secret intelligence, rising to the post of deputy director.

In 1984, the new foreign minister, Yitzhak Shamir, had appointed him director general of the foreign ministry. Kimche was liked and admired by the Americans. He was highly regarded as a cultivated, professional intelligence agent and diplomat. Over the past decade, he had established close ties with McFarlane, now in a position of similar influence on the American side.

Khashoggi was no newcomer to Nimrodi and Schwimmer. According to Israeli sources, the two had known Khashoggi for some years past in various business-political ventures that were their specialty. In 1981–82, a group including Nimrodi, Schwimmer, Kimche, and Israeli Defense Minister Ariel Sharon met with President Nimeiri of the Sudan at a safari resort in Kenya owned by Khashoggi. The plan was to arm the Sudan as a center of subversion for covert operations against the new Iranian regime and elsewhere in Africa and the Middle East. If the plan had gone through, Khashoggi, Nimrodi, and Schwimmer would have acted as middlemen in arranging the deals necessary for pouring arms into the Sudan. It did not go through, apparently because higher officials in Israel decided that the risks were too great.[40]

The Sudanese plan was a dress rehearsal for the injection of this trio into the Iran affair. As usual, we have more than one version of how the Iran scheme was hatched.

According to Nimrodi, Khashoggi called him and Schwimmer in early 1985. Khashoggi asked Nimrodi to meet with Ghorbanifar. When the two came together in Geneva in February 1985, Ghorbanifar said: "Look, I want to buy Israeli arms. We can do a lot together. I am a close friend of the Iranian Prime Minister. There are pragmatists in the leadership who want to bring Iran back to the West, I am ready to bring Israel together with them."

Back in Israel, Nimrodi reported this conversation to Schwimmer, and both went to see Prime Minister Peres. "I felt there was a real opportunity to make an opening again with Iran," Nimrodi related. "We asked Peres if we could sell Israeli arms. He said, 'No. Offer to sell them food.' " In continued discussions with Ghorbanifar the next month, the Iranian came up with a special inducement—to give Israel one of the three Soviet T-72 tanks captured by Iran. Ghorbanifar also claimed to have $50 million to pay for Israeli arms. Nimrodi related:

> This got people's attention. But first everyone wanted to make sure that Ghorbanifar was for real. He was brought to Israel in early March and checked out by all the intelligence experts. They listened to him speaking on the phone with high officials in Tehran. Some of them said that he is obviously well connected, but he is also a liar. Sure he is a liar, but what do you expect to find in this business? Sons of rabbis?[41]

Segev tells a different story. He has Khashoggi first getting in touch with Ronald Furer, an Israeli businessman living in London, about inducing Israel to sell arms to Iran. Furer, not Nimrodi, brought the proposal to Peres. With Peres's permission, Nimrodi and Schwimmer soon met in London with Khashoggi, Ghorbanifar, and Cyrus Hashemi, a naturalized U.S. citizen of Iranian extraction (not related to General Manucher Hashemi). Khashoggi repeated Ghorbanifar's line that "moderate elements" in Iran wanted to open channels of communication with the United States. Ghorbanifar mentioned Iran's desire for food and arms, but emphasized that the main thing was to begin talking with the United States. Khashoggi asked the Israelis to sound out the Americans.

Ghorbanifar and Nimrodi met again in Geneva in March 1985. Ghorbanifar is said to have told Nimrodi the story of his life—born in Isfahan in September 1945, making him ten years younger than Khashoggi. He had served in the Iranian military intelligence, then SAVAK, and in the 1970s had set up the Black Star Shipping Co. in partnership with an Israeli, Dr. Yoram Almogi. This business tie had opened Ghorbanifar to suspicion in Iran that he was an Israeli spy, which Segev says he was not. In any case, the fall of the Shah in 1979 forced Ghorbanifar to move to Hamburg, West Germany, with his wife, two sons, and a daughter. In Hamburg, he went into business as an importer of carpets, which is how, in Khashoggi's version, he may have met Khashoggi and Furmark buying carpets in Hamburg.[42]

Segev also tells a story of how Khashoggi succeeded in getting the Israelis to believe in Ghorbanifar's reliability. It seems that Ghorbanifar, in a conversation with Khashoggi on May 16, 1985, had revealed that Iran's president, Ali Khamenei, and prime minister, Mir Hussein Moussavi, had organized a plot to assassinate the emir of Kuwait, Sheikh Jaber Ahmed as-Sabah. Such an attempt was actually made, though not successfully, on May 25. Khashoggi passed the story on to his Israeli friends, Schwimmer and Nimrodi, as evidence that Ghorbanifar possessed extraordinary powers of penetration into the highest ranks of the Iranian government.[43]

Another Israeli version comes from the journalists Dan Raviv and Yossi Melman. They say that Khashoggi began the "Irangate scandal" in April 1985 by putting in an urgent call to Nimrodi and Schwimmer to come to London to meet with him and some Iranians "who are worth meeting." Prime Minister Peres authorized Schwimmer to attend, at which time Schwimmer met with Cyrus Hashemi, whom Khashoggi introduced as "a man of influence" and a cousin of Iranian Speaker Rafsanjani. Unlike his former plan to use the Sudan to overthrow the Khomeini regime, Khashoggi now urged Israel to befriend "specific elements in the regime," and Hashemi wanted Israel to renew arms sales to Iran, previously cut off as a result of U.S. pressure. Khashoggi soon introduced Nimrodi and Schwimmer to Ghorbanifar, "whom he identified as a Hamburg-based

Iranian businessman authorized by Iran's Prime Minister to pursue better relations with the West—again, through Israel." Later that same month, Hashemi and Ghorbanifar came to Israel to be "tested."[44]

Raviv and Melman say that they have read a report, dated May 2, 1985, which Ghorbanifar wrote in a Mossad guesthouse near Tel Aviv in order to impress the Israelis—and the Americans to whom it was soon sent—with his inside knowledge of Iranian affairs. Its main contribution was an analysis of the Iranian political lineup under the Ayatollah Khomeini. It was an elaboration of the story that Ghorbanifar had told Khashoggi and Furmark in the Hamburg restaurant the month before. While Khomeini was still the "sole ruler," three "lines" or factions were competing for power after his departure: a "rightest" Line One, a "leftist" Line Two, and a middle-of-the-road Line Three. Ghorbanifar named names and seemed to command an intimate knowledge of Iranian political tendencies and rivalries.[45]

Whatever the merits of Ghorbanifar's analysis, it served to convince the Israelis that they had an inside track into the hitherto secret world of Iranian politics and persuaded them that they could profitably share their newfound knowledge with the Americans.

Michael Ledeen, later the first American intermediary, has still another story of how Khashoggi and Ghorbanifar came to the attention of the Israelis. He makes David Kimche the main protagonist. In his Mossad period, Kimche had allegedly sought to open a secret channel to the Saudi royal family. For this purpose, he used Khashoggi, which, if true, would explain Khashoggi's previous dealings with the Israelis. Kimche appointed Schwimmer as Khashoggi's Israeli contact in a relationship that lasted more than fifteen years. For this reason, Khashoggi first turned to Schwimmer to introduce Ghorbanifar to the Israelis. Khashoggi was responsible for setting up the first Israeli meeting between himself, Ghorbanifar, Schwimmer, Nimrodi, and an important Iranian official in Hamburg—evidently Karoubi—in March 1985, not the accidental meeting among Khashoggi, Furmark, and Ghorbanifar described by Khashoggi. Ledeen also has a carpet story—that Khashoggi went to a bonded warehouse full of Persian carpets, not that Khashoggi and Ghorbanifar met looking at carpets. At this Hamburg meeting, Ghorbanifar told the Israelis that many Iranian leaders wanted to improve relations with the West and that the only way for the West to accept Iran was through the sale of weapons.[46]

Finally, an official Israeli chronology states that Schwimmer and Nimrodi met with Ghorbanifar and Cyrus Hashemi in London, Geneva, and Israel in early spring 1985. They discussed weapons sales, without any concrete result. In late April, Ghorbanifar proposed to one of the Israelis that he could obtain the release of the hostage most sought after by the CIA, William A. Buckley, in return for permission to purchase U.S.-made TOW antitank missiles from Israel.[47]

Furmark says that in mid-June 1985 in Israel he heard Ghorbanifar, Schwimmer, and Nimrodi discuss how to get U.S.-made spare parts to Iran. On the way back to Paris, Ghorbanifar excitedly told Furmark that he hoped to get U.S. approval for Israel to supply the spare parts to Iran.[48]

Clearly, there is fact and folklore in all these versions. What emerges from them is one fact basic to all that followed. In the first three or four months of 1985, Khashoggi and Ghorbanifar conceived a plan to sell arms to Iran, for which purpose it was necessary to use Israel as the intermediary and eventually to bring the United States into the transaction. The whole theoretical underpinning of the plot, based on a three-fold factional struggle in Iran, had already been worked out. If it succeeded, Khashoggi and Ghorbanifar saw themselves as the main financial beneficiaries as well as having realized their political ambitions.

Khashoggi and Ghorbanifar were not philanthropic in their motives. They saw millions of dollars ahead in future trade with Iran if only the United States could be made to abandon its embargo against Iran. According to Furmark, Khashoggi had visions of getting trade contracts in the billions, "because he thought once the war would be stopped, Iraq and Iran would probably spend 20, 30, 40, 50 billion a year to rebuild for the next 10 years."[49] The perfect combination was Khashoggi, with his money, financial experience, and statesmanlike ambitions, and Ghorbanifar, with his apparent inside knowledge and high-level contacts in Iran. As Khashoggi told Michel Clerc: "I was risking a great deal, but the game was worth the candle."[50]

7

Another interloper in the Iran-hostages entanglement at about this time was Cyrus Hashemi, the naturalized U.S. citizen of Iranian extraction who figures in some of the Israeli versions of this period. He was another deal maker, in everything from oil to arms. In May 1984, Hashemi was charged with violation of the U.S. ban on exporting weapons to Iran and was desperately trying to extricate himself from the indictment. By this time, he was well known to U.S. authorities and could hardly have played the supposed role that Khashoggi attributed to him.

In Hamburg, Hashemi got in touch with Casey's friend John Shaheen in an attempt to make a deal over Hashemi's indictment. Shaheen promptly informed Casey that Hashemi had offered information about a possible change in Iranian policy if the U.S. government "would be able to get him a nolle prosequi." Shaheen had told him that he had no power to do that but then asked "whether Hashemi's contacts with the Iranian government were good enough to spring the hostages if he could be gotten off the hook." Hashemi soon called back, apparently after having checked with his Iranian sources, and added the release of sev-

enteen Da'wa terrorists imprisoned in Kuwait and TOW missiles for Iran
to his own personal case. Shaheen said that he had told him to dismiss
the idea of freeing the Da'wa terrorists and getting U.S. weapons, whereupon Hashemi countered with another offer to bring a high-ranking
Iranian representative for a conference with a U.S. official to find out
what the Iranian government wanted.[51]

The Da'wa terrorists were so called from their membership in one of
the most extreme of the Iranian-influenced factions in Lebanon, *al Da'wa
al-Islamiyya* or the Islamic Call. On December 12, 1983, six bombs
exploded at intervals in the small city-state of Kuwait, killing six and
injuring more than eighty. U.S. and French targets, including the U.S.
embassy compound, were the main objectives. Seventeen of the terrorists
were caught and held as prisoners in Kuwait, with the result that their
organization was determined to use every possible means to force Kuwait
to free them. The determination of the United States to free its own very
different hostages in Lebanon gave the Da'was an opportunity to make
a trade through arms-for-hostages deals, first put forward by Hashemi and
Ghorbanifar. The Da'was were evidently able to act through the Hizballah
or Party of God movement in Lebanon, which is believed to have been
inspired or even organized by the Revolutionary Guards of Iran.[52]

A cat-and-mouse game with Hashemi went on for weeks. The CIA's
Near East Division did not believe that Hashemi was acting on his own
and believed that Ghorbanifar was behind his moves. The chief of the
division said that it had been "stiff-arming" Hashemi's proposal, because
it believed that "you have a fabricator once again coming up, this time
he is coming through Cyrus Hashemi."[53]

Casey did not let the matter drop and put it up to Assistant Secretary
of State for Near Eastern and South Asian Affairs Richard W. Murphy,
who in turn consulted the Justice Department. Despite a reluctance to
deal directly with the Iranians, Murphy felt that an intermediary should
be used to listen to but not negotiate with the alleged Iranian representative.[54] Shaheen was told that no meeting could be held with Ghorbanifar
alone, because he was "a fabricator and unreliable."[55] At this time Ghorbanifar was supposed to be "a high-ranking Iranian intelligence officer."[56]
As negotiations continued, Hashemi claimed that "the Iranians are more
interested in a change of course than in any other *quid pro quo*" and that
seven hostages could be freed if the prosecution against him was
dropped.[57] Nothing came of all this. Hashemi died in 1986 without
getting his case dropped or coming through with any of his engagements.

Yet Hashemi's attempt to use the hostages in his own interest was
significant. He, like Ghorbanifar and others, realized that the hostages
could act as bait to hook the Americans in behalf of personal or financial
gain. The Iranians' later demands, including freedom for the Da'wa
prisoners in Kuwait and the sale of U.S. weapons, were fundamental
Iranian requirements which did not go away; they reappeared at a later

date—sometimes, as in the case of the Da'wa prisoners, when the Americans least expected or wanted it.

From all that we know about the activities of this exotic group of international deal makers, some things are clear. The original idea of trading arms for hostages originated within a relatively small circle that included Khashoggi, Ghorbanifar, Hashemi, Schwimmer, and Nimrodi, largely for personal, commercial, or financial gain. All the later elements of the Iran initiative were already present in the first half of 1985 before the active intervention of Israel or the United States. In fact, the two governments were drawn in as the ringleaders gradually worked out a modus operandi to get what they wanted.

It became increasingly clear that Iran would be most interested in obtaining U.S.-made weapons, that they could most easily come via Israel, and that Israel would need U.S. approval to make them available. On the American side, a trade for hostages was the most likely bait to get such approval. The influence of Iranian exiles, such as Hashemi and Ghorbanifar, added a larger political dimension to the arms-for-hostages scheme. They introduced the idea of assisting Iranian "moderates" to overthrow or succeed the Khomeini regime. With a U.S. government still smarting over the humiliation suffered in connection with the downfall of the Shah, the political and strategic stakes reinforced the intense desire to free the American hostages in Lebanon. In this way, arms, hostages, Iranian "moderates," the United States, Israel, and Iran were bound together in a still incipient commercial-military-political strategy.

It still had far to go. The one who emerged as central to the entire operation was Ghorbanifar, whose reputation for truth-telling and reliability was unfortunately very low. It would have been easier for him if he had entered the game as a new player. His great disadvantage was that the Americans had known him too well, at least since 1980. The one U.S. agency that could do him the most good or harm was the CIA, and it was his greatest obstacle.

Thus, by mid-1985, much remained to be done. Israel still had to be drawn in, the United States lured into following suit, and Ghorbanifar somehow had to find a way to get into the good graces of a U.S. center of power outside the CIA. All this was as yet preliminary to moving weapons to Iran and freeing hostages whom Iran did not even admit having or controlling. Yet events moved in all these directions with remarkable speed.

7

Catalysts

By the summer of 1985, pressure from various sources began to move U.S. policy on Iran into a new phase.

The unlikely catalyst who first brought all three elements—Israel, the United States, and Ghorbanifar—together was a part-time consultant to National Security Adviser McFarlane, Michael A. Ledeen. He was one of those bright, ambitious young men who had gravitated to Washington to share in the power that flowed into the American capital with the Reagan administration.

Ledeen had spent several years in Italy, where he had developed "a modest career in journalism," as he put it. Returning to the United States in 1977, he was ready for bigger things and obtained a job as "special adviser" to Reagan's first secretary of state, Alexander Haig. He was taken on primarily to report on the affairs of the Socialist International, in which capacity he became acquainted with the future Israeli prime minister, Shimon Peres, the leader of the Israeli Labor Party, which belonged to the Socialist International. When Haig was forced out in 1982, Ledeen lost his patron but continued on as a consultant for the State and Defense Departments, where he did various chores, such as making a study of the documents captured in Grenada. At the beginning of 1985, Ledeen, now in his mid-forties, was taken on as a part-time consultant by National Security Adviser McFarlane, who knew him from the days when both had worked for Haig. Ledeen spent much of his time reading intelligence reports on terrorism.[1] He had been assigned administratively to North's counterterrorism office but did not keep North informed of what he was doing.[2]

As Ledeen later told the story, the beginning of his active involvement in the Iran affair was fortuitous. Sometime in March–April 1985, he happened to be talking to an intelligence official of a Western European country who had recently returned from Iran. This official told him that the situation in Iran was more fluid than at any time since the Khomeini revolution and that the United States could profitably play a role in Iran. Ledeen asked him "how we could best learn more about Iran." The answer was that "the Israelis knew everything, or words to that effect, that the Israelis had a terrific intelligence organization inside Iran, and that they undoubtedly knew more about Iran than any other country in the Western world, and that we should talk to them."[3]

Ledeen's problem was how to find a niche for himself as a part-time consultant to McFarlane. The meeting with the intelligence official gave Ledeen an opening to report the conversation to McFarlane and suggest that he should go to see Peres, who had recently become Israeli prime minister, to find out what the Israelis knew. On March 21, 1985, Ledeen saw North, who recorded in his notebook that Ledeen "wants to make trip to Israel."[4]

Ledeen's proposal was not appreciated in some quarters. Howard Teicher, in the Near East and South Asia Directorate, later recalled: "I questioned the ability of Michael to serve in this sensitive a function given his persona in public and his tendency to talk and not necessarily be as discreet as one needed to be." Teicher added guardedly: "He tended to be verbose and to, I would say, describe his functions in an official capacity to the maximum extent possible which might not have been accurate."[5]

After discussing the matter with others, including Teicher, Deputy National Security Adviser Donald R. Fortier informed McFarlane: "None of us feel Mike should be our primary channel for working the Iran issue with foreign governments, and we think you should probably should [sic] not provide a formal letter." Nevertheless, Fortier suggested that it would be useful for Ledeen to see Peres but to limit himself to two points— that it was necessary "to begin to develop a more serious and coordinated strategy for dealing with the Iranian succession crisis" and to get Peres's ideas "on how we could cooperate more effectively."[6]

Both McFarlane and Fortier were worried that Ledeen's trip to Israel might disturb the State Department. McFarlane told Fortier: "I want to talk to [Secretary] Shultz so that he is not blindsided when [Ambassador] Sam Lewis reports—as he will surely find out—about Mike's wanderings."

In any case, McFarlane decided to let Ledeen go. To guard against some of the misgivings raised by Teicher, according to Ledeen, Mc-Farlane "told me specifically what to say and what tone of voice I was to use when I said it to Peres." McFarlane told Ledeen to say that "it was a research project, and that while it was a project undertaken for the National Security Council on which I would report directly to Mc-Farlane, it was nonetheless not a policy initiative but simply a search for better information about Iran."[7]

Ledeen met with Peres in the first week of May 1985.[8] Ledeen says that he asked three questions: Was Peres satisfied with Israel's own information and understanding of Iran? If he was, would Israel be willing to share its intelligence with the United States? Did Peres have any "bright ideas" about Western policy toward Iran?

Peres is said to have replied that he was personally dissatisfied with Israel's intelligence on Iran. It might be better than that of the United States but not at all sufficient for policymaking purposes. Basically, they didn't have any great understanding of the situation. But the subject was undoubtedly important; he suggested that the two countries should work together to develop better information about and a better understanding of Iran.

All this belied the original reason for Ledeen's mission to Israel—that Israel knew everything about Iran and had a "terrific intelligence organization inside Iran," as he had allegedly been told by the Western European intelligence official. All that Ledeen had learned from Peres was that none of this was true. Yet a false lead and an apparently unenlightening interview with Peres enabled Ledeen to find a niche for himself in the still nascent "Iran initiative."

Peres, however, went beyond answering Ledeen's questions. Peres decided to appoint Shlomo Gazit, the former chief of Israeli military intelligence and then president of Ben-Gurion University in Beersheba, to meet with Ledeen and arrange for intelligence sharing on Iran. Peres also brought up an even more delicate matter. According to Ledeen, he said that he had recently received a request from Iran to sell it artillery shells, which Israel was prepared to do if the United States did not object. Ledeen says that he demurred at becoming the channel for this request, but Peres insisted, and Ledeen finally agreed to do it for him this one time. Ledeen also met with Gazit and agreed to come back within a month with a U.S. evaluation of "Iranian matters."[9]

All this—the weapons request and the arrangement with Gazit—went considerably beyond Ledeen's original instructions from McFarlane to do nothing more than to listen and learn. Ledeen says that contacts with Iran and the American hostages in Lebanon were never discussed on this first trip. An Israeli official, however, recalled that Ledeen had told him about offers by various Iranians to help get the hostages released.[10] Ledeen's story is that he had not yet met any Iranians.

What Ledeen did not know was that Peres had already been drawn into the Khashoggi-Ghorbanifar net through the previous contacts with Nimrodi, Schwimmer, and Kimche. In April 1985, Peres had authorized Nimrodi and Schwimmer to meet with Khashoggi in London and had permitted Ghorbanifar and Hashemi to come to Israel to be "tested." According to Israeli sources, Ghorbanifar had persuaded the Israeli Defense Ministry to sell $40 million worth of Israeli-manufactured weapons, none of them missiles, to Iran. Later that same month, when the arms were loaded aboard a ship sailing from Eilat in Israel to Bandar Abbas in Iran, Ghorbanifar received a call from Tehran canceling the order and seeking instead U.S.-made TOW missiles from Israel. The deal was off, and the Israelis realized that they were faced with an Iranian demand that could not be legally satisfied without the approval of the United States.[11]

If the authorities in Tehran had not changed their minds, it appears, Israel would have sent mortars, shells, and air bombs to Iran in late April 1985, before Ledeen's arrival. When Peres told Ledeen, according to the latter, that Israel wanted to sell "artillery shells" to Iran if the United State did not object, Peres was not telling Ledeen the whole story, or Ledeen somehow misunderstood what he had been told.

Ledeen's trip almost provoked a serious breach between a long-suffering Secretary of State Shultz and McFarlane. Shultz was infuriated because he had not been told in advance about the trip. Ambassador Lewis heard about it from Israeli Defense Minister Yitzhak Rabin and quickly called Shultz's executive assistant to ask: "Do you know anything about it?" only to receive the answer: "No, we don't know a thing about it."[12] When he was informed of Ledeen's trip, Shultz, then in Lisbon, shot off a "hand-carried, eyes-only," cable to McFarlane.

Shultz first took issue with what he understood Ledeen's purpose to have been—"pursuing the possibility of getting us access to Iran." He strongly criticized Israel's past policy of dealing with Iran, and then went on to make clear that he was skeptical about whatever Israel might contribute:

> Israel's agenda is not the same as ours. Consequently doubt whether an intelligence relationship such as what Ledeen apparently has in mind would be one which we could fully rely upon and it could seriously skew our own perception and analysis of the Iranian scene. We of course are interested to know what Israel thinks about Iran but we should treat it as having a bias built in.

Then he turned to the embarrassment which the use of Ledeen had caused:

> Second: I believe it is deleterious to encourage or even merely acquiesce in someone like Mr. Ledeen undertaking a mission such as this without our Ambassador in Israel being informed. The results are predictable. The emissary does not cover his tracks, rumors start, and the President's representative on the scene appears to lack the confidence of the White House or in the worst case simply is made to look foolish.

Shultz concluded by treating the incident as if it were a personal affront and a case of official misconduct:

Finally, I personally am unhappy to learn of this matter as I have. Embassy Tel Aviv was told by the Israeli Ministry of Defense that Rabin would raise the Ledeen request when Rabin was in Washington. He did not do so, at least not with me. All in all, I am mystified about the way this situation has been handled and am concerned that it contains the seeds of further embarrassment and serious error unless straightened out quickly. I would appreciate hearing from you what you know about it.[13]

McFarlane was evidently not prepared for such an onslaught. His reply of June 7, 1985, betrayed signs of hasty improvisation:

I received your cable concerning Israel. I suppose I am a little disappointed in its prejudgements. Be that as it may, the facts in sum are: The GOI [government of Israel] posed the question of possible cooperation to the visitor who was there on his own hook. He passed it on to me last week. I had intended to talk to you about it, but time did not permit before you left town. Basically I intend now to send unequivocal instructions that we have no interest at all. I must tell you that I am not convinced that that is wise. The state of our intelligence on the country in question is deplorable, and surely we ought to be sensible enough to discern between intelligence and self-serving filtration. But be that as it may, I am turning it off entirely (and, of course, would never have turned it on without talking to you).[14]

Virtually nothing in McFarlane's reply was true. Ledeen, not the government of Israel, had posed the question of possible cooperation. Ledeen had not gone to Israel "on his own hook," McFarlane had not sent unequivocal instructions that we had no interest at all, and he did not turn it off completely. Later, McFarlane admitted that he had asked Ledeen to visit Israel to find out what the Israelis knew about Iran.[15] Yet McFarlane's clumsy effort to deceive the secretary of state betrayed a diseased condition among the leading officials in the administration that was already grave by mid-1985 and that was not going to get any better.

2

Shultz's high dudgeon interfered with Ledeen's next move. Ledeen was held up by the contretemps with Shultz and waited impatiently to get going again.

For two months, nothing had come of Ledeen's initiative. Ledeen had not returned to Israel to meet with Gazit, as had been agreed, and no progress had been made on U.S.-Israel collaboration. In fact, Gazit had decided to remove himself from the operation, because he allegedly objected to Peres's preference for dealing through the Israeli arms dealers Nimrodi and Schwimmer instead of through the official Mossad intelligence service.[16]

For these two months, May–June 1985, Peres and Foreign Minister Yitzhak Shamir were faced with the problem of what to do with the opportunities that had apparently opened up through the contacts with Khashoggi, Ghorbanifar, and Ledeen. They had to evaluate how seriously to take the overtures from Khashoggi and Ghorbanifar and the opening to the United States implied by Ledeen's visit. Early in July, the Israelis decided to act. They sent David Kimche to Washington.

On July 3, 1985, Kimche met with McFarlane and gave him a report of the Israelis' thinking as a result of their recent experiences. It was such a fateful meeting that it bears describing in detail, on the basis of the various versions we have of it.

The first version appeared in a message which McFarlane sent to Shultz on July 13. McFarlane considered it to be of such great moment that he requested Shultz not to share the information with anyone else. Written with evident haste, McFarlane's account jumbled together Ledeen's original visit to Israel in the first week of May, Kimche's meeting with him on July 3, and another meeting with an unnamed Israeli emissary on July 10.

According to McFarlane, he had learned of a proposal "by an Iranian official endorsed by the Government of Israel." The proposal had a short-term dimension concerning seven hostages and a long-term dimension involving "the establishment of private dialogue with Iranian officials on a broad relation." Ledeen, McFarlane added, had previously reported that Peres had told him of this "interest." McFarlane still insisted that "Ledeen had been in Israel on his own and without any sponsorship from me but he did report the contact." McFarlane stated that he had told Ledeen to tell the Israelis that he did not favor a "process" of opening a dialogue with Iran. When Kimche had met with him on July 3, Kimche had said that the Israelis were puzzled by this "disinclination" to open a dialogue with Iran and wanted to determine its accuracy. Kimche again received a "flat turndown" but asked that it should be raised again with the appropriate authorities and reconfirmed. At this stage, McFarlane seemed to have cut short the Israeli overture.

Ten days later, however, McFarlane related that he had been visited by a private Israeli emissary who asked to convey a message from Prime Minister Peres. This portion of McFarlane's report is important enough to give in full; from it flowed the main phases of the Iran affair for the next year and a half.

Reduced to its essentials, the oral message expressed the Israeli position that their access to Iranian officials (which became clear has involved extensive dialogue for some time) had surfaced serious interest among authoritative persons in the Iranian hierarchy in opening a dialogue with the west . . . He stated that Israel has for some time been conducting meetings with high level persons in Iran. At a recent meeting in Germany attended by Kimche, a man named Al Schwimmer (Father of the Israeli aircraft industry), and on the Iranian side [several words deleted] and an advisor to the Prime Minister named Gorbanifar, the Iranians presented a picture of contemporary Iran that was extremely pessimistic: continued economic decline, stalemate on the war front; no improvement even assuming Khomeini's passing without having an "option." Their hope and that of what they portrayed as a significant cadre of the hierarchy was to develop a dialogue with the west. At this point and often throughout the conversation, Kimche reminded them that they were talking to Israelis who aren't the "west" and what did they have in mind? The interlocutors stated emphatically that they sought a dialogue with the United States. The Israelis pressed (in the interest of vetting the bona fides of the Iranians with the real power in Iran) for some tangible show of their ability "to deliver" in such a dialogue. The Iranians stated that they were very confident that they could in the short term achieve the release of the seven Americans held hostage in Lebanon. But in exchange they would need to show some gain. They sought specifically the delivery from Israel of 100 TOW missiles. But they stated that the larger purpose would be the opening of a private dialogue with a high level American official and a sustained discussion of US-Iranian relations.

All the leading themes that were to run through the entire course of the Iran affair are here brought together—dialogue with the West, political change in Iran, hostages, missiles. McFarlane now was faced with decisions that went beyond sending Ledeen to Israel ostensibly to ask for no more than information.

In the same message to Shultz, McFarlane made an effort to think through the nature of such decisions. He was acutely mindful of Shultz's recent skepticism about setting up an intelligence arrangement with Israel. McFarlane called it a "very reasonable concern" and recognized that "one has to consider how such a 'trialogue' would be affected over time by sustained Israeli involvement. Surely we ought to expect that Israel's fears over any Arab (as opposed to Iranian) fallout would not always necessarily coincide with our own."

McFarlane also foresaw some of the larger problems ahead:

Then one has to consider where this might lead in terms of our being asked to up the ante on more and more arms and where that could conceivably lead, not just in the compromise of our position, but to the possible eventuality of the Iranians "winning" and where that would put the security of the neighboring Gulf States. Clearly that is a loser. But I would think that, given the vulnerability of the Iranian interlocutor to our discreet blowing of his cover with Khomeini, ought to enable us to control that.

This last assumed that the Israelis were really dealing with an Iranian official. The threat of exposure came up in another connection:

At the end of the day, our long term interest remains in maintaining an ability to renew ties with Iran under some more sensible successor regime. Whether or not this contact is connected to viable, stable parties in Iran remains to be seen. It could be that these people are no more than self-serving, self-promoters who seek to curry favor with an element of the military—those who happen to want TOWs right now. But I would think their risk of exposure again provides some insurance against that. And Israel is not noted for dealing with fools and charlatans.

Finally, McFarlane confessed: "George, I cannot judge the equities on this." But he leaned in the direction of doing something to keep the connection going:

On balance my instincts are to see our larger interest in establishing an entree to someone in Iran and the check provided by the Iranian interlocutor's vulnerability to being "blown" as giving us some insurance against perfidy. We could make a tentative show of interest without commitment and see what happens. Or we could walk away. On balance I tend to favor going ahead.[17]

McFarlane cannot be said not to have seen at this early date the pitfalls in any "trialogue" or "dialogue." He had little to work on except for what Kimche and Ledeen had told him, and he had too much confidence in Israeli intelligence to discount it. As long as the Americans themselves did not have contact with the "high level persons in Iran" dangled by the Israeli emissary, they were groping in the dark.

In one respect, McFarlane's message to Shultz was a pretense. McFarlane had not actually spoken to this Israeli emissary. He was actually Schwimmer, who had come to see Ledeen, not McFarlane. McFarlane later admitted that he had written to Shultz on the basis of what Ledeen had told him about the latter's meeting with Schwimmer, not that he himself had "received a private emissary."[18] Kimche, according to Ledeen, had previously asked McFarlane whether Ledeen was the proper channel of communications between Israel and the United

States, and McFarlane had said yes. Schwimmer, therefore, had flown to the United States to brief Ledeen.[19]

The degree of McFarlane's confusion may be gathered from his belief, presumably based on what Schwimmer had told Ledeen and Ledeen had told McFarlane, that Ghorbanifar was an "advisor to the Prime Minister" of Iran. The Israelis at that point were no nearer to high-placed "Iranian officials" or Prime Minister Moussavi than Ghorbanifar and Khashoggi. All the inside information about what was happening in Iran came from them. If McFarlane had known as much about Ghorbanifar and Khashoggi as he later learned, he would hardly have taken the Israeli proposal so seriously or put so much stock in Ghorbanifar. McFarlane's message to Shultz was largely based on Ledeen's tête-à-tête with Schwimmer, and McFarlane's information about Ghorbanifar came to him third-hand.

In his congressional testimony two years later, McFarlane gave a rather different and more detailed account of his July 3 meeting with Kimche:

> He came to report the existence of contacts with Israeli officials and Iranian officials that had gone on for some time, and through these contacts the interest on the part of Iranian officials in establishing contact with the United States.
>
> The largest part of the conversation focused upon my asking why he had the confidence in these people, why was it we shouldn't believe that they were self-serving, opportunistic people, and he went to some length to explain the basis to [sic] which he and his associates in Israel had concluded that these people were legitimate and sought over time to be able to influence change in Iran away from the rather extreme policies of the time to a more, a less violent coexistence with their neighbors.
>
> He stated at the time that the people with whom they had dealt who were at some risk understood that the United States had no reason to believe in them, we had not dealt with them and accordingly their bona fides would have to be demonstrated.
>
> Mr. Kimche said, they, understanding they would see if they couldn't influence the captors of the United States and other countries' hostages in Lebanon to release them. And, in fact, in that first encounter stated that they had thought it through and with some confidence only wanted to know two things: Were we interested in talking to them; and how would we prefer that they release the hostages.[20]

The first version, in the message to Shultz, must take precedence, because it was written soon after the event. In it, the only matter in question was undertaking a dialogue with Iran. Nevertheless, the second version is so circumstantial that it may well be equally credible and is certainly more informative. In this version, Kimche not only had referred to such a dialogue but had concretely connected it with "Iranian officials" with whom Israeli officials had been in contact for some time and who they had concluded were "legitimate." Two of the main themes in the entire affair now came to the surface—a change in Iranian policy and release of the hostages. The immediate question was whether the United States was interested in talking to these so-called Iranian officials. Both versions made a "dialogue" the most pressing matter for American decision.

Kimche apparently emphasized that the decision was for the United States to make. "It seems to me," McFarlane testified, "that there was never any suggestion on the part of Mr. Kimche that Israel was seeking to subvert us or to influence us unduly." Kimche had repeatedly stressed that "this doesn't make any difference. If you all want to have nothing to do with it, we certainly would understand. We bring it to your attention as an ally. If you wish to do it, good. If you don't, good. It is there for you to consider." Kimche had also said: "Obviously, Israel's interests are very different from your own," and McFarlane added that Kimche had "pointed out they have an interest in sustaining the conflict. We don't."[21]

3

We know from Ledeen how Schwimmer happened to come to Washington. Early in July, Ledeen received a telephone call from Kimche. A friend of his named Al Schwimmer, Kimche said, was coming to Washington, and he would appreciate it if Ledeen could listen to what Schwimmer had to say. A few days later, Schwimmer, whom Ledeen had not previously known, invited Ledeen to lunch. Ledeen relates:

> Schwimmer told me that he was a close friend of Shimon Peres, that he had been the president of Israel Aircraft Industries, now retired, but that he still was active in some matters on behalf of the Prime Minister and that in that connection, he had been introduced a short time before by Adnan Khashoggi to a very interesting Iranian by the name of Ghorbanifar, and that Ghorbanifar had a lot of very interesting things to say both about Iran and about the intentions of leading figures in the Government of Iran, and that he thought under the circumstances it was worthwhile for me to come as quickly as could possibly be managed to meet with Ghorbanifar and that this could be done either in Europe or in Israel.[22]

This was Ledeen's introduction to the name of Ghorbanifar. From Ledeen's account, Ghorbanifar had come to the attention of the Israelis through Khashoggi, with whom they had done business for some years. Schwimmer was also introduced to Oliver North for the first time by

Ledeen. Schwimmer gave Ledeen a report on Iran that had been sent to McFarlane by Khashoggi, one section of which, according to Schwimmer, had been written by Ghorbanifar and which he and other Israelis had found to be particularly interesting. Schwimmer mentioned that Ghorbanifar was interested in discussing the subject of hostages in Lebanon and had indicated that the government of Iran could be helpful in obtaining their release.[23]

In another version by Ledeen, Schwimmer had told him some other things that Ghorbanifar thought there were good chances to accomplish. One was establishment of contacts with high-level officials of the Khomeini regime in order to work toward "normalization of relations." A second was contacts with opponents of current Iranian policies, in the hope of strengthening such elements in Iran and eventually changing the policies themselves. A third was gaining Iranian assistance for the release of the hostages in Lebanon.

The third, however, was not unconditional:

But such a gesture—which would be a step along the road toward rapprochement—would have to be accompanied by an American gesture of equal significance. Ghorbanifar proposed that we permit Israel to sell several hundred TOW antitank missiles to the Iranians. This would demonstrate that the president himself was committed to a new relationship with Iran (despite his formal public policy of Operation Staunch, which was designed to prevent anyone from selling weapons to Khomeini's regime).[24]

Thus Schwimmer again brought all the main pieces of the Iran puzzle into place—normalization of relations with the existing Iranian regime; changing the policies through opponents of the existing policies; release of the hostages; American missiles for Iran. But the first three were still uncertain eventualities; nothing had as yet happened to give them any reality. The fourth was payment in advance for nothing more than alleged "good chances." The Iranian "gesture" of assisting in the release of the American hostages was still hypothetical and untested; the American gesture "of equal significance" was no less than several hundred non-hypothetical, tested U.S.-made missiles. The president of the United States was expected to make a commitment "to a new relationship with Iran" by permitting Israel to sell the missiles without any similar or comparable commitment from the other side, except for Ghorbanifar's pretensions.

It was a peculiarly one-sided proposal. Yet, as Ledeen passed it on, he apparently saw nothing strange about it. He says that he immediately reported the conversation with Schwimmer to McFarlane and asked if McFarlane wanted him to meet with Ghorbanifar. Ledeen was now bent on meeting Ghorbanifar, since all that he had heard from Schwimmer led back to Ghorbanifar.

McFarlane and Ledeen were clearly receptive to the unsupported and unverified news brought by Kimche and especially by Schwimmer. The reason for their responsiveness was given by McFarlane. "One of the problems which led us to consider listening to someone out of Iran was that our intelligence was so poor that we didn't know what was going on," he said. "The fact that we did not know seven years after we had gotten run out of there, is kind of a shame; isn't it?"[25]

The American intelligence vacuum was largely responsible for the inclination to lean on any reed that presented itself. This inclination was further encouraged by the respect with which Israeli intelligence was then held in Washington circles, especially in Israel's own region of the world. Peres had not been encouraging about Israeli superiority, but as soon as the Israelis learned from Ledeen that the Americans were avid for information, the Israelis themselves were apparently inspired to seize on whatever and whoever came their way to satisfy the American need.

It was a situation made to order for someone with the glibness and perseverance of Ghorbanifar. Israeli receptiveness fed into American receptiveness, and they reinforced each other.

4

At about this time, in mid-1985, two different paths opened before the Americans and led them toward considering whether to deal with Iran in a new way. One came from Israel. The other came from within the American government itself.

A reconsideration of U.S. policy on Iran had not waited for Ledeen. A halting start had been made, from the spring of 1982 through the summer of 1984, by various interagency groups that had attempted, evidently without notable success, to formulate a "security strategy" for Southwest Asia.

In January 1984, as previously noted, Geoffrey Kemp had told McFarlane that he regularly communicated with Iranian exiles who said that they wanted to replace the Khomeini regime with a pro-Western government and hoped to get foreign help.[26] If so, Ghorbanifar and Karoubi were contributing nothing new along this line.

In August 1984, McFarlane asked for a formal interagency analysis of U.S. policy toward a post-Khomeini government in Iran.*[27] This study, completed in October 1984, raised the possibility of resuming arms shipments to Iran on condition that Iran was willing to restore normal relations. It was most pessimistic about the ability of the United States to

---

* By interagency was meant the State Department, Joint Chiefs of Staff, CIA, and NSC staff.

influence events in Iran and saw little prospect of any change in the relationship.[28]

In December 1984, the State Department prepared a draft of a highest-level National Security Decision Directive (NSDD) which was no more hopeful. It is said to have "produced no new ideas which any of us involved considered to be of great value in terms of significantly affecting our posture in the region."[29] It was received with so much dissatisfaction that it never moved beyond its draft status.[30]

Thus about three years had gone by without any perceptible progress in getting a more promising Iran policy for the United States. Some things were already in the air—Iranian exiles who were seeking to get U.S. help for the overthrow of the Khomeini regime; U.S. arms might be used as an inducement for Iran to reestablish "normal relations"; Operation Staunch was less sacrosanct within some circles in the Reagan administration than it appeared to be in official declarations on the highest level.

After so much frustration, Ledeen's report from Israel in May 1985 brought a glimmer of hope. If the United States could not penetrate the Iranian wall of secrecy and hostility, perhaps Israel could. However little Ledeen had learned, there seemed to be no point in giving up a chance that he might lead to something more.

Soon after Ledeen's return, McFarlane decided to open up U.S. policy on Iran for reconsideration. He asked Donald Fortier, then the NSC staff's senior director for political-military affairs, to direct the CIA to prepare a special intelligence estimate on Iran. Fortier turned for help to Graham Fuller, the CIA's national intelligence officer for the Near East and South Asia, and Howard Teicher, who worked in the Near East and South Asia Directorate of the NSC staff. Fuller submitted a five-page memorandum entitled "Toward a Policy on Iran" to Director Casey on May 17. It was the first semblance of a new U.S. policy on Iran.

Fuller assumed that the Khomeini regime was "faltering." He saw Iran as preferring to "come to terms with" Soviet Russia, which, he believed, had far better Iranian cards to play than did the United States. Fuller argued that there was no longer any need to respond with force if Iran engaged in a terrorist attack or to deny arms to Iran. Of all the possible means of getting back into some relationship with Tehran, he preferred to "have friendly states sell arms," without affecting the Iran-Iraq strategic balance.[31]

The CIA largely accepted this estimate. On May 20, it issued a revision of its basic analysis of Iran in which it also stressed the competition with the Soviets for Iran's favor. It was rather pessimistic about a direct approach by the United States; its favored course was indirect influence through European and other friendly states, including Turkey, Pakistan, China, Japan, and even Israel, "to help protect Western interests." To achieve this objective, the provision of arms to Iran was envisioned: "The degree to which some of these states can fill a military gap for Iran will be a critical measure of the West's ability to blunt Soviet influence."[32]

A new Iranian policy was now moving quickly through the bureaucracy of the CIA and NSC staff. Fortier argued that "the Israeli option is one we have to pursue, even though we may have to pay a certain price for the help." On June 11, Fortier and Teicher presented what they themselves described as a "provocative" proposal in the form of a draft National Security Decision Directive. This document reflected the thinking of those who were pushing for a new Iran policy.

It stressed the Soviet advantage in Iran as a reason for "movement towards eventual normalization of U.S.-Iranian" diplomatic, cultural, trade, and commercial relations. It professed to see a decline of the Khomeini regime's popularity and the emergence of a power struggle. Radical, conservative, and ultraconservative factions were beginning to compete for the succession. In the power struggle, the most likely faction to shift Iranian policy toward the West were the "conservatives working from within the government against the radicals." The regular armed forces represented a potential source of pro-Western influence. The U.S. position in Iran was "unlikely to improve without a major change in U.S. policy" with the aim of getting "a more conservative regime, still Islamic." To block the Soviets, they advocated encouraging Western allies and friends to provide "selected military equipment as determined on a case-by-case basis."[33]

The Fortier-Teicher analysis was so "provocative," as they themselves called it, that they advised showing it to Secretary of State Shultz and Secretary of Defense Weinberger.

Shultz's response to the new Iran line was measured. He agreed that the time had come to reassess U.S. policy. But he differed on two points. He thought that the "current anti-regime sentiment and Soviet advantages over us" in Iran were being exaggerated. He also believed that "we should not facilitate the supply of weapons from Western Europe" to Iran, on the ground that the flow was likely to become uncontrolled and come as a shock to Saudi Arabia, the Persian Gulf states, and Iraq. Instead, he put forward a two-track policy: continued restraint of the arms flow and more efforts to mediate the Iran-Iraq war.[34] Despite the balanced tone of his response, Shultz was understood to be strongly opposed to the new line.[35]

Weinberger's reaction was explosively hostile privately and emphatic but more diplomatic officially. On the note that came to him with the NSDD from his military assistant, Major General Colin L. Powell, Weinberger wrote:

This is almost too absurd to comment on. By all means pass it to Rich[ard Armitage], but the assumption here is: 1) that Iran is about to fall, and 2) we can deal with that on a rational basis. It's like asking Qadhafi to Washington for a cozy chat.[36]

Weinberger's formal reply, however, gave assurances that he agreed "with many of the major points in the paper" but proceeded to disagree with the main ones. He came out against a "policy reversal" on the ground that it "would be seen as inexplicably inconsistent by those nations whom we have urged to refrain from such sales, and would likely lead to increased arms sales by them and a possible alteration of the strategic balance in favor of Iran while Khomeini is still the controlling influence." He concluded that "changes in policy and in conduct, therefore, must be initiated by a new Iranian government," not by the United States.[37]

Casey, on the other hand, was all in favor of the provocative proposal. He wrote McFarlane that he strongly endorsed the draft NSDD of Fortier and Teicher. It appealed to him as a way "to ensure that the USSR is not the primary beneficiary" of change and turmoil in Iran, though he wanted a more complex analysis of Soviet motives and actions.[38]

The opposition of Shultz and Weinberger was enough to prevent the proposed new line from going forward. Teicher tried to get Fortier to back a "decision memorandum" to President Reagan to get him to decide between the rival viewpoints. Fortier thought better of it and advised Teicher to "stand down."[39]

In the end, nothing came of all this effort to rethink U.S. policy on Iran, except for a clarification of what the main questions and problems were and where the leading officials in the government stood on them. It was already clear that a struggle for power over policy was opening up between the CIA and NSC staff on the one hand and the two senior cabinet members on the other. There was nothing bureaucratically wrong, in principle, with NSC staffers putting forward new, admittedly provocative ideas about beating out the Soviet Union in a race to gain the favor of a post-Khomeini Iran. All their premises and prescriptions may have been absurdly wrong, as Secretary Weinberger thought, but no one higher up was forced to accept them.

5

One of the leading premises in the Fortier-Teicher proposal of June 11, 1985, was that there were three Iranian factions competing for the succession—radical, conservative, and ultraconservative. Neither Fortier nor Teicher was in a position to know from his own knowledge or experience or from the virtually nonexistent U.S. intelligence whether there were such factions. The formula was suspiciously similar to the ideas which had recently been put forward by Adnan Khashoggi.

In his guise as statesman, Khashoggi sent around a document of 43 pages, dated July 1, 1985, containing an analysis of the situation in Iran.[40] It was largely based on the report of May 3, 1985, written by Ghorbanifar for the Israelis. Khashoggi sent it to the rulers of Saudi Arabia and Jordan, Israeli Prime Minister Peres, and National Security Adviser McFarlane. One of its leading ideas was the three-faction theory. All three were said to be blindly loyal to the Ayatollah Khomeini and the Islamic revolution; the differences among them were primarily tactical.

Khashoggi's Iran factions were extremist, moderate, and something in between. The extremists, with 53 members in the Majlis or Iranian parliament, were supposedly led by President Ali Khamenei, Prime Minister Mir Hussein Moussavi, Minister for Intelligence Affairs Hojatolislam Mohammed Reishari, and Chief of Intelligence Operations Mohsen Kangarlou. They allegedly favored large-scale agrarian reform, a nationalized economy, export of the revolution, and continued terrorism in Lebanon.

The moderate faction, with 63 members in the Majlis, was supposedly led by Hassan Karoubi, built up as Khomeini's adviser for the past fifteen years, whom Khashoggi soon introduced to the Israelis Kimche, Schwimmer, and Nimrodi. Its most prominent adherent in the Majlis was a former prime minister, Mohammed Reza Kani. It was supported by the commander of the army's ground forces, the commanders of the police and gendarmerie, and the deputy commander of the Revolutionary Guards. They allegedly favored free enterprise and a cautious reorientation toward the West, and they opposed export of the revolution.

The largest faction, with a solid majority in the Majlis, was allegedly headed by its speaker, Ali Akbar Hashemi Rafsanjani. With him were Khomeini's heir apparent, the Ayatollah Hussein Ali Montazeri, Deputy Speaker Ayatollah Mehdi Karoubi (brother of Hassan Karoubi), and Colonel Mohsen Rezai, commander of the Revolutionary Guards. This faction apparently did not have fixed aims; Montazeri was said to favor exporting the revolution, but the group generally decided each case on its merits.[41]

In his covering letter to McFarlane, Khashoggi explained that part of the document had been written by "a single senior individual who is in charge of Iranian intelligence in Western Europe." This individual, none other than Ghorbanifar, was not in charge of Iranian intelligence in Western Europe—or of any official Iranian business in Western Europe or anywhere else. It is highly unlikely that Khashoggi did not know better; if Ghorbanifar had gulled even Khashoggi, the former's powers of deception were truly formidable.[42]

The only one in the document's three factions whose voice can be heard at all is that of Hassan Karoubi, the alleged leader of the moderates. On July 8, 1985, he met for four hours with Khashoggi, Ghorbanifar, Kimche, Schwimmer, and Nimrodi in a Geneva hotel. The Israelis helpfully made a tape recording of the meeting.

Oddly, Karoubi asked as many questions as he answered. He first asserted that his group wanted Iran to adopt a pro-Western orientation, sought an "honorable" end to the Iran-Iraq war, desperately needed anti-tank missiles, and pledged itself to act to get the hostages released. On the other hand, he seemed most uncertain about basic policy.

Should the goal be working toward the moderation of the Khomeini regime or its overthrow in favor of a more liberal system? Kimche told him that a moderate government was preferable. What should his group do to cooperate with the others present? Kimche assured him that they, together with Khashoggi, were prepared to cooperate and plan joint actions. Nimrodi, however, turned the question back to Karoubi and asked him "what to do and how to help you." Karoubi said little more to this than that his group was ready for a detailed and practical discussion to work out "joint lines of action." Strangely, Karoubi also asked the Israelis to provide him with information on the activities of the Left and the Soviets in Iran, as if they were in a position to know what was going on there. Kimche and Karoubi disagreed on the strength of the Iranian Left; Kimche suggested that it had been all but eliminated, Karoubi insisted that it was still a substantial force.

For one who—according to Ghorbanifar—was supposed to be Khomeini's most important adviser, Karoubi asked some disconcerting questions about the very nature of the regime: "Sometimes I wonder—what is the real color of the Iranian government? What is its identity? Are we really opposed to the Soviet Union and the Left, or do we in effect stage shows against the U.S. and the West?" Khomeini himself, he said, was clearly anti-Soviet and anti-Western. If so, it was not clear why he was so puzzled about the orientation of the Khomeini regime.

One other thing that Karoubi asked for was money. We are not told where it was supposed to come from or what came of this request. In a follow-up memorandum, Karoubi again asked for "financial aid" to test "your sincerity and seriousness." He expected, it said, to return in a week to Tehran, where the distribution of a few riyals to clergy and merchants "could be very productive."[43] Whether Karoubi received any money is not stated.

The transcript of the discussion and the text of the memorandum seem hardly to bear out the image of a leader of the "moderate" faction who was in a position to engage in a struggle for post-Khomeini power. He appeared to need far more help from the West than he could give in return. About the only concrete aspect of the meeting with him was his request for money and missiles.

Yet, it is said, the three Israelis were favorably impressed by him; Kimche recommended that contacts with him should be continued. This meeting with Karoubi led Prime Minister Peres to send Schwimmer to Washington to meet with Ledeen, with the result that Schwimmer suggested to Ledeen that he should come to Europe or Israel to meet with Ghorbanifar.[44]

Just what substance there was to the dealings with Karoubi is far from clear. He was introduced to the Israelis by Khashoggi and Ghorbanifar, who were the only ones to attest to his importance and legitimacy. Kimche admitted that he did not know whether Karoubi was telling the truth or not.[45] Whatever that truth may be, Karoubi's dubious authority was exaggerated by Schwimmer in his conversation with Ledeen, by Ledeen in his report to McFarlane, and by McFarlane in his message to Shultz.

McFarlane claimed that he never saw Khashoggi's document, so it is difficult to say what immediate influence it had on him.[46] Schwimmer, however, gave the document to Ledeen, for whom it was an additional source of inside information on Iran. In any case, the basic three-faction schema in it soon became the conventional wisdom on Iran in U.S. policy circles. Since the Americans did not even pretend that they knew from their own people what was going on in Iran, they were dependent on the outsiders who made such a claim. McFarlane, the key to the emerging U.S. policy at this time, was so impressed with what Ledeen had told him that he immediately passed it on, with evident excitement, to Shultz—and Ledeen knew only as much as Schwimmer had told him, and Schwimmer knew only as much as Ghorbanifar had told him.

And yet we are on the verge of the first real American decision in the Iran affair. It was precipitated by this strange confluence of one American, Ledeen; three Israelis, Kimche, Schwimmer, and Nimrodi; two Iranians, Ghorbanifar and Karoubi; and one Saudi Arabian, Khashoggi. The official who had to tie all these threads together was McFarlane, and he was in no position to judge how accurate his information was. In the end virtually everything went back to Ghorbanifar and Karoubi, whom even the Israelis had only recently encountered. Karoubi, like Ghorbanifar, had to be taken on faith. The CIA's only expert on Iran, George Cave, later testified that Ghorbanifar had been reported as having dressed Karoubi as an ayatollah, evidently to pass him off as someone of consequence. Cave did not find this story at all "incredible."[47]

8

The First Deal

Much of the trouble that beset the Americans in any effort to work out a new policy for Iran, in order to achieve a "strategic opening" or to liberate the hostages or both, resulted from an almost total American ignorance of what was going on in Iran. All the lines of intelligence had been cut off by the fall of the Shah. The absolute hostility of the Khomeini regime and the equally complete rejection of Iran implied by Operation Staunch made it peculiarly inaccessible to the Americans.

This estrangement was a boon to any third party who claimed to be able to fill the vacuum. It was a situation made to order for someone like Ghorbanifar, who had known pre-Khomeini Iran from the inside as few Americans did and professed still to have lines into the bureaucracy and especially the armed forces. As the Americans had long ago learned, Ghorbanifar did know something but never as much as he claimed to know; it was generally impossible to check on his sources or reliability; and in the end he disappointed too frequently to be trusted. Yet he was an artful intelligence resource, especially since he was clever enough to tell his interlocutors what they wanted to hear. When Ghorbanifar said that he represented "moderate" Iranians in the government and armed forces who wanted to establish friendly relations with the West in general and the United States in particular or that he knew what it would take to free the hostages, it was hard to resist wanting to believe that he might be able to do what could not be done by any other means.

This disruption of the old U.S.-Iran connection also worked in favor of Israel. Its intelligence capability was then held in the highest esteem, and the CIA had long since established the closest relations with its Israeli counterpart. On Israel's part, any service that it could provide to the United States was to be welcomed in consideration for all the financial and diplomatic benefits it owed to the United States. Thus a situation was set up that was peculiarly apt to bring Israel into the forefront of U.S. preoccupation with Iran. Two things worked together—Ghorbanifar and his confederates decided to get the attention of the United States via Israel, and the United States was disposed to look to Israel as a way of making contact with Iranians who could help the American cause.

Ghorbanifar needed the Israelis, and to impress the Americans with their helpfulness the Israelis needed someone like Ghorbanifar.

2

The three-sided game played by the United States, Israel, and Ghorbanifar soon gathered momentum. The first decision to make U.S. arms available to Iran was imminent.

On July 3, 1985, it will be recalled, Kimche had come to see McFarlane with news of alleged "Iranian officials" who wanted to engage in a "dialogue" with the United States, with the prospect that they could arrange for the release of the American hostages in Lebanon.

On July 10, Schwimmer had come to see Ledeen in order to pass on Ghorbanifar's proposal that Israel sell several hundred U.S.-made TOW missiles to Iran as an earnest of President Reagan's commitment to a new relationship with Iran.

On July 13, 1985, President Reagan entered the Bethesda Naval Hospital for abdominal surgery.

Three days later, as the president was recovering from the operation, McFarlane visited him in the hospital. To get to him, McFarlane had to get permission from Chief of Staff Donald Regan, who had to get permission from Nancy Reagan. "He had been asking from day one," according to Regan, "to get to see the President, saying he had something important regarding the intelligence finding. But on the second day he told me it was regarding the hostages." Regan also recalled McFarlane saying repeatedly: "I've just got to see the President," though he did not tell Regan why. Regan told him to keep it short; the doctors wanted McFarlane to get in and out; the president was still uncomfortable. So far as Regan could remember, McFarlane told the president that "they had been approached by the Israelis, who had had a contact that they would put us in touch with that could lead to a breakthrough in reaching elements in the Government of Iran" and "that this could lead to some help in the hostage situation because we suspected that the Iranians were in some way connected in to the group who had abducted the Americans."[1]

McFarlane gave more than one version of what the president said to him in the hospital. At the congressional hearings, McFarlane related:

> Well, the President said that he could understand how Iranians who wanted to achieve a change in policy would be vulnerable to the more radical Iranians affiliated with Khomeini, and so the idea

of strengthening this by giving them the means to rally the army or revolutionary guards to them was not an outrageous notion, but that we hadn't met them and we didn't know them and their bona fides were very uncertain, and so at the time there could not be any U.S. owned items from the United States proper shipped to them in this kind of arrangement, and I conveyed that back to Mr. Kimche. . . . we can't do that [ship U.S.-owned arms to Iran].[2]

In an earlier interview, McFarlane had given a somewhat different emphasis to the president's reply:

And while it [Kimche's suggestion that eventually arms transfers would become an issue] wasn't linked to the hostages, the President said, well, it seemed to him that the Middle East experience well beyond Iran is that elements to succeed ultimately to power do need to strengthen themselves, and that the currency of doing that is usually weapons. And he said the key element is not denying history, but deciding whether or not our doing that or somebody else doing that can be distinguished as a political matter of policy between the natural perception of people that weapons are going to people portrayed as terrorists. Iran is identified as a terrorist state. He said the key element is whether or not these people are indeed devoted to change and not just simply opportunists, self-serving radicals.

In a subsequent interview, McFarlane recalled:

I briefed him on the new information received from Mr. Schwimmer, there is a vividness in my recollection . . . and the President says words to the effect that gee, that sounds pretty good.

The weapons issue is a problem, and our discussion of that, and he says: I guess we can't do the weapons or something like that ourselves, but isn't there a way that we can get at trying to keep this channel going or something like that?

After this rambling recital, McFarlane was asked:

Rhett Dawson [Director of Staff]: And that's tied in to the hostages at that point? It is clear that one of the purposes of this is not so much a strategic opening as you might have otherwise stated, but it is an attempt to get arms for hostages through the transfer from Israel to Iran?

McFarlane: Well, I think that was foremost in the President's mind.

Dawson: So if he didn't state to you in so many words, Bud, go ahead and do it, he clearly led you to believe from the outset that here was a chance to bring some hostages out through a third country?

McFarlane: It was unambiguously clear.[3]

This version makes the president's attitude in the hospital toward arms for Iran much less unqualified. He seems here to accept the necessity or advisability of giving weapons to opponents of the Khomeini regime, perhaps through "somebody else," so long as they were going to "people [who] are indeed devoted to change" and were not radicals or terrorists. "Somebody else" in this context pointed to Israel.

In a third version, McFarlane reminded his successor, Poindexter, that the president "was all for letting the Israelis do anything they wanted at the very first briefing in [the] hospital."[4]

And in a fourth version, McFarlane said: "As I recall he said that he could understand how people who were trying to overthrow a government would need weapons, but we weren't yet sure about whether they were legitimate. So he said that we, the United States, could not do it."[5]

There is also a recollection by Regan, the only other person present at this encounter.

And what McFarlane wanted was the President's authority to make this contact [with Iranians], to see if it could be developed and what it could lead to. There was a discussion of the importance of Iran as far as its strategic location . . . and the fact that it seemed worthwhile to McFarlane that this be pursued.

The President, after asking quite a few questions—and I would say the discussion lasted for perhaps 20, 25 minutes—assented and said yes, go ahead. Open it up.[*6]

Finally, the president himself told three different stories. In 1987, he said that he could not even remember meeting with McFarlane on that July day.[7] But in February 1990, he was interrogated in preparation for the Poindexter trial and this exchange took place:

Dan Webb [Office of Independent Counsel]: As far as the Iran initiative was concerned, Mr. President, am I correct that your best recollection is that the first time that you became aware that certain elements in Iran had approached the United States to have discussions was in July of 1985 while you were in the hospital when Robert McFarlane came to see you; is that correct to the best of your recollection?

---

* In his book, Regan says that the question of Iran took up no more than ten or twelve minutes out of a total of twenty-three minutes. Regan strongly doubts that there was any discussion of "the idea of swapping arms for hostages" (*For the Record*, pp. 20–21).

Reagan: Well, that is to the best of my recollection, although I don't have a really clear memory of these events and how they were—the days that they were transpiring.[8]

That Reagan did not have a clear memory of these events was less surprising than his less than clear memory of other events. He was just recovering from surgery when he was told for the first time about the murky dealings with the Iranians and Israelis.

Oddly, Reagan's memory of this episode had miraculously improved by the time he wrote his autobiography. In it he related that McFarlane had informed him then and later that Israeli representatives had "contacted him secretly to pass on information from a group of moderate, politically influential Iranians." These Iranians were "disenchanted members of Iran's government" who "wanted to oust the tyrannical theocracy imposed on them by Khomeini and his cohorts." They also wanted to establish "a quiet relationship with U.S. leaders as a prelude to reestablishing formal relations between our countries following the death of the Ayatollah Khomeini." These Iranian "moderates" had offered to persuade "the Hizballah terrorists to release our seven hostages."[9]

All this went much further than anything McFarlane had earlier remembered. In one of his versions, McFarlane had apparently described the Iranians as representing an opposition to the Khomeini regime that needed weapons in order to overthrow it. McFarlane had said nothing about actual members of the Iranian government or getting the release of seven American hostages. In any case, by the time Reagan composed his autobiography, the lone Iranian figure of Manucher Ghorbanifar had been transmogrified into "disenchanted members of Iran's government."

McFarlane's various versions and Reagan's autobiography agree on one thing—Reagan agreed to permit Israel to sell U.S.-made arms to Iran in August–September 1985. "The truth is," Reagan writes, "once we had information from Israel that we could trust the people in Iran, I didn't have to think thirty seconds about saying yes to their proposal." Reagan's conscience about selling arms to Iran was eased by the thought that the United States was doing it through Israel and not directly. Yet, even on his own account, this was an indirect arms-for-hostages deal. "But I said," Reagan writes, "there was one thing we wanted: The moderate Iranians had to use their influence with the Hizballah and try to get our hostages freed."[10]

Reagan's decision in the hospital was critical, because it was the opening move that set going all the others in the next two years. Yet McFarlane did not make any record of his hospital conversation with the president. It was a decision made on the spur of the moment and without consultation with any other senior adviser or cabinet member.

Some things seem clear. That McFarlane should have insisted on bringing the matter of Kimche's and Schwimmer's alleged revelations to the president in the hospital before he had fully recovered indicates how excited or enthusiastic McFarlane must have been about his good tidings. McFarlane could not have chosen a more unlikely place and less propitious moment to bring up a serious question for immediate attention. If McFarlane's report to the president was the same as the one he had sent to Secretary Shultz three days earlier, the president must have received the impression that a major decision was immediately required because a major opportunity had offered itself. A decision could not have been made on the basis of an accurate, realistic account of the existing circumstances. If, as McFarlane said, the president had responded with "words to the effect that gee, that sounds pretty good," McFarlane must have made the opportunity appear to be "pretty good."

It was clear to McFarlane that the president had agreed to encourage a "dialogue" with those who purported to represent Iran and that he had leaned to the side of letting the Israelis carry on. It is less clear that the president thought of using weapons to gain the release of the American hostages or whether weapons were discussed at all. McFarlane recalled it in two ways—that the president had definitely rejected the idea of using weapons and that he had merely ruled it out on the part of the United States. Regan could not recall that the subject had come up and thought that he would have remembered it if it had.

In practice, what the president had agreed to was less important than what McFarlane thought he had agreed to. For McFarlane, not the president, was in charge of what to do next. He was not serving a president who was likely to keep a close check on him or give him carefully thought-out instructions. This first step on the way to a new American policy on Iran was easy; it entailed nothing more than advising Israel that the United States agreed to a continuation of the "dialogue" between Israelis and Iranians. The door was opened a crack, but it was a door that would not close.

3

It is now necessary to follow events simultaneously in places thousands of miles apart—Tel Aviv and Washington. Each reacted to the other.

Ledeen was itching to get back to Israel. Ever since he had heard about Ghorbanifar from Schwimmer, he had been eager to meet the Iranian. The idea of getting together with Ghorbanifar had come to Ledeen from Schwimmer, who, according to Ledeen, had "thought under the circumstances, it was worthwhile for me to come as quickly as could possibly be managed to meet with Ghorbanifar and that this could be done in Europe or in Israel."[11] McFarlane agreed to the meeting when Ledeen told him that he was going to be in Israel anyway at that very time on a midsummer vacation with his family. Ledeen left for Israel on July 16, the very day that McFarlane spoke to the president in the hospital. Ledeen says that McFarlane authorized him to meet with Ghorbanifar but gave him no instructions beyond telling him to listen and collect information. McFarlane is supposed to have said: "Go ahead and talk to this guy and let's see what happens."[12]

Toward the end of July 1985, Ledeen met with Ghorbanifar in Tel Aviv in the presence of the Israeli triumvirate, Kimche, Schwimmer, and Nimrodi. Ghorbanifar told them of desperate conditions and growing unrest in Iran; he assured them that "several of the most powerful figures in the government" were interested in achieving better relations with the West; he held out the possibility that the Iranian regime could be changed by working with these figures. Ghorbanifar also proposed the same kind of deal that Schwimmer had previously outlined to McFarlane in Washington. Iran would make "a series of gestures," including a different public rhetoric toward the United States, an end to terrorist attacks against U.S. targets, and an effort to convince the hostage holders in Lebanon to release one or more U.S. hostages. Ghorbanifar was sure that Iran had enough influence to get the hostages released, especially the CIA's station chief in Beirut, William Buckley. In return, the American "gesture" would take the form of enabling Iran to obtain U.S. weapons—namely, TOW missiles.[13]

After the meeting with Ghorbanifar, the four others conferred among themselves and decided that his advice was so important that it had to be reported without delay to McFarlane. Kimche, who planned to leave for Washington, was given the assignment.

On this occasion and others, Ledeen acted together with the three Israelis as if they made up a joint U.S.-Israel commission. Of the Israelis, only Kimche had official status; the other two could not be held accountable for anything. Ledeen's behavior was strangely amateurish. He thought that his vacation was more important than his mission and that he did not need to report to McFarlane in person, or that Kimche could do it just as well, as if Kimche represented the United States as well as Israel.

Ghorbanifar, in effect, was now manipulating the group. Kimche and the others knew only as much as Ghorbanifar told them. If Ghorbanifar was as yet unable to negotiate with the United States directly, he was going to do so indirectly through Kimche.

4

On August 2, 1985, Kimche again met with McFarlane in Washington. Again McFarlane, at least as he remembered it, seems to have gained a wildly exaggerated notion of the Iranians with whom the Israelis had presumably been dealing. He later said that "generically the Iranians involved represented the highest level decision makers, but the principal advisers to them as well, both civilian, clerical, and military, and that the circle of people of this persuasion—that is interested in change, included military, cleric, and government officials."[14]

This time the issue brought forward by Kimche was more than a dialogue; it was purely and simply arms for Iran. As McFarlane understood him, the heart of the matter was: "Will you or won't you condone or endorse the sale of weapons to Iran?"[15] According to McFarlane, Kimche said that the Iranians were "more concerned about the bona fides of our side and specifically whether or not we would provide weapons right away, not for a threat, not for expanding the war, but, as it was cast, for the expansion of and consolidation of the faction with military elements, of arms elements specifically."[16] Weapons in this sense were supposed to benefit the faction Ghorbanifar and Khashoggi had described as "moderate," later to be known by some as "pragmatic," not the Khomeini-controlled forces.

McFarlane turned down the proposal of a direct U.S. transfer of arms to Iranians on the ground that the proposed recipients were not known to the United States. Whereupon Kimche asked the more difficult question: What would the United States say to the transfer of U.S.-made weapons by Israel?

We are here at the turning point of the new U.S. policy. Operation Staunch had forbidden all weapons from anywhere for whatever reason going to Iran. If Israel was permitted to sell weapons to Iran, Operation Staunch was fatally breached, especially if Israel was understood to be acting as an American surrogate in a deal to get back what the United States most wanted—its hostages in Lebanon.

McFarlane says that he asked Kimche why it was in Israel's interest to sell weapons to Iran. Kimche, according to McFarlane, replied:

> Well, we in Israel have our own interests. They are basically to ensure a stalemate of the conflict with Iran, but also to get the United States back into Iran, and that helps us if the United States' position in the Middle East is strengthened; and separately, to reduce the Iranian support for terrorism, and so we might very well do this as a matter of Israeli interests.
>
> I pose it for us doing that, because ultimately if we provide things we're going to have to come and buy other ones, and I need to know, are we going to be able to do that or not, whether it's Hawks or TOWs or whatever else?

This question plagued the U.S.-Israel relationship for months to come. McFarlane says that he replied to Kimche:

Well, that really isn't the issue. Israel has bought weapons from the United States for years and always will, and so you don't need to ask whether you can buy more weapons. It is a matter of whether or not the support of the idea of providing weapons to anybody in Iran is in policy terms sensible. But I will get you our position.[17]

On another occasion, McFarlane recalled that he answered Kimche in a way that went to the heart of the issue. It was, McFarlane said, the question of "weapons going to Iran, not so much the matter of who sends them." To which Kimche asked pointedly: "Well, if we do it, could we buy new ones from you?" McFarlane replied: "David, that's not the point. You've been buying missiles from us for a long time and you always can. You know that. The issue is, and I will get you an answer, is whether it should be done at all."[18]

Kimche and McFarlane seem to have misunderstood each other on this point. Kimche apparently wanted to know whether the United States would quickly replace any Israeli weapons sent to Iran; McFarlane understood replacement as going through the usual procedure of U.S. sales to Israel.* Both agreed on the principle of replacement or replenishment, but not on how it was to be done. New weapons were likely to be more expensive than old ones; sales could depend on America's own needs and inventory. The Israelis did not wish arms transfers to Iran to deplete their own stock of weapons for any length of time, especially if, as they were apt to think, they were acting in behalf of the United States.

In any case, Kimche's visit on August 2, 1985, lifted the incipient new policy onto a much higher plane. Arms to Iran had now become an open, urgent, immediate issue, even if through the mediation of Israel.

According to an official Israeli source, Kimche's visit had been preceded by an Israeli consideration of the issue on the highest level. Defense Minister Yitzhak Rabin had insisted on receiving assurances that Secretary of State Shultz knew of the plan to send TOWs to Iran and that President Reagan unequivocally approved of it. The Israelis were worried about getting all the blame if a transfer of arms by them without U.S. approval should become public knowledge. To protect themselves, they held a meeting with Ghorbanifar on July 25, 1985, at which he stressed the Iranian need for 100 TOWs and for the first time mentioned spare parts for antiaircraft missiles, as well as other weapons. He was told that the price for such arms was complete secrecy of the transaction and release of the hostages. Ghorbanifar had promised the release of the hostages or most of them within two or three weeks of the arms delivery. On July 28, Ledeen had been informed of the result of the meeting with Ghor-

* McFarlane later said that "the expectation was that there would be a sale by Israel based upon their costing of what it required for them to come to the United States and purchase an equivalent replacement item and that we would sell the items from defense stocks at cost in a normal kind of FMS [Foreign Military Sales] pricing system" (100-7, Part II, p. 224).

banifar and the Israeli decision to require unequivocal U.S. authorization. Ledeen is said to have told them that President Reagan had given sufficient authorization in his hospital meeting with McFarlane. This was not good enough for the Israelis, who insisted on confirmation.[19]

From this and other indications, it would appear that the initiative for a new U.S. policy on Iran came from Israel, which did not have an Operation Staunch to contend with, but that the Israeli influence was exerted with all due respect for U.S. prerogatives and procedures. Schwimmer's report had sent McFarlane to consult the president in the hospital. Now Kimche's visit induced McFarlane to get the highest-level U.S. decision on permitting U.S.-made arms to go to Iran. The Israeli feelers could have been rebuffed at any time; the United States must have responded to them for reasons other than that they came from Israel.

From August 2, 1985, the question of arms to Iran in exchange for the freedom of some or all hostages was squarely posed. Just how many arms was at first not fully clear. McFarlane once told the president that the price for a "dialogue" was 10 TOWs.[20] Ghorbanifar is said to have told the Israelis that the U.S. hostages would cost 100 TOWs.[21] Finally the figure was lifted to 500. The number of hostages to be released and what Iran could do about them were never clear. Ghorbanifar sometimes spoke of all, sometimes of some. Sometimes Iran had enough control to be sure of getting them released and sometimes only intended to make the effort.

Despite this unclarity, the choice for the Americans was sufficiently clear: Should arms be traded for hostages? Would arms help to bring about a moderation of Iranian policy or a normalization of U.S.-Iran relations? In what way could arms conceivably assist or strengthen the so-called moderate faction in Iran?

5

Just how and when these questions were answered depends to some extent on who is giving the answers. The final decisions had to come from President Reagan, and his peculiar method of making decisions is as significant as the decisions themselves.

The president, according to McFarlane, made an unusually serious effort to deal with the problem of authorizing Israel to send U.S.-made arms to Iran. He is said to have spent about ten days from late July to early August consulting with his chief advisers both singly and in groups. He convened an informal meeting of the top-level National Security Planning Group (NSPG), including Secretary of State Shultz, Secretary of Defense Weinberger, CIA Director Casey, Chief of Staff Regan, McFarlane, and possibly Vice President Bush. All the implications and ramifications of the proposed action were forcefully argued, with Shultz and Weinberger strongly expressing their opposition.

At the end, McFarlane said, the president gave his opinion:

> Well, as he had said before, that his inclination was not to have any U.S.-owned weapons or our inventory involved in this, but that he believed that it was possible over time, if these people's standing and authority and intentions were reformist, if you will, that he could see the need to support them, and with weapons, although at the time he said, right now I'm inclined not to have any U.S. weapons involved, U.S.-owned, but if Israel, whose judgment on this is based on a track record of dealing with these people, believes that it is sensible to do it and does transfer weapons, then ultimately their wish to buy replacements we should honor and we should sell to them.

McFarlane says he warned that people might think it was all an arms-for-hostages deal. The president took this into consideration and replied:

> Well, you're right, the risks of misunderstanding are quite high, and the question is are these people valid interlocutors or not, dealing in good faith or not. And he says: We have no way of judging it, really, except the track record of the past seven years, and it is only this report, really, and other things, the corroborating work we have done, focused upon intelligence hard copy that had been provided by these Iranians to the Israelis and Israel and ultimately to us—that it was basically—an order of battle is the wrong word. It was the names of the leadership of the Iranian armed forces from about the battalion level up, and that is nothing novel, but identifying those who were disposed to support these elements and those who were not.[22]

This somewhat jumbled account in McFarlane's words indicates that the president's thinking was based on what Kimche and Schwimmer had told McFarlane about what they had heard from Ghorbanifar and Ka-roubi. No "track record of the past seven years" existed, and the United States had been able to do little or no "corroborating work." Since the president was getting all his information from McFarlane, and McFarlane had not shown an undistorted grasp of what he had been told by Kimche and Schwimmer, it was little wonder that the president's reasoning was largely confused. Yet what comes through most strongly here is the dependence on Israel and the inclination to go along with some sort of arms deal through Israel.

A more formal meeting on the same subject soon took place. In this case the versions are so many and so varied that we have an embarrassment of riches.

6

On August 6, 1985, the president's principal advisers were called to the White House. Those present were President Reagan, Vice President Bush, Secretary of State Shultz, Secretary of Defense Weinberger, Chief of Staff Regan, and McFarlane. The meeting was held in the president's private quarters, where, dressed in pajamas and a robe, he was still recovering from his operation.

As McFarlane later observed, "what was being asked was approval for someone else to do something, not for us. However, it seemed clear to me that the linkage was very apparent and that we had an obligation not to be naive that this did engage U.S. interests in a major way. . . . What was discussed was that Mr. President, it is Israel who is going to be doing it, not the United States; that is true."[23]

McFarlane is said to have reported to the group that three meetings had taken place between Israelis and Iranians, at which it was claimed that "Iran was in a shambles and a new government was inevitable." The Iranians had reported that the military and the people were "still pro-American" and "want a dialogue with America." The Iranians wanted arms from the United States and 100 TOW missiles from Israel, in return for which they could produce four or more hostages. "All would be totally deniable." Israeli Foreign Minister Yitzhak Shamir had allegedly told Kimche that he wanted to know explicitly whether Shultz had been informed.

This version of what McFarlane told the group comes from Secretary Shultz.[24] We have no such account from McFarlane himself, except for his stress on Israel's role. Shultz's account was given sixteen months later and need not be taken literally. The "Iranians" in question had probably not told the Israelis that "a new government was inevitable" (though McFarlane may have understood it that way), and Rabin, not Shamir (according to the official Israeli chronology), had told Kimche that Shultz had to be informed. Nevertheless, Shultz's recollection contains the main elements of what was going on and reveals the confused nature of the information at the disposal of the most senior officials. Shultz and the others could not have known that the "Iranians" amounted to Ghorbanifar and Karoubi, as filtered through Kimche and Schwimmer to Ledeen and McFarlane.

In any case, Secretary Shultz himself came out strongly in opposition to any deal. He later recalled that he had said that "I thought this was a very bad idea, that I was opposed to it, that we were just falling into the arms-for-hostages business and we shouldn't do it."[25]

Secretary Weinberger gave two versions of what occurred. In one, he said that the meeting had turned mainly on the previously proposed National Security Decision Directive of June 1985, drawn up by Fortier and Teicher, which had suggested encouraging other Western countries to provide some weapons to Iran as a way of blocking the Soviets. Weinberger had previously called it "almost too absurd to comment on" and now repeated his objections to it, which were very much like Shultz's.[26] On another occasion, Weinberger said that only U.S., not Israeli, arms to Iran had been discussed. He could not remember any talk about resupplying Israel but noted that "McFarlane could have mentioned that the Israelis did this."[27]

Regan, however, thought that the effort was worth pursuing.[28] He seems to have been the only one present, besides McFarlane, who wanted to go ahead.

As for President Reagan's own view at the meeting, impressions differed so much that they seem to have mirrored what each one present wanted to hear. The only agreement is that no decision was made at this meeting, but there is little agreement on what the president said or indicated.

Shultz recalled that "he didn't seem to push one way or the other. He listened and it seemed to be relatively new information for him."[29]

Weinberger, however, thought that the president had agreed with him in opposition to the proposal. "My clear impression was that the idea [of arms to Iran] was set aside, or finished, that that was the end of it. The president seemed to agree."[30]

Regan gave three versions of what the president had said. In one, Reagan had told McFarlane "to go slow on this and let's make sure we know who we are dealing with before we get too far into this."[31] In a second, he had authorized McFarlane to "explore it further."[32] And in a third he had expressed concern over "this one-for-one type of swap and not wanting to get into arms sales through people that he at this point did not have enough assurance from Bud [McFarlane] that they were (a) reliable or (b) could deliver on anything, and that we should go slow on this but develop the contact."[33]

What McFarlane heard—or thought he heard—the president say was quite different. Reagan, according to McFarlane, was inclined to permit arms to be sent to Iran, so long as they went to anti-Khomeini forces.

The President's points were foremostly that he could imagine that if these people in Iran were legitimate and their interest of changing Iranian policy, and were against terrorism, that to provide them arms would not be at variance with his policy since he wasn't providing arms to Khomeini, but to people opposed to Khomeini's policy.

And that he would be willing to take the considerable public heat that would inure [sic] if this were tried and it failed because he could make that distinction.[34]

Of those present, McFarlane's impression was the most important, because he was going to carry out any policy that the president might opt for. The Israelis were waiting for the president's decision, but they were going to get it through McFarlane.

The different impressions of this meeting with the president suggest that he had not yet made up his mind about the essential aspects of the proposed new Iran policy. It presented him with grave choices, which he was taking his time to figure out. He behaved on August 6, 1985, in the manner described by Regan:

> Never did he issue a direct order, although I, at least, sometimes devoutly wished that he would. He listened, acquiesced, played his role, and waited for the next act to be written. From the point of view of my own experience and nature, this was an altogether baffling way of doing things.[*][35]

Nevertheless, some things seemed clear immediately after the August 6 meeting. An arms-for-hostages deal was not authorized. The two senior secretaries were dead set against it. McFarlane was more willing than the others to go ahead. Whatever the president said, it was open to different interpretations, from Weinberger's impression that the plan was "finished" to McFarlane's impression that Israel could go ahead with an arms deal so long as the weapons went to the right parties. But if the arms-for-hostages deal was not immediately approved, it was not rejected. The question was left open—and the fact that it had become an open question was a decided change from the adamant position of Operation Staunch.

We should now have a better idea of how such matters were handled in the Reagan administration. The record keeping of this affair was often so deficient or nonexistent that even at key moments we have only the memories of participants to fall back on. These memories can differ so much that one can almost believe that they were present at different meetings. The August 6 meeting is one of the worst cases, not only because of a lack of records but because the participants were clearly groping in a mist of information and misinformation. Everything was coming through McFarlane, who was getting everything from Kimche and Ledeen, who were getting everything from Khashoggi, Ghorbanifar, and Karoubi. The president and his advisers had no real idea of who the "Iranians" were with whom they were supposed to be dealing. The re-

---

* McFarlane gave a somewhat different version of the president's decision making: "Generally speaking the president would reach decisions only at the time of a meeting only if there was unanimity. Where there was disagreement it was his habit almost never to make the decision there but to wait and then convey it to me later on" (TR, p. B-22).

liance on Israel was forced on them if they wanted to do anything to save the hostages, and Israel was only too willing to act as intermediary, both in its own interests and in order to do the United States a good turn.

7

In fact, the plan as it speedily worked out was an arms-for-hostages deal, though not the way the Americans or Israelis had expected.

As soon as McFarlane informed Kimche of the U.S. decision, the Israelis prepared to send 100 TOWs to Iran. It was not easily arranged, because the weapons had to be paid for, and neither side was willing to put up the money by itself without the other. The Israeli Ministry of Defense demanded payment for the TOWs before they were flown to Iran, which refused to pay for them until they were delivered. The impasse was broken by the ever helpful Khashoggi.

Furmark, Khashoggi's American associate, happened to be present when Ghorbanifar came aboard Khashoggi's yacht in Marbella, Spain. Furmark described how Ghorbanifar had come aboard in great excitement to say that he needed $1 million to make a prepayment on the delivery of the 100 Israeli-owned TOWs. Khashoggi agreed to provide the money as "bridge financing" until Iran paid Israel for the missiles. It was established that Khashoggi posted the $1 million on or about August 7, 1985, and got back the money on or about August 29, 1985.[36] According to the official Israeli chronology, the $1 million went into an Israeli intermediary's account—either Schwimmer's or Nimrodi's.[37]

The haggling that went on was monumental. The deal was managed through intermediaries, Ghorbanifar for Iran and Schwimmer-Nimrodi for Israel, to shield both countries from direct contamination. At first, according to an Israeli source, an Iranian official, Mohsen Kangarlou, told Ghorbanifar that Iran did not want to pay for the missiles, because he thought that the release of William Buckley was enough payment. Only when the Israelis informed Ghorbanifar that this demand was out of the question did Kangarlou agree to payment for the arms. Kangarlou did not let on that Buckley was already dead.[38]

Iran agreed to pay Ghorbanifar $8,000 per missile. Ghorbanifar agreed to pay the Israelis $10,000 per missile. The Israeli Ministry of Defense wanted $12,000 per missile, which it expected to be the replacement cost. Schwimmer and Nimrodi pleaded that they could pay only $6,000 per missile, because they needed the remainder of what they received from Ghorbanifar for shipping and other expenses. In the end, the Israeli Ministry of Defense received about $5,500 per missile.[39]

With Ghorbanifar on board, the first plane with a load of 96 TOW missiles flew from Israel to Iran on August 20, 1985. A week later, Ghorbanifar was paid $1,217,410 by the government of Iran. On August

29, Ghorbanifar repaid Khashoggi the loan of $1 million. Whatever profit there was went to Ghorbanifar and probably some of it to Schwimmer and Nimrodi.

All that remained was the release of hostages, as Ghorbanifar had promised. But Ghorbanifar soon served notice that this part of the deal was unlikely to be honored. He informed the Israelis that he was not certain how many hostages would be released, but certainly not the CIA's William Buckley, on whom the Iranians put a "special value" and intended to return last.[40] Later, McFarlane received a call from Kimche, who said that only one hostage was to be released. Kimche asked McFarlane to choose the lucky one. McFarlane chose Buckley, who was still presumed to be alive.[41] Later, Ghorbanifar told the Israelis that Buckley was too sick to be released.[42] As a result, no hostages were immediately released.

With the first installment of missiles delivered on August 20, 1985, and with no hostages released, the deal seemed to have come unstuck at the expense of the Israelis.[43] They asked Ledeen to come to Paris on September 4 to find a way out of the impasse. When Ledeen was asked who had been there, he answered half jokingly: "The usual suspects"— namely, Kimche, Schwimmer, Nimrodi, Ghorbanifar, and himself. Ghorbanifar explained that the missiles had been seized by the extremist Revolutionary Guards instead of going to his "moderate" faction and "therefore, were unusable as a symbolic gesture by the people that Ghorbanifar had in mind and on whose behalf he was speaking." But Ghorbanifar, always the optimist, insisted that "with just a few more TOWs, this whole unpleasant problem will be solved."[44]

The failure of Iran and Ghorbanifar to make good on the release of any hostages for the first delivery opened the Israelis and Americans to something close to blackmail. The Israelis were faced with admitting the loss of almost 100 missiles, for which they had not yet been paid, with nothing to show for them. An official Israeli source says that severe arguments broke out at the Paris meeting. Ghorbanifar demanded an additional 400 TOWs for the release of only one hostage.[45] Ledeen says that Ghorbanifar passed on a proposal from the Iranian regime—"send the remaining four hundred missiles and hostages would be freed." When Ghorbanifar was challenged, he went to the telephone and called the office of Iranian Prime Minister Moussavi, with Nimrodi, who knew the language from his years in Iran, listening in on an extension and confirming that Ghorbanifar's demand was indeed the official Iranian position.[46]

On September 15, 1985, an Israeli-chartered plane delivered 408 more TOW missiles to Iran for a total of 504.[47] Only on that same day was a hostage, the Reverend Benjamin Weir, released. Weir was a Presbyterian missionary who had spent about twenty years in the Middle East; he came out of his ordeal expressing sympathy for his captors. In fact, Weir told the U.S. ambassador in Beirut, Reginald Bartholomew, that he had been released only to bring pressure for the release of the Da'wa prisoners in Kuwait, the longtime objective of the Lebanese hostage holders.[48] Weir's release was hardly what had been intended. McFarlane later admitted that "it was very clear that this was not a—the kind of exchange that was proper."[49]

On September 17, the Israeli intermediaries received an additional $290,000 from Ghorbanifar for the expense of transporting the 504 TOWs to Iran. On September 18, Iran transferred $5 million to Ghorbanifar's Swiss account for the additional TOWs.[50]

The details are less important than the control of these financial transactions; they were largely entrusted to Ghorbanifar for Iran and Schwimmer-Nimrodi for the Israelis. Because each country wished to hold itself formally aloof from the deal, it was transacted by these freewheeling middlemen who were interested in profiting from it, even if other motives entered into their actions. The line between profit and patriotism was another very fine one, especially in the case of Ghorbanifar, who always seemed to need money and to take considerable risks to get it.

8

The first Israel-to-Iran transaction in August–September 1985 was clearly an arms-for-one-hostage deal. The larger issues, such as a potential change in Iranian policy or a new strategic relationship between Iran and the United States, had little bearing on the outcome. In this as in other ways, the first deal was basically the prototype of all the others.

It was a foretaste of what was to come. For one thing, dealing with Iran was a tortuous, treacherous business. Agreements were made, broken, made again, and finally carried out in a manner that ultimately satisfied no one. The men in power in Iran cared about one thing—arms with which to fight Iraq. All other issues, such as a change in the long-range relationship with the United States, were at best to be left to an indefinite future. For arms, the Iran authorities had to turn to the United States, because the Shah's forces had been built with American weaponry. For the sake of TOWs, the Iranian rulers were even willing to compromise their hostility to Israel.

The one thing that Iran had to trade for arms was the American hostages. But they were in Lebanon, not under direct Iranian control. Just what hold Iran had on the Lebanese who held the hostages was never satisfactorily established. Yet the release of the Reverend Weir showed that Iran could use its influence in Lebanon if the price was right. The strategy of trading arms for hostages, however, required that there should always be hostages to be traded. The single hostage who came out in September 1985 was a signal that any engagement to release all the hostages was bound to be a snare and a delusion. All hope for an arms-for-hostages deal should have been extinguished in September 1985. If it was not, the intense desire of President Reagan to get the hostages out, as transmitted to McFarlane, was largely responsible. Everything else, such as whether the arms were going to extremists or moderates, had to be taken on faith and mainly served to alleviate the guilt, or provide a pretext, for sending arms.

This complex of needs, emotions, and inhibitions made intermediaries and "plausible deniability" necessary on all sides. Ghorbanifar was the main beneficiary. He succeeded in making himself temporarily indispensable to Iran, Israel, and the United States, each of which used him for its own purposes. Whatever Ghorbanifar's checkered past in Iran may have been, by accompanying the first installment of TOWs to Iran on September 20, 1985, and by telephoning the office of Prime Minister Moussavi in the hearing of Nimrodi, he showed that he was persona grata in some Iranian circles or they were willing to use him. The Iranian need for weapons was so great that the Iranians could feel about him in the same way as the Israelis and Americans—they used him because they did not have a better way to get what they wanted. By selling himself to the Israelis, Ghorbanifar was able to convince both Iran and the United States that he was indispensable—to Iran, because Israel alone could get it U.S.-made weapons, and to the United States, because Iran alone could get back the hostages. Whatever the misgivings about him, there was always the sense that no one else could take his place.

That Ghorbanifar was able to play one side off against the other testifies to an extraordinary cunning and resilience on his part. He failed his first test by not getting any hostage out in exchange for the August 1985 shipment of 96 missiles; he then succeeded in bartering one hostage—and not the one wanted—for another 408 missiles. Despite the disappointment both times, he survived to put himself at the center of even greater expectations and disillusionments. He was so free and easy with the truth that only desperation can explain how he could get away with beguiling and betraying ordinarily sensible and responsible people.

An Israeli source tells a story about Ghorbanifar that perhaps best conveys the effrontery of the man. It is said that Ghorbanifar and Nimrodi had met in Nice, France, on August 27, 1985, soon after the delivery of the first missiles. Ghorbanifar related that he had talked to Speaker Rafsanjani a few days earlier in Tehran and had revealed a "hidden secret" to him. The secret was that the emir of Kuwait had asked Vice President Bush to sell weapons and planes to Iraq to enable it to destroy the Iranian Kharg Island oil-storage and other facilities. Ghorbanifar was happy to inform Rafsanjani that Bush had rejected the request. Nimrodi asked Ghorbanifar how he had found out about this confidential exchange between the emir of Kuwait and Vice President Bush, who was in any case unlikely to have made such a decision. Ghorbanifar did not blink an eye and replied: "I made it up as I went along."[51]

The source of this story was probably Nimrodi. It was so characteristic of Ghorbanifar that it is retold by an Israeli source without any indication that it might not be credible. Ghorbanifar might have done better and gone further if a flaw in his character had not made it difficult for him to hold his tongue in check. Yet he came through just well enough to keep his Israeli and American handlers off balance, hoping for better luck next time. He was the joker in the pack, without whom nothing might have happened and with whom nothing right ever happened.

9

Horror Story

Until the fall of 1985, North was chiefly useful to McFarlane as the "principal action officer" holding the Nicaraguan contras together "body and soul." North worked endless hours, attended innumerable meetings, helped raise funds indefatigably, looked after the needs and intrigues of the contra leaders, unceasingly impressed his superiors with his ability to get things done and his devotion to the call of duty. By this time, however, McFarlane had begun to worry about North's staying power, and when he resigned in December 1985, McFarlane suggested to North that they should work together outside the government.[1] Nothing came of this proposal, and North continued to do as much—and more—for McFarlane's successor, Poindexter.

As if his responsibility for the contras were not enough, North was soon thrust into the Iran affair, a task that was easily as demanding and for which he was even less qualified by training and experience. The beginning came during McFarlane's last days in office. When McFarlane heard that the Reverend Weir was going to be released, he gave North the task of arranging for Weir to be brought to the United States from Lebanon. North arranged for a ship to bring Weir to Norfolk, welcomed him there in the name of the president, and carried out his assignment with his usual efficiency.

This episode brought North unwelcome attention from the news media. An NBC news broadcast on September 17, 1985, reported that North had met an Israeli official, David Kimche, in London. At 5 p.m., North wrote in his notebook: "Call from JMP [Poindexter] re leak," followed by: "Kimche/Schwimmer—Israel."[2] These names were soon to become more familiar to him.

On October 4, North put another Israeli name in his notebook: "Call from Nir.* No confirm re Buckley." On October 5, North talked to

---

* This is a reference to Amiram Nir, who soon replaced David Kimche as the main Israeli representative and of whom we will soon learn more.

McFarlane about a meeting with Kimche the next day.[3] During the same month, North authorized the FBI to monitor the conversations of "Iranian agents who purportedly had knowledge about or were involved in hostage negotiations."[4]

These preliminaries suggest that North was not yet fully embroiled in the Iran affair. North's next opportunity to inject himself into it was nearly missed by him. After Weir's release, North was supposed to meet with Ghorbanifar, Schwimmer, and Nimrodi, who had been invited to come to Washington. As soon as they arrived, North arranged for the FBI "to undertake electronic surveillance of two Iranian agents, Mr. Asgary and Yakov Nimrodi, who arrived in Washington on October 7 to assist in negotiations regarding the American hostages."[5] Evidently, at this early stage, North was still unsure of the personae of this drama; he did not know that "Asgary" was one of Ghorbanifar's aliases, and he made Nimrodi into an Iranian agent instead of an Israeli.

At this very time, North was busy with the capture of the Palestinian hijackers of the Italian cruise ship *Achille Lauro*. As a result, he seems to have had one meeting with Ledeen, Ghorbanifar, Schwimmer, and Nimrodi on the morning of October 8, but to have left further discussions to Ledeen.[6]

Ledeen was no longer willing merely to listen and report. He now assumed a more active role. "Ghorbanifar," Ledeen related, "conveyed from his Iranians the promise of more hostages for weapons." Besides TOWs, he now wanted Phoenix missiles, Hawks, Sidewinders, Harpoons. "And for each bundle of advanced weapons, they were offering one or more hostages."[7] As usual, Ghorbanifar also held out the prospect of future contacts with "conservative" Iranians willing to cooperate with the United States.

At this point, Ledeen says, he expressed a personal antipathy to the entire business of arms for hostages. "My argument was that, if we continued to sell arms to the Iranians, we would never be able to evaluate their real intentions, since they would do almost anything in order to lay their hands on the weapons." He wanted the participants to recommend to their governments that the hostage question be abandoned in favor of the long-range objective of changing the policy or nature of the Iranian regime.[8]

Schwimmer and Nimrodi were appalled by the suggestion. They brought up the Israeli concern for a dozen Israeli Jews and two Israeli soldiers held prisoner in Lebanon. Ghorbanifar, however, is said to have surprised Ledeen by agreeing with him. He allegedly told the group that "if we continue in this manner, we shall all become hostages to the hostages."[9]

In this peculiar way, the issue of more arms for more hostages was raised. Ledeen described some of the discussion as "so many weapons, so many hostages, so many weapons, so many hostages, a kind of alternating swap."[10] We are told that Ghorbanifar proposed the swap but advised against it. Ledeen also advised against it but had nothing more concrete to offer. Ledeen was right that the Iranians would do almost anything to get arms, even dangle a vague possibility of discussion of other, substantive aspects of future U.S.-Iran relations. Ghorbanifar was right to warn that they were bound to become hostages to the hostages if they continued on the arms-for-hostages track that he himself was always proposing and in which he had the most self-interest.

As Ledeen describes this exchange, there was something unreal about it. The meeting, after all, consisted of one U.S. part-time consultant supposedly authorized to do no more than to listen to others; two Israeli businessmen with no official status; and one Iranian exile of dubious motives and interests. The Israelis, according to Ledeen, were still ambivalent about Ghorbanifar; they felt that he had very good contacts but were suspicious that he might simply be "some kind of a provocateur."[11]

Yet these four sat around in the conference room of the Old Executive Office Building, where North had his office, discussing the fate of the hostages and future U.S.-Iran relations as if they represented Iran, Israel, and the United States. Ghorbanifar and Ledeen professed to be against arms-for-hostages deals and that is all they discussed. It is typical of this period that we should be wholly dependent on Ledeen for information about this meeting. He was one of those who deliberately made no notes, and all we have is his memory, long after the event.

Ledeen says that he soon reported to McFarlane about what the Iranians wanted and asked to get out of the "hostage business." McFarlane, according to Ledeen, readily agreed "that the whole hostage question was a bad question, and he used the expression 'I have a bad feeling about this whole operation,' and he said that his intention was to shut the whole thing down."[12]

McFarlane also claimed that he had been clairvoyant about where this type of negotiation was bound to lead.

> As I speculated earlier, I was surprised by the move from 100 to at least 400 [TOWs] and by the release of only one [hostage]. The President was pleased by the release of one and/or the continuation of the relationship. But that seemed to me a very clear evidence of bad faith, and I said so to Mr. Kimche, probably because I met with Mr. Ledeen, although I don't know that, but I made it very clear, and I think he's testified to the fact that I had a "bad feeling" about this program in October.[13]

If we can believe Ledeen and McFarlane, the first arms-for-a-hostage deal of September 1985 would have been the last one if their views had prevailed. If they are right, someone else must have been the force behind the continued effort to get more arms-for-hostages deals. After the disappointment following the Weir release, it was abundantly clear that a "continuation of the relationship" was likely to end in the same way, buying the release of one hostage at a time for ever increasing amounts of arms. So long as the president was "pleased" by the release of any hostage, McFarlane was in no position to "shut the whole thing down."

2

Into this delicate American balance of hopes and fears stepped Ghorbanifar with another tempting offer—a meeting with a "senior Iranian official." Ledeen learned that such a meeting had been arranged in Geneva for October 7, told McFarlane about it, and received permission to attend. The "usual suspects" were there—Ghorbanifar, Kimche, Schwimmer, Nimrodi, and Ledeen.

Ghorbanifar's bait was Hassan Karoubi, the same "ayatollah" whom Ghorbanifar had introduced to the Israelis the previous July as the alleged leader of the Iranian "moderates" and who was now passed off as a "senior Iranian official."* We have no fewer than four versions of this meeting, two of them so different that they might almost refer to different meetings. These versions tell us how deceptive one or another account can be and that a measure of truth can be obtained only by closely analyzing all of them.

In one version, Ledeen says that Karoubi told them that, with enough support and cooperation from the United States, "a significant degree of change could be achieved in Iran peacefully through elections." This meant that Karoubi and his supporters "could place their people in a series of key positions in the government" if they could demonstrate that "he had the support of the United States." Karoubi asked to be provided with "secure communications" in order to supply information to the Americans and get advice from them. Ledeen makes no mention of the feasibility of such elections in Khomeini's Iran or any assurance that the United States was so popular in Iran that its support could sway an election.

---

* Karoubi is referred to as the "First Iranian" in FR, p. 175. Segev makes him an "ayatollah" and says that Ghorbanifar "described Karoubi as Khomeini's 'right-hand man' " (*The Iranian Triangle*, p. 155). Ledeen refers to Karoubi as a "Senior Iranian Official" and says that he had met with Theodore Shackley and Ghorbanifar in Hamburg in late 1984 and had been with Khashoggi and Ghorbanifar when they talked with Schwimmer, Nimrodi, and Kimche in Europe in early July 1985 (*Perilous Statecraft*, p. 139). Taheri refers to Hassan Karoubi as a mullah, not an ayatollah, and a member of the Majlis (*Nest of Spies*, p. 193). He will be called "Hassan Karoubi" here, with the understanding that his name and rank are less important than the role which Ghorbanifar ascribed to him and which was all the Americans knew about him.

In this version, Karoubi allegedly went Ghorbanifar one better. Karoubi is said to have "vociferously opposed" providing arms to Iran. He said that they had strengthened the Khomeini regime, that it was a "terrible thing" to have done so, and that he "did not like that at all." Finally, Karoubi gave Ledeen a "signed letter" in which he expressed a willingness to cooperate in various ways, together with the names of "all the other Iranians who felt the same way, and for whom he spoke."[14]

In a second version, Ledeen added that Karoubi had gone so far as to say that the Iranian "radicals" had been "saved" by the August–September arms shipment. To the surprise of Ledeen and the three Israelis, Karoubi did not ask for financial support and called for no more than "an orderly working relationship" with the United States. He merely asked for some small arms "to defend themselves, along with some training in their use."

Karoubi may not have asked for financial support, but Ledeen and the Israelis thought that some sort of financial backing might be necessary. "We talked about the possibility," Ledeen says, "that it might be necessary to provide people like him with some expense money, or something like that from time to time, and it might be a useful idea to create an account in the event that became necessary." Schwimmer opened such an account in a Swiss bank and gave Ledeen the number.[15] Ledeen later testified that Ghorbanifar had told him that he had given Karoubi about $300,000. When Ledeen asked him how he expected to recoup such a large payment, Ghorbanifar had replied that he hoped to get it out of future arms sales by Israel to Iran.[16]

Ledeen was so impressed with Karoubi's line that he promised—apparently without authorization, as he had previously promised the Israeli Shlomo Gazit—that they would meet within thirty days, at which time Ledeen would give him the U.S. government's response. For Ledeen, Karoubi's claim "to speak for a powerful coalition of national leaders" who were allegedly trying to establish a working relationship with the United States raised the first "serious, strategic questions."[17] It seemed to be overlooked that some American missiles would not have been a life-and-death matter for a truly powerful Iranian coalition.

The third version of the same meeting in Geneva comes from the Israeli journalist Samuel Segev. Karoubi is said to have told the group that "he and his men were now in key positions," if they had enough support and cooperation from the United States. They were so influential that they could bring about the release of the remaining five U.S. hostages—without Khomeini's knowledge. Karoubi described himself as a "pragmatist" who knew that compromise was necessary.

There is nothing in Segev's version about Karoubi's allegedly vociferous opposition to providing the Iranian regime with arms. Instead, Karoubi is said to have demanded arms in no uncertain terms:

In exchange for the release of the American hostages in Lebanon, Karoubi demanded 150 Hawk missiles for the defense of the holy city of Qom and for shooting down high-flying Soviet intelligence planes entering Iranian airspace. He also asked for 200 Sidewinder missiles and 30–50 Phoenix missiles. As with the TOWs, Karoubi did not want to pay for the Hawks and argued that the release of the hostages was payment enough.[18]

Ledeen allegedly took these demands—so inconsistent with his own and Karoubi's professed views—in stride:

> Ledeen answered that he was not authorized to give Karoubi an immediate answer, and that he would have to present the matter to his superiors in Washington. He made it clear, however, that if the U.S. decided to supply Iran with the Hawk antiaircraft missiles and the other arms, Iran would have to pay for them. Ghorbanifar persuaded Karoubi to agree. Ledeen also insisted that Iran free all the hostages at the same time, and not one by one. After their release the U.S. would be willing to enter a new era of relations with Iran, supply it with arms and intelligence and send it technicians and advisers in various fields.[19]

This version of Ledeen's response presumably comes from the Israelis present. It is so distant from Ledeen's own accounts that there seems to be no way to reconcile them. To add to the confusion, we have one more version from Ledeen—this one given to Oliver North on October 30, 1985, on Ledeen's return from Geneva. North noted that Karoubi "wants to be U.S. ally—has support in Tehran." Karoubi "can have people meet w[ith] U.S." To get the hostages out, Iran demanded a "blanket order" of 150 Hawk missiles, 200 Sidewinder missiles, and 30 to 50 Phoenix missiles. The exchange of hostages and missiles was to be staggered, as North's notes have it:

> 1, 3, 5—ship hostages
> 2, 4—ship weapons[20]

North also heard from Ledeen that Israeli Defense Minister Rabin was "complaining about 500 TOWs"—those sent to Iran by Israel in August–September 1985, which had not been replenished by the United States.

Another meeting was held the same day between McFarlane, North, and Ledeen. McFarlane, according to North, felt that there were "very few sensible people" in the Iranian Army. Ledeen, on the other hand, urged a willingness "to deal with Israelis to bring out credible military and political leaders" in Iran. McFarlane then insisted that "not one single item" wanted by Iran should go without the release of "live Americans."[21]

These notes were put down only three days after the meeting in Geneva, long before the other versions by Ledeen and Segev. The number of missiles in North's notes coincides exactly with those given by Segev. The most significant omission in both of Ledeen's later versions is any mention of Karoubi's demands for weapons. By leaving out this aspect of Karoubi's proposals, Ledeen made it appear that Karoubi was "vociferously opposed" to an arms deal and was exclusively interested in long-range U.S.-Iran relations. Like Ghorbanifar, it seems, Karoubi was willing to talk about all manner of vague plans for the future, but in the end he came down hard on the immediate Iranian demand for arms and the only thing that Iranians had to offer in exchange—hostages.

Yet, in this period, the only one who spoke for the United States in dealings with Iranian and Israeli middlemen was Ledeen. We have no means of finding out what actually happened between them other than these versions, of which only North's contemporary notes bring us close to the event. They show that the Iranian strategy from the outset was based on a staggered or sequential exchange of arms for hostages. North was cognizant of this Iranian demand from October 1985 on, and he could have had no illusions about it as it was repeated time after time the following year. This meeting on October 30 also indicated that North had moved into a key position in the Iran as well as the contra affair, mediating between Ledeen and McFarlane, while the latter had other things on his mind. As North's notebooks show, he was still primarily occupied with the care and feeding of the contras, but North was not one to give up an opportunity to rush into new and dangerous territory where other bureaucrats might fear to tread.

3

By this time, the Iranians pulling the strings at home had sharply escalated their demands from TOW missiles to Hawks, Sidewinders, and Phoenixes, the latter the most advanced and restricted missiles in the U.S. armory, not even entrusted to Israel. The Iranians may well have reasoned that, if they could get TOWs for one hostage, the United States was so bent on getting back the hostages that the price could go up sharply. There was still so much suspicion on both sides that neither side was willing to make a payment without assurance of a return, but the meeting with Karoubi showed that a method had been worked out to get over this obstacle by staggering the shipments of missiles and hostages.

In early November 1985, Ledeen says, he again urged McFarlane to forget about the hostages and concentrate wholly on Karoubi's allegation that he spoke for "a powerful coalition of national leaders" in Iran who wanted nothing more than to achieve friendly relations with the United States. Ledeen also wanted the United States to stop thinking about what to do after Khomeini died and instead to deliver "some kind of blow to Khomeini before he died." In fact, if Ledeen can be believed, it was time for both Ghorbanifar and himself to step aside and leave the rest of the so-called Iran initiative to others. Ghorbanifar, he told McFarlane, no longer wanted to be an intermediary, and Ledeen thought that the "professional intelligence service" should take over from him. McFarlane, Ledeen says, never gave him a response.[22] For Ledeen, the failure to pursue contacts with Karoubi and others like him was the "great blunder" of the entire Iran affair.[23] Just how such contacts could have been pursued if the Iranians preferred to act sub rosa through types like Ghorbanifar and Karoubi is not clear.

Meanwhile, Ledeen learned that McFarlane, for personal or other reasons, was contemplating resignation as national security adviser. Ledeen says that he prevailed on Kimche to come to Washington on November 8, 1985, to persuade McFarlane to stay on the job and to go on with the Iran initiative.[24] It would seem odd for a part-time U.S. consultant to enlist an Israeli official to come all the way to Washington to strengthen the "resolve" of an American superior, but that is the way things were done in this highly unorthodox affair.

In the next few days, another Israeli official came to Washington to play a leading role in the Iran affair. He was Amiram Nir, then in his mid-thirties, who had been known to the Israeli public as a military correspondent of Israeli television. Political ambition had led him to resign in 1981 to work in an election campaign for Peres's Labor Party. After engaging in research at Tel Aviv's Center for Strategic Studies, Nir was appointed as Peres's adviser on counterterrorism in 1984. By this time, Nir was no stranger to North. They had worked closely together in October 1985 in the interception of the Egyptian plane carrying four Palestinian terrorists after the *Achille Lauro* hijacking. North said that the feat could not have been accomplished without Nir's contribution.[25]

On November 14, 1985, Nir met with North in Washington. They talked about Lebanon, where, both agreed, the United States and Israel had "similar views, liabilities, vulnerabilities."[26] It also seems that they discussed a joint covert operation which would cost at least $1 million a month. In his notebook, North listed questions which indicated how close U.S.-Israel collaboration was:

> How to pay for
> How to raise $
> How use Israel as conduit?
> Have Israelis do all work w[ith]/U.S. pay?
> Set up joint/Israeli cover op[eration]?[27]

These options showed the various ways the United States was prepared to use Israel as a surrogate in covert operations. They ranged from letting Israel do all the work, as a "conduit," to working jointly.

While North was meeting that day with Nir, McFarlane was meeting with Casey, his deputy, McMahon, and McFarlane's deputy, Poindexter. McFarlane told Casey afterward—and Casey told McMahon about it—that the Israelis planned "to move arms to certain elements of the Iranian military who are prepared to overthrow the government."[28]

There was another important meeting on November 15, when Israeli Defense Minister Rabin came to see McFarlane in Washington. This meeting lasted only ten minutes and was interrupted by a two-minute telephone conversation. Rabin's purpose, according to McFarlane, was "to reconfirm that the President of the United States still endorsed this concept of Israel negotiating these arms sales [with Iran]." McFarlane replied that "based upon recent questions and reaffirmations by the President that I had received, yes, he does, and he [Rabin] said all right." McFarlane agreed he had told Rabin that Israel was authorized to continue to sell arms to Iran "subject to replenishment." Thereupon Rabin expressed misgivings about the reliability of the Iranians with whom they were dealing, a sentiment with which McFarlane concurred.[29]

North now took over the details. The problem was how Israel was going to pay the United States for the missiles to be replenished. On November 15, North got in touch with Avraham Ben-Jousef, the Israeli purchasing agent in New York, to discuss the price. It was decided that the original price was "O.K.," if the missiles were "taken from stock."[30] Ben-Jousef called North on November 19 to get prices and to figure how the transaction could be carried out without attracting attention. North's notes read: "Request for LOA will attract attention. Normally do with FMS$ [Foreign Military Sales]. Cash transfer will create severe visibility."[31]

In effect, the Israelis planned, with U.S. approval, an arms-for-hostages deal similar to the one in August–September 1985. It came in mid-November, a bad time for McFarlane, who was leaving for Geneva on November 16 for the first "summit meeting" with the new Soviet General Secretary, Mikhail Gorbachev. Chief of Staff Regan, who made it his business to stay close to the president, recalled that McFarlane had spent a moment prior to his departure telling the president that "there was something up between Israel and Iran" which might lead to getting some of the hostages out.[32] Secretary of State Shultz said McFarlane had told him on November 18 that four hostages were to be released on November 21 in exchange for 100 Hawk missiles and that Israel was to buy replacements, for which Iran was to pay. "I complained to Mr. McFarlane that I had been informed so late and it was impossible to stop this operation,"

Shultz recalled. "I nonetheless expressed my hope that the hostages would in fact be released."*[33]

Shultz mentioned this transaction to his executive assistant, Charles Hill, who made a written note of it.

To complicate matters, we have two contradictory versions from McFarlane. In his public testimony on May 12, 1987, McFarlane related that "Mr. Rabin had made clear they were going to make a shipment and they would need to replenish whatever they shipped."[34] In a private deposition on July 2, 1987, however, McFarlane declared that "there hadn't been any forewarning from Israel to me or to the staff that I know of" of an intention to send any more weapons by way of Israel to Iran prior to his departure for Geneva.†[35] Everything else points to a forewarning, but apparently he did not pay much attention to it because it was primarily an Israeli operation.

We have been looking as closely as possible into the circumstances of this intended second shipment of arms to Iran in late November 1985 for a very special reason—it was to prove to be the crucial factor which led to the political upheaval over the Iran operation almost exactly a year later. Without Shultz's memory in November 1986 of what McFarlane had told him in November 1985, supported by Hill's note, there might very well not have occurred the occasion for searching through North's papers and finding what the investigators were not looking for—the telltale memorandum about the "diversion" of Iranian funds to the Nicaraguan contras.

It has been necessary to anticipate the climax of this strange story in order to prepare the way for the emphasis that was later given to the shipment of November 1985. If all had gone according to plan, it would have gone off as quietly as the previous one of August–September 1985, and no one would have been the wiser. Just how the November 1985 shipment came to haunt the Iran affair may be left for later; it is enough now to find out why the second shipment did not go off according to plan.

---

* At the congressional hearings, Shultz said that he had received a telephone call from McFarlane "about a hostage release and arms sales to Iran." Shultz saw it as "a straight out arms-for-hostages deal." Shultz also said: "I told him I hoped the hostages would get out, but I was against it, and I was upset that he was telling me about it as I was just about to start [to go to a meeting] so there was no way I could do anything about it. But anyway, if it was happening, I hoped the hostages would get out" (100-9, pp. 28–29).

† On this occasion, McFarlane could only recall that he talked about replenishment with Kimche in August 1985 and that he did not learn from North about the proposed Israeli shipment of arms until November 18, 1986. McFarlane's memory was especially confused in this deposition, which he partially explained by saying that in Geneva he had focused almost entirely on Soviet-American relations. The matter of the missiles to Iran, he said, "was not important. This was not going to lend one whit to whether the president of the U.S. succeeded in his central responsibility in bringing stability to East/West relations" (B-16, p. 640). Yet this does not explain why McFarlane told two different stories within less than two months; he knew what Rabin had made clear to him in his public testimony on May 12, 1987, and he had totally forgotten it by July 2, 1987.

4

We can follow the unfolding of this drama day by day with the help of North's notebooks, other contemporary documents, and the detailed testimony of almost all the actors in it. The blight which it cast over the whole enterprise and the political price ultimately paid for it make the effort worthwhile.

November 17, 1985

At 5:26 p.m.—we know the exact time, thanks to North's notebook—Israeli Defense Minister Rabin, who was in New York, called North to discuss "funding arrangements" for 80 Hawks. North apparently told Rabin to call McFarlane in Geneva to settle the matter.[36] At first the U.S.-Israel problem seemed to turn on replenishment for the Israeli missiles to be sent to Iran and how much they would cost.

At 5:47 p.m., McFarlane called North to tell him to return Rabin's call and assure him that the Israelis could get their missiles replenished. McFarlane also told North to see Ben-Jousef and to keep the Israeli order "under $14M[illion]."[37] The figure was significant, because any weapons purchase over $14 million had to be reported to the congressional oversight committees.

November 18, 1985

North put in a call to Al Schwimmer in Tel Aviv. Schwimmer was in charge of the operation there, while Nimrodi was in Geneva with Ghorbanifar and Mohsen Kangarlou representing the Iranian government.[38] North learned from Schwimmer that the Israelis were planning a series of deliveries of the weapons to Iran in the next three or four days, starting with a first load consisting of one-sixth of the total that had been approved by the Israeli government.

North also conveyed to Ben-Jousef the requirement about paying $14 million or less for the U.S. weapons. In addition, North heard that Schwimmer had moved $1 million to Secord's Lake Resources account in Geneva, which had heretofore been used exclusively for Nicaraguan contra business.[39] By this crossover of funds, the two affairs were intermingled for the first time.

Thus far, Rabin had seemed to be concerned with the old problem of replacements and their cost. On this day, however, something far more serious developed.

The original plan called for an Israeli 747 to fly 40 or 80 Hawk missiles from Tel Aviv to Lisbon, Portugal, there to unload, store, and reload the weapons on other, ostensibly non-Israeli, planes at the airport for the flight to Iran, in order to cover up the Israel-Iran character of the transaction. For this purpose, the Israeli operators, headed by Schwimmer, needed special clearances to land the cargo of arms at the Portuguese airport. Unfortunately, Schwimmer had neglected to get such clearances in advance. When he applied for them at the last moment, he found that the Portuguese authorities were reluctant to grant them.

This seemingly minor, technical problem of the Portuguese clearances set off the entire series of slip-ups that finally resulted in a monumental fiasco and the ultimate exposure of the Iran affair. As North later put it, "it is a bit of a horror story."[40]

Sometime on November 18, Rabin learned that something had gone dreadfully wrong with the operation. When Schwimmer found that he could not handle it, he appealed to the Israeli Ministry of Defense, which passed it on to Rabin in New York. Rabin called McFarlane in Geneva for help, and both of them called North.

As McFarlane told the story, Rabin told him "we have a problem in getting through a European country. Can you help?" McFarlane replied that he would put one of his staff in touch with Rabin, whereupon McFarlane notified Poindexter and North that Rabin was going to call for help.[41]

According to North, Rabin called to say McFarlane had told him that North was the one who would "fix it." Just as North hung up, McFarlane called him to expect Rabin's call. North says he told McFarlane that Rabin had described the problem "in altogether too specific terms over the open telephone. And I am concerned about that." McFarlane said: "You go take care of the problem. Just take care of it." North asked "if the President had approved, does the President know?" McFarlane replied: "Yes, just go take care of it."[42]

North flew to New York, met with Rabin, and got a detailed briefing on what the problem was—"which was basically finding a place in the European country to change airplanes and on-load and off-load weapons." At that meeting, North said, "they told me that they were going to manifest, they were going to—in other words, the shipment that they were planning would be manifested as oil drilling equipment." North added: "It was an operational nightmare, is what it was."[*][43]

By getting into trouble, Schwimmer and Rabin put the United States in a new position in the transactions with Iran. "This was a dramatic change of role for the U.S. Government," North later recognized. "Up until now the Israeli Government had been handling everything."[44]

It also changed North's role. North had previously preoccupied himself with the contra affair and had been only marginally engaged in the Iran

---

* At the Poindexter trial, North said that Rabin had told him the number of missiles they were trying to ship and some overflight clearance problems they were having. North told Rabin he would get back to him after checking for authorization (PT, pp. 1350–51). Thus North knew at this time that the cargo was made up of missiles, not oil-drilling equipment.

affair. "My role until November 1985 was simply one of collecting intelligence on it and trying to position U.S. assets to recover or receive the American hostages as they were released. In November 1985, Mr. McFarlane had me get directly involved in the operation of this and conducting it and so at that point I became operation engineer. I didn't know the details of who he worked it out with, except the persons that he sent to me, first of all, in the case of Mr. Ledeen and second of all, in the case of those who came from overseas to meet with us."[45]

Just as McFarlane changed North's role in the Iran affair, North changed Secord's role. Secord had previously devoted himself exclusively to supplying the contras. Now both North and Secord were plunged into another and even more confused affair, the full measure of which neither could hardly imagine when they took their first step into it.

November 19, 1985

From Washington, North could do little for the Israelis in Lisbon. Instead of going there himself or using someone else on the NSC staff or elsewhere in the government, he again turned to Secord. One advantage Secord had was his close ties with a leading Portuguese arms dealer, Defex, which had obtained arms for him for the contras.

On November 19, North sent Secord this message:

Dear Major General Secord:
Your discrete [sic] assistance is again required in support of our national interests. At the earliest opportunity, please proceed to [Lisbon] and other locations for the transfer of sensitive materiel being shipped from Israel.
As in the past, you should exercise extreme caution that this activity does not become public knowledge. You should ensure that only those whose discretion is guaranteed are involved.[46]

This message was signed by "Robert C. McFarlane," who had not authorized it.[47] It confirms that North understood the "transfer of sensitive materiel" to be in "our national interests" as well as Israel's. Yet he still considered the operation to be an Israeli one that the United States had been pulled into inadvertently and for a limited purpose.

Secord met with North on November 19 to be briefed on what assistance was required of him.[48] As Secord later related, "he told me that there was a secret operation that had been underway which was running into difficulty and the difficulties he described were what I would say were logistical difficulties involving the transfer of some missiles from Israel to Iran and this was a sanctioned—meaning sanctioned by the United States—operation and that it involved among other things, the possibility of getting some of our hostages out of Lebanon." North told him that "what they wanted to do was transship these missiles through Portugal, that is bring them to Portugal and put them on a different aircraft and fly them to Iran. Obviously, Israel cannot deal directly with Iran."[49]

Secord called for his associate Thomas G. Clines, who had been handling Secord's business in Portugal, and both flew to Lisbon on November 19, arriving the next day. Secord settled down in an office at Defex, which he expected to get him access to the Portuguese Foreign Ministry and the office of the prime minister. In return, Defex was supposed to get the job of handling the transshipment arrangements.[50]

November 20, 1985

North was so confident that he knew what was going on that he reported to Poindexter, who was taking charge in Washington in McFarlane's absence, on the exact nature of the transaction. It was another straight arms-for-hostages deal.

Basically, as North understood it, 120 Hawk missiles were going from Israel to Portugal and from Portugal to Iran. The first 80 were to go on November 22 aboard three planes at two-hour intervals, followed by a release of hostages, whereupon the remaining 40 were to follow. North assured Poindexter that "the appropriate arrangements have been made with the proper Portuguese air control personnel." As soon as the first aircraft had been launched, Ghorbanifar was to call his contact in Tehran, who was to call someone in Damascus, Syria, who was to direct the Hizballah in Lebanon holding the hostages to deliver them to the U.S. embassy in Beirut. No aircraft was to land in Tabriz, Iran, until all the hostages had been handed over.[51]

In his notebook for November 20, North was busy recording how he was putting all the pieces of the Portuguese puzzle together. In a telephone conversation with Rabin in New York, he guaranteed U.S. replenishment of the Israeli missiles. In return, North was told that $18 million had been deposited for 80 Hawks at a price of $225,000 each. They also seem to have discussed a plan other than the one that North had outlined to Poindexter. It provided for a sequential pattern—a delivery of 27 missiles followed by the release of two hostages; 27 more missiles and three hostages released; the remaining 28 missiles for the last American hostage and possibly one French hostage. In this plan, the hostages would not be released all at once before the landing of the first plane, as North put it to Poindexter, and the release of the hostages would depend on a succession of deliveries.

In another call from Ben-Jousef in New York, North again heard that $18 million had been deposited. He was made acutely aware of the "bill of lading problem": "Bill of lading should not show real name of equipment."

Still another notation that same day contemplated a different exchange. This plan called for delivering 40 more Hawks, 200 Sidewinders, and 1,900 TOWs. After enumerating these missiles, North wrote: "120 Hawks = (1) 5 Amcits [American citizens] (2) Guarantee that no more." These cryptic figures suggest that North was contemplating a somewhat different formula to get all the American hostages out, with a guarantee that no more hostages would be taken, which would make this deal the last one.

The last note on November 20 was foreboding. It indicated that Secord was not doing well in Lisbon and was calling for high-powered assistance. It read: "Bud [McFarlane] or George [Shultz] need to tell P.M. [Portuguese prime minister]."

November 21, 1985

At noon, North hears from Schwimmer in Tel Aviv that the clearance problem was still unsolved. The money that was supposed to have been deposited in the Swiss bank had not yet cleared. How soon could North say the Israeli missiles would be replaced? The answer was: "80 can be replenished in 1 mo[nth]—6 wks." But Israel would need 40 more.

1 p.m.: Schwimmer calls again. An Israeli flight clearance request in Lisbon for a rented 747 aircraft has been turned down. The Portuguese airport officials insist that only the foreign minister can give authorization. Nevertheless, Schwimmer gives North a proposed schedule for the flight to Tabriz, Iran, starting at noon.

1:20 p.m.: Kimche in Tel Aviv calls North. The Israeli plane which had been sent out to Lisbon has been recalled.

1:40 p.m.: Clarridge calls North and is advised of the aborted Israeli flight.

2 p.m.: Secord calls North. He wants to get the U.S. chargé d'affaires in Lisbon to intercede. He urges North to get Under Secretary of State Michael H. Armacost to send a cable to the chargé.

2:50 p.m.: Poindexter calls North. Secretary of State Shultz is aware of the proposed deal. Poindexter does not want Armacost to send a cable.

3:10 p.m.: North discusses options with Clarridge.

4 p.m.: Secord calls North. Portuguese prime minister has been given a message about clearance.

5 p.m.: North calls McFarlane to ask him to call the Portuguese foreign minister.

5:30 p.m.: NSC staff counsel Paul Thompson calls North and says that McFarlane has just made contact with the foreign minister, who has allegedly agreed to permit the landing in Lisbon the next morning.

Between 5:00 and 6:00 p.m.: U.S. chargé calls to say that the Portuguese cabinet requires a formal diplomatic note and would consider the request only if full information about the flight and its lethal cargo is given in the note.

6 p.m.: Secord calls North. He has instructed the chargé not to send a note.

8 p.m.: Secord calls North. Nothing can move without clearance.

9 p.m.: Secord calls North. He wants McFarlane to call the Portuguese foreign minister.[52]

This frenzied telephoning gives some idea of the efforts and frustration on November 21. Secord was obviously having trouble convincing the Portuguese authorities or even getting to them and had to call for help. In this way, the State Department in the person of the chargé d'affaires in Lisbon and the CIA in the person of Clarridge were dragged into the operation. By the end of November 21, no progress had been made and the Israeli 747 was still waiting in Tel Aviv to take off.

An unlucky incident also took place on this day. The first effort to get a clearance had been made by a Defex partner, who was the brother-in-law of an official at the Portuguese Foreign Ministry. The official was told that Defex was working with a retired American general who wanted to arrange for a shipment of arms to Iran. This request baffled the Portuguese officials, who had been told firmly that the United States was opposed to all shipments of arms to Iran, according to the letter and spirit of Operation Staunch.[53]

As a result, the political counselor in the Lisbon embassy, James F. Creagan, was called to the Foreign Ministry the same day and was asked to explain why a retired American general wanted an urgent flight clearance. The operation was so secret that Creagan had not been told about it and replied that "our policy was to discourage such shipments."[54] From then on, the Portuguese authorities suspected that something dubious was going on and became increasingly determined to give no clearance until they knew exactly what it was for.

This mishap made Secord realize that he had to go higher on the diplomatic ladder and bring in the chargé d'affaires, who happened to be in charge of the embassy in the temporary absence of the ambassador, Frank Shakespeare. When Secord was told about the contretemps, he called North for permission to get the chargé to get in direct touch with Portuguese Prime Minister Anibal Cavaco Silva and Foreign Minister Pedro Pires de Miranda to induce them to intervene.[55]

November 22, 1985

We now come to one of the most peculiar episodes in this melodrama. Schwimmer decided to send an El Al plane loaded with 80 Hawk missiles out of Tel Aviv toward Lisbon—without a clearance. The plane was sent on a "go/no go" basis, meaning that it would turn back at a certain point if a clearance was not obtained in time for its landing. This risky maneuver set off panicky measures in Lisbon and Washington to make it possible for the plane to land.

In Washington, North mobilized both the State Department and the CIA.

At the State Department, North went to see Robert B. Oakley, director of the Office of Counterterrorism and Emergency Planning, North's counterpart in the department. According to Oakley, North told him that the secretary of state was "aware" of the matter and that McFarlane was in overall charge of the operation. North said that McFarlane had been contacted in Geneva and had agreed to help get the flight clearance, if necessary by his personal intervention. On the basis of these assurances, Oakley authorized North to communicate with the Lisbon embassy and advise that it could request clearances from the Portuguese government.[56]

A peculiarity in Oakley's account is a story told to him by North that reflected unfavorably on Israel.

> North stated that he was aware of Israeli arms shipments to Iran in exchange for certain intelligence [deleted]. North indicated that he had discovered this relationship when "one of his people" went to an arms warehouse in Portugal to obtain arms for the Nicaraguan Resistance, and learned that the Israelis had been obtaining arms from the same source for shipment to Iran.[57]

This story seems to have had no foundation.[58] It may have been a gratuitous effort on North's part to show how much he knew about what went on in Lisbon.

For some time, Oakley was fed optimistic reports by North. On November 22, Oakley informed Secretary Shultz, who had returned to Washington from Geneva, "that the hostages would be released that afternoon in exchange for 120 Hawks at $250,000 each—worth $30 million in all." Shultz is said to have "regarded it as a $30 million weapons payoff," but observed that "Bud [McFarlane] says he's cleared [it] with the President."[59] One day later, Shultz was told that no hostage had been released and that it was "over"—when it was not.[60]

At the CIA, North enlisted Dewey R. Clarridge, the flashy chief of the European Division. Clarridge, North, and Charles Allen, the CIA national intelligence officer for counterterrorism, assembled in Clarridge's office, as if it were a command post, to deal with the Portuguese crisis.[61]

At 3 a.m., the Lisbon station received a "flash message," the highest in urgency, from Clarridge, requiring the immediate presence of the chief of station. A follow-up message at about 4 a.m. directed him to assist "Richard Copp," whose real name it said was General Richard Secord, on personal assignment from the National Security Council.[62] A later message that day gave fuller information—the operation was intended to obtain the release of the Western hostages; it was of "great interest to the highest levels of the USG [U.S. government]"; five flights were contemplated from Israel to Iran; Portugal was asked for overflight clearances and refueling; the U.S. ambassador need not be informed.[63]

As a result of Clarridge's urging, the CIA chief of station and the U.S. embassy's chargé d'affaires went to see the Portuguese foreign minister, whom they found in a cabinet meeting. They tried to get him out of the meeting; waited an hour; repeatedly called the Foreign Ministry, which refused to act without the foreign minister. Finally it was clear to them "that the foreign minister was not going to come out of the cabinet meeting to respond to our request."[64]

Even McFarlane, by that time in Rome, put in a telephone call to the Portuguese foreign minister to get him to agree to clearance for the Israeli plane.[65] He was no more successful than the others, though there is disagreement about whether the foreign minister at any time had agreed with McFarlane's request.[66]

Secord was so desperate that he once tried to intercept the prime minister and foreign minister at the Lisbon airport as they were returning from a meeting in Brussels. According to the chargé, Secord's idea was to persuade them "to go ahead and agree with all this without going through normal channels." Unfortunately, Secord waited for them at the VIP lounge, and they landed at the military side of the airport. Instead of bearding the Portuguese leaders in the airport, Secord made himself conspicuous in a high-security area and brought on himself "suspicions is probably a gentle word, but suspicions, antagonism" from the Portuguese authorities.[67]

Meanwhile, the Israeli plane had reached the "no go" point on its flight and had turned back to Tel Aviv. Schwimmer's gamble had failed.

Still hopeful that Secord would get Portuguese permission, North wanted to try again with the same plane and route. With this in mind, North asked Kimche to put the operation "on hold until we could iron out the clearance problem in Lisbon." Schwimmer, however, acted precipitately and canceled the charters for the three planes he had intended to use. North scornfully informed Poindexter: "Schwimmer released them to save $ and now does not think that they can be re-chartered before Monday [November 25]."[68]

Recriminations were now in the air. The Americans were poised to blame Schwimmer for the plane holdup in Tel Aviv, and the Israelis to blame North and Secord for failing to get the Portuguese clearance.

After this disappointment, another type of "diversion" occurred to Secord and was approved by North. When North informed Secord that Schwimmer no longer had a plane at his command, Secord suggested that they could use a Lake Resources plane then in Lisbon picking up ammunition for the Nicaraguan contras. Secord planned to repaint the plane and get it ready for service to Iran by November 23. When North informed Poindexter of Secord's intention, he added: "So help me I have never seen anything so screwed up in my life." North was unhappy about the proposed diversion of Secord's plane, because it was set to make the first direct flight with ammunition from Lisbon to contra forces inside Nicaragua. To Poindexter, North lamented: "One hell of an operation."[69]

Secord's new idea did not work out any better than the old one.[70] It merely served to show how the Iran and contra affairs were likely to be jumbled together by North and Secord if they were desperate enough for a solution to some problem in either one.

Secord was still left with the problem of the Portuguese flight clearance. He soon informed the CIA chief of station of a new plan for three flights by two planes to arrive between November 23 and 27.[71] The next move came from the Portuguese Foreign Ministry, which demanded a formal diplomatic note, including characteristics of the aircraft, routes, and cargo.[72] It was an awkward request, because the embassy officials were not permitted to divulge the nature of the operation. The Portuguese evidently wanted to make sure they would not later be charged with violating Operation Staunch and sought, according to the U.S. chargé, "formal acknowledgement they were being asked to help in a weapons shipment." An unresponsive reply, described as "skimpy," did not satisfy the Portuguese.[73]

After all this trouble, the Portuguese authorities were rudely told not to bother any more. The U.S. chief of mission handed them a note from Washington which made the Portuguese "very upset because it was in a sense impolite. Also, we had turned them inside out for about 24 hours, and now we were simply saying 'thanks, but no thanks,'—we don't—we are not proceeding down this track."[74]

The luckiest person in this story was Ambassador Shakespeare. When he returned to Lisbon and was told what had happened in his absence, he exclaimed: "Thank God, I wasn't here."[75]

November 23–25, 1985

As the Portuguese route become more and more questionable, North and Clarridge prepared a fallback position. The new plan took the procurement of planes and delivery of Hawks to Iran out of the hands of the Israelis and put it into the Americans'.

On the afternoon of November 22, while the Portuguese route was still being worked on, Clarridge took the initiative to get a new plane for Schwimmer. He called in the CIA air branch chief and told him to find a commercial Boeing 747 for "a very sensitive mission in the Middle East." This official reported that he could not get so large a plane very quickly but suggested a smaller Boeing 707 from a CIA "proprietary" in Europe.[76]

A "proprietary" airline was one owned or controlled by the CIA, but, as in this case, it did not work exclusively for the CIA. It operated as if it were an ordinary business doing straight commercial operations but was available for special assignments by the CIA whenever it was considered desirable to conceal the official U.S. source of the operation. Such a proprietary had a CIA agent in ultimate control, especially if a CIA clearance was necessary, as in flights to Iran. If the flight was sufficiently sensitive, it was referred to Washington for approval.

That same day, Clarridge sent word to the CIA's proprietary charter airline in Frankfurt, West Germany, to be prepared to take over the flights to Iran. It was the same airline that had been used by the Israelis on a commercial basis to deliver the first missiles to Iran on August 20, 1985, with the knowledge and approval of the CIA.[77]

When Clarridge decided to use the proprietary, he called its CIA controller in Frankfurt and told him to expect to hear from someone about an urgent flight which it was in the interest of the U.S. government to perform. He stipulated, however, that it was to be regarded as a commercial flight paid for by one "Richard Copp" and not the responsibility of the CIA. That evening, the controller received the expected call from Secord, using the name of "Copp," who told him that "there had to be three flights done as quickly as possible" from Tel Aviv to Iran. They agreed on a price of $60,000 plus the cost of fuel and other expenses per flight.[78]

A proprietary Boeing 707, flown by a West German pilot, arrived in Tel Aviv on November 23. It was beset by one bedevilment after another. The plane could load no more than 18 missiles, far short of the 80 that the Iranians expected. Secord said that it would take two hours to load the missiles; it took twenty-four. A dispute broke out between the CIA controller in Frankfurt and Schwimmer in Tel Aviv. While the plane was being loaded, it was belatedly realized that it was U.S.-registered. Word came from Washington to withdraw the plane and substitute a different one with a Western European registration.[79] The cargo had to be removed to a second plane and a new crew sent in. Schwimmer's proposal to paint a different registration on the plane was turned down. The plane's captain reported to the CIA controller about Schwimmer that "this guy on the ground there must be crazy."[80] All the stops and starts were costly. The proprietary's manager demanded a down payment of $30,000 to the plane's captain for landing fees and fuel. With difficulty, Schwimmer managed to raise $8,000.*[8] After more such hold-ups, the plane took off on November 24, with no more than 18 missiles.

---

* The version in Raviv and Melman is: "Schwimmer was muttering curses all day at 'those American crooks,' because Lieutenant Colonel Oliver North of the U.S. National Security Council had sent an airplane with no money for aviation fuel. The Israeli had only around five hundred dollars in his pocket, and he quickly drove to the homes of wealthy friends to borrow the rest of the nine thousand dollars the pilot said he needed to refuel" (*Every Spy a Prince*, pp. 325–26).

Segev has an even more lurid account: "The plane arrived at Ben-Gurion Airport on Saturday morning, November 23, flown by two Germans. It was a small craft, and the missiles were loaded onto it only with difficulty. Nimrodi and Ghorbanifar spoke with the Iranian Prime Minister several times from Geneva, and promised the Hawks would arrive. Ghorbanifar and Kengarlou were being threatened by Iranian army officers [in Geneva!], and Nimrodi was worried about the Revolutionary Guards at the door to his hotel room" (*The Iranian Triangle*, p. 202).

The agony was far from over. The first destination en route to Iran was Turkey, but the Turks also proved to be too curious about the nature of the cargo. The CIA chief of station in Ankara cabled Clarridge that the Turkish government was friendly but insisted on getting "some idea of what the aircraft would carry as presumably they would not be empty." Clarridge replied with the cover story that the plane was carrying "sophisticated spare parts for the oil industry."[81] Suddenly, Turkey was given up in favor of Cyprus. The change necessitated defueling in Tel Aviv, because the fully loaded plane was too heavy to land in Cyprus. After more delay, the plane finally took off.

Cyprus was another close call. The plane lacked all documentation and was apparently not expected at the airport. When the plane landed, the local authorities refused to let it go on unless proper documents were produced and the cargo inspected. The plane's captain concocted a false cargo manifest and managed to talk his way into the air again.

But he still had to fly over Turkey, for which he had no overflight clearance. The Turkish ground controllers repeatedly demanded a diplomatic clearance number. Again the ever resourceful captain made one up for the occasion. When it was rejected, the plane flew about at different altitudes and positions for an hour and a half, while the captain and flight controllers argued the point. Finally, the captain talked his way out of Turkish airspace and departed for Iran.

The plane landed in Tehran on November 25. The local officer directing the unloading of the missiles revealed that the plane was not expected and that its arrival came as a surprise. A civilian carrying a machine gun, thought to be a member of the Revolutionary Guards, ordered that no one should be told that the plane had come from Israel. Despite these hazards, the plane left uneventfully the same day.[82] Secord's Lake Resources account in Geneva paid $127,000, more than twice the original $60,000, to the proprietary for the delivery.

Again there was blame enough for everyone. The Americans blamed Schwimmer for his mismanagement and behavior. The CIA's proprietary controller reported to his superiors in Washington about "a certain Mr. Schwimmer" who was "very pushy with the military, sometimes to a point where he was insulting, but he did not understand their special aviation problems and did not have things under control."[83] Schwimmer's apologist blames Secord for not getting landing rights in Lisbon and in general for not doing anything right, besides scheming to take the Iranian business away from Schwimmer and Nimrodi. These two, who are described as blameless, "suddenly realized that the people the White House had assigned were incompetent."*

---

* Segev, *The Iranian Triangle*, pp. 200–1, 210. Segev's account here is largely distorted in order to absolve Schwimmer of all responsibility and put all the blame on Secord.

After all this, far more serious trouble broke out in Tehran and Washington.

5

In Tehran, it was soon discovered that the wrong missiles had been sent.

As the Israelis tell the story—and they were in a position to know because Nimrodi was with Ghorbanifar and Kangarlou in Geneva receiving word from Tehran—the slip-up was quickly discovered by an Iranian officer who had some experience in the U.S. factory that manufactured the Hawks. When the boxes were opened before the crew and plane were released, he immediately spotted the trouble—the missiles were obsolete types and not capable of hitting high-flying planes. With him was Prime Minister Moussavi. As soon as he heard the bad news, Moussavi rushed to a telephone and called Kangarlou in Geneva.

We have two Israeli versions of the denouement, obviously coming from Nimrodi. Segev relates:

Moussavi was furious. He notified Kengarlou that he had ordered the plane delayed, the missiles confiscated, and the crew arrested until "the last toman" of the money was returned. He blamed Kengarlou for the fraud. Kengarlou knew what that meant. He fainted, and was rushed to the hospital, where he remained for four days. Ghorbanifar told Moussavi that Kengarlou had fainted, and the Prime Minister responded curtly, "May he go to hell." Ghorbanifar broke down and screamed at Nimrodi: "You're thieves, cheats!" Then he began wailing and worrying about the fate of his father and mother in Tehran.[84]

Raviv and Melman tell the same tale in different words:

Moussavi dialed Kangarlou's suite and screamed, "Who is trying to treat us as fools? I am standing here with the Hawk missile expert of our army, and he sees that these are old Hawks—totally out of date and worthless to us!" . . . Moussavi yelled on, and Kangarlou turned white as a sheet and fell to the floor. He had fainted from the pressure. His bodyguards feared it was a heart attack and began pounding Kangarlou's chest. . . . an ambulance took Kangarlou to a Swiss hospital, and the next morning Nimrodi was accompanied by burly Iranian bodyguards to a branch of Crédit Suisse to transfer $18 million back to Iran's account.[85]

The first American to hear the bad news was Ledeen. Later that day he received a "frantic" telephone call from Ghorbanifar. As Ledeen later recalled, Ghorbanifar, "on the very edge of hysteria," said that

the most horrible thing had happened. That those missiles had arrived and they were the wrong missiles. That it was a provocation and that it was an Israeli provocation because not only were they the wrong missiles, but they came with Israeli markings all over them. And you can imagine what effect this has had on our people and so on and so forth and that various high Iranian officials may go into cardiac arrest within hours and here is a message from the Prime Minister for the President of the United States and he read it to me and I copied it down and I carried it into Poindexter later that evening.[86]

When North learned of the Iranians' displeasure, he sent Secord to Israel to find out what had gone wrong.* Secord learned from Schwimmer that the deal had been made with Ghorbanifar, who had told Schwimmer, Nimrodi, and Ledeen that Iran needed a weapon to deal with high-altitude reconnaissance aircraft coming from the Soviet Union and bombers from Iraq. The Israelis had sent Hawks specifically designed for low-altitude aircraft. Secord concluded that the fault had been with the civilians—Schwimmer, Nimrodi, Ghorbanifar, and Ledeen—who had discussed Iran's needs without knowing the difference between one missile and another. Iran already had low-altitude Hawks and therefore quickly recognized that it was getting what it did not want.[87] An official Israeli source contends, however, that Ghorbanifar, not the Israelis, had made promises to Iran about the capability of the missiles.[88] Wherever the blame should be placed, the Iranians felt cheated and responded accordingly.

Low altitude was not the only thing wrong with these missiles. Money was also a cause of understandable Iranian concern. The Iranians had expected 80 Hawks but had received only 18 in the first and only delivery on November 25, 1985. Iran, however, had paid Ghorbanifar in advance for 80. On November 22, 1985, Iran had transferred $42.72 million to Ghorbanifar's account in Switzerland, assuming a price per Hawk of $300,000. On the same day, Ghorbanifar transferred $24 million to Schwimmer's account in Switzerland. Ghorbanifar, according to the official Israeli source, paid only $18 million for the 80 Hawks, with $6 million more to be held in trust by the Israelis at Ghorbanifar's request. The Israeli source also says that the $6 million was later paid back to

---

* In his garbled account of the entire episode, Segev has Secord leaving for Israel on November 18, 1985 (The Iranian Triangle, p. 197). This slip-up has the effect of making Secord responsible for the "mishandling of the arrangements" from the outset and helps to absolve Schwimmer of all blame for the mishaps.

Ghorbanifar, who intended to keep $1 million for himself and use the remainder for payments to "certain Iranians."[89] There were no lack of temptations along the money trail. Schwimmer paid the Israeli Ministry of Defense only $11.2 million for the hypothetical 80 missiles, at a cost of $140,000 per missile, not the $300,000 Ghorbanifar charged the Iranian government. Schwimmer thus received $11.8 million more from Ghorbanifar than he paid the Israeli Ministry of Defense (plus $1 million to Secord's Lake Resources, about which more later). Of this $11.8 million, $6 million was supposed to be held in trust for Ghorbanifar and the remaining $5.8 million was to cover expenses for the entire operation.

Once it became apparent that no more than 18 missiles were going to be delivered and that they would have to be returned, the money started going backward. The Israeli Ministry of Defense paid $8.17 million to Schwimmer, or $3.03 million less than Schwimmer had previously paid to the same ministry. The difference was ascribed to a prorated charge of $140,000 per missile for the 18 Hawks delivered to Iran and a charge of $510,000 for general expenses. Schwimmer then transferred $18.6 million to Ghorbanifar's account. Over $5 million was still held out by Schwimmer, although most of it was repaid to Ghorbanifar and to the Israeli Ministry of Defense after 17 (not 18, because Iran had shot one off) of the luckless missiles were returned to Israel in February 1986.[90] Schwimmer says that he also paid $700,000 to "various other Iranians," in which case a good deal of bribery and other forms of baksheesh had greased the whole operation.[91]

It is hard to say from the data at hand who—except for the bribe takers—benefited from the fiasco. What is clear is that a great deal of official Iranian money was invested in the undelivered 80 missiles and that it must have weighed heavily on Iranian officials when they discovered that they had only 18 of the wrong missiles. By hiding behind intermediaries, who were—whatever else they were—businessmen with a keen nose for profit, the Iranian, Israeli, and U.S. governments opened themselves up to double-dealing and mutual suspicions. When Iran was bitterly resentful about the delivery of the wrong missiles, Prime Minister Moussavi did not complain about Ghorbanifar or Schwimmer; he charged the president of the United States with having cheated him.

Moussavi's criticism showed that the missiles had been going to the Iranian government and its armed forces, not to some dissident or opposition faction. It should have been clear by now that Ghorbanifar had been dealing on behalf of the ruling circles in the Khomeini regime, which had provided the large sum of money and which had reacted speedily the very day the first 18 missiles were received.

6

Ledeen was the messenger who paid for bringing the bad news from Moussavi. Ledeen was probably on the way out anyway, but his fate happened to be settled at this time of discontent.

Ledeen had wanted to bring Moussavi's wrathful message to McFarlane. Unfortunately, McFarlane was not available, and Ledeen brought it to Poindexter instead. The deputy national security adviser, soon to take McFarlane's place, merely nodded and abruptly informed Ledeen that he was being taken off the entire project. "We need people with more technical expertise," Ledeen remembered Poindexter saying. Ledeen speculates that Poindexter considered him to be "unreliable, incompetent, or both."[92] Poindexter himself explained that he was "never completely comfortable with Mr. Ledeen, because he talked too much and I didn't think he was a particularly discreet emissary to be using" and "we were concerned with Ledeen not really being very knowledgeable about what he was dealing with." Ledeen asked to be retained to work on what he considered to be the long-range U.S.-Iran relationship, which Ledeen identified with Karoubi, but Poindexter only stared blankly at him and gave no sign that he knew who Karoubi was.[93] After Poindexter replaced McFarlane, Ledeen tried on several occasions to talk to Poindexter about Iran but was always rebuffed. Dismayed at the time by his unceremonious dismissal, Ledeen was later grateful that he had inadvertently been saved from further responsibility for the ill-fated Iran initiative.[94]

Ledeen's departure ended the first phase of the Iran initiative. For six months he had been the only American in direct touch with the Israeli and Iranian middlemen. That a part-time consultant, who was not likely to be content merely to listen, as he had been instructed to do, should have been let loose on his own in Israel and Europe, far from the supervision he might have had in Washington, was a quintessential example of "perilous statecraft," the title of Ledeen's book. If Ghorbanifar was responsible for much of the havoc caused by the Iran initiative, Ledeen was responsible for having been Ghorbanifar's most ardent American sponsor.

Finally, there is the mystery of the $1 million.

At an early stage of this operation, even before he had arrived in Lisbon, Secord figured that the entire operation would take about five flights at a cost of $1 million. That sum was deposited on November 20 by the Israeli operators in the Secord-Hakim Lake Resources account in Geneva, previously used solely for Nicaraguan contra purposes.[95]

This $1 million has never been fully explained. North's notebook for November 18 contains the words: "Schwimmer move $1M[illion] to Lake." North testified that the money was supposed to pay for "the movement of Hawks to Iran."[96] Secord also said that the $1 million was to be used to transport the Hawks to Iran.[97] Both North and Secord were unable to explain why North should have arranged with Schwimmer as early as November 18 to put $1 million in the Lake Resources account, when Secord did not arrive in Lisbon until November 20 and supposedly came there only to get clearance for an Israeli plane.

The mystery of this $1 million deepened when it turned out that $850,000 of it was admittedly used by North to support the Nicaraguan contras, not to pay for moving the Hawks to Iran.[98] Only $150,000 was used to pay for legitimate expenses in the Hawk operation. Ordinarily the remainder should have gone back to the Israelis, but when it did not, according to North, he "told them we used it for the purpose of the contras, and they acknowledged that"—and never asked for the money back.[99]

In effect, the "diversion" of funds to the contras from the Iran operation started in November 1985 and did not originate with Ghorbanifar's suggestion to North in January 1986, as North was to claim. As North himself told the story, he simply decided to appropriate $850,000 of Israeli money for the contras, told the Israelis he had done so, and did not give it back because they did not ask for it. The original diversion was North's doing, whatever he may have been advised later by Nir or by Ghorbanifar. It was not a new idea.

For good reason, then, those who tried a year later to concoct a false account of the Iran initiative and those who tried to find out whether there was any truth in it came to realize that the weakest link in the chain of events had taken place in November 1985. The "horror story" came back to haunt the characters in it, especially the one who called it that—Lieutenant Colonel Oliver L. North.

The cruelest thing about all the bungling was that it was ostensibly done to get the American hostages released. For all the toil and trouble, November 1985 came and went without a single hostage released.

Another by-product of North's desperate efforts to get the Israeli planes in and out of Portugal was the improvised extension of his network. McFarlane had called on him as if he could have done the task by himself. Then North called on Secord as if he could get it done by pulling a few wires. When nothing worked for them, they were forced to get the cooperation of the CIA station and embassy officials in Lisbon. In this way, as with the contras, North brought about a quasi-conspiratorial tie-in with agencies and departments beyond the NSC staff on the strength of his assumed position in the White House. The bureaucracy, for all its rules and regulations, was vulnerable to someone like North who had nothing but contempt for bureaucrats.

7

The aftermath of the "horror story" was not one of horror. It was rather an almost immediate decision to repeat the operation, but next time more successfully and under U.S. management.

On the morning of November 26, North met with Poindexter from 9:40 to 10:50, an unusually lengthy meeting for Poindexter, who was short on words. North made the following notes about what Poindexter told him:

—RR [Ronald Reagan] directed op[eration] to proceed
—If Israelis want to provide diff[erent] model, then we will replenish
—We will exercise mgt [management] over movmt [movement] if
   yr [your] side cannot do
—must have one of our people in on all activities

On November 26, then, Reagan and Poindexter talked about reviving the operation under different auspices. They were persuaded that the fault lay with the Israelis who had been in charge, not with the inherent folly of trading arms for hostages. According to an official Israeli source, later that day North told an Israeli official, evidently David Kimche, that the United States wanted to carry on even if Israel needed additional American arms.[100] What the Israelis did not immediately realize was that the Americans planned to take over.

At 3:30 p.m. the same day, North met with Poindexter again. North noted:

Copp [Secord] or D.K. [David Kimche] tell Iranians we are disappointed that they perceive we were dealing in bad faith. Not the case, we had nothing to do w[ith] the implication that we did not deliver what had been agreed to

Change of team to ensure that . . .

Must have *all* [hostages] on 1st Delivery. Sit[uation] in Lebanon could prohibit delivery of others

Reiterate commit[ment] for no more terror

Commit to no more than 120 [Hawks]

Dick [Secord] to check [unclear][101]

These notes indicate that Poindexter and North had been working out a strategy to get back into the good graces of the Iranians by telling them that the fault had not been with the United States. The "change of team" referred to the elimination of Kimche, Schwimmer, Nimrodi, and Ledeen in favor of Nir and North. The next approach was going to offer a maximum of 120 Hawks—40 more than the Israelis had contemplated sending—in exchange for all the hostages, hypothetically to be released all at once to prevent a slip-up in Lebanon, and an Iranian promise not to engage in more terrorism.

Far from taking the "horror story" as a sign that such a deal with Iran was bound to go wrong and that it was time to stop, Reagan and Poindexter were persuaded that the Israelis had bungled it and that Americans could do the same thing, only better. The effect of the fiasco was thus to draw the United States more deeply and directly into more deals with Iran. In practice, this meant that North was let loose to take personal charge of the next American moves. With his usual zeal, he wasted no time.

Within a few days of President Reagan's decision to proceed with the operation, North sent his alter ego, Secord, to Paris to meet with Ghorbanifar, Kimche, Schwimmer, and Nimrodi, the latter three in one of their last appearances in this story.[102]

In Paris, Ghorbanifar carried on as if nothing had changed. According to Secord, he held forth on "how he thought the game should continue in the future." Ghorbanifar's game was always the same—arms for hostages in a staggered or sequential pattern. This time, however, Ghorbanifar was interested in the more advanced Harpoon and Phoenix missiles as well as TOWs and Hawks. Secord regarded Ghorbanifar's overture as "blatantly a set of proposals of arms for hostages"—for example, "so many Phoenixes for so many boxes," Ghorbanifar's word for hostages.

Ghorbanifar volunteered five options:

> (1) 600 TOWs = 1 release
> H + 6 hrs later = 2000 TOWs = 3 release
> H + 23 hrs = 600 TOWs = 1 release
> (2) Same as option (1) except substitute [unclear] for
> TOWs
> (3) 2000 TOWs = 3 host[ages]
> 50 [unclear] = 2 host[ages]
> (4) 600 TOWs
> (5) Bombs, spares, F-4 parts, comm[unication] gear
> Maverick—spares; test equip[ment][103]

Ghorbanifar, it seems, came well prepared to ask for one weapon if he did not get another. Secord's shrewd impression of Ghorbanifar was not flattering:

> He had a boilerplate kind of salesmanship pattern, which he put out very glibly, which talked about the strategic setting and things that he knew Americans would like to hear. The Russian threat,

the Iranians were being held hostage by the hostages themselves, and they needed to move on. But it was my impression that Ghorbanifar was more interested in business than he was in foreign policy.[104]

Secord reported back to North, who told him that he had agreed to meet with Ghorbanifar and the Israelis in London on December 6. Ghorbanifar's game was afoot again.

10

Finding No. 1

Still more haunting is what happened in Washington as a result of the horror story.

In the renewed effort to get arms to Tehran, North's chief confederate in the CIA was Dewey R. Clarridge, head of the European Division. Clarridge had formerly headed the Latin American Division—though he had had no prior experience in Latin America—and had supervised the first efforts of the Reagan administration to use the Argentine military to support the Nicaraguan contras. The idea of planting mines in Nicaraguan harbors in 1984 was Clarridge's. It was Clarridge who had first introduced North to the contra leadership.[1] Clarridge had also been sent to South Africa in 1984 in one of the first, ultimately aborted, attempts to get a foreign country to subsidize the contras. Personally, Clarridge looked the part of a maverick spymaster; he dressed fancily and flaunted his taste for expensive cigars and fine food. The austere North and the flashy Clarridge had one thing in common—they were willing to take risks.

When North had come to see Clarridge on November 22 to get a new plane to fly the missiles to Iran, Clarridge did not think it necessary to get approval from any higher authority in the CIA.[2] He took it upon himself to order the CIA's proprietary airline in Frankfurt, West Germany, to be prepared to take over the flights to Iran. Yet Clarridge had made one precautionary move that later set off alarm bells among the top leadership of the CIA. Before communicating with the proprietary airline, Clarridge had gone to see the associate deputy director of operations, Edward S. Juchniewicz, who worked under the deputy director, Clair George. Clarridge asked Juchniewicz about the use of the proprietary airline. Juchniewicz says that he knew nothing about "what Colonel North had in mind or what anyone else had in mind," and replied that anyone could charter an aircraft from the proprietary, because it was "a bona fide commercial venture." So long as no one was asking for the

use of CIA funds, Juchniewicz saw no problem.[3] North called Juchniewicz on November 24 about the same thing and received the same
advice: "I said look I've already explained it to Dewey Clarridge and if
you people are that hard up and you need to charter an aircraft, I mean
this is a commercial enterprise, you can go out and put your money on
the table and charter the airplane. He asked me for no specific assistance.
He just said thank you and hung up."[4]

It appears from this that North and Clarridge were not sure about the
propriety of using the proprietary. In any case, they did not go beyond
Juchniewicz, who did not know all the ramifications of the missiles deal
and thought that Clarridge and North were somehow interested in helping
a private commercial enterprise. Juchniewicz seems to have been mystified about why they came to him at all.

Chance played a part in the imminent blowup. Casey was traveling
abroad. McMahon and George happened to be away during most or all
of the period of the proprietary crisis. North had wanted to talk to George,
with whom he was accustomed to deal, and was apparently ill at ease
with Juchniewicz.[5] Whether North or Clarridge would have gone to
Casey for approval if he had been available, and what he would have
done about it, will never be known. They could have reached McMahon
or George before November 23 if they had tried, but they did not try.
On their own, events moved relentlessly.

2

John N. McMahon was deputy director of the CIA, second only to
Director Casey. Compared with McMahon, Casey was a Johnny-come-
lately in the Agency. Casey's only intelligence experience went all the
way back to the OSS, the CIA's World War II predecessor, after which
he had gone on to other, more lucrative occupations, mainly making
money as a lawyer and getting ahead in Republican politics. He had
continued to be interested in intelligence and had served on the president's
Foreign Intelligence Advisory Board. But his chief rewards—as chairman
of the Securities and Exchange Commission in 1973–74, as head of the
Export-Import Bank in 1975, and especially as campaign manager of
Ronald Reagan's presidential candidacy in 1980—had to do with money
and politics far more than with intelligence gathering or covert activities.
In contrast, McMahon had left law school to go into the CIA in 1952
and had spent three decades working his way up in the Agency. Casey
asked him to stay on as deputy director of intelligence in 1981 and made
him deputy director of the CIA the following year.

Casey's background and temperament tended to make him bend the
rules as far as they would go. There is no telling what Casey would have
done if confronted with the problem of the unauthorized proprietary

flight to Iran. But McMahon happened to return before Casey and, as acting director, faced the problem alone. As a professional intelligence officer of long standing or perhaps because it was native to him, he was accustomed to play by the rules. In any case, McMahon was soon put to the test.

McMahon says that all he knew at this point about the Iran affair was that Israel was involved in an initiative to gain the release of the American hostages and was dealing in arms with Iran. On September 19, 1985, McFarlane had told Casey and McMahon that there had been no arms-for-hostages deal to obtain the release of the Reverend Weir four days earlier.[6] Afterward, Casey told McMahon, who had left the room earlier, that McFarlane had told him "the Israelis either had or proposed to ship arms to Iran."[7] McMahon did not know much more because, he said, it was an "NSC operation" and the CIA knew only as much as it was told or could glean from the cable traffic, the distribution of which was restricted.[8]

McMahon came back to his office on November 23, two days before the proprietary's plane took off for Tehran. According to McMahon, Juchniewicz said: "Do you know what these guys are up to?" and handed him a cable to the U.S. chargé d'affaires in Lisbon "bemoaning the fact that the [Portuguese government] would not help out on this humanitarian mission."[9] McMahon apparently did not get the full implications of the cable and said to Juchniewicz: "Look, it's okay to send cables. We do that all the time for Secretary of State or Defense or what have you, use our channels because they are more secure. But I said make sure we don't get involved." At this time, McMahon still knew nothing about the use of the CIA proprietary.[10]

There had still been time on November 23 to get approval for the proprietary's flight from one as high up as McMahon, but North and Clarridge did not try. If Juchniewicz or McMahon had inquired more deeply into what was going on, they would have had the authority to stop the flight.[11] The opportunity passed without their interference, for one reason because North and Clarridge had not confided the nature of the operation to them.

Two days later it was too late. On November 25, the proprietary plane took off from Tel Aviv to Tehran. At about the same time, the horror story came to haunt the CIA in Washington.

At about 7 a.m. on November 25, McMahon arrived as usual in his office. As he told the story, fifteen or so minutes later Juchniewicz again hailed him with: "Hey, do you know what those guys did?" The rest of the story is best told by McMahon:

And I said what guys, and he said Secord. Now that's the name I heard. And I said what was that? And he said they used our proprietary to send over some oil supplies, and I said goddam it, I told you not to get involved.

And he said, we're not involved. They came to us and we said no. And they asked if we knew the name of a secure airline and we gave them the name of our proprietary. I said, for Christ's sake, we can't do that without a Finding. So then I went back to my office and I punched a button and I said you get those guys together with Sporkin.[12]

Stanley Sporkin was the general counsel of the CIA. He had been brought into the CIA in 1981 by Casey after long service in the Securities and Exchange Commission, where Casey had come to know him.

Somewhat later that same morning, McMahon walked in on Clair George, who had just returned, and said: "I am just trying to find out what went on. You make sure you get some guys over to brief Sporkin on what happened." Later McMahon told George: "Hey, you pull together all the cables and see what the hell is involved here."[13]

In a "Memorandum for the Record" on December 7, McMahon recalled the events of that day with less equanimity. After he had learned about the proprietary flight, he wrote: "I went through the overhead pointing out that there was no way we could become involved in any implementation of this mission without a Finding."[14]

Juchniewicz told a slightly different story about how McMahon came to see the necessity for a Finding. On November 23, Juchniewicz said, McMahon had popped in on him to see if anything was happening in the Operations Directorate. Juchniewicz mentioned that North had called him the previous evening, and then Juchniewicz said: "John, guess what? The NSC wants to charter our airplane."* McMahon stopped, paused, "became very contemplative," and left. After thinking about it, McMahon came back and said: "I think that we need a Presidential Finding before we can do anything further." He also told Juchniewicz to get a reaction from Stanley Sporkin.

Juchniewicz's version puts McMahon's statement about a Finding on November 23 instead of November 25 and makes it appear to refer to a future use of the proprietary, not one that had already taken place.[15] The essentials, however, are similar—McMahon learned about the proprietary flight from Juchniewicz and quickly saw that it required a Finding.[16]

Clair George added some color to McMahon's story:

I came back Monday morning, Monday afternoon [November 25]. McMahon was in a rage. He told me to pull together the traffic, meaning the telegrams, that took place, went back and forth. I got

---

* It will be seen that the NSC staff was referred to as the NSC, as if there was no difference between them.

them in, put them in a little folder and took them to John [McMahon] and read them when I took them, and that was when I first knew about it.

Later John came in, again quite upset and terribly concerned, talking to Juchniewicz, and his remark, which is burned in my mind, was not only did we send the goddam telegrams, but the goddam airplane went in. Now obviously we know that that was the famous proprietary flight. [17]

George said that McMahon told him "there will be no more activity in support of this without a Finding."[18] North also learned from George on November 25 that further flights were off.[19] North's notebook says that he called Schwimmer, with whom he had been in constant contact, to say that there were to be no more flights "until we tell you."[20]

One gets the impression from all this that if it had not been for McMahon, the horror story might have turned out differently in Washington. It does not seem to have occurred to anyone else in the CIA that a Finding was necessary. Another striking aspect of the event is that almost no one in the CIA knew much about what was happening and why. McMahon and George, who should have known the most, say that they knew little or nothing. Clarridge knew the most, but he claimed that he knew only as much as North told him, which, if Clarridge can be believed, did not include the information that the proprietary aircraft was carrying arms to Iran. Clarridge told George that "it was Ollie North that told him, that it was Ollie North that wanted the airplane, that it was Ollie North that was frantic."[21]

Paradoxically, McMahon's reasoning for the Finding had nothing to do with arms. When he called for a Finding, he did not know and he did not care whether the proprietary plane had carried arms to Iran. He was actually told by Juchniewicz that it had carried oil-drilling equipment, which was what North had told Clarridge.[22] For him oil-drilling equipment was just as much war matériel as weapons. The critical point for him was that the CIA could not take part in such an operation without a Finding. "The focus in CIA for me, because I was the noisiest," he explained, "centered around the use of a proprietary, and I don't think anyone in CIA was going to discriminate what was in that box: whether it was an arm, a baby carriage or oil drilling equipment, that wasn't the issue at the time. The issue was if we did something wrong, we would have to fix it." The use of the proprietary plane, not what it carried, was wrong; that was what had to be fixed by a Finding.*[23]

---

* McMahon also said: "I just felt we had violated the law, and it didn't matter what was in it. Even if I knew it was weapons at the time, they wouldn't have rang a different bell to me than oil drilling equipment. . . . oil drilling equipment is probably far more important to the Iranians than weapons. Because they live and prosecute the war by oil" (B-17, pp. 288–89).

McMahon's anxiety about getting a Finding was well founded. As it happened, the Reagan administration had itself issued a highest-level National Security Decision Directive in January 1985, which specified in detail the requirements for a presidential Finding. It provided that Findings had to be issued "in writing" and subject to "Congressional reporting procedures." It further gave the CIA jurisdiction over all covert actions "unless the President specifically designates another agency," in which case its extent and nature had to be included in a Finding.[24] The CIA's participation in the covert action to send missiles to Iran clearly came within the scope of this directive.

When Casey returned, according to McMahon, he agreed that a Finding was necessary.[25] Of Casey in general, McMahon said: "I would say Casey by nature is forward leaning, but I don't think he's dumb enough to do anything that's against the law and I don't think he would ask the agency to do anything that was against the law . . . In fact, he used to proclaim quite proudly that he took a view [vow?] of political chastity when he was sworn in as the DCI [Director of Central Intelligence]."[26] Nevertheless, it was one thing for Casey to have agreed on the Finding with McMahon once the latter had made such an issue of it; it may have been another thing for Casey to have raised the issue himself without McMahon's initiative.

3

The larger question is why the CIA, in McMahon's absence, permitted itself to be dragged into this apparent violation of the law on Findings. All it took to get the use of the proprietary was the determination by one member of the National Security Council staff, Oliver North, and the resources of the CIA were made available to him.

This question was frankly and sometimes ingenuously answered by several of those implicated in the CIA's intervention. The answers generally invoked two aspects of the Iran initiative: that it was an "NSC operation" and that it was a function of "compartmentation."

In the first case, much confusion resulted because so often no distinction was made between the National Security Council and the staff. The statutory members of the NSC, such as the secretaries of state and defense, were not consulted and knew little or nothing about the frantic efforts to transport missiles to Iran. Yet members of the NSC staff, such as North, benefited from the association with the NSC and identification with the White House. As far as other agencies and departments were concerned, a call from North was a call from the White House, to be treated with proper deference and dispatch. North habitually exploited this association.

Compartmentation was an elementary rule in both the NSC staff and the CIA, whereby each sector or division was largely insulated from every other in order to guard against unauthorized or unwitting disclosures and, in the worst case, defections. Compartmentation, Poindexter once explained, was the way to keep secrets.[27] As Clarridge put it: "You learn in this business you don't ask a lot of questions. You know, you—there are certain things of compartmentation."[28] When North asked him to do something, Clarridge explained: "My instinct on something like this would be to respect his compartmentation, and I would ask him—I would ask him no questions other than what else he—what other support he might need, but I would let him volunteer what he wished to volunteer."[29]

Compartments were sometimes compared with boxes. Lieutenant Colonel Robert Earl, North's aide, once spoke of the Iran initiative as "a sensitive program, compartment, very few people were in the box, and so, therefore, security was extremely important and . . . the need-to-know principle was ruthlessly applied in this compartment." He also explained "that there is a big box, referring to the whole Iran operation, and that there are boxes within that or parts of that."[30]

The rule of asking no questions was particularly adhered to for anything that was presumed to have come from the White House. When the CIA air branch chief involved in the procurement of the proprietary aircraft was asked about whether he knew what the cargo was, he replied: "Just the dimensions of the cargo, and you don't ask unnecessary questions when it comes out of the White House. I presume it was something sensitive, obviously; they wouldn't be doing it otherwise."[31] Clarridge interpreted "our attitude toward compartmentation" as "we will not—we operations officers [in the CIA] will not investigate an NSC sensitive operation."[32] Clair George explained the CIA's role by pointing out that "this was the White House, and the White House was calling the CIA and they were asking for help."[33] When Juchniewicz was asked why he had made no inquiries about the reason for the proprietary flight, he explained: "I was not one of those privileged few who were privy to this activity."[34]

One more factor enabled Oliver North to manipulate the CIA and other forces far beyond his relatively modest rank. As McMahon explained, the CIA regarded the Iran initiative as an NSC operation, with the CIA in a strictly supportive role. "You must bear in mind," he said, "that this was an NSC operation and that the CIA was in a you call/we haul mode, that we weren't doing the planning or anything like that, and that the NSC had all the contacts. They had the wiring mechanisms through their go-betweens, the Iranian go-betweens, the Israelis." However, "if someone came to the CIA and said take this planeload of TOWs and deliver it to the Tehran airport on such and such a date and we have that wired, we could do that."[35]

McMahon attributed the role of the NSC—shorthand for the NSC staff—to the frustration with the CIA's inability to rescue the hostages.[36] President Reagan, he thought, "would look to CIA to solve this, and we weren't solving it," whereupon "the NSC finally grabbed the ball and said well, those guys out at the Agency can't hack it, so we'll do it ourselves."[37] McMahon traced the CIA's problem to its inability to get good intelligence on the plight of the hostages, enabling the NSC staff "to move into a vacuum."[38] Nevertheless, McMahon was "dumbstruck that the National Security Adviser didn't realize that when you call upon CIA to conduct something, that you need a Finding to do it. And most people in CIA will, you know, salute and go do something because that is the nature of the beast, especially when it comes from the NSC."[39] In effect, the entire mix-up brought on by the CIA's necessity for a Finding would have been avoided if North had not gone to Clarridge for an aircraft and ended up with a CIA proprietary.

Clair George expressed a similar view. "Every Administration in this country has finally run either big and terrible, or small and unsuccessful covert actions out of the White House," he said. "Every Administration finally decides that its spy service just can't do it, and whether it's [former President] Carter with poor Hamilton Jordan wandering around in a red wig trying to free the hostages, or whether it's under Reagan trying to sell arms to Iran. Finally, there is some guy in the National Security Council says, who formed that really stupid spy service we have? Let's get a good one. Let's set it up ourselves."[40]

The impression in the upper reaches of the CIA, then, was that the NSC staff had grabbed the initiative to free the hostages because the CIA had failed when it had had the chance. From this point of view, the subordination of the CIA to the NSC staff was no vote of confidence in its director, William J. Casey.

The traditional role of the CIA had been operational, that of the NSC staff policy coordination. Now, in effect, there were two operational agencies, with the NSC staff in the forefront in at least the hostage-Iran affair. The NSC's operational role had been coming on for some time, notably during the TWA and *Achille Lauro* hijackings earlier in 1985, in both of which Israel and the United States had worked intimately together, and in the second of which Oliver North had played a prominent role. For North, his activities in behalf of the contras and in the *Achille Lauro* case were dress rehearsals for his takeover of the Iran affair. As McMahon observed, however, never before had the NSC—or rather its staff—mounted an operation of such magnitude. In the past, he said, the NSC staff had usually trespassed on "State Department turf, not CIA's turf."[41]

4

The horror story was more than a misadventure about missiles to Iran. It also tested the relationship between the CIA and the NSC staff and the internal workings of the NSC staff.

Lieutenant Colonel Oliver L. North—the "action officer" on the National Security Council staff, responsible for both the Iran and contra affairs

Retired Air Force General Richard V. Secord—North's chief associate in the Iran and contra affairs

Albert Hakim—Secord's financial partner, the unlikely negotiator with Iranian representatives of a 9-point agreement

National Security Adviser Robert C. McFarlane—with his successor, Admiral John M. Poindexter, and President Ronald Reagan, as McFarlane publicly announced his resignation on December 4, 1985

CIA Director William Casey—as he arrived to testify before the House Intelligence Committee on November 21, 1986, near the climax of the Iran-contra affairs

Attorney General Edwin Meese III—who stumbled into the contradictions in the official story prepared for congressional committees and disclosed the secret of the "diversion" out of fear of possible presidential impeachment

Elliott Abrams—Assistant Secretary of State for Inter-American Affairs, who negotiated a contribution from the Sultan of Brunei of $10 million, which was never received as a result of two wrong bank-account numbers

Carl R. (Spitz) Channell—the contras' champion fund-raiser, who specialized in getting rich old ladies to part with their money

Retired Major General John K. Singlaub— the contras' free- lance money-raiser and arms supplier

Michael A. Ledeen—in 1985, the part-time consultant to National Security Adviser McFarlane and the only American who never lost his faith in Manucher Ghorbanifar

Manucher Ghorbanifar—the Iranian go-between who more than anyone else kept the Americans embroiled in the Iran affair

Adnan Khashoggi—the Saudi entrepreneur (with his wife, Lamia), Ghorbanifar's banker, who was in on the original conception of arms-for-hostages deals

By chance, the head of the staff, McFarlane, was in either Geneva or Brussels during the entire fiasco. He seems to have done little more than to set North going by telling him to help Israeli Defense Minister Rabin and by making a fruitless telephone call to the Portuguese foreign minister. There is no evidence that North consulted McFarlane on anything more or that the latter was aware of what was taking place in Washington. In any case, McFarlane was coming to the end of his tether and soon after his return he resigned on November 30, 1985; it was announced on December 4, 1985, from which date Poindexter actually functioned as national security adviser.[42]

The reversal of roles between the CIA and NSC staff especially suited one of North's abilities and temperament. He was clearly an operational rather than a policy-coordinating type. When he threw himself into anything, he recognized no limit on the means for getting what he wanted. Compartmentation, the no-questions-asked code, the mystique of a personal visit or telephone call from someone in the White House, the CIA's acceptance of a "you call/we haul mode," all worked in favor of North's ascendancy. Only the sternest and strictest supervision could have held him in leash. With McFarlane missing and Poindexter not yet officially in charge, supervision was lacking.

In these days of the horror story, North was frenetic. His notebooks show that he was dealing with Schwimmer in Tel Aviv, planning delivery of the missiles, managing Secord, working with Clarridge, carrying on for the contras, and doing all sorts of other chores.[43] He worked days and nights without respite, driving himself to the breaking point. In McFarlane's absence, he reported to Poindexter methodically to show that he was on top of the situation.

On November 20, he sent Poindexter a message giving all the details of the proposed arms-for-hostages exchange, recommending a medal for Secord "for his extraordinary short notice efforts," commenting that "it isn't that bad a deal," and expecting the hostages to be out in a matter of three or four days.[44] On November 21, North again had good news— Secord had heard that the Portuguese prime minister had approved the transaction in Lisbon for November 22 and the foreign minister was "aware and supportive"—none of which was true.[45] On November 22, North told Poindexter about Clarridge's arrangement for a proprietary plane to work for Secord, though Secord did not know it was a proprietary. With his usual enthusiastic belief that everything was in good hands, North praised his collaborators: "Clarridge deserves a medal—so does Copp [Secord]." Later that same day, North added that Kimche had been told "how screwed up his people are in planning something like this on such short notice" and that "we have now taken charge of that phase of the operation." Only later that evening had North expressed alarm that he had never seen "anything so screwed up in my life" and that it was "one hell of an operation."[46] From then on, it was all downhill.

There do not seem to be any more reports from North to Poindexter between November 23 and November 25, when the first missiles were delivered and the entire operation fell through. There are no messages of instruction or advice in this period from Poindexter to North. North appears to have been very much on his own, desperately improvising and clutching at straws. North put all the blame for the fiasco on the Israelis, and the whole incident might have passed as but another disappointment if McMahon had not caught the absence of a Finding. But North was apparently not criticized for having made use of the proprietary without a Finding and went on to ever greater domination of the Iran affair.

5

Superficially, the problem of the Finding appeared to be no more than a slight embarrassment. It went back to the Intelligence Oversight Act of 1980, which obligated the president to "find" that a covert operation by the CIA was important to the national security of the United States and to report it "in a timely fashion" to the appropriate committees of Congress. It was understood that a Finding had to come before, not after, the operation in question and that it had to derive from the president himself. When McMahon demanded a Finding for the use of the CIA proprietary aircraft, all that seemed necessary was to produce one.

Yet the scramble for such a Finding had such embarrassing consequences that they came to be more important than the flaw which the Finding was supposed to correct. The Finding led to one contretemps after another and haunted the Reagan administration to the bitter end of the Iran affair.

For one thing, Findings were supposed to be anticipatory, not retroactive. One way to get around this awkward requirement was to pretend that President Reagan had made a "mental Finding" that had covered the proprietary but that he had somehow neglected to put it in writing. There is a mysterious notation by North on November 21, 1985, at an early stage of the effort to get the missiles to Iran, which reads:

RR [Ronald Reagan] said he w[oul]d support "mental finding."[47]

It would appear from this that North knew or was told that President Reagan had been informed of the Israeli transport of missiles and had "mentally" covered it with a Finding or that the question of a Finding had been raised in some quarters and that it had been answered by a reference to a possible later "mental finding" by the president. North's note gives no clue to the origin of this citation. In any case, the pretense of a "mental finding" was tentatively advanced by Attorney General Meese a year later but was not taken seriously.

What did happen after McMahon had taken his stand was that Juchniewicz, on McMahon's demand, sent two aides to brief CIA General Counsel Sporkin.[48] McMahon met Sporkin soon afterward and the following discussion ensued:

"You need a Finding [Sporkin said], but not necessarily for the eyes of the proprietary." I [McMahon] said, "What are you talking about?" He said, "Well, for the influence that our overseas personnel had." I said, "You mean like getting landing rights and things like that?" And he said, "Yes." I said, "Okay, then prepare a Finding, and I want it made retroactive." He said that he was going down and talk to the White House Counsel and Justice. And I said, "Great," and he walked away.[49]

In this version by McMahon, Sporkin's support for a Finding came not from the use of the proprietary but from the activity of the CIA's station in Lisbon in trying to get landing rights "and things like that" from the Portuguese government. McMahon had started the Finding going for one reason and Sporkin had sped it on for another. Sporkin himself recalled that he had considered a Finding to be "prudential" and not required necessarily.[50] In that event, the complications that followed were even more unlucky. On another occasion, however, Sporkin said that he had decided a Finding was needed because, according to the law, the CIA could not expend funds on activity other than the collection of intelligence without a Finding.

Sporkin came through with a draft of the Finding in a hurry. It was sent to Casey on November 26, only about twenty-four hours after McMahon had given Sporkin the task.

This draft raises troublesome questions about the comportment of General Counsel Sporkin. The function of a general counsel is not merely to do what he is told to do; it is essentially to determine the legality of what is proposed and to guard against whatever is illegal or illegitimate. General counsels are not supposed to be legal rubber stamps. This draft posed such problems of legal propriety and later led to such a questionable action by National Security Adviser Poindexter that it is worth giving in full.

Finding Pursuant to Section 662 of The Foreign Assistance Act of 1961. As Amended, Concerning Operations Undertaken by the Central Intelligence Agency in Foreign Countries, Other Than Those Intended Solely for the Purpose of Intelligence Collection.

I have been briefed on the efforts being made by private parties to obtain the release of Americans held hostage in the Middle East, and hereby find that the following operations in foreign countries (including all support necessary to such operations) are important to the national security of the United States. Because of the extreme sensitivity of these operations, in the exercise of the President's constitutional authorities, I direct the Director of Central Intelligence not to brief the Congress of the United States, as provided for in Section 501 of the National Security Act of 1947, as amended, until such time as I may direct otherwise.

SCOPE	DESCRIPTION
Hostage Rescue— Middle East	The provision of assistance by the Central Intelligence Agency to private parties in their attempt to obtain the release of Americans held hostage in the Middle East. Such assistance is to include the provision of transportation, communications, and other necessary support. As part of these efforts certain foreign materiel and munitions may be provided to the Government of Iran which is taking steps to facilitate the release of the American hostages.
	All prior actions taken by U.S. Government officials in furtherance of this effort are hereby ratified.[51]

This draft of the Finding by Sporkin raises some awkward questions. It was entirely addressed to the role of the CIA, which was admittedly not in charge of the Iran operation but had seen itself as playing a role subordinate to the NSC staff. McMahon had merely wanted to get a Finding to cover the specific actions taken by the CIA for the transport of missiles to Iran on November 25. Sporkin produced a Finding of far greater scope and general applicability to the release of the American hostages.

Even more questionably, Sporkin committed the president to postpone reporting the Finding to Congress for as long as he might please and not "in a timely fashion," as the law required. In the event, the final version of the Finding was not reported for almost a year, which could hardly be said to have been "in a timely fashion."

A third anomaly was the retroactive nature of this draft. There is some question whether a retroactive provision had ever been used before. Sporkin later admitted that the retroactive provision was so rare that "it might have been used one other time in my tenure," but he could not recall any.[52] Senator William S. Cohen found that the Senate Intelligence Committee had never received a single retroactive Finding.[53] Yet Poindexter considered this its main feature.[54] Sporkin was so little proud of this provision that he later said it was "probably the first and only time, and probably the last time it's ever going to be done, because if I realized this would get me my 15 minutes in the sun, I think I would have given up on that opportunity."[55] Sporkin later explained the retroactive character of the Finding on the ground that the CIA personnel needed "protection," as if he could protect them by perverting the very purpose of Findings.[56] Attorney General Meese admitted that "a finding after the fact of something having been done by the President would be of questionable legality and would certainly raise questions." A Finding, according to Meese, "would be a condition precedent to the activity going forward." Meese also said that he had known nothing about the 1985 Finding and that it had not gone through the Department of Justice.[57]

It is also noteworthy that the draft named the government of Iran as the recipient of "foreign materiel and munitions," not "moderates" or opposition elements in Iran. Indeed, North soon recognized this aspect as a matter of fact. In a message to Poindexter on December 4, he noted "the fact that any supplies delivered [to Iran] will undoubtedly have to be examined by an Army or Air Force officer."[58]

Above all, this draft showed that Sporkin had understood the real purpose of the Finding—to sanction a straight arms-for-hostages policy. Sporkin later testified that he had been told by CIA officials "about a CIA proprietary having shipped missiles."[59] The draft said nothing about any larger considerations, such as a general improvement in U.S.-Iran relations. Sporkin was not the only one to see the Finding in this light. He submitted his draft to Casey, who quickly sent it on to Poindexter on the same day, November 26, with this advice: "Pursuant to our conversation this should go to the President for his signature and should not be passed around in any hands below our level."[60] Casey saw nothing wrong in Sporkin's draft. Both Casey and McMahon wanted to have it signed without delay.

6

A strange fate awaited this draft.

Poindexter, now acting as national security adviser, put the draft before President Reagan on December 5. The president read it and signed it.[61] Like Casey, he evidently saw nothing wrong in it. As a result, it admittedly remained in effect until another Finding on the same subject was also signed by the president on January 6, 1986.[62] Poindexter then gave the December 5 Finding to his counsel and military assistant, Commander Paul Thompson, who put it in an envelope which went into his safe.

At the same meeting on December 5, Poindexter told the president of another arms-for-hostages deal in the making. His note of their meeting reads: "Hostages—1 to Tehran 22—2," which meant that one shipment of arms to Tehran on December 22 would produce two hostages.[63] This discussion at the same time as the signature on the Finding gives reason to believe that the two were interrelated and that the president and Poindexter were still considering nothing more than an arms-for-hostages deal.

It was this December 5, 1985, Finding that Poindexter tore up a year later on the ground that it was bound to be "politically embarrassing" if it ever came out publicly.* He could not have realized what a good prophet he was going to be.

Destroying a Finding was unprecedented; Poindexter himself had never done so before.[64] Poindexter's explanation tried to have it both ways—that the Finding was not "an important document" and that it would be misconstrued if it had leaked out.[65] In addition to its potential for political embarrassment, Poindexter gave two other reasons for his action: that the Finding had not been fully "staffed" and that it was merely one of three such Findings, with the last the only one that counted. By improper staffing, he meant that it had not been fully discussed by other members of the National Security Council, including the secretary of state, secretary of defense, Attorney General Meese, and CIA Director Casey.[66]

The December 5, 1985, document was as legitimate a Finding as any other; it was in force for almost six weeks before another, temporarily more satisfactory Finding took its place. If the first was an improper Finding, it should never have been submitted by Poindexter to the president, and he should not have signed it. When Poindexter was asked why he had permitted this Finding to go to the president, all he could say was that he regretted it and that he had acted "under pressure" from McMahon.[67] He did not explain why the pressure had taken so long to work on him. The Finding had been submitted to him on November 26, and he had not brought it to the president to sign until December 5; then it had been permitted to remain in effect until January 17. Moreover, its "staffing" had included Casey; the two secretaries had already expressed their opposition to the transfer of U.S. arms to Iran. The afterthoughts cannot explain why the Finding was initially acceptable to Casey, McMahon, Poindexter, and the president.

The trouble with the Finding of December 5, 1985, was that it clearly and unequivocally provided for a simple arms-for-hostages deal. When Poindexter brought it to President Reagan, he was still at the beginning of his education in the Iran affair. The more he knew, the more he regretted it.

---

* "When I destroyed that Finding, I didn't really think that it was an important document from the standpoint of the process that we had been going through. I viewed it as being superseded by the final Finding; and the reason I destroyed it was simply because if it leaked out, it would be misconstrued and present a picture that was not accurate as to the President's thinking at the time" (Poindexter, 100-8, p. 395).

11

Finding No. 2

Except for having been McFarlane's deputy for the previous two years, Poindexter was not an obvious choice for national security adviser. Nothing in his background had especially prepared him for the job. He was the product of a small farming community in Indiana, from which he had gone to the U.S. Naval Academy in Annapolis. He was an exemplary student and had graduated first in his class of about 900. In 1959, he seemed to have found his métier by obtaining a doctorate in nuclear physics at the California Institute of Technology. From 1976 to 1978, he had served as executive assistant to the chief of Naval Operations, Admiral James Holloway. His "fitness report" for promotion from captain to rear admiral by Admiral Holloway seemed to destine him for a distinguished naval career. "I know of no one of his contemporaries," Holloway wrote, "who can equal his potential to serve with effectiveness now in a wide range of flag assignments."[1]

But Poindexter did not go on to flag assignments or use his knowledge of nuclear physics. Promoted to rear admiral in 1980, he was recommended to President Reagan's first national security adviser, Richard Allen, by a retired admiral, James W. (Bud) Nance. Allen appointed him his military assistant in June 1981; McFarlane made him his deputy in October 1983. In 1984, after the usual three-year term away from the navy, he was offered command of the Sixth Fleet, no small prize. Yet, like North, he chose to stay on the NSC staff, and McFarlane recommended him to be his successor in November 1985.

Whatever Poindexter's virtues were in subordinate roles, he hardly seemed to possess the kinds of political talents expected in a national security adviser. He had "to bring before the president the policy options," as Poindexter himself understood his main task to be, and policy had never been Poindexter's strong point.[2] The adviser had to mediate in the struggles over foreign policy among the secretary of state, the secretary of defense, and others—a burden that had worn down and discouraged

McFarlane. He had to cope with the president's chief of staff, Donald Regan, who always liked to know everything that was going on and usually considered the national security adviser something of a rival for the president's attention. As we shall later see, Poindexter's most notorious decision—to withhold knowledge of the so-called diversion of funds from the president—was admittedly political; he explained that "I was essentially in a political position."[3] Nothing in his past seemed to have prepared him for such a position.

Poindexter's personality worked in his favor because it was not threatening to other high officials. He was seclusive, remote even from his own staff, closemouthed, self-effacing. He preferred to communicate, even with North, by sending written messages. He avoided the press as if it were the enemy. He described himself as "a very low-profile person. I don't feel that I need a lot of acknowledgement in order to get any sort of psychic income."[4] Regan had no objection to him, because "with his phlegmatic nature, [he] seemed unlikely to be a source of trouble or embarrassment."[5] Poindexter impressed the longtime presidential confidant Michael K. Deaver as "loyal and well balanced, a career military man who was limited by his political inexperience . . . not someone who relished power or saw covert action as a sport."[6] President Reagan was cavalier about appointments, even at the top, as Regan's own transfer from Treasury to chief of staff showed. Poindexter had no enemies, as good a recommendation in this case as having friends.

Like North, Poindexter was an indefatigable worker. The job was all-consuming, and he was willing to sacrifice himself. After arising between 5:30 and 6 a.m., he arrived at his office by 7 a.m. He met with the directors of the NSC staff at 7:30 a.m. He attended the chief of staff's daily operations meeting at 8 a.m. He met, usually for a half hour, with the president at 9:30 a.m. Only then did his working day begin, at 10 a.m. He regularly handled whatever needed his attention or attended various meetings until about 9 p.m. He ate most of his meals at his desk. On Sunday, he attended church in the morning—his wife was an ordained minister—and spent the afternoon or evening on paperwork.[7] In May 1986, his deputy, Donald Fortier, was stricken with cancer and went into the hospital, never to return. His successor was not appointed during Poindexter's term, as a result of which Poindexter took on an additional load.

The Iran and contra affairs constituted only a small part of his responsibilities. In 1986, he had many more problems to occupy him—among others, the post-Marcos regime in the Philippines, the raid on Libya, the Tokyo summit, the overthrow of the Duvalier regime in Haiti, U.S.-Soviet relations, especially the U.S.-Soviet summit at Reykjavík, Iceland, and virtually everything else that happened around the world.[8] It was a killing and often thankless job, especially for a man who worked for an indolent president and with a labyrinthine bureaucracy that he held in contempt. Again and again McFarlane and Poindexter pleaded that they had been overwhelmed by so many problems at once that they had had little time or mind left over for the Iran conundrum.

Poindexter's estrangement from the rest of the bureaucracy derived from—as he saw it—its reluctance to engage in high-risk operations. He explained his view of it in these terms:

> Now, because the cost of failure is very high, the bureaucracy is not willing to recommend, often recommend, or certainly endorse high-risk operations, because [of] their fear of failure and the resulting harangue that comes about because of failing. Therefore, they don't make those kinds of hard options available to the President. And I think one of the roles of the NSC staff has got to be to bring these options to the President, and because the bureaucracy is often not willing to push them once a decision is made, push them vigorously, I feel that in the very real world that we live in, the NSC staff has got to be the catalyst that keeps the process moving forward, keeps the President's decisions moving along, and helps to make sure that they are implemented, and that often involves an operational role for the NSC staff. Their only loyalty is to the President.[9]

The NSC staff, as Poindexter often put it, was the president's "personal staff."[10] In addition, Poindexter believed that the president totally controlled American foreign policy, and even that Congress should not use its power over appropriations to restrict the president on foreign policy.[11] In effect, Poindexter regarded himself as the head of an American version of a Roman praetorian guard around the president, loyal and responsible to him alone, embattled against Congress and the bureaucracy, invested with the authority to make the "hard decisions" and to see them through. He was a strict devotee of compartmentation and secrecy: "My philosophy was the way you keep a secret is you don't tell anybody."[12] He was especially determined to practice his philosophy at the expense of Congress: "I didn't want Congress to know the details of how we were implementing the president's policy"—not the nation's policy but only the president's policy or the policy made for the nation by the president alone, without checks and balances.[13] He was willing to admit that he deliberately withheld information from Congress and that it could be regarded as telling Congress an "untruth."[14]

Poindexter was not the only one to espouse this credo. Oliver North also asserted that the NSC staff was the president's personal staff, to do with as he pleased.[15] North boasted that he had lied to both Congress and the CIA.[16] His expression of fealty to the president resembled that of a vassal in a feudal age:

This lieutenant colonel is not going to challenge a decision of the Commander in Chief for whom I still work, and I am proud to work for that Commander in Chief, and if the Commander in Chief tells this lieutenant colonel to go stand in the corner and sit on his head, I will do so. And if the Commander in Chief decides to dismiss me from the NSC staff, this lieutenant colonel will proudly salute and say "thank you for the opportunity to have served," and go, and I am not going to criticize his decision no matter how he relieves me, sir.[17]

North also evoked the Roman example by saying: "Every centurion had a group of shields out in front of him, a hundred of 'em," and he alluded to himself as the person "to take the spear."[18]

The fidelity of Poindexter and North to what they considered to be the president's commands was thus based on a curious amalgam of extremist ideas about the nature of the American political system and the place of the presidency and Congress in it. Their risk taking and self-righteousness were not merely personal aberrations. They were not ordinary officeholders or bureaucrats, and they gloried in their deviation from the norm. They were, in their own eyes, a breed apart.

2

The Finding of December 5, 1985, revealed that Poindexter's contempt for the bureaucracy extended even to the CIA. He blamed McMahon for having "pestered" him to get it signed and called it a CYA (cover your ass) act on the part of the CIA.[19]

Poindexter had not caught the allegedly fatal defect in the Finding when he had first presented it to the president for his signature. But events soon made him alert to other factors in the Iran affair that put the Finding in a different light.

During McFarlane's tenure, Poindexter had not been responsible for either the Nicaraguan contra activity or the Iran operation and had only a general knowledge of them when he took over from McFarlane.[20] His inadequacy made North more important than ever in both fields. In August 1985, Poindexter had already given North extraordinary access to himself. The messages to him from other members of the staff were required to go through the executive secretary. North was given the privilege of communicating with him directly by using the code word "Blank Check."[21] It was an apt characterization of their relationship.

North was a glutton for responsibilities. He worked even more ceaselessly and feverishly than Poindexter, sometimes getting no more than two or three hours of sleep a night. The Iran affair presented him with another world to conquer. He plunged into the turmoil of the most

perplexing country in the Middle East, for which he had as little preparation as Poindexter, with his usual enthusiasm and optimism. Poindexter admittedly gave him little supervision or, as Poindexter put it, he
gave North "a very broad charter."[22] Poindexter flattered himself that
"micromanagement" was not his style.[23] By giving North almost total
custody of both the Iran and contra operations, Poindexter violated a
cardinal rule of covert activities—not to mix them. North had already
mixed them by calling on Secord to help get the Hawk missiles from
Israel to Iran in November 1985. Once started on this course, North was
not one to stop.

North was also a quick study. On December 4, the day that Poindexter's
succession as national security adviser was announced, North sent him
an extraordinarily long and detailed analysis of the entire Iran affair to
date. The horror story had concluded only a few days earlier, and North
was already poised to instruct Poindexter on what had happened and what
needed to be done. This communication marked North's emergence as
Poindexter's mentor in the Iran affair.

North was able to report on discussions in Geneva that had taken place
that same day between Kimche, Secord, Ghorbanifar, and Karoubi, the
latter making his last appearance in this story. North referred familiarly
to "Gorba." North blamed Schwimmer and Ledeen for their unfamiliarity
with the range of the Hawk missiles as the reason for the Iranians' disappointment and distrust. Ghorbanifar had explained that a different kind
of missile was needed to stop regular Soviet reconnaissance flights along
the Iranian-Soviet and Iranian-Iraqi borders. Kimche had expressed the
fear that "the credibility of the Gorba/[Iranian] mission had probably
seriously been called into question." Ghorbanifar had charged that "this
whole thing was a 'cheating game' on the part of the Israelis."

But all was not lost. Secord and Kimche had thought of a way to renew
the dialogue in order to achieve three objectives:

—support for a pragmatic-army oriented faction which could take
 over in a change of government
—return of the AMCIT [American citizen] hostages
—no more terrorism directed against U.S. personnel or interests

For the rest, North showed an appreciation for Iranian grievances,
which put it up to the United States to appease their distrust. "In short,
they have been 'scammed' so many times in the past that the attitude of
distrust is very high on their part." But Secord and Kimche had decided
that the Iranian military situation was "desperate" and the Iranians desperately wished to conclude "some kind of arrangement in the next 10
days."

North went on to interpret Israeli policy for Poindexter. North had
had discussions with Kimche and Major General Menachem Meron,

director general of the Israeli Ministry of Defense, which he thought had given him an insight into Israeli thinking. Israel aimed at encouraging the Iran-Iraq war to continue as a stalemate, to obtain a more moderate Iranian government in the end, and to get Jews out of Iran. North saw the first two goals as "generally congruent with our interests," and the return of the hostages as only "a subsidiary benefit." He seemed to ignore that the stated U.S. policy was to be neutral in the Iran-Iraq war and to try to bring it to an end without a victor, not to encourage both sides to drag it on to a stalemate.

North let on where he was getting all this by mentioning that Kimche, Meron, Secord, and he all agreed that while "there is a high degree of risk in pursuing the course we have started, we are now so far down the road that stopping could have even more serious repercussions." This reasoning became North's refrain in justifying striking more deals, in opposition to the Shultz-Weinberger desire to call a halt. North himself had not yet had direct contact with Iranians, but he had learned enough to instruct Poindexter that "none of us have any illusions about the cast of characters on the other side." They were "a primitive, unsophisticated group who are extraordinarily distrustful of the West in general and the Israelis/U.S. in particular." Ghorbanifar was particularly ignorant of how the American system worked. To overcome the Iranians' distrust and lack of political sophistication, North urged that the next step had to be "confidence building" on both sides. He saw indications that the Iranians were already making such efforts and implied that the United States should do the same.

These ruminations, North said, were merely a "lengthy preamble" to an immediate plan that had allegedly been worked out by the Israelis and Iranians in the past two weeks. This plan turned out to be nothing other than an arms-for-hostages deal, but of a somewhat different kind. North recognized that the United States had always demanded the freedom of the hostages as a precondition for any negotiation or agreement with Iran. He now proposed to waive this condition on the ground that "mutual distrust" made it impracticable and that a different approach was necessary.

The new approach substituted a sequential or phased release of the hostages in return for successive deliveries of arms. North gave the formula as follows:

—The total "package" from the Israelis w[oul]d consist of 50 I [improved] HAWKs w[ith]/PIP (product improvement package) and 3300 basic TOWs.
—Deliveries wd commence on or about 12 December as follows:
   H − hr: 1 707 w/300 TOWs = 1 AMCIT
   H + 10s: 1 707 (same A/C [aircraft]) w/300 TOWs = 1 AMCIT
   H + 16hrs: 1 747 w/50 HAWKs & 400 TOWs = 2 AMCITs

H + 20 hrs: 1 707 w/300 TOWs = 1 AMCIT
H + 24hrs: 1 747 w/2000 TOWs = French Hostage

This schedule had Israel delivering 300 TOWs in return for the release of one American hostage; then 300 more TOWs for one more hostage; 50 Hawks and 400 TOWs for two hostages; 300 TOWs for a fifth hostage; and, finally, 2,000 TOWs for a French hostage—all deliveries to be staggered in a single day. The date set for this transaction was on or about December 12, only eight days away.

North assured Poindexter that precautions were being taken to avoid a repetition of the fiasco in November. The first hostage was to be released before the aircraft crossed into Iranian airspace. The Israelis were supposed to give up so many TOWs that they were to be quickly replaced by the United States. Kimche, Secord, Schwimmer, and North planned to meet in London on December 6 to review the arrangements. Secord and Kimche would get together with Ghorbanifar in another London hotel "to finalize the plan." Kimche and Secord were to meet with the Iranians on December 9 to tell them that the United States had agreed to it. Secord was put in charge of the flight arrangements and was able to stop them if the Iranians did not abide by the scheduled release of hostages. Detailed plans were also made for the pickup of the hostages and their debriefing in Wiesbaden, West Germany.

North concluded with another intimidating warning that some or all of the hostages were likely to be condemned to death and another wave of Islamic holy-war terrorism unleashed if "we do not at least make one more try at this point." Like Poindexter and McFarlane, he found "the idea of bartering the lives of these poor men repugnant." But there was nothing else to do.[24]

This extended document has been cited at length because it was North's first major bid for assuming personal command of U.S.-Iran policy and because it contained the germs of what became U.S. policy. It was a peculiar mixture of theory and practice, with the primary theoretical aim of a new U.S.-Iran relationship put off until the secondary practical objective of freeing the hostages was fulfilled. It showed that North had no inhibitions about flying in the face of established policy. He used the plight of the hostages as a club to get what he wanted, making his superiors feel guilty if they did not give in to him. Above all, he stood out from others by the shock methods he was willing to use on colleagues and by his willingness to take on the most daunting responsibilities.

North followed up this lengthy message the very next day, December 5, with another. Entitled "Special Project Re Iran," it went over the same ground, stressing that the Iranians were anxious to make another deal owing to their military desperation and that time was running out for the hostages. North now paid particular attention to the arguments he foresaw might be raised against an immediate delivery of 3,300 TOW missiles and 50 Hawk missiles from Israel in exchange for six hostages, five of them American. He recognized that it was contrary to U.S. stated policy to make concessions to terrorists or those who sponsor them, that the arrangement might be a "double-cross," that it was repugnant to barter lives of innocent human beings, and that the Israelis would require very prompt replenishment of their diminishing stocks. At the same time, he brandished the fear of condemning the hostages to death and the risk "of abandoning both the longer term goals and the likelihood of reprisals against us for 'leading them on.' "

In the previous message of December 4, North had mentioned that Poindexter had suggested sending McFarlane to meet with the Iranians "in an effort to obtain release of the hostages before starting on an effort to undo the present regime in Tehran." In the message of December 5, North suggested that McFarlane's mission might change and, if the hostages were released according to his immediate plan, McFarlane "would then step in to supervise achieving the longer range goals."[25]

North was not the mastermind of these ideas and plans. They had mainly come from Ghorbanifar, on the occasion of his meeting with Secord in Paris on December 1.

The follow-up meeting in London did not take place on December 6, because a different and more important meeting in the White House was called for December 7. It was considered necessary because McFarlane, at the time of submitting his resignation to the president in California, had given him a discouraging report of past dealings with Iran. The president's reaction was: "Fine. When we get back to Washington, let's have a meeting of the guys."[26] The "guys" were the statutory members of the National Security Council. The meeting happened to come on the day before North had planned to leave for London to review his plans with Ghorbanifar and the Israelis, and North waited for its outcome.

Another reason for the meeting was given by Richard L. Armitage, the assistant secretary of defense for international security affairs. Armitage says that he began to hear rumors toward the end of November about discussions going on with Iran about which the Defense Department had been kept in the dark. Told to find out what was going on, he decided that North was most likely to know and invited him for a lunch on December 3. North confirmed that such meetings had taken place, whereupon Armitage gave him some homely advice:

> As best I remember, I told him that I knew my boss [Secretary Weinberger], I felt my boss, didn't know anything about it. I didn't think the Secretary of State knew anything about it. I thought he was way out of line. I think I used the term that his ass was way out on a limb and that he ought to get everyone together quickly to discuss this problem.

Armitage also told North that he needed to get the "elephants" together as soon as possible, the term he used for the principal advisers, such as the secretary of state, the secretary of defense, and the national security adviser. North seemed to be shocked by Armitage's statement.

Armitage went back and reported the conversation to Secretary Weinberger. The news was so disconcerting to Armitage that he decided to "strategize," as he put it, with Arnold Raphel, the principal deputy assistant secretary for the Near East and South Asia in the State Department. They agreed to work on Shultz and Weinberger to get the two secretaries to form a "united front" on the issue and confront the president with roughly the same arguments. Armitage also met with Weinberger and went over the "down sides" of the Iran issue with him, including why arms sales were barred by the Arms Export Control Act.[27]

In this peculiar way, two assistant secretaries conspired against the Iran arms deal, secure in the knowledge that their superiors were of the same mind.

Poindexter knew what was in Shultz's mind two days before the high-level meeting. Shultz says that Poindexter called him on December 5 and gave him a lengthy account of plans to make more arms sales to Iran—more information than Shultz had ever received from McFarlane. "Well, I told him," Shultz recalled, "that I thought it was a very bad idea, that I was opposed to it. That doesn't mean I was . . . not in favor of doing things that had any potential for rearranging the behavior of Iran and our relationship with Iran, but I was very much opposed to arms sales in connection with Iran."[28] At the same time, Shultz complained that the State Department had been cut out of cable traffic relating to the hostages. Despite the complaint, the traffic did not come to the department.[29] In effect, the State Department was permitted to know only as much as Poindexter decided that he wanted to tell it.

Another thing of future interest may have happened before the meeting. On December 6, North met with Israeli officials, whom he allegedly told that the United States wanted to use profits from expected arms sales to Iran to pay for U.S. activity in Nicaragua. One Israeli official later made handwritten notes of this meeting, on December 12; two others did not take notes and did not remember whether North had made such a remark.[30] North himself professed to have no recollection of the incident.[31]

3

The meeting on December 7, 1985, was the first time the highest-level policymakers in the government had come together to discuss a concrete policy for the Iran problem. The meeting took place in the president's family quarters in the White House; the discussion is described as unusually "free-wheeling." Present were President Reagan, Secretary of

State Shultz, Secretary of Defense Weinberger, Deputy Director McMahon of the CIA (in the absence of Director Casey), Chief of Staff Regan, McFarlane (who was still nominally the national security adviser until January 4, 1986), and Poindexter.

It is impossible to put together an altogether faithful account of this critical meeting, because again no record was kept. The best that can be done in this and similar cases is to search out what each participant says he said or says others said. At the risk of taxing the reader's patience, this is the only way to judge the nature of the evidence at a critical juncture.

The meeting opened with a report by McFarlane. He was more opposed to dealing with Ghorbanifar than to dealing directly with Iranian officials. "I said essentially," he recalled, "that I believed that the intermediary was unreliable and that we should not do business with him. That if ultimately we could get in contact directly with officials in Tehran that that might offer some hope. But I recommended against continuing to deal with Mr. Ghorbanifar."[32]

Thereafter, the discussion was dominated by Shultz and Weinberger, who came armed for combat.

Shultz made a strong attack on deals with "terrorists" to rescue the hostages. He had prepared "talking points," which show that he warned presciently that "the whole story will come out someday and we will pay the price." He doubted that influence in Iran could be bought. He was worried about moderate Arab and allied reactions. He came out for putting "this operation aside" and reconsidering "where we are going with Iran."[33]

Weinberger was equally or even more strongly emphatic in his opposition to any deal making. Before Weinberger spoke up, a peculiar exchange seems to have taken place between him and the president. According to Shultz, Weinberger started off by saying something to the effect: "Are you really interested in my opinion?" Only after the president had said "Yes" did Weinberger continue.[34] The implication was that the president already knew of Weinberger's opposition and that Weinberger was not sure that the president wanted to hear it again.

Weinberger says that the specific subject at the meeting was another arms deal—"to transfer some weapons to the Iranians and why this would produce a good result." Weinberger made many of the same points as Shultz, including another prescient one that "we would be subject to blackmail, so to speak, by people who did know it in Iran and elsewhere." Weinberger made a special point of criticizing the legal basis of any arms deals—it undermined the arms embargo against Iran, and for U.S. arms to be reexported to Iran by any other country was a violation of the Arms Export Control Act.[35]

Regan first told two different stories about his role. In one, he said that he, together with the CIA and the NSC, had favored "keeping the channel open, if necessary selling a modest amount of arms" in order to make contact with Iran and influence the release of the hostages. He thought that this was probably the president's view.[36] In another, he first said that he had taken the position that after five or six months of effort, "we weren't getting anywhere," and it was time to "cut your losses and get out of it."[37] Under questioning, Regan explained the contradiction by saying that President Reagan and Secretary Shultz had told him that the second version was the true one.[38]

McMahon recalls that he spoke up to dispute the premises which had been stated by Kimche. McMahon said that he was unaware of any moderates in Iran; most of them had already been slaughtered by Khomeini; arms to the so-called moderates would end up supporting the Khomeini regime and be used against Iraq.*[39]

Poindexter says that "I had very little comment." Another version is that he had supported going ahead in a sentence or two.[40] It seems that Poindexter preferred to keep his views to himself until he knew where the presidential winds were blowing.

McFarlane gives the impression that he agreed with the "consensus" at the meeting—that "our attitude should be one of openness to purely political discourse, but that we should not agree to sell weapons or to encourage others, like Israel, to do so."[41]

Casey, in absentia, supported another deal with Iran. Poindexter says that he had been told by Casey before the meeting that the CIA chief supported such a proposal and had even given Poindexter his "proxy" to say as much to the president.[42]

It is clear that the opposition to any further arms deals with Iran, directly or indirectly, was predominant, especially from the two senior cabinet members, who otherwise were not known to agree very often. Secretary Weinberger was so confident that the idea had been squelched that he went back to the Department of Defense and told his military assistant, General Colin Powell: "I believe this baby had been strangled in its cradle, that it was finished." Weinberger also commented that "my strong impression was at the end of this meeting that the conclusion had been reached that we couldn't do this."†[43]

Shultz is less sure that the baby had been strangled. He says only that he felt "we had made a real dent" and "perhaps we had won the argu-

---

* The range of different views of what McMahon said is typical of what one faces in reconstructing this entire affair. Poindexter said that McMahon merely "commented a little bit about some of the technical aspects of the initiative" (100-8, p. 25). Shultz said that McMahon seemed to be "rather passive" (100-9, p. 31). Regan said that McMahon had stirred up the meeting by asking, in effect: "What the hell are we doing here? Arms are being sent. Where is the formal authority? You know, what are we doing here? Is this going to be policy?" (TR, p. B-45). McMahon gave much the same version of his intervention in TR, p. B-45, as in his B-17.

† This was also the impression in the State Department. Under Secretary of State Michael H. Armacost reported to Shultz after the meeting: "Bud's [McFarlane's] recommendation upon returning from his latest discussions was to drop the enterprise. That has now been agreed. But the President wants other possible avenues for securing the release of the hostages to be energetically pursued" (100-9, p. 526).

ment." But the president did not seem to be pleased. "The president, I felt," Shultz also noted, "was somewhat on the fence but rather annoyed at me and Secretary Weinberger, because I felt that he sort of—he was very concerned about the hostages, as well as very much interested in the Iran initiative." Shultz "could feel his sense of frustration."[44]

Weinberger evidently thought that he had won the president over. But Shultz quotes an exchange between Weinberger and Reagan that suggests something else. When Weinberger said: "There are legal problems here, Mr. President, in addition to all of the policy problems," Reagan replied: "Well, the American people will never forgive me if I fail to get those hostages out over this legal question." Shultz then adds: "And Secretary Weinberger—'but,' he said, 'visiting hours are Thursday,' or some such statement."[45]

The reply to Weinberger implies that, for Reagan, sending arms to Iran was primarily bound up with rescuing the hostages. They evidently weighed so heavily on the president's mind that he was willing to bend or somehow get around the legal obstacles raised by Weinberger. Regan also suggests that the president was troubled by the tenor of the discussion—"he was disappointed that there was no success," and "I know that he still wanted something."[46]

McFarlane gave more than one version of how the meeting went. In the first one, he said:

> And it was unanimous in the meeting that this really had gone badly off course and that we should say yes, still be open to talking to Iranian officials, authorities, and have a concrete political agenda to describe. . . . But because of how things had gone up until then we ought to also tell them that we were not going to allow or encourage anybody else to do so. And I don't recall anybody disagreeing with that at all.
>
> The President wasn't terribly—didn't terribly intervene in the meeting, as I recall, very much on one side or the other, but at the end said well, okay. That's what you should say. And I left that evening and was in London the next morning, and we took off from there.[47]

In another, McFarlane gave a somewhat different version of the president's attitude. He said that Reagan had first repeated a view that he had expressed earlier "about distinguishing between Iranians of genuine opposition to terrorism and Khomeini, and his [Reagan's] willingness to try to identify and establish dialogue with those who were truly opposed to terrorism, and that strengthening them to include with arms [sic] was a legitimate thing to do." This line of thought suggests that Reagan had been led to believe that there was a serious moderate opposition to the Khomeini regime and that it could be strengthened by giving it arms.

Though McFarlane could not be definite about it, he also thought that the president had possibly repeated something that he had more than once said before—that "he was willing to take the heat for making a decision to try to save the hostages."[48]

It was typical of these meetings that there were several different versions of what came out of it—if anything did come out of it. Weinberger thought that the arms deal in any form had been strangled. Shultz was not so sure. McFarlane thought that the president had gone along with the consensus against arms sales, though the president "was not pleased by it."[49] McMahon believed that the president had been "countering" Shultz and Weinberger and that "the whole thrust of the president's pitch was that we ought to pursue a policy of trying to win the Iranians back," without making a definite decision.[50] Regan sensed that the president probably agreed with him in favor of some more arms sales.

Only much later, in his autobiography, did President Reagan reveal that he had felt "inside" that the initiative with Iran should go on. Again his main concern was with the hostages—"I felt a heavy weight on my shoulders to get the hostages home." Outwardly, however, he did not fully show his hand at the meeting on December 7. In his mind, as he put it in his diary that day, the weapons were to go to the "moderate leadership in the army"—as if he knew that there was such a leadership in the army as well as "disenchanted members of Iran's government."[51] Peculiar things happened on the way from Ghorbanifar to the Israelis, the Israelis to McFarlane, and McFarlane to Reagan.

The meeting on December 7, which should have set the Iran policy of the United States on a definite course, was inconclusive. It left the participants guessing about what was in the president's mind, with the president himself squirming between the uncompromising views of his two senior cabinet members and his own inclination to make some kind of deal with Iran.

4

President Reagan's way out of making an immediate decision took the form of going along with the idea, first broached by Poindexter to North, of sending McFarlane to London to "check out this Israeli channel," meaning Ghorbanifar.[52] The idea was to bring back an independent assessment of what the "Iranians" wanted.

The Americans who came to the London meeting were McFarlane, North, and Secord; the Israelis were Kimche, Schwimmer, and Nimrodi; the "Iranians" were Ghorbanifar. On December 8, the meeting took place in Nimrodi's town house near Hyde Park.

Secord had arrived first and had gone over the ground with Ghorbanifar and Nimrodi, who on this occasion talked a great deal. Secord found that they "wanted to keep the game going, they wanted to continue in their dealings with Iran and they were seeking ways in which they could continue." The ways invariably turned out to concern U.S. high-technology military systems, including Harpoon and Phoenix missiles, which Israel itself did not have, as well as TOWs, which Israel did have. Secord says that he advised them to forget about the Harpoon and Phoenix, because the United States was unlikely to transfer them to any other country, but that they continued to bring them up in later meetings.[53]

On the morning of December 8, McFarlane first met with Kimche alone and found that they were not in agreement.[*] When McFarlane told him that his instructions barred further arms shipments to Iran and required immediate release of all the hostages, Kimche expressed disappointment. According to McFarlane, the conversation was rather acrimonious.

> [Kimche] was upset and he said: I think you're missing a big opportunity; that you have to have some patience; that these movements take time to consolidate; and these people are delivering to us important items, information basically; and that we see signs from our intelligence that they're making headway and beginning to lock up and arrest radical elements and put their own people in more responsible positions, and the gradual evidence of their growing influence and ability to act.
>
> And I said: Well, we don't see that; and further, we think it is being skewed off in the wrong direction. So he said: Well, we disagree.[†][54]

One gathers from this account that the Israelis were unduly optimistic about what they were getting from Ghorbanifar and such Iranians as Karoubi, whom Ghorbanifar had introduced to the Israelis. A breach was opening between the Israelis and the Americans on how far to go with the Iranians, with McFarlane determined to stick to his instructions. The main confrontation between McFarlane and Ghorbanifar took

---

[*] This meeting at the Hilton Hotel was "bugged" by MI5, the British intelligence service, according to Geoffrey Smith in his book, *Reagan and Thatcher* (The Bodley Head, 1990). As a result, the British learned "that something very strange had been happening." Two high British officials, Sir Antony Acland, permanent under-secretary of state at the Foreign Office, and Sir Percy Cradock, the prime minister's special adviser on foreign affairs, made a trip to Washington to ask Poindexter what was going on between the United States and Iran. Poindexter's answers were "opaque." It seems that senior officials at the U.S. embassy in London were also asked for information and professed ignorance.

[†] In a second interview, McFarlane said that he had told Kimche "if they are open to dialogue, we are too, and if not so be it, but under no circumstances are we prepared to sell arms nor to allow anybody else to either" (TR, p. B-46). In his congressional testimony, McFarlane merely says that Kimche "expressed his concern and stated that we needed to be patient, that these things weren't concluded" (100-2, p. 56).

place in the afternoon. We have at least three accounts, from McFarlane, Ghorbanifar, and Secord.

McFarlane says that he sharply challenged Ghorbanifar by accusing the Iranian side of "bad faith." McFarlane put Ghorbanifar on the defensive by posing two sharp questions: "Is there good faith at all?" and "Is there real authority? Can you take decisions and change things?" McFarlane also flatly declared that "the President has decided that there can be no sale of U.S. weapons nor will we approve the sale by others of weapons." All the United States wanted was a "political dialogue."

Ghorbanifar, according to McFarlane, accepted the challenge in such a way that he revealed what was really at stake:

And he replied in a kind of cursory fashion, accepting that his superiors in Tehran were in fact interested in changing Iranian policy and forming a government with better relations with the West, but that I had to understand that their vulnerability was quite high and that they needed badly to maintain their own support from within the military and that the coin of that relationship and support and strength within Iran was the weapons.

McFarlane came away from the meeting with the impression that "it was very apparent that his agenda was buying weapons and his interest in our political agenda [was] very superficial."[55]

McFarlane gave another version in which the argument with Ghorbanifar came out as having been much more bitter. McFarlane now said that Ghorbanifar's insistence on an arms-for-hostages deal had "revolted" him. At one point, Ghorbanifar had angrily reminded him of the wrong Hawks in the horror story two weeks earlier and had warned McFarlane that such incidents jeopardized the continuing U.S.-Iran relationship. To this McFarlane "told him to go pound sand, that is too bad."[56]

Ghorbanifar's version indicates that he was in no mood to be lectured.

McFarlane gave a lecture that we want to know the importance, strategic point of Iran, we know the people, we know we had bitter relations before, and so on and so on, and we want a better one.

I said what are you talking about? You just left a mess behind and you want something else? I was tough. I explained, I explained to him that what is the situation inside Iran between the rival groups, between the politicians, what is this mess, what the hell a problem has brought this one, this issue has presented to this big policy. . . .

I told him what the hell is this, what is the problem, you leave a mess behind, and if you want to continue this way, I said, just is better you cut off and don't put us, the blame on us, and by the fire on your side because then there will be fire back on your interests. [57]

It appears that Ghorbanifar had been so shaken by the episode of the wrong missiles in November and had as a result lost so much face in Tehran that he did not think he had much to lose by putting up a fierce front against McFarlane's obdurate demands. McFarlane had closed the door on the only thing that really mattered to Ghorbanifar as a businessman and as an intermediary—more arms for Iran. By cutting him off at the outset from "the coin of that [U.S.-Iran] relationship," McFarlane gave him no room to maneuver. If the meeting was intended to be no more than a "political dialogue," excluding arms, Ghorbanifar was the wrong man.

Secord's account blames the meeting's disaster on Ghorbanifar's insistence on talking about arms for hostages:

The meeting went on for quite a long while, several hours and there was—it was badly seated, I may say, because they had Mr. McFarlane seated at a table smaller than this, directly across from Mr. Ghorbanifar. They were practically nose to nose throughout this entire session. And then the rest of us were seated around the room, essentially listening.

McFarlane said that he was there to listen to what had happened and listen to any proposals that they might have. Ghorbanifar ran through again the whole litany of things . . . He started with his overview, his strategy setting. As I said, it was very good. I have heard him make that address several times. He almost has like a tape [sic].

Very quickly that meeting degenerated. It degenerated into propositions of U.S. arms for U.S. hostages in Lebanon. Ghorbanifar pursued that line with Mr. McFarlane for a long time, far too long. I was glad when the meeting was over, and McFarlane was very, very unhappy with this session. [58]

On the way back to Washington, McFarlane was so unhappy that he told Secord and North that Ghorbanifar was "one of the most despicable characters I have ever met." Secord cynically commented that "I found that interesting because he [Ghorbanifar] was far from the most despicable character I have ever met." McFarlane was so unyielding that Secord thought that the Iran initiative was as good as dead. [59] Later, McFarlane was still so angry with Ghorbanifar that he referred to him as a "borderline moron." [60]

The London meeting should have helped to strangle the arms-for-Iran baby. If it did not, it was because both sides were caught in their own contradictory objectives. The Americans wanted to change the Iranian government and rescue the hostages but found themselves faced with doing business through the Israelis and Ghorbanifar, who could only make headway by trading in arms. Ghorbanifar wanted arms but could only hope to get them by dangling the reform or overthrow of the Khomeini regime and piecemeal release of the hostages.

The decision to send McFarlane to London and exclude arms from any discussion with Ghorbanifar was, in effect, a decision to end the Iran affair. The Israelis understood this and therefore kept on trying to use arms to achieve the American objectives. Secretaries Shultz and Weinberger were willing to face the consequences of their rejectionist position. The trouble was that they could not offer any practical, alternative means of exchange. President Reagan was caught in this dilemma without immediately knowing how to solve it.

5

McFarlane's intransigence in London faced North with a delicate problem. It threatened the entire program of action that he had been advocating to Poindexter. Yet McFarlane had been North's superior and protector for the past five years, the one North had been accustomed to regarding as his chieftain and authority figure.

North had been chafing in London at the way McFarlane had handled Ghorbanifar, and he went back to Washington with the alternative of submitting or fighting. North decided to fight.

On December 9, soon after returning from London, North shot off one of his lengthy messages to both McFarlane and Poindexter. It was his declaration of independence. Entitled "Next Steps," it broke decisively with McFarlane's tutelage and represented another large step in the emergence of North as the arbiter of Iran policy.

North saw that McFarlane's loathing for Ghorbanifar threatened to undermine North's program. If Ghorbanifar was out as the Iranian interlocutor, the tie with Iran, however frail, was broken and the Israeli link to him endangered. Despite his own qualms about what he had heard about Ghorbanifar from Secord and others, it became necessary for North to defend Ghorbanifar as the only way to save his own arms-for-hostages proposal.

At this point it is well to stop and compare what North said at the congressional hearings in July 1987 with what he actually wrote to McFarlane and Poindexter on December 9, 1985. The comparison illustrates the difference between documentation and testimony.

At the hearings, North described the meeting in London as follows:

> It was wide ranging, rambling, very disconnected in some respects. He [Ghorbanifar] clearly mentioned, and I recall it because

he is an effusive man, talking about the fact that there were potential openings that could be achieved, talked about terrorism as did Mr. McFarlane in the meeting.

But it was very clear that Mr. Ghorbanifar was trying to establish a price which, as you know from my records, I found to be most unpalatable for a number of weapons for a number of Americans.

North was asked whether McFarlane had not told him that he was going to recommend to the president to have nothing more to do with Ghorbanifar. North replied:

My recollection is that the outcome of that meeting was that unless we could get beyond Ghorbanifar and establish direct contact with the Iranians, that this was probably not going to work in the long run, that we were not going to achieve our objective.

And I shared that belief.[61]

What North wrote to McFarlane and Poindexter on December 9, 1985, was quite different. He first declared that the meetings with Ghorbanifar and the Israelis in London had been "inconclusive." Ghorbanifar, he said, had refused to return to Geneva to give an Iranian emissary "our message that no further deliveries would be undertaken until all the hostages were released." If such a message were passed on to the Iranian prime minister, according to Ghorbanifar, one or more hostages were sure to be executed.

Then North came to the central issue of Ghorbanifar's role:

Much of what we decide to do in the days ahead depends upon whether or not we can trust Gorbanifar [sic]. The Israelis believe him to be genuine. Gorbanifahr's earlier game plan delivered Reverend Weir. He has proposed that we "deliver something" so that we retain credibility with the regime in Tehran. He even suggested that the weapons delivered be useful only to the Army or Air Force (not the Revolutionary Guards) and that they be "technically disabled." He urged that, if improved Hawks were not feasible, to at least keep the door open by some kind of delivery between now and the end of the week. He said we must recognize that if TOWs are provided that they will probably go to the Revolutionary Guards.

If North can be believed, Ghorbanifar had made some peculiar proposals. If the weapons were "technically disabled," they were hardly calculated to retain the credibility of the regime in Tehran. If the purpose was to avoid sending TOWs because they would go to the extremist Revolutionary Guards, the implication was not to send the more technologically advanced missiles that the United States had not even entrusted to Israel. In the face of McFarlane's adamant position, Ghorbanifar had apparently begged for anything "to keep the door open." North then went on to state his own view:

Whether we trust Gorbanifahr [sic] or not, he is irrefutably the deepest penetration we have yet achieved into the current Iranian Government. There is nothing in any [deleted] which contradicts what he has told us or the Israelis over the past several months. Much of our ability to influence the course of events in achieving a more moderate Iranian Government depends on the validity of what Gorbanifahr has told us—and his credibility as one who can "deliver" on what the Iranians need. While it is possible that Gorbanifahr is doubling us or simply lining his own pockets, we have relatively little to lose in meeting his proposal, i.e., the Israelis start delivering TOWs and no hostages are recovered. On the other hand, a supply operation now could very well trigger results he claims.

North next put his finger on what the real American problem was: "Our greatest liability throughout has been lack of operational control over transactions with Gorbanifahr." Schwimmer had bungled the previous delivery. The question now was "should we take a relatively small risk by allowing (encouraging) a small Israeli-originated delivery of TOWs and hope for the best" or do nothing? According to the new Ghorbanifar-Schwimmer "game plan," the maximum risk was 1,100 TOWs from Israeli stocks to be repaid and replaced by the United States. Or Israel could deliver 400–500 TOWs "in effort to show good faith to both factions in Iran" and possibly induce Iran to deliver a hostage. The most dangerous thing, he suggested, was for the United States to do nothing and "ignite Iranian fire," with the sacrifice of the hostages "our minimum losses."

Finally, North made a proposal that no one else had yet put forward.

We could, with an appropriate covert action Finding, commence deliveries ourselves, using Secord as our conduit to control Gorbanifar and delivery operations. This proposal has considerable merit in that we will reduce our vulnerabilities in the replenishment of Israeli stocks and can provide items like the Improved Hawk (PIPII) which the Iranian Air Force wants and the Israelis do not have. Finally, Secord can arrange for third country nationals to conduct a survey of ground and air military requirements which is what Gorbanifahr has been attempting to obtain from the Israelis for nearly three months.*[62]

* North consistently spelled Ghorbanifar's name with the "h" displaced. North confirmed that he was the author of this document, entitled "Next Steps" (100-7, Part I, p. 284).

This approach was hardly consistent with North's testimony that he had shared the belief in London on December 7, 1985, or immediately thereafter that it was necessary for the United States to "go beyond" Ghorbanifar. At that time, he did not think that it was feasible as yet to do without Ghorbanifar and, despite some qualifications, he had made a circuitous appeal to go along with him. He had hinted at making direct contact with the Iranians, but only in the sense of assuming operational control over transactions with Ghorbanifar. North's new line was designed to edge out the Israelis, not Ghorbanifar.

Yet North had here made some striking advances in American policy—the substitution of U.S. for Israeli control of arms deliveries to Iran and, above all, a new covert Finding to cover the changeover. As matters stood, with Ledeen gone, North had become Ghorbanifar's most effective champion, even if he recognized that going along with Ghorbanifar was not without risk. Ghorbanifar's hold on him grew out of North's desperation to do something, anything—and his conviction that there was no one and nothing else to turn to.

The confrontation with McFarlane arose from the different approaches to Ghorbanifar. McFarlane despised and distrusted the Iranian with such passion that he was willing to do nothing if doing something meant doing it through Ghorbanifar. North was willing to do what Ghorbanifar proposed in order to avoid doing nothing. Whatever the merits of the case for each side, the break with McFarlane over what policy to follow took North into another dimension of influence and self-importance. McFarlane was now a lame duck and could safely be defied. McFarlane had not done much to hold North in check, and Poindexter was prepared to do even less.

6

McFarlane reported to President Reagan on his London mission on December 10, in the presence of Casey, Regan, Poindexter, and North.[63] He had come back with the same view as before, only more so, about Ghorbanifar's undesirability.

Weinberger thought that the December 7 meeting had strangled the Iran baby, and three days later McFarlane thought the same thing. McFarlane recalled:

I said: Whatever may be the case in Iran, this fellow is a person of no integrity and I would not do any more business with him, the Iranian Ghorbanifar. And I left the government believing that it was discontinued.

McFarlane also said that "it is conceivable some day that our original point, the political dialogue, they may come back to you on. I doubt it, but I recommend that you have nothing further to do with this person nor with these arms transfers."[64]

Casey confirmed that McFarlane had said this much but added something more:

> Other options which Bud had suggested were to let the Israelis go ahead doing what they would probably do anyway, and hope that we get some benefit.[65]

The main interest at this meeting was President Reagan's reaction. McFarlane said that he was "rather pensive" and made this comment on the president's behavior:

> [The president] was, however, of a mood that was not uncommon when he was uncomfortable with the situation, when in this case everyone else in the room seemed to be of one view and he didn't want to oppose that view. I don't recall his having been emphatic about an opposing point of view.
>
> The President was always very hopeful, optimistic and on almost every issue, and I think on this one on that day, was disappointed that he [sic] hadn't turned out so far, but always looking for the bright side or the possibility that it could be salvaged. But concretely did he say anything by way of decision? I don't believe so.[66]

McFarlane also said that the president had seized on McFarlane's suggestion to let the Israelis do it for the United States as a halfway house to avoid giving up all hope of getting back the hostages. According to McFarlane, "the President made the point, I believe, of why couldn't we continue to let Israel manage this program, and was expressing and searching for, I think understandably, ways to keep alive the hope for getting hostages back, and it is quite true that the President was profoundly concerned for the hostages."[67]

This was not only McFarlane's impression. Casey wrote a memorandum on the meeting for McMahon which probably best described the president's attitude:

> The President argued mildly for letting the operation go ahead without any commitments from us except that we should ultimately fill up the Israeli pipeline in any event, or the Congress will do it for us. He was afraid that terminating the ongoing discussions, as Bud had speculated they might, could lead to early action against the hostages. The trend of the succession of this was that it was a little disingenuous and would still bear the onus of having traded with

the captors and provide an incentive for them to do some more kidnapping, which was the main burden of the argument against going forward on the program. The President felt that any ongoing contact would be justified and any charges that might be made later could be met and justified as an effort to influence future events in Iran. I did point out that there was historical precedent for this and that was always the rationale the Israelis had given us for their providing arms to Iran.

Casey added: "As the meeting broke up, I had the idea that the President had not entirely given up encouraging the Israelis to carry on with the Iranians. I suspect he would be willing to run the risk and take the heat in the future if this will lead to springing the hostages."[*][68]

Regan's memory of the meeting also made the president unwilling to let go, primarily for the sake of getting the hostages out:

> [T]he President urged that, as a matter of fact, that we try some-thing else or abandon the whole project, because he wanted to keep it open not only for geopolitical reasons but also the fact that we weren't getting anywhere in getting more hostages out. And we were going to spend another Christmas with hostages there, and he is looking powerless and inept as President because he's unable to do anything to get the hostages out.[69]

One gathers that the president was primarily moved to hold on in the interest of "springing the hostages," that their fate threatened his presidency, and that he was mindful of "geopolitical reasons" as a vague possibility in the distant future. These purposes were intertwined in such a way that the second could not get anywhere until the first was accomplished. Yet the danger was there that the Iranians, through their Lebanese allies who actually held the hostages, might dole them out one by one and need a supply of hostages to keep the exchange for arms going. Ever since the Israelis had made the first deliveries of missiles to Iran in August–September 1985, they had served as a surrogate and shield for the United States. President Reagan now fell back on using them again to lessen his own political risk, which he recognized was considerable. He was willing to take the heat, if necessary, but not if he could help it.

---

[*] Poindexter said that this report by Casey was "a very accurate description of the President's—what I perceived of as the President's thinking at the time" (100-8, p. 337).

7

Poindexter took the hint. He was, as he put it, "pretty well convinced in my own mind that the President would want to go ahead with it, and do as much as we could, and if we were going to do that, I wanted people involved that I was, frankly, more comfortable with." He was impressed with the legal arguments of Shultz and Weinberger against arms deals and decided that it was necessary to bring Attorney General Meese into the deliberations.[70] According to North, only he and Casey were backing Poindexter's efforts to do what the president wanted—to "go ahead with it."[71] Poindexter's next moves were dictated by his desire to get different people to work with and a different legal basis for selling arms to Iran.

The old hands in the Iran affair were the Israelis Kimche, Schwimmer, and Nimrodi, and the lone American, Ledeen. The three Israelis were now eliminated and replaced by Amiram Nir. Ledeen was unceremoniously dismissed, though McFarlane had already thought of taking him out of the operation.[72]

Nir's takeover of the Israeli side of the U.S.-Israel collaboration on Iran was an innovation in Israeli covert operations. Israeli sources agree that the Mossad never had any confidence in Ghorbanifar and had stayed aloof from the early negotiations with him. Kimche, however, was an old hand from the Mossad, and both Nimrodi and Schwimmer had similar ties, official and unofficial. Nir was an interloper. The Mossad resented his sudden prominence in an operation traditionally assigned to it. "The situation was truly abnormal," two Israeli journalists write. "In other times if the Mossad said no, a proposal would be canceled. Now, after thirty years of dominating covert operations on Israel's foreign horizons, the Mossad was completely locked out from a covert project abroad."[73]

In both countries, a risky, arcane, complex operation was carried on by two young men outside, and sometimes against, the normal channels of government. Nir was Peres's man, and Peres took it upon himself to handle the Israeli operation without the Mossad and, with Kimche out, the Foreign Ministry.

The American who benefited most from Poindexter's reshuffling was North himself. The only American who had had a direct connection with the Israelis and Ghorbanifar in previous months, Ledeen, had been cast aside. North now had no competition and little supervision. He virtually had a blank check from Poindexter and moved into the bureaucratic vacuum with his usual whirlwind enthusiasm.

As for the new legal basis for selling arms to Iran, Poindexter decided that it needed a new Finding. The old one of December 5, 1985, was still in effect, though hardly anyone in the top echelon had been told about it—not Secretary Shultz or Secretary Weinberger. As a result, it was easy for Poindexter to set about replacing it with something that he thought would satisfy the legal concerns of the two secretaries. This was how the Finding of December 5, 1985, came, in his mind, to be obsolescent, not because he had suddenly realized it had not been properly staffed or did not truly represent what was in the president's mind at the time it had been signed.

North's new eminence was shown by the way Poindexter went about getting a new Finding. Poindexter gave the task to North, who had no legal or similar training for the job.* North promptly went to see the obliging CIA general counsel, Stanley Sporkin, the author of the previous Finding.[74] It was a peculiar way to go about it, because though the operation was being managed by the NSC staff the Finding was ostensibly sought for the CIA. As Sporkin himself understood what was happening, it "was an operation not mounted by the CIA. This was an operation that was mounted by, I guess, the NSC where the CIA somehow happened to be standing around when somebody needed their help."[75]

When North first saw Sporkin on December 9, 1985, the CIA's role seemed to be in some doubt. North made clear, according to Sporkin, that he preferred the CIA to stay out of the affair, and Deputy Director McMahon was even more emphatically opposed to dragging the CIA in again.[76] Actual work by Sporkin's aides on the new Finding, however, did not start until January 2, 1986, when North telephoned Sporkin to say that he wanted an "expanded Finding" and told him what to put in it.[77] In the draft drawn up in Sporkin's office, all reference to the hostages was omitted and stress was put on the broader aims of the Iran policy. Sporkin also put in two versions about notifying Congress, one for and one against, with the choice to be made by the president.[78]

Sporkin soon realized that he was taking too much on himself. By chance, Casey was playing golf in Florida, and McMahon was abroad. Sporkin delivered his draft to North, who called him to a meeting on January 3. At this, Sporkin decided to get Casey off the golf course and succeeded after three or four tries. Casey told him to go to the meeting but to keep him advised. When they met in North's office, North had reworked the Finding and had eliminated the clause about notifying Congress in favor of the nonnotification version. Finally, on January 5, North and Sporkin met with Casey at the latter's home in Washington. North handed Casey his redrafted Finding together with an explanatory memorandum, which he had written; Casey merely nodded "Okay."

There was one last change. Sporkin had noticed that North's draft, unlike the previous Finding, made no mention of the hostages. As they stood in the hall, Sporkin asked North to "tell me why we're not putting hostages in this document." North replied that they were omitted because

---

* "I asked Colonel North to work with the appropriate people at CIA and in Ed Meese's office, if not Ed Meese himself, on resolving that issue [a legal way to send arms to Iran]" (100-8, p. 128).

the secretary of state or secretary of defense did not want them in. The two engaged in a little argument:

> He [North] was presenting what I believed he thought was the Department of State's position, that they didn't want it in. I think he gave all the arguments, that it looks like a hostage for arms shipment. My argument was but that's the fact, we are going with a very—this is going to be a very sensitive Finding, this is a very important element of that Finding—there is a proposal not to disclose this—not to notify Congress and nobody wants to put in what is in my view a very important element of that and I said I think it ought to be in there.

They went back to Casey, who agreed with Sporkin that the hostages should be put in the Finding. They made changes in handwriting on the typewritten draft for submission to the president the next day.[79]

Thus was Finding No. 2 conceived. It was a collaborative effort between North and Sporkin, another odd couple. North made the final revisions and decisions except in the matter of the hostages, which was decided by Casey. By this time, the arms-for-hostages issue had become so embarrassing that it would have been eliminated from polite conversation if Poindexter and North had had their way. Sporkin and Casey knew better, and North could only tell them lamely that the Department of State was opposed to it. The difference was that the Department of State opposed the policy in fact, and North merely opposed putting it down on paper.

8

Another strange fate awaited the new Finding.

Whereas the old one had been addressed to the CIA, the new one mentioned it in only one connection—to direct the director of the CIA to refrain from reporting it to Congress until the president directed him to do so. In this respect, it was like the old one.

Its main purpose was to give a different rationale for working with "third parties" (inserted in handwriting) and "selected friendly foreign liaison services and third countries"—in order to establish a connection with "Iranian elements, groups, and individuals sympathetic to U.S. Government interests." The "third parties" were intended to cover individual agents such as Secord, and the rest was a guarded reference to Israel.

The arms-for-hostages deal outlined in the old Finding was now put third in a listing:

(1) establishing a more moderate government in Iran,
(2) obtaining from them significant intelligence not otherwise obtainable, to determine the current Iranian Government's intentions with respect to its neighbors and with respect to terrorist acts, and
(3) furthering the release of the American hostages held in Beirut and preventing additional terrorist acts by these groups.

For these purposes, approval was given to providing "moderate elements" in and out of the Iranian government "with arms, equipment and related materiel in order to enhance the credibility of these elements in their effort to achieve a more pro-U.S. government by demonstrating their ability to obtain requisite resources to defend their country against Iraq and intervention by the Soviet Union."[80]

This language made releasing the hostages a "subsidiary benefit" of a larger program to change the Iranian government through military and other support of supposedly "moderate" Iranian elements. By so doing, it sought to take the sting out of the Shultz-Weinberger accusation that the United States was wrong to engage in illegal or illegitimate arms-for-hostages deals. Sporkin took credit for putting in the clause about furthering the release of the hostages. Sporkin said that North told him that Secretary of State Shultz or the State Department was opposed to it "because they did not want this to look like a swap of arms for hostages."[81] Sporkin was evidently not sufficiently impressed by their objection.

Poindexter brought this Finding to the president for his signature on January 6, 1986. But again something went wrong. The president duly signed it, presumably after he had read it, as Poindexter said he always did. Legally, it superseded the Finding of December 5, which only now became defunct.

After the new Finding was signed, however, Poindexter again had second thoughts. When he came to explain why the Finding of January 6, 1986, had not been enough, he once more fell back on the excuse that it had not been fully staffed—that is, submitted for their views to the secretaries of state and defense and the attorney general.[82] He did not explain why, after having had a month to consider what had been wrong with the previous Finding, he should have been guilty of the same oversight a second time. Apart from that, he already knew what the secretaries of state and defense thought about providing arms to Iran. In this case, unlike the previous one, Casey had approved the Finding in advance, and the attorney general was not usually included in such foreign-policy decisions.

Poindexter gave another reason for disregarding this Finding. He said that he had not wanted the president to sign it, but that "when the President is reading something, whether it is a final or a draft, if he agrees with it, he will often sign it, and so that's why this particular version of the Finding was signed."[83]

At least this tells us that the president had agreed with the Finding of January 6, even if Poindexter did not think that he should have signed it. It does seem that Poindexter had not intended the president to sign it immediately. A memorandum, which Poindexter included with the proposed Finding, had advised the president to discuss it with Shultz, Weinberger, Casey, and Meese and to sign it "based on their input."[84]

In any case, Finding No. 2 went the way of Finding No. 1. It was signed inadvertently and never went into effect.

9

Findings came with accompanying memoranda that explained their backgrounds and purposes. The Finding of January 6, drawn up by North on behalf of Poindexter, came with a particularly revealing memorandum.

This memorandum began with the words:

> This week, Prime Minister Peres of Israel secretly dispatched his special adviser on terrorism with instructions to propose a plan by which Israel, with limited assistance from the U.S., can act to bring about a more moderate government in Iran.[85]

The entire memorandum was based on a visit to North and Poindexter on January 2 by Amiram Nir. It was Nir's first major appearance as the official Israeli go-between in the Iran affair. North's memorandum showed that Nir was the source of his sudden burst of knowledge and wisdom about how to achieve a more moderate Iranian government and free the hostages as an incidental benefit.

One paragraph in North's memorandum gave what he understood to be the Israeli raison d'être for the plan Nir brought to Washington:

> The Israeli plan is premised on the assumption that moderate elements in Iran can come to power if these factions demonstrate their credibility in defending Iran against Iraq and in deterring Soviet intervention. To achieve the strategic goal of a more moderate Iranian government, the Israelis are prepared to unilaterally commence selling military materiel to Western-oriented Iranian factions. It is their belief that by so doing they can achieve a heretofore unobtainable penetration of the Iranian governing hierarchy. The Israelis are convinced that the Iranians are so desperate for military materiel, expertise and intelligence that the provision of these resources will result in favorable long-term changes in personnel and

attitudes within the Iranian government. Further, once the exchange relationship has commenced, a dependency would be established on those who are providing the requisite resources, thus allowing the providor(s) to coercively influence near-term events. Such an outcome is consistent with our policy objectives and would present significant advantages for U.S. national interests.[86]

This grandiose perspective captured North's wishful political imagination. A unilateral Israeli delivery of limited weaponry could set in motion a process bringing about nothing less than long-term changes in the Iranian government and a dependency on the donors enabling them to "coercively influence" immediate Iranian policy. North was clearly oblivious to the inherent contradiction in this fanciful plot.

The scheme assumed that the governing hierarchy would give way peacefully to the "moderate elements" or permit those elements to penetrate the hierarchy merely because the moderates could provide needed arms to the hierarchy's armed forces. The Israelis could not ensure that the arms would go to the moderate elements; the Israelis and Americans could only hope that the armed forces would put the moderates in power because those forces were grateful for a few hundred missiles. A confrontation between the governing hierarchy and the allegedly moderate elements was far more likely to be a struggle for power and not a smooth subversion of the governing hierarchy through the provision of arms, however desperately needed in the struggle against Iraq.

The entire memorandum accompanying Finding No. 2 was bound up with this curious reasoning. Every paragraph was based on what the Israelis allegedly thought or expected the United States to do. The document showed that North was completely dependent at this time on Israeli tutelage and that he counted on the prestige of Israeli intelligence to make the Finding acceptable to both Poindexter and the president.

In fact, Nir's actual plan did not stand or fall on the larger by-products that North ascribed to the Israelis. It was at bottom a simple arms-for-hostages deal. Nir had carefully worked it out in preparation for his visit to Washington and had first submitted it to Prime Minister Peres and Defense Minister Rabin. It essentially provided for the direct sale to Iran of Israeli-owned but U.S.-made TOWs in exchange for the simultaneous release of the American hostages in Lebanon. The only condition was American replacement of the missiles. Israel proposed to handle the details of the entire operation in such a way as to enable the United States to deny any involvement in it. A cover story would explain the release of the hostages and other prisoners held by the Southern Lebanon army.

Nir had brought this plan to Ghorbanifar and Nimrodi in London in late December. The three had refined it, and the Israeli government had authorized Nir to bring the plan to Washington. The official Israeli

Historical Chronology, which relates this story, adds that the Israeli government insisted that the United States had to agree to the entire concept of the plan and that Israel would assist in whatever way the United States requested but not play a leading role.[87] How Israel could fail to play a leading role if it handled the entire operation by itself is not explained.

When Nir saw Poindexter on January 2, he laid out the plan in a way that made it particularly attractive. In the first place, it was presented as a "unilateral" Israeli action, in which the United States was not directly involved. It proposed the delivery of 500—later changed to 1,000—unimproved TOWs from Israeli stocks by an Israeli 707 in exchange for all five American hostages. If all went well and the Iranians lived up to their commitment to get the release of the hostages, Israel would follow with the delivery of 3,500 more TOWs. The Iranians were expected to confirm Ghorbanifar's assurance that there were to be no more hostages or acts of terror.

The beauty of this plan is that the Israelis were originally prepared to risk only the loss of 500 of their TOWs in the first exchange. If Iran did not obtain the release of all the hostages, it would not get the remaining 3,500 TOWs. If the operation went through as planned, the United States would get back all the hostages at the cost of replacing 4,000 TOWs. These made up as much as one-third of Israel's reserve of TOWs, making replacement necessary. The United States was not asked to risk anything in advance unless the plan leaked out. In that case, the United States was supposed to acknowledge that it was aware of the plan and had approved it for long-term reasons of state or some similar explanation.[88] Poindexter's notes of this conversation concluded with a reference to a "Covert Finding" and thus probably prompted North to call Sporkin that same day and ask him for an "expanded Finding."[89]

In effect, all Israel asked for was U.S. approval of the operation and replacements if it worked.[90] The risk of losing the first 500 TOWs was to be entirely Israeli; the prospective gains were entirely American. One merit of this procedure was that the Israelis could be made wholly responsible if the operation was exposed. When North was asked whether this factor played a role in working through the Israelis, he replied that it would have enabled the United States "to pursue it in such a way as part of the plausible deniability, that is correct," and that "we did not want the U.S. Government's hand or role in this activity exposed."[91]

In addition to the TOWs, one more thing was soon added to the missiles offered to Iran. It was U.S. intelligence information on the state of the Iran-Iraq battlefront. On January 14, General Powell questioned North about it and asked whether providing Iran with intelligence was a "prerequisite" for the deal. North replied that it was probably something that could be negotiated and in any event was not a Defense Department matter.[92] Later that month, North asked the CIA to provide him with a map revealing the order of battle on the Iran-Iraq border, showing units, troops, tanks, electronic installations, "and what have you," as McMahon put it in a message to Casey, who was in Pakistan.

Throughout this critical period in the last days of December 1985 and the first days of January 1986, during which an anguished debate turned on the questions whether to renew arms sales to Iran and how to do it with a Finding, almost all the thinking and planning were done by North, with the approval of Poindexter, in conjunction with the Israelis. They had pushed themselves forward because they had been the first to exploit Ghorbanifar, because they were anxious to do the Americans a good turn, and because they had a greater geopolitical imperative of helping Iran against Iraq. They regarded Iraq as the main immediate enemy and had most to gain by keeping both sides fighting. They did not make their motives a secret and carefully tried to protect their American rear by getting antecedent approval of their plans and replacements for their weapons. All the Israeli persuasion in the world would not have done any good if the Americans had not been willing to use them and to overlook differences in outlook. Yet the Israeli persuasion was too successful for its own good; it went much too far in its claims of what could be achieved through Ghorbanifar and underestimated the cost of ultimate exposure and disappointment.

The American role was reactive and hesitant. The United States was inhibited by its past statements of policy against arming Iran, by the adamant opposition of the two senior cabinet members, by the hostility of McFarlane toward the only Iranian intermediary, Ghorbanifar, and by President Reagan's hesitation. Casey, Poindexter, and North were the only real advocates for going ahead even if it required an arms-for-hostages deal, but they were not yet in a position to speak up and take the lead openly. North, like nature, abhorred a vacuum; his only way of filling it quickly was to repeat what the Israelis told him. The decision was still unclear and could have gone either way. The decision was up to President Reagan, and he could not delay much longer making it.

12

Finding No. 3

In January 1986, President Reagan faced a problem of the greatest delicacy at the summit of his administration. On Iran policy an irreconcilable split had opened up between his secretaries of state and defense on one side and his director of the Central Intelligence Agency and national security adviser on the other. One side wanted to have nothing to do with arms deals with Iran and the other saw arms deals as the only way to save the hostages or change the Iranian government. A breach between them had been developing for months, but the president had avoided choosing between them by saying little or by wavering.

This indecision came to an end on January 7, only one day after he had accidentally signed Finding No. 2. One more indication that it was accidentally signed was the decision at the same time to hold another meeting of the National Security Council to discuss the issue all over again.[1] The President, Vice President Bush, Secretary Shultz, Secretary Weinberger, CIA Director Casey, Chief of Staff Regan, and National Security Adviser Poindexter gathered together for the second time in a month. The only new figure present was Attorney General Meese, who had been made a nonstatutory member of the NSC by President Reagan.

Only one new factor was introduced at the meeting. Weinberger and Shultz had previously challenged the legality of providing arms to Iran. Now Attorney General Meese was primed to get around the main legal obstacle, the Arms Export Control Act. The chief problem raised by the act was a requirement to report arms exports to Congress. Meese came to the meeting with a letter written to Casey by Reagan's first attorney general, William French Smith, in 1981. In this letter, Smith said that the State Department's legal adviser, Davis R. Robinson, had informed him that the United States could sell weapons to foreign countries outside the Foreign Assistance Act and Arms Export Control Act, both of which contained reporting requirements. The president could instead use the

Economy Act and the National Security Act, which did not have these requirements for such sales.[2]

The reporting requirement was thus put off by Meese, but he understood at the time that it would not be delayed for longer than thirty to sixty days.[3] If that course had in fact been followed, it would probably have prevented the later argument over whether the president had intended to report to Congress "in a timely fashion."

Though the group was not informed of Finding No. 1 or the Finding that the president had apparently accidentally signed only the day before, the arms sales it referred to was the critical issue. The immediate question was whether to permit the sale of 4,000 Israeli TOWs, starting with the provisional 500, in exchange for all American hostages in Beirut.

At the previous meeting on December 7, Weinberger had come away thinking that the president was with him in opposing it, and Shultz had had a similar, if somewhat less optimistic, impression. This time neither of them left the meeting with any illusions. Something had happened to make up the president's mind. He was no longer sitting on the fence.

Weinberger recalled:

> I made the same points. George Shultz made the same points. Bill Casey felt that there would be an intelligence gain, and there was also talk of the hostages as one of the motivating factors, but not the motivating factor, but the responses of the President seemed to me to indicate that he had changed his view and now had decided he wanted to do this.

Weinberger said that no formal decision was made but that he felt the president had "pretty well decided, yes."[4]

Shultz told the same story:

> Well, it seemed to me that as people around the room talked, that Secretary Weinberger and I were the only ones who were against it. And so that included everybody who was there on the other side of the issue, which surprised me, and it almost seemed unreal, and I couldn't believe that people would want to do this. I thought it was a bad idea.

It was also clear to Shultz that the president "wanted to push in that direction," though "there was no doubt in the President's mind about my opinion. It wasn't as though there was something that I had missed or that I felt he hadn't quite gotten. I felt I had made myself very clear."[5]

Casey and Poindexter had always favored an arms deal. On January 7, Regan changed sides and joined them.[6]

Meese came down on the side of the new majority. He later said that he had made a 51–49 decision, swayed by thinking that "the risks would be fairly short-term because if it did not work we would be able to stop it; if this didn't produce results after, say, the first foray, that the thing would be stopped." The start-and-stop aspect of the plan was evidently one of its most appealing features, though Meese and others did not object when the operation became long-term and one foray was followed by another. Meese also believed that by this time President Reagan knew what he was doing: "The President had an adequate understanding of the arguments for and against the project."[7]

No one seems to remember what Vice President Bush said. But Secretary Shultz testified that "it was clear to me by the time we went out that the president, the vice president, the director of Central Intelligence, the attorney general, the chief of staff, the national security adviser all had one opinion and I had a different one and Cap [Weinberger] shared it."[8]

Weinberger and Shultz had correctly read Reagan's mind, though he had still failed to speak it at the meeting. Later, he divulged that he had decided "to proceed with the initiative despite a deep division within the cabinet and staff." As Reagan put it, Weinberger and Shultz "argued forcefully that I was wrong, but I just put my foot down."[9] This was one decision which Reagan made on his own and for which the responsibility was entirely his. Weinberger's impression that Reagan had changed his mind between December 7 and January 7 was mistaken. It seems rather that Reagan had inwardly tended to go along with using arms to free the hostages on December 7 and had made a final decision by January 7— always telling himself that it was not an arms-for-hostages deal.

2

Immediately after the January 7 meeting, North charged into action to carry out Nir's plan. On the same day, North told Nir the good news, exaggerating it somewhat. He informed Nir that both Reagan and Weinberger had agreed to the plan, that he was taking care of the ever present problem of replenishment, and that the president wanted both sides to adopt a policy of "no comment" if the operation was publicly disclosed. Much of North's effort was spent working out what Israel would pay the United States for the TOWs and how to get them transferred without attracting attention.[10]

The replenishment of the U.S.-made missiles sold to Iran by Israel tells a great deal about the way North operated, about U.S.-Israel relations, and about Weinberger's extreme repugnance to the whole deal. To get the missiles from the Defense Department, North had to manipulate officials from outside his narrow circle, just as he had dragged in Clarridge from the CIA and the chargé d'affaires in the Lisbon embassy in the effort to get clearance for the Israeli plane in November 1985.

To get the missiles for replenishment, North went to Noel C. Koch, the principal deputy assistant secretary of defense for international security affairs, and asked him to negotiate the price with the Israeli purchasing agent in New York, Avraham Ben-Jousef. North thought that the previous price had been too low and wanted Koch "to make that price better."[11] As Koch explained, it was necessary to keep the price within $14 million, above which level arms transfers had to be reported to Congress, and yet high enough so that it "would go through the system without raising eyebrows"—that is, raising awkward questions about who was getting what for whom.[12]

To get information for his negotiation with Ben-Jousef, Koch turned to two other officials in the Defense Security Assistance Agency, Glenn A. Rudd, the deputy director, and Harold H. Gaffney, director of plans.[13] In this way, North's net came to enclose an increasingly large number of officials, without most of them knowing it. Koch himself explained that "my practice was not to try to be overly curious about what was going on. I assumed if people wanted me to know something they would tell me."[14] Koch also reflected a common impression of North: "Ollie was one of those peculiar people who would work, and so we all know how bureaucracies run and you find somebody that's willing to work and there's a hell of a lot of work to do."*[15]

Koch and Ben-Jousef haggled over the price as if they were competing businesses, not allies engaged in a joint enterprise. While Koch wanted to get it up, Ben-Jousef tried to bring it down. It was commonly assumed in the Defense Department, from Secretary Weinberger to Koch, that the Israelis were making a profit on the resale of the missiles to Iran. Koch, in fact, asked Ben-Jousef "if they were making money on the deal" and said that he had received a noncommittal answer.†[16]

General Powell and Koch thought it best to tell Secretary Weinberger about the negotiations with Ben-Jousef.[17] Weinberger, according to Koch, became "extremely agitated" about it, "made it clear he didn't like Iran and he hated the Ayatollah," and said "this is a disaster and it should be stopped and so forth." Koch half humorously asked: "Are we apt to go

---

* Koch also said: "You know, Ollie was always—I mean he worked himself. He just worked very, very hard and one always had a sense that you just sympathized with the guy never getting any rest and not seeing much of his family, and having to carry the load that everybody shoveled off on him. So that I said at some point how are you doing or how do you feel or whatever, and whatever it was, he said that the hostages, that it's driving the President nuts, and words to that effect. And he's on me all the time and he's driving me nuts. And he said he [the president] wants them back by Christmas [1985]" (B-15, p. 63). This was one of the times North pretended that the president had personally addressed him.

† Koch described this conversation as: "I said, Christ, you know, we don't know what you guys are making on this thing. I can't believe you're doing it for nothing, or something like that. And he didn't say. I mean, he may have said I don't know, and he may not have known" (B-15, pp. 52–53).

North told Koch—apparently without justification—that he thought Ledeen had "screwed up" the Iranian deal in November 1985 and that Ledeen "was making money on the deal" (ibid., p. 29).

to jail over this?" whereupon Weinberger said: "Something like, yes, we could go to jail, or somebody could." Koch had arrived at a price of $4,500 per missile, which was more than the original U.S. cost, whereas Weinberger wanted to charge the replacement cost, which could go as high as $13,000. Koch defended his figure by saying that it was his "understanding that the president wants this" and Weinberger "confirmed that, yes, he does, but it's wrong. He [Weinberger] said this is crazy."[18]

The replenishment of the Israeli missiles was a symptom of the U.S.-Israel relationship in the entire Iran affair. An inordinate amount of time and effort was spent deciding when and how to do it. Each side jockeyed with the other in a way that annoyed both of them. There never was any doubt that the United States had committed itself to the replacement of the missiles. The Israelis wanted it done directly and simply by exchanging the missiles sent to Iran for a similar number of American missiles. The trouble was that North had to get the missiles from the Department of Defense, which could not send missiles to Israel without an explanation and accounting. McFarlane had hoped to overcome the difficulty by using ordinary procurement procedures, but he had not made this clear to the Israelis.*

As a result, the replenishment of the missiles was caught up in the bureaucracy of the Defense Department, which was suspicious of the entire arrangement. North inherited the problem from McFarlane, with the result that he was forced to work through Koch and others whose own understanding of the whole affair was necessarily limited by the rules of compartmentation and deniability. It was a recipe for mutual misunderstanding and mistrust.

3

The best minds in the Office of the General Counsel of the CIA finally came up with the answer to a momentous problem—how to evade the obstacles placed in the way of third-country arms transfers by the Arms Export Control Act and the Foreign Assistance Act. By third-country transfers was meant a sale of arms, such as the one to Iran through Israel.

The lawyers were still worrying about how to get around both these acts, which, as they said, "require Presidential consent to a third country transfer and certification to Congress where certain dollar amounts and specific types of equipment are involved."[19] They decided that the way to bypass these inconvenient requirements was to do what Attorney General Meese had already recommended—use the Economy Act. It provided for the following procedure: first, for the Department of Defense to sell

---

* On January 15, 1986, North's notebook shows that he discussed the replenishment problem with McFarlane. North recorded: "over time, we will *sell* requisite TOWs to replace the TOWs that they sent for Weir. There *is* an obligation to replenish" (Part III, p. 412).

the weapons to the CIA; second, to have the CIA sell the same weapons to the third country, in this case Israel; and third, resale by Israel to still another country, Iran. This procedure, it was recognized, required a presidential Finding to the effect that it was important to the national security of the United States.[20]

How complicated all this could be was shown in a detailed explanation to Casey on January 13 of two options for making the transfer.

> Under this option [to sell directly to Israel], the idea was that the Israelis would buy the improved version of the TOW and ship to the Iranians the basic TOWs they now have. The Israelis would then replace those basic TOWs by buying the improved version. Unfortunately, there is not enough money available to do this. The Iranians have placed $22 million in an account in Switzerland. This is enough for the basic TOWs, but for the Israelis to buy the improved version it would cost about $44 million.
>
> Therefore, they want to use the second option under which the CIA would buy 4,000 basic TOWs from DoD [Department of Defense] for $21 million. As far as Defense is concerned these purchases would be for general CIA uses for assistance in [deleted] etc., and other purposes. The money for the Iranian account would be transferred to the Israelis. The Israelis would transfer that money to a CIA account to pay for this purchase of the TOWs from DoD, the shippers would move the TOWs to the Israelis who would then move them to the Iranians. The Israelis would keep their basic TOWs and the problem of upgrading them to the new TOWs would be handled in the normal DoD-Israeli relationship.[21]

The two options reflected an implicit struggle between the CIA and the Defense Department. Each one wanted the other to assume the responsibility for the transfer of arms to Iran. The CIA's legal counsel, Sporkin, favored the first option of a direct sale by the Defense Department to Israel in order to keep the CIA out of what was here explicitly described as a "TOW for Hostage deal." Defense favored going through the CIA in order to hold itself as aloof as possible from the deal.

On the very day these options were explained to Casey, North met with Ghorbanifar at Ledeen's home to work out the details of Nir's plan. The discussion showed how the U.S.-Israel-Iran operation was intimately connected with Ghorbanifar's business interests. North's notes of the meeting recognized that the subject was a TOWs-for-hostages "deal"— the word used by North. Most of the time was spent going over how much Ghorbanifar was willing to pay for the TOWs, how much he wanted from Israel, and how the profits were to be split. One of North's notations on January 13, 1986, reads: "Jacob [Nimrodi] gets 30%." Another is "$500k [$500,000] for Gorba."[22]

Secretary of Defense Weinberger's reluctance to participate in the deals was well known to Secord and Nir. North made a note during his meeting with Secord: "Have President *tell* Cap [Weinberger] 'make it work.' " The next day, in a conversation with Nir, North wrote: "force CAP."[23]

Secord was again essential to North's plans. North wanted to use Secord the way the Iranians used Ghorbanifar. The intention was never to sell the missiles directly to Iran; they were to go through Ghorbanifar, who was acting as if he were Iran's agent, thus shielding the Iranian government from direct contamination by Israel and the United States. Now North suggested to Koch that the United States should use Secord, whom he had first brought into the Nicaraguan contra supply operation and then into the ill-fated Lisbon rescue effort, in the same way. North proposed that the United States should sell the TOWs to Secord, who would then sell them to Ghorbanifar for ultimate sale to Iran.[24]

Koch knew, however, that Secord was persona non grata with Secretary Weinberger. Koch called North the next day to warn him that the "Secretary will blanch," as North put it in his notebook.[25] But Weinberger's disapproval was no longer enough to blackball Secord. In a matter of hours, North heard from Casey that "Secord Op [is] O.K."[26] With Casey behind him, North did not have to defer to the secretary of defense.

January 14 was one of North's strenuous days. After talking with Koch, Casey, and others, North met with Poindexter to work out the details of Secord's employment. They decided to tell Casey that they were going to use Secord—as North's notes put it—"as agent for CIA." Israel would pay Secord for the replacements. Secord would buy the TOWs from the Defense Department and move them to Israel for the CIA. All the hostages were to be released after the first delivery to Iran.[27] Strangely, however, when North conferred with Secord on January 14, they discussed various "options," one of which was to make Secord an agent of the Israelis instead of the CIA.[28]

That evening, North went out to Fort McNair for a conference at which Weinberger gave a speech. There he met with Casey, and he reported their revealing conversation to Poindexter:

> Casey's view is that Cap [Weinberger] will continue to create roadblocks until he is told by you that the President wants this to move NOW and that Cap will have to make it work. Casey points out that we have gone through three different methodologies in an effort to satisfy Cap's concern and that no matter what we do there is always a new objection. As far as Casey is concerned our earlier method of having Copp [Secord] deal directly with the DoD as a purchasing agent was fine. He did not see any particular problem w[ith] making Copp an agent for the CIA in this endeavor but he is concerned that Cap will find some new objection unless he is told to proceed.[29]

The following day, North was still worrying about missile prices. North and Nir talked about 25 percent going to other Iranians and 15 percent to the "accountant" (Schwimmer). They also agreed that Secord would pay $5,300 to the Defense Department and get $7,500 for each TOW.[30] On the basis of the 4,000 TOWs ultimately contemplated in Nir's plan, Secord would make a profit of $8.8 million.[31] But North also told Poindexter that the use of Secord could work only if the Israelis came up on their price to $10,000 per TOW, apparently because Ghorbanifar had informed North that he had paid $10,000 per TOW and had "pocketed" $500 for each one delivered.[32] The latter sum seems very modest for one of Ghorbanifar's ambitions, but it refers to the missiles sent by the Israelis in August–September of the previous year when Ghorbanifar was first trying to make himself useful to the Israelis. In any case, it told North that Ghorbanifar always had to get a rake-off, and one that had increased considerably since he began dealing with the United States.

By January 15, Nir's original proposal had been hanging fire for two weeks. On that day, North's reports to Poindexter were increasingly bleak. Nir, according to North, believed that the Israeli government was about "to formally withdraw its offer to assist on this matter so that it cannot be blamed when the AMCITS [American citizens] are killed." Nir himself, North reported, "is both so exhausted and in such jeopardy of losing his job over this that he may no longer be functional." Of Nir, North remarked: "He doesn't sleep either."[33]

This Israeli pressure made North all the more anxious to find ways to make the deal work. His latest plan was for Nir to make a direct deal with Ghorbanifar, "cutting out Schwimmer and Iranian officials." Ghorbanifar would get $10 million for the first 1,000 TOWs sent from Israel to Iran. "Hopefully the hostages are then released." Ghorbanifar would then pay Secord out of the $10 million to enable him to purchase the 504 missiles necessary to replenish the Israelis for those still outstanding in the 1985 transaction.[34]

This farfetched plan by North shows how labyrinthine the desperate effort to make a three-sided U.S.-Israel-Iran deal could become. In principle, the exchange was a simple one—U.S.-made missiles for U.S. hostages. Because the American and Iranian governments refused to deal with each other, Israel, Ghorbanifar, and Secord were used to bridge the gap. The replenishment of the 1985 missiles plagued the transfer of the 1986 missiles. North was indefatigable in concocting all sorts of intricate schemes to get the missiles out of the Defense Department to the CIA, from the CIA to Secord, from Secord to Ghorbanifar, and finally from Ghorbanifar to Iran.

But nothing was simple anymore. If North had not been so obsessive in his determination to make a deal with Iran at all costs, this effort might well have ground to a halt, as some indeed thought it had done in the past few weeks. Once wound up, however, North was unstoppable except by a direct order from the president or possibly Poindexter—and neither of them said the word.

4

By bringing in Secord, North gave a great deal of extra work to the CIA's lawyers. Casey saw no particular problem in making Secord an "agent for the CIA," but his lawyers were greatly disturbed by it. On January 15, North came to see General Counsel Sporkin about Secord's role. Sporkin called George W. Clarke, the associate general counsel, and asked whether he saw

> any problems or reporting requirements with a proposal to have DoD provide weapons to a CIA "agent" who would pay for the weapons with money supplied by a friendly country. The agent would then supply the weapons to the intended recipient country. The agent would have no connection with CIA other than to act as a "middle man" with our authority.

Clarke was far more troubled than Sporkin. Clarke said that he had never had any experience with "the third party cutout, commercial guy [who] was the whole operation." As Clarke saw it, the CIA was handing over its authority to someone who would not be under its control and with little direct involvement of the CIA.[35] He told Sporkin that he "would feel more comfortable if CIA were directly involved in the activity and that it would be essential that we act in furtherance of a traditional covert action objective." Clarke could foresee problems "if this activity were merely intended to rotate a specific country's stock of weapons." One reason for this indefinite reference is that the case was so closely held that Sporkin never gave his lawyers its full details.

Sporkin put North on the phone to "clarify the hypothetical facts"— hypothetical, because North also refrained from telling Clarke the real facts of the case. Clarke was repeatedly urged "to concur in variations that would have DoD provide the weapons without other than token CIA involvement." Clarke refused and in the end told Sporkin that he could not make the legal determination the general counsel wanted without all the facts.[36] Compartmentation had its legal drawbacks.

After much deliberation, Sporkin advised Casey how to get around the legal obstacles to transferring missiles from the Defense Department to the CIA. Sporkin favored using the Economy Act instead of the Arms Export Control Act to get the missiles to Secord via the CIA rather than from the Defense Department. But he recognized that "this entire matter revolves around whether or not there will be reports made to Congress." Here he recommended the possibility of not reporting the activity "until after it has been successfully concluded." He added, however, that the chairmen and ranking minority members of the two congressional oversight committees should be briefed. He also suggested that action should be taken only after discussion with the attorney general, secretary of defense, secretary of state, and national security adviser.[37]

Sporkin's advice concerning the timing of the report to Congress stretched both the law and previous practice. As Clarke noted, "generally, the notification is made prior because we notify significant anticipated intelligence activities which by statutes covert actions are."[38] The intent of the law and previous practice had been to give prior notification of a covert action and to give delayed notification in a timely fashion only if an emergency situation made prior notification impossible. In the latter case, the president was required to provide a statement of reasons for not giving prior notification. Sporkin's formula stretched the term "timely" to extend indefinitely, even if he did not expect it to do so; it made reporting retroactive instead of anticipatory; and it made no provision for a statement of reasons to explain the delay. As for Sporkin's other recommendations, they were largely ignored.

In any case, Sporkin produced the rationale for getting around the "timely fashion" reporting requirement. "Timely" was now construed to mean "after it has been successfully concluded," whether it took a month or a year or whenever. At that time, however, Sporkin says that he expected the operation to be accomplished "at some short date," though his formula had no necessary temporal limitation.*[39]

This was Sporkin's last important contribution to the legal aspects of the Iran affair. He was made a federal judge the following month and turned future developments over to Clarke.[40]

5

At last, on January 17, 1986, Poindexter had the Finding he said he had been seeking for a month. He later insisted that it was not Finding No. 3, because he regarded all three Findings as really a single one, of which the January 17 one was only the final version.[41]

The real mystery of the Findings is why No. 3 was necessary. A careful examination of No. 2 and No. 3 shows that they were almost identical or even, in one copy of No. 2, identical. The only possible difference appeared in the opening phrase about assisting "selected friendly foreign liaison services, third countries" to which was added "and third parties." This addition had been made in handwriting by Sporkin in No. 2.[42] He

---

* Sporkin also said that he would have expected "disclosure maybe 30 or 60 days down the road" (100-6, p. 180).

later said that he had put in the addition only because "third parties" had already been mentioned in the third paragraph of the same Finding and he wanted the two paragraphs to be symmetrical. Sporkin also said that he had thought of Ghorbanifar, not Secord, as the "third party."[43]

In effect, No. 3 was virtually the same, word for word, as No. 2. Even if No. 2 had been accidentally signed by the president on January 6, it could have served as the true Finding without going through the formality of another Finding on January 17. Sporkin said that he had been told about getting No. 2 back to the president merely to put in the missing three words but that he did not think it was absolutely required.

As usual, a memorandum, written by North for Poindexter, accompanied Finding No. 3. Most of it was similar to that written by North for No. 2, but there were some interesting changes. One difference was a reference to the newly devised method of getting the CIA to purchase arms from the Defense Department under the Economy Act, whereupon the CIA would use an "authorized agent" to deliver them to Iran. It was further explained that Israel would make the necessary arrangements for the sale of 4,000 TOW weapons to Iran; the payment for these weapons would go to an agent of the CIA, after which the CIA would purchase them from the Defense Department; and finally, the weapons would be delivered to Iran by the CIA through the authorized agent. It was another extravagantly roundabout scheme to avoid a direct deal between Iran and the United States. One more addition was significant—it reminded President Reagan that Secretary Shultz and Secretary Weinberger were opposed to the plan and that Attorney General Meese and CIA Director Casey favored it.[44]

Poindexter noted in handwriting at the bottom of his copy of the memorandum: "President was briefed verbally from this paper. VP[Bush], Don Regan and Don Fortier were present."[45] This time there is no doubt about what President Reagan understood and did. He told the Special Review Board that he had understood the January 17 Finding to have changed the original Nir plan in only one essential—the United States had undertaken to become a direct supplier of arms to Iran instead of going through Israel. On January 17, the president wrote in his diary: "I agreed to sell TOWs to Iran."[46]

In a press conference on November 19, 1986, Reagan took full responsibility for selling weapons to Iran:

> Several top advisers opposed the sale of even a modest shipment of defensive weapons and spare parts to Iran. Others felt no progress could be made without this sale. I weighed their views. I considered the risks of failure and the rewards of success, and I decided to proceed. And the responsibility for the decision and the operation is mine and mine alone.[47]

In his deposition at the Poindexter trial on February 17, 1990, Reagan seemed hopelessly confused about his decision to sell arms to Iran. First, Reagan said that he had agreed to permit private Iranian citizens to buy the TOWs:

Well, talking to private citizens and so forth working to get the freedom of hostages—well, yes, the private people were the Iranians, and the arrangement that we had made was that, yes, we would accede to their request to buy the TOW missiles if they would use their influence to try to free the hostages from the Hezbollah. So yes, there was no involvement of the government of Iran in this at all, and so, it was private citizens, but not ours. It was theirs. And our reward to them for taking that action was to sell them the missiles shipment that they asked for.

At this point, Reagan was reminded that the Finding had referred to providing materiel and munitions to "the Government of Iran." Whereupon, Reagan replied: "Well, yes, through the government which is taking steps to facilitate the release."[48] It may well be that Reagan's apparent confusion in 1990 came from his first intention to resort to the old cover story about dealing with private Iranians and not the Iranian government, though he seems to have quickly changed his mind as soon as he was pressed about it.

One of the most startling things about Finding No. 3 was that half of the four statutory members of the National Security Council were kept in ignorance of it. President Reagan met with Secretary Shultz on the afternoon of that same January 17, after having signed the Finding in the morning, and never mentioned it to him. Shultz testified that he did not find out about Finding No. 3 until November 10, 1986, almost ten months later.[49] Since he thought that the Iran initiative was at that time dead, he was not given the opportunity to discover that it was very much alive.

Secretary Weinberger was put in an even more embarrassing position. In the fall of 1985, he had learned that instructions had been issued from the White House cutting him out of the distribution list of cables and other information about the early phase of the Iran affair. He was forced to admit having known nothing about the 508 U.S.-made missiles sent to Iran in August–September of that year. As an additional indignity, Weinberger had been tipped off by foreign intelligence sources that mysterious negotiations were going on about weapons between American officials and Iranian representatives. Worse still, the reports had been kept from him by the intelligence agency in his own Defense Department. Weinberger had taken "very strong umbrage at that," as he put it, and had ordered his military assistant, General Powell, "to remind the Agency for whom they were working" and to make it "very clear to the defense agency involved that they took instructions from us and they certainly were under no circumstances ever to accept instruction that we were not to be on the distribution list for any of this for intelligence material." Weinberger assumed that the instructions to exclude him had come from the National Security Council, which in this context pointed to Poindexter. When Weinberger protested, he was merely told that it had been a "mistake."[50]

Like Shultz, Weinberger also did not know that a presidential Finding had been signed on January 17.[51] Yet on that day Weinberger and Shultz had had their usual weekly luncheon meeting with Poindexter.[52] On the following day, however, Poindexter called and told him, in Weinberger's words: "The President has decided this and there's no more room for argument, something along that line." This referred to the sale of 4,000 TOWs by the Defense Department to the CIA. Weinberger had had enough. "I had made all the arguments I could think of at the two meetings, and having been told in very flat, uncompromising terms that the President had decided, and that they were anxious to have the order carried out, I did not [reargue it]."[53] Yet Weinberger was President Reagan's oldest and closest friend in the cabinet, a political ally for over twenty years, going back to the California days. The president did not give him the courtesy of a personal call about the new turn of events. Weinberger was obviously too hurt to call the president and again argue against the decision. The order came peremptorily from Poindexter, who was nominally inferior in rank to a secretary of defense.

In his autobiography, Weinberger says that he "seriously contemplated resignation" when Poindexter told him to transfer the weapons to the CIA for them to go to Iran. He was "greatly attracted to the idea," but decided against it because he could not see what he could accomplish by resigning. As a result, he permitted himself to be humiliated in office and to watch helplessly as a policy was adopted and carried out that he knew "could never work" and "could only bring great harm and damage to the President and America." In his retelling of the Iran story, he incomprehensibly places almost all the blame on McFarlane and hardly mentions Poindexter or Reagan, as if they had not known what was going on or could do nothing about it.*[54]

Shultz made no secret of his opposition but did not consider it worth risking his office. His self-restraint in the Iran affair was noteworthy, because he had offered to resign previously for much more trivial reasons.

---

* Weinberger devotes most of his chapter on Iran and the hostages to 1985, when McFarlane was national security adviser but only the first steps had been taken to get into the Iran affair. Weinberger performs the extraordinary literary feat of largely ignoring 1986, when most of the decisions were made and actions taken. Weinberger goes so far as to make McFarlane responsible for giving the Iranians U.S. military intelligence, a gift for which Casey, Poindexter, and North should be given credit (*Fighting for Peace*, p. 379). In a reply to Weinberger, McFarlane called this charge "an outright lie" and deplored Weinberger's effort to make him a "scapegoat" ("Why Cap Is Wrong," *National Review*, June 11, 1990, pp. 44–47).

He had offered to resign the first time because he had been denied an Air Force plane for one of his trips. He blamed "a character in the White House," Johnathan Miller, for that affront. Shultz was so upset that he went to President Reagan with a letter of resignation, which the president shrugged off, telling him he was tired and needed a vacation.*[55]

In 1983, Shultz again resigned, because McFarlane had gone on a trip to the Middle East without his knowledge. Shultz says that he told Reagan: "Mr. President, you don't need a guy like me for Secretary of State if this is the way things are going to be done, because when you send somebody out like that McFarlane trip, I'm done."[56] Shultz also demanded a meeting with the president's top aides, at that time Clark, Meese, and Baker, whom he notified that he could not be an effective secretary of state if they did such a thing and that he wanted to leave. Shultz changed his mind when he was given assurances that it would not happen again.[57]

Shultz resigned yet a third time in late 1985 in protest against lie detector tests in his department. Again the president refused to accept his resignation, and Shultz bethought himself that it was not "fair" for him to leave at the same time as McFarlane.[58]

Even more resignations by Shultz were later revealed by President Reagan. In his autobiography, Reagan disclosed that "more than once, Shultz threatened to resign because of Casey. I had to bring them together several times, and they worked out most of their differences and I convinced George not to resign." On a later occasion, Shultz wanted to resign because he thought that Weinberger, Casey, and Poindexter "were ganging up on him and pushing foreign policy issues that he opposed behind his back." Assured that Reagan had not lost faith in him and that he could stay in office as long as Reagan stayed, Shultz again held on to his job.[59]

The difference between the Shultz of these resignations and the Shultz of the Iran affair is not easy to understand unless one assumes that the Iran affair was less important than the others. The disparities among Shultz's levels of indignation makes one wonder what his standard of acceptable humiliation for a secretary of state was.

6

The lines were now unmistakably drawn.

President Reagan did more than sign a Finding to sell weapons to Iran. He also divided the top leadership of his administration into those who were permitted to take part in the Iran affair and those who were not.

---

* Miller said that he was "a bit flabbergasted" when he heard Shultz tell this story, because Miller did not have the authority to approve or disapprove such a trip by Shultz (B-18, pp. 693–94).

One group, headed by the secretary of state and secretary of defense, was henceforth excluded from a major sphere of U.S. foreign policy. The other group, made up of a small number of officials, was given control of it. This group was so small that it could be counted on the fingers of one hand. It considered itself beholden to President Reagan alone as his "personal staff." It undertook not only to make policy but to carry it out. It was given a license to act as if it were a junta, his junta.

The operational inner circle was located in the National Security Council staff, though compartmentation largely restricted knowledge and decision even there to Poindexter and North. The president's notorious lack of interest in details gave them something in the nature of a blank check, once they had obtained his general agreement to a course of action. Their main accomplice—retired Air Force Major General Richard V. Secord, under a cloud because of his past dubious associations—was not even in the government. Yet Poindexter and North could have done little on their own. They were largely dependent on the complicity and co-operation of the CIA, which was itself ambivalent about its role. Poindexter acknowledged that the NSC staff and not the CIA was operationally in command in this affair. Poindexter could not think of any other case in which the NSC staff had played such an "operational role"; it was indeed an aberration in the normal functioning of the government.[60] The key Finding of January 17 did not mention the NSC staff as the controlling factor; the only name specifically mentioned in it was the director of the CIA. Findings, moreover, were meant to apply to the CIA as the agency in charge of covert operations. By referring to the CIA and not the NSC staff, the Finding was in this respect fraudulent.

Nevertheless, the CIA was soon drawn in collectively by Poindexter and North. The day after the Finding was signed, they lost no time putting it into effect. They called together a group that included CIA General Counsel Stanley Sporkin; CIA Deputy Director of Operations Clair George; Deputy Chief of the Near East Division (DC/NE) Tom Twetten; Secord; and perhaps one or two others.[61]

The principal purpose of the meeting, as one participant put it, "was to start CIA support for the NSC operation. So the main focus was here we have this Finding and this is what we are going to have to do." The Finding, which had been kept from the secretaries of state and defense, was handed around to be read. Poindexter explained what they were there for. The main problem was how to get the missiles to the CIA.[62] It was understood that they were going to be exchanged for the hostages.[63]

The most unusual aspect of the meeting was Secord's presence. Poindexter had called him in earlier to invite him to take part in the operation. According to Secord, he had told Poindexter that his previous experience with Ghorbanifar had led him to believe that it was "a swap of American arms for American hostages in Lebanon, and that, to me, was not acceptable, and I thought he knew that." Poindexter won him over by saying that this was an entirely new initiative "founded on strategic objectives" to make contact with so-called moderate elements in Iran. Hostages were also an important element in the initiative, and a small amount of arms "could be used successfully as bona fides in this initiative." Secord signed on.

It soon became clear to Secord why he had been invited. He recalled:

> There was a discussion of one change that had been made in which they inserted into the language that in addition to the normal action agencies, that the Government would work through third parties in third countries, and that is why I was at the meeting.
>
> I was the third party. I was to be the commercial cutout, if you will. It was their intention to, in some respects, mirror the previous Israeli operation. The previous Israeli operation dealt from the Israeli Government through an Israeli company to an Iranian commercial operator, Ghorbanifar, and then to the Government of Iran, and it was in that fashion that the Israelis dealt with the matter.

Secord then described the new plan:

> Additionally, it was decided that the United States—this is a very important point—the United States would have to directly ship the weapons rather than taking them from Israeli stocks.
>
> They decided that they would have to do this because of the various statutes that applied to the sale of arms, and it was decided by the lawyers that the Economy Act would have to be utilized whereby one agency in the U.S. Government can purchase from another agency, and so, the plan was for the CIA to buy the materials from the Defense Department stocks, and then to sell them to my organization which in turn would sell them to Ghorbanifar, who in turn would sell them to Iran.

But, Secord explained, it was still to be a joint U.S.-Israel venture:

> The Israelis were to provide the base from which to ship, a secure base, and they were also to provide cover. It was planned that part of the cover for this operation would be that if it were discovered that the Israelis could take the hit, if you will.[64]

A "commercial cutout" was a person or company used by the government to carry out its policy in such a way that the government itself was not openly linked with the operation and could make it seem to be an ordinary commercial transaction. "Cutouts" served "deniability." Ordinarily, the CIA had "proprietaries" for just such a purpose. In this case, Secord and his company were used because he further removed the CIA from implication in the operation and had the expert knowledge and experience to move arms to Iran by plane, as he had been doing for the Nicaraguan contras.

Secord had been repeatedly referred to as an "agent of the CIA." He was more nearly an agent of the NSC staff who worked with CIA officials in the course of the operation. Secord later maintained that he had had no intention of making a profit, which implied that he was not an ordinary businessman. Nevertheless, he also insisted he did not feel that he was part of the government and that it was nothing more than a commercial operation.[65]

Secord's status permitted him to have it both ways when it suited him. He admittedly took on a government assignment and carried it out in the spirit of a good soldier. He agreed that he had had "a moral obligation to follow the direction of the CIA" and was "an instrument of the [government] policy." But he also protested that he was not an agent of the government, because "I wasn't paid a nickel by the Government. I had no contract, there were no terms of references, no instructions, no nothing."[66] In fact, what he wanted was not so much money as a reward for his service but rather to be forgiven for his past indiscretions and welcomed back into the government, apparently into the CIA itself.

It should be noted that this critical meeting was presided over by Poindexter. He alone, acting in the name of the president, was able to commandeer high-ranking CIA officials to do his bidding. North sometimes pretended to have personal relations with the president; Poindexter had no need to pretend. He more than anyone else in the administration was the president's alter ego in these affairs.

But whatever Poindexter was able to do at this time was made possible by President Reagan's Finding of January 17. It was his Finding, and he had had plenty of time to know what he was doing. Ever since his secretary of state and secretary of defense had voiced their opposition more than a month earlier, only his stubborn determination to continue dealing with Iran made all that followed possible.

13

Ghorbanifar

Whatever the plan, there was still Manucher Ghorbanifar. His chief capital was his wits. His stock-in-trade was his ability to tell others what they wanted to hear or believe. He was so shady that he inevitably aroused a suspicion that he was congenitally incapable of telling the truth or dealing in good faith. Yet he regularly managed to overcome others' doubts and stage a comeback as the indispensable middleman. He repelled some Americans like McFarlane and charmed others like Ledeen. Even those who were convinced that he was a liar and con artist found themselves in the position of thinking that they could not do without him.

Ghorbanifar lived well, with a house and family in Paris, another house in Nice, and a "girlfriend" in California. Whatever his financial resources, he seemed to have a constant need for money. He had to overcome a past in which he was said to have worked for SAVAK, the Shah's feared secret police, in order to turn himself into a self-proclaimed spokesman and middleman for "moderate" elements in Khomeini's Iran. The CIA considered him an unusable fraud. Oliver North thought that he was an "Israeli agent" and said that Casey had told him as much.[1]

North explained why Ghorbanifar had so many political lives. By 1985, when he first came to know about Ghorbanifar, he said that he had had no illusions about him:

> We—and throughout, I knew, and so did the rest of us who were dealing with him, exactly what Mr. Ghorbanifar was. I knew him to be a liar. I knew him to be a cheat, and I knew him to be a man making enormous sums of money. He was widely suspected to be, within the people I dealt with at the Central Intelligence Agency, an agent of the Israeli Government, or at least one of, if not more, of their security services.
>
> That is important in understanding why we continued to deal

with him. We knew what the man was, but it was difficult to get other people involved in these activities.

North admitted that he had been relying on the judgment of the Israelis in deciding to deal with Ghorbanifar and those he represented. The reason, he said, was that the United States had no intelligence sources in Iran, and Israel had them.[2]

North was now instrumental in bringing Ghorbanifar to the United States. The occasion was a rumor in September 1985 that William Buckley, the CIA's chief of station in Beirut, was about to be released, which was then followed by an announcement on October 3 that he was going to be executed. North decided that it was important for Ghorbanifar to come to Washington to determine whether there was still a chance to save Buckley.[3] Ghorbanifar arrived on October 7, having traveled with a Greek passport bearing the name of "Nicholaos Kralis," accompanied by Schwimmer and Nimrodi. To make matters more mysterious, North notified Charles E. Allen, the CIA's national intelligence officer for counterterrorism, of Ghorbanifar's expected arrival but referred to him as "Ascari," another of Ghorbanifar's aliases.[4] Ledeen had already told North that Kralis-Ascari was Ghorbanifar.[5]

North told Allen that he had "made some very strong remarks to Ascari about the need for success in obtaining the release of the American hostages" and had warned him to "keep his commitments and not deceive in any way the U.S. Government in this effort."[6] By this time North evidently knew of Ghorbanifar's reputation.

Ledeen, who was closest to Ghorbanifar, met with him, Schwimmer, and Nimrodi the next day, October 8. According to Ledeen, they talked about "Hawks, Phoenixes, Harpoons, Sidewinders, every missile known to man or beast." Paradoxically, Ghorbanifar is also said to have agreed with Ledeen that it was time "to get out of this hostage business."[7] Ledeen does not explain why they should have talked about every missile known to man or beast if they agreed that arms should play no part in release of the hostages.

2

Like Ghorbanifar, Ledeen was a hard man to hold back. The two of them had come together again by chance, and as a result Ledeen also staged a partial comeback.

Ledeen says that he accidentally met Ghorbanifar again early in December 1985 in Paris as both were getting Air France tickets. Ledeen told him about his removal from the Iran affair and his impression that it had come to an end. Nevertheless, he questioned Ghorbanifar about the latter's troubles with the CIA. When Ghorbanifar indicated that he still wanted to stay in the game, Ledeen told him that he would have to do something about the CIA's unfriendly attitude toward him. "OK," Ghorbanifar is quoted as saying, "I am coming to America later in December in any case, and I will talk to them."[8]

No sooner did Ledeen get back home than he asked for a meeting with Clarridge and Allen on December 4 to tell them about a sensational story that Ghorbanifar had told him in Paris. It was the tale of the "Libyan scam." It seems that Ghorbanifar had friends who knew about an alleged offer of $10 million by the Libyan dictator, Muammar al-Qaddafi, for the murder of a Libyan émigré leader named al-Mugarieff. This news gave Ghorbanifar an idea—for the CIA to stage a fake funeral for al-Mugarieff, after which he would appear in public to the great humiliation of Qaddafi. Qaddafi would lose $10 million and presumably suffer extreme loss of face. Ghorbanifar did not have the resources to stage a phony funeral and had hit on the CIA to carry it off. Ledeen said that he had already discussed the operation with North, who had allegedly favored undertaking it.[9]

Ledeen had previously been told by McFarlane to tell the CIA nothing about his activities. Now that McFarlane was gone and Poindexter had dismissed him, Ledeen felt free to go to the CIA and work that quarter, using his experience in the Iran affair as his entering wedge. Ledeen says that he obtained North's approval for his overture to the CIA.[10]

At the same meeting on December 4, Ledeen told Clarridge and Allen at length about his experiences in the Iran affair, including what he knew about Ghorbanifar and the internal Iranian political situation. According to Allen, Ledeen said that "Ghorbanifar was a good fellow, praised Ghorbanifar to the hilt."*[11] Ghorbanifar, Ledeen said, traveled to Iran once a month, at great personal risk, to discuss weapons procurement; Ledeen had allegedly arranged for him to come to Washington in October; Ghorbanifar's visit had greatly enhanced his credibility with senior Iranian officials, including Speaker of the Majlis Rafsanjani, the alleged leader of the moderates.

Mention of Rafsanjani brought a curious bit of intelligence from Ledeen, whose only source was Ghorbanifar:

[Rafsanjani] believes that Vice President Bush is orchestrating the US initiative with Iran. In fact, according to Subject [Ledeen], Rafsanjani believes that Bush is the most powerful man in the US because in addition to being Vice President, he was once Director of CIA.[12]

---

* Allen also said that "each time Mr. Ledeen met with me or Mr. Ghorbanifar or anyone else he always praised Mr. Ghorbanifar, and I anticipated that he would strongly urge that Mr. Casey endorse Mr. Ghorbanifar's efforts" (B-1, p. 510).

If this was Rafsanjani's belief, and both Ghorbanifar and Ledeen thought it worth passing on, it did not bode well for realistic U.S.-Iran relations. Two days later, on December 6, another memorandum showed that the CIA officials had been indoctrinated in the threefold division of Iranian factions—radicals, conservatives, and moderates, with Montazeri and Rafsanjani described as "pragmatists" who supported the conservatives on some issues and the radicals on others. The most effective opposition to the radicals was supposed to come from a moderate-conservative coalition. [13]

According to Ledeen, who merely "liked" it, Casey "loved" the idea of the Libyan scam but did not want to go ahead with Ghorbanifar until the Iranian had "cleared up" the problem of his previous CIA polygraphs, two of which he had failed to pass in 1984. [14] On the other hand, Allen, who was much closer to Casey, did not think that "Mr. Casey was enthused about it," and said that Casey told him "it just wasn't going to happen." [15] In fact, it did not happen.

Ledeen again held forth on December 22 for the benefit of the chief of the CIA's Iran branch on his relations with Ghorbanifar. Ledeen mentioned that the Iranians had been purposely overcharged in November and that Ghorbanifar had used around $200,000 of the profit to support his political contacts inside Iran. This official's report cited Ledeen's praise of Ghorbanifar: "Ledeen is a fan of Subject [Ghorbanifar] and describes him as a 'wonderful man . . . almost too good to be true.' "[16]

By now, Ghorbanifar was Ledeen's personal asset, whom Ledeen used to gain another foothold in the Iran affair. On the evening of December 22, the same CIA official interviewed Ghorbanifar for two hours at Ledeen's home; North dropped by to talk to Ghorbanifar about retrieving the unwanted TOW missiles sent to Iran in November. As usual, Ghorbanifar went into the political divisions in the Iranian government, which the official dutifully recorded as "line one—rightist; line two—hardline; line three—balancers," with the last two allegedly working more closely together than in the past. Ghorbanifar also demanded from CIA Director Casey a guarantee that he would be given a key role in dealings with Iran. [17]

Ghorbanifar was willing to take a polygraph test, because he thought that it had been set up in such a way that he could not fail it. Ledeen says that it was supposed to be a brief, friendly affair, with a Farsi-speaking interrogator who was not going to ask any awkward questions about recent events. Instead, the questioner spoke English only, concentrated on recent events, and went on for five hours. [18]

Ghorbanifar's polygraph on January 11 was another disaster. It indicated deception on his part in thirteen of the fifteen questions, and was inconclusive in the remaining two. The report on his test concluded: "Ghorbanifar is clearly a fabricator and wheeler-dealer who has undertaken activities prejudicial to U.S. interests."[19] North's notebook for January 13 records a call from the CIA's Clair George: "Gorbanifar lying on 13 of 15 items." Presumably the news should have made North lose confidence in the Iranian, but it had no such effect. Ledeen and Ghorbanifar reacted angrily, feeling that he had been led into a trap by enemies in the CIA.[20]

On January 13, North recorded another proposed deal with Ghorbanifar.

[$]6–7M[illion] available on return of Hawks
$40M avail[able] for 4000 TOWs
$500K [$500,000] for Gorba
Two weeks to deliver 4K [4,000] TOWs
Pay $10M in advance
1st plane must deliver "flashy intelligence"

This deal, whatever its merits, suggested that Ghorbanifar expected to get $500,000 for his trouble, only two days after his polygraph had made him appear totally untrustworthy. In another note made that day, North recorded: "Jacob [Nimrodi] gets 30%."

North met with Poindexter the next day and gave him a detailed plan for the next deal.

Copp [Secord] to serve as agent for CIA
Is[rael] to pay Copp for purchase of replacements
Is[rael] to buy T[OW]s from DoD [Department of Defense]; move
    to Is[rael] for CIA
Copp to pay DoD for Basic T[OW]s
Is[rael] to prov[ide] T[OW]s to I[ran] for op[eration] to begin
1st shipment to Is[rael] coincides w[ith] 1st Is[raeli] shipment to
    I[ran]
All to be released immed[iately] after 1st delivery
Lahad release of 25 Hizb[allah] to coincide w[ith] 1st Delivery[21]

Notable in this scheme was Secord's assumed role as agent for the CIA, not merely the NSC staff. Only by representing the CIA could Secord buy TOWs from the Defense Department and sell them to Israel, which in turn was supposed to transfer them to Iran.[22] The entire transaction was still predicated on the immediate release of all the American hostages together with twenty-five of the prisoners held in southern Lebanon by Colonel Lahad's forces allied with Israel. It was the classic arms-for-hostages deal with no pretense of including a strategic dimension. North's record of the meeting with Poindexter has a notation: "Call Casey," who soon called North to say, as North recorded, "Secord

Op[eration] O.K." The process indicates how closely North, Poindexter, and Casey were intermeshed in all this planning.

Casey was also reluctant to shake Ghorbanifar off. Casey, moreover, had a special problem within the CIA about Ghorbanifar. The Operations staff was specifically in charge of covert activities, and Ghorbanifar fell well within its exclusive sphere. Yet the greatest opposition to using Ghorbanifar came from Operations, and especially from its deputy director, Clair George. "At that time," George related, "we were being urged to establish an operational relationship with Mr. Ghorbanifar to try to get it—quite correctly, to be fair to everybody—by the director, who had been informed by people in whom we had some trust, above all the Israelis, who said Ghorbanifar was the greatest thing since bagels, Michael Ledeen, who visited the director and told him he was a great guy, and the White House, which, as we now know, was obviously quite interested in the Israeli idea." By the White House, George indicated that he meant Poindexter.[23]

The trouble was that the Operations Directorate thought that Ghorbanifar was "a cheat and a crook and totally dishonest."[24] George says that he went to Casey and told him: "Bill, the guy is really no good" and "Bill, old pal, this isn't really worth it." But Casey insisted on going ahead with Ghorbanifar and having Allen meet with Ghorbanifar. George later regretted having been replaced by Allen, who was an intelligence officer: "I should have stormed into Casey's office and said, Bill, take it."[25]

The Operations Directorate was not the only source of CIA opposition to Ghorbanifar. According to Clarridge, "word that we were going to send somebody to have a chat with Ledeen and Ghorbanifar was greeted by the NE [Near East] Division with more than a little consternation." Despite the internal resistance, "there are some things that you can turn Mr. Casey off and some that you can't, and it was pretty clear to us that he was not going to stop entirely on that one."[26]

On January 13, Ghorbanifar and Allen again talked in Ledeen's home for another five hours. Despite his fury at the unfortunate polygraph, Ghorbanifar offered his services to the CIA to work on freeing the hostages and preventing more terrorism. To listen to him, Ghorbanifar had exceptional influence at the highest levels of the Iranian government. He boasted that he had convinced Iranian Prime Minister Mir Hussein Moussavi and Oil Minister Gholam Reza Aqazadeh "to trust the United States with Israel acting as an intermediary." He had given the prime minister the deadline of January 24, only eleven days away, to reach a U.S.-Iran agreement or he, Ghorbanifar, would no longer wish to serve as an intermediary in dealing with the United States. Moussavi, President Ali Khamenei, and Aqazadeh owed him substantial sums of money. One of them had been photographed in "compromising situations" with Western women and would be finished if it became known. Ghorbanifar volunteered that he was currently engaged in assisting the Iranian purchasing agent in Europe "with procurement of arms for Line Two"—the "hardline"—though he also said that he was "secretly part of the conservative 'Line One' faction in Iran." Never far from the subject of money, Ghorbanifar made clear that he expected to be paid millions of U.S. dollars for his services.[27]

Also on January 13, Ghorbanifar made some remarks to Allen that the latter had considered so "farfetched and trivial" that he had failed to note them down and recalled them a year later only after their full significance had become apparent. Ghorbanifar had said that some of his projects could generate funds for "Ollie's boys in Central America."[28] In his notes taken down at the time, Allen had handwritten: "can fund Contras."[29] Allen said that he had made little of these remarks at the time, because he had been interested in terrorist plots and thought that Ghorbanifar was merely adding something to make himself "a contractor to the CIA."[30] Though Allen virtually ignored this overture at the time, it suggests that Ghorbanifar had had the idea in his mind before dangling it in front of Oliver North.

When Allen reported to Casey on this conversation, the CIA chief showed him photographs of alleged terrorists that Ghorbanifar had supplied and that had impressed Casey. Allen then related this exchange with Casey:

> I said it was very hard to pin down the individual in any concrete way. He is very flamboyant. He's very clever, cunning. I described him as a con man to the Director. I said it doesn't mean that, properly managed, and it might take a lot of effort, that you cannot manage a con man to do this. And I remember the Director joking and saying well, maybe this is a con man's con man then.[31]

As a result, Ghorbanifar was back. For months to come, he bedeviled the Americans more than anyone else in this affair. They felt that they could not do without him and could not do with him. Casey, North, and Poindexter, who were mainly responsible for holding on to him, were not without misgivings. Even Clair George declared that "Mr. Ghorbanifar didn't turn out to be a total phony, but he is untrustworthy in our books."[32] If he had been a total phony, he would have been easier to shake off. He was used by the Iranians as well as by the Americans and thus had access to bits and pieces of useful information for both sides. The difficulty was that he did not know when to let well enough alone, and neither side was able to check on him. In part, the problem with Ghorbanifar came from a clash of cultures; one of the worst things the Americans could say about him was that he was a typical "rug merchant," which meant that he dealt with them in a way that his own countrymen would have understood and appreciated.

Only Ledeen was totally devoted to Ghorbanifar, and he apparently influenced Casey. Allen, who was subjected to Ghorbanifar's presence for hours, summed up his feelings in this way:

It is our feeling there are bits of valid information in Subject's reporting but he has embellished and projected his own feelings in presenting this information as hard fact. This has been a persistent problem throughout the four years we have known him. His reporting has sometimes been useful but it is extremely difficult to separate the good from the bad information. It is hard to find in the file any instance where his reporting in fact resulted in a solid development.[33]

Ghorbanifar's political line appealed to the Americans, because it told them that providing Iran with arms was a way of strengthening the "moderates." This proposition was inherently implausible. It presupposed that the regular army and air force were under moderate leadership, and the Revolutionary Guards were extremist. In fact, the war against Iraq indicated that the regular forces as well as the Revolutionary Guards were firmly controlled by the central government. The central government, not a few moderates, was behind Iran's response to the delivery of Israeli and American arms. When the TOWs were rejected in November 1985, the complaints came from the top. The considerable amount of Iranian money invested in the expected delivery of 80 missiles came from the same source, not from a faction. The whole operation was clearly known to and approved by the responsible leadership.

Ghorbanifar repeatedly took credit for having arranged for a temporary cessation of terrorist threats from Iran in exchange for the early arms shipments. This concession, if real, was made by the Iranian government as a whole and not by a few moderates. It also implied that the Iranian authorities were willing to refrain from making public threats only so long as arms kept coming, and that the threats could be renewed if the arms stopped.

Finally, Ghorbanifar and Ledeen frequently pointed to the release of the Reverend Weir and later the Reverend Lawrence Jenco as proof of what Ghorbanifar could accomplish in obtaining the release of hostages. This ignored the true function of hostages for Iran, which was to convince the United States that Iran could obtain enough releases of hostages to make any hostages-for-arms deals credible but could always dole out hostages in such a way as to continue with such deals indefinitely. For this reason Poindexter tried vainly to get all the hostages released at once and never succeeded—for if he had, it would have put an end once and for all to arms-for-hostages deals.

3

Meanwhile Ghorbanifar was the principal figure in the incident that was destined to be considered the most serious of all the malfeasances in the Iran affair. It came to be known as the "diversion" or the "residuals."

It will be recalled that something of this sort had already happened during the November 1985 "horror story." At that time, the Israelis had deposited $1 million in Secord's Lake Resources account for the purpose of sending Hawk missiles to Iran. In the end, according to North, only a small portion of the money had been spent, whereupon the Israelis had asked about the rest of it. North told them that it had been spent in support of the Nicaraguan contras, "and they acknowledged that," by which North meant that they had never asked for the money back.[34]

An official Israeli source also reports that North had met with Israeli officials in New York on December 6, 1985, and had remarked that the United States wanted to use profits from future arms sales to Iran to fund U.S. activity in Nicaragua. North could not recall this conversation but did not rule it out.[35] This alleged incident, together with the fate of the remainder of the $1 million, suggests that the idea was somehow in the air.

Something definite—still according to North—was said and done in January 1986. The first occasion was the visit to North by Amiram Nir on January 2, when the Israeli emissary had brought his new plan for consideration. Nir is said to have broached the idea that "there be a residual and that the residual be applied to the purpose of purchasing replenishments and supporting other activities." By replenishments, Nir meant the 508 missiles in the August–September 1985 shipment to Iran that had not yet been recovered by Israel, and the allusion to "other activities" was not spelled out.[36] The idea seems to have been that there was a prospect of making a profit—which North liked to call a "residual"— in arms deals with Iran, and that the profit could be used for other, unstated purposes.

The next step, as North told the story, was far more definite. It was taken by Ghorbanifar during a meeting with North in London on or about January 22, 1986.[37] This is how North recalled the famous incident:

> Mr. Ghorbanifar took me into the bathroom and Mr. Ghorbanifar suggested several incentives to make that February transaction work, and the attractive incentive for me was the one he made that re-siduals could flow to support the Nicaraguan Resistance.
>
> He made it point blank and he made it by my understanding with the full knowledge and acquiescence and support, if not the original idea of the Israel intelligence services, if not the Israeli Government.[38]

From this it appears that Ghorbanifar had left it up to North to choose the contra incentive out of several possibilities, in which case Ghorbanifar would not have made "it point blank." North also believed that Ghorbanifar was a mere mouthpiece for the Israeli intelligence services or government, as shown by North's opinion that Ghorbanifar was an "Israeli agent." This assumption was almost certainly unfounded, despite the use made by the Israelis of what they considered to be their valuable Iranian intelligence asset, a different category from agent. By the time he testified, North may well have been displeased with himself for having been so credulous for so long about Ghorbanifar's indispensability; more than once North made it seem that the Israelis had led him astray. Ghorbanifar was capable of finding ways to lure North without Israeli inspiration.

In fact, North made a tape recording of this meeting with Ghorbanifar. It appears from this tape that Ghorbanifar coolly boasted of the money that could be made from the deals with Iran and laughingly offered to use the profits to pay for what the United States wanted, even in Central America. The dialogue gives some idea of Ghorbanifar's language and approach:

> *Ghorbanifar:* I think this is, Ollie, the best chance we (garbled), we never will find such a good time again, never get such good money (garbled), uh, we do everything, we do hostages (laughs) free of charge, we do all terrorists free of charge, Central America free of charge, American business free of charge, [deleted] everything (laughs) free.
>
> *North:* I would like to see. . . . some point this, uh, idea, in the [deleted] thing, and maybe, you know, if there is some future opportunity, w[ith] Central America, you know that there is a lot of Libyan, a lot of Libyan *and* Iranian activity with the Nicaraguans.[39]

In retrospect, North jumbled together the Nir and Ghorbanifar approaches as if they were one and the same. In the Poindexter trial, he said that "as I remember it today, it was a product of a discussion with Amiram Nir and Manucher Ghorbanifar."[40] Yet, as North also told the story, Nir and Ghorbanifar had put the idea into his head on two different occasions and in markedly different ways.

North revealed that he was instructed to tape-record all meetings with Iranians and various intermediaries. He carried a covert tape-recording device and, on some occasions, a covert video-recording device. He also used the FBI to monitor, covertly, all meetings in the United States. To the National Security Agency he passed telephone numbers for the purpose of close monitoring.[41]

As for the "residuals," North later said that they had come from four arms shipments to Iran in 1986.[42] It is also said that the total sum came to $16 million, roughly $6 million from the sale of TOW missiles and as much as $8 or $9 million from the Hawk missiles.[43] North said that he had cleared each transaction with Poindexter in advance.[44]

The diversion was not the only "incentive" that Ghorbanifar offered to North. Another one was more lucrative for North personally. "Mr. Ghorbanifar," North said, "offered me a million dollars if we could make this prosper"—"this" being the prospective arms deals. North told him that if he pursued this kind of bribe, "he would be out of the picture very quickly." Evidently it was not too much for North that Ghorbanifar made such a blatant approach; North prided himself on knowing all about baksheesh in the Middle East and was not offended. Then came the other incentive—the diversion—and Ghorbanifar was back in business.[45]

Whatever the circumstances when the diversion was broached, North quickly made the idea his own. He testified:

> I must confess to you that I thought using the Ayatollah's money to support the Nicaraguan Resistance was a right idea. And I must confess that I advocated that. To this day, you have referred to it as a diversion. My understanding of the word "diversion" is that what we did is we took something off the course that was originally intended and what we did is we diverted money out of the pocket of Mr. Ghorbanifar and in the enormous files of intelligence that I had received from our intelligence agencies, it was very clear that Mr. Ghorbanifar and perhaps others had made enormous profits on the September and November [1985] transactions.
>
> They didn't make them on the November transaction because it was never completed, but they certainly had in the August–September transaction. And I saw that idea of using the Ayatollah Khomeini's money to support the Nicaraguan Freedom Fighters as a good one.
>
> I still do. I don't think it was wrong. I think it was a neat idea and I came back and I advocated that and we did it; we did it on three occasions.[46]

This curious rationale assumed that it was right for North to make a profit from the Iran arms sales for the benefit of the contras because Ghorbanifar had made a profit for himself out of past sales. North believed, of course, that he was acting from a higher motive in transferring the profit to the contras. The means were the same but the ends differed. By mixing the Iran and contra operations, however, North put the former at risk. As a result of the November 1985 horror story, the Iranians had just recently screamed that they had been cheated by being overcharged for the missiles. At every turn they were suspicious of the Americans. If the aim was really to achieve a long-term understanding with Iran, the utmost care was necessary to treat the Iranians scrupulously, especially in financial matters. North liked to joke about the "Ayatollah's money," but it was the government's or the Iranian people's, not the Ayatollah's.

If North was capable of questionable judgment, Poindexter was no better. Here again, the larger responsibility belonged to North's superior. According to Poindexter, North had just come back from London and at the end of his report had said something to the effect: "Admiral, I think we can—I have found a way that we can legally provide some funds to the Democratic Resistance . . . through funds that will accrue from the arms sales to the Iranians." North presented the plan as if it were his own, without mentioning Nir or Ghorbanifar.[47] Poindexter had never thought of it before but "in the end I thought it was a very good idea, the end of this conversation, and I personally approved it."*[48]

To justify his approval, Poindexter explained that the Iranian profit could be characterized as "private funds" or "third-country funds."[49] If the profits were "private funds," he said, they belonged to Secord. But Secord had been acting as an American agent, not as an ordinary businessman. If they were "third-country funds," they must have been contributed by Iran, without its knowledge. In fact, the profit or residual that went to the contras was the result of a decision made by North, not by Secord or Iran.

Poindexter also explained why he had deliberately failed to tell President Reagan about North's diversionary funds for the contras. On the one hand, he said that he had never made such a decision before.[50] In that case, this decision must have been one that deserved to be referred to legal counsel to make sure of its permissibility. On the other hand, he insisted that he could not see much difference between the diversionary money and third-country money.[51] If so, it is difficult to understand why Poindexter carefully kept the diversion from the president, unlike the third-country contributions.

Something else was illuminating—the relationship between Poindexter and the president. If we can believe Poindexter, once Reagan gave him a general mandate, he did not tell Reagan how, and Reagan did not bother to ask him how, it was being implemented. As Poindexter said:

> So after weighing all these matters, and I also felt that I had the authority to approve it, because I had a commission from the President which was in very broad terms, my role was to make sure that his policies were implemented. In this case, the policy was very clear, and that was to support the Contras.
>
> After working with the President for 5½ years, the last 3 of which were very close, probably closer than any other officer in the White

---

* Poindexter also related: "he [North] said that he thought that he had figured out a way to transfer residual funds from the arms sales that Dick Secord was making to the Contras. . . . I thought about it for several minutes while he was standing there . . . at the end of the conversation I told Colonel North to go ahead because I thought it was a good idea" (100-8, pp. 251–52).

House except the Chief of Staff, I was convinced that I understood the President's thinking on this and that if I had taken it to him that he would have approved it.

Now, I was not so naive as to believe that it was not a politically volatile issue, it clearly was, because of the divisions that existed within the congress on the issue of support for the Contras, and it was clear that there would be a lot of people that would disagree, that would make accusations that indeed have been made.

So although I was convinced that we could properly do it and that the President would approve if asked, I made a very deliberate decision not to ask the President so that I could insulate him from the decision and provide some future deniability for the President if it ever leaked out.[52]

Poindexter's role as political protector of the president came out in another connection:

I think that it's always the responsibility of a staff to protect their leader, and certainly in this case, where the leader is the Commander in Chief, I feel very strongly that that's one of the roles, and I don't mean that in any sense of covering up. But one has to always put things in the President's perspective and to make sure that he is not in a position that can be politically embarrassing.[53]

It is not easy to get behind the contradictions and contortions in Poindexter's explanations of why he had made a point of keeping the diversion from President Reagan. The one thing that comes through clearly is the identification of Poindexter with a commander in chief, not with a constitutional order, the government as a whole, or a civilian president who is among other things a civilian commander in chief. As Poindexter put it: "The decision for me to accept responsibility for what I did was made in February, 1986, when I decided to approve Colonel North's plan for providing funds to the Contras. I accepted that responsibility then and knew that if it became public, I would have to leave. Simple as that."[54]

Yet it was not so simple. The most striking thing about Poindexter's motive, as he himself tells it, was that it was so political in nature. The national security adviser, however, was one official who should be insulated from ordinary politics. The adviser's traditional task, after all, was to coordinate the policy options presented to the president by the different departments of the government without preempting their views and determining in advance that there was only one option to be considered. In this case, Poindexter did not present even a single option and made the presidential decision by himself, because he was convinced, as he said, "that I understood the President's thinking on this and that if I had taken it to him that he would have approved it." This presumptuousness was not a mere identification of Poindexter with the president on this issue; it also came from a deeper sense that both of them belonged to a privileged inner circle that made it possible for anyone in it to know what any other wanted and to act for him. It betrayed the mentality of a band under siege, dug in on the highest ground in the government.

4

More happened during North's meeting with Ghorbanifar in London on January 22, 1986, than the curious conversation in the hotel's bathroom. Nir and Secord also attended the meeting.

The meeting had been called to put the finishing touches on the latest plan to trade arms for hostages. By this time, it had been decided at the Army headquarters that handled the TOWs to sell them to the CIA for $3,469 per missile; the figure should have been $8,435 per missile, but a slip-up in the paperwork somehow resulted in the lower figure.[55] Since Ghorbanifar had already offered to pay $10,000 per TOW, Secord, to whom the CIA was selling the missiles, could make a profit of $6,531 per missile instead of $1,565. Ghorbanifar, who was selling the missiles to Iran, could make even more by charging, according to North, from $13,000 to $14,000 per missile.[56]

In effect, once the Army and CIA established the price that they wanted for the missiles, Secord and Ghorbanifar were able to decide between themselves what they wanted for the same weapons.* The Army price was so low that both of them were given enormous leeway for profit taking. So long as the Army was paid what it asked for, Secord—with North's blessings—could act as if the missiles belonged to him. In this way, a U.S.-Iran deal became a Secord-Ghorbanifar deal, with the two middlemen under no constraints from the countries they were nominally serving. This arrangement subsequently enabled Secord to claim that he had owned the missiles that he sold to Ghorbanifar, and Ghorbanifar to overcharge the country he was ostensibly trying to save from the Khomeini tyranny.

Neither Secord nor Ghorbanifar was risking any of his own money. They were acting as "cutouts"—a setup which so confused patriotic duty with private profit in conditions of secrecy that it was bound to get into trouble.

The deal as North saw it on the day that he met with Ghorbanifar, Secord, and Nir in London was recorded by him as follows:

---

* This is exactly how North understood the transaction: ". . . he [Secord] became the person with whom Mr. Ghorbanifar negotiated prices, delivery schedules, arrangements, and General Secord then became the person who went back and paid the Government of the United States, through the CIA, exactly what the Government of the United States wanted for the commodities that it provided" (100-7, Part I, p. 115).

Phase I
A—Provide small piece of Intel[ligence]
B—Iranian Govt will release 40M[illion]
C—$10M sent to [blank]
D—1000 TOWs, Basic Intel[ligence] Package
E—Hizb[allah] Prisoners from [Southern Lebanon Army]
    [All above] = hostage release.[57]

These notes indicate that Iran was expected to pay $10,000 per missile for 4,000 missiles and that it would get a first installment of 1,000 TOWs plus some military intelligence, in return for which the hostages were to be released as planned.

North went to London with instructions to get beyond Ghorbanifar and to arrange for a face-to-face meeting with Iranian officials. Though Ghorbanifar was still regarded as the only way to make direct contact with those officials, he was already viewed with such disfavor in Washington that it was thought necessary to escape from his clutches. The catch was that Ghorbanifar had to be used to get rid of Ghorbanifar, a maneuver which did not escape his notice.

When North talked about wanting to meet Iranian officials face to face, Ghorbanifar promptly promised to arrange just such an encounter in Europe the following month.[58] Ghorbanifar's offer had the desired effect on North. He says that he had gone to London with "grave reservations" about the entire process. He came back, however, advocating that it should be continued, for which he gave two reasons—Ghorbanifar's "incentive" to use profit from the Iran sales to support the contras and his promise to arrange a meeting with Iranian officials.[59] Ghorbanifar was still the impresario.

We have another version of this London meeting from Secord. He remembered it as full of complaints. He said that Ghorbanifar complained about being owed $5.4 million on the November 1985 sale to Iran of the wrong missiles. Nir agreed to see what he could do about it; the money was evidently returned by Israel soon afterward. Nir complained that Israel had not yet received replacements for the 508 missiles that it had sent to Iran in September–October 1985. They decided to charge Iran enough for the 4,000 TOWs to pay for 4,508. Secord confirmed North's urgent wish to get a high-level government-to-government meeting with Iranian officials. In this account, Ghorbanifar merely agreed to take the matter up with his contact in the Iranian prime minister's office. Secord made sure to nail down Ghorbanifar's offer of $10,000 per missile. Everyone agreed that it was necessary to get around the issue of the hostages, but no definite plan was adopted. The main result of the meeting was a decision to meet again in London on February 6. When the time came, however, North, Secord, and Nir assembled but Ghorbanifar stayed away.[60]

As soon as North returned to Washington, he sent Poindexter an extraordinary plan or, as he called it, "Notional Timeline for Operation Recovery." It set forth a daily schedule of actions, starting on January 24, which provided for the preparation and delivery to Iran of American military intelligence. It also stipulated just how much money was to be transferred from Ghorbanifar to the Israelis, from Secord to the CIA, and from the CIA to the Defense Department. It set forth how and when the first 1,000 TOWs were to be sent from Kelly Air Force Base in San Antonio, Texas, to Eilat, Israel, and from there to Bandar Abbas, Iran; the return of the 18 luckless Hawks from Iran to Israel; the release of all American hostages; and other details of what was, in effect, a fulfillment of the original sequential or staggered arms-for-hostages scheme. Most remarkably, North even noted that on February 11, the anniversary of his seizure of power, "Khomeini steps down." North assured Poindexter that his plan was known to only nine people—Poindexter, Fortier, North, McMahon, George, Clarridge, Secord, Nir, and Peres.[61]

This plan showed North at his best and worst. It meticulously worked out each step for the accomplishment of what had been agreed with Ghorbanifar and Nir in London. North was able to marshal all the details and manipulate all the factors in the far-flung scheme. He was also gullible enough to believe that Khomeini had decided to relinquish power on February 11 and that Iran was willing to obtain the release of all the hostages at once, thereby surrendering its best hope for future arms deals with the United States.

Ghorbanifar was North's source for the prediction of Khomeini's imminent resignation. On January 22, the day of the alleged bathroom incident, North's notebook reads: "Khomeini: stepping down Feb 11." Allen taped a conversation with Ghorbanifar and Ledeen in London on January 25, during which Ghorbanifar broke the news to them:

Ghorbanifar: You know the Khomeini has decided to step down.

Ledeen: Hmmm.

Ghorbanifar: On the 11th of February. And to, to resign and to bring the new leader in charge to settle for a time. You know, he wants everything be fixed when he dies.

Ghorbanifar spoke as if he were actively engaged in the struggle for the succession. "We are holding our own very well. This is a big fight."[62] If Ghorbanifar had been right about Khomeini's resignation, he would have demonstrated his intimate political connections in Tehran. Though he was not right, it was not held against him.

Allen met with Ghorbanifar again the next day. After complaining bitterly about the way the CIA had treated him, Ghorbanifar launched into his set piece on how important he was and what influence he had in Tehran.

Subject [Ghorbanifar] claimed that he had worked with other Iranians for the last six years at great personal expense and sacrifice, endeavoring with others to build an organization inside and outside of Iran that is capable of challenging the Line Two. Subject recounted how much he had suffered since the Khomeini regime had come to power. He said that he had lost "his best friends" and that his sister had been tortured.

Subject claimed that his organization had such influence he could get subjects inserted into the debates in the Majlis. He also asserted that he could get a subject discussed at the Friday prayers by President Khamenei. He claimed that "we control the President like a chicken." He noted that his organization is not "a broker of change" but "an architect." He stated he had put his personal fortune and the lives of his family at stake in order to seek such change in Iran.

Ghorbanifar also boasted that "as an [sic] procurement agent for the current Iranian Government, he could write checks for millions of dollars, and displayed a checkbook as well as records of deposits of large amounts of money." He seemed to know what others thought of him by assuring Allen that he was " 'an unusual individual' who is straightforward in his dealings. He said that he would not 'trick' anyone, unless he found himself dealing with deceptive individuals or organizations."*63

While Ghorbanifar was holding forth in London, North's plan was meeting with resistance in Washington. One of the nine in the know was not happy with it. He was again McMahon. On January 25, the day after he had received the plan, McMahon sent Casey, who was in Pakistan, a cable making known the opposition of everyone else in the CIA. What troubled McMahon most was the provision to Iran of a map depicting the order of battle on the Iran-Iraq border showing units, troops, tanks, electronic installations, "and what have you." McMahon protested:

Everyone here at headquarters advises against this operation not only because we feel the principal involved is a liar and has a record of deceit, but, secondly, we would be aiding and abetting the wrong people. I met with Poindexter this afternoon to appeal his direction that we provide this intelligence, pointing out not only the fragility in the ability of the principal to deliver, but also the fact that we were tilting in a direction which could cause the Iranians to have

---

* In this interview, Ghorbanifar said that he was having problems with the Israeli Nimrodi. "He commented that Nimrodi claims to be worth $75 million, including 10 million pounds in the UK Midlands Bank. Nimrodi, according to Subject, is unhappy over being excluded from certain business arrangements with Subject and has threatened him (Subject)" (B-1, p. 1035).

a successful offense against the Iraqis with cataclysmic results. I noted that providing offensive missiles was one thing but when we provide intelligence on the order of battle, we are giving the Iranians the wherewithal for offensive action.[64]

McMahon also informed Casey that Poindexter "did not dispute the rationale of our analysis but insisted that it was an opportunity that should be explored." Poindexter told McMahon that "the most we could lose if it did not reach fulfillment would be 1,000 TOWs and a map of order of battle which is perishable anyway." As a result, McMahon said that the CIA was going ahead to prepare the map and deliver it to North.[65]

This incident was another manifestation of the relationship between McMahon and Casey and between North and Poindexter. McMahon protested, Casey consented; North proposed, Poindexter disposed.

After North had made known his full plan to Poindexter on January 24, over three weeks passed before the first 500 TOWs were delivered from Israel to Bandar Abbas, Iran, on February 17. The interval was spent getting the money transferred from Ghorbanifar to Secord to the CIA to the Defense Department, and the weapons from Texas to Iran.

The next day, Ghorbanifar informed Secord that the long-awaited Iranian official and five others were soon going to arrive in Frankfurt, West Germany. Ghorbanifar also put new stress on the transfer of intelligence data. The Iranians, he said, wanted 500 more TOWs on February 21 but "they say they will release all hostages, if intelligence is good . . . Gorba repeatedly stressed need for good current intelligence . . . They want focus on current fighting."[66] In North's plan, the release of all the hostages had hinged on the delivery of the first 1,000 TOWs, not on good intelligence.

Ghorbanifar had some good news. The Iranians "envision a future meeting in Iran with us to consider next steps while we are delivering balance of TOWs (3,000)." North immediately listed his proposal for attendance at the meeting:

Nir (Office of Israeli Prime Minister)

MGEN Adams (Director, Current Intelligence—DIA (AKA—Secord)

William Goode (Office of President)

Albert Hakim (Support Assistant to Director DIA)[67]

At the meeting in Frankfurt, however, Nir was passed off as an American official, an impersonation which did not bother Ghorbanifar, who knew who he was.[68] Secord masqueraded as "Major General Adams," director of current intelligence of the Defense Intelligence Agency. William Goode was Oliver North's alias. Hakim, Secord's business partner, pretended to be a "Support Assistant" to the director of the defense intelligence agency. North explained that the CIA's Clarridge had been asked to produce false documents for Secord in order to avoid having him use his own passport and that Hakim, a native Iranian, was going along because he was fluent in Farsi.[69] By the time North set out for Frankfurt, he had added one more to his retinue, the chief of the CIA's Near East Division, Tom Twetten, to provide, as he put it, an " 'objective' account."[70]

Why North needed to use an assumed name is not clear. Secord presumably needed a false name and position to give him prestige and perhaps to hide his past career in Iran. Hakim, on the other hand, was not changing his name but was given a false position in the government, again probably to explain why he was important enough to go along. Yet these fictitious names and official positions were oddly inconsistent with the stated American objective of arriving at a serious long-range understanding with Iran. The Iranian side was being asked to negotiate seriously with make-believe Americans, who could not have negotiated in good faith if they had presented themselves as they were. Yet Ghorbanifar, for one, knew who they really were and could easily have tipped off his Iranian compatriots. There seems to have been an element of youthful playacting in North's makeup that added excitement to his adventurism. This element was noted by Twetten,* who spoke of North's two sides— "one is sort of secret and compartmented, and another one is sort of boyish and boastful."[71]

In his notes for the meeting, North put down the way he intended to appeal to the Iranians. The United States expected to have the American hostages released "promptly and safely." President Reagan was prepared to send a special emissary to Iran to discuss "further steps we can take together once this first phase is completed." More remarkably, North planned to reveal differences within the U.S. government. "It is important," he stressed, "that you recognize that there are many senior officials in our government who do not believe that this can work—and want to see it fail. We must act to prove them wrong." He also explained that he was bringing "highly accurate" intelligence information but nothing on the southern Iran-Iraq front "because of the opposition that exists in our govt." If the Iranians could assure the prompt, safe release of the hostages, however, "it will be possible to do much more."[72] In effect, the Iranians were going to be told much more than almost all Americans knew about the disagreements at the highest levels of the U.S. government.

---

* Twetten was deputy chief of the CIA's Near East Division until May 1986, when he was promoted to chief. He is sometimes cited as DC/NE (deputy chief) and as C/NE (chief), depending on the time and source. He gave his deposition as C/NE and is cited here as such, though much of his testimony deals with the previous period as DC/NE.

5

The long-awaited meeting in Frankfurt started out disastrously.

North's delegation arrived on February 19. But there was no new Iranian official to meet them. Ghorbanifar, as Twetten recalled, said that "he would be coming the next day, probably the day after that, but certainly coming at any moment." North was so angry that he immediately ordered a return to the United States and refused to come back until the Iranian official was physically seen to be on the ground in Frankfurt.[73]

While North was waiting for word of the Iranian's arrival, a crisis brewed between Ghorbanifar and Hakim. When Ghorbanifar learned that Hakim was coming with the American delegation, he realized that the Americans would no longer be entirely dependent on him as the sole translator and intermediary for both sides. On February 23, Allen taped a conversation with Ghorbanifar that vividly expresses, in his idiosyncratic English, Ghorbanifar's type of come-on as well as his animus against Hakim, who he had discovered was Jewish, apparently because his first name was Albert.

First, Ghorbanifar exuded his usual confidence that now, really, everything was going to be settled:

> Tell him [North] this is a real breakthrough. They have made up their minds, and we have brainwashed these people and have instigated them against the northern neighbor so they are ready to make a real firm response and collective cooperation for the future. They should also be ready to be "large" and to play the game just to make them show off. I think this time with all the strings I have pulled now it is going to work out.

Then Ghorbanifar warned darkly against Hakim:

> We hope it works out but there is something which could not only upset these arrangements but could also be really bringing the end of the life of those people which we are working on. That brought to me a very critical and deliberate mistake the name of an individual as a member of your delegation which has such a bad name in my place. He's a real Jewish gangster. He has one of the heaviest files in that organization which is following up the people. This is a very dangerous mistake; I don't know who made it on your side to give up such a Jewish name at such a critical time for such

an important meeting. If I didn't know about this, then it could be the end of everything."[74]

It seems that Secord had inadvertently told Nir that Hakim was coming to act as the American translator. Nir told Ghorbanifar, and Ghorbanifar was ready to take aim at Hakim.[75]

Finally, the Iranian official came, and the first meeting was held on February 25 at the airport hotel. He was Mohsen Kangarlou, a shadowy figure who continued to play a major role in meetings with the Iranians. Whoever he really was—and he has been identified as everything from the Iranian official in charge of arms purchasing to a high official in the Iranian prime minister's office to chief of Iranian intelligence—the Americans then understood that he was a Foreign Ministry official.[†] He was accompanied by Ali Samii, said to be a Revolutionary Guard intelligence official, and two colonels who were said to be military intelligence officials.[‡] We are going to encounter Samii again.

North was sufficiently impressed by Kangarlou to report to McFarlane that the Iranian had "authority to make his own decisions on matters of great import. He does not have to check back w[ith] Tehran on decisions take[n]."[76] In his notebook, North wrote: "Major breakthrough w[ith] an honorable religious man who we can trust— Relationship based on honesty."[77] North, as usual, was probably overdoing it. Nevertheless, if North was right, he was not negotiating with enemies of the Khomeini regime or with a "moderate" faction that had its own interests at stake, as Ghorbanifar pretended. Kangarlou's mission was clearly to negotiate for the Iranian government as a whole, with the Foreign Ministry and armed forces represented in his group. That he was someone with the right credentials was shown by the fact that he remained a factor in the negotiations for many months as the "First Channel," which is how the Americans thought of him.

* Ghorbanifar also said: "His name started with 'Albert'—a Jewish man—which I told him if it came up it could be the end of everything" (B-1, p. 1052). This was evidently said to Nir, who was also Jewish.

† He is referred to as the "Second Iranian Official" in FR, p. 219. The name is also spelled Kengarlou or Kangarlu with a first name of Mohsen or Ahmed; it was probably Mohsen. Among the Americans, he was sometimes called the "Australian." In a document entitled "1986 Chronology of CIA Involvement in NSC Iran Program," which was inadvertently made public and then withdrawn, the following item appears: "24 February: Twetten and North meet in Frankfurt with Ghorbanifar and Iranian MFA [Ministry of Foreign Affairs] official Kangarlu, and return with shopping list of spare parts for Hawk missile batteries." The date should have been February 25.

‡ The name "Ali Samii" is handwritten in 100-8, pp. 635–36 (Hakim's nine points). Woodward gives it as "Samaii," a Revolutionary Guard intelligence director in Prime Minister Moussavi's office (Veil, p. 496). Jane Mayer and Doyle McManus have "Ali Samaii," a Revolutionary Guard intelligence officer (Landslide, p. 276). Ledeen uses "Semai'i," again a Revolutionary Guard intelligence officer in the prime minister's office (Perilous Statecraft, p. 234). He is also called "the Engine" by Hakim, owing to his presumed influence, and "the Monster" by other Americans, who apparently disliked his behavior. For his presence in Frankfurt in February 1986, see FR, p. 254. The two colonels are mentioned in Secord, 100-1, p. 108.

Nothing went right from the very start. An immediate crisis between Ghorbanifar and Hakim was averted as if they were taking part in a comic opera. In their hotel room, North, Secord, and Twetten sat around debating what to do about Ghorbanifar's expected denunciation of Hakim. Hakim was a most amusing witness, and the reader should not be deprived of his own account of how he managed to fool Ghorbanifar.

And so there I'm sitting there and said to the group, I certainly would remember Ghorbanifar. There is no reason that he would not remember me. So how do you want me to go into this meeting?

So they turned to the CIA official and said, do you have somebody that can disguise Albert, and the guy said, by the time I go through the bureaucracy, it will be the end of the meeting.

So Oliver North turned around to me and said, I've heard from Richard [Secord] that you're very resourceful, why don't you go and disguise yourself. I said, thanks.

So I left the hotel, came down to the concierge, said I need to buy a gift for my father and I want to get a wig for him. Where is the best place to go?

So a lady is looking at me, said—gave me a couple of addresses, recommended one. I got a cab. I went to the place and the lady started to go through all kinds of salesmanship to sell me the best wig and if I wanted to swim, I didn't want to swim, and I'm sitting there knowing that the meeting is going to start very soon and I cannot—lady, let's get on with it, I don't give a damn, just give me a wig.

So she goes and brings me a number of wigs to select from. This has that advantage, this one this. Finally, to make a long story short, I said, this is beautiful, just let's try it on. And so we tried it on and I looked at myself, I said, oh, this is not good enough. I said, I don't like the style of this. Do you have a barber? They sent me to the basement. There was another lady. I said, I would like my hairdo in this form. We managed to shape it in such a way that it didn't look like me.

And I normally don't wear eyeglasses, but I have a pair of folding eyeglasses that I carry in my briefcase. I put that on and walked into the room and those three guys were just shocked, amazed. They didn't think that there was a chance for Ghorbanifar to know who I was.[78]

And that is how Hakim saved the meeting at the very outset. He was also given a change of name to Ebrahim Ebrahimian, with which he feigned to be an Iranian of Turkish descent.[79] To make the credentials of Hakim-Ebrahimian even more impressive, he was presented to the Iranians as the special translator of the president of the United States.[80]

Hakim also says that Nir wanted to look older in order to impress the Iranians, who, Nir claimed, respected people with white hair. So Hakim took Nir to the place where he had obtained his wig, bought some spray, and gave Nir white hair.[81]

Ghorbanifar's troubles with Hakim were not over. As Ghorbanifar was translating from Farsi, Hakim interrupted to charge that Ghorbanifar was deliberately distorting what both sides were saying to each other. Hakim made matters worse by taking over most of the translating. It seems that the Iranians were now more interested in talking about the more advanced Phoenix missiles—because Ghorbanifar had assured them that the Americans had promised to supply them. Tempers and confusion rose as North declared that he had never heard anything about Phoenix missiles, which the Iranians wanted because they were air-to-air weapons.[82]

The contretemps was caused, according to Twetten, by "Ghorbanifar having lied to both sides to get them to the table. He then was at the table to watch us have a fight." Yet he gave Ghorbanifar credit for "working like crazy to try and put it together. He had successfully done what he had set out; he got us to the table, not a minor achievement. But he then had a lot of work, and I will have to say in fairness to him that he was working harder than anybody else there."[83]

The main problem was still the same—both sides were talking at cross-purposes. North wanted to get the hostages out of the way as impediments to a strategic arrangement. The Iranians had their hearts set on Phoenix missiles, which the United States had not even given Israel. The Iranians dangled the hostages as bait without making commitments but demanded a commitment on the missiles before anything else was decided. The CIA representative paraphrased Kangarlou's strategy as "if you do something really big, get those Phoenix missiles for us, we might need only a couple thousand, and there might be some other things—but there was much more forthcoming, yes, there is a strategic plan here; yes, we will deliver; yes, we will start on the hostages. You might not get them all immediately, but we will at least start on it."[84]

Another incident showed how far apart the Americans and Iranians were in their ways of doing business. Kangarlou took Hakim aside in a corridor and gave him a message for the president of the United States. He told Hakim to whisper in the president's ear that he would make a lot of money if he took care to get the "Volkswagens"—meaning the missiles—to Iran right away. That is not the way things are done in the United States, said Hakim virtuously.*[85]

In the end, the meeting was not a total disaster for both sides. Secord and the CIA representative gave the two Iranian colonels an intelligence briefing in which details of the order of battle on a small section of the

* Hakim said that it had been his impression that he had been asked to "tell the President of the United States that he would get a personal payment if he arranged for the Phoenix missiles to be sold to Iran" (100-5, pp. 285–86).

Iran-Iraq border were described. The Iranians were also shown but not given an annotated photograph of the front to give them an idea of what the United States could provide if the two countries entered into an intelligence exchange agreement.[86]

The Americans went home with an agreement for high-level delegations of both countries to meet in the near future on Kishm Island, off the coast of Iran.[87] This had long been an American objective and represented the principal gain from the Frankfurt meeting.

North's reaction to the encounter with Kangarlou came in a message to McFarlane. "If nothing else," he wrote, "the meeting serves to emphasize the need for direct contact with these people rather than continue the process by which we deal through intermediaries like Ghorbanifar." North complained: "Throughout the session, Ghorbanifar intentionally distorted much of the translation and had to be corrected by our man on occasions so numerous that [deleted, probably Kangarlou] finally had Albert [Hakim] translate both ways."

Otherwise, North gave McFarlane his customary optimistic appraisal. The Iranian government "is terrified of a new Soviet threat. They are seeking a rapprochement but are filled w[ith] fear & mistrust." All the hostages "will be released during rpt [repeat] during the next meeting." Kangarlou "recognizes the risk to both sides—noted need for secrecy." North was again riding high:

> While all of this could be so much smoke, I believe that we may well be on the verge of a major breakthrough—not only on the hostages/terrorism but on the relationship as a whole. We need only go to this meeting which has no agenda other than to listen to each other to release the hostages and start the process.

There was one final somber note:

> Have briefed JMP [Poindexter] and Casey—neither very enthusiastic despite [Twetten]-North summary along lines above. Believe that you sh[oul]d be chartered to go early next w[ee]k or maybe this weekend—but don't know how to make this happen. Have not told JMP that this note is being sent. Help.[88]

As this implies, McFarlane had been chosen to head the American delegation to the projected high-level meeting provisionally set for Kishm Island, though he was a former rather than an active American official. McFarlane's reply to North showed that the former national security adviser had been infected with North's exhilaration:

> Roger Ollie. Well done—if the world only knew how many times you have kept a semblance of integrity and gumption to US policy,

they would make you Secretary of State. But they can't know and would complain if they did—such is the state of democracy in the late 20th century. But the mission was terribly promising. As you know I do not hold Ghorbanifar in high regard and so am particularly glad to hear of [Kangarlou's] apparent authority.

McFarlane also had good news. He had received a note from Poindexter asking whether he could go on the mission sometime next week "and that the President is on board." McFarlane needed no urging: "I agreed. So hunker down and get some rest; let this word come to you in channels, but pack your bags to be ready to go in the next week or so." Incidentally, he added, Ledeen had been requesting him for assistance in getting visas for Ghorbanifar to come to Switzerland, but he had refused. McFarlane advised North not to tell Ledeen "any of this new info."[89]

North soon added to the good news in a reply to McFarlane. He had met with Casey, Poindexter, and Clair George, and "all had agreed to press on. Believe we are headed in the right direction." Always irrepressibly hopeful, North reported that he had received a message from Secord that "once we have set a date [for the top-level meeting] we shall have a very pleasant surprise. Dick [Secord] and I believe that they may be preparing to release one of the hostages early." Even more exciting, McFarlane's "counterpart at the mtg [meeting] w[oul]d be Rafsanjani," the speaker of the Iranian parliament. Then came one of North's boyish jokes: "Nice crowd you run with!" He followed with more optimism: "God willing Shultz will buy onto this tomorrow when JMP [Poindexter] brief[s] him. With the grace of the good Lord and a little more hard work we will very soon have five AMCITS [American citizens] home and be on our way to a much more positive relationship than one which barters TOWs for lives."[90]

McFarlane sympathized with Poindexter. "My part in this," he wrote to North, "was easy compared to his. I only had to deal with our enemies. He has to deal with the cabinet." In a follow-up message, he added: "And I fully understand the narrow path he is trying to walk between those who want to go balls out for the wrong reasons (Regan) and those who don't want to do it at all (GPS [Shultz] and Cap [Weinberger])."[91]

Thus North returned from Frankfurt all fired up again. In mid-February, 500 TOWs were delivered to Iran. Forgotten or ignored was the plan that he himself had sent to Poindexter on January 24 and that he had taken to Frankfurt to put into effect. That plan had provided for the delivery of 1,000 TOWs by February 8 and the release of all American hostages on February 9.

Another 500 TOWs were delivered by February 27. Not a single hostage was released the next day or for many weeks afterward. Yet North was as buoyant as ever. He looked forward irrepressibly to the next meeting with higher-level Iranian officials, at which he was confident that everything was going to be put right, again.

Money also changed hands. Secord paid $3.7 million to the CIA, which paid it to the Defense Department for the 1,000 TOWs. He received $10 million from Ghorbanifar, who received even more from Iran. Some of Secord's profit went to support the Nicaraguan contras, or what North called the "residuals" and others called the "diversion." The only loser was the Defense Department.

14

The Diversion

The holy grail of American Iran policy was always just within reach and yet tantalizingly unreachable. The highest hopes had been held out for the meeting in Frankfurt in February 1986, when at last a real Iranian official had come to negotiate with North and his entourage. For a while, North had thought that the official, Kangarlou, was important enough in the Iranian hierarchy "to make his own decisions."[1]

But Kangarlou was a minor bureaucrat interested mainly in obtaining the unobtainable Phoenix missiles and unable to commit himself on what the Americans most wanted. Yet his agreement to another meeting on the highest official level, the main outcome of the Frankfurt discussion, was seized on as putting the grail again within reach. This time Ghorbanifar had led North to believe that a major Iranian figure, Speaker of the Majlis Rafsanjani, was going to attend and enable the Americans to make the long-awaited breakthrough.

North seems to have expected the Kishm Island meeting to take place within days or no more than a week after his return from Frankfurt. McFarlane, the designated American negotiator, was put on the alert and told to be ready to depart at any moment. He waited three months. In that time, all sorts of new obstacles appeared that might have disheartened someone less dogged than North.

The first signal of trouble came from Secord and Hakim on March 2, 1986. Hakim had talked with Kangarlou, who had led him to believe, as he informed North, that "situation is not right for mtg [meeting] in Kish[m]." Nevertheless, the Iranians wanted Phoenixes. North quickly got in touch with Nir, whom he told "no way we can delay this much further." He asked Nir to get "Gorba [to] pull out all stops."[2]

Next came disquiet in the CIA, which now significantly increased its investment in the Iran affair. Though it still considered the NSC staff to be in charge of the operation, the CIA could not resist getting more deeply embroiled in it, if only to help North out of trouble.

On March 5, the CIA contributed one more of its own to North's entourage. He was George Cave, a retired CIA veteran, who had been called back as a consultant on Iran owing to his fluency in Farsi. Cave had first known Ghorbanifar in 1980 and the following year had recommended breaking off with him. Ghorbanifar, Cave said, had provided information that did not check out and had demanded exorbitant financial payments. When Ghorbanifar was apparently taken on again in 1984, Cave's suspicions had led to the polygraph tests which Ghorbanifar had failed and to the "fabricator notice" which had warned all and sundry against any dealings with him. In January 1986, when he heard that Ghorbanifar was back again, Cave had again made his distrust known and had helped to design the new polygraph test, which Ghorbanifar had again failed. Cave thought that that was the end for Ghorbanifar—prematurely, as had been the case with so many other rumors of Ghorbanifar's downfall.[3]

The CIA was instrumental in putting Cave into North's operation. The Near East Division's Tom Twetten was disturbed by the use of Hakim, who had allegedly been involved in some illegal arms or technology sales to Iran. Twetten went to Clair George, the Operations chief, to get Hakim out and Cave in; George went to Casey; Cave came in, though Hakim was also a hard man to get rid of.[4] With Cave, Allen, and Twetten working with North, the CIA had no trouble monitoring the Iran affair—and bearing more responsibility for it.

When he was called in on March 5 and told about the Iran operation, Cave says that it was "quite a shock" and that he was "very alarmed."[5] He met that same day with North, whom he had not previously known, and came in for an even greater shock.

Two days later, they were on a plane together heading for Paris—to meet with Ghorbanifar.

2

On March 7, 1986, North, Cave, and Twetten met Ghorbanifar and Nir in the French capital. As usual, Ghorbanifar claimed to have everything under control and said that there was nothing to worry about. He was, Cave wrote in a memorandum that same night, "very relaxed and said that everything was arranged." He spent at least a half hour talking about how indispensable he was—"how careful we must be in dealing with these guys and how we needed such a person as him to guide the way he knew how to handle them."[6]

Twetten recalled that in an early exchange of recriminations about which side had been most at fault in the past, Ghorbanifar was not abashed. The Americans were unhappy because no hostages had been released. Ghorbanifar countered that the Iranians were so unhappy with the Americans that Kangarlou was accusing them of bad faith and broken promises. The American intelligence that had been brought to the Frankfurt meeting was "garbage" and not what they had asked for. Twetten interpreted these grievances as "typical Middle Eastern tactics—whatever you do isn't any good, and whatever deposit you have made doesn't really count until you start walking out of meetings and then they have to call you back in to complete the purchase of the rug. It was really kind of low-level merchant tactics."[7]

To Nir at this time, North complained that "up to now [,] primary purpose is on arms, not political change."[8] The "merchant tactics" were designed for nothing else.

Two new things emerged from the meeting in Paris. The Iranians had changed their minds about TOWs and Phoenixes; they now, according to Ghorbanifar, wanted nothing so much as spare parts for Hawk missiles. He presented a list of 240 line items, which, from their knowledge of them, made no sense to the Americans.[9] Ghorbanifar also told them that Kishm Island as the place for the high-level meeting was out; the Iranians had decided to move it to Tehran. Otherwise, Ghorbanifar was still full of confidence. He held forth on how he had talked to the conservative Line 1 leaders and had found that certain military leaders were enthusiastic about relations with the United States.[10]

One more item later attracted a good deal of attention. In Cave's memorandum on the meeting, this final sentence occurs: "He also proposed that we use profits from these deals and others to fund [other operations]. We could do the same with Nicaragua."[11] This remark would tend to corroborate North's statement that Ghorbanifar had broached the use of profits to support the contras in the London bathroom in January, or at least that Ghorbanifar had had such a "diversion" of the profits very much on his mind.

The Paris meeting did not live up to expectations. All the Americans learned from it was that they were going to Tehran, not to Kishm Island, and that the Iranians now wanted Hawk spare parts the Americans thought they did not need. North returned to Washington uncertain what to think of the new state of affairs. He confided to McFarlane:

> Per request from y[ou]r old friend Gorba, met w[ith] him in Paris on Saturday. He started w[ith] a long speech re how we were trying to cut him out, how important he is to the process and how he c[oul]d deliver on the hostages if only we could sweeten the pot w[ith] some little tidbits—like some arms, etc.

After this, North turned to the Soviet threat, which was emerging as a major theme in the American approach to Iran:

The real problem facing Iran—that of Soviet intervention was becoming a reality and the Iranians are in no position to deal w[ith] this problem. We can help—and are willing to because a free, independent Iran is in our best interests. Unless the hostage issue is resolved quickly and favorably, U.S./Iranian cooperation on opposing the Soviets is out of the question. . . . We probably won't know for a couple of weeks whether this "the Russians are coming" approach will have any effect, but it does have the merit of being mostly the truth—and something about which their military people expressed great concern during the Frankfurt meeting the week before. We shall see.[12]

To which McFarlane replied:

Gorba is basically a self-serving mischief maker. Of course the trouble is that as far as we know, so is the entire lot of those we are dealing with. The Soviet threat is the strategic menace and I would guess that they would like to avoid having Russians in Iran. But it is going to take some time to get a feel for just who the players are on the contemporary scene in Teheran. So the sooner we get started the better.[13]

Ghorbanifar and the Russians preoccupied North in his answer to McFarlane:

In re the Gorba prob[lem]: He is aware of the Kish[m] mtg [meeting] and is basically carrying our water on the mtg since he is still the only access we have to the Iranian political leadership. It w[oul]d be useful, I believe, for you to talk w[ith] George Cave, the Agency's Iran expert. He shares our concern that we may be dealing only w[ith] those who have an interest in arms sales and their own personal financial gain and believes the "Russians are coming" approach is about the only way to broaden the perspective. So w[oul]d do well to explore other contacts if they can be opened.[14]

After all the optimism, then, came another letdown. The Americans were no longer taken in by Ghorbanifar's smooth talk; he was now a necessary evil—"the only access we have to the Iranian political leadership." The lesson seemed to be that the Americans had to get to Iran to negotiate with responsible Iranian leaders over the head of Ghorbanifar. The catch was that they still needed him to get them to Iran. Yet Ghorbanifar clearly knew the game that was being played and had no intention of making himself obsolete.

The Paris meeting was typical of North's hectic arrangements. The American delegation arrived at the airport early in the morning, immediately went to the hotel, where they arrived at about 8 or 8:30 a.m., met with Ghorbanifar and Nir until noon, and North took the afternoon flight back to Washington.[15]

3

What to do with Ghorbanifar continued to haunt the Americans.

Opinions differed. Allen saw no way out of continuing to work with him. The CIA's counterterrorist intelligence officer had been given the assignment of staying in close touch with Ghorbanifar, as a result of which we have Allen's memoranda of his telephone conversations with Ghorbanifar all through the month of March. The substance of these conversations permits a rare insight into the relations with Ghorbanifar in this period.

March 9, 1986: Ghorbanifar said that the recent discussions in Paris on the "principal matter" [hostages] had gone well, though more work had to be done. Allen told him that this "principal matter" must be resolved before working with him on other issues. Nevertheless, Allen noted that Ghorbanifar seemed "unusually subdued and less sanguine" than before.[16]

March 11, 1986: Ghorbanifar said he planned to travel to Tehran "at some personal risk but claimed to have good friends there who would protect him."[17]

March 17, 1986: Ghorbanifar called from Paris; said that he has just returned from Tehran; had met with key people; had had a difficult time, but believed he had achieved most of the trip's objectives. He requested another meeting with North and Nir to discuss the "principal matter"; claimed he had made "certain unspecified arrangements for this meeting"; implied other Iranians might attend; had other unspecified "good news" for North.[18]

March 20, 1986: Ghorbanifar said he had just returned from a meeting with Nir. He again talked about his trip to Tehran: he had met with Prime Minister Moussavi, Speaker Rafsanjani and Ahmed Khomeini, son of the Grand Ayatollah. He predicted significant changes in the Iranian government in the next ten days, claimed to know just who was going to be the next Prime Minister and had given a photograph of him to Nir.

Later that day, Allen spoke with Nir, who confirmed meeting Ghorbanifar. Nir stated that Ghorbanifar "needed the help and support of all parties at this critical time, pointing out that Subject [Ghorbanifar] remains the central thread in this entire initiative." Nir urged the United States "to be more responsive in support of

Subject, again noting that he remains the best hope for a successful US initiative."

Summing up these conversations, Allen commented: "I tend to agree with Adam [Nir] that we should work with Subject concurrently on 'the main problem' as well as on assisting him in terrorism, regardless of whether we find his information at this stage credible. He remains the single link to significant Iranian leaders who may be able to accomplish a major Administration objective."[19]

March 24, 1986: Allen talked to Nir about Ghorbanifar. Nir said Ghorbanifar showed signs of being "under pressure to produce" and needed financial assistance. Nir reiterated his view that Ghorbanifar should be supported "inasmuch as Subject's credibility apparently is at stake with some of his associates."[20]

March 27, 1986: Ghorbanifar called to say that his "financial situation was currently precarious" because he had covered the bad debt of a friend. He stated that an important meeting was to be held in Tehran the next day, at which Khomeini himself would be consulted. He expected "very positive" developments, in which case North and Ghorbanifar would have to travel to Tehran "fairly quickly."[21]

March 27, 1986: Cave talked to Ghorbanifar in London and reported that Ghorbanifar is so "extremely unhappy" with the CIA that he has decided not to work with agency on terrorism. Ghorbanifar blamed the CIA for entering the apartment of his girlfriend in California and for rifling through her personal effects.[22]

March 28, 1986: Allen told Ghorbanifar, who had called him, that "it was important for him to know that we intended to continue to do business with him and that we would provide him with appropriate support in some of his endeavors. From conversations that he had earlier with me and a consultant to the NSC [Cave], I had discerned that he believed that there was no interest in a long-term relationship. I assured him this was not the case . . ."[23]

March 28, 1986: Allen called Ghorbanifar, who was in London, because North had heard from Nir that Ghorbanifar was "emotionally upset" and had told Nir that "he [Ghorbanifar] had learned he was being shoved aside from participation in the 'principal matter.' " North had requested Cave to tell Ghorbanifar that "this was not our intention at all" and to invite Ghorbanifar to come to Washington on March 31. As a result, Cave asked Ghorbanifar "to stay in close touch" and to call "on a daily basis if possible."[24]

March 30, 1986: Nir called Cave to say that Ghorbanifar "wanted reassurance that the US side would not attempt to bypass him in dealing with his fellow countrymen." Nir stated that "it was unwise to try to eliminate" Ghorbanifar, who "was not always truthful but that, with patience, the principal matter could be resolved by keeping Subject involved as originally envisioned."[25]

These conversations show how disturbed the relations between Ghorbanifar and the Americans had become. He had read the signs of American disaffection and made no secret of his resentment. Not knowing how to do without him, the Americans were forced to disavow their intention to go over his head and to reassure him that they were still determined to maintain their old ties with him. Pressure to hold on to Ghorbanifar also came from Nir, who was somewhat in the same position as Ghorbanifar. If the Americans succeeded in striking a direct bargain with the Iranians, both the Israelis and Ghorbanifar saw themselves as no longer essential go-betweens. Nir's insistent interventions on behalf of Ghorbanifar served to make the Americans even more convinced that Ghorbanifar was an "Israeli agent," though the probability is that Nir was reluctant to see Ghorbanifar go because he was his main source of alleged intelligence from Iran. Without Ghorbanifar, Nir had little to contribute to the Americans, for whom he was serving as middleman to the Iranian middleman.

Two telephone calls by Hakim to Kangarlou made Ghorbanifar even more suspicious. It seems, according to Ghorbanifar, that Hakim, who claimed to speak for President Reagan, had taken it upon himself to tell Kangarlou that there was no need for Ghorbanifar to be involved in U.S.-Iran affairs. Kangarlou promptly reported the calls to Ghorbanifar, who fumed about them to Allen.[26]

Hakim's continuing role is another of the curiosities of North's operation. Hakim had entered the contra affair merely because he was Secord's business partner. In the Iran affair, he was drafted for the Frankfurt meeting because he spoke Farsi and could check on Ghorbanifar. He had checked so well and so enthusiastically that he had upstaged Ghorbanifar and had earned the latter's undying hatred. Hakim's call to Kangarlou to get Ghorbanifar shut out was more than the latter's all too human nature could bear. Hakim seems to have made these calls on his own, as if he were conducting a feud with an Iranian rival. By bringing in a character like Hakim, who was not responsible to anyone and had only a faint idea of what was permissible in covert operations, North extended his little band of secret agents far beyond his ability to control them. After Ghorbanifar complained to Allen about Hakim's calls, there is no indication that Hakim was called to account for his meddling. The record simply shows that Ghorbanifar complained to Allen and that Allen reassured him that all was well between them. This was not the last time that Hakim was permitted to play at being an American spokesman.

4

Cave had never put any trust in Ghorbanifar and saw no reason to change his mind as a result of his latest experiences. When he was brought in to help out in 1986, he examined some of the material on Iranian terrorist activities that Ghorbanifar had given Allen and said that he "didn't believe it. It was similar to the kind of things he told us before. A mixture of truth. When Ghorbanifar does something like that, he is setting you up or somebody up to make—not necessarily you—to make a lot of money."[27]

Cave was troubled not only by Ghorbanifar but by the Israelis, who, he thought, had "different goals" from the United States. Israel, he believed, was so hostile to Iraq that it was even willing to see an Iranian victory over Iraq, whereas the United States did not want either side to win. In addition, he argued that the Israelis had had such good relations with the Shah's Iran that they wanted to return to a similar status with Khomeini's Iran and needed the United States "to do some brokering for them."[28] When Cave met Nir in Paris, he asked him whether the Israelis had ever made an intelligence assessment of Ghorbanifar to justify their faith in him. When Nir asked him what he meant by this, Cave replied: "Well, we have some doubt, and I think if you haven't done it, you ought to."[29]

Cave's assessment of Ghorbanifar was unsparing:

> The Israelis, particularly in the person of Nir, insisted on Ghorbanifar, for one thing. I was at the other end of it, insisting that he couldn't be trusted. There were other people that felt that you had to keep him in because since [sic] he—because he would probably blow the whole thing.
>
> He was investing a lot of money in this operation, so that he had to be kept in it. I was more concerned that, knowing Ghorbanifar, that Ghorbanifar works for Ghorbanifar, period, which is basically what we found out when we got to Tehran.[30]

Secord was another who later said that he had wanted Ghorbanifar out. Secord had a special grievance because Ghorbanifar had deposited a bad check in Secord's account at the Crédit Suisse bank in Geneva, leaving Secord and Hakim temporarily without money. Secord told of the incident:

> So, I was having a rather acid conversation with Mr. Ghorbanifar on the telephone, and I told him that I thought that he had behaved very poorly, that he was promising the moon always, but never producing, and that I was going to recommend that he be termi-

nated. He misinterpreted that, and he—I don't mean to be funny—
he took it the wrong way and he told Mr. Nir that I was going—
trying to have him killed. I think I even said later it was not a bad
idea, but it was not what I had in mind.

From this time onward [February 1986], I was complaining, and
so were my colleagues, about the Ghorbanifar connection. It seemed
to me to be too fraught with problems. It was just a big operational
security problem and it was a very inefficient connection, and a
very indefinite connection.[31]

Whatever others may have thought, the decision to hold on to Ghorbanifar was largely made by North, who had similar misgivings but could
not find a viable substitute. It was generally understood on the American
side that the American and Israeli purposes were not entirely the same;
Cave was not the only one to hold this view. The more important question
was whether they were sufficiently compatible to justify working closely
together. Here again, the Americans were fatally handicapped by their
intelligence vacuum in Iran and thought that they could not afford to
give up whatever the Israelis could provide. Nevertheless, there was a
tendency in some American quarters to make a scapegoat of Nir, as if
he had some power over the Americans to make them do what they did
not want to do.

To appease Ghorbanifar, North again invited him to come to Washington, where he arrived on April 3, 1986. Ghorbanifar, carrying $50,000
in cash, was met at the airport by Cave and Allen, who put him up at
a hotel. North and Cave spent most of the time with Ghorbanifar discussing the coming trip to Tehran. Ghorbanifar offered to provide false
passports, a genuine driver's license, and a bank account to the Americans—for a price. The most troublesome subject was still the exchange
of arms for hostages. Ghorbanifar had to come up with money in advance
to pay the CIA for the Hawk spare parts and TOWs; only after this
condition was satisfied could the Americans begin to get everything "pre-
positioned" for delivery to Iran. Ghorbanifar evidently did not have the
money at hand and said that he was raising it "through his bankers."
The Americans insisted on the preliminary release of all the hostages,
after which a plane loaded with the Hawk spare parts would be launched
and 3,000 more TOWs brought over ten days later. Ghorbanifar as usual
pressed for more—new batteries no longer in inventory and radars that
would have to be sent by ship.

The Americans, according to Cave, depended on Ghorbanifar "to play
the key role in making it all work." Ghorbanifar for his part "spent a lot
of time telling us how essential he was to the operation" and gave them
a clearer idea of whom they were going to meet in Tehran. He suggested
that the Americans should take "presents" to Tehran—Korans and one
unit of spare parts. North and Cave thought that they were really "getting

somewhere" when Ghorbanifar began talking about "his cut." North told him that "he could add on whatever he thinks right for his cut to the final price," at which Ghorbanifar said that he had already spent $300,000 "to grease the skids, etc."

Ghorbanifar was still his old, confident self, pretending to be very much in the know about what was going on in Tehran. The whole thing, he confided, "is being masterminded by Rafsanjani behind the scenes." The speaker might at some point put in a personal appearance but in any case would be following everything closely. Ghorbanifar warned against Prime Minister Moussavi, "who may be our primary senior contact" and who did not like or trust Americans. Cave, however, did not think that the Iranians had given much thought to how to maintain a continuing relationship.[32]

The upshot of Ghorbanifar's Washington visit was what North had hoped for—a determined effort to convince Ghorbanifar that he was not being cut out and preparation for the long-delayed mission to Tehran.

But Ghorbanifar was not North's only problem. Nir had come to suspect that he was being eased out of the now predominantly U.S. operation. In a talk with the Israeli on March 7, North found it necessary to assure him, as his notes state, that there was "no intention to cut you out or go around you." In the same conversation, North confessed: "We cannot verify that there is anyone else in G.O.Ir. [government of Iran] aware or even interested in talking to USG [U.S. government]."[33]

Later that month, the man who had been responsible for the fateful Finding to cover the CIA's participation in the "horror story" had had enough. John McMahon resigned on March 26, 1986. For the past year, right-wing organizations had carried out a letter campaign defaming him. "This was a public campaign," Twetten testified, "thousands of letters to Congressmen attacking John McMahon for being soft on Communism and not letting the Muj[ahadeen in Afghanistan] push back the Russians. It was nasty stuff."[34]

5

We now come to the most famous or notorious of North's literary works— the "diversion memorandum." It was composed for Poindexter and the president soon after Ghorbanifar's departure from Washington on April 4, 1986.[35] Apart from the diversion aspect, the memorandum has a special interest, because in it we can follow what North understood had been happening in the Iran operation.

About a quarter of the memorandum was devoted to background, as if North wanted to make sure that it was properly understood. He recorded as a simple fact that the Israeli shipment of arms to Iran in September 1985 had been carried out "with the endorsement of the USG [U.S.

government]." He then explained that the United States had been frustrated "due to the need to communicate our intentions through an Iranian expatriate arms dealer in Europe" and, therefore, in January 1986 had decided to demand a meeting with "responsible Iranian government officials."

North also wanted to get straight the relation between the two main American objectives—the need to establish a long-term connection between the United States and Iran "based on more than arms transactions," and the hostage issue. The latter was merely a "hurdle" which had to be overcome before the improved relationship could prosper. North accused Ghorbanifar of having inaccurately transmitted to the Iranian government the U.S. conditions and demands that had been agreed upon at the meeting with Kangarlou on February 20, 1986:

> The United States had established "its good faith and bona fides" by providing 1,000 TOW missiles on February 21 to Iran, "using a private U.S. firm [Secord] and the Israelis as intermediaries."
> A later meeting of senior U.S. and Iranian officials in Iran during which the U.S. hostages would be released.
> Once the hostages were released, the United States agreed to sell an additional 3,000 TOW missiles to Iran "using the same procedures employed during the September 1985 transfer."

After which, North related, in early March, Ghorbanifar had raised the ante and had demanded 200 Phoenix missiles and an unspecified number of Harpoon missiles in addition to the 3,000 TOWs as the price for releasing the hostages. When this demand had been turned down at the Paris meeting on March 8, North claimed that no further American effort had been made to get in touch with Ghorbanifar or the Iranian government—ignoring the many telephone conversations between Ghorbanifar and Allen that very month.

The rest of the memorandum—with the exception of the diversion paragraph—dealt with the arrangements for the Tehran meeting. It is most revealing of North's persistent will to believe that he had finally settled once and for all the exact details for the release of the hostages. The schedule, as he had worked it out, was:

> April 7, 1986: Iranian Government transfers $17 million to an Israeli account in Switzerland. The Israelis will in turn transfer $15 million to the Secord-Hakim Lake Resources account in Switzerland.
> April 8, 1986 (or as soon as above transactions are verified): Lake Resources will transfer $3.651 million to CIA account in Switzerland. CIA will then transfer this sum to Department of the Army in the United States.

April 9, 1986: CIA will commence procuring $3.651 million worth of HAWK missile parts and transferring them to [deleted].

April 18, 1986: A private U.S. aircraft will fly missile parts to a covert Israeli airfield, where they will be transferred to an Israeli military aircraft with false markings.

April 18, 1986: McFarlane, North, Teicher, Cave, Nir [deleted] and a SATCOM communicator board a CIA aircraft in Frankfurt, Germany, en route to Tehran.

April 20, 1986: U.S. party arrives in Tehran, met by Rafsanjani, as head of the Iranian delegation. U.S. hostages released seven hours later in Beirut. Israeli military plane with HAWK missile parts aboard lands in Bandar Abbas, Iran, fifteen hours later.

This plan tells us a number of things of special interest. A great deal more money was intended to reach the Secord-Hakim Lake Resources account than was ever meant to go the Department of the Army, which was supplying the missile parts. It is also clear that the joint U.S.-Israel–Iran operation was still very much in force. Ghorbanifar had convinced North that Speaker Rafsanjani was so fully behind the meeting that he intended to head the Iranian delegation and meet the U.S. delegation on its arrival in Tehran. And North still expected all the American hostages to be released before the Iranians had received their newly demanded missile parts.

This memorandum also betrayed North's anxiety to persuade the Iranians of American good faith. In this respect he was always defensive, as in this typical example:

The Iranians have been told that our presence in Iran is a "holy commitment" on the part of the USG that we are sincere and can be trusted. There is great distrust of the U.S. among the various Iranian parties involved. Without our presence on the ground in Iran, they will not believe that we will fulfill our end of the bargain after the hostages are released.

Another theme struck by North played up the Soviet menace:

We have convinced the Iranians of a significant near term and long range threat from the Soviet Union. We have real and deceptive intelligence to demonstrate this threat during the visit [to Tehran]. They have expressed considerable interest in this matter as part of the longer term relationship.

Toward the very end of this lengthy discourse, North came to the subject of "residual funds," by which he meant the profit earned by the Secord-Hakim combine in the sale of the spare parts. He implicitly recognized that the profit was so great that it could not be considered normal or reasonable.

North foresaw two uses for the residuals. One was to use $2 million to pay for the replacement of the 508 TOWs "sold by Israel to Iran for the release of Benjamin Weir." This statement incidentally acknowledged that the first shipment of weapons by Israel to Iran had been a straight arms-for-hostage deal.

The second use was the diversion from the Iran to the contra operation:

> $12 million will be used to purchase critically needed supplies for the Nicaraguan Democratic Resistance Forces. This materiel is essential to cover shortages in resistance inventories resulting from their current offensives and Sandinista counter-attacks and to "bridge" the period between now and when Congressionally-approved lethal assistance (beyond the $25 million in "defensive" arms) can be delivered. [36]

These few lines created more future trouble for North than anything else he ever said or wrote. The diversion at this stage was a declaration of intention, not a statement of fact. Its importance at the time it was discovered was that the statement of intention led to an inquiry about the fact.

There is a good deal of confusion about the fate of this memorandum. It ended with the usual request for the president to approve it, but no copy was found with the president's signature. Yet North told McFarlane that he had written it at Poindexter's request for the benefit of the president. [37] North also said that he had written five or six memoranda seeking the president's approval for the diversion. [38]

Poindexter told two stories about the diversion memorandum within minutes of each other—that he could not recall having seen it before it was divulged in November 1986 and that he had probably destroyed it at the time it was submitted to him. [39] He could not have destroyed it very effectively; five copies were later found. [40] North added to the confusion by saying that the diversionary plan in this memorandum was "never executed or implemented"—presumably implying that it was executed or implemented later. [41]

As might be expected, the diversion memorandum was not a favorite subject with North or Poindexter; they did not exert themselves to remember much about it. In any case, it exists, and the diversion occurred. North's diversion memorandum was written for the president and Poindexter, whatever they may have done with it.

At about this time, another document, entitled "Terms of Reference: U.S.-Iran Dialogue," was drawn up as policy guidance for the American delegation at the projected meeting in Tehran. Its main drift may be gathered from these lines:

We view the Iranian revolution as a fact. The U.S. is not trying to turn the clock back. . . .
Your influence in achieving the release of *all* hostages and the return of those killed (over time) is essential. . . .
In essence, we are prepared to have whatever kind of relationship with Iran that Iran is prepared to have with us. . . .
Moscow has designs on Iran. . . .
We may be prepared to resume a limited military supply relationship. . . .
However, its evolution and ultimate scope will depend on whether our convergent or our divergent interests come to loom larger in the overall picture. . . .
What does Iran want?[42]

North was so much in charge of the entire operation that these political pronouncements largely represented his thinking or the thinking that he shared with Poindexter and McFarlane. North was not content to be the "action officer" of the operation; he gradually took it upon himself to oversee its every phase, intellectual as well as operational. He attempted and largely succeeded both in making policy and in carrying it out. His only arbiter was Poindexter, who had the power to give him his head or restrain him. In an operation so closely held, the policymakers in the State Department were totally excluded, and North's adjutants in the CIA acknowledged his ascendancy. Unlike others in the bureaucracy, he recognized no limits to his range of activity and authority. The CIA's Near East chief, Twetten, said of him that "he was clearly the most hectically pressed member of the U.S. government I had ever met."[43] He was never more hectically pressed than in these weeks before the long-expected hegira to Tehran.

6

We are in the first week of April 1986. Ghorbanifar had led North to expect that the Tehran meeting and the release of the hostages would take place on or about April 19, as North told McFarlane.[44] Yet so many problems remained that the appointed day came and went without any sight of Tehran.

One problem was whether to take Nir along to Tehran, something which Nir virtually demanded and the Americans initially opposed. On April 3, North met with McFarlane and Cave, with the result that he wrote in his notebook: "Plan to go to Tehran. Mention nothing about Israel. No Israeli presence."[45] On April 7, North received a call from

Nir and North recorded: "Nir very upset that Israel might be 'cut out' of the Iran trip. Very bad if cut out."[46]

If Cave had had much to do with it, Nir would have been cut out. According to Cave, "I made the point I thought it would be a terrible error for Nir to go to Tehran and it was decided that because of the way the Israeli pressure on this issue, that the only way that you could get him out was for the President to call Peres and ask him to say that he just can't go." The issue seems to have been left to McFarlane, who decided: "Well, he has worked so hard on it, let him go."[47]

For another thing, there was disagreement about the wisdom of going to Tehran without a preparatory meeting to make sure that both sides understood what they were getting into. North admitted that "we did not know all of the expectations of the Iranians as to what it would take to make things go well." He said that he had wanted an advance-party trip "because I knew Ghorbanifar to be what he was. I knew he was a duplicitous sneak." North said that he had advocated an advance trip by Secord and himself but that Casey had prevented it on the ground that North had been involved in too many operations and would have to be prepared to take his own life if he was tortured.[48] Yet McFarlane testified that North as well as Poindexter had assured him that the existing arrangements, without an advance party, were going to work.[49]

Cave, Secord, and Nir favored an advance party to agree on an agenda and work out the logistical details. A preliminary trip by North and Cave as well as one by North and Secord seems to have been contemplated but never came off.[50] Cave said that a preliminary meeting was not a bad idea, "because having—with all my Iranian experience and my distrust of Ghorbanifar, I thought there was an awful lot of risk in us going in."[51] Secord thought the trip was "not well organized" for lack of an agenda; he had never before been to an international meeting "where there wasn't some preparatory work done in advance."[52] Nir told Allen that he was not "too happy" about the cancellation of the preliminary meeting. Nir thought that such a meeting was one way "to have complete assurance that both sides were in agreement on the terms of the arrangements."[53]

Ghorbanifar was another who wanted to have a preliminary exploration of the conditions in Tehran. He said that he had proposed that he and North should go ahead to prepare the way and that the Iranian officials were amazed that McFarlane would agree to come without adequate preparation.[54]

Poindexter had the last word on this, as on other matters whenever he chose to have it. He revealed that he had vetoed the idea of an advance trip because he had thought "that that was more dangerous and that if we had a more senior person there with the group that there was less risk to the whole group."[55] The logic may escape some; if the Iranians wished to hold anyone for ransom or for any other reason, a more senior person would seem to have been more desirable to them than a lesser one.

Once Poindexter decided against an advance party, the details had to be arranged at long distance, with Ghorbanifar the only intermediary. When April 19 had come and gone without any meeting in Tehran or hostages released, the rest of April was spent by the Americans still getting messages from Ghorbanifar about what the Iranians allegedly wanted and by the Americans trying to decide what they wanted from the Iranians.

What the Americans supposedly heard from Iran went from Ghorbanifar to Allen. On April 14, Ghorbanifar called from a restaurant near his hotel in London, because he was convinced that the British were conducting electronic surveillance of his room. As usual, he professed to know just what was needed for a successful mission. He suggested that McFarlane should carry messages from President Reagan to the president and prime minister of Iran, and other messages should be brought from the speaker of the House of Representatives or head of the U.S. Senate. In return, McFarlane would be permitted to meet with the three top officials in the Iranian government, who, Allen understood, were Speaker Rafsanjani, Prime Minister Moussavi, and President Khamenei.

Of greater significance was the latest arms-for-hostages deal allegedly put forward by the Iranian authorities. It provided for the release of one American hostage upon the arrival of the American delegation; followed by the delivery of one-half of the spare parts about ten to twelve hours later; and if the negotiations proceeded successfully, the other hostages were to be released over the next four or five days.

This scheme went back to the sequential or staggered system that had once been accepted by North. Nevertheless, this time Ghorbanifar surprised Allen by telling him to advise North to reject the Iranian approach, as if he knew that it did not stand a chance. When Allen called him the next day to say that North had rejected it, Ghorbanifar was not at all discouraged. He resumed his old air of confidence and said that a small "miracle" had been achieved by getting the hard Line 2 to accept the release of any hostages and that with North's proper backing he could successfully pressure Prime Minister Moussavi, the main obstructionist, to adhere to the original plan.[56]

At issue, however, was a fundamental difference of strategy. The Americans were willing to pay for the hostages, but only once, and then they wanted to go on with the more substantive "strategic opening" without the blackmail of the hostages hanging over them. The "hurdle" theory, which the Americans continually urged, assumed that the hostages were merely obstacles in the way of achieving the larger political understanding both sides supposedly wanted.

At this point, the decision was up to Poindexter. On April 16, in response to the new Iranian sequential feeler, he sent unequivocal instructions to North:

You may go ahead and go, but I want several points made clear to them. There are not to be any parts delivered until all the hostages are free in accordance with the plan that you layed [sic] out for me before. None of this half shipment before any are released crap. It is either all or nothing. Also you may tell them that the President is getting very annoyed at their continual stalling. He will not agree to any more changes in the plan. Either they agree finally on the arrangements that have been discussed or we are going to permanently cut off all contact. If they really want to save their asses from the Soviets, they should get on board. I am beginning to suspect that Kangarlou doesn't have much authority. [57]

Poindexter was so firm in his resolve that he sent a similar message to McFarlane:

[Kangarlou] wants all of the parts delivered before the hostages are released. I have told Ollie that we cannot do that. The sequence has to be 1) meeting; 2) release of hostages; 3) delivery of Hawk parts. The President is getting quite discouraged by this effort.

This will be our last attempt to make a deal with the Iranians. Next step is a Frankfurt meeting with Gorba, Kangarlou, North and Cave. Sorry for the uncertainty. [58]

McFarlane was equally determined to stick to the original plan of all the hostages or none:

Roger, John. Your firmness against the recurrent attempts to up the ante is correct. Wait them out; they will come around. I will be flexible. [59]

Nir evidently suspected that waiting out the Iranians might not be easy. On April 21, in a mood of resignation, he talked to Secord, who reported to North: "He [is] quite pessimistic re Gorba-[Kangarlou] cabal. He know[s] time is nearly over."[60] On April 22, however, North was told by Nir what the sequence of events in Tehran was going to be:

> U.S. arrives—Iranians to Beirut
> W[ith]in 24 h[our]s all host[ages] released
> Disc[ussions] begin on arrival
> After hostages—240 [spare parts] arrive[61]

This schedule led the Americans to believe that they would get the release of the hostages before they had turned over any more spare parts. Two days later, North wrote: "Delegation from Tehran to Beirut as soon as we arrive . . . [Iranian] 'Authority' probably does not want G[horbanifar] in on political decisions/discussions."[62] North's expectation was questionable. If an Iranian delegation did not go to Beirut until the Americans had arrived in Tehran, was it certain or even likely that the hostages could be released within twenty-four hours? Did the Iranians have such control of the Lebanese hostage holders that they could get the hostages out by merely appearing in Beirut?

One of the pessimists was the CIA's Allen. The most recent information suggested to him on May 5 that "the White House initiative to secure release of American hostages in Lebanon remains dead in the water." He surmised that Kangarlou had not been able "to provide the assurances and to make the arrangements demanded by our side." Allen believed that the Iranian government had not been able to persuade the Lebanese holders of the hostages to release them to Iranian custody. He saw Ghorbanifar's failure to deposit funds to pay in advance for the spare parts as an indication that the Iranian middleman had doubts about the release of the hostages. Allen also directed attention to what always came between the Americans and the Iranians—"that we have insisted that the spare parts will [be] delivered eight hours after the release of the hostages and *only* after the release of the hostages."[63]

If anything seemed to be firm before the Tehran meeting, it was the American determination to deliver no more arms until all the hostages were released.

7

At about the same time, Ghorbanifar figured in a strange episode in London.

Except for speaking his mind against arms deals, Secretary Shultz had not been looking for trouble once the president had decided against his view of the matter. Instead, trouble came to him.

When Poindexter had first told Secretary Shultz on February 28 that McFarlane might meet with high-level Iranian representatives, at which time the hostages would be released, Shultz said that he had responded with: "Well, that sounds almost too good to be true, but anyway, if that's the case, I'm in favor of it." Shultz had also agreed to the "Terms of Reference," in which the sale of weapons to Iran had been so underplayed that Shultz had thought he might belatedly have won the argument with the president against a weapons deal.*[64]

In May, this amicable interlude was suddenly broken off. Shultz, in Tokyo with the presidential party for an economic summit, received a cable from Under Secretary of State Michael H. Armacost, who relayed

---

* The "Terms of Reference" statement had been: "We may be prepared to resume a limited military supply relationship."

disconcerting information from the U.S. ambassador in London, Charles H. Price II. The story, as told by Price, began sometime at the end of April 1986, when a delegation made up of Ghorbanifar, Nir, and Adnan Khashoggi came to see Rowland W. Rowland (better known as "Tiny," because he was not), the head of the far-flung Lonrho group of companies, extending from mining to textiles to hotels.

The trio allegedly told Rowland of a plan to sell grain, spare parts, and weapons to Iran, with Lonrho acting as "some sort of umbrella company" in return for 7 percent of the profits.[65] Rowland said that he was not inclined to get involved but might reconsider if it became a U.S. government operation. Nir allegedly told him that it had been cleared by the White House and that a very limited number of people knew about it.[66]

Rowland soon disclosed the visit to Bob Frasure, a U.S. aide attached to the embassy.[67] On May 2, Price called Armacost about the puzzling approach to Rowland, and Armacost thought it important enough to send word of it to Secretary Shultz. Price also talked to Poindexter about it and made a memorandum of the conversation, part of which reads:

> John [Poindexter] then said there was a "small shred of truth" in Nir's contention regarding White House involvement. He added that Nir was "up to his own games." Originally the USG [U.S. government] became involved because "we caught the Israelis red-handed delivering arms to Iran in the middle of last year." There was only "a small connection," he reiterated, but claimed that the story was "out of all perspective." He recommended that I advise Rowland not to get involved.

Poindexter was admitting something but not much. His equivocation gave evidence of an increasing tendency to blame Nir and the Israelis for any embarrassment in this affair. Poindexter must have known that the Israelis were not caught "red-handed" in August–September 1985 delivering arms to Iran but had done so in consultation with and with the approval of the United States, then speaking through McFarlane.

Poindexter said something else of future interest. When Price maintained that the whole thing "could blow up" and be "very damaging to the President," Poindexter replied that the president "is completely aware of everything that has been done" and "is very sensitive [to the potential for a blowup]."[68]

After receiving Price's call about the bid to Rowland, Poindexter sent a message to North about Price's "wild story." Nir again came in for most of his wrath: "What the hell is Nir doing? We really can't trust those sob's."[69]

After all this, it turned out that North and Casey had known all the time about this attempted transaction. North replied to Poindexter:

I agree that we cannot trust anyone in this game. You may recall that nearly a month ago I briefed you to the effect that Tiny Ro[w]land had been approached and we went back through Casey to tell those guys that the whole thing smelled very badly, do know that Khashoggi is the principal fund raiser for Gorba.

Even more startling was North's disclosure that Price had been given a "cover story," not the real one.

The story you had relayed to you by Price was the one made up by Nir to cover the transaction and Clair George reported it to me when the issue first came up several weeks ago. At the bottom line, this typifies the need to proceed urgently to conclude this phase of the operation before there are further revelations. We all know that this has gone on too long and we do not seem to have any means of expediting the process short of going to Iran.[70]

North had more news for Poindexter. He was leaving for London the next day to meet with Ghorbanifar, Nir, and Cave. Ghorbanifar had not yet made a deposit in the Swiss bank to pay for the spare parts; North intended to tell him that "unless a deposit is made by the end of the week, the whole operation is off." North reiterated the plan that was going to be put to Ghorbanifar—all the hostages released after the Americans' arrival in Tehran, followed by delivery of spare parts.[71]

Not knowing what North had revealed to Poindexter, Shultz took the news from London seriously. After reading Armacost's cable, he walked from his part of the Tokyo hotel in which they were all staying to the part occupied by the president, Regan, and Poindexter. He could not reach the president but found Regan and Poindexter. Regan seemed "very upset" about the news and promised to take it up with the president; he later told Shultz that the president was also "upset." Poindexter said something like: "We are not dealing with these people. This is not our deal."[72]

It thus appears that all the confusion about the Rowland story was a comedy of errors. Poindexter had forgotten what North had told him weeks earlier, and Shultz had never been let in on it. In reality, the plot seems to have been a way to make some money for Ghorbanifar, who had been making known for some time that he needed money desperately. The "shred of truth" is that the Americans knew that Nir was trying to find ways to make Ghorbanifar solvent, though North apparently did not like the way it was being done through Rowland. Just what it was all about is still unclear; what is clear is that it came as no surprise to North. If Nir, Ghorbanifar, and Khashoggi had been trying to put something across secretly, they had made a fatal mistake in going to Rowland, who promptly upset their applecart by making their scheme known to a U.S.

aide in the London embassy, who told the political counselor, who told the ambassador, who told Armacost, who told Shultz, who told Poindexter and Regan, who told President Reagan.

The Americans had been aware of Ghorbanifar's financial plight for almost two months. On March 24, 1986, Nir had told Allen that Ghorbanifar was in such trouble that he had had to utilize funds from his wife's account and that the Israelis were attempting to support him financially.[73] Four days later, Ghorbanifar told Allen that his financial condition was so precarious that his credit had been shut down in Geneva and he found himself without a "cash flow."[74]

The following month, Ghorbanifar came to the attention of the CIA in another connection. On April 22, 1986, he was arrested in Switzerland with eighteen other arms dealers as the result of a U.S. Customs "sting" operation. It seems that Cyrus Hashemi—the same Hashemi who had been indicted in April 1985 for having attempted to sell arms to Iran— had cooperated in the sting against the other arms dealers, who were trying to do the same thing as he had done, in order to get off more lightly in his own case. Ghorbanifar had been picked up with the others but was held by the Swiss police for only twenty-four hours, evidently because he had merely invested some money in the scheme. Oddly, the CIA had known nothing of the U.S. Customs' action and was caught by surprise. The incident was apparently regarded as nothing more than another attempt by Ghorbanifar to get into a money-making deal.[75]

8

Oliver North might have been a character in a play entitled *Waiting for Ghorbanifar*.

The all-important mission to Tehran depended on the delivery of American spare parts for Hawk missiles at the same time as or soon after the arrival of the American delegation. But—once more—the spare parts had to be paid for in advance in order for the Defense Department to release them. Defense had to get its money from the CIA, the CIA from Secord, and Secord from Ghorbanifar. But Ghorbanifar could not get his money from Iran, which refused to pay in advance on the ground that it had been tricked once too often.

Until Ghorbanifar put up enough money to start the payments going in reverse, the mission to Tehran could never be sure of coming off. Since Ghorbanifar was strapped for money, everything depended on his coming up with it. This was not the only financial consideration. Ghorbanifar was also in these deals to make as large a profit as possible. As a result, the prices of the weapons and spare parts were always in dispute. The only fixed prices came from the Defense Department, which set them so low that they presented no problem. Once the materiel left

Defense and the CIA, however, the prices were subject to bargaining. The Americans constantly ran the risk that the Iranian government would learn that it was being outrageously overcharged. The Americans could do little about it, because they were never sure what Ghorbanifar was charging.

On May 6, 1986, North, Nir, Cave, and Ghorbanifar came to London for one more of these sessions. Before leaving, North received instructions from Poindexter: "Do not let anybody know you are in London or that you are going there. Do not have any contact with Embassy."[76] Poindexter had already received the call from Ambassador Price about the Rowland imbroglio and evidently did not want any more inquiries from the U.S. embassy about anything that had to do with Ghorbanifar.

Cave later analyzed the trouble with Ghorbanifar's methods. As Cave put it, "the problem you get into with Gorba—he was involved with so many arms deals with them." The result was such "egregious overcharging that it could queer the whole deal with the Iranians."[77] North's notebook for May 6 shows that the U.S. price for what the Iranians wanted was $12,688,173 and the proposed price to the Iranians was $23,663,911.[78] Significantly, North, who claimed that he was not interested in financial matters and left them wholly to Secord and Hakim, was the only American who set the prices in London. Cave said that "they were very careful not to talk about the costs in my presence" and that North had set them with Nir and Ghorbanifar alone. When Cave pointed out to North that Ghorbanifar's markup was more than the 60 percent he had previously fixed for himself, North agreed but "really didn't have much to say at that time."[79]

Allen later learned that Ghorbanifar had raised the money for the spare parts in such a way as to go even more deeply in debt. It was at this time that a story was concocted to account for Ghorbanifar's debt. According to this version, Khashoggi and some Canadian investors had lent him $15 million to finance the deal. Khashoggi had put his assets in jeopardy by putting up collateral to cover at least part of the loan. The interest on the $15 million, which was repayable in thirty days, came to 20 percent, forcing Ghorbanifar to pay a minimum of $16 million.[80] Ghorbanifar's debts—of which no one on the American side could be sure—haunted the Iran operation from then on.

Still in London, Ghorbanifar told them about arrangements for the Tehran trip. According to Cave, he assured them that the Americans would meet with Prime Minister Moussavi, Speaker Rafsanjani, President Khamenei, and possibly Ahmed Khomeini, the Ayatollah's son. When Cave talked on the phone with Kangarlou, however, the old trouble reappeared. Cave described what he was up against:

> We run into our first major snag and Kangarlou is insisting we bring all of the Hawk spares with us. I told him we can't do that.

And we haggled, typical, like you are buying a rug. Finally, I said, Okay, we will bring a small portion, what we can carry with us on the one plane, given the fuel, which would be about one pallet. He agreed.

They also agreed that the Iranians would make an effort to get the release of all the hostages and meanwhile the remaining three pallets of spare parts would arrive.[81] On May 7, North recorded: "We get our 4 items [hostages] w/in [within] 24 hrs. 8 hrs later we deliver the 240 parts."[82] All through this period, the Americans thought that they had an arms-for-hostages deal nailed down.

Like so many meetings with Ghorbanifar, this one in London seemed to settle everything and nothing. Both sides talked as if the Iranians were going to produce the U.S. hostages and the Americans were going to give them spare parts in return. But Iran did not have the hostages; they were in Lebanon, held by the Hizballah, who presumably were beholden to Iran and could be prevailed upon to give them up—but no one could be sure. Ghorbanifar said that the Americans were going to be met by the three top Iranian officials—Rafsanjani, Moussavi, and Khamenei—but everything still went back to Ghorbanifar.

The London meeting was followed on May 9, 1986, by a strategy session in Washington attended by North and his aide, Lieutenant Colonel Robert Earl, together with four CIA officials, including Clair George, George Cave, and Burt Dunn, the newly appointed assistant deputy director of Operations (ADDO). It was called to decide on three outstanding questions: the Israeli role, overall strategy in Tehran, and the intelligence information wanted by Iran. North and George did most of the talking.

North reported that the Israelis wanted to be represented at Tehran. "North pointed out," reads the memorandum for the record, "that the Israelis provide some degree of plausible deniability if the project unravels." Whereupon George agreed to Israeli participation in the person of Nir. In effect, the Israelis were being set up to take the blame in the name of "plausible deniability."

On overall strategy, North pointed out that the long-term objective was to end the Iran-Iraq war, and a short-term aim was to get Iran to cut off its oil to Nicaragua.

On the intelligence offering: "North wants it jazzier, more photos, more reports of evil Soviet deeds against Muslims and mosques, etc. . . . The objective is to string this out (not just a two-hour slam bam, thank you ma'am). George suggested the theme that the Soviets are 'one idea' people and that you (Iran) are OK now so long as the Soviets are preoccupied in Afghanistan. But afterwards, watch out."

George asked what was to be done if the Iranians could not deliver the hostages. North replied: "We probably don't give them the parts and radars, but we also probably don't want to 'go away mad' and give up the opportunity to develop some sort of on-going relationship."

George also wanted to make sure that Secretaries Weinberger and Shultz and Director Casey would be briefed on the project, especially on the subject of long-term goals.[83]

As of May 9, it was noted, Ghorbanifar had not yet deposited any money. Three days later, however, Secord sent word that $10 million had been put into his Lake Resources account in Geneva with $5 million more to come.[84]

Following George's suggestion, North urged Poindexter to meet with McFarlane and added: "You may also want to include Shultz, Weinberger and Casey."[85] Poindexter peremptorily replied: "I don't want a meeting with RR [Ronald Reagan], Shultz and Weinberger."[86]

Only after the CIA had been paid on May 16 was it possible to set a date for the trip.[87] On May 19, North sent Poindexter a schedule of events from May 22 to May 24 on just how the spare parts and TOWs were to be moved from Kelly Air Force Base to Israel.[88] On May 22, North sent another schedule for May 24 to May 29: Americans to arrive on May 25; hostages released on May 26; spare parts delivered; Americans depart on May 29.[89] Everything was neatly laid out, even to the timing of the State Department's notification to the hostages' families and the issuance of the White House press statement.

Poindexter went over these plans with care. He objected to the use of a military aircraft for a flight to Israel and suggested a CIA proprietary plane.[90] As a result, North made other arrangements.[91] Poindexter was always there in the background, intervening when he saw fit. North took the initiative so often that he can be given too much credit for what occurred. He was an inveterate writer of reports, down to the least detail, always asking for approval and almost always getting it. But Poindexter was finally responsible; when he gave an order, North obeyed.

Finally, the American party, with McFarlane at its head, was put together. It was first intended to be a three-man delegation, made up of McFarlane, North, and Cave.[92] One more, Howard Teicher, who had just been appointed senior director for political-military affairs on the NSC staff, was added as a regional policy expert and note taker. In the end, the entire delegation consisted of these four plus a CIA communicator who was to remain on the plane and forward messages to Poindexter in Washington and Secord in Tel Aviv. Nir was passed off as a quasi-member of the American delegation, described to the Iranians as another American, though Ghorbanifar knew who he was. Ghorbanifar had gone on ahead to Tehran to be the inevitable intermediary between the two sides. Secord in Tel Aviv was to oversee the delivery of the remaining spare parts. All the Americans carried false Irish passports, evidently to enable them to deny their origins if the wrong Iranians took them hostage. North masqueraded as "Goode," Teicher as "McGrath,"

Nir as "Miller," and Cave as "O'neil."[93] According to Cave, Ghorbanifar protected himself by telling the other Iranians who Nir really was.[94]

It was a peculiar mission. The only American who could lay claim to any political stature was McFarlane, who came with a presidential commission but no longer had an official position. He was chosen, according to Cave, precisely because he was not an active American official.[95] Cave was later told that the Iranians did not even know who McFarlane was.[96] Yet this relatively low-level American delegation expected to be greeted by and to negotiate with the highest-level Iranian officials on matters of the greatest moment to both countries. The entire pilgrimage had been prepared so imprudently that no one knew what to expect in Tehran, and it was even regarded as an act of maximum physical risk to go on the trip. McFarlane was thought to be the one in greatest danger and was prevailed on to carry a poison pill to be used if he was tortured to give away vital American secrets. U.S. naval forces might have been able to protect the delegates if the meeting had taken place as originally planned at Kishm Island but they were bound to be helpless in Tehran. McFarlane and the others showed considerable courage or foolhardiness in making the trip under these circumstances, which were hardly conducive to diplomatic deliberation.

Whatever the merits of the mission as planned, it was not one of those events in this affair about which President Reagan could plead ignorance. On May 12, 1986, Rodney McDaniel, the executive secretary of the NSC staff, noted that the president and Poindexter had discussed the hostages and McFarlane's coming trip. McDaniel, who was present, later recalled that Reagan had said it was important to maintain secrecy throughout the entire operation.[97] On May 15, the president specifically authorized McFarlane's mission to Iran and its "Terms of Reference." On May 21, the trip was discussed again.[98] The president evidently was briefed on all such activities, gave them his blessing, and was responsible for the extreme secrecy with which they were carried out.

If all had gone as planned, Tehran would have delivered the holy grail to the Americans.

15

Tehran

The Americans arrived in Tehran at 8:30 on the morning of May 25. They came in an unmarked Israeli aircraft, repainted to look like another country's plane and furnished with false flight plans. It was flown by an American crew selected by Secord from his Lake Resources organization. The group did not wait long for their first letdown.

Though Ghorbanifar had led them to believe that Speaker Rafsanjani would greet them, and McFarlane had even thought that they might have a motorcade, there was no one at the airfield who knew they were coming.[1] Ghorbanifar appeared a half hour later and explained that they had not been expected for another hour. The Americans had brought gifts with them—two pistols and a chocolate-covered cake from a Tel Aviv bakery. The cake could not have come at a worse time, because the visit had been thoughtlessly arranged to coincide with the fasting holiday of Ramadan. Throughout the meetings, the Iranians were "frazzled," because they could not drink or eat anything during the heat of the afternoon.[2] Irish passports, gifts, and the pallet of spare parts were taken away by security guards—the spare parts much to the dismay of the Americans, who had thought that they would be delivered after the hostages had been released. The group was brought to the fifteenth floor of the former Hilton Hotel, renamed the Istiqlal, or Independence, and sequestered on the entire top floor, which they and the security guards had to themselves.

The Americans, it is said, narrowly escaped being taken prisoners in the hotel by Revolutionary Guards, who came there to arrest them. Other Iranian guards fought them off in the parking lot and prevented an incident that would have recalled the seizure of the U.S. embassy in 1979.[3]

The first meeting took place at 5 p.m., with three Iranians, one of whom has been described as an intelligence officer. One of the Iranians seems to have been called "Ali Najavi."[4] The names and identities of these Iranians are so uncertain that it is enough to know when an Iranian spoke and what he said. Cave, the only American who spoke the native language, assumed that all the Iranians used aliases, which would make their names of no great use in any case.*[5]

McFarlane's opening statement was conciliatory. President Reagan, he said, had asked him to "try to find common ground for cooperation." The United States acknowledged the Iranian revolution and had no interest in or intention of trying to reverse it. Among other things, he suggested exchanging information on Soviet intentions and capabilities in that part of the world.[6]

The Americans had rehearsed their Soviet line on the plane. McFarlane, North, and Teicher had concocted a story—Cave called it "play acting"—about a Soviet plan to invade Iran. The source of the plan was allegedly a Soviet major general, whose identity could not be revealed but who was dubbed "Vladimir" by North and who had taken part in two war games on the invasion of Iran.[7]

The Iranian spokesman told the Americans the best way to build "a bridge of confidence": "The U.S. will supply physical support to Iran. U.S. support will be with us. This is the best way to build confidence. For the U.S.A. to demonstrate that it is with Iran." After more talk, he came back to this theme: "We expect anyhow to receive more items from you so that we will be in a better position with our leaders. I want to make this point very clear. Iran has been at war for six years . . . We are expecting more equipment."[8] According to North's notes, the Iranian

---

* Yet this has not stopped some sources from giving names and positions. Mayer and McManus say that the first Iranian to greet the Americans was Ahmed Kangarlou (*Landslide*, p. 231). Later, they say that Kangarlou appeared with Ali Najavi, whom they identify as a deputy to Prime Minister Moussavi (p. 232). On the second day, they have Hossein Najafabadi, called a closer adviser to Speaker Rafsanjani and a leading member of the Majlis (p. 235).

According to Segev, four Iranians met with McFarlane's group: Mohammed Ali Hadi Najafabadi, chairman of the Majlis Foreign Affairs Committee; Ali Mohammed Bisherati, senior deputy to Prime Minister Moussavi; Hossein Sheikh El-Islam Zadeh, deputy foreign minister; and Mohammed Lavassani, head of the Foreign Ministry's political department (*The Iranian Triangle*, p. 273). Segev introduces Kangarlou toward the end (p. 278).

Amir Taheri in *Nest of Spies* says that McFarlane's party was first greeted by Abbas Kangarloo. To him were added Ali Reza Moayeri, an assistant to Prime Minister Moussavi, and an unnamed junior Foreign Ministry aide. Finally, there came Muhammad-Ali Hadi Najaf-Abadi, chairman of the Majlis Foreign Relations Committee (pp. 196–98).

Ben Bradlee, Jr., in *Guts and Glory* refers only to an unnamed junior deputy prime minister and Naja Fabadi, a leading member of the Majlis (pp. 374, 379).

Still others appear in the record. One Iranian, called by Hakim "the Monster," probably Kangarlou in this context but elsewhere called "Samii" or "Samai," came to some meetings (Cave, B-3, p. 846). Teicher's notes list "a deputy prime minister," an "assistant to the Prime Minister"; and a "Senior Foreign Affairs Advisor" at various meetings. These alleged identifications were deleted in A-1, but were restored in TR, pp. B-103–17. Ghorbanifar said that he had arranged for "the head of the Majlis foreign relations committee," who was probably meant to be Najafabadi, to meet with McFarlane (ibid., p. B-120).

It will be seen that the names and spelling vary wildly in these sources. The two Iranians who appear most often and were undoubtedly the main negotiators were Kangarlou and Najafabadi, as their names will be spelled here. I will refer to them whenever it can be safely established that they were the interlocutors.

held out the freedom of the hostages as a reward: "Iran is in position to make possible their release."

This exchange of views starkly disclosed the gulf between the Iranians and the Americans on a critical issue. The Iranians were interested in the hostages only as a means to an end; the end was their successful prosecution of the war against Iraq. They were not merely seeking one or two deliveries of missiles or spare parts. They looked upon the United States as wanting to curry favor with them and accordingly expected American military support on a vastly greater scale than the Americans had ever envisaged. The official U.S. position of neutrality in the war and its desire for a speedy conclusion without a victor were never accepted by the Iranians and was not their idea of how to gain their "confidence." The Iranians were desperately fighting a holy war, in which they had suffered a heavy loss of lives. They had been attacked by Iraq, which had a decisive advantage in weaponry. For the Americans, a relatively small amount of arms was mainly a bargaining point to get the release of the hostages and enter upon a vague "normal relationship" with Iran to prevent the Soviets from getting to them first.

A related complaint also came from the Iranians. They were disappointed that McFarlane's plane had brought only one pallet of spare parts whereas they had expected half of the entire purchase. This charge was unexpectedly linked with what Iran was prepared to do about the hostages: "What Iran expected is not here, but as a humanitarian gesture, Iran will send a delegation to Beirut to solve that problem while expecting Iranian logistics needs to be met."[9]

In effect, this meant that the Iranians had barely begun to do anything to get the release of the hostages. Yet the entire U.S. calculation had been based on rescuing all the hostages before any spare parts were handed over. McFarlane tried to put up a brave front in the face of this blow: "Let's be clear. I have come. There should be an act of goodwill by Iran. I brought some things along as a special gesture. So far nothing has happened on your side. However, I am confident it will." The Iranian tried to relieve the tension by emphasizing that he and his colleagues were not decision makers: "We just give you a message and take your message. But we told our leaders that you would bring one-half of the items."

McFarlane had been restraining himself. He now blew up angrily: "I have come from the U.S.A. You are not dealing with Iraq. I did not have to bring anything. We can leave now!" The Iranians responded that they were in trouble with their superiors because they had promised one-half of the items and that they had done all that could be expected of them by sending a special delegation to Lebanon to deal with the humanitarian problem of the hostages.[10]

The first meeting, lasting almost four hours, had gone badly. Cave, who was in a position to understand the Iranians better than anyone else in the U.S. delegation, summed up his impression: "This initial meeting was hostile with the Iranians listing past sins of the United States etc. The meeting ended with what appeared to be little chance of any progress. Basically the American side insisted on adherence to the agreement as we understood it, and the Iranians insisting that America must do more to atone for its sins." Cave and Ghorbanifar translated, the latter, as usual, twisting what each side said to favor whatever he thought best, until Cave could stand it no longer and rebuked him.[11]

McFarlane's report to Poindexter was less pessimistic but did not hide his misgivings. He realized that he had been dealing with third- and fourth-level officials who were "uncertain, fearful and timid." It was also clear to him by this time that Ghorbanifar had caused much of the misunderstanding between the two sides: "It has become more and more clear that while Gorba has brought us to the beginning of a dialogue with the GOI [government of Iran], he has done it with considerable hyperbole, occasional lies and dissembling." McFarlane had made up his mind that serious business could not be done with the Iranians present at the first session and that it would be necessary to get beyond their level. Nevertheless, he told Poindexter that "the meeting ended on a harmonious note."[12]

That night, another crisis erupted. The Iranians decided to remove the crew member who remained on the plane to take care of communications with Washington and Tel Aviv. McFarlane's reaction was to pack up and leave if the Iranians carried out their threat. The crew member was forced to leave the plane, and another was not permitted back until the next day. Cave thought that the Iranians had merely intended to search the plane. The incident did not contribute to McFarlane's peace of mind.[13]

Another meeting, which at first McFarlane did not attend, took place on the afternoon of the next day, May 26. The issue for McFarlane was that he had counted on meeting with Iranian ministers, not underlings; he felt that the impasse of the first day should not be repeated. As a result, North did the speaking for the Americans and gave the Iranians a strange reprimand. His notebook reads at this point: "Insulted Presidential Emissary. Rob. will be President next 8 yrs." That McFarlane expected to follow Reagan as president must have been North's idea of impressing the Iranians with McFarlane's importance. North also complained that the Americans' documents had been taken and that the Iranians had not come through on their promise to release the hostages in twenty-four hours. He reminded the Iranians that time was running short and that the Americans were going to stay in Tehran for only two more days and intended to leave early in the morning of May 28 at the latest.[14]

According to Teicher, North also said:

We are confused and concerned. We have tried for months to come to a point where we could talk government-to-government. Some in our government opposed. McFarlane favored. I was convinced that necessary arrangements had been made. We received President Reagan's permission to proceed. We have now been here for over a day and no one will talk with us. Where are we going? Nothing is happening.

The Iranian who replied wondered

why we came to this situation. We were both happy last night. Why are you now confused? We are working to make things happen. We have similar problems with our people, but don't see any insurmountable problems. I understand McFarlane is unhappy about something. I want to see McFarlane.[15]

At this, McFarlane was prevailed on to attend. He gave the Iranians a deadline, saying that he had to depart the next night. To mollify him, the Iranian offered to return the Americans' passports and to produce someone of greater authority. McFarlane insisted on meeting with Iranian ministers, asserting that his staff was good enough for the proposed new Iranian. "We have to build up to that stage," McFarlane was told defensively. When McFarlane refused to relent and insisted on having the newcomer work with the staff, the Iranian declared that his government had now appointed "a high authority to follow up." McFarlane repeated that he had to return to Washington the following night and exclaimed: "As I am a Minister, I expect to meet with decision-makers."[16]

2

That evening, a second meeting took place, at which the promised Iranian "high authority" made an appearance. He was Hossein or Hadi Najafabadi, said to be an adviser to Speaker Rafsanjani and a prominent member of the Iranian parliament.[17] At this session, which lasted over four hours, North did most of the talking for the American side. The Iranian was conciliatory and made an effort to soothe the flustered Americans.

Much of the time was spent discussing the Soviet danger, on which both sides could agree. Najafabadi was most anxious to explain why McFarlane was not meeting with Iranian ministers, a disappointment which had become the main sticking point. The Iranian recalled the collapse of the government of former Prime Minister Mehdi Bazargan in the spring of 1980 as a result of his single meeting with former National

Security Adviser Zbigniew Brzezinski. This allusion to Bazargan's fate was made to show how difficult it was for Iran to permit its ministers to meet with McFarlane. When North stated that he had told McFarlane that he would be meeting with Speaker Rafsanjani, Prime Minister Mousavi, and President Khamenei, Najafabadi asked North why such a promise had been made. North replied that Ghorbanifar had made the commitment in George Cave's presence. "We did not agree to such meetings for McFarlane," the Iranian said flatly. North wanted to know whether a secret meeting could be arranged for McFarlane and was told that more positive steps could be taken after the hostages were freed and the arms deliveries completed. As for the hostages, Najafabadi was merely hopeful. Asked by North whether the Iranians could convince their Lebanese captors to release the hostages, he replied: "They're difficult to deal with. But anything we start we are hopeful about."[18]

Again and again, Najafabadi put off to the future what the Americans wanted the most—release of the hostages and meetings with Iranian ministers. On the other hand, he never missed an opportunity to remind the Americans that Iran needed and wanted more American weaponry without delay. "I am sure," he said, "official trips and high-level meetings will take place." But "speed up what has been agreed. A few 747s can carry a lot in one day." The Iranian attitude seemed to be that it was up to the United States to gain Iran's favor by providing it with arms or at least all the spare parts that had already been agreed to. From the American point of view, the spare parts were there to be delivered, but only if Iran kept its part of the bargain—the immediate release of all the hostages. The two sides were ostensibly not that far apart in principle—in the short term, arms for hostages. What separated them was that the United States had the arms but Iran did not have the hostages—or it was not in Iran's interest to release them all at one time even if it could get them.

Nevertheless, the second meeting on May 26 brought renewed hope that something could be worked out. The Americans were encouraged by the superiority of Najafabadi over their former interlocutors. McFarlane informed Poindexter that he "was a considerable cut above the bush leaguers we had been dealing with."[19] Cave took him to be "several cuts above the other members of the Iranian side. He is obviously well educated and very cultured."[20] Both sides now recognized that they had been gulled by Ghorbanifar to expect more than either side was prepared to offer. The Iranians realized that they had to justify their reluctance to have McFarlane meet with their ministers. McFarlane, on the other hand, came to appreciate "the extreme paranoia that dominates the thinking of the political leadership here" and explained to Poindexter that Rafsanjani, Moussavi, and Khamenei were "each traumatized by the recollection" of Bazargan's debacle after his meeting with Brzezinski. Still, by the end of May 26, McFarlane believed that we "have finally reached a competent Iranian official—and that's good." He also cautiously foretold that "we are on the way to something that can become a truly strategic gain for us at the expense of the Soviets. But it is going to be painfully slow."[21]

After two days of meetings, McFarlane's impression of the Iranian regime made him think that "we must take a step back from the history of the past 8 years and put our task in a different light." His report to Poindexter put this task in a curious light: "It may be best for us to try to picture what it would be like if after nuclear attack a surviving Tatar became Vice President; a recent grad student became Deputy Secretary of State; and a bookie became the interlocutor for all discourse with foreign countries. While the principals are a cut above this level of qualification the incompetence of the Iranian government to do business requires a rethinking on our part of why there has been so many frustrating failures to deliver on their part."[22]

3

At the next meeting, on the morning of May 27, the mood swiftly changed. The Iranians reported bad news from Beirut. Their messenger had made contact with the hostage holders and had received "heavy conditions" for the hostages' release. These were: Israel to withdraw from the Golan Heights and southern Lebanon; Lahad prisoners must return to East Beirut;* the Da'wa prisoners in Kuwait freed; and, to top it all, all expenses incurred in the hostage taking to be paid by the United States. (Of the last, McFarlane commented to Poindexter: "How's that for chutzpah!!!"[23]) The news was passed on apologetically; Iran had told the captors that these conditions must be reduced, was negotiating about them, and was willing to pay for the hostages.

The two sides then settled down to quarreling once more about the spare parts. The Iranians wanted all of them immediately, not merely the small portion brought along on the American plane. They were impatient with the American explanation that Iran had to pay in advance for the spare parts, which Iran could or would not do. The Iranian waved aside such a formality: "In the same way we can finance your hostages you can find a way to finance our purchases."[24]

The demands of the Lebanese captors put the problem of releasing the hostages in an altogether different light. The American position had been that the hostages-for-arms deal was strictly with Iran. As both sides haggled over who was to deliver its part of the bargain first, this relatively simple transaction was proving to be difficult enough. But now the deal had

---

* Colonel Lahad was the leader of the pro-Israeli Southern Lebanon army, which had taken Shiite prisoners.

become three-sided. The Americans had to negotiate with the Iranians and the Iranians with the Lebanese. The latter had their own demands, which went far beyond the mere payment of arms to Iran. The American hostages were being used to extort far-reaching concessions from two other countries, Israel and Kuwait, neither of which was remotely likely to agree.

The Americans had been working on the premise that the hostages were Iran's to release, or at least that Iran had enough influence with the Lebanese captors to get them released if Iran was paid enough. Here again the vacuum in American intelligence was costly. Without knowing who the Lebanese captors were, it had been necessary to assume that they were Iranian-inspired or -financed in order to get any purchase on how to free them. The Iranians, with Ghorbanifar's help, had played along with this assumption in order to make possible any kind of arms-for-hostages deal. The release of the Reverend Weir in September 1985 after the delivery of 508 TOW missiles had further encouraged this assumption.

After the revelation on May 27, 1986, that the Lebanese captors had interests in the hostages apart from Iran, no one could be sure of anything. There was no telling whether Iran was using or even inventing the impossible Lebanese demands to increase its own leverage on the Americans or what the relationship between Iran and the Lebanese was. If taken seriously, the news from Beirut cut the ground from under anything resembling the arms-for-hostages deal that the Americans had been prepared to offer or accept.

Meanwhile, the old arguments went on. At a private session between McFarlane and Najafabadi lasting three hours on the morning of May 27, the critical point was again the different perceptions of the two sides on what each had previously agreed to. When McFarlane repeated the American litany about the prompt release of all the hostages as soon as the American delegation had arrived in Tehran with some of the spare parts, Najafabadi became "somewhat agitated," according to McFarlane, and wanted to know who had agreed to these terms. Ghorbanifar, he was told.[25] Najafabadi denied that these were the terms as he understood them; the basic difference was that the Iranians expected all the arms deliveries to occur before any release took place and the Americans expected all the hostages to be released before they delivered any spare parts. According to North, McFarlane was only willing to give this assurance: "All items that have been paid for *will* be delivered within 10 hrs of hostage release."[26]

Too late, the Americans learned that Ghorbanifar had sent a letter to Iran committing the United States to the delivery of all the spare parts.[27] At one point, Najafabadi drew Cave aside and showed him letters from Ghorbanifar "giving them all this stuff that we had never heard about." It was clear, Cave said, that "Ghorbanifar was telling the Iranian side one thing and us another."[28] The irony is that the Americans might never have got as far as Tehran if Ghorbanifar had not deceived both of them.

After three days of intense discussions, the two sides were still going around in a circle. McFarlane sought to "build a little fire under them," as he put it, by warning Najafabadi that he had to leave that very night, which in fact was not the case. McFarlane had made up his mind to stick to his original instructions; he told Poindexter that he intended to leave if the Iranians did not bring word of the release of the hostages in the next six or seven hours.[29]

Still another meeting took place at 5 p.m. on May 27. Najafabadi had some good news. The Lebanese captors had withdrawn all their demands except for the release of the Da'wa prisoners in Kuwait—the most difficult for the Americans to satisfy. He also confirmed that documents attesting to the American version of the prior understanding were in Ghorbanifar's handwriting. His tone was again conciliatory. McFarlane took a strong line. He insisted that he had received instructions from President Reagan to break off the talks if the hostages were not released and he intended to abide by them. Najafabadi pleaded for the delivery of the remaining spare parts; he even offered to have the hostages freed by noon if the next plane arrived before the next morning. When McFarlane seemed to relent, Najafabadi suggested that the two staffs should first reach an agreement, a preliminary that would have required the Americans to extend their stay. McFarlane this time softened his attitude and agreed to seek permission from President Reagan.[30]

This hopeful interlude was short-lived. After reconvening at 9:30 p.m., the two sides faced a final breakdown. It came over an American statement that had been drawn up to test the Iranian offer to produce the hostages a few hours after the delivery of the remaining spare parts and to reach an agreement between the two staffs. On the essential point, this document committed the United States to launch an aircraft with the spare parts at 1 a.m. on May 28 to arrive in Tehran at 10 a.m., while Iran agreed to deliver the hostages at 4 a.m. the same day. It was clearly designed to save face for the Americans by having the hostages delivered six hours before the arrival of the spare parts; the Iranians, on the other hand, could take some satisfaction from the departure of the plane before the release of the hostages. If, however, the hostages were not released by 4 a.m., it was understood that the aircraft would turn back and the American delegation would leave immediately.[31]

This draft proposal was submitted to the Iranians at 9:30 p.m. on May 27. It produced consternation among them. One asked: "How are we supposed to free the hostages by 4 a.m.?" Another Iranian was forced to admit that there was no telling when the hostages might be released: "We are negotiating. There is still a lot of work to do. We cannot make the final decision on when they will be released!" North reminded them that McFarlane had been told earlier that the hostages could be freed by noon, as if the Iranians were able to determine their release. At this an Iranian countered with: "What can you say about those held in Kuwait?" This demand was obviously the most intractable, because the United States could not guarantee the release of prisoners held in Kuwait, but North presented a formula that obliged the United States to make an effort through third parties "to achieve the release and just and fair treatment for Shi'ites held in confinement, as soon as possible."

During the night, a peculiar falling-out took place between North and McFarlane. North and Nir were far more reluctant than McFarlane to abide by the original instructions that bound the Americans to accept the release of all the hostages or nothing. Faced with total failure of the mission, they were willing to compromise on the Iranian offer of two hostages.[32] The Iranians sensed that something could be worked out with North and proposed that he and Cave should stay behind to receive the hypothetical hostages even if McFarlane and the others left. McFarlane was obdurate; all had to leave together. Cave thought that McFarlane was showing "a little bravado," because the plane at that time had no fuel in it and there was no telling when the Iranians might permit it to leave.[33]

During a late-night discussion with the Iranians, including Ghorbanifar, North and Nir agreed to go along with the revised Iranian plan. While McFarlane was sleeping, North ordered a plane with spare parts to take off from Tel Aviv. When McFarlane heard of North's order, he angrily countermanded it and turned the plane, already in the air, back. McFarlane said that President Reagan had backed his recommendation against delivering the arms.[34]

North had a different version. He claimed total innocence; he had merely followed the original plan to send the plane out from Tel Aviv in plenty of time to call it back. His story was that McFarlane had awakened at 6 a.m. and had been told by North about the departure of the plane when it was still two hours from the turnaround point. They had allowed the meeting to go on a little longer, "and then both of us reluctantly agreed to turn the plane around." North even denied that he had made the decision to send the plane out; he made it seem that it had been launched "in accord with a previously established schedule."[35]

McFarlane and North cannot both be right. McFarlane testified that "I was upset and very abrupt with him, and short."[36] If North can be believed, there was no reason for McFarlane to have been upset and very abrupt and short with him. After McFarlane had awakened at 6 a.m., the meeting on May 28 began at 7:50 a.m., according to Teicher's notes, at which point the plane was only ten minutes from its turnaround point. If the meeting had been permitted to go on a little longer before the decision to recall it was made, it would have been a very close call. Moreover, according to Teicher, the meeting began as follows: "Regarding the hostages, he [Iranian] says, they think two [hostages] can get out now but it will require 'joint action' on the other two." McFarlane's reply was: "It is too late. We are leaving."[37] Thus the issue was whether the Americans would settle for the possible release of two hostages instead of four—and even two appeared to lack all signs of credibility. North's original schedule had never contemplated an arms delivery for two hostages; the sequential arms delivery had always been based on an assured release of all the hostages.

It seems most likely that North, with Nir's backing, was willing to take the risk of sending out the plane with more spare parts in exchange for the immediate release of possibly two hostages and, far more problematically, two more in the indefinite future. North was saved from outright insubordination by virtue of the plane's two-hour turnaround time; he was able to give McFarlane the last word before it was too late. The fact remains that he was putting the plane in a position to deliver the spare parts if two hostages were released, in defiance of McFarlane's adamant rejection of a partial release and Poindexter's instructions to make no deal without the freedom of all the hostages. McFarlane did not report the incident, and it did North no harm. Irrespective of who was right or wrong, North's temerity testified to his willingness to make up his own rules as he went along unless he was caught short by superior authority.

In any case, the end came at 11:30 p.m. McFarlane, as Teicher's notes put it, "concludes that they're just stringing us along. He gives the order to pack and depart."[38]

Another version by Cave says that the Iranian spokesman asked to see McFarlane shortly before 2 a.m. on May 28. The Iranian wanted assurances that the Americans would deliver the remaining spare parts two hours after the hostages were released and would stay after the arrival of the spare parts to discuss additional Iranian needs. He also asked for more time to get the hostages, and McFarlane gave him until 6:30 a.m. on May 28. The next Iranian move was an offer to release two hostages immediately and two more after the delivery. The Americans replied that they intended to leave for the airport after finishing breakfast, during which time the plane was being refueled. The refueling had worried the Americans, because the Iranians had been stalling and could have held the Americans hostage by the simple expedient of withholding fuel for their plane.

The scene at the airfield was anticlimactic. As the Americans were standing near the plane, an Iranian asked McFarlane for more time, saying that releasing the hostages was a very delicate and time-consuming effort. McFarlane somehow informed him that the plane with the spare parts was in the air but would turn around and return to its base if no word on the hostages came by 9:30 a.m. In one last exchange with Cave, the Iranian admitted that the hostages were not under Iranian control. Cave advised him to get them under Iranian control, to which the Iranian said they would seek to do this and intended to send Ghorbanifar to

Europe to maintain contact with the Americans. The plane took off at 9 a.m.[39]

We have an additional version of the last hours from Teicher. An Iranian pleaded with the Americans as they were boarding the aircraft: "Why are you leaving?" McFarlane told him to tell his superiors "that this was the fourth time they had failed to honor an agreement. The lack of trust will endure for a long time. An important opportunity was lost." The plane left at 8:55 a.m.[*40]

4

After Tehran came the postmortems: What went wrong?

One commonly held view was that a grave mistake had been made in failing to send an advance party to work out an agreement or at least an agenda. North thought belatedly that that had been an error and explained it on the ground that he had trusted assurances from Ghorbanifar and from the Israelis, who, he hastened to add, had got them from Ghorbanifar.[41]

In the end, all trails led back to Ghorbanifar. He had lured the Americans to Tehran by assuring them that they would be welcomed by Speaker Rafsanjani, if not by two other principal leaders, Prime Minister Moussavi and President Khamenei. He had assured them that the Iranians could obtain the release of all the hostages if the Americans did their part by providing all the spare parts. He had told the Iranians that the Americans were willing to deliver all the spare parts before any hostages were released. If he had not deluded each side about what the other was prepared to give, they might never have come together. But by deluding them he made sure to disillusion both sides once each had to deliver to the other. Ghorbanifar was glib and cunning, but not glib and cunning enough to carry his intrigues to a successful conclusion.

The wonder is that the Americans still trusted him enough to go to Tehran at his behest after all the disappointments they had earlier suffered at his hands. This incongruity was most ingenuously expressed by North. When he was asked whether he knew that the Iranians had agreed to the release of all the hostages prior to the American arrival in Tehran, North replied:

> It turns out that the Iranians did not. Manucher Ghorbanifar told us that they had agreed to that. And what had happened is we had

---

* Reagan later wrote that McFarlane had twice called him from Tehran. Soon after his arrival, McFarlane said that he had been misled by Ghorbanifar and had doubts about the Iranians he had met. Toward the end, McFarlane reported that the Iranians had made "outrageous demands" for the release of the hostages. Reagan confided to his diary: "It was a heart breaking disappointment for all of us" (*An American Life*, pp. 520–1).

gone too far down the line with Ghorbanifar. What was his process, if you will, was to tell the Iranians one thing and tell us another. Then let the two sides sit down and duke it out.

Well, as I said, we knew Ghorbanifar for what he was. We did not know of the letters that he had sent to Tehran committing us to certain things until after we got there.

When we exchanged letters face to face with the Iranians in Tehran, it was very obvious that he had lied to both sides and we knew that he did this, but we didn't know that the lie was quite so blatant.

We had expectations from him, communicated to us directly and through the Israelis, that that would be the outcome if things went well in Tehran.

We did not know all the expectations of the Iranians as to what it would take to make things go well. And thus, when we got there, both sides were surprised at the intransigence of the other side's opinions. And that is why I had advocated, despite the risks, despite the deep concern of Director Casey, that information about a very covert program would be revealed if I went on the trip and were tortured, despite all of that, I was a proponent of the advance party trip because I knew Ghorbanifar to be what he was.

I knew he was a duplicitous sneak, and I thought we could do better by General Secord and I going to Tehran.[42]

This explanation makes the dependence on Ghorbanifar all the stranger. The Americans knew what he was, a liar and duplicitous sneak, but still believed him sufficiently to base their expectations and plans on what he had told them. They were surprised not that he had lied but that he had lied so blatantly, as if a mere lie was not enough to explain how he had taken them in.

Yet one thing rings true—that "we had gone too far down the line with Ghorbanifar." Ghorbanifar had drawn them into his net bit by bit, despite all the polygraph tests and almost unbroken string of disappointments. Two things were necessary for his success—the American unwillingness to give up the quest for the hostages whatever the odds and the lack of an alternative to him. As long as he was capable of dangling one hope after another, American gullibility was seemingly endless.

Ghorbanifar gave his version of the Tehran events to aides of the Tower Board who went to Paris to question him. He blamed the lack of preparation for the failure of the mission. He had proposed, he said, that he and North should go to Tehran first to prepare the way, but the Americans had refused. He claimed that McFarlane had promised to come with all the spare parts as the precondition for a welcome by the Iranians. He criticized the Americans for having attempted to resolve the hostage issue before progress could be made on other matters.

The Ayatollah Khomeini, according to Ghorbanifar, had played a key role behind the scenes. He had allegedly approved the meetings and had been the main concern of Ghorbanifar and the other Iranians. Najafa-badi, who Ghorbanifar said was head of the Majlis Foreign Affairs Committee, had urged McFarlane to give them time—in Ghorbanifar's exotic English—"that we cook the way we want the Ayatollah Khomeini to pave the ground for this, to make it ready, prepare for him." But McFarlane was intransigent, insisting that "we have nothing to discuss and nothing is going on to get to this agenda if the whole four American hostages are not released."

McFarlane was the villain of Ghorbanifar's story. At 7 p.m. on May 26, Najafabadi had allegedly agreed to the American demands and had prepared the "old man" to accept them. Khomeini had agreed to release all the hostages first. Forgetting that the Americans had always called for release of all the hostages, Ghorbanifar quickly contradicted himself by recalling that Najafabadi had offered two hostages immediately. Mc-Farlane had behaved as if he were giving a Russian-style ultimatum. The Iranians had pleaded; North and Nir had betrayed "panic" at McFarlane's refusal. When it was all over, "I saw the tears in the eyes of North, Nir, and everybody."

Finally Ghorbanifar accused McFarlane of having taken advantage of him in order to get rid of him and of having treated the Iranians as poor, helpless victims. Again, in Ghorbanifar's language:

> Why he did so? I know why. I tell you why. Number one, he had $15 million in his pocket. We were a hostage to him. Number two, the Iranians, they are not real politicians. The people came to him. They were so soft and they were so open to him; they explained to him deeply how they are in disaster. They need the help of the United States financially—I mean the support-wise, logistic-wise, military-wise. And he is a smart guy.
>
> He found out that in such a catastrophe and that situation they are. They are really in need of it. And, besides that, he says what the hell is this. I know now all the big shots. I have their telephone number. We have relation. We go out. We have the money. We have them. We know their need. They will follow. Who needs this man, middle man? Who is he?[43]

Ghorbanifar and the Iranians had a case about the $15 million. He, on behalf of Iran, had already deposited that much for all the spare parts in the account of the Secord-Hakim Lake Resources in Geneva. To make matters worse for Ghorbanifar, he had borrowed the money from Adnan Khashoggi, who had allegedly borrowed much of it from two Canadian businessmen. When McFarlane ordered the withdrawal from Tehran, only one pallet of the Hawk parts had been delivered; the remaining twelve pallets stayed in Tel Aviv. Thus Iran, through Ghorbanifar and Khashoggi, had paid in advance for spare parts they did not receive. Secord was left with the money, some of which was spent on supporting the contras, leaving him in a position of what he called "financial jeopardy," because he could no longer return all the money. As a strictly business proposition, this procedure was bizarre; it was justified by the Americans not on business grounds but because the Iranians had failed to gain the release of the hostages. To Ghorbanifar and the Iranians, they were being swindled out of most of the $15 million by unscrupulous Westerners who refused to deliver what had been paid for. In the end, it took almost three months for Iran to get all the spare parts—and then the Americans obtained less than the Iranians had offered in Tehran.[44]

The U.S.-Iran failure at Tehran was also Ghorbanifar's failure; he knew that he was being blamed for it by both sides. After Tehran, his days as the indispensable middleman were numbered. Nir was another loser. Secord talked to Nir on his return from Tehran and found him bitterly disappointed. "He felt," Secord said, "that it had not been handled correctly. He felt they should have stayed longer, thought they were making progress, thought that the Iranians—that it was fair to give the Iranians more time because the Iranians were disorganized, Ghorbanifar's preparations had been inadequate and so on."[45] According to Cave, Nir kept insisting after Tehran that Ghorbanifar had to be used.[46] The more the Americans wanted to get rid of Ghorbanifar, the less useful Nir was to them. He, too, was fearful of what the future had in store for him.

5

But other, more basic factors had doomed the mission to Tehran.

One was that McFarlane had been given no negotiating room. Poindexter, who had the last word, had sent him with instructions to get out all the hostages or make no deal on weaponry. North may have been willing to settle for two in the hand, but he as well as McFarlane knew that it would have been in flagrant violation of Poindexter's instructions.

The Iranians had acted as if either they did not know whether they could get the hostages out or they were trying to keep the Americans on tenterhooks. Their first story was that they had sent an emissary to Beirut to find out whether the hostages could be brought out. This opening move stunned the Americans; it told them that the Iranians were using something they did not have to bargain for something the Americans had. Moreover, the Lebanese demands to free the Da'wa prisoners went far beyond any deal on which the Americans could deliver.

The two sides allegedly had a common interest against the Soviet Union. Here, too, problems presented themselves. The Iranians wanted weapons to fight Iraq, not the Soviet Union. The Americans felt impelled to impress the Iranians with how much the Soviets threatened them. Yet all this was taking place in 1986 at a time when the new Gorbachev regime was increasingly embroiled in its program of domestic economic and political reform. It was not a convincing time to speak of a planned Soviet invasion of Iran. A "strategic treaty" between Iran and the United States, which North mentioned as one of the aims of the Tehran mission, would have been anti-Soviet in its objective. Such a treaty was so far-reaching in its ramifications that it would have required preparations and negotiations for which the McFarlane group was ill equipped and unprepared.

The larger question is whether it was wise to mix two such different aims as release of the hostages and a strategic realignment between Iran and the United States. The first was immediate and concrete, the second distant and complex. It was just as well that McFarlane cut short the futile game of Iranians asking Americans for what they were not willing to give and Americans asking Iranians for what they did not have. Ghorbanifar exacerbated the frustrations of both sides, but he did not create the conditions which were bound to be frustrating. For their credulity, the Americans had only themselves to blame.

The return from Tehran was notable for an unpremeditated act on the part of North. As McFarlane and North walked away from the plane in the airport at Tel Aviv, where they stopped on the way home, North tried to cheer up McFarlane, who was sadly aware of the failure of his mission. McFarlane later recalled that North "told me that I shouldn't be too disappointed, that some of the proceeds or the dollars from the sale of weapons to the Iranians was going to be available in Central America."[47]

Irrelevant though this confidence was to what they had been trying to do in Tehran, McFarlane thus joined Poindexter as North's confidant in the secret of secrets—the "diversion."

On May 29, the day after their return, McFarlane reported to President Reagan, Vice President Bush, Chief of Staff Regan, and Poindexter on what had happened in Tehran. "We did not succeed in gaining the hostages' release," McFarlane said, according to Teicher's memorandum. "The current state of government in Iran lacks competence. The competents were decapitated. One hundred thousand or more are gone. The tentative overtures to U.S. result from a recognition of their declining circumstances."

McFarlane also described "the bazaar-style negotiating tactics and apparent fear of failure" on the part of the Iranians. He noted some areas of agreement, as on the Soviet threat and Afghanistan, but criticized the Iranians for having "never stepped up to the reality of [the] hostage release process." Ghorbanifar had been responsible for misunderstandings. Still, McFarlane felt that the Iranians did not wish to give up "the opportunity to restore ties to serve their strategic and economic interests." He concluded: "They will be back in touch with us. They have now met with North and Teicher. I recommend no more meetings until the hostages are released. A lot may be possible. You have begun to open the door to these people."[48]

McFarlane also talked about the meeting some months later. He said he had told Reagan that "I thought that there were people legitimately oriented toward change that they had not yet gotten to a position of confident ability to act. I had not met with Rafsanjani. He must have felt vulnerable, as Mr. Brzezinski's meeting with Bazargan had led to certain consequences, and he probably was fearful about it. But that ought to tell us something and that I thought it was unwise to continue anything further."

Reagan's reaction to McFarlane's report was noncommittal. "The President didn't comment really, but that was not untypical. He would often hear reports, say that he would think about it, and that was—and he didn't react to me and I left, and that's the last I heard about it."[49]

In effect, McFarlane had little encouraging to bring back from Tehran. His report, given about twenty-four hours after his arrival, showed how closely President Reagan and Vice President Bush were kept abreast of these negotiations.

16

Narrow Escapes

By mid-1986, the contra operation seemed to be working better than ever. A new southern front was taking shape. In May, the Costa Rica-based Southern Opposition bloc and the Honduras-based United Nicaraguan Opposition (UNO) agreed to form the Nicaraguan Resistance, with a fifty-four-member assembly and a six-member directorate. Arms had increasingly been coming to the contras—about 90,000 pounds of arms worth $504,000 in January and February, over $1.3 million in late April and late May.[1] Robert Dutton's reorganized resupply operation was beginning to make airdrops to both the northern and southern fronts.[2] On May 16, North informed Poindexter that more than $6 million was available for immediate disbursement to the contras.[3] On June 10, North told him that "an extraordinary amount of good has been done and money truly is not the thing which is needed at this point."[4]

Even more favorably, the administration at last persuaded Congress to appropriate more money to the contras. On June 25, the House of Representatives passed a bill providing $100 million in military and humanitarian aid to the contras. The vote was 221–209, close enough to show how divided the House was. The Senate passed the same mixture of lethal and nonlethal aid on August 13. On October 17, both the Senate and the House approved a conference agreement providing $100 million in contra aid, of which $70 million was unrestricted. Legislation authorizing the appropriation was signed by the president on October 27. A final, corrected version of the legislation was signed into law on October 30.

Thus, if nothing else had happened, the contras could again have expected to become full wards of the United States, as they had been under the CIA. The divisive period of private and third-country aid was about to come to an end. The belated appropriation was evidence of Congress's confusing role in the entire contra affair. It had been a struggle between the Reagan administration and Congress as well as one between Nicaraguan factions, and Congress had blinked first.

Yet foreboding clouds had been gathering for some time. The darkest of them again hovered over Oliver North.

2

North's name again appeared in print on January 18, 1986.[5] He was singled out in *The Miami Herald* by Alfonso Chardy, the most enterprising and knowledgeable journalist on the trail of the contras. On December 2, 1985, a Sandinista helicopter was shot down by a Soviet-made SAM-7 missile, killing twelve Nicaraguan soldiers and two Cuban pilots. Chardy reported that the missiles had been purchased for the contras from European arms dealers through the efforts of General Singlaub, who freely admitted his role in order to show how much he was doing for the contras. Singlaub said that the contras had been trained in the use of the missiles by U.S. experts and that he had discussed the subject with North, but he denied that North had guided him to the arms dealers. Chardy cited unnamed "administration sources," including one "administration official," a "prominent contra fund-raiser," a "congressional source," and Adolfo Calero, who had made a statement that the money had come from a "rich lady" outside the United States who had provided $1 million for more such weapons.

North was said not to have been directly responsible for telling the contra leaders, Calero and Bermúdez, where to get the missiles. He was implicated by name for having indirectly suggested "to private contra fund-raisers the possibility of steering the guerrillas toward an arms market source." Despite the guarded reference to North, the story again paid unwelcome attention to him and was soon followed by others that brought him into sharper focus.

On April 30, 1986, Chardy and *The Miami Herald* again closed in on North in an article headed "Colonel's Actions May Have Broken Contra Aid Ban." The article stated that Philip Mabry, a Fort Worth security consultant, said that North had invited him to the White House in February 1985 after North had heard that Mabry wanted to help the contras. North had subsequently set up a meeting for Mabry with Andy Messing, executive director of the National Defense Council, a private anti-Communist group. According to "administration sources," North "organized and supervised an informal system to locate and screen private donors and then arranged for supplies and contributions to reach the contras." Singlaub and Robert Owen were specifically mentioned as "conservatives closely associated with the contras" who frequently met with North. Owen was even identified as a $51,000-a-year consultant to the contras who was paid by the State Department's NHAO.

The Miami Herald put out a follow-up story by Chardy on page one on June 8. This one, headed "Despite Ban, U.S. Helping Contras," again featured North, who, it was said, supervised the system of secretly "finding weapons and plotting military strategy through a network of private operatives overseen by the National Security Council (NSC) and the CIA," according to administration and contra officials. Singlaub and Owen once more came in for special mention. The article was more knowledgeable about Owen than about Singlaub. A U.S. official was cited as saying: "Owen was the messenger boy and Gen. Singlaub the military commander, chief fund-raiser and arms adviser and broker." Singlaub was his own best promoter.

The Associated Press picked up the same story, which ran in *The Washington Post* on June 11. So long as it appeared only in Miami, the political damage was limited. Washington was different.

On June 22, *The Miami Herald* again publicized bad news for North. Marine Lieutenant Colonel Oliver North, according to Chardy, had "continued to oversee" a supply network for the contras after it had been set up in 1984. Legislative critics of President Reagan's Nicaraguan policy "are scrutinizing North's role and it could be the target of a congressional investigation." As usual, Singlaub and Owen were prominently mentioned.

The news media were onto something and would not let go. At about this time, North received a disturbing message from Karna Small, on the NSC staff in charge of liaison with the media. She warned him of a "blast" coming on the CBS program *West 57th*. It was asking for an "NSC comment on the fact that somebody named Robert Hull had been boasting to friends that for a while he was receiving weekly checks from the NSC." The correct name was John Hull, not Robert, but he was a link to the secret airstrip in Costa Rica. She told North that she had declined a request to interview him. She did not know what to do about it, because "I can't just give them the 'bullshit' response."[6]

The program on June 25 charged that "the White House secretly directed a private aid network to arm the Contras when it was illegal for the White House to do that." It named John Hull, who had been instrumental in setting up the Costa Rican airstrip, and Robert Owen, now described as "the bag man for Ollie North." Among those interviewed for the program were Edén Pastora and Jack R. Terrell, a self-described disillusioned former mercenary for the contras.[7] The program also gave the official line: "The White House today quoted Colonel Oliver North as calling the private aid network 'nonsense.' The White House also said, quote, 'The President never approved any such plan [to aid the contras].' "

The private aid network was, of course, not "nonsense," and the president had by his presence at its briefings in the White House implicitly approved it. Yet North felt it necessary to send an impassioned, blanket denial to Karna Small:

I have just had a chance to watch the W 57th piece. As far as I am concerned, it is the single most distorted piece of "reporting" I have ever seen. Hull does not allege that he knows me, does not confess to receiving money from me or anyone else at the NSC. The only charges made about the NSC are made by people who are in jail, on their way to jail or just out of jail. If this is supposed to be credible, then I'll eat my shirt. I have never met ANY of the accusers or had anything to do with any of them. Obviously I know and have met several times with Eden Pastora. He does not allege any wrongdoing. I know Robert Owen—he was, up until the time it went out of business—a consultant to the State Dept. NHAO. He was not "paid off" $50k [thousand], as alleged by an anonymous accuser, he was paid a salary and expenses for services he provided in delivering humanitarian aid for the USG on a State Dept. contract. Finally, their main "witness," Mr. Terrell was not called to appear before Sen. Kerry's inquisition—apparently because people have learned that Mr. Terrell was not, as he claimed, a former Special Forces Officer, nor a CIA agent, nor a "contra combat leader." In short, neither the witnesses nor the slanderous piece that CBS produced have any credibility whatsoever.[8]

This program, as was usual in such circumstances, was a mixture of the true, the half-true, and the untrue. Its credibility was general rather than specific. Owen had delivered money to Central America given to him by North and was far more than a mere NHAO "consultant." North had known of Terrell's activities though he had never met him.*[9] Whatever the merits of the program, it came dangerously close to what Poindexter and North were doing.

North finally cracked. Another CBS program on July 14 and an item in *The Washington Times* the next day seem to have unnerved him completely. Instead of trying desperately to hold on to his job on the NSC staff, he was now ready to quit. He wrote to Poindexter on July 15:

In view of last night's CBS piece and this morning's appalling Washington TIMES item, I can understand why you may well have reservations about both my involvement in Nicaraguan policy and even my continued tenure here. Since returning a few minutes ago I have been told that even my luncheon engagement with my sister yesterday is in question. Under these circumstances, and given your intention that I extricate myself entirely from the Nicaragua issue, it probably w[oul]d be best if I were to move on as quietly, but

---

* The FBI report contains this statement by North: "He stated that he is not involved with any covert operations being run in the United States" (A-1, p. 857).

expeditiously as possible. I want you to know that it is for me deeply
disappointing to have lost your confidence, for I respect you, what
you have tried to do and have enjoyed working with you on a number
of issues important to our nation. On the plus side of the ledger we
have had a close relationship on several initiatives that could not
have been accomplished without absolute trust between two professionals. At the same time you should not be expected to retain on
your staff someone who you suspect could be talking to the media
or whom you believe to be too emotionally involved in an issue to
be objective in the development of policy options and recommendations.[10]

This was North almost out of control. His message was virtually a
confession that he had reached the end of his emotional resources. He
suspected that Poindexter wanted him out and preferred to leave before
he was told to go. He also thought that by taking the initiative he would
make it easier for the tight-lipped, stone-faced Poindexter to make the
move. A word from Poindexter at this juncture would have been enough
to send him back to the Marines and save him from further public
exposure and self-questioning. The reference by North to the *Washington
Times* item concerned a story headed "Going After North," in which
North's position on the NSC staff was said to be "precarious" and "NSC
soft liners" were attempting "to edge him out."

Instead, Poindexter decided that it was easier to keep North than to
let him go. He replied to North the same day:

> Now you are getting emotional again. It would help if you would
> call Roger Fontaine and Jerry O'Leary [of *The Washington Times*]
> and tell them to call off the dogs. Tell them on deep background,
> off the record, not to be published that I just want to lower your
> visibility so that you wouldn't be such a good target for the Lib[eral]s.
> . . . I do not want you to leave and to be honest cannot afford to
> let you go. . . .[11]

Later, Poindexter explained that this episode had come about because
"I wanted to lower Colonel North's profile on the contra support activity
and his operational roles in general." He had expected the CIA to take
over, "and as CIA phased back into the contra operation, Colonel North
I wanted to phase out." But, Poindexter explained, "it became public
that he was going to be phased out, and I frankly was getting a lot of
static from Colonel North's supporters on the Hill as to why I was trying
to take him out of the program. And I think Ollie misunderstood what
I was trying to do."[12]

This explanation suggests that Poindexter was engaged in a supposedly
subtle plot to keep North for a while and to take him out as soon as the

CIA came in again. Poindexter himself was suspected of having leaked the story to *The Washington Times* about North's "precarious" position on the NSC staff.[13] In any case, North was soon mollified and carried on as before. His offer to move on quietly and expeditiously was not put to the test.

North's ultimate downfall began with the failure of his covert operation to remain covert. From January to July 1986, attention was repeatedly drawn to him in the press, mainly in *The Miami Herald*, which far outdid the larger newspapers in New York and Washington in covering the contra-support operation. At this stage, the threat to his position came from the contra rather than from the Iran side of his activity. The contra operation had become so far-flung that too many people knew bits and pieces of it—and were not averse to letting on that they knew. The indications are that inquisitive journalists were getting their information from contra sources, contributors of funds to the contra cause, Singlaub, and officials within the administration itself who were not altogether in sympathy with North's activities or methods.

By mid-1986, U.S. clandestine support for the contras was an open secret. Yet it could not be admitted or defended publicly without confessing to flagrant violation of the Boland Amendment, which still remained in force. North was the likeliest target only because he had taken so much of the operation upon himself and turned up in every aspect of it, from military operations to fund-raising. The lines were tightening around him.

3

While the news media were paying renewed attention to North and preparing trouble of one kind, another threat came from a different quarter—the Marine Corps.

In the spring of 1986, North was again ordered to report to the 2nd Marine Division at Camp Lejeune as battalion commander. After still another verbal request for an extension, General Kelly tried to block it once and for all with the words: "I will not accept any more discussions."[14]

When North heard that the Marine Corps intended to order him to take over the 2nd Battalion at Camp Lejeune that summer, he took counsel with McFarlane. North was clearly torn by conflicting obligations and ambitions. "This is a situation (like so many others)," he confided to McFarlane, "fraught w[ith] opportunity and risk. I, quite frankly[,] don't know what to do about the situation, but will have to take some kind of action in the next few weeks." He asked for McFarlane's "good counsel on the merits/liabilities of such an assignment and advice on how to proceed."[15]

McFarlane's reply reflected some of the danger ahead for North:

"Frankly, I would expect the heat from the Hill to become immense on you by summer. Consequently it strikes me as wise that you leave the White House. At the same time, there will be no one to do all (or even a small part of what) you have done. And if it isn't done, virtually all of the investment of the past five years will go down the drain." McFarlane then gave North a "self-serving scenario" about what they could do together: "1. North leaves the White House in May and takes 30 days leave. 2. July 1st North is assigned as a fellow at the CSIS [Center for Strategic and International Studies] and (lo and behold) is assigned to McFarlane's office. 3. McFarlane/North continue to work the Iran account as well as to begin to build other clandestine capabilities so much in demand here and there."[16] McFarlane's daydream revealed how difficult it was for both of them to tear themselves away from "clandestine capabilities."

In May 1986, when the order to report to Camp Lejeune at the end of that month was still pending, North found a new reason to get around his departure from the White House. He grasped at an opening given to him by the Palestinian terrorist Abu Nidal, who had recently vowed to revenge himself against those who had been responsible for tracking down the *Achille Lauro* terrorists. One of those mentioned by him as marked for retribution was North, who heard the threat on a television news program. By linking Abu Nidal's threat with the Marine Corps order to send him to Camp Lejeune, North made it appear that the order was somehow in response to the threat. In an agitated message to Poindexter, North went all out to get the order rescinded:

> W[ould] you please call either SecDef [Secretary of Defense] or SecNav [Secretary of Navy] or Gen[eral] Kelley [Paul X. Kelly, Commandant of Marine Corps] to advise them that North will not be detached from the NSC. The incredible answer to the current Abu Nidal threat is to immediately PCS [assign] North to Camp Lejeune, N.C. I cannot imagine putting my tail between my legs and running in the face of this provocation. I do not believe that this is what you or the President want but cannot say so myself. It w[oul]d be best for you or the President to do this—if it is indeed what you want. Otherwise, I have been ordered to detach no later than 30 May and proceed for duty at Camp Lej[eune]. I am here to serve as you and the President so direct. Pl[eas]e advise y[ou]r wishes in this regard.[17]

North had his wish. He did not go to Camp Lejeune and stayed on the NSC staff long enough perhaps to regret that he had resisted the effort to get him back into the marines. Later, at the congressional hearings, he challenged Abu Nidal in his best mock-heroic style: "Now, I want you to know that I would be more than willing—and if anybody else is watching overseas, and I am sure they are—I will be glad to meet

Abu Nidal on equal terms anywhere in the world. OK? There is an even deal for him."[18]

Abu Nidal was also the ostensible reason for North's embarrassing decision to put a security system at his house. The security expert on the job, Glenn A. Robinette, who had previously worked for the CIA, testified that he had been hired at the end of April 1986 by Secord to install the system.[19] As Robinette testified, it was designed to protect against vandalism rather than terrorism.[20] Secord paid for the entire job with cash and a check amounting to $16,000, the latter from a Geneva account implicated in the Iran operation.[21] The embarrassment to North came after his dismissal from the NSC staff in November 1986, when he realized that he had violated a federal law prohibiting government officials from accepting gifts or compensation other than salary.

In December 1986, North telephoned Robinette and pretended to be surprised that he had not received a bill for the security system. Robinette realized that North wanted to cover up the gift from Secord and, with this in mind, sent North two false, backdated invoices, to which North responded with two misleading, backdated letters. North had not paid for the system and merely tried to make it appear that he had done so.[22]

At the congressional hearings, North said that "I did probably the grossest misjudgment that I have made in my life. I then tried to paper over that whole thing by sending two phony documents back to Mr. Robinette. It was not an exercise in good judgment."[23] When North explained his security system as a defense against Abu Nidal, Senators Cohen and Mitchell say: "We shook our heads in disbelief. That fence might keep out the neighborhood dogs or some anti-contra activist who had poured sand in his car's gas tank. But Abu Nidal? Hardly. Still, the theater was far more compelling than our doubts."[24]

In any case, Abu Nidal served North as a convenient excuse for asking Poindexter to prevail on Secretary of Defense Weinberger, Secretary of the Navy John F. Lehman, Jr., and General Kelly to save him from duty at Camp Lejeune and to keep him on the NSC staff. The excessively emotional character of his appeal was not lost on Poindexter, who was soon given reason to remark on North's repeated exhibitions of emotionalism.

4

Meanwhile, Poindexter had cause to worry about a breakdown in the covert nature of North's operations. On May 15, 1986, Poindexter took the unusual step of rebuking North and ordering him to change his ways. Poindexter's outburst was brought about by a strange deal on the part of North, Secord, and Hakim.

In April, as if he did not have enough to do in managing the Iran and contra affairs, North had apparently conceived the idea of using an off-shore ship to transmit propaganda messages into Libya.[25] At the request of North, Hakim was sent to Copenhagen, where he bought a Danish-registered ship, the *Erria*, for about $350,000.[26] At one point, North apparently offered the ship to the CIA on a six-month lease but was turned down on the ground that the CIA could outfit one of its own vessels for the mission more cheaply than it could the *Erria*.[27] It appears that the ship was actually used for the transportation of weapons to the contras through two Central American countries.[28] In September, the ship was also the subject of a curious conversation between North and Israeli Minister of Defense Rabin, during which the latter proposed that the *Erria* should be used to carry Soviet-bloc weapons from Israel to the contras, an offer that was apparently accepted.[29]

North and Rabin met again in September and discussed an Israeli transfer of Soviet-bloc weapons to the contras. Rabin wanted "to know if we had any need for SovBloc weap[on]s and ammo he could make avail[able]." Rabin asked whether the *Erria* had left the Mediterranean. When North responded that it was in Lisbon, Rabin suggested that it dock at Haifa and "have it filled w[ith] whatever they c[oul]d assemble" of a "recently seized PLO shipment captured at sea."[30]

Back in May, the *Erria* had been the accidental cause of Poindexter's show of irritation with North. As such things will in Washington, word about the ship reached the ears of another member of the NSC staff, Kenneth deGraffenreid, senior director of intelligence programs, who promptly passed it on to Poindexter. North soon heard from Poindexter:

> In a memo from Ken to me today he talks about your offering a Danish ship under your control to CIA for broadcasting into [Libya]. I am afraid you are letting your operational role become too public. From now on I don't want you to talk to anybody else, including Casey, except me about any of your operational roles. In fact you need to quietly generate a cover story that I have insisted that you stop.[31]

Poindexter later explained that he had included Casey among those to be kept in ignorance of the ship's purchase and purpose because Casey was always liable to be questioned by congressional committees.[32] "The problem, as I have stated," said Poindexter, "I didn't want Congress to know the details of how we were implementing the President's policy."[33] His other reason had a significant bearing on his view of the Boland Amendment. Though he professed to believe that the amendment did not apply to his staff, he realized that Congress might "tighten it up" if it "became obvious what we were doing."[34] In effect, Poindexter acknowledged that Congress would have explicitly included the NSC staff in its enumeration of agencies involved in intelligence activities if Congress had anticipated what the staff was going to do.

At this time, North betrayed an uncharacteristic desire to shift his burden to others. On May 16, 1986, he gave Poindexter an optimistic financial report on the contras but added a personal cry for relief from further responsibility. He reported that the contra support organization had more than $6 million for immediate disbursement, with the result that there was less need to go to third countries for help. This news led him to make an unexpected proposal:

> It does not, however, reduce the urgent need to get the CIA back into the management of this program. . . . Unless we do this, we will run increasing risks of trying to manage this program from here with the attendant physical and political liabilities. I am not complaining, and you know that I love the work, but we have to lift some of this onto the CIA so that I can get more than 2–3 hrs of sleep at night. The more money there is (and we will have a considerable amount in a few more days) the more visible the program becomes (airplanes, pilots, weapons, deliveries, etc.) and the more inquisitive will become people like [Senator John] Kerry, [Representative] Barnes, [Senator Tom] Harkin, et al. While I care not a whit what they say about me, it could well become a political embarrassment for the President and you. Much of this risk can be avoided simply by covering it with an authorized CIA program undertaken with the $15M[illion]. This is what I was about to say in the [NSPG] meeting today and a point that I believe Shultz does not understand in his advocacy of Third country solicitation. I have no idea what Don Regan does or does not know re my private U.S. operation but the President obviously knows why he had been meeting with several select people to thank them for their "support for Democracy" in CentAm [Central America].[35]

Poindexter's reaction to North's appeal for relief by the CIA was: "He [North] has wanted CIA to get back into the management of the problem and we need to lower Ollie's visibility on the issue."[36] To North himself, Poindexter wrote that "I still want to reduce your visibility."[37]

North's anxiety to unload on the CIA went so far that he wanted all of the "assets" in Central America accumulated by Secord and his associates to be sold at bargain rates to the CIA. He told Poindexter that the total value of the aircraft, warehouses, supplies, maintenance facilities, ships, boats, leased houses, vehicles, ordnance, munitions, communications equipment, and the airstrip came to over $4.5 million. He was willing to offer the whole lot to the CIA for $2.25 million.[38] At his trial in 1989, North left little doubt that he had thought he had reached the end of his endurance. He had told Poindexter, he said, that "there was no way physically humanly possible to carry this on in the way it was going and that what we really needed was not just funding from the Congress, we needed the authority from the Congress to have the CIA back in this effort."[39]

North did not let the issue drop. On June 10, 1986, he wrote to Poindexter: "An extraordinary amount of good has been done and money truly is not the thing which is most needed at this point. What we most need is to get the CIA re-engaged in this effort so that it can be better managed than it now is by one slightly confused Marine LtCol."[40]

This unwonted modesty on North's part was apparently the result of growing fatigue and depression. It was not like North to confess that he needed more than two to three hours of sleep at night and was suffering from political confusion. If ever there was a time when Poindexter should have relieved him of at least part of his duties, it was now. Instead, Poindexter let him go on as before, and North continued to carry the full responsibility for both the contra and Iran affairs.

From the sidelines, McFarlane watched the growing pressure on North with increasing alarm. McFarlane sensed that North had been stretching himself too thin and could not go on in the face of so many demands on him. McFarlane was worried most that North's condition was bound to grow worse as he attracted more attention from the media and political critics of the Nicaraguan policy. On June 11, McFarlane wrote to Poindexter:

> I am getting very worried in Ollie's behalf. It seems increasingly clear that the Democratic left is coming after him with a vengeance in the election year and that eventually they will get him—too many people are talking to reporters from the donor community and within the administration. I don't [know] what you do about it but in Ollie's interest I would get him transferred or sent to Bethesda for disability review board (apparently the Marine Corps already tried to survey him once [)]. That would represent a major loss to the staff and contra effort but I think we can probably find a way to continue to do those things. In the end it may be better anyway.[41]

Instead of taking McFarlane's advice, Poindexter merely advised a "lower visibility" for North, for whom the injunction came too late.

Yet North soon recovered his nerve sufficiently to protest at what seemed to him to be a reduction of his influence. In July 1986, Congress was expected to authorize the resumption of CIA support for the contras. A directive was prepared establishing an interagency group to oversee the new setup. According to Rodney McDaniel, executive secretary of the NSC staff, it was normal practice to assign someone from the Intelligence Directorate to the proposed agency. When the assignment did not go to North, he complained bitterly and made known that he wanted the job.[42]

Another occasion when Poindexter seemed to be fed up with North's "emotionalism" came in September. North had sent him a message in which he had complained that he was having trouble getting White House transportation. He had needed a car to get to an appointment with Israel Defense Minister Rabin and had been a half hour late because he had had trouble getting one. In another incident, he had almost missed a flight to Miami because he could not get a car at the White House and on his return late at night had been forced to wait two hours for a taxi to pick him up and return him to the White House. He had other grievances:

I have never whined before and do not mean to do so now, but it is becoming increasingly difficult to do my job. Not only can I not get my secretary promoted, I cannot even get regular staff badges for two of the finest staff officers on the NSC.

Poindexter did not give him much sympathy. He appended a hand-written note to Paul Thompson, the counsel, in which he made no concessions to North and ended with the words: "Tell him to quit bitching."[43] Nerves were wearing thin.

5

If the media showed an unusual interest in the NSC staff's tie-up with the contras, Congress could not be far behind. So it was again in June 1986.

The oversight committees in both the Senate and the House of Representatives were supposed to be kept informed of and to stand guard over covert activities. In fact, the committees had no sources of information of their own and knew only as much as the administration chose to tell them. So long as the CIA was the only agency legally charged with conducting covert activities, the committees could always call its director and question him. By ostensibly staying out of the Iran and contra operations, the CIA avoided giving any information to the committees for almost two years.[44] In this way the secret shift of the operations to the NSC staff created a dilemma for the committees. The president considered the NSC staff to be his personal staff and thereby, according to the doctrine of the separation of powers, exempt from congressional oversight. As a result, the committees were charged with overseeing covert activities but were prevented from overseeing the very staff that was carrying them out.

In 1985, when McFarlane had been faced with congressional questions about his staff's activities in aid of the contras, he had finessed the inquiry by pretending to answer it. He had answered untruthfully, but he had answered. At that time, Poindexter had wanted, in principle, to withhold all information from Congress, thereby making untruthful answers unnecessary. In McFarlane's temporary absence, he had admittedly appointed North to compose the first responses precisely in order to withhold information.[45] Now Poindexter was faced with the same sort of congressional questions as McFarlane had been.

On June 24, 1986, in the midst of the flurry of exposés in the media, Representative Ronald Coleman of Texas introduced a Resolution of Inquiry that directed the president to provide the House of Representatives with "certain information concerning activities of Lieutenant Colonel Oliver North or any other member of the staff of the National Security Council in support of the Nicaraguan resistance." North's name was mentioned three more times in the body of the resolution, together with Singlaub's, Owen's, and Hull's.[46] On June 25, Representative Dante B. Fascell, chairman of the House Committee on Foreign Affairs, requested comments on the resolution from President Reagan, again mentioning North by name. On July 1, Representative Lee H. Hamilton, chairman of the House Permanent Select Committee on Intelligence, made the same request, also mentioning North by name.[47]

Poindexter replied on July 21. True to his previous attitude, he refused to give the committees any information. His stonewalling took the form of saying that the information had already been provided by McFarlane the year before, and that the staff was "in compliance with both the spirit and letter of the law regarding support of the Nicaraguan resistance."[48] Poindexter's reply was curt and defiant. It hid behind McFarlane's former misrepresentations; repeating them did not make them any more truthful. When he was questioned at the congressional hearings, Poindexter insisted that his reply was "accurate" but "clearly withh[eld] information."[49]

Poindexter's treatment of this incident reflected the inflexibility or the insensitivity of the man. "I have always felt," he testified, "that the Boland Amendment did not apply to the NSC staff and that the NSC staff was complying with the letter and spirit of the law."[50] Poindexter tried to explain how his staff had complied with the letter and spirit of the law: "We were clearly helping the contras. But we were also trying very hard to stay within the letter and spirit of Boland by keeping the other departments that were covered by the Boland Amendment out of the issue."[51] In effect, he made the tactical bureaucratic maneuver that made the NSC staff's doing what the other departments were forbidden to do into proof of the NSC staff's virtuous behavior. Poindexter also testified that "we had been running this [contra] operation on our own for a long period of time because there was no other alternative in order to keep the contras alive."[52] Whatever the reason, running this operation alone no more complied with the letter, let alone the spirit, of the law than would running the operation in cooperation with other departments.

In his deposition at the Poindexter trial, President Reagan was asked about Poindexter's reply to the congressional committees. "I am in total agreement," Reagan said. "If I had written it myself, I might have used a little profanity."[53]

In the end, however, even Poindexter compromised. He refused to give the committees documents or any other information in his possession, but he made North personally available to the House Intelligence Committee for questioning. In effect, Poindexter avoided facing the committee himself, as might have been expected from a superior officer, and deliberately pushed North out in front.* The meeting took place on August 6, 1986, in the White House Situation Room. Eleven members of the committee, an unusually large number, two officials of the NSC staff, and two staff members of the committee attended.

North could not refuse, as he had put it in connection with the 1985 inquiry, "to show Congress a single word on this whole thing," but he did the next-best thing—he gave the assembled congressmen a trumped-up version. According to committee notes taken at the meeting, he said that he had merely given the contra leaders advice on human rights and on their need for an improved civic image. He had given the contras no military advice and knew of no specific military operations.[54] As Representative Lee Hamilton later testified, North said he had not violated the Boland Amendment in any way, had not assisted contras by raising money for them, and had not provided any kind of military advice. North even blamed a "Soviet disinformation campaign" for the things that had happened to him.[55] Thomas Latimer, the House committee's staff director, recalled that North had denied having had any dealings with Singlaub for the past two years, had never given Owen any guidance, and had not been involved in any fund-raising for the contras.[56]

North's performance was an unqualified success. Some representatives present, especially Dave McCurdy of Oklahoma, were so impressed by North's testimony that they immediately expressed the hope that their committee would adversely report on the Coleman Resolution of Inquiry. Representative Hamilton, the committee chairman, closed the meeting by indicating his satisfaction with North's responses and predicting the full committee's satisfaction.[57] When Poindexter received a report of the meeting, he sent North a congratulatory message: "Well done."[58]

Later, North was belligerently unapologetic about his admitted deception of the committee. In his testimony before the congressional com-

---

* Earl testified that North had had difficulty getting guidance on his meeting with the committee from Poindexter, who was on leave at that time. Earl's impression had been that Poindexter's leave was "not accidental. The timing of the leave was just not a coincidence" (B-9, pp. 856–57). Poindexter virtually admitted that he had deliberately avoided giving North guidance: "Obviously with hindsight, it would have been prudent to have sat down and talked to him about it before he did it to provide more detailed guidance, but that was not the manner in which I was managing and directing Colonel North at the time . . . I did not expect him to lie to the committee. I expected him to be evasive, say that he didn't want to answer the question, be uncooperative, if necessary, but I rather think that with his resourcefulness, I thought he could handle it" (100-8, pp. 153, 155).

mittees in 1987, he said: "I will tell you right now, counsel, and all the members here gathered, that I misled the Congress" and made false statements about his activities in support of the contras. He also admitted that "I participated in preparation of documents for the Congress that were erroneous, misleading, evasive, and wrong, and I did it again here when I appeared before the committee convened in the White House Situation Room and I make no excuses for what I did."[59]

Still later, at his own trial in 1989, North was somewhat more contrite, as the occasion demanded. After admitting that he had not told the truth at the meeting of the House Intelligence Committee on August 6, 1986, North confided: "I was not honest in that meeting. I'm not proud of that. It's not something I feel good about."[60]

Neither had the members of the House Intelligence Committee reason to feel good about it. They had been satisfied to listen to North's creative imagination and to decide to drop the subject. It was as if law enforcement officers were to do nothing but interrogate a suspect, politely listen to his denials of wrongdoing, and straightway let him go. First, the committee members did not know any more than they read in the newspapers, and then they did not want to know any more than North chose to tell them. Oversight was the right designation for the committee in more than one sense.

Thus, for the second time in two years, an opportunity to intervene before the contra operation blew up was lost. Poindexter, North, and administration policy could not be saved from themselves.

It could also not be saved by Congress. This missed opportunity was followed by the far more serious congressional reversal of policy between June and October 1986, which opened Congress to the criticism that it had been guilty of confused and contradictory policies. Congress's inability to stay on a steady course throughout the contra affair puts one in mind of James Bryce's observation almost a hundred years earlier—that the U.S. Congress "does not impress the nation by either its intellectual power or its moral dignity."

6

A month after his appearance before the congressional committee, North was suddenly confronted by another emergency. As luck would have it, the Santa Elena airstrip in Costa Rica did not become fully operational until May 1986. In that very month, an election brought in a new president, Oscar Arias Sánchez, who quickly revoked permission to use the airstrip.[61] The airstrip was so remote that the Costa Rican government had not known what was happening there until an accident brought it unwelcome attention.

The villain was mud. On June 2, 1986, a plane tried to make an airdrop, could not locate the troops inside Nicaragua, and made an emergency landing at the Santa Elena airstrip. In the rainy season, the plane, loaded with heavy military cargo, went down and stuck in the mud. Tambs said that he was not surprised, because he assumed that the plane had not been loaded to drop "Band-Aids."[62] After Arias had made known that he did not want the airstrip any longer, Tambs related, he had told Fernandez "to tell North and the Udall Corporation to shut it down" and had thought that it had been shut down.[63] Nevertheless, as Tambs admitted, it was still used by planes needing to refuel.[64] Fernandez realized that there could be trouble ahead with the Costa Rican government, not only because the incident showed that the airstrip was still being used but because "we had a plane in neutral Costa Rica loaded with lethal supplies." Castillo claimed that he had told the airstrip's operators to close it down but they had ignored him.[65]

It took about a day to get the plane out of the mud, after which Secord triumphantly reported to North: "All aircraft out of mud and back."[66] Nevertheless, this incident and the increasing uneasiness of the Costa Rican government convinced North that the airstrip was too risky to maintain. On August 13, 1986, Secord received a message from North's aide, Lieutenant Colonel Robert Earl, instructing him:

> 1. Conduct emergency recall immediately. Bring the mainte-nance and aircrews out of there quietly, but quickly. Leave all the equipment, including airplanes.
>
> 2. Destroy registration plates on A/C [aircraft] if possible. But don't damage the A/C. . . . Perhaps this thing can be patched back together for the transition. But for the moment the people must be gotten out of there.[67]

For once, Secord refused to take orders. Since the Udall Research Corporation was registered in his name, he regarded himself as its owner and saw its material assets endangered by Earl's instructions. Secord quickly struck back:

> 1. There is more than 1 million dollars worth of equipment, spares, located at the airfield. I presume your msg [message] results from telecon with Ollie. If so I must remind you that these assets are owned by Udall Research and there is no intention of aban-doning them.[68]

Secord later insisted that he could sell these assets and keep the pro-ceeds, even though the money had come not from him but from private donations to the contras. His private little band had "sweated over" the airstrip project for so long that he was loath to abandon it.[69] As a result, the operation continued—until it was hit by another near disaster.

Late at night on September 5, 1986, North learned that the secret of the Santa Elena airstrip in Costa Rica was about to be blown wide open. He was informed by Joe Fernandez, the CIA chief of station in San José, that Costa Rican Minister of Public Security Garrón planned to hold a press conference to denounce the airstrip as a violation of Costa Rican law. Worse still, he intended to name North and Secord among those responsible for the violation.[70]

Early the next morning, North passed the startling news on to Poindexter and reported that he had already taken action. He claimed that he had conferred with Ambassador Tambs, Assistant Secretary of State Elliott Abrams, and the head of the CIA Central American Task Force, Alan Fiers, and they had agreed on the following counterattack: North was to call President Arias and warn him that he would be punished in two ways: he would never be permitted to meet with President Reagan and "w[oul]d never see a nickel of the $80 million that [M. Peter] McPherson [director of Agency for International Development] had promised him" on Friday, the day before.* Tambs and Abrams had called Arias with the same message. All this pressure on Arias had worked, and he had called back to say that the press conference had been canceled.

North clearly meant to tell Poindexter that he had actually put in the planned call to Arias in the form of this halfway apology for his action:

> I recognize that I was well beyond my charter in dealing w[ith] a head of state this way in making threats/offers that may be impossible to deliver, but under the circumstances—and w[ith] Elliott's concurrence—it seemed like the only thing we could do. Best of all it seems to have worked.[71]

This was one of the strangest messages ever sent by North. Poindexter knew only as much as North had told him and congratulated him: "Thanks, Ollie. You did the right thing, but let's try to keep it quiet."[72] In fact, North had not done the right thing. He had never called Arias, and his threats had never been delivered to Arias. This incident makes one wonder what there was about North that made him concoct a totally fictitious telephone call to Arias in order to take credit for having called off the Costa Rican press conference.

Tambs, not North, had called Arias. According to Tambs, he had been called by North about midnight on September 5, told about the threatening press conference, and asked to call President Arias to dissuade

---

* In his notebook, North wrote: "Conf. call to Elliott Abrams and Amb. Lew Tambs; —Tell Arias; —Never set foot in W.H. [White House]; —Never get 5¢ of $80M[illion] promised by McPherson" (NN, September 6, 1986). North told Tambs to call Arias with a similar message, and Abrams advised the ambassador "to advert to the visit [to Washington] in a way which made it clear to President Arias that his visit was at risk" (Abrams, 100-5, p. 25).

him from holding it. Tambs succeeded in getting to Arias, who was at dinner, and suggested to him that it would not be prudent for such a press conference to take place, especially in view of a pending case against the United States by Costa Rica in the International Court of Justice at The Hague. Tambs said nothing about whether Arias would be permitted to meet President Reagan or about the money from the Agency for International Development. Arias told Tambs that he would see what he could do about it and later called to say that he had spoken with Garrón and that the press conference had been called off. Tambs informed North and Abrams of the outcome in a three-way conference call. So far as Tambs knew, North had never called Arias.[73]

Abrams recalled that North had called him about the imminent Costa Rican press conference and had asked him to get Tambs to call Arias to stop it. Arias apparently expected to make an official visit to the United States, and Tambs was told to warn him "diplomatically" that the visit "was at risk." Tambs had reported an hour or two later that the press conference had been canceled. Abrams also knew nothing about a threatening call from North to Arias.[74]

North's own explanation of his note to Poindexter about his mythical call to Arias was as peculiar as everything else in this episode. At the congressional hearings, he admitted that he had never made the call to Arias but had pretended to have done so "to protect the other two parties engaged."[75] The other two parties were Tambs and Abrams. In his report to Poindexter, North had already implicated them as having cooperated in planning the approach to Arias. The only question was whether North or Tambs had made the call to Arias. The even more mysterious question is why Tambs and Abrams needed to be "protected" in a communication to Poindexter.

Poindexter was asked why he had congratulated North for having done "the right thing" in having made a telephone call to Arias to threaten him with political and economic reprisals if the press conference was held. In one of his dimly evasive replies, Poindexter appeared to think that an NSC staff member could have been right to call the head of state of another country, depending on the circumstances, on who the head of state was, and on "what sort of acquaintance the staff officer has." Almost a year after North's fictitious call, Poindexter still professed to believe that it might have been made, or at least that he did not know that it had not been made.[76]

When Secretary of State Shultz was questioned about the incident, he was sure that there were no circumstances to warrant a call by an NSC staff member to a head of state.[77] Apparently Poindexter did not see any impropriety in an invasion of the State Department's traditional territory by a subordinate member of his staff without his own prior knowledge and approval.

The CIA's Fiers, who North said had participated with Abrams in the decision to call Arias, had another sidelight on North's touch of fantasy on this and other occasions:

> As the committee is aware, North was full of bombast. He met with a lot of people and did a lot of things, and I always wondered how he could do them because he didn't speak to Spanish speakers. Look at the famous call to Arias, I was sure he didn't do that. There were other people that he said that he spoke with from time-to-time and I always wondered how a non-Spanish speaker got through to Spanish-speaking people only. [78]

At another point in his testimony, Fiers said:

> I never knew Colonel North to be an absolute liar, but I never took anything he said at face value because I knew that he was bombastic and embellished the record, and threw curves, speed balls and spit balls to get what he wanted, and I knew it, and I knew it well. . . . I have seen Colonel North play fast and loose with the facts. But, on the other hand, I believe there is a, from where I sit, from glimpses I saw of this thing as the train windows went by, there was a lot of fact in what he said too. [79]

In any case, the Santa Elena airstrip's days were numbered. On September 10, a message arrived in Washington that Costa Rican security forces had "raided" the airstrip and had impounded seventy-seven drums of gas. It concluded: "Alert Ollie Pres. Arias will attend Reagan's dinner in New York Sept. 22nd. Boy [Arias] needs to be straightened out by heavy weights."[80] On September 25, the dreaded press conference was held in San José, Costa Rica, and the secret Santa Elena airstrip was no longer a secret. North informed Poindexter that Costa Rican Minister of Public Security Garrón had announced that "Costa Rican authorities had discovered a secret airstrip in Costa Rica that was over a mile long and which had been built and used by a Co. called Udall Services for supporting the contras." He had "named one of Dick's [Secord's] agents (Olmstead) as the man who set up the field as a 'training base for U.S. military advisors.' "[81] When the affair of the airstrip was duly reported in *The New York Times*, the story could not be ignored in Washington. [82]

Poindexter angrily queried North: "Why didn't Lew Tambs know that this was coming?"[83] Instead of blaming North, who had supposedly intimidated the Costa Rican president into changing his mind, Poindexter blamed Tambs. In return, North gave Poindexter a "damage assessment":

> Udall Resources, Inc., S.A. is a proprietary of Project Democracy. It will cease to exist by noon today. There are no USG [U.S.

government] fingerprints on any of the operation and Olmstead is not the name of the agent—Olmstead does not exist.

We have moved all Udall resources ($ [unclear]) to another account in Panama, where Udall maintained an answering service and cover office. The office is now closed as are all files and paperwork.[84]

As usual, such embarrassments required "press guidance." North said that this one was composed by him in coordination with Abrams of the State Department, Armitage of Defense, and the CIA. North's version was another exercise of creative imagination. It attributed the airstrip to an offer by the Monge administration in Costa Rica for use "as an extension of the civil guard training center" at a nearby site. The land was "reportedly" made available by "the owner of the property who had apparently decided to abandon plans for a tourism project." Finally, the press was guided to ask the question: "Was the airstrip intended for use by the contras?" The answer was: "The Government of Costa Rica has made clear its position it will not permit the use of its territory for military action against neighboring states. The U.S. Government respects that position."[85]

Thus the secret Santa Elena airstrip came to an inglorious end. It was another narrow escape for North. So long as Poindexter saw no evil, heard no evil, and spoke no evil, the system could not regenerate itself from within. Alarm bells had to be set off from outside.

17

The Unraveling

We have been following the Iran and contra affairs as they unfolded independently of each other. Yet they were intertwined in the persons of Lieutenant Colonel Oliver North and former Air Force General Richard V. Secord, with the result that a single slip in either one was enough to threaten both. In retrospect, North himself admitted that "the operational mistake was to cross the two operations in the person of perhaps this guy here and the others who are having to carry it out."[1] It was as elementary a mistake as could be made.

The cost of the operational mistake began to come in fortuitously.

At 11 p.m. on October 5, 1986, Colonel Samuel J. Watson III, the deputy assistant for national security affairs to Vice President Bush, received a telephone call from Felix Rodriguez in Miami. Watson made this record of the call: "Subject: A C-123 is missing, possibly in Nicaragua."[2] Rodriguez had heard about the missing plane from a friend in the area, where the flight had taken off, who told him that it was overdue. Rodriguez had asked his friend to make sure that the plane had not made an emergency landing somewhere. On the following morning, Rodriguez heard the Havana radio broadcast a report that a plane had been shot down in Nicaragua and that one crew member had been taken prisoner. He called Watson again with the news, which was how official Washington first learned about it.[3]

That Rodriguez should have called the vice president's military aide was not accidental. Like Rafael Quintero, Rodriguez—who used the alias "Max Gomez"—was a native Cuban, who had taken part in the Bay of Pigs invasion, had worked for the CIA, and had been recruited by North in September 1985 to assist in the contra resupply operation in El Salvador. Rodriguez, however, was much closer to Donald P. Gregg, the vice president's national security adviser, under whom he had fought in Vietnam and who regarded him as an intimate and valued friend. In August 1986, Rodriguez had met with Gregg and Watson to accuse virtually everyone in the leadership of the operation—Secord, Dutton, Gadd, and Quintero—of fraud and profiteering.[4] Gregg had introduced Rodriguez to Vice President Bush, whom he had met three times—and to whom, surprisingly, Gregg claimed he had told nothing about Rodriguez's charges. North and his henchmen had turned against Rodriguez, and in Gregg's absence it was Watson to whom Rodriguez entrusted his grim news.

Watson passed it on to the Situation Room in the White House and the NSC staff.[5] It was soon learned that the plane belonged to Secord's organization under the direct command of Dutton and that it had been shot down with a surface-to-air missile by Sandinista forces in northern Nicaragua. In it had been the pilot, William J. Cooper, the copilot, Wallace "Buzz" Sawyer, a seventeen-year-old Nicaraguan to handle radio communication with the ground forces, and a "kicker," Eugene Hasenfus, who pushed the cargo out of the plane. Only Hasenfus had survived.

Hasenfus was a forty-five-year-old Wisconsin man with a wife and three children. He was a former Marine who had served in Vietnam, specializing in aerial resupply.[6] After leaving the Marines in 1966, he had worked for six years for Air America, a CIA proprietary, in Southeast Asia. One of the chief pilots for Air America, whom Hasenfus had met at that time, was Cooper.

After an interval of fourteen years as a construction worker back in Wisconsin, Hasenfus suddenly received a telephone call from Cooper in June 1986. Cooper told him about a job which, as Hasenfus put it, would be "the same as we were doing in Southeast Asia, different geographic location, different time period." The pay was $3,000 a month. Hasenfus signed on the next month to work for "Corporate Air Services," which Cooper told Hasenfus was a "front" for "the CIA and the government."[7] The operation was actually managed by Southern Air Transport under Dutton's direction. Hasenfus heard from Cooper that "this is being run directly out of the White House," and Vice President Bush's name was mentioned.[8]

After making about sixty drops, the operation with Cooper and Hasenfus ran out of luck. A Caribou plane, loaded with jungle boots, ammunition, and AK-47s, was sent out on the morning of October 5 to resupply a contra group located in northern Nicaragua. It was shot down at 12:38 p.m. After twenty-four hours of wandering about in the jungle, Hasenfus was captured. He spent two and a half months in confinement and was released on December 17.

Joseph Fernandez, the CIA station chief in Costa Rica, attributed the disaster to a recent shift, owing to the plane's lack of navigational equipment, from nighttime to daytime airdrops. The CIA, he said derisively, would never have run an airdrop operation in the middle of the day in enemy territory using the same flight plan several times in a row.[9]

Also on October 5, Dutton heard from El Salvador that an aircraft was overdue. He called North's office the next morning and talked to Earl, who informed him that Rodriguez had already called Vice President Bush's office. [10] North was not in Washington to receive Dutton's message, because he was just then in the air flying to Europe for a meeting in Frankfurt with the Iranians, set for October 6. As soon as North heard of the Hasenfus incident, he cut short his stay in Frankfurt and boarded a plane for Washington. North was now caught between the conflicting demands of his two affairs and chose to give the contra crisis his immediate attention.

Dutton had all the aircraft flown out and sent the maintenance and air crews back to the United States. [11] Dutton blamed Rodriguez for having caused the downed airplane to fly alone and advised North: "He should be taken out of this net." [12]

When North was asked at the congressional hearings about his connection with the unlucky plane, he made no attempt to deny it:

The flight happened to have been paid for by General Secord's operation, the airplane was paid for by his operation. The pilots were paid for by his operation. Those were not U.S. Government moneys, but those were certainly his activities, and I was the U.S. Government connection. [13]

According to North, Assistant Secretary of State Elliott Abrams called him to take care of getting the bodies of the two dead U.S. pilots, Cooper and Sawyer, home and to raise the money to pay for funeral services. [14] North began to shred documents in his office, because "I certainly knew that I would be leaving the NSC shortly, and I took steps to go through my files and cleaning things out that no longer would be pertinent." [15] His mood was so lugubrious that he spoke to Poindexter of the necessity for a scapegoat: "All this was going to result in somebody having to be offered up, as it were." [16]

At this point, the ruling minds of the Reagan administration were faced with questions inherent in every covert operation—whether to play for time, plead ignorance, disown it completely, or defend it publicly as the best option in the circumstances. If it was disowned, could the denial be made to stick?

The reaction of the administration to the incident was the first test of its ability to cope with an unmistakable disclosure of its covert operations, either Nicaraguan or Iranian. The previous publicity had not brought on such a crisis, because the congressional committees had been easily talked out of doing anything about it. Yet the existence of an armed anti-Sandinista resistance in Central America and its support in the United States had been an open secret for over a year. In these circumstances, a panicky reaction to the plane incident was surprising.

2

As might have been expected, a denial reflex took over in official circles. The immediate reaction in Washington was to disavow any connection with the plane. Secretary of State Shultz said that it had been "hired by private people" who "had no connection with the U.S. government at all."[17] Assistant Secretary of State Abrams later testified that he had assured Shultz that no government official had been "engaged in facilitating this flight or paying for it or directing it or anything like that," so that Shultz's misleading public statement was Abrams's doing.[18]

Abrams exhibited the most bravado in his first public statement on October 7. He said that "some very brave people" had been willing to bring materiel into Nicaragua, and added: "God bless them . . . If these people were involved in this effort, then they were heroes."[19] On October 8, President Reagan denied that there was any U.S. government connection with the flight; he praised the efforts to arm the contras and compared them to the Abraham Lincoln Brigade in the Spanish Civil War—a strange allusion to a Communist-organized and -led force for a devoutly anti-Communist president.*[20]

Some denials took refuge in claiming what was not in question. Senator David F. Durenberger, chairman of the Senate Select Committee on Intelligence, said that the CIA had assured his committee "there is absolutely no connection between that plane, what was in that airplane, the pilots or anybody else [on board] and a U.S. government-financed or -sponsored effort such as the so-called contra operation."[21] If he had been better informed, Durenberger would have known that the North-Secord operation, which was under the direction of a U.S. government official, was designed for the very purpose of acting as a surrogate for a U.S. government-financed or -sponsored effort.

The chief figure in the "damage control" that followed Hasenfus's capture was Abrams. His most costly defect was that he grossly overestimated his own cleverness. On this occasion, he went out on the longest public limb, as if he were immune to being caught out. Abrams was chairman of the Restricted Interagency Group (RIG), made up of representatives from all the interested departments, though it was effectively managed by a trio from the State Department, the NSC staff, and the CIA—Abrams, North, and Fiers.

At a meeting of the RIG on October 8, which North did not get back from Europe in time to attend, decisions were made on how to handle the subject of the "Downed Plane." In effect, the group adopted a strategy of putting all the responsibility on the contras themselves. The two most important decisions were:

* The "International Brigade" in Spain had an "Abraham Lincoln Battalion."

Press Guidance was prepared which states no U.S.G[overnment] involvement or connection, but that we are generally aware of such support contracted by the Contras.

UNO to be asked to assume responsibility for flight and to assist families of Americans involved. Elliott will follow up with Ollie to facilitate this.

The UNO was also to be asked to engage legal counsel for Hasenfus. Some U.S. officials, however, did not look favorably on Abrams's aggressive line: "Elliott said he would continue to tell the press these were brave men and brave deeds. We recommended he not do this because it contributes to perception U.S.G. inspired and encouraged private lethal aid effort."[22] A few days later, the contra leadership took full responsibility for the incident and denied that there had been any U.S. government connection.[23]

Abrams now stepped forward as the chief government spokesman on the whole affair. With his usual temerity, he went on the Evans-Novak television show on October 11 to explain what had happened. He made these categorical statements:

Evans: Mr. Secretary, can you give me categorical assurance that Hasenfus was not under the control, the guidance, the direction, or what have you, of anybody connected with the American government?

Abrams: Absolutely. That would be illegal. We are barred from doing that, and we are not doing it. This was not in any sense a U.S. government operation. None. . . .

Novak: Now, when you[,] say[,] gave categorical assurance, we're not playing word games that are so common in Washington. You're not talking about the NCS [sic], or something else?

Abrams: I am not playing games.

Novak: National Security Council?

Abrams: No government agencies, none.[24]

Abrams wriggled and wiggled through many more such questions. He even blamed Congress for the deaths of the Americans in the plane incident. He cited members of the congressional intelligence committees—who were told that there was no U.S. involvement—as confirmation that there was no such involvement. In the end, Novak was taken in and agreed that "this doesn't look like a cover-up, and it doesn't because there is no equivocation."[25]

To put forward sophistries on television might be considered a venial sin in Washington, but Abrams did not stop there. On October 10, he repeated the performance for the Senate Foreign Relations Committee and on October 14 for the House Intelligence Committee, on which occasion he was accompanied by the CIA's Clair George and Alan Fiers.

The House Intelligence Committee was treated to this kind of testimony:

> *Abrams:* I will say that no American intelligence or Defense or any other kind of government officials was engaged in facilitating this flight or paying for it or directing it or anything like that, there is no U.S. Government involvement, no government involvement, including anybody in the Embassies overseas.[26]

Later, at the Iran-contra congressional hearings, Abrams declared that this and similar statements were "completely honest and completely wrong." The question of his honesty mainly turned on whether he had asked North about the latter's connection with the flight and whether North had denied having had any such involvement. Abrams was not one to give a straight answer:

> *Question:* At that time, sir, wasn't it the fact that you believed there was someone in government who would know, who organized, or paid for the Hasenfus flight?
>
> *Abrams:* No. To say that Colonel North was the person who knew the most about the private benefactors—which I thought, and think to be the case—is not to say that he could tell you the name of every one of them and could tell you everything that every one of them was doing each day. . . .
>
> *Question:* So you did not ask Colonel North in so many words if he was involved or if he knew if there was any official U.S. involvement, it was because you decided not to ask him that question in so many words, isn't that right, sir?
>
> *Abrams:* No. I think it is because I believed I knew there was no U.S. Government involvement, had checked around, was aware of the fact Colonel North would not be involved in this because of previous statements of his and others that he would not be involved in this kind of activity.
>
> Then he came back to town—I believe I had already spoken publicly about this—and did not say wait a minute, stop.
>
> *Question:* Sir, let me go back to my question. If you did not ask Colonel North in so many words, "Ollie, were you involved with this flight?" "Ollie, did you know who paid for this flight?" If you didn't ask him any of those questions in so many words, it was

because you decided not to ask him any such question, isn't that correct?

Abrams: Sure. That is logically correct. [27]

On another occasion, Abrams explained that asking questions, such as the one about the flight, was not fashionable in his circles:

I think most of us were careful not to ask lots of questions, other than once in a while, to say is this all okay, is this stuff legal—once in a while. [28]

On the basis of such investigation, Abrams had given categorical assurances to the general public, to the congressional committees, and to Secretary of State Shultz that there was no U.S. government connection with the Hasenfus flight. All North had had to do to cover his tracks was to tell Abrams and others that he was not breaking any laws. This is how Abrams explained how he thought he knew what North had been doing:

Question: And you were willing to give categorical assurances to the Secretary of State, under oath to Congress, to the public and the press without ever asking the question point blank of the man you knew knew the most in the Government; isn't that right?

Abrams: That is correct. Not only was I willing, Mr. Belnick, I did it because I was confident that there was no such activity going on.

Question: And you turned out to be wrong?

Abrams: That is correct.

Question: And as a result of that, you ended up making false statements to the Congress, the public, and the press?

Abrams: Making wrong statements is the way I'd put it. . . .

Question: Well, sir, didn't you testify to the Tower Board that you were careful not to ask Colonel North too many questions?

Abrams: I was careful not to ask Colonel North what questions I thought I did not need to know the answers to. I was also careful to see that he worked through channels. I was careful to see that Colonel North was doing what he appeared to be rightly doing, while assuring me and other members of the U.S. Government that he was not violating the law in any way. *[29]

---

* Abrams was not the only one who claimed to be satisfied when North told him he was not violating the law. Assistant Secretary of Defense Richard Armitage recalled: "Several of us in those groups said, Ollie . . . you are not involved in all this, are you? And he said . . . I have broken no laws."

In testimony before the House Intelligence Committee on October 14, 1986, Abrams claimed to have had "complete knowledge" of the private groups contributing money to the contras but only to the extent of publicly encouraging them.

> *Chairman Hamilton:* Just to be clear, the United States Government has not done anything to facilitate the activities of these private groups, is that a fair statement? We have not furnished any money. We have not furnished any arms. We have not furnished any advice. We have not furnished logistics. . . .
>
> *Abrams:* Yes, to the extent of my knowledge that I feel to be complete, other than the general public encouragement that we like this kind of activity.[30]

In another statement on December 19, 1986, he explained his ignorance in these terms:

> We did not engage in nor did we really know anything about this private network. We knew that it existed. We knew it in part because somebody was giving the contras guns . . . they were instructed to kind of stay away, as the Agency people were, on the grounds that if you got too close, you would end up being accused of facilitating and so forth.[31]

Whether Abrams was honestly mistaken or not, the two high CIA officials who accompanied him, Clair George and Alan Fiers, knew that something was wrong with Abrams's testimony.

3

As deputy director of operations, in direct charge of covert operations, Clair George was the third-highest official in the CIA. He was a thirty-one-year veteran, twenty of them spent abroad. George himself had assured the House Intelligence Committee on October 14 that the CIA was not involved directly or indirectly in arranging, directing, or facilitating resupply missions conducted by private individuals in support of the contras, for which he later apologized in testimony at the Iran-contra congressional hearings.[32] He also testified that he had been "surprised" at Abrams's statements and explained why he had not said anything at the time:

> The question is, should I leap up and say, "hold it, Elliott, what about—excuse me, all you members of HPSCI [House Permanent

Select Committee on Intelligence], but Elliott and I are now going to discuss what we knew about"—I didn't have the guts to do it or I didn't do it.[33]

George was again pressed to explain his reaction to Abrams's statements and gave two more reasons. He said that he was "almost megalomaniacal in trying to prove one thing"—that the CIA "was not involved in that activity because it would have been illegal." He was also impressed by how "categorical" Abrams's statements had been, so that "it was the sort of thought that went through my mind—excuse me, Elliott, but maybe you are the only guy in town that hasn't heard this news."[34]

When George was asked about an attempt by North to get the CIA to buy three of Secord's airplanes, he replied:

> God bless poor Colonel North. Everything was his, the world is mine, I'm going to see the President, I'm going to see the King, I'm going to fly down to Central America and have a private con- ference. How would you like to have some tickets to the Redskins game? Christ—Colonel North calls me up and says, "How would you like to buy my airplanes?" I guess what I'm saying, counsel, is, I'm not sure he could even produce any airplanes.[35]

Fiers had put in nineteen years in the CIA. He had learned enough in that time to develop a strategy of keeping out of trouble:

> I knew from the very beginning of my time in the task force that I wanted to stay away from harm's way and backed away from things that were, in my view, controversial either politically or questionable legally; and my tack was to play a passive role, to not seek things out and look the other way.[36]

Fiers had also been "taken aback" by Abrams's categorical denials of any U.S. connection with the Hasenfus flight, but had said nothing, because, he said, "the pieces weren't together" in his mind. He explained his personal problem in this way:

> I could have been more forthcoming to the committee, but I frankly was not going to be the first person to step up and do that. You may call that a cowardly decision, some may call it a brave decision, it is a controversial decision, but so long as others who knew the details, as much as I, who knew more than I, were keeping their silence on this, I was going to keep my silence. That may be false loyalty, it may be folly, but I said before that I worked for the

administration, and I was to support the administration, and to stay within the bounds of the law.[37]

Fiers also tried to tell how his mind had worked:

Frankly, when that was said, my mind was racing. I was figuring how is Elliott getting from A to B. And he must have it worked out in his own mind so that that statement is technically correct or is correct. And I sat and was silent. I walked out of that—there is no excuse for it.[38]

According to Fiers, Casey had once convened a meeting with George, Fiers, and North. Casey had confronted North: "Ollie, are you operating in Central America." North had replied: "No, I'm not operating in Central America."[39] It may be hard to believe that Casey was so easily satisfied with North's answer, but Fiers recalled the incident to show how he and George had been influenced by it.

Ignorance was highly prized. Fiers told a story about a conversation with Casey in which the latter asked him: " 'What do you know about those, about the funding for the Resistance forces?' And sort of how it's being done and what Ollie is doing. And I said, 'Not very much, I don't know where it's coming from, I have stayed away from it.' He said, 'So have I, I haven't asked any questions about it, I don't want to know about it, I've kept myself ignorant.' "[40] One doesn't quite know what to make of such denials, especially on the part of Casey, but "protection" of the Agency, even if feigned, was as all-important to him as to his underlings.*

Another such story has North telling Fiers: "You don't want to know." And Fiers says that he replied: "You're right, I don't want to know."[41]

The cases of George and Fiers show how loyalties and self-interest influenced behavior. The rules of the game did not motivate them to demonstrate a higher degree of civic courage, which might have embarrassed their agency and endangered their careers if they had spoken up more clearly and candidly. They were products of a system that rewarded "team play" and "CYA" (cover your ass). They felt themselves caught, as Fiers repeatedly expressed it, in a "nutcracker," threatened with dire consequences no matter what they did.† In these circumstances, they could hardly be expected to be more high-minded and courageous than their superiors.

---

* Fiers told another story of how Casey could deceive himself or others about a personal matter. "You know," Casey said to Fiers, "so and so said that I had terminal cancer. Isn't that preposterous? Isn't that the most ludicrous thing you heard? Do I look like a man with cancer?" Fiers answered: "No, you don't." To which Fiers later added: "Well, he did."

† Of Fernandez in Costa Rica, Fiers said that he "was in the most difficult position of any of us, he was in a nutcracker as well as me, as well as others" (B-3, p. 185).

4

Behind the scenes, Hasenfus's capture brought on more than denial and equivocation. The entire operation began to unravel. Panic set in where it might have been least expected.

According to North, he and Casey first talked about "this operation coming unraveled" right after the Hasenfus shoot-down.[42] Casey told North to shut down the entire Central American operation, get the airplanes out, and close the safe houses.[43]

Shortly afterward, Casey received a visit from an old friend, Roy Furmark, who further unnerved him with a story about a threatened exposure of the Iran affair—about which more later. North gave various versions of his conversations with Casey after the Hasenfus and Furmark episodes. North says that both events in early October 1986 led them to have "a lengthy discussion about the fact that this whole thing was coming unraveled and that things ought to be 'cleaned up,' and I started cleaning things up."[44] To "clean up" his files, North began shredding the paperwork in them. Sometime between October 13 and November 4, Casey is said to have told North: "Get rid of things, get rid of that book because that book has in it the names of everybody, the addresses of everybody. Just get rid of it and clean things up."[45] "That book" was the ledger which Casey had allegedly given North to keep an account of all those who had been given money to support the contras and which North thinks was destroyed by him on November 4 or 5.[46]

Also in early November, apparently alarmed by Furmark's disclosures, Casey told North: "Look, this revelation that is either occurring or about to occur is the end. You ought to go out and get a lawyer."[47] Another version of what Casey said is: "Look, you have had the shoot-down of the Hasenfus airplane, that operation is in trouble, Furmark has now come and told me that other people are aware of the fact that the arms sales to Iran have generated funds that have gone to support the Contras, and it is getting out."[48]

That the contra and Iran affairs should have come together at this time was only a coincidence, yet they somehow intersected in Casey's mind and influenced him to want to close down both operations. Others besides Casey had the same premonition of disaster and tried to head it off.

Poindexter saw North soon after Hasenfus's capture. North reported that "there had been a lot of identifying information aboard the aircraft." Poindexter expressed his extreme displeasure, and said that "these guys needed to shape up in terms of maintaining deniability and carrying identifying information aboard the aircraft was just not acceptable." Poindexter also said he might then have said something to North "about getting rid of his records."

Later, according to Poindexter, he heard from Kenneth deGraffenreid, the senior director of intelligence programs on the NSC staff. De-Graffenreid, in whose office the documents were kept, was worried about newspaper articles naming North and wanted to know whether to get rid of memoranda by North "that would be very damaging to the administration" if they got out. Poindexter told him to see North and work something out.[49] At about this time, moreover, North went to see Poindexter and said "that I knew things were coming down and that I was prepared to leave at any point."[50]

The unraveling of the Nicaraguan operation ostensibly came about as the result of a single unlucky incident that might have been avoided if one man, Eugene Hasenfus, had not been captured or if incriminating documents had not been found on the plane. Yet it was an incident that was waiting to happen at any time, given what Fernandez, the CIA agent in Costa Rica, called the "Larry, Moe and Curly" character of the entire operation, referring to the three bumbling comedians.[51]

It is conceivable that the incident might have been brazened out, as Abrams tried to do, or that the Reagan administration might have decided to make a public defense of what had been a covert operation. That such an operation had been going on was, after all, no longer a secret or a surprise.

Yet Casey and North were so overcome by the incident that they almost immediately decided that the end had come and retribution might not be far behind. North was never asked, and Casey could not be asked, why they had reacted with such fatalism to a single mishap of this kind. It may be that they were victims of their own trust in "deniability" as a cardinal principle of covert operations. Hasenfus's living presence in Nicaragua could not be denied, and, to them, that may have made the pretense no longer tenable. "Cover-up" had become a dirty term in American politics and, after Hasenfus, it may have seemed that one more time was once too often.

Or it could be that both Casey and North were tired and depressed, willing finally to give up the long and grueling struggle to hold the contras together "body and soul." Casey was only two months away from his death, and North had been seeking to unload his burden on the CIA for some time. In any case, the Hasenfus incident seemed to be the last straw for them.

5

Abrams was also a key figure in another miscarriage, one of the strangest in the entire story. It began before the Hasenfus incident and ended afterward.

An amendment to the Intelligence Authorization Act, passed in December 1985, opened the door to an initiative by the State Department that closely resembled the previous covert activities of the NSC staff. Section 105 of the amendment prohibited the solicitation of third-country funds for the contras by most agencies and departments of the government but did not restrict solicitation by the State Department, so long as it was for humanitarian assistance only. However, it provided for two conditions on giving such assistance: that it should be furnished from the third country's own resources and that the United States could not enter into any express or implied arrangement making U.S. provision of assistance to the third country contingent on the third country's assistance to the contras.

This amendment was one of the congressional compromises that envenomed U.S. policy vis-à-vis the contras. It could not be administered effectively, especially if the assistance took the form of money, because it made the State Department responsible for making sure that the money was actually spent on humanitarian or nonlethal as opposed to military or lethal assistance. If the money was given directly to the contras, the State Department had no machinery to monitor the way it was spent. If it was given indirectly, it was bound to be even harder to tell what happened to the money before it reached the contras. The amendment also barred a simple "quid pro quo" between the United States and the third country, as if third-country donors were really interested in supporting the contras and not in gaining U.S. goodwill for future use. Section 105 was an invitation to intrigue and chicanery.

For about six months, the State Department stalled and did nothing to take advantage of this amendment. The opportunity came in mid-1986.

On May 6, a meeting of the top-level National Security Planning Group (NSPG) brought together—in the absence of the president and vice president—Donald P. Gregg, Bush's national security adviser; Secretary of State Shultz; Assistant Secretary of State Abrams; Secretary of Defense Weinberger; CIA Director Casey; the chairman of the Joint Chiefs of Staff, Admiral Crowe; White House Chief of Staff Regan; National Security Adviser Poindexter; Oliver North; and others. Its main purpose was to get additional support for the Nicaraguan contras. A background paper drawn up by North and Ray Burghardt of the NSC staff proposed, among other things,

a direct and very private Presidential overture to certain Heads of State who are financially and politically capable of "bridging" the resistance needs until a more favorable Congressional environment prevails. Such a step would likely allow us to demonstrate the viability of the resistance without having to endure further domestic partisan political debate. This option has two significant liabilities:

—Public exposure would exacerbate the current partisan atmosphere.

—The foreign contributors would ultimately expect that their largesse would result in some kind of USG[overnment] concession in their favor.[52]

This proposal was essentially an effort to repeat the still secret contribution by Saudi Arabia. It clearly sought foreign "largesse" as a way of evading domestic debate on the issue. It recognized that any foreign donor was bound sooner or later to expect to get some sort of "quid pro quo" for doing the Reagan administration a favor.

We know what happened to the proposal from notes exchanged between North and Poindexter. North informed Poindexter that Abrams had called him to find out "where to send the money." North told Abrams to do nothing until he had talked to Poindexter. "As you know," North continued, "I have the accounts and the means by which this thing needs to be accomplished. I have no idea what Shultz knows or doesn't know, but he could prove to be very unhappy if he learns of the [probably Saudi] and [probably Taiwanese] aid that has been given in the past from someone other than you. Did RCM [McFarlane] ever tell Shultz?"[53]

Poindexter's reply showed how delicate the handling of Shultz had become:

> Out of the last NSPG on Central America Shultz agreed that he would think about third country sources. I wanted to get an answer from him so we could get out of the business. As I understand the law there is nothing that prevents State from getting involved in this now. To my knowledge Shultz knows nothing about the prior financing. I think it should stay that way. My concern was to find out what they were thinking so there would not be a screw up. I asked Elliott at lunch. He said he had recommended [Brunei] where Shultz is going to visit. They have lots of money [several words deleted]. It seems like a good prospect. Shultz agrees. I asked Elliott how the money could be transferred. He said he thought Shultz could just hand them an account number. I said that was a bad idea not at all letting on that we had access to accounts. I told Elliott that the best way was for [Brunei] to direct their embassy here to receive a person that we would designate and the funds could be transferred through him. Don't you think that is best? I still want to reduce your visibility. Let me know what you think and I will talk to George [Shultz]. I agree about CIA but we have got to get the legislation past [sic].[54]

This note was another indication that Poindexter and North were tired of bearing the contra burden alone and desired to shift at least part of it to the State Department or the CIA. It was awkward for them to ask Shultz to get third-country money for the contras, because he had never been informed of the previous third-country contributions. In this foreign affair, Poindexter and North knew more than the secretary of state and could not trust him with their knowledge. A national security adviser and an assistant secretary of state were reduced to plotting how to transfer money as if they were engaged in an illicit "laundering" operation.

As Abrams later told the story, he had the idea of getting "humanitarian" aid for the contras from third countries in line with Section 105 and raised the question with Secretary Shultz.[55] Shultz agreed, but set two conditions: no solicitation from right-wing dictatorships or from any government that was dependent on and was getting much foreign aid from the United States, because "it could appear that we had twisted their arms in some way." In this way, Abrams took on a money-raising responsibility for the contras that had long been North's métier. Unfortunately for Abrams, he did not know how to go about it without North's help.

Abrams's next move was to make the rounds of other regional assistant secretaries to ask them if they knew of a country with the necessary requirements—rich, without U.S. foreign aid, and amenable to U.S. wishes.[56] Abrams first thought of the Middle East and went to see Richard W. Murphy, the assistant secretary of state for the Near East and South Asia. Murphy told him that "Central America was not an area of the world that was on the map as far as Middle Eastern countries were concerned."[57] Murphy's reaction was a telling commentary on Saudi Arabia's contribution to the contras, which neither he nor Abrams as yet knew about.

Abrams was luckier with Gaston J. Sigur, the assistant secretary of state for East Asian and Pacific Affairs, who had already served as an intermediary for the contribution by Taiwan. In the end, Abrams hit on tiny Brunei, from which he decided to ask $10 million. The touch was going to be made when Secretary Shultz visited Brunei, a tiny enclave on the island of Borneo in the South China Sea, in June 1986.

Sultan Haji Hassanal Bolkiah Mu'izzaddin Waddaulah of Brunei was the absolute ruler of about 240,000 people in an area not much larger than the state of Delaware. Like Khashoggi, he has been publicized as the richest man in the world; Khashoggi, in fact, was one of the Sultan's sometime intimates and agents. Brunei owed its wealth to the discovery of oil at the turn of the century. It had been a British protectorate, was occupied by the Japanese in World War II, and did not obtain full independence until 1964. As an unofficial biography puts it, "Brunei is a private country run like a private possession."[58] A country with less reason to show an interest in the Nicaraguan struggle would be hard to imagine.*

Shultz was thinking of making the approach to the Sultan of Brunei himself for the $10 million to the contras, but Sigur, who made the plane trip with him, did not think that it was befitting for the secretary of state to ask for money from a foreign government. "I thought you had to kind to [sic] talk to other people around him, that you just can't talk to him directly like that," Sigur later explained. "So anyway, that was given up, the idea of doing that."[59] Instead, the U.S. ambassador was instructed to make the direct approach to the Brunei foreign minister, Pengiran Muda Mohammed Bolkiah, but this method unexpectedly encountered another difficulty.

To Abrams's dismay, the ambassador thought that "considerable groundwork" of more than a month or two would be required for a reasonable chance to get the money out of the Sultan. Abrams refused to delay and proposed an early meeting with the Brunei foreign minister. After many cables between Washington and Brunei, the foreign minister agreed to a meeting in London with Abrams, who sent word ahead that he was going to identify himself on the telephone as "Mr. Kenilworth." Secretary Shultz was brought into the negotiations to thank Brunei for "this endeavor which we believe has great importance for the overall security of the free world."[60]

Before Abrams set out for London, he made arrangements for the transfer of the money from Brunei to the contras. Abrams, however, did not know how to set up a secret account and went to North and Fiers to arrange it for him. A week later, both gave him account numbers on index cards for the deposit of the Brunei money. Abrams says that he intended to have the money deposited in a contra account, not in a North-controlled personal account. Whatever he had intended, he never told North what to do. Yet Abrams decided to use North's account, unaware that North was using the Secord-Hakim account at the Crédit Suisse in Geneva. North had months ago taken control of the money raised with his help out of the hands of the contras and had turned it over to Secord, who did nothing without North's approval.

Abrams admitted that he did not ask North what his Swiss account was for or who was authorized to draw on it. Abrams was not even suspicious that a presumptive contra account should have been put in a Swiss bank and not in Miami or somewhere closer to contra operations. Later, Abrams explained why he had chosen North's account: "I think in my mind it was more the question of why should we work with the Agency? We're always trying to build power at the State Department as opposed to the power of the Agency in this respect, not build the power

---

* The Sultan had already made a relatively small contribution to the contras. North's notebook for February 11, 1985, reads: "Sultan Brunei—100K [$100,000] for Calero."

of the Agency." On such "turf-fighting," as Abrams called it, did this affair of state turn, though Abrams never explained why in this case he had turned to the CIA's Fiers in the first place.*[61] Thus Abrams chose an account which he could not monitor and about which he admittedly knew nothing. Abrams was asked:

> *Counsel:* And my question is, did you do anything to assure yourself that there was no connection between this Swiss account that Colonel North gave you and any activities of the private network or private benefactors that were supplying lethal assistance to the Contras?
>
> *Abrams:* No.[62]

Abrams also had the problem of accounting for the way the State Department could be sure that the Brunei money would be used exclusively for humanitarian aid, as the law required. Despite his avowed ignorance of anything to do with North's account, Abrams made an effort to explain how he had thought the transaction was going to work out.

> What I had in mind was a sort of post hoc vouchering system, that is, this was not supposed to be our money. My understanding was that that would have been a—had it been deposited in a U.S. Government account, it would have had to go to the Treasury and all sorts of complications would ensue, and it was not supposed to be U.S. Government funding.
>
> My understanding was that this would go into—my thought was this would go into a separate account in which there would be no other money; therefore, it would be obvious any money withdrawn was being spent on humanitarian purposes and we would get vouchers, you know, bills, whatever you want to call them, documents demonstrating what the money had been spent on.
>
> In that way we would know that we were complying with the congressional provision this was to be humanitarian aid.[63]

When Abrams was asked what made him expect to get $10 million dollars' worth of vouchers from North attesting to the compliance with the humanitarian provision, he answered plaintively: "Trust." Abrams said that he had thought the money was going into North's personal secret Swiss account, which would have made it almost indistinguishable—in

---

* In his testimony at the congressional hearings, Abrams said that "we were having a bit of tug of war throughout this period about the relative roles of the State Department and the CIA, and did not really want to—this would be a situation where, in essence, the CIA would be in charge of this account were we to use—I don't know who had opened it, which UNO representative had opened it, and so forth, and we weren't really keen on, I think, on that idea of enhancing the role of the CIA in what was supposed to be a State Department initiative" (100-5, p. 46).

view of North's official position—from the kind of U.S. government account that Abrams was ostensibly trying to avoid.[64] In effect, Abrams had intended to use a subterfuge for a U.S. government account in order to be able to get the vouchers to prove after the $10 million was spent that he had complied with the congressional provision.

If Abrams's plan had gone through as planned, his Brunei money would have become North's Swiss money, which was not likely to be devoted to humanitarian assistance. Abrams himself later admitted that "the line between feeding and clothing a resistance force and helping it to fight is a difficult one to administer."[65]

A little slip of the typewriter kept the money from both of them. In Abrams's presence, North asked his secretary, Fawn Hall, to type the necessary information on his secret Swiss account on an index card—account number, name of bank and branch, bank official, telex.[66] Abrams copied this information on a slip of paper and went off to meet the Brunei Foreign Minister at a hotel in London on August 8, 1986.

As they walked in a nearby park, Abrams delivered a lecture of about fifteen minutes on the nature of his mission—U.S. policy in Central America, how strongly President Reagan felt about it, the troublesome congressional legislation. When Abrams mentioned $10 million as the sum requested from Brunei, the following discussion took place, in Abrams's own words:

> He said to me.
> What do we get out of this? What is in it for us?
> And I said, "Well—I actually had not thought about that question much, and I said, Well, you will—the President will know of this, and you will have the gratitude of the Secretary and of the President for helping us out in this jam."
> And he said, "What concrete do we get out of this."
> I said, "You don't get anything concrete out of it."[67]

This dialogue more than anything else explains the motivation of Saudi Arabia, Taiwan, and Brunei for their contributions to the contras. The money was an investment in the gratitude of President Reagan and Secretary Shultz, because the three countries did not have the slightest interest or stake in the fate of Nicaragua. After Abrams's recital, the foreign minister told him that the decision and money would have to come from Brunei, because he did not have access to such funds during his travels.

What Abrams did not know was that Fawn Hall had accidentally transposed the first three numbers of the account. On August 19, Brunei duly deposited $10 million in the right bank but the wrong account.[68] For weeks afterward, the mystery of the missing $10 million baffled and frustrated Abrams and North. By September, they were worried because no word had come from Geneva that the money had been deposited. Abrams called North to say: "Could you check and see if the money has come in?" A day or two later, North told Abrams: "No." Every time Abrams repeated this request, North said: "Not there." When Abrams asked the government of Brunei about the transfer, he received an answer to the effect: "Relax, these things take time." Abrams was so alarmed that, as he put it, he sent a cable to the ambassador: "Would you ask them, hey, where is the money, what is happening?" In one cable late in November, Abrams drafted a message which used the word "embez-zlement," because by this time he suspected that some skulduggery had prevented the money from reaching North's secret Geneva account. This cable was not sent, owing to the public disclosure of the "diversion memorandum" and the attendant government panic on November 25.[69]

The $10 million snafu finally came to an end on December 1, 1986. Secretary Shultz sent a cable to the ambassador in Brunei instructing him to stop the deposit of the money in Geneva "in light of recent events."[70] When the ambassador did as he was told on December 3, he cabled back that the Brunei foreign minister had been "surprised and visibly shaken." The latter's only comment was: "We did this as a good faith gesture to a friend. Let us hope that as a result, [Brunei] does not become part of a public scandal." The ambassador was informed the following day that the money had been transferred to the Geneva account as Abrams had instructed and could not be withdrawn except on orders of the recipient—whose identity was not known for some additional months and who had fallen heir to a mysteriously bestowed fortune.

The finale of this comic-opera fiasco came at hearings of the Senate Select Committee on Intelligence on November 25 and December 8, 1986. At the first meeting, Abrams was asked by Senator Bill Bradley of New Jersey: "Were you completely ignorant of all fund-raising activities by the contras?" Abrams's reply was a classic case of evasion and decep-tion. He first talked about General Singlaub, as if he were the only one in question, and righteously protested that he did not know just what Singlaub had been doing. "I was, until today," Abrams went on, "fairly confident that there was no foreign government contributing to this. But I knew nothing, still don't know anything about the mechanisms by which money was transferred from private groups that have been raising it, to the contras." He also said: "We don't engage—I mean the State De-partment's function in this has not been to raise money, other than to try to raise it from Congress."[71]

This meeting took place on November 25, 1986, the very day President Reagan and Attorney General Meese held their startling press conference about the "diversion." Soon afterward, Abrams apparently realized that his testimony might get him into trouble with the committee and turned to two members of the department, Nicholas Platt, the executive secre-tary, and Charles Hill, the executive assistant to the secretary, for advice.

Platt went to Secretary Shultz, who, according to Abrams, said: "Yeah, you probably should [correct your testimony]." Abrams then spoke to a member of Senator Bradley's staff about his desire to clarify his previous testimony, and the committee held another meeting on December 8 to permit him to explain.[72]

At this meeting, the senators were in no mood to be trifled with. The Iran-contra affairs had become a national scandal and enough information had come out publicly to make the congressional oversight committees realize that they had been systematically duped and deceived. Instead of coming quickly to the point and admitting that he had misled the committee, Abrams at first tried to double-talk his way out of his predicament and to pretend that the discussion had been limited to the Middle East and funds raised by the contras. In fact, the discussion had not been limited to the Middle East, had been about any foreign government contribution, and had touched on whether the State Department was in the fund-raising business.

Abrams's sparring with the committee members finally brought an outburst from Senator Thomas F. Eagleton of Missouri, who heatedly accused him of having lied to the committee on November 25. "Well, I resent the remark, Senator," said Abrams. "I have never lied to this committee." Soon, however, Abrams explained that he had gone back to the department after his appearance on November 25 and had discussed whether he should call Senator Bradley and say: "You didn't ask about this, but we have been trying to get money from another government. Haven't succeeded, but we have been trying."

As Abrams continued to defend his previous testimony, some of the senators became increasingly irate, until this exchange took place:

Senator Eagleton: Page 15 [of the November 25 transcript]. We're not, you know, we're not in the fundraising business. No one intimidated that out of you. That was your answer.

Abrams: Senator, I can always say to you that I am—

Eagleton: You're not in the fundraising business. Today I asked were you at any time in the fundraising business.

Abrams: We made one solicitation to a foreign government.

Eagleton: Were you then in the fundraising business?

Abrams: I would say we were in the fundraising business. I take your point.

Eagleton: Take my point? Under oath, my friend, that's perjury. Had you been under oath, that's perjury.

Abrams: Well, I don't agree with that.

Eagleton: Oh, Elliott, you're too damn smart not to know—

Abrams: I think that the—

Eagleton: We're not in the fundraising business. You were in the fundraising business, you and Ollie. You were opening accounts, you had account cards, you had two accounts and didn't know which account they were going to put it into.

Abrams: You've heard my testimony.

Eagleton: I've heard it, and I want to puke.

Abrams: Well, I would state again, Senator, that if you can find anything that the Department of State did here that is a violation of the letter or the spirit of the law in soliciting these funds—

Eagleton: The letter and the spirit of your brain and your honesty and forthrightness with this committee. You did not tell us the truth. You did not respond to Bradley's questions. You lied to us.

Abrams: I just can reject that, Senator, and say that had Senator Bradley asked the direct question, I was going to respond that I needed to talk to the Secretary before I can respond to that question.[73]

This statement touched on the heart of the committee's oversight problem. Under questioning by Senator David L. Boren of Oklahoma, Abrams admitted: "I was trying to duck what I hoped was a question that would not be asked and felt had not been asked." To this Senator Boren gave him some fatherly advice and received a grudging admission:

Boren: But, Elliott, in terms of your credibility and your future credibility before this Committee, this kind of splitting of hairs and the possibility of leaving wrong impressions is a tragic mistake. It just is, because in the future people will always ask the question, "Well, were they splitting hairs? Were they being technical? Were they stopping just short of giving the information and allowing the wrong impression to be created?"

Abrams: I thought, Senator, I must say, that I was failing to volunteer information, and in a situation which ordinarily would have called for the volunteering of it.

Boren: Rereading this transcript, wouldn't you say you went beyond failing?

Abrams: Yes, I would. I agree.[74]

In effect, the senators had to know enough to ask exactly the right questions in order to get the information they were seeking. They were, however, dependent on Abrams and other officials to give them the information they needed even to ask the right questions. In this case, the senators did not specifically know about Brunei, but they suspected that Abrams knew a good deal about the solicitation of funds for the contras. He tried to mislead them by talking about Singlaub and the Middle East, waiting apprehensively to see if he would get a direct question about Brunei or its area. When the right question did not come, he did not volunteer anything more. It took repeated prodding by the committee to get Abrams to express his conditional "regret" about his previous testimony and to "apologize to the extent that that testimony was misleading to any or all members of the Committee present or who have read the transcript."[75]

Abrams was guilty of misleading Congress in both the Hasenfus and Brunei cases but did not suffer any penalty for his misconduct. Secretary of State Shultz even came to his defense as "a very able, energetic fine person . . . the country needs people like that . . . he is good, really good."[76] With this standard of forgiveness, it is hard to see why anyone should have been punished for misbehavior in the Iran-contra affairs.

In its own way, the Brunei fiasco was part of the unraveling. Nothing seemed to go right after the Hasenfus incident. In retrospect, Abrams did not think highly of his Brunei escapade. At the congressional hearings, he confessed: "I can only describe the solicitation of foreign governments for financial contributions as I have today as tin cup diplomacy."[77]

18

End Run

We must now return to the Iran part of the Iran-contra affairs. We had left it after the frustrated return of McFarlane and North from the abortive meeting in Tehran in May 1986. It was not clear after this disillusionment how or when the negotiations could be revived and more hostages released.

The prospect seemed so bleak that serious consideration was given to using direct force to rescue the hostages, as President Carter had tried to do with tragic results in April 1980. Another such plan was discussed in President Reagan's presence even while McFarlane's delegation was still negotiating in Tehran.[1] After the return from Tehran, Poindexter wrote to North: "I am beginning to think that we need to seriously think about a rescue effort for the hostages. Is there any way we can get a spy into the Hayy Assallum area?"[2]

This question raised the problem of how to mount a rescue effort if the location of the hostages was not known. North's response was reserved. He would only go so far as to tell Poindexter that "if the current effort fails to achieve release then such a mission should be considered." But he recalled the failure of previous efforts of the same kind and informed Poindexter that Secord and Nir were working on a similar scheme, in which they rated the possibility of success as no more than 30 percent. The Joint Chiefs of Staff, North reported, had "steadfastly refused to go beyond the initial thinking stage unless we can develop some hard intelligence on their whereabouts."[3]

Poindexter, however, seems to have been pushing for a rescue mission. On June 6, he obtained the approval of President Reagan for the military planning of such a venture. Poindexter himself urged Casey to intensify efforts to locate the hostages.[4] Nothing came of these projects.

Instead, a more or less concrete plan had been worked out through the private resources of H. Ross Perot, the Texas tycoon. This was Perot's second intervention in the hostage crisis. In June 1985, he was supposed to provide funds for a scheme to get two hostages out at a cost of $2 million in bribes and other payments—"ransom" being a forbidden word. The contacts were to be made in Cyprus by two Drug Enforcement Administration officers, who were to pay $1 million for each hostage.[5] North asked Perot to deposit $2 million in a Swiss bank for the operation, which finally failed to come off.

A year later, North again counted on Perot. This new plan had been worked out in May 1986, before McFarlane and the others had set off for Tehran. It was based on the use of private aircraft, personnel, and vessels to convey the hostages out of Lebanon and bring one or more to Cyprus. As North informed Poindexter on June 10, when the operation had been called off, Perot had "dispatched one of his personal staff to oversee the mission and maintained communications between his offices in Texas and the forward operating team in Cyprus." The operation had been aborted, North said, because "the security situation inside Beirut deteriorated before this plan could be put into effect." President Reagan sent Perot a letter telling him that he had been briefed "on your effort over the past several weeks on behalf of our Americans abducted in Beirut" and "on behalf of the American people, I want to thank you for your discreet assistance in this regard."[6]

This "private" scheme, which went forward with the knowledge and approval of Reagan, Poindexter, and North, was evidently an effort to get around the reluctance of the Joint Chiefs of Staff to use U.S. forces for such a mission. It was also conceived as a way of shielding the government from direct responsibility and thus avoiding the price the Carter administration had paid for its misfortune. That serious consideration and preparation had gone into the Perot plan indicates how frustrating the deals with the Iranians had become and how desperately Poindexter and North were casting about for almost any means to rescue the hostages.

2

In the aftermath of Tehran, Ghorbanifar was not so easy to cast off.

For him, another deal with Iran was financially indispensable. He had allegedly borrowed $15 million from Adnan Khashoggi to pay for all the Hawk missile parts which Iran expected to get from a successful exchange. Khashoggi had in turn borrowed the money.* Iran had a small fraction of the parts, those which McFarlane had brought with him, and refused to pay until the rest were delivered. Khashoggi leaned on Ghorbanifar for the money, and Ghorbanifar could not afford to let much time pass

---

* It appears that Khashoggi made a deposit of $15 million in the Lake Resources account about May 14, 1986, before the Tehran mission. Two days later, Secord put $6.5 million into a CIA account, apparently giving Secord a profit of $8.5 million (A-1, p. 661).

without making another effort to get the remaining parts to Iran in order to get paid in full. The Americans were temporarily less driven to action; they seemed to have come to a dead end and did not know what to do next except to demand that all the hostages should be released first.

According to an official Israeli source, Ghorbanifar made the first move. He telephoned Nir and tried to explain away what had happened in Tehran. He blamed internal rivalries within the Iranian government and McFarlane's refusal to accept the offer of two hostages in return for the missile parts. The Israeli is said to have restated the U.S. position—no further discussions without the release of all the hostages.[7] For some time, Nir, Ghorbanifar, and the Iranians in Tehran were the only ones who actively pursued the matter.[8]

For the time being, North stayed out of the dealings with the Iranians and let the CIA's expert on Iran, George Cave, take the initiative. North was still the "point man" in the operation, and Cave coordinated all his moves with North.[9] Cave had left Tehran more optimistic than the other Americans and had afterward told Casey that he expected two more, maybe three, hostages to come out if the Americans kept at it.[10]

Cave and Kangarlou spoke repeatedly on the telephone between Washington and Tehran in an effort to revive the deal after the deadlock in Tehran. Their conversations, of which we have either a transcription or Cave's notes, showed how the two sides jockeyed endlessly for what they wanted—Cave the hostages, Kangarlou the spare parts. Neither side was willing to give way, and neither side was willing to give up. They bullied, blustered, and bargained.

On June 13, Cave telephoned Kangarlou in an effort to break the deadlock. Cave proposed a meeting in Europe, after which the American group would again go to Tehran, where the rest of the missile parts would be exchanged for two hostages.[11] Kangarlou countered with a proposal for the 240 spare parts to arrive with the Americans, two hostages to be turned over, and two Hawk radars to come next in return for two more hostages. After more haggling, they agreed to meet in West Germany; Kangarlou said encouragingly that it was not so important which side did what first.

Cave and Kangarlou both projected bald arms-for-hostages deals. At one point, Cave asked Kangarlou if the hostages were still under Iranian control. Kangarlou, according to Cave, hesitated but answered that the Iranians could get them. Cave said: "Then they are in your hands." Kangarlou replied that they were, although Cave doubted it.[12]

A deadlock seemed to develop between them on June 17. Cave insisted that the Americans were not willing to change the position they had taken in Tehran. If they returned to Tehran, he said, all the hostages would have to be released the same day, whereupon the rest of the spare parts would be delivered immediately and the two radars a little later. That was nothing new, so we will not be able to do anything, Kangarlou hit back. The verbal tug-of-war went typically as follows:

> *Kangarlou:* I'll tell you now as much as I know. You want us to do something for you. You do something for us. When you have done this thing for us, we'll do something for you.
>
> *Cave:* Fine. I know. I mean. I understand your position very well. You told me that several times before. But the officials here said that it has to be this way, and they are not willing to change their minds. [13]

In another telephone conversation on June 22, the Iranian told Cave that his people wanted to go through with the deal but that they were having "enormous difficulties" with those who opposed it. The opposition was allegedly numerous and made it necessary to "appear to have a good deal." Cave again stressed that "the chief of our company was insisting" on the release of the four American hostages, to which the answer came that the United States had to deliver what it had promised in arms at the same time as the four hostages were delivered. In reply to a direct question by Cave as to whether the Iranians had control of the hostages, Kangarlou hesitated and admitted that "they could not specifically say exactly when the 4 million [code word for the hostages] would be transferred, but this was still in their power, despite the fact that the situation where the 4 million are held [Lebanon] was continually deteriorating." [14]

One reason Cave did not believe Kangarlou was that the Iranians in Tehran had essentially admitted to him that they did not have control over the hostages. The Iranians' attitude in May had been that they had influence, but not control, over the Lebanese hostage takers. [15] The difference between control and influence came up repeatedly in this battle of wits between the Iranians and the Americans, with the Iranians sometimes implying one, sometimes the other. So long as the Americans were willing to hang on to any hope of recovering their hostages, the Iranians could stretch their links with the hostage takers as loosely or as tightly as they pleased.

3

On June 23, North received more disturbing news from Iran. It had found a microfiche of prices charged in the past for Hawk spare parts and had discovered that the new prices were far higher than the old. For the Iranians, it was more evidence that they were being cheated and could not trust the Americans. As a result, the prices of the spare parts continued to block any understanding between the two sides. North tried to explain the difference in prices as due to several reasons—the actual price plus packing, handling, transportation, and other costs, the Iranians were using a 1985 microfiche, and there were fifty-four different manufacturers.[16]

Cave and Kangarlou argued some more about prices on June 30. Neither could think of anything new to say but could not stop saying it for fear of breaking off contact, which neither was willing to do. Kangarlou wanted the Americans to be responsible for the prices, and Cave insisted that it was up to Ghorbanifar. They commiserated with each other:

> *Cave:* Mr. Goode [North] and I are in a bad situation here.
>
> *Kangarlou:* Why?
>
> *Cave:* Because the head of our company is very tired of this deal; he wants to break it off.
>
> *Kangarlou:* It's the same for me here.
>
> *Cave:* Then both of us are in the same boat. . . .
>
> This time, it has to be this way. The head of our company is very tired of this. He's angry, he said, "if they don't want to deal, break it off."
>
> *Kangarlou:* Look, the problem is the price. . . . The price is an important matter for us. . . . But six or seven times the cost? This is not right. This is having an effect on the deal—on your good will that you wish to establish. An adverse effect. They are saying: If they want us to do this service, why are they charging six times the price? We have no problem with our friend [Ghorbanifar] that he is asking this. We have no problem with him. We see this as your fault. . . . We have no quarrel with a 5 or 10 per cent markup. But 600 per cent—no.

Whereupon they continued arguing some more about whether it was 600 percent or less than that. When they seemed to have exhausted every way of saying the same thing over again, Kangarlou tried to be more encouraging:

> *Kangarlou:* Look. Try to keep things going there. We've brought this thing to the final stages and are on the verge of a solution. Don't let the issue of price destroy what we've done. We don't have any problem with anyone; not with our friend or anyone else.
>
> *Cave:* And I am in the same bind here. Because I've worked a lot on this. And now it has gotten nowhere. We haven't attained our goal.
>
> *Kangarlou:* We must try to pursue the right course. . . .[17]

They had not, of course, brought this thing to the final stages, and Kangarlou was merely trying to get a better price. Every time he seemed to push the Americans too far, he drew back in order to continue dealing another day. This preoccupation with pricing was the price paid for using Secord and Ghorbanifar as intermediaries in the sale. Whatever else they were, they were businessmen out to make a profit. The quarrel was really between Iran and Ghorbanifar, but the Iranians chose to blame the Americans for anything that went wrong.

The whole affair was mishandled. If the stakes were as high as the United States and Iran claimed they were, such obstacles as the price of a few hundred spare parts were ridiculously paltry. If the two countries had dealt with each other directly, the United States at least might have decided not to let a relatively small sum of money stand in the way of consummating the deal or at least forcing Iran's hand. Instead, after the Tehran meeting, weeks were wasted haggling over the cost and selling price of the spare parts. The Americans permitted Ghorbanifar to set the price and then insisted that it could not be changed, because he alone had the power to set it. In addition, they did not know what price he was setting. They threatened repeatedly to cut off negotiations if all the hostages were not immediately freed—without cutting off negotiations and without the freeing of the hostages. The Iranians were being told that they could buy the arms on condition that they freed the hostages. But they behaved as if it were a purely business deal in which they were determined to get the best possible price, probably because they were never sure that they could meet—or did not wish to meet—the American demand for all the hostages.

4

The telltale microfiche was another cause célèbre. On June 30, Kangarlou told Cave that Iran had a microfiche with 1985 prices. Cave did not believe him and thought that it was much older, but the problem refused to go away.[18]

North tried to get around it by telling Nir to inform Ghorbanifar that the microfiche contained prices for one-time items manufactured years ago and were very costly to remanufacture, as a result of which the spare parts had to come out of more expensive current stocks. Later, North suggested faking a new price list with inflated numbers, and a new little pink card with spurious prices was made up for the special benefit of Iran.[19] Another record of a call by Ghorbanifar to the CIA's national intelligence officer for counterterrorism, Charles Allen, has the Iranian middleman "screaming" that he had increased the price of the spare parts by only 41 percent.[20] To make matters worse, the Americans could not judge whether it had been exorbitant, because they did not know just what Ghorbanifar was charging Iran.[21] The Americans, however, knew that the Department of Defense had sold the parts for only $4.7 million, much less than whatever Secord had charged Ghorbanifar, and far less than whatever Ghorbanifar had charged Iran.[22] In addition, Nir, for some reason not clear to the Americans, added $1.7 million to the price charged to the Iranians to pay for debts incurred by the Israelis.[23]

Meanwhile, on June 5, Casey and Poindexter conferred on freeing the hostages in a different way. Poindexter told Casey of a suggestion to ransom them for a sum that might be as much as $10 million. The administration's public policy prohibited using ransom to free the hostages, but Poindexter agreed to talk to President Reagan about it.[24] It was another example of how closely the president was expected to follow developments in this affair.

The Israeli source says that Amiram Nir hoped to obtain the release of at least one more hostage by July 4, 1986, the hundredth anniversary of the Statue of Liberty.[25] Ghorbanifar allegedly told Nir that he could bring one out, and Nir called North on July 2 to expect him the next day.[26] North immediately sent a team to Wiesbaden, West Germany, to receive the freed hostage—an effort which proved to be another disappointment. North, according to Allen, blamed Nir for having failed to check out the story and for having opened him to a dressing-down by Poindexter. Incensed by Nir, North cut off all contact with him for a time, and Nir's messages went to Allen, who passed them on to North. Allen says that Nir's superiors "were quite disturbed and almost frantic over the fact that they had lost this fine link to the White House."[27]

The CIA was now, in effect, deeply implicated in the Iran affair. Allen and Cave recognized North, with Casey's blessings, as, in fact, their immediate taskmaster. Allen reported to Casey, who was able to follow events through various channels, including North himself. North seems to have used the CIA staff far more than his own NSC staff, whose resources were far more limited. Casey went along because he did not want the CIA to bear the formal responsibility for such a "high-risk operation," as Casey was said to view it, but it could not have gone far without him.[28] Another very thin line separated the CIA from the NSC staff, so thin that it was virtually ignored in practice.

5

Ghorbanifar was desperate for some relief from his financial predicament.

On July 8, he could wait no longer and allegedly made a move that betrayed his extreme anxiety. Instead of complaining to the Americans, he vented his displeasure at the way things were going to the Iranians. His distress was ostensibly expressed in a letter to Kangarlou that came into the possession of George Cave later that month.[29]

Ghorbanifar blamed the Iranians for not taking advantage of the right opportunity "to get concessions" from the Americans. He reminded them that he had advised them, without result, to get the release of one hostage, an American clergyman, in time for the Fourth of July celebration as a way of inducing "the Americans to accept many of our demands." He listed a number of "positive and constructive steps" taken by the Americans, such as the U.S. vote in the United Nations condemning Iraq for the use of chemical weapons in the war against Iran. In return, he complained, the Iranians had not made "the slightest attempt nor shown the smallest sign—even discreetly—to improve relations." He even seemed to blame the Iranians for having failed to make a real effort to gain the release of all the U.S. hostages during the Tehran meeting in May.

After this preamble, Ghorbanifar gave the Iranians three different "solutions." One was for Iran to pay immediately for all the spare parts and obtain the release of two hostages, to be followed by American delivery of all the spare parts and two radars in return for the other two hostages, after which the Americans would study how to provide helicopter spare parts and all other needs of the Iranian army.

The second method was similar, except that one hostage would be released, then two, and finally the other two. In this case, Ghorbanifar promised to deliver to Iran 3,000 TOW missiles at a cost of $38.5 million, plus 200 Sidewinder missiles—allegedly at cost, but only if Iran let him make a profit—"not like this [last] time when you did not leave anything for me."

The third option assumed that the other two were unacceptable to Iran. If so, Ghorbanifar proposed that the spare parts delivered by the McFarlane mission in May should be immediately returned and the whole effort wiped out as if, as in the Persian saying, "no camel arrived and no camel left." In conclusion, Ghorbanifar virtuously hoped that a "good and generous God will compensate" him for his "friendship, good intentions, honesty, belief, and trust."[30]

Whether written by Ghorbanifar or for him, this letter indicated where the long-suffering deal was bound to go. The months of June and July were the low point of the entire initiative. North was so discouraged that he could not bring himself to take part in it personally. Yet neither side could bear to give it up. Ghorbanifar seemed to want to tell both sides that something had to give or neither side would get anything. This alternative evidently helped wonderfully to concentrate the minds, at least of the Iranians.

While both sides were trying to wait each other out, the Americans received some encouraging news. On July 10, North informed Poindexter about the visit of two senior foreign government officials to Tehran in mid-July. They reported that the highest levels in the Iranian government, including Speaker Rafsanjani, were more concerned about the Soviet threat; some of its members foresaw that Iran could possibly "cause the release" of the American hostages "given the right conditions"; and a suggestion for direct U.S.-Iran discussions was not rejected.[31] On July 17, North passed on a message given to Secretary of State Shultz by a foreign official who had talked to Iranian Deputy Foreign Minister Mohammed Javad Larijani. The latter had observed that Iran and America shared similar strategic interests and had indicated that Iran "wanted an easing of relations on substantive matters with USA."[32]

North seized on these apparent overtures to recommend an even stronger bid to the Iranians. He proposed that they should be told "the highest levels of the American Government are prepared to open direct and private discussions with responsible officials who are empowered to speak on behalf of the Iranian Government." The United States, he added, was prepared to take steps leading to "a normalization of relations" between the two governments. A senior American official was prepared to meet with a responsible Iranian "at the time and place of your choosing." The Americans were also prepared "to make an appropriate gesture of goodwill."[33]

Events now moved quickly. According to North in a later report to Poindexter, the decision to release Father Lawrence Jenco, who had been director of Catholic Relief Services in Lebanon, was made in Tehran on or about July 21.[34] Jenco had been a hostage since January 1985. Two days later, Nir advised North that if, as hoped, a hostage was released, it would be the Reverend Jenco. On the same day, Nir told Ghorbanifar that the United States government was breaking off all contact on this matter. A somewhat different version of Nir's ultimatum claims that the issue was forced by Nir, who had told Ghorbanifar that the U.S. initiative was over unless a hostage was soon released.[35] George Cave was dispatched to Frankfurt to meet with a high Iranian official and another Iranian go-between apparently named Tabatabai.[36]

North also reported that the Iranian government had paid Ghorbanifar $4 million as partial payment for the Hawk missile parts that had been removed from the U.S. aircraft during the McFarlane mission in May. Ghorbanifar, North added, had borrowed more than $15 million to pay the Israelis for all the previously committed Hawk parts and "has been under threat of death from his creditors." The Israelis, North said, were interpreting the payment of $4 million as further evidence that the Iranians were anxious to maintain contact with the United States on the hostage issue.[37]

It soon turned out that Ghorbanifar had obtained the release of the Reverend Jenco by making a commitment that the United States had never agreed to. The Iranians took the position that what they had agreed to with Ghorbanifar was also what the United States was obliged to follow through on. In effect, Ghorbanifar was again at his old game of telling both sides different stories and confronting them with a fait accompli.

Ghorbanifar's latest scheme was another version of his favorite strategy—the sequential deal. As North put it, Ghorbanifar had "acted on what he considered to be the following arrangement":

Step 1: One hostage released and $4 million to Ghorbanifar for items removed from the aircraft in Tehran during the May visit (Ghorbanifar received the $4 million on July 28).
Step 2: Remainder of 240 parts plus full quota of electron tubes (Item 24 on Iranian parts list) and 500 TOWs delivered to Iran.
Step 3: Second hostage released and Ghorbanifar paid for remainder of 240 parts.
Step 4: 500 TOWs and 1 HIPAR radar delivered.
Step 5: Third hostage released and Ghorbanifar paid for one radar.
Step 6: Meeting in Tehran to discuss future followed by release of the last hostage and delivery of second HIPAR radar.[38]

In effect, this arrangement was a sequential hostages-for-arms deal and nothing else. It was a blatant violation of the policy which the United States had repeatedly claimed to uphold—no arms could be delivered to Iran until all the hostages had been released. On behalf of this principle, McFarlane had broken up the Tehran meeting in May after he had been offered two hostages. Now Ghorbanifar maneuvered to get Iran to obtain the release of the Reverend Jenco and then put it up to the United States to carry out the other half of the deal that he had sold to Iran.

6

Ghorbanifar's end run around the Americans put North in an uncomfortable position, but one for which he had a way out—playing up the fatal consequences of refusing to deal.

In his report to Poindexter, North admitted: "It is obvious that the conditions for the release of the hostages arranged between Ghorbanifar and [deleted, probably Kangarlou] are unacceptable." But North hastened to find an acceptable reason for not rejecting Ghorbanifar's conditions. If Iran received nothing for the release of Father Jenco, the Iranian official who had ostensibly made the deal with Ghorbanifar "will be killed by his opponents in Tehran." Ghorbanifar "will be killed by his creditors (they are the beneficiaries of a $22M[illion] life insurance policy)." And "one American hostage will probably be killed in order to demonstrate displeasure."

The upshot was that North recommended holding another meeting with the Iranians in Europe to make a new effort to reach a mutually beneficial agreement. As if it were always possible to start all over again, he adroitly ignored Ghorbanifar's sequence of moves and blandly proposed aiming at "a concrete schedule that is agreeable to both parties and which allows all remaining hostages to be released simultaneously." In effect, North was willing to forgive the unacceptable and reward it with another meeting in Europe.

This recommendation was approved by Poindexter, who added in his own handwriting: "President approved."[39] Here again, Reagan had been informed and had agreed to a move of this nature; it is hard to believe that Poindexter would have bothered to deceive North about the president's action in a confidential message between the two of them.

Poindexter saw through Ghorbanifar's intrigue. On the day the Reverend Jenco was released, Poindexter received a congratulatory message from McFarlane:

> Bravo Zulu on Jenco's release. Do you correlate this to the anxious calls that have come since the trip to Iran [by him in May] and our insistence that they move first? Or is it really a Syrian effort?[40]

Poindexter's reply showed that he knew what Ghorbanifar was up to but, like North, could not entirely resist it.

> Gorba finally convinced [his Tehran contact] after numerous telephone calls that they should come forward with a humanitarian gesture. Gorba either on his own or as Nir's agent is out a lot of money that he put up front for the parts. [The Tehran contact] has been unwilling to pay him since all of the material has not been delivered. Gorga [sic] has cooked up a story that if Iran could make a humanitarian gesture then the US would deliver the rest of the parts and then Iran would release the rest of the hostages. Of course we have not agreed to any such plan. Nir and Gorba are in London. [The Iranian official] is enroute. I am trying to decide whether to send Ollie and George Cave. The problem is that if parts aren't delivered, Gorba will convince [his Tehran contact] that we welched on the deal. Although through several conversations Cave has repeated to [the Tehran contact] what our position has been—all the hostages out before anything else moves[,] I have about decided to send Ollie to make certain our position is clear. It seems to me that we may have some leverage over [the official in the prime minister's office] now since he is out on a limb in Tehran and may fear for his own safety.[41]

Of all the comments we have on Ghorbanifar's machinations, Poindexter's comes closest to the reality—that Ghorbanifar had "cooked up a story that if Iran could make a humanitarian gesture then the US would deliver the rest of the parts and then Iran would release the rest of the hostages." In effect, Ghorbanifar had cooked up a story which had broken the stalemate and had sent both sides into action. Only the first half of Poindexter's analysis came out as planned, but it was enough for Ghorbanifar's purposes. Whether or not the United States had agreed to Ghorbanifar's scheme, Poindexter could not resist doing something to prevent Ghorbanifar from convincing the Iranians that "we welched on the deal."

The Reverend Jenco's release and its implications were important enough to bring Casey out of the shadows and put himself on record. In a written communication to Poindexter, he, more than anyone else, supported going ahead with Ghorbanifar's plan. "It is indisputable," he asserted, "that the Iranian connection actually worked this time, after a series of failures." He interpreted Kangarlou's persistent contact with "one of my officers, George Cave," as indicative of the Iranian's "desire to arrange a 'deal' with Washington through Ghorbanifar or, if necessary, with Cave." He paid tribute to Amiram Nir for having "played a critical role in a determined effort to force Iran to begin the release of American hostages"—as if Nir or the Americans had done anything to "force" Iran to act. Casey also commended the support of Israeli Prime Minister Peres and Defense Minister Rabin and noted that Israel had independently offered additional arms to Iran "to sweeten the deal."[42]

Casey then set forth "how we see the current situation":

> The Ghorbanifar-[Kangarlou] connection has worked for the second time—and another American has been released.[43]
>
> Ghorbanifar is an uncontrollable factor, but appears to respond generally to Nir's direction.
>
> Nir has every reason to work for further releases of our hostages. Peres and Rabin have put their reputation on the Ghorbanifar-[Kangarlou] connection and support Nir fully in his endeavors. There would be a considerable loss of face for Nir and his superiors if the link were broken. This connection appears to be the only hope they have for recovering their own missing soldiers.
>
> [Kangarlou] has now acted and likely expects the United States to respond quickly in turn by delivering most of the remaining Hawk spare parts. He probably believes the United States is also supplying the additional military equipment that has been promised.
>
> If the deliveries do not occur, [Kangarlou] will lose badly with his superiors in Tehran and matters could turn ugly, especially since the Lebanese Hizballah captors probably are not pleased with the Jenco release.
>
> If there is no USG [U.S. government] contact as a result of Jenco's release, it is entirely possible that Iran and/or Hizballah could resort to the murder of one or more of the remaining hostages.

This reasoning led Casey to recommend:

In summary, based on the intelligence at my disposal, I believe that we should continue to maintain the Ghorbanifar-[Kangarlou] contact and consider what we may be prepared to do to meet [Iranian] minimum requirements that would lead to release of the rest of the hostages. Although I am not pleased by segmented releases of the American hostages, I am convinced that this may be the only way to proceed, given the delicate factional balance in Iran. I also see resolution of the hostage issue as potentially leading to contacts with moderate factions in Iran that we may be able to deal with in the longer term.[44]

Much of this analysis raises troublesome questions. Did the Iranian contact act without the authorization of his superiors and therefore risk losing badly with them? Since Father Jenco was a hostage of the Lebanese Hizballah, how could Kangarlou or any subordinate Iranian official obtain his release from them without the approval and cooperation of his superiors? Why should the Hizballah have released Father Jenco if it was probably not pleased? What kind of fruitful deal was possible with people who were supposedly ready to carry out one or more murders if Iran did not get more American arms?

These questions suggest that Casey was willing to use almost any arguments, however questionable, to keep the deals going. There was no reason to believe that Kangarlou—or anyone else in his place—had acted on his own or had had so much power that he could obtain the release of Father Jenco by himself. There was also no reason to believe that the release of Father Jenco would lead to the early release of the rest of the American hostages any more than the release of the Reverend Weir in September the previous year had led to more releases. Casey's expectations were not borne out and appear to have been inspired more by special pleading than by sober calculation. Casey was clearly using the same strategy as North to prolong the existing setup—predictions of retribution on the part of the Iranian authorities, as if they were not behind Kangarlou and the rest.

The only qualms about the Jenco deal seem to have come from an official in the State Department. On July 2, Under Secretary of State for Political Affairs Michael H. Armacost advised Secretary Shultz of rumors that one hostage might be released. Armacost appeared to think that Amiram Nir, who he said "is not very discreet," might have tipped off a Washington columnist, Jack Anderson. On the larger issue, Armacost stated: "The NSC rationale for a deal goes well beyond getting the hostages back. They argue that Iran is the strategic prize in the area, and that sub rosa provision of arms can pave the way to a broader rapprochement." Armacost was apprehensive:

The concept has merit to a point. Certainly we should keep our options open vis-à-vis Tehran. . . . this seems scarcely a propitious moment to send arms to Tehran. And it has never been clear that the Iranians we are dealing with on this affair are going to possess any clout in a post-Khomeini Iran.

In the meanwhile, as this story surfaces, we are going to sow more and more confusion among our friends, who will recall our frequent lectures on no deals for hostages and no arms for Iran.[45]

This warning came at an early stage and was apparently not followed up by Secretary Shultz.

After Jenco's release, North and Cave met with Ghorbanifar and Nir in Frankfurt on July 27. Ghorbanifar, as usual, had a ready explanation for what had gone wrong in the past. North's notebook on that day reads:

Gorba: The Iranian radicals cheated Hizballah
    —Told Hizb[allah] that way to get 17 [Da'wa prisoners in Kuwait] free and US out of ME [Middle East]—take hostages.
    —Has not worked—Angry w[ith] Iran

Prob[lem] in Tehran
    —Good guys/ Bad guys
    —Two who want to give most
    —Rafsanjani: wants to *milk* U.S.
    —Musavi: Hates U.S. . . .

RR [Ronald Reagan] sh[oul]d not be misled
    —Criminals are leading Iran
      They hate U.S.
    —This [unclear] should not end w[ith] any advantage for Iran
    —If it does, the Radicals will be in power forever. . . .
    —Man captured in Tehran questioned about Gorba accused of being [U.S./?] spy . . .
    —The longer this goes on—the worse things will be . . .
    —Host[ages] dead
    —No dialogue w[ith] existing regime
    —Prob[ably] no dialogue w[ith] Repl[acement/?] regime
    —Major crisis for exist[ing] gov[ernmen]t[46]

These sometimes cryptic notes indicate that Ghorbanifar was capable of seeming to give the Americans a detached insight into Iranian conditions. Yet he continually urged them to make a deal quickly, on pain of suffering even worse reverses if they did not follow his advice. Since they were wholly at his mercy for information, they were never in a position to know what was real and what was not. North ended his version of what Ghorbanifar had told them with the words: "Need CIA analysis."

The Americans also reported that they had held a discussion with Kangarlou by telephone which had produced these "salient points":

> [Kangarlou] believes he had demonstrated his ability to perform and has expectations we are now prepared to deal. Despite our earlier and current protestations that we want all hostages before we deliver anything, this is clearly not the way they want to proceed. They see clearly that the ball is now in our court. In discussion with [Kangarlou] he repeatedly asked quote—"When are you going to deliver." While [Kangarlou] made no specific threat, he noted that he was under intense pressure and could not totally control events.
>
> Bottom line, is that, if we want to prevent the death of one of the three remaining hostages, we are going to have to do something.[47]

Doing something actually meant sending the 240 Hawk spare parts that Iran had long demanded. On July 30, President Reagan approved "further shipments of arms to Iran in response to the release of Rev. Jenco."[48] On August 3 or 4, they were flown to Iran by one of Secord's crews aboard an Israeli airplane.[49]

In the end, Ghorbanifar had trapped the Americans into doing what he had "cooked up" for them. His first sequence had worked out just as he had intended. For almost a year, the Americans had made it a cardinal principle to refuse to deal with Iran unless all the hostages were released. This principle was now sacrificed to the only deal that Iran was willing to entertain. The Americans tried to tell themselves that they were still committed to it—always next time—but with diminishing conviction. In fact, they had engaged in a purely arms-for-hostage deal at the rate of one hostage for 240 Hawk spare parts. This deal was a victory for Casey and North, who had been most firmly in favor of it, even as they recognized that it fell far short of American policy. It would not have been possible if President Reagan had not approved it.

At stake in a larger sense was an understanding of Iran-Hizballah strategy. The Casey-North approach preferred to believe that all the American hostages could be rescued one at a time or at some indefinite time all at once. The Weir and Jenco releases ten months apart were taken to be grounds for believing in this method. Yet both releases had come about as a result of an impasse which Iran was determined to overcome in order to get more of the arms it desperately needed. The problem for Iran was that all it had to bargain with was the hostages. If it surrendered them all at once, the game was up. The sequential strategy was a way out of this dilemma. It gave up one hostage with the promise of more if the United States did what Iran wanted it to do. There was never any assurance of more or of an end to the hostage taking. Every hostage released was a hostage saved, but every hostage released was no guarantee that others would not be seized in order to keep the deadly game going. So long as the United States was willing to trade arms for hostages, it could be sure that there would be hostages to be traded for arms. Ghorbanifar had gambled that neither side could bring itself to renounce such deals—and he had won.

7

The Iran strategy was no mystery. Vice President Bush received a lecture on it from Amiram Nir during a visit to Jerusalem on July 29, three days after Father Jenco's release.

The meeting with Nir had been set up at the request of North, apparently because Prime Minister Peres had had a recent briefing by Nir and had thought that Bush should have the same thing.[50] Nir gave Bush and his chief of staff, Craig L. Fuller, a detailed account of the Iran affair, going back to the previous year, together with his views on Iran's strategy. We have Fuller's unusually full notes on the meeting, lasting twenty-five minutes, during which Nir did almost all the talking.

According to Fuller, Nir told them that the reason for Iran's delay in gaining the release of any hostages

> is to squeeze as much as possible as long as they have assets. They don't believe that we want overall strategic cooperation to be better in the future. If they believed us they would have not bothered so much with the price right now.

Turning to the Iranian strategy of "sequencing," Nir said:

> Should we accept sequencing? What are the alternatives to sequencing? They fear if they gave all hostages they won't get anything from us.

This analysis was exceptionally blunt. It suggested that Nir at least did not share the optimism of his American colleagues that the Iranians would one day part with all their hostages. Yet Nir posed the old dilemma, as if a year's experience had not been enough to disclose Iran's strategy:

> He reviewed the issues to be considered—namely that there needed to be a decision as to whether the items requested would be delivered in separate shipments or whether we would continue to press for the release of the hostages prior to delivering the items in an amount agreed to previously.

Nir also gave Bush a surprising insight into the Iranian side of the deal. The American assumption had been—ever since Adnan Khashoggi and Ghorbanifar had instilled it in them in 1985—that the best hope of freeing the hostages and getting a long-range realignment with Iran rested with the "moderates," whoever they were. But now Nir had altogether different news for Bush:

We are dealing with the most radical elements. The Deputy Prime Minister is an emissary. They can deliver . . . that's for sure. They were called yesterday and thanked [for Jenco's release] and today more phone calls. This is good because we've learned they can deliver and the moderates can't. We should think about diversity and establish other contacts with other factions. We have started to establish contact with some success and now more success is expected since if these groups feel if the extremes are in contact with us then it is less risky for the other groups—nothing operational is being done—this is contact only.

From this, it appears that Nir thought that he and the Americans had been dealing with the Iranian deputy prime minister, which was considerably above Kangarlou's official station. In any case, according to Nir, the deals had been made with the "most radical" faction, suggesting that he was no longer taken in by Ghorbanifar, who had pretended to represent the "moderates." If Nir was right, the only motive of the Iranians had been to obtain arms, because the most radical faction was least likely to want to get any closer politically to the United States. Nir, so far as one can tell, gives no reason to believe that he now knew much more about internal Iranian political forces than he had known previously, but his startling about-face does give a very different meaning to all that had happened earlier.

In the end, Nir summed up:

The bottom line is that we won't give them more than previously agreed to. It is important that we have assets there 2 to 3 years out when the change occurs. We have no real choice [other] than to proceed.

In effect, for all his hard-boiled diagnosis of the problem, Nir had no new policy to propose. He, too, had invested too much in the enterprise to let it slip away. Nir also took credit for what the Israelis had done in behalf of the United States:

We activated the channel; we gave a front to the operation; provided a physical base; provided aircraft. [All this to] make sure the U.S.

will not be involved in logistical aspects. [Nir indicated that in the early phase they] began moving things over there. [51]

Except for asking a question or two, Bush listened and said nothing. In the aftermath of the Iran affair, he tried to shield himself by insisting that he had known little or nothing about it. His attendance at various high-level meetings at which the policy was discussed and this extensive briefing by Nir tell a different story.

8

Whatever Vice President Bush may or may not have known, one branch of the government that was long kept in ignorance of the transfer of arms to Iran was the Joint Chiefs of Staff. Its chairman, Admiral William J. Crowe, Jr., learned about it almost by accident.

In late June or early July 1986, not long before the Jenco release, Crowe's special assistant, Lieutenant General John Moellering, attended a meeting of the Terrorist Incident Working Group (TIWG), headed by Oliver North. Moellering heard references to arms transfers to Iran which puzzled him, because he had never known of them before. When Moellering raised some questions at the meeting, he was told by Assistant Secretary of Defense Armitage, who was there: "I will talk to you about it later, John." After they had returned to the Pentagon, Armitage gave Moellering a general sense of what had been going on with Iran, including the arms transfers.

Moellering went to Crowe and reported what Armitage had told him. Crowe was "startled." Moellering's information was still so confused that they did not know exactly what arms and how much had been sent. Subsequently, in the summer of 1986, Crowe tried to get more information from Secretary of Defense Weinberger. Crowe told of this conversation in this way:

> Well, I was interested in whatever background he could tell me and why I had not been kept informed, and he told me that he had known about it for some time and that he had opposed it and that the decision had been made by the President and that there had been some transfers in a specific way in order to keep distribution to a low level, and that it was his understanding that a conscious decision had been made that it was not a military matter so it was not necessary to bring in the military and that he had made strong representations opposing it, and that it was an accomplished fact and we talked in [sic] a few more minutes and both agreed that the

Commander-in-Chief of the United States can do what he wants to do. That is within his purview.

Whether it is wise or not is a separate question.

So long as the full responsibility rested with President Reagan as commander in chief, Crowe was satisfied. He felt relieved that the decision to overrule Weinberger "had been a deliberate and conscious one and that it just had not been made because people got out of the way, it had been made in the face of opposition—the decision was." Except for the bits and pieces that Moellering had brought him, Crowe still did not know about the President's Finding, the financial details, or Israel's role. In fact, Crowe did not learn about the 1985 transfer of TOWs until he read about it in newspapers in November 1986, shortly after the Iran-contra affair was publicly exposed. Crowe's ignorance was the result of a deliberate decision to bypass the usual channels by which information came to him—the only time that it was ever done and a development that confronted him with a "unique surprise." Crowe resented the power that military personnel on the NSC staff, such as North, had arrogated to themselves:

> . . . it was my reluctant conclusion that there were military people on the NSC that in certain circumstances were willing to, in order to keep something closed for whatever the purpose, would say, well, we will provide the military advice. So you have the military input and you don't need to worry about going further afield outside of this very small select circle and I didn't necessarily appreciate that. . . .
>
> Now, from my perspective, if an item came to the National Security Planning Group or to the National Security Council, I was invited and I attended the meeting, and I immediately knew something was afoot or what the decision was and what was being discussed, and I had an input. But as in so many things in this town, the top level was sort of the tip of the iceberg, there is a whole huge iceberg of things going on at the working level, and so forth.

The reason he was kept out this time, Crowe thought, was "to keep dissent out of the decision-making calculus." He declared that he should have been informed about the transfer of intelligence information to the Iranians. As for the service of military officers, he wanted to reexamine it, "primarily with a view to putting some kind of fixed limit" on the term of service. He felt that it was better for an officer who stayed on the NSC staff for an extended period to leave the service instead of expecting to be given promotions for nonmilitary duty. North's long stay and promotions on the NSC staff obviously rankled and had caused some serious soul-searching in the high command.[52]

That the chairman of the Joint Chiefs of Staff should have been kept so deliberately in ignorance of a transfer of arms and military intelligence to Iran tells as much as anything else how very small the "select circle" was. A lieutenant colonel on the NSC staff knew more about these events, and could have vastly more influence on them, than the highest-ranking officer in the U.S. armed forces. The humiliation of the chairman of the Joint Chiefs of Staff was part of the price of the Iran initiative.

19

The Second Channel

Despite his great gifts as a con man, Manucher Ghorbanifar fell on hard times. After his successful deal exchanging Father Jenco for 240 Hawk spare parts, nothing seemed to go right for him.

One reason was that neither side was altogether happy with the deal. The Iranians were still fretting over the price, to which they were never reconciled and which caused them to hold up payment to Ghorbanifar. They had been challenged to produce the microfiches with the lower prices, and in July or early August they finally did.[1] These microfiches turned out to be authentic, as of November 1, 1985, and could no longer be ignored.[2]

North had first tried to deal with the problem by getting the CIA to print fake microfiches with higher prices. Apparently this ruse did not work, because the CIA's Office of Technical Services proved to be incapable of preparing a credible forged list.[3]

We have two versions of how North finally handled the problem. According to Charles Allen,

> he insisted again that we had to maintain the integrity of our stories relating to the price, that we don't know what Ghorbanifar was charging; therefore, you know, let's just ensure that we all make it clear to Mr. Ghorbanifar and, in the case of Mr. Cave, to [an Iranian], that it was very difficult to obtain these parts and the costs were very high.[4]

Cave put it somewhat differently:

> the basic position we took with them [Iranians] was that he [sic] should haggle it out with Ghorbanifar since Ghorbanifar was the man that actually sold the stuff to them.[5]

In both versions, it appears that North decided to avoid the pricing issue by hiding behind Ghorbanifar. Yet at this stage everything seemed to hinge on satisfying the Iranians that they were paying a fair price. They were excessively suspicious of everything the Americans did or wanted, and the exorbitant prices became for them a test of trust and confidence. In their minds, they were dealing primarily with the Americans, even if Ghorbanifar was the go-between and, in fact, the only one who decided on what the price should be. It was a hopeless, seriocomic squabble on both sides; the Iranians complained to the Americans when they should have addressed their complaints to Ghorbanifar, and the Americans referred them back to Ghorbanifar. By refusing to deal directly with the price-microfiche issue, North permitted Ghorbanifar to envenom the relations between Iranians and Americans over a matter that might easily have been settled to the satisfaction of both sides if Iran and the United States had been dealing directly. For months, the arms-for-hostages deal had been degenerating into an arms-for-profit deal, with Ghorbanifar determined to make the most profit.

North may not have wanted to get in Ghorbanifar's way, because Ghorbanifar was not the only one out for profit. North later admitted that "although we had certainly run the charges up, Mr. Ghorbanifar had almost doubled it on top of that."[6] The charges had been run up as much for the benefit of Secord's operation as for Ghorbanifar's. Secord testified that he had taken in about $30 million from the Iranians; had paid $12 million to the CIA for arms; had diverted $3.5 million to the Nicaraguan contras; had $8 million left after other expenses in the Swiss account controlled by his partner, Hakim; and had $2.5 million more not accounted for.[7] These were among the profusion and confusion of figures offered by Secord and others, with the actual financial accounting still in doubt. They leave no doubt, however, that in the end the Secord-Hakim enterprise came out far ahead in all the transactions with Iran and Ghorbanifar.

Indeed, Ghorbanifar ended up the chief loser. After the whole affair was over, some Iranian representatives admitted to Cave that Iran still owed Ghorbanifar $10 million—just as Ghorbanifar had claimed—and that he owed Iran 1,000 TOWs, which he did not have.[8]

The 1,000 TOWs represented another of Ghorbanifar's overclever maneuvers. When the Iranians had complained about the price of the spare parts, Ghorbanifar had appeased them by throwing in the promise of 1,000 more TOWs to make up the difference. Unfortunately, Ghorbanifar had made the commitment without the knowledge or approval of the Americans who had to honor it. North told Nir that Cave had never heard of these TOWs and that he thought Ghorbanifar was lying about them. North's instructions to Cave were: Iran could not get the TOWs free and would have to buy them.[9]

At this point, North revealed that a new threat had come up. He informed Nir that Cave was instructed to tell the Iranian representative that "if there is no payment" to Ghorbanifar by Iran, the United States would have to stop selling arms to Iran because "those who loaned the merchant [Ghorbanifar] the money will make the whole thing public."[10] This danger, which loomed larger and larger as time passed, had appeared for the first time in early August 1986. It apparently referred to Adnan Khashoggi and his backers, who had lent Ghorbanifar the money to pay for the spare parts.

Ghorbanifar was caught between Khashoggi, who demanded his money; Iran, which refused to pay the full $15 million until the price came down;[11] North, who thought that Ghorbanifar had lied to the Iranians about the extra 1,000 TOWs and saw no reason to give them to Iran for nothing; and Secord, who had Ghorbanifar's money and had no intention of giving it back to him. The great fixer had outsmarted himself.

On August 8, North, Nir, and Ghorbanifar met in London to work out their differences. North and Ghorbanifar saw each other for the last time. Ghorbanifar's debts still haunted them. North noted: "Gorbas [sic]: Creditors want $19.5M[illion]."[12] Judging from North's notes, they agreed that the sequential exchange of hostages and arms was the only way to go. It was no new departure for North, who had long ago made up his mind that no other arrangement was possible. One of North's notes apparently reflects a statement by Ghorbanifar citing the Iranian speaker on why all the hostages could not be released at once: "Rafsanjani: If all the Americans are released at once, everyone knows that a deal was made w[ith] Iran." The main outcome of the meeting was a "proposed next step," which provided for the usual sequential arms-for-hostages deal:

1. 40 Tubes [Hawk Radar Parts]
   500 TOWs
2. [Hostage]
3. 500 + HP [Hawk Radar] + 137 missing items
4. [Hostage]
5. Meeting
6. Remaining for disc[ontinued]:
   —[Hostage]
   —HP
   —[William] Buckley location
   —Pay us $15.5M[illion]
     for 1000 TOWs
     177 missing units
     40 Tubes
     2 HPs[13]

This list is chiefly interesting for the continued trading that took place at these sessions—so many arms for so many hostages at so many intervals. If this plan had gone through, everyone in Iran might still have been able to deduce that a deal had been made; a sequential deal releasing one hostage after another was not likely to fool anyone any more than a once-for-all arms-for-hostages deal. For their part, the Iranian authorities could afford to let Ghorbanifar hold out hopes for a full-scale sequential deal which they did not necessarily intend to carry through. No one could ever be sure that Ghorbanifar was speaking for the Iranians and even less for the Lebanese who actually held the hostages. As always, the great beauty of a sequential deal for the Iranians was that it enabled them to get arms for one hostage without immediately exhausting the supply of hostages.

Still more trouble awaited Ghorbanifar. On August 20, North received a disturbing call from Nir. The Iranians had reported that they were sorely dissatisfied with the Hawk spare parts that they had received on August 4. The list of complaints included many parts with something missing, others that were nonfunctioning, 299 parts that had not been received, and 63 other items that the Iranians wanted to return.[14]

By this time, Ghorbanifar confronted two problems—the charge that he had unconscionably tried to get a profit of 600 percent on his sales to Iran, and his inability to collect from Iran. He put in a "frantic call" to Allen in an effort to clear himself—his markup had been no more than 41 percent and he had borrowed $15 million from Adnan Khashoggi at 20 percent interest.[15] It appears that he had received $5 million from Iran for the Hawk spare parts of August 4, but still fell short by $10 million.[16]

The financial transactions were, as usual, labyrinthine. All of them were carried out in Switzerland. In April 1986, the Iranian government transferred $17 million to an Israeli account. The Israelis transferred $15 million to the Secord-Hakim Lake Resources account. Lake Resources transferred $3,651,000 to a CIA account. The CIA transferred the latter amount to a covert Department of the Army account in the United States.[17]

No way had been found to get Ghorbanifar out of trouble. On August 27, Nir called North to say that Ghorbanifar was angry and had accused the Americans of "trying to play games with him." This message was accompanied by a threat: "If by Monday [September 1] the merchant [Ghorbanifar] does not have a clear pic[ture] of what we are going to send, merchant is out."[18] By September 3, Nir told North that Ghorbanifar had received a total of $8 million, had paid $5 million to Iran, and still owed Khashoggi $10–$11 million.[19] On September 4, North received two calls from Nir. North wrote: "Merchant going off the res-ervation." Ghorbanifar was receiving threats from lenders. His financial affairs with Khashoggi were "our problem."[20] On September 15, Nir gave

North information on Ghorbanifar's *"Financial Arrangements*: Merchant says that for $20M[illion], he needs $24M to cover financial charge of 20%." On September 30, Nir told North: "Merchant very mad."[21]

After all his schemes and scams, Manucher Ghorbanifar faced disaster. His downfall had come about because he had lost the trust of both the Iranian authorities and the Americans. His greatest mistake had been not to follow the American example of getting paid first and delivering afterward. The weakest link in the plan had been his own country, which demanded deliveries first and made payment afterward, if at all.

2

For the Americans, Ghorbanifar had been a necessary evil for some time. On February 27, 1986, North had written to McFarlane that "Gorba tells Mike [Ledeen] everything and that is an additional reason to get Gorba out of the long range picture ASAP [as soon as possible]."[22] Cave had always worried that Ghorbanifar had been relied on too much and "cannot be trusted."[23] Except for Casey, everyone in the CIA had advised against giving intelligence information to Iran because—as McMahon had put it—"we feel the principal involved [Ghorbanifar] is a liar and has a record of deceit."[24] At Tehran in May 1986, the Americans had blamed Ghorbanifar for much of the misunderstanding with the Iranians.

Still, Ghorbanifar had held on. Whenever a hostage was released, he received the credit and managed to stage a temporary comeback. Ghorbanifar was Nir's chief stock-in-trade, and he in turn benefited from Israeli backing. Despite North's earlier wish to get rid of him, North continued to be dependent on Ghorbanifar's sequential arms-for-hostages schemes and invariably gave him one more chance to show what he could do.

Secord says he was the one who took the initiative in looking for a substitute for Ghorbanifar. Soon after the unsuccessful Tehran meeting, he discussed the matter with his partner, Albert Hakim, and notified North that they were going to search for a "Second Channel."[25] Secord and Hakim saw the new channel as an opportunity to make greater profits for themselves as well as to serve the larger cause of bringing Iran and the United States together. "I had enough imagination and self-confidence," Hakim said, "that somewhere along the line, in the future, I would be making a bundle of money." Hakim saw a $15 billion-a-year future market in Iran and wanted "a chance to get a stab at it."[26]

Secord left the search for the Second Channel to Hakim, who as a former businessman in Iran had Iranian contacts in Europe. Hakim conceived of a plan to use his commercial connections as a means of getting to influential Iranian political circles. His first move was to get in touch with a former acquaintance in Iran, Sadegh Tabatabai, an Iranian businessman in London, who is known as "Number One" or

"First Contact."[27] North described him as "allegedly well connected to Rafsanjani and several other of the so called 'pragmatists.' "[28] To find out about Tabatabai's "real access and willingness to act as an interlocutor," North sent Cave to see him in Frankfurt and to assure him that the Americans were willing to meet Iran halfway if a hostage could be released.[29]

Hakim's inducement to Tabatabai was a partnership with Secord and himself to sell pharmaceuticals to Iran. Hakim proposed gaining the goodwill of Iran by creating a line of credit and providing medicines at cost or even getting medical donations for it.[30] The idea was, as Hakim explained, to obtain "a penetration into Iran through supply of medical business in Iran" as "a good way to get into the Iranian network quickly, efficiently and gain some credit."[31]

Through Tabatabai, Hakim met another expatriate Iranian businessman, known as "Number Two."[32] Hakim dangled before them a fund of $2 million from his Swiss account to start the venture off.[33] In the end, Hakim brought together three or four Iranian exiles, and Tabatabai brought a number of others into the scheme, all of them promised a share of the expected profits.[34]

To make sure of Tabatabai's reliability, Hakim brought him to Washington, where he met with North on June 27.[35] Hakim had Tabatabai take a private lie detector test, which was managed by the Glenn A. Robinette who had also made the arrangements for North's security system.[36] On July 10, 1986, Tabatabai met with Hakim and Cave and told them that he kept in touch with representatives of important Iranians who traveled abroad on business. Tabatabai assured them that the vast majority of "senior Iranians," with the exception of a "radical" group, wanted to reestablish some degree of political relations with the United States.[37] Tabatabai met with them again the next day and discussed how best to get in touch with Speaker Rafsanjani, who had clearly emerged as the Americans' best hope for getting what they wanted from Iran. Money, however, was never far from Tabatabai's mind. "During the course of the evening," Cave noted, "[Tabatabai] said quite frankly that he wasn't going to do this for nothing and Hakim told him that if anything goes through he would get a good commission."[38]

Hakim's strategy paid off. According to Cave, Tabatabai made contact with Iranians who were engaged in a purchasing operation in London, and through them he learned that a relative of Speaker Rafsanjani had come out of Iran and had asked for an American contact.[39] On August 19, North was told that a meeting with him had been set up in Brussels, that he had come with instructions to act as an intermediary, and that he was even willing to come to the United States.[40]

On August 25, the Second Channel became a reality. At a meeting in Brussels, Secord and Hakim were introduced to the new Iranian emissary, dubbed "the Relative," because he was allegedly a nephew of

Speaker Rafsanjani. His name was apparently Ali Hashemi Bahramani.*
He spoke no English, which made Hakim's presence necessary. He seems
to have been younger than North but, as an officer in the Iranian Revolutionary Guards, on a level senior to North's.[41] After all the talk about
dealing with "moderates," the long-awaited Second Channel came from
the allegedly extremist Revolutionary Guards.

Hakim's two business contacts, who had led him to Bahramani, were
also present in Brussels, though they did not take part in the meetings
with him. In the end, Hakim did not give them anything for their pains.
As soon as they had served their purpose, Hakim forgot about his $2
million fund and medical supply business.[42] They badgered and threatened Hakim to get some financial reward out of him, but he seems to
have held them off by assuring them that they would get their share when
"his bundle of money" came through.[43] Ghorbanifar was not the only
artful dodger in this story.

Secord's report to North about the meeting in Brussels was altogether
favorable. They had met three times for a total of eight hours. Bahramani
was "very sharp." Secord called their talk a "comprehensive tour de force
regarding Iran/Iraq War, Iranian views of U.S. and other western policies,
Soviet activities, activities of nearly all important Iran government figures,
hostage matters, activities in the Hague, and Iranian forces' equipment
and materiel shortages." Rafsanjani, it was said, headed the Supreme
War Council and wanted to terminate the war as soon as the military
situation was more favorable to Iran. Bahramani knew all about Mc-
Farlane's mission to Tehran in May; Ghorbanifar, whom he called a
"crook"; and the Israeli connection. Secord told him that everything was
negotiable "if we can clear the hostage matter quickly." Secord concluded
his message optimistically: "My judgement is that we have opened up
new and probably much better channel into Iran. This connection has
been effectively recruited and he wants to start dealing."[44]

In this peculiar way, a new quasi-negotiation began between the United
States and Iran. On the one side were Secord, whose authority came
from North, and Hakim, whose authority came from Secord. On the
other side was a young Iranian officer whose authority came mainly from
his purported family relationship with Speaker Rafsanjani. Each side
assumed that the other was speaking with authority—which, in fact,

---

* North notebook for November 15, 1986, contains a reference to "Bahr." Virtually all sources
agree that the name was Bahramani or Bahremani, but there is a difference of opinion about his
first name and relationship. Segev says he was Mehdi Bahremani, the eldest son of Speaker Rafsanjani
(*The Iranian Triangle*, p. 297). Robin Wright calls him Ali Hashemi Bahramani and says he was
Rafsanjani's nephew (*In the Name of God*, p. 147). Jane Mayer and Doyle McManus also call him
Ali Hashemi Bahremani and again a favorite nephew of Rafsanjani (*Landslide*, p. 263). Bob Woodward repeats Ali Hashemi Bahramani, a nephew of Rafsanjani (*Veil*, p. 496). Ledeen refers to Ali
Hashemi Bakhramani, a Revolutionary Guards officer and Rafsanjani's nephew (*Perilous Statecraft*,
p. 234). Amir Taheri prefers Mehdi Bahramani, the eldest son of Rafsanjani (*Nest of Spies*, p. 218).
He will be called here Ali Hashemi Bahramani, with the understanding that he may also be
encountered as Mehdi Bahremani.

neither side had. In effect, the Americans were shaking off Ghorbanifar only to fall into increased dependence on Hakim as the new intermediary. Cave, the only American able to speak with Iranians in their own language, had a much higher opinion of Hakim than of Ghorbanifar. When Cave was asked about Hakim, he said: "He's head and shoulders above Ghorbanifar, but you gotta remember, he's gonna look at this initiative as a business opportunity."[45] The Second Channel gave Hakim the opportunity of his life to play the dual role of businessman and diplomat, both of which he clearly relished.

3

But Ghorbanifar was still not finished. The Second Channel was only in its opening stage, without anything concrete to show for it, whereas a definite deal had been put forward to North and Nir by Ghorbanifar in London on August 8. In Washington, no one had as yet taken the measure of young Bahramani, and Ghorbanifar's proposal was the only real issue before Poindexter, Casey, and North.

On September 2, North reminded Poindexter of the "sequential delivery process" that Ghorbanifar had put forward in London. He summed it up in seven simplified steps:

> Deliver 500 TOWs and the 39 electron tubes for the Hawk system previously requested.
> Sutherland released.*
> Deliver 500 TOWs and one of the Hawk radars previously requested.
> Anderson released.†
> Meeting in Tehran to discuss broadened relationship, Soviet intelligence, etc.
> Deliver remaining radar and 1000 TOWs while we are in Tehran.
> Jacobsen released and [Buckley's body] delivered.‡[46]

This was another staggered or sequential plan. Poindexter was still hesitant. "If we get into a sequential arrangement," he wrote North, "we really have to be prepared to deliver a lot more material and arrange a rather continuing technical arrangement. Of course that could all be

---

* Thomas P. Sutherland, acting dean of agriculture at the American University in Beirut, was kidnapped on June 8, 1985.
† Terry A. Anderson, chief Middle East correspondent for the Associated Press, was kidnapped in Beirut on March 11, 1985.
‡ David P. Jacobsen, director of the American University Hospital in Beirut, was kidnapped on May 28, 1985.

done, but after the hostages are released. I just can't see how we can have such a continuing relationship until that is happening."[47]

The main pressure for accepting the sequential deal came from North and Casey. North informed Poindexter:

CIA concurs that the [Kangarlou]-Ghorbanifar connection is the only proven means by which we have been able to effect the release of any of the hostages. Though the sequential plan is not what we prefer, the commodities and quantities are within the framework of our original understanding. CIA believes that we should proceed expeditiously with the Ghorbanifar connection and pursue the other five alternatives as subsidiary efforts.[48]

Casey wanted to proceed so expeditiously that North also wrote: "CIA is seeking 'go/no go' guidance by the end of this week."[49] To McFarlane, North complained:

We still have no response f[ro]m JMP [Poindexter] re proceeding w[ith] the sequential release proposal outlined to you some time back. Have now undertaken to have Casey raise same w[ith] JMP tomorrow at th[ei]r weekly meeting. The things one must do to get action. Am hopeful Bill [Casey] can push hard enough to move on the matter. Nir will be here next week and will raise enough hell to move it if it hasn't all fallen apart by then.[50]

While North was pushing Ghorbanifar's sequential plan, he was also preparing the ground for meeting with the Second Channel. On September 2, he told Poindexter that Bahramani had clearly indicated to Secord that he had a specific mandate to meet with U.S. officials to seek a means for "getting beyond the hostage issue" and to start a U.S.-Iran dialogue. Bahramani, according to North, was prepared to proceed with further discussions and appeared to be "a bona fide intermediary seeking to establish direct contact with the USG for Rafsanjani's faction within the Government of Iran."[51] On September 8, North sent word that Secord had learned from Bahramani that "the several factions in Tehran have agreed to a serious discussion with American officials, preferably in Europe next week."

At the same time, North reported that efforts to get Kangarlou of the First Channel to obtain the release of all three U.S. hostages simultaneously had failed. The demand had been rejected because of "the intransigence of the captors and Iranian inability to ensure results." North himself was so deeply committed to Ghorbanifar's plan that he was pleased to advise that the CIA and Army Logistics had located more Hawk parts for Iran, as a result of which "we now believe that the total 'package' will be sufficient to entice the Iranians to proceed with the sequential release pattern proposed in the London meetings."

North continued to stress Casey's view that the "Ghorbanifar connection" was still the only proven means to get any hostages released. The CIA, according to North, wanted to proceed with Ghorbanifar's sequential plan "with hopes that we could improve on it in discussions with Rafsanjani's representatives when they arrive in Europe." The CIA also thought that Rafsanjani was "moving to take control of the entire process of the U.S. relationship and the hostages." North saw in all this that "our window of opportunity may be better than it will ever be again."[52]

In effect, a two-track policy was contemplated for U.S. policy—to get as much as possible out of Ghorbanifar's First Channel and to hold Hakim's Second Channel in reserve. Signs and portents from Iran were taken to mean that the United States was at last dealing with Rafsanjani, the alleged leader of the alleged "moderates."

Yet, at this very time, two more hostages were taken. Frank H. Reed, director of the Lebanese International School, was kidnapped on September 9. He was apparently taken by "Mughniyyah's group," whose leader had a brother-in-law among the Da'wa prisoners in Kuwait.[53] This connection helps to explain the insistent Lebanese demand for the release of the Da'wa prisoners. Joseph J. Cicippio, the acting comptroller of the American University in Beirut, was seized on September 12.

North first thought that the American reaction would be to cut off further deals. When he heard of Reed's kidnapping, he was so alarmed that he feared President Reagan and Poindexter would close down the Bahramani or Second Channel in reaction to one more hostage.[54] But nothing of the kind happened. On September 9, Poindexter consulted the president on what to do about the Second Channel, the prospects for a hostage release, and the possibility of a rescue operation.[55] We know the outcome from a report by Allen to Casey after Allen had talked to North that same night. The decision went in favor of the new channel and conditionally against Ghorbanifar:

> Ollie is to continue to develop links to the Iranian Government through Albert Hakim and Dick Secord of Stanford Technology Associates . . . (The [new channel] apparently is attempting to arrange for Ollie and George Cave to meet with Rafsanjani, presumably with the next shipment of arms to Tehran.)
>
> Ghorbanifar will be cut out as the intermediary in future shipments of cargos to Iran, if at all possible. To cut Ghorbanifar out, Ollie will have to raise a minimum of $4 million.[56]
>
> If there is no other channel for financing future arms shipments, then Ghorbanifar will be used as a last resort.

Allen added: "Ollie is greatly relieved by Poindexter's decision because he feared that John and the President would shut down completely this back channel to Iran because of the kidnapping yesterday of Frank Reed."[57] The Lebanese and the Iranians may also have been relieved, because the decision showed that the Americans were willing to go ahead even if they had to worry about one hostage more instead of one hostage less.

The reference to $4 million to pay off Ghorbanifar puzzled Allen, who later said that "little wheels clicked in my mind, that all my fears were probably true." Nevertheless, he did not put this remark in his memo to Casey. "I probably should have," he admitted, "but these were my own private musings at that stage, and my own worries that the security—I guess what focused my mind with the opening of the new channel was that Colonel North was moving rapidly into this channel and that he had not shut down the first channel in a way that would be damage-limiting." It also occurred to Allen that North might get the money from the Israelis to "take care of" Ghorbanifar.[58]

It does not seem to have occurred to Allen that North's "reserves" were held by Secord and Hakim in their secret Swiss bank accounts. Allen apparently worried most of all about the security problem that was opening up as a result of going into Hakim's Second Channel without shutting down Ghorbanifar's First. For all his worries, Allen seems to have missed an opportunity to find out what North was up to and how he could have had access to a mysterious $4 million.

Allen might have been less puzzled if he had understood that the new turn of U.S. policy was meant to favor the Second Channel while holding Ghorbanifar in reserve. It was recognized that getting rid of Ghorbanifar without paying him off was dangerous. By claiming that he had not been paid enough, whether $4 million or $10 million, and threatening to blow the entire operation wide open, Ghorbanifar was still able to influence the fate of the Iran initiative.

The Americans opened themselves to blackmail because they had no fallback position in the event that the initiative was made public. A covert operation which cannot be defended openly, if necessary, is always in danger of becoming a political scandal. By sanctimoniously preaching to the world that Iran was a terrorist state to which no other state should sell arms, and then not only selling arms but also engaging in discussions aiming at no less than a strategic tie, the Americans cut off their line of retreat. The covert operation was in such blatant contradiction to the overt policy that it could not be divulged without risking ridicule and dishonor.

All these circumstances worked in favor of Ghorbanifar as soon as he sensed that he was being shunted aside in favor of the Second Channel. It would have been difficult enough to make the shift from one to the other even without Ghorbanifar's claim that he was owed millions of dollars. But money was handled so cavalierly in this operation that no one else knew just what he was owed, or why, or who was responsible for paying him back, if at all. Yet North, who was ultimately responsible for managing Ghorbanifar, considered the money end of the operation beneath his dignity or beyond his capability.

4

Ghorbanifar was not the only factor put at risk by the new American policy.

Ghorbanifar had long been the Israelis' chief card in this three-cornered game. They had introduced him to the Americans, and he had introduced the Americans to the First Channel. If Ghorbanifar was on the way out, so were the Israelis. A visit to Washington by Amiram Nir and Prime Minister Peres in the second week of September made clear what the Israelis were worried about.

Nir came first on September 10. North prepared Poindexter for the visit by telling him that Nir had already "become partially aware" of the contact with the Second Channel.[59] In fact, Ghorbanifar had apparently tipped Nir off that the Americans were seeking a new channel into Iran and that at least one meeting had already occurred with someone representing it.[60] North also led Poindexter to expect a meeting with an Iranian delegation headed by Speaker Rafsanjani's brother, Mahmoud Rafsanjani, the former Iranian ambassador to Syria—another indication that the Americans thought they were going to deal directly with Rafsanjani.[61]

The U.S. side was coming close to a crisis in its relations with Israel over the Iran affair. North warned Poindexter that the Israelis still backed Ghorbanifar's sequential scheme: "The Israeli government has been anxious to consummate the hostage release plan worked out with Iran." Nir had already made clear that Israel expected to continue to be treated as a partner in the Iran initiative. The word "joint" had come up twice in Nir's recent statement of his government's position:

> The Government of Israel has supported this joint effort for over a year and has not at any time acted unilaterally.
> The Government of Israel expects that the effort in Lebanon will continue to be a joint endeavor and include U.S. demands for the release of the Israeli hostage.

It was a delicate hint that Israel did not expect the United States to act unilaterally. North said that Nir had been told that the United States "will continue to support these two objectives and that the U.S. and Israel will work together to that end."

Nevertheless, North knew that the American side had gone ahead unilaterally to make contact in Brussels with Bahramani, the putative representative of Rafsanjani, and had decided to freeze out Ghorbanifar if possible. In his brief for Poindexter, North was faced with the awkward problem of explaining "how contact was established with Rafsanjani and how we expect to proceed." He advised Poindexter to say:

> In the process of investigating a possible illegal diversion of TOW missiles to Iran, Copp [Secord] made contact with an agent in [country deleted] working the sale.
>
> The European agent indicated that [Bahramani] was involved with the purchase. Copp met with [Bahramani] in Brussels on August 25, 1986 and advised him that it will not be possible to obtain TOW missiles without the help of the USG.

This story was a product of North's imagination. It had nothing in common with Hakim's feelers through his old business acquaintance in London or how the meeting in Brussels had actually come about. Another imaginary touch was North's tale that Bahramani "had been probed by Senator Kennedy and former Secretary of State Haig concerning the possible release of the hostages." North also wanted Nir to know that President Reagan had approved "proceeding with a meeting with the Rafsanjani representative."[62] Poindexter seems to have followed North's recommendations.[63]

Israeli Prime Minister Peres came to Washington a few days later, and again North advised Poindexter how to handle him. North said that Peres had several weeks earlier expressed concern that the United States might be contemplating the termination of "current efforts with Iran." Since the Israelis had not been informed of the moves to get a Second Channel, this could only mean concern that the Americans might be thinking of dropping "current efforts" in which Ghorbanifar would continue to be a prime factor.

"It is likely," North told Poindexter, "that Peres will seek assurances that the U.S. will indeed continue with the current 'joint initiative' and ensure that we will include the two missing Israelis in the [hostage] process. In that neither Weir nor Jenco would be free today without Israeli help (particularly in logistics), it would be helpful if the President would simply thank Peres for their discrete [sic] assistance." To which Poindexter appended a handwritten note to tell the President to say: "Thanks for assistance on Weir & Jenco. Will continue to work Iran with you. Include two missing Israelis in it."

In his advice to Poindexter, North added:

> *Israeli Arms:* On Friday night, Defense Minister Rabin offered a significant quantity of captured Soviet bloc arms for use by the

Nicaraguan democratic resistance. These arms will be picked up by a foreign flag vessel this week and delivered to the Nicaraguan resistance. If Peres raises this issue, it would be helpful if the President thanked him since the Israelis hold considerable stores of bloc ordnance, compatible with what the Nicaraguan resistance now uses.

To this, Poindexter had written a marginal note: "Rabin. Very tightly held."[64]

North and Poindexter exchanged two other messages about this Israeli arms shipment:

North to Poindexter: Re the Israeli arms. Orders were passed to the ship this morning to proceed to Haifa to pick up the arms. Loading will be accomplished during one night and the ship will be back at sea before dawn. Loading will be accomplished by Israeli military personnel.

Poindexter to North: I think you should go ahead and make it happen. It can be a private deal between Dick [Secord] and Rabin that we bless.

Poindexter soon cautioned:

Absolutely nobody else should know about this. Rabin should not say anything to anybody else except you or me.[65]

Here again, the contra and Iran operations were linked in a peculiar way. At the very time the Israelis were trying to be helpful in the contra operation, they were being eased out in the Iran operation. In effect, the Israelis had sensed that something was suddenly amiss in the U.S.-Israeli "joint initiative." Ever since Secord had been brought into the Iran initiative, he had understood that it was a "joint venture" with Israel.[66] Nir and North had been acting together as if they were colleagues; they went together to meetings, even one so risky for Nir as the one in Tehran in May; they were incessantly on the telephone exchanging ideas and information. Yet final decisions had always been made by the Americans, as at Tehran, where Nir had disagreed with McFarlane's decision to break off negotiations. The Israelis were so deeply indebted to the United States that they felt obliged to be helpful in every possible way, as Rabin's offer of arms to the Nicaraguan contras showed. In effect, the initiative had been "joint" but not equal.

How touchy U.S.-Israel relations had become was shown in a message from North to Poindexter on September 17, after Peres had left Washington. North's problem was how to get Bahramani to Washington without the need of visas or making it known to the Israelis:

> We are planning to bring him [Bahramani] into the U.S. at the end of the week, via parole papers thru Istanbul. Iranians can go to Turkey w/o [without] visas and parole papers avoid the necessity of stamping a visa in his passport—a complication which frequently causes major problems for those living in Iran. We (Cave, Clarridge, C/NE [Twetten], North) decided to honor their request to keep this meeting private (w/o Nir/Israelis) and to have it here so that they can confirm that they are indeed talking to the USG [U.S. government]. We knew this when you and Nir met on Monday, but I had not yet had the chance to brief you. We will have a follow-up mtg [meeting] with [Bahramani] in Europe and we will work Nir back into this op[eration] then.

But there was a hitch in the CIA that needed Casey's personal intervention:

> In the interim, Clair [George] has put a hold on bringing [Bahramani] in because he does not know whether you have "approved the operation." W[oul]d you pl[ea]s[e] call Casey and tell him to get on with moving the guy in so that we don't embarrass the hell out of ourselves w[ith] Rafsanjani. [67]

Poindexter had already obtained Casey's approval and assured North: "If Clair has a problem, he should talk to Casey." [68] On the other hand, Casey was worried about Secretary of State Shultz. According to North, Casey differed with him on how to handle Shultz.

> He [Casey] said he planned to tell Shultz in general terms that we were talking to another high level Iranian and that we would fill him in after the interview [with Bahramani]. I protested that experience showed that Shultz would then talk to ★ ★ ★ or ★ ★ ★ who would in turn talk to ★ ★ ★—and that ★ ★ ★ could well be the source of the Jack Anderson stuff we have seen periodically.* Casey Agreed [sic] to proceed with the INS parole paperwork for the Relative [Bahramani] and the visa for his escort but noted that he would still talk privately to Shultz about this.

In the same message, North praised Secord for doing what the CIA was allegedly not able to do:

* Jack Anderson's newspaper column caused official annoyance because it seemed to be based on "leaks" from inside the administration.

We are now underway with getting [Bahramani] aboard a chartered jet out of Istanbul. CIA could not produce an aircraft on such
"short notice" so Dick has chartered the a/c [aircraft] thru one of
Project Democracy's overseas companies. Why Dick can do something in 5 min[utes] that the CIA cannot do in two days is beyond
me—but he does. How the hell he is ever going to pay for it is also
a matter of concern, but Dick is a good soldier and never even
groused about it. You may want to talk to Sec Shultz about [Bah-
ramani] before Casey does.[69]

It appears from this that North was just as suspicious of confiding in
the secretary of state as he was of confiding in the Israelis. The reference
to Project Democracy, which was supposed to apply to the struggle of
the Nicaraguan contras, showed how intertwined it had become with the
Iran operation, for Secord was able to switch funds from one to the other
whenever the need arose.

On the same day, September 17, Secord told North what to expect
from the imminent arrival of Bahramani. Secord urged North to be ready
to hand over intelligence information, OB (Order of Battle) data, and a
secure voice device for use in "telecoms" (telecommunications). It would
also be necessary to talk about "war material and its relation to a long-
term connection from U.S. to Iran." The short and the long always came
together:

My opinion is that he and his group are attaching more importance to a long-term relationship than to any short-term quick fix,
such as a few thousand TOWs. He will, however, have a list of
needed items and will no doubt suggest some kind of shipment to
clear the hostage matter and to firmly establish direct USG [U.S.
government] to GOI [government of Iran] transactions and to eliminate the Gorbas and [deleted]. Thus, if I'm right, CIA must deliver
the goods re good OB [Order of Battle] and come up with suitcase
secure phone service.[70]

Whatever the importance attached by the new channel to the short-
term and long-term relationship, the former always came first as a necessary condition for anything else. To the Iranians the short-term meant
arms; to the Americans, hostages. The long-term relationship might be
talked about by Bahramani, but he could do little about it; a new strategic
and political relationship between the two countries was something for
their governments to negotiate—and their governments were not even
on speaking terms. Still, Secord's reports raised the highest hopes in
Washington among the very small select circle that knew about them—
mainly North, Hakim, Cave, Poindexter, and Casey.

The U.S.-Israeli connection was significantly changed by the emergence of the Second Channel. North and Poindexter had deliberately decided to go ahead without the Israelis and, in North's case, to deceive them. Secord and Hakim had taken the place of Ghorbanifar, with the result that the Israelis no longer had a privileged position in the action.

5

At last, Bahramani, accompanied by two aides, came to Washington to meet with North, Secord, Cave, and Hakim on September 19 and 20.[71] North had the meetings secretly taped, with the result that we have an exceptionally full record of what took place. Bahramani alone spoke for Iran, and the United States was represented by North, pretending to be "Colonel Goode," Secord as "General Kopp," and Cave as "Colonel Sam O'neil."[72]

Bahramani satisfied them that he had come with the approval of four leading Iranian officials. He named Rafsanjani, Mohsen Rafiq-Dust, Mohammed Hosein Jalalai, and Moussavi-Khamenei (evidently a conflation of Prime Minister Moussavi and President Khamenei). They had told him to be sure to talk to "the top of the U.S. government"—instructions that he was not able, or did not know enough, to carry out. He also said that Foreign Minister Velayati, alleged to be relatively close to Rafsanjani, had participated in meetings regarding earlier American approaches to Iran and had evaluated them as "sincere," though Velayati had not been present at the final sessions which had authorized Bahramani's trip to the United States.[73]

The two-day meetings filled the Americans with more optimism than ever before. The Iranian immediately said all the things the Americans hoped to hear. Iran recognized the increasing Soviet threat. His government wanted strategic cooperation between Iran and the United States. The Ayatollah Khomeini was absolutely opposed to terrorism and hostages. The Iranian leadership thought of forming a "joint committee" to resolve all problems between the two countries step by step.*

Ghorbanifar was another link between the two sides. North said that he was not acceptable to both the Iranians and the Americans. Bahramani had as little use for him as the Americans now had. He flatly said that

---

* At the outset, Bahramani made some strange remarks about various "approaches" to Iran: "They also were curious about the approaches from Senator [Edward] Kennedy and [former Secretary of State] Alexander Haig. The Haig approach blew their mind because it was via an Iranian hair dresser in Europe" (in the copy produced at the North trial; deleted in Part III, p. 1224).

The reference to Kennedy and Haig had already been brought up at the Brussels meeting on August 25. Secord had then reported to North: "Special interest items included claim that an 'Al Haig gp [group?]' and 'a Senator Kennedy gp' have recently tried to meet with [the Relative]—he has declined—he wants to deal with the Presidents [sic] representative" (in TR, p. B-149, deleted in A-1, p. 1349).

These allusions to Kennedy and Haig have not been explained.

the Iranians mistrusted Ghorbanifar. The Americans agreed but were worried "about his going public and destroying everything." Bahramani rejoined that "they think they can take care of Gorba. He was almost executed in 1981. They have a lot on him and he also has family back in Tehran." But the Americans were doubtful and believed "this remains a problem since Gorba has told Nir that he would go public."[74]

According to another American version of the meeting, Bahramani said that someone close to Ghorbanifar's contact in Tehran was believed to be working for the KGB, the Soviet secret police. He expressed great concern that the Soviets could make the contact public, if it was confirmed, by "doing great mischief in Iran and the U.S. and by rapidly escalating their assistance to Iraq or even intervening in Iran." To which North says that the Americans responded helpfully: "We did all we could to feed this anxiety."[75]

When they came to discussing arms for hostages, North pointed out that TOWs and Hawk spare parts had been delivered, but Ghorbanifar was complaining that he had not been paid in full. "Ghorbanifar," North said, "always claims to be borrowing and then getting paid in part and rolling debts forward and raising costs and it is very, very confusing and it's impossible for us to follow exactly what it is that he is doing. However, Ghorbanifar knows a great deal and he could be harmful to us if he were to go public and this is a problem which we wish to address. We think Iran should pay him whatever they owe him so he will be quiet and stay off the air."

The Iranian answer was that Ghorbanifar had received all his money but it will be looked into. At a later point in the meeting, Bahramani said that "they [Iranian authorities] want to get him out of the loop as soon as they can. He's been profiteering and people in Iran fear that they will be accused of being profiteers." North remarked that "Ghorbanifar has some strong Tehran connections that we know of and this remains a problem that needs to be solved."[76] North noted a way to get rid of Ghorbanifar: "Tell G. [Ghorbanifar] that 2 new hostages have made proceeding *impossible*."[77]

Religion also entered into the discussion.

On a number of occasions he was told that RR [Ronald Reagan] believed deeply in the teachings of our Holy Book, a copy of which was on the table, and reference was made to a number of pertinent passages (e.g. Gen. 15:7–21; Gal. 3:7; etc.). At one point he [Bahramani] noted to George [Cave] that RR being a man of God had removed the only argument they had—that Allah was supposed to be on their side.[78]

This reference to President Reagan's alleged religiosity was apparently intended to show how much the two sides had in common spiritually.

The hostage issue was downplayed by both sides. The Americans took the line that it was an obstacle, not the key to arriving at a strategic relationship. North recognized that the Iranian government did not have absolute control over the Lebanese groups but believed that Iran could help resolve the issue. Bahramani assured Cave that he was certain the matter could soon be settled. "He has promised prompt action on the hostages," North told Poindexter, "is looking for assurances that we will not walk away once they use their influence to get them free." As a token of Iran's new antiterrorist policy, North pointed to a recent Iranian refusal to permit the landing in Iran of a hijacked Pan American plane at the Karachi airport. In return, Bahramani was promised that a Voice of America broadcast the following week would mention Iran favorably as one of the states that had taken a courageous stand against the hijacking. As for the Da'wa prisoners in Kuwait, North said, the United States could not make a direct approach to Kuwait but believed that the government of Kuwait was prepared to release the prisoners gradually if the government of Iran approached Kuwait privately with a no-terrorism promise.[79]

On the Soviet Union, North said that the United States did not want to see Iran lose but neither did it want to see an attempt against Iraq "which will bring in the Soviets." Soviet anxiety "could be quickly raised if they knew that we are trying to reestablish relations," so that absolute secrecy was necessary. It was advisable to set up a secure communication station with two American technicians in Tehran to thwart the KGB. As a gesture of his own, Bahramani offered to hand over to the United States a captured Soviet T-72 tank.[80] If there was to be a U.S.-Iran strategic relationship, it was clearly aimed more at the Soviet Union than at Iraq, which the United States did not wish to see lose any more than it wished to see Iran lose. The two sides' attitudes toward the Soviet Union were not identical. North spoke as if the Soviets were the common enemy. According to North's notes, Bahramani said: "Before I came here, responsible officials wanted me to make clear that while we do not want to be an enemy of Soviets, we are not about to be friendly toward them."[81]

Iran's view of the Iran-Iraq war, according to Bahramani, was bound to be troublesome. Iran, he said, needed some kind of victory against Iraq, though not necessarily "a big, decisive military victory." More important for Iran was the removal of Iraq's strongman, Saddam Hussein. "Iran," he said, "agrees completely with respect to an honorable peace with Iraq; however, Saddam Hussein must go from the Iranian point of view." He knew that it was not U.S. policy to overthrow Saddam Hussein, but he also claimed to know that the United States could influence Arab nations which had it in their power "to get rid of Saddam Hussein." How Iraq could get an honorable peace if Saddam Hussein had to be overthrown was an Iranian secret.

North tried to temporize. The United States, he said, wanted to ensure the territorial integrity of Iran and had no interest in an Iraqi victory. He could "make no commitment about getting rid of Hussein," but "there is a need for a non-hostile regime in Baghdad." This conciliatory position was not enough for Bahramani, who kept coming back to the demand for U.S. pressure on Arab states to overthrow Saddam Hussein, a particular obsession of Ayatollah Khomeini's. North's formula was double-edged: "The United States does not wish to see Iran lose. We do not want to see an attempt against Iraq which will bring in the Soviets."

On the other hand, North complained about Iran's support of the "Communist government" of Nicaragua. He charged that Iran planned to ship 10,000 rifles and other munitions to Nicaragua through North Korea. These activities, he maintained, "serve Soviet interests and in the long-term jeopardize Iran and the United States."[82]

Despite such differences, the two sides substantially agreed on the immediate issue of arms for hostages. North accepted the Iranian strategy of a stage-by-stage or step-by-step process.[83] He undertook to provide Iran with military "items which will help in her defense," so long as Iran paid for them. Secord had drawn up a list of Iranian military needs, and the Iranians had their own ideas of what they wanted. The Iranian "wish list" included Hawk spare parts and radars as before, plus intelligence information against Iraq, artillery, and other weapons, not all of them defensive. Bahramani gave intelligence information a higher priority than any other military assistance by the United States.[84] In principle, North said to him, "to the extent that items are available either here or elsewhere there isn't a particular problem."[85] North even chided the Iranians for wanting nothing more than arms and offered American aid in support of new Iranian housing, oil production facilities, and medical supplies.[86]

At the end of the first day, North was so gratified by the progress they had made that he took Bahramani on a complete tour of the White House. Hakim, who had not attended the business sessions, was now pressed into service as translator. They went as far as the president's Oval Office, into which they peered from behind the rope barrier. North was so exuberant that he stopped before one painting, and as Hakim later related:

> North, by this time, was also impressed by this gentleman, and he was feeling, after many months of frustration, he was feeling upbeat. It is interesting to know while we were passing by one of the corridors, stepping down the stairs, we came across a picture that was hanging on the wall. It portrayed the table and like a conference table and there were dogs sitting around the table and I remember one of the dogs I think was taking a little nap, and Ollie was feeling very upbeat and he asked me to translate for our guest that this represented our Cabinet, and that Mr. Casey was taking a nap. That broke the ice.[87]

Hakim related another curious incident. One of the two Iranians accompanying Bahramani was thought to be a government official.[88] On the second day of the visit, he made Hakim aware that they expected "financial remuneration" for their services in opening the Second Channel. Hakim went into the room in which North and Bahramani were conferring and talked to them about it in such a way that he "made sure that this issue would not be forgotten," either for himself or for the Iranians. Hakim says that the conferees agreed, "in principle," to remunerate them, but that the amount and method were left to the future. "It was too early to be specific."[89]

The entire meeting was mainly an exchange of views and had not been very specific. From the American point of view, however, it was a huge success. North and Bahramani had hit it off splendidly together. Each had tried as much as possible to say the right things to the other. Where they had not fully agreed, they had never come to any real clash. The Americans felt that they had finally made direct contact with Speaker Rafsanjani, their great hope for achieving the dual tasks of rescuing the hostages and arriving at a new long-term relationship with Iran. North exuberantly informed Poindexter:

> We appear to be in contact with the highest levels of the Iranian Government. There is no doubt that [Bahramani] is far more competent and better "connected" than our other interlocutor [Kangarlou]. It is possible that the Iranian Government may well be amenable to a U.S. role in ending the Iran-Iraq war. This, in and of itself, would be a major foreign policy success for the President.[90]

In another reference to the president, North exulted: "Sincerely believe that RR can be instrumental in bringing about an end to Iran/Iraq war—a la Roosevelt w[ith] Russo-Japanese war in 1904. Anybody for RR getting the same prize?"[91]

Yet nothing had actually been settled. The only concrete result was an agreement to meet again after Bahramani had reported to his superiors in Iran. On the immediate issue of American arms for Iran, Bahramani had reason to be satisfied. North had accepted the Iranian plan for a sequential exchange of hostages for arms. But the larger questions about a U.S.-Iran strategic understanding, the fate of Saddam Hussein, and the like were not about to be settled soon. North's repeated pronouncements that the hostages were merely an obstacle in the path of larger aims and had to be cleared away first represented an obstinate refusal to recognize how distant those larger aims were. Historically, theologically, politically, geographically, and in almost every other way, the United States and Iran were so far apart that anything resembling a strategic realignment was bound to be a distant and highly dubious goal.

Even if the long-term aim had been more feasible, it would have had to be negotiated, in the usual way of carrying on American diplomatic business, by the Department of State, not by a junior lieutenant colonel on the NSC staff. Both Casey and North now began to think about giving some role to the State Department. On September 22, just after the departure of Bahramani, North informed Poindexter:

> Casey has asked what we are doing ab[ou]t bringing Sec State up to speed on results. I told him this was your call. Casey is urging a mtg [meeting] on Weds. among you, Casey, Cave and me to discuss situation prior to discussion w[ith] Shultz. Can we schedule same?[92]

Two days later, North himself put this question to Poindexter: "Who, if anybody, at the State Department should be brought into this activity?"[93] Only a week earlier, North had protested against Casey's intention to tell Shultz in general terms about the contact with Bahramani.[94] Shultz himself later testified that he had heard nothing about it—or about anything related to the Iran operation.[95] It appears that Poindexter was not yet willing to bring in anybody from the State Department.

The Israelis were also left out of the new developments. North told Poindexter that Amiram Nir had been calling daily—"often several times"—to urge the Americans "to get on with the process in our 'joint venture.' " North decided to "stall," because Bahramani had asked him to leave the Israelis out for the time being. While Nir and Ghorbanifar were put off with a fictitious story that the Americans could not proceed without holding a meeting with Kangarlou, whom they had already cast out, Nir continued to encourage Ghorbanifar to raise the necessary funds for another arms delivery.[96] In effect, North, with Poindexter's knowledge, began to deceive Nir and to treat Bahramani as if he were more to be trusted than the Israeli.

In some ways, North and Bahramani were two of a kind. Both were young military officers doing work generally left to senior diplomats or high-ranking government leaders. They talked effusively about matters that they could not have decided by themselves, and neither could be sure that the other fully represented the official views of the ruling circles. Both might be expected to report back that they had made great strides forward, while neither really knew how the other country's system functioned.

Ghorbanifar was more disaffected and suspicious than ever. On September 24, Nir told North that the sense he was getting from Ghorbanifar was that he was "getting very worried."[97] On October 1, North heard from Nir that Ghorbanifar had complained bitterly about the way he had been treated. Cave had told Kangarlou in one of their telephone conversations that the United States did not trust Ghorbanifar—a message which Kangarlou promptly passed on to Ghorbanifar. Nir forwarded

Ghorbanifar's complaints—he had spent $2 million "out of pocket"; his credibility in Iran was "severely damaged" and his "ability to raise money ruined." He had decided "to get out of the game" unless shown the "tape and script of the conversation" between Cave and Kangarlou. With "crooks like us," said Ghorbanifar, apparently referring to the Americans, he "does not want to do this any more."[98]

By now, Ghorbanifar was the time bomb that seemed most likely to go off. He seemed to have good reason to explode publicly—he had been displaced, and he owed, if he can be believed, about $10 million that he expected the Americans to make good for him. But Ghorbanifar had waited too long, and other events rushed forward to the climax.

20

Out of Control

North was now a man in a hurry. He had found his good Iranian and meant to make the most of him. Few things had ever worked for North in the Iran initiative before; the golden opportunity had arrived.

After the meeting in Washington, Secord kept in touch with Bahramani. On October 2, 1986, the latter called Secord to say that he wanted to meet with the Americans in Frankfurt, West Germany, on October 6. He indicated that he had "good news"—an "internal consensus" in Iran on how to deal with the hostage problem—and wished to get past the "obstacle" as quickly as possible. He intended to bring with him one of the Iranian officials who had been present in May at the Tehran meeting, whom the Americans believed to be a Revolutionary Guard intelligence official. He also asked them to bring "a definite sample" of the intelligence information previously discussed in Washington—the information which he had considered to be of the highest priority. As a gesture, he was going to bring a Koran for President Reagan.[1]

North clutched eagerly at all these straws. As a reciprocal gesture, he purchased a Bible for Bahramani to take back to Tehran. In it he wanted President Reagan to inscribe a passage, which, as he explained, "is important in that it is a new testament reference to Abraham, who is viewed by Moslems, Jews and Christians as the progenitor of all the world's nations." North had most difficulty with the request for intelligence information, the sensitive nature of which he recognized. But he reminded Poindexter that they had previously agreed "it was unlikely that providing such information would change the course of the war." His additional reason for giving Iran intelligence information was strange, in view of the importance he attached to a long-term friendly relationship:

> Further, we all recognized that the information need not be accurate and that it was highly perishable given the dynamic nature of the conflict. In short, we believe that a mix of factual and bogus

information can be provided at this meeting which will satisfy their concerns about "good faith" and that we can use the "perishable argument["] as an incentive for the Iranians to accept a CIA communications team in Tehran.[2]

North knew that he was dealing with an Iran still smarting over the microfiches and the alleged overpricing of their missiles and spare parts. Yet he was willing to risk disaffecting Iran again should they discover that they had been given inaccurate or bogus intelligence information.

North again returned to the problem of Nir. He informed Poindexter that "we made a conscious decision not to apprise him of our near-term efforts with Rafsanjani's [relative]." Nir had been informed earlier of the contact but not about what had come of it. Kept in the dark, Nir had persistently tried to find out what was going on, even calling Cave's home and office several times daily. Ghorbanifar, it seems, had offered to purchase the remaining Hawk spare parts and 500 TOWs, without getting anywhere, and Nir wanted to know why.

North now proposed a way of getting rid of the Nir problem. Its worst aspect, North said, was that Nir essentially controlled American access to Ghorbanifar and Ghorbanifar's Iranian contact. The solution was to reduce Nir's role.

> We believe that we now have an opportunity to change the relationship in such a way that Nir is placed in a supporting role rather than acting as a primary source of control. We also recognize that Israel's participation in this activity is both politically and operationally important. In altering Nir's status, we need to do so in such a way that he and those officials in his government who are cognizant continue to perceive that this is still a "joint venture."[3]

To dispose of the joint venture without the Israelis knowing that it was being done, North had a simple proposal. Nir had been able to communicate with the five main Americans—North, Cave, Allen, Secord, and Twetten—in the Iran operation. North suggested cutting the number down to one or two besides himself, with daily reports going to him. The move was to be cloaked by a "cover story." The scheme seemed to be to make it more difficult for Nir to communicate with anyone but North, Cave, and Secord and put North in tight control of the other two.[4]

Yet North was not sure enough of Bahramani to be willing to give up Ghorbanifar and his Iranian contact. North took the precaution of sending Secord to Israel on October 4, two days before the meeting in Frankfurt, "to ameliorate Nir's *angst*," as he put it, without telling Nir that North himself was en route to the German rendezvous. To make sure that Nir could not get to Frankfurt, North planned to tell him only the night before about the meeting, "which he (Nir) will be unable to make due to lack of connecting flights to Frankfurt."

This elaborate plot was conceived in order to shift over to the Second Channel without breaking all ties with the First:

> The steps above are designed to give us a chance to make the new relationship through the [Relative] function without destroying the Ghorbanifar-[Kangarlou?] channel. We would, in effect, put Ghorbanifar-[Kangarlou?] on "hold" until we see what [Bahramani] produces.[5]

Before Secord went off to Israel to see Nir, instructions were drawn up for him. The main objective was to explain why Ghorbanifar had to be removed as the intermediary between Iran and the United States and why Nir had been left out of the dealings with Ghorbanifar's successor. Ghorbanifar, it was charged, had made commitments the United States could not meet, and he was no longer to be trusted by either side. More difficult was the problem of how to explain away the failure of the Americans to keep the Israelis informed of, if not involved in, the Second Channel.

This delicate feat required some creative sophistry. Secord was told to say that he had been empowered to act as the U.S. intermediary with the new Iranian channel, Rafsanjani's alleged nephew, and to seek a second meeting with him. Nir would be introduced "into this process under the same conditions as obtained when you went to Tehran with us," but only when U.S. government officials had made direct contact with the new channel—as if such contact had not already been made. Secord was reminded that Nir had already been told the tall story that Secord had happened upon "the Relative" while looking into the possible diversion of TOWs in late July and early August. Meanwhile, the Americans wanted to keep the Ghorbanifar-Kangarlou channel "on hold." Secord intended to meet with Bahramani somewhere in Europe or Turkey, he hoped the same week, and to attempt to have Nir included in the following meeting. But Nir was to be cautioned that Bahramani and others in Tehran had known that Nir was an Israeli even during the May meeting in Tehran and that the Americans did not want the new contact to fail because of Nir. In any case, Secord was to expect all of them to meet with Bahramani the following week.[6]

On October 5, Secord met with Nir in Tel Aviv and presented him with a letter from President Reagan to Prime Minister Peres thanking him for his efforts in furthering the Iran initiative and praising Nir's work.[7] After much discussion, Secord concluded that "we clearly have problem to confront re promise to Nir and inclusion in 'next' meeting with [Bahramani]."[8]

North's optimism about the new channel was so infectious that Poindexter caught some of it. On October 3, after receiving North's report on the coming meeting with the Relative in Frankfurt, Poindexter wrote cheerfully to McFarlane:

We have quite a bit of news on that front. It looks promising. We have made contact with Rafsanjani [Relative]. Two meetings so far. One here in US. Ollie, Cave and Secord meet with him this weekend in Frankfort. Your trip to Tehran paid off. You did get through to the top. They are playing our line back to us. They are worried about Soviets, Afghanistan and their economy. They realize the hostages are obstacles to any productive relationship with us. They want to remove the obstacle. [Deleted] has been in Beirut, says he has good news for Frankfort. We shall see. Still insisting on group release. If this comes off may ask you to do second round after hostages are back. Keep your fingers crossed.[9]

This hint was all that McFarlane needed. A day later, he responded to Poindexter: "Roger; anytime John." To which he added:

If you think it would be of any value, I might be able to take a couple of months off and work on the problem. No guarantees and no need for any sponsorship (except for airfares and hotels) but I might be able to turn something up. Think about it.[10]

McFarlane was evidently still caught up in the Iran project, as if he regretted that he had prematurely removed himself from it. A second Tehran meeting might enable him to make up for the first.

2

But a second meeting in Tehran was still distant. Meanwhile, North, Secord, Cave, and Hakim went to Frankfurt for a second meeting with Bahramani.

The Frankfurt meeting took place October 6–8. With Bahramani came another Iranian representative who proved to be of particular interest. He was the Ali Samii, who had attended the first meeting with Ghorbanifar in Frankfurt in February 1986 as well as the Tehran meeting with McFarlane's group in May 1986. He seems to be someone in whom the top Iranian leadership put the utmost confidence and who was used by it as a watchdog over both Ghorbanifar and Bahramani. We know little more about him than that he was considered to be a Revolutionary Guard intelligence official and a tenaciously hard bargainer. He described himself as the "extraordinary representative of the cooperative that has been assigned to deal with the relationship with the United States."[11] The Americans also dubbed him "the Monster" and "the Engine."[12] North apparently referred to him as "the general."[13] Hakim was particularly impressed by him, for one reason because he had refused to take gifts from Hakim even for his children. At times, he seemed to be a more important Iranian spokesman than Bahramani.[14]

We have an unusually full record of this meeting because it was surreptitiously recorded and almost twenty printed pages of the tape are available as well as an extensive report in North's notebook.[15] As a result of this largesse, we have a much better idea of the liberties North permitted himself to take in these meetings. North's imagination or fantasy was never more unrestrained than in his encounters with Bahramani. On this occasion, he was most creative in inventing meetings with and statements by President Reagan, as if North imagined himself to be the president's stand-in.

They went through the by now familiar questions—arms, hostages, money, Ghorbanifar, Iraq's Saddam Hussein, Kuwait's Da'wa prisoners, Iran-Iraq peace, and the hypothetical U.S.-Iran strategic relationship. The difference is that we now know what was actually said, as if we were present in the room.[16]

The Iranian request for arms and intelligence brought from North imaginary instructions from President Reagan and familiar references to the secretaries of state and defense.

North: What the President told me to do was to build the best possible intelligence . . . We didn't give you a full intelligence package back in February.

Hakim interprets for the Iranians.

North: He only put one constraint on what I did. "You will not," he said to me, "recommend items that would allow or encourage the Iranian Army or the Pasdaran [Revolutionary Guards] to seize Baghdad."

Hakim (interprets): Isn't it your understanding from everything that you have seen that Baghdad is not one of their objectives?

North: My friend, I understand that. I actually believe that, but I have one hell of a time convincing people like Caspar Weinberger and George Shultz.

Hakim (interprets): He says that they did not believe that they could seize Faw,[17] but they did.

North: That's what scared the hell out of Caspar Weinberger and George Shultz (laughs).

Hakim (interprets): He says they are not going to wait for Shultz and Weinberger to seize Baghdad.

North (laughing): I understand that.[18]

Secord was also privy to what President Reagan had allegedly authorized.

Secord: Based upon previous official requests of the Iranian Government, i.e. [deleted] and verified, and I would underline, desperate requests from him, for TOWs, for Hawk parts and for high-powered radars, we have achieved presidential authority for immediate air delivery of those items. . . . And the President of the United States has approved a secret operation to deliver these items immediately.[19]

As the discussion proceeded, North's version of what President Reagan had told him became more and more expansive:

North: That Saturday when [the Relative] was in Washington, and I flew up to Camp David to talk to the President, and I showed him the list [of requested arms], and he said, "Why are you thinking so small?" He took the list, that list right there, and he went like this with it—I was sitting across the table—and he said, "For someone who has seen so much war as you have, North, you should understand that I want to end that war on terms that are acceptable to Iran. I don't want to simply help[,] go out and kill more Iranian youngsters. What about the 2 million people without homes? What about the oil industry which is already in ruins? What about the industrial base which is being destroyed? Stop coming in and looking like a gun merchant." And he banged on the table, "I want to end the war."[20]

At a later stage of the meeting, the Iranian request for howitzers produced unorthodox suggestions from Secord and North. Cave said that the 100 towed howitzers and 500 howitzer barrels desired by Iran constituted such a large order that they would necessitate opening a production line.[21] Secord thereupon advised the Iranians to go to a friendly third country to buy them. North interjected: "Go tell some allied, some country, that we will look the other way." Cave pointed out that another country would have to open a production line. "Look," North rejoined, "all of this is to say that all of this and more can be done, but we need to fireproof our President by removing the obstacle [of the hostages]."[22]

The Iranians pleaded that they were not sure they could get the hostages, on which, for the Americans, everything else hinged. Samii said, in Hakim's translation: "And I want you to know that even today, as I'm sitting here, we do not have a guarantee that the Lebanese would 100 per cent listen to what we have to say." Even "up to this date," he said, we are still "in a mess" with respect to the hostages.[23] Later an Iranian protested that "you must understand that they are going to try their best. They are not in a position to make any promises because they don't know where they are."[24]

North gave the Iranians some apocryphal information and advice on the release of the Da'wa prisoners in Kuwait:

> We recognize that those who hold the hostages most want their brethren who are held in Kuwait as convicted terrorists freed. Very, very privately with the Kuwaitis, last Friday, we helped to try and set the stage for that kind of thing to happen in a direct dialogue between Iran and Kuwait. We have assured the Kuwaitis—a very, very experienced foreign minister—that the Da'wa prisoners are their business. But you should know, very, very privately, that what that means is that if the Kuwaitis decide to release them over some length of time or for some religious reason, that we are not going to criticize them.[25]

North was also ready to provide Iran with "very sensitive intelligence." But it had to be done "in such a way that we will not be known to have given them to you." If it ever became known, North warned, "we would be finished in terms of credibility as long as President Reagan is President."[26]

North again posed as if he were the president's confidant:

> The President has said—and I said this to you—and I flew up to Camp David to talk to the President. And he said, "I understand why we should do everything possible to insure an honorable peace for Iran."[27]

Whenever the problem of Iraq's Saddam Hussein came up, North made some of his most astonishing statements. The transcript reads:

> *North:* He [President Reagan] knows that Saddam Hussein is a (expletive).
>
> *Hakim:* Do you want me to translate that?
>
> *North:* Go ahead. That's his word, not mine.[28]

North again spoke of Saddam Hussein in this vein:

> Saddam Hussein. Okay. And I don't know exactly how that's all going to work. Okay? One of the things that we would like to do is that we would like to become actively engaged in ending this war

in such a way that it becomes very evident to everybody that the guy who is causing the problem is Saddam Hussein.[29]

There was also much talk, mainly by North, about the primary American aim to arrive at a long-term relationship with Iran. It came up in a peculiar exchange:

North: Ronald Reagan is going to be President of the U.S. for two more years and will never again serve as President.

Iranian: There is McFarlane.

North: He wants to be president?

Iranian: They are very active in trying to make McFarlane president (laughter).

North: That's not beyond reason. It could happen. (Continues with previous thought.) This President would like to have—I can tell you because I've listened to him—his vision is that when he leaves office in 1989 we will have full diplomatic relations between your country and ours.[30]

At other times North said that "our objective is to assure the political sovereignty and territorial integrity of Iran."[31] North also assured the Iranians that "we are working for a military balance in the region—a political solution and honorable solution to the Iran-Iraq war."[32] North seems to have made up American policy as he went along; no decision had been made in Washington on how the United States was going to "assure" Iran's political sovereignty and territorial integrity.

This meeting, like the others, tended to wander into political areas in which both sides knew that little if anything could be done by themselves. The real business of the Frankfurt meeting was still what it had always been—an arms-for-hostages deal. On the way over, North had handwritten a seven-point program, headed "U.S. Proposal," which he had presented toward the end of the first day. It read:

1. Iran provides funds for 500 TOWs and remainder of Hawk parts.
2. Within 9 days we deliver [Hawk] parts and TOWs (500) plus medical supplies.
3. All American hostages released.
4. Iran provides funds for 1500 TOWs.
5. Within 9 days we will deliver:
   ★1500 TOWs
   ★Technical support for Hawks
   ★Updated intelligence on Iraq
   ★Communications team

6. Iran will then:
  ★Release Pattis*
  ★Provide body of [William] Buckley
  ★Provide copy of Buckley debrief [by Lebanese captors]
7. U.S. will then
  ★Identify sources for other items on [Iranian arms] list
  ★Iran will then work to release other hostages.[33]

The striking thing about this proposal was its American-style arms-for-hostages approach. It differed from an Iranian-style deal in that it required the one-time release of all the American hostages rather than release in a sequential pattern. North admitted that he had not talked to his superior, Poindexter, or anyone else in the administration about these points.[34] In any case, they were not what the Iranians were looking for.

For one thing, the Iranians could not guarantee that they would be able to obtain the release of the American hostages. All they were willing to do was to "promise" to use their influence with the Lebanese captors. It appears that the various American hostages were not necessarily held by one Lebanese group and that the Iranians did not have influence with all of them. In fact, the Iranians claimed that they did not even know where the latest two American hostages were being held and merely agreed to try to find out.[35]

In any case, the Iranians wanted the Americans to promise on behalf of Kuwait to gain the release of the Da'wa prisoners. It had become more and more apparent that the fate of the American hostages was inextricably wound up with that of the Da'wa prisoners. North's previous suggestion about how they could be freed, for which he had had no warrant, was not enough for the Iranians, who apparently needed something much stronger for the Lebanese. The issue was now more clearly drawn than ever before, especially since the Iranians noted that North's seven points had said nothing about the Kuwaiti problem.[36]

By the second day of the meeting, the two sides were drawing further and further apart. Samii countered North's seven points with his own seven-point proposal, which has been reconstructed in the following way:

1. The United States would establish a timetable for the delivery of the arms on the Relative's list, thus committing itself to providing offensive and defensive arms.

2. One hostage would then be released.

3. A timetable and a location would be established for the exchange of intelligence; and the United States and Iran would evaluate the Russian, Afghanistan, and Iraq situation.

* John Pattis was an American citizen who had been arrested in Iran as an alleged spy several months earlier.

4. Iran would "only promise" to gain the release of the remaining two American hostages but this was to be linked to American progress on the Da'wa prisoners. The Engine made clear that the release of the Americans and the Da'was would have to "wash." "They would have to coincide or have some logical correlation."

5. Shipment of the eight items on the Relative's list would proceed based upon mutually agreed-upon priorities and quantities. Iran would try—but not promise—to locate and arrange the release of the other two hostages.

6. The United States would contact Kuwait to make sure that there are no problems with the release of the Da'wa prisoners.

7. The United States and Iran would agree to work within the framework of the Hague settlement process to provide Iran with military items, such as F-14 spare parts, that Iran had paid for under the Shah's rule but that had been embargoed after the Embassy seizure.[37]

The Iranian and American proposals differed sharply. Instead of obtaining the release of all the American hostages at one time, the Iranians agreed to the immediate release of only one hostage, followed by an exchange of two American hostages for the Da'wa prisoners in Kuwait. The Iranians also brought into the deal the Iranian funds sequestered by the United States after the fall of the Shah, a factor North was not prepared to deal with. Curiously, the Iranians complained that the Americans were guilty of always seeking to trade hostages for arms, whereas the Iranians wanted both sides to take everything on trust.[38] This riposte would have been more convincing to the Americans if the Iranians had not obviously been trying to avoid committing themselves to the release of the American hostages and had not been so determined to force the Americans to commit themselves to specific arms deliveries.

By the middle of the second day, the outlook for an agreement was so dark that even North was ready to give up. Once both sides had presented their proposals, it was clear that they were not talking the same political language. Of his own seven points, North said that "this list was given to me by the President of the United States of America. And there's no way on God's green earth that I'm going to violate my instructions. . . . That's the President's authorized list. That's all he authorized . . . In fact he told me, he said, you know, 'Don't give away more than you have to.' That is everything he authorized me to talk about."[39] North was so pessimistic that he saw the two countries "pass each other like two ships in the night . . . my sense is that I have failed in my mission . . . we are missing each other; we are not understanding each other."[40] He felt, he said, "very much like I did the last time you and I saw each other in Tehran," when everything had fallen apart at the end.[41]

Even the Bible had not been able to bring both sides together. When

Bahramani had said at their Washington meeting that he was going to bring a Koran for the president, North had decided to reciprocate with a Bible for the Iranians with a suitable inscription in the handwriting of President Reagan. He chose a passage, Galatians 3:8, which read: "And the Scripture, foreseeing that God would justify the Gentiles by faith, preached the gospel beforehand to Abraham, saying, 'All the nations shall be blessed in you.' "[42] The passage was intended to show how much Moslems and Christians had in common.

As North presented the Bible, he said these words:

> We inside our Government had an enormous debate, a very angry debate inside our government over whether or not my President should authorize me to say, "We accept the Islamic Revolution of Iran as a fact . . ." He [the president] went off one whole weekend and prayed about what the answer should be and he came back almost a year ago with that passage I gave you that he wrote in front of the Bible I gave you. And he said to me, "This is the promise that God gave to Abraham. Who am I to say that we should not do this?"[43]

When North was asked about this and other statements which he had made to the Iranians in Frankfurt and elsewhere, he said that "they were blatantly false" and that "I lied every time I met the Iranians."[44] It was as if he thought that his lies would never catch up with him and that lies could be made the foundation of a "long-term strategic relationship."

Other matters dealt with at Frankfurt concerned Ghorbanifar and Iraq's Saddam Hussein. According to North's notebook, the Iranian side said: "Gorba & Israel must be out. We cannot be sure that Israel will be fully out. In a near term—must keep Gorba [from] going public." As before, Iraq's ruler was a particular Iranian bugbear and it was emphasized that "an honorable peace means that Saddam Hussein must go."[45]

3

The crisis of the second day was made all the worse by something totally unforeseen by either side. It added a still more extraordinary episode to the annals of American intercourse with other countries.

North had flown to Frankfurt on October 5, 1986. On that very day, the plane carrying Eugene Hasenfus was shot down, and he was captured by the Nicaraguan Sandinistas the next day.

This coincidence brought the Iran and contra affairs together as never before. North received word of the Hasenfus debacle on the second day of the meeting, October 7, and immediately made plans to leave for Washington.

This abrupt departure required some more tall stories. North explained to the Iranians that he was forced to leave for Iceland "to meet with the President this afternoon" and then "go down south." He suggested November 2 or 3 for another meeting.[46] To Hakim, North said that he had to meet with the president in Washington.[47]

Shortly afterward, Secord announced that he had to leave briefly for a business meeting in Brussels. Cave also left. Only Hakim remained— a recently naturalized American citizen who had spent most of his life in Iran, a businessman admittedly out to make as much personal profit as possible, without even as much unofficial status as Secord.

It was Hakim's great moment. It was also a reductio ad absurdum of the entire affair. Hakim says that he was told by North to continue negotiating with the Iranians, but that North gave him a deadline of only the six hours it would take North to get to Washington to come up with "something acceptable" or North was going to put an end to the Second Channel.[48] Before leaving, however, Secord had given him advice on what to do about North's seven-point proposal, of which Secord did not approve. Secord wrote down six points that went far beyond North's seven:

[1]—[North's] List will be seen as disengenuous [sic], i.e., dishonest
[2]—US interests are only strategic
[3]—Hostages are of no value to Iran
[4]—US already pressing Kuwait; will not tie this to US hostages
[5]—As I said in Brussels, US will fight Russians in Iran in case of invasion with or without gov't of Iran assistance
[6]—We will cooperate to depose S. Hussein[49]

Just as North had done, Secord was now making American policy out of his own head. Whatever the dubious authority of North's proposal, it was at least presented by someone in an official capacity, as Secord and Hakim were not. The United States had put such stress on the hostages that its interests could not be said to be "only strategic." Nor was the United States "pressing Kuwait." But the fifth point was the most extravagant. It committed the United States to a war against the Soviet Union whether the Iranian government wanted American intervention or not. Point six went much further than North's, who had merely called Saddam Hussein a bad name; Secord's version implicitly made the United States an ally of Iran in achieving the deposition of the Iraqi chieftain.

Hakim was asked by an incredulous senator about the last two points:

Senator Sam Nunn: But did we tell them if the Russians invaded we are going to basically defend them whether the Iranian Government cooperated or not?

Hakim: That, I believe, was discussed not in a way to threaten the Iranians, rather as a U.S. policy that led the Iranians to believe that the United States had a policy that if ever the Russians tried to invade Iran because of the geopolitical importance of Iran, the United States would fight the Russians there.

Nunn: And that is put forth as the policy of the United States?

Hakim: That was set forth to lead the Iranians to believe that that was the policy.

Nunn: Did you think it was then an effort to deceive Iran? Were you trying to deceive them or did you really believe this was the policy of the United States?

Hakim: I could not tell sir. But—

Nunn: What about—

Hakim: I don't know what was is the policy.

Nunn: The next point, "we will cooperate to depose Hassan [sic]." Was that put forth to deceive the Iranians or was that what you understood our policy to be?

Hakim: I really don't know. If I have to—and I am trying to recall the circumstances—if I have to guess I would say that it was more along the lines of deceiving the Iranians.[50]

Another senator asked Secord general questions about his authority to make national policy:

> *Senator David L. Boren:* Did you not wake up some mornings and think, how did I, as a private individual, start exercising all this responsibility to make foreign policy of the United States of America in lieu of the Congress, the Secretary of State, the President of the United States, members of the National Security Council? Did you not have even a moment of humility about your judgment in sub-stituting yourself for the constitutional process of this country?
>
> *Secord:* I don't agree with what you are saying about what I did. I thought I was doing the right things at the time, but I can tell you I was troubled all along the way, troubled all along the way.[51]

For both Secord and Hakim, it seemed enough that they had the authority of North, who, they assumed, spoke for the president.

Alone, Hakim worked out a new agreement with Samii, who had now apparently taken command for the Iranians. They had before them North's original seven points, and Hakim had Secord's six points. With North's deadline of six hours pressing Hakim, they managed to put together an agreement of nine instead of seven points. Hakim's nine points, in his own translation from the original Farsi, read:

1. Iran provides funds to Mr. Hakim for 500 TOWs and, if willing, Iranians will provide for the HAWK spare parts which remain from the previous agreement.

2. Nine working days from now the 500 TOWs and the HAWK spare parts (if accepted by Iran) and the gifted medicines will be delivered to Iran.

3. Before executing Item 4 below, Albert [Hakim] will provide the plan for the release of the Kuwaitis [seventeen persons].

4. 1½ (1 definitely and the 2nd with all effective possible effort) American hostages in Lebanon, through the effort of Iran, will be released by the Lebanese.

5. Using the Letter of Credit method (three to four days after delivery of shipment stipulated in Item 2) additional 500 TOWs (together with a maximum of 100 launchers), within four days after the execution of Item 4 above, will be delivered to Iran. The method of Letter of Credit will be reviewed between Albert [Hakim] and [Ali Samii] by tomorrow night. Iran will pay the funds for 1500 TOWs (the 500 TOWs mentioned above plus an additional 1000 TOWs) and the 1000 TOWs will be delivered to Iran within nine days.

6. The United States will with the technical support of the HAWKs (material and know-how), update of the military intelligence and maps, establishment and commissioning of the special communication link.

7. Before the return of Mr. [Samii] to Tehran, the subject of the Moslem prisoners (Shia) in Lebanon and the manner of their release by the involved parties will be reviewed by Mr. Secord.

8. Iran will continue its effort for creating the grounds for the release of the rest of the hostages.

9. The steps for delivery of items referred to in the second part of Item 6 above will start.[52]

Some of Hakim's nine points were obviously based on North's seven points but made them more explicit. The main differences came in Hakim's points 3 and 4. In point 3, he promised to provide a plan for the release of the seventeen Kuwaiti prisoners, which North had refrained from doing. In point 4, he agreed to the release of "one and one-half" American hostages instead of all the hostages, as demanded by North. Both plans were clearly arms-for-hostages deals, with the arms to go to Iran before any hostages came back to the Americans.

As Hakim later told the story, the one and one-half hostages baffled North. Hakim had quickly called North's secretary, Fawn Hall, with the good news about his agreement with the Iranians and was told that North had called from the airport and was on the way to his office. Hakim called again and this time talked to North, but lack of a secure connection inhibited him. "I could not compromise our telephone conversation," Hakim recalled. "I tried to talk to him in riddles and he couldn't understand it, especially when I said we have agreed on one and a half hostages, he thought I was drunk."[53]

Hakim explained in greater detail:

> He [North] said, "Are you drinking?" I said, "No, I am not drinking, that is what it is." He was very frustrated. The man hadn't slept for a long time, just caught him as he landed. I said, "Ollie, wait until we send you a god-damned message." Richard [Secord] came in later and had to explain the concept behind the nine points. We sent the message. Richard kept on saying, "Albert, the more I read this package of yours, the more I like it, and it is even better than the seven points that Ollie put together."[54]

Hakim was inordinately proud of his diplomatic triumph. He was questioned about it by the Senate committee's chief counsel, Arthur L. Liman:

> *Liman:* When you were told that this agreement that you had negotiated had been approved by the President of the United States, you must have felt very proud?
>
> *Hakim:* I felt proud throughout, sir. I felt proud being part of the team.
>
> *Liman:* Did you feel like you had been the Secretary of State for a day?
>
> *Hakim:* I would not accept that position for any money in the world, sir.
>
> *Liman:* Well, you had it better than the Secretary of State in some sense. You didn't have to get confirmed; correct?
>
> *Hakim:* I still believe that I have it better than the Secretary.
>
> *Liman:* And—
>
> *Hakim:* I can achieve more, too.
>
> *Liman:* And if this initiative had succeeded, did you ever make any calculation as to how much you and General Secord would make?
>
> *Hakim:* In what period of time, sir?
>
> *Liman:* People tend to think in terms of three-to-five-year plans.
>
> *Hakim:* Many millions.

Liman: Did it bother you at all that here you—and I say it respect-fully—a private citizen was left with this kind of task of negotiating an agreement in which if it succeeded, you stood to benefit very substantially?

Hakim: Mr. Liman, what bothered me was that we didn't have the competence within the Government to do what I could do. That still bothers me. [55]

North also admired Hakim's handiwork. He adopted the nine points when he understood that the one and one-half hostages meant one hostage to be certainly released and another possibly. Once North received word from Secord and Hakim that an agreement had been reached with the Iranians, he recovered his nerve, which had virtually deserted him in Frankfurt. Instead, he gave Poindexter a report which hid the true dimensions of the trouble he had had with the Iranians and made it seem that he had come out the victor.

> Copp [Secord] has just returned from Frankfurt. According to both he [sic] and Sam [Hakim], my donkey act with [Bahramani and Samii] had quite an effect. [Samii] told Dick [Secord] that if he returned home without the hope of further help that he "would be sent back to the front." [Samii] gave Dick a proposal closer to the line in my original seven points and asked Dick if there was any way that he could get us to meet before the 3 Nov. meeting I had suggested.

This version of what had occurred in Frankfurt was largely imaginary. North's "donkey act" had not impressed the Iranians and had brought the meeting to a virtual breakdown. It had been salvaged by Hakim, who had made the necessary concessions to the Iranians, but not by an Iranian proposal closer to North's seven points. Nor was this proposal given to Secord. North later admitted that he had lied to the Iranians, to Secord, and to Congress. [56] He might also have admitted lying to his immediate superior, Poindexter.

After this preliminary falsification, North still kept back from Poindexter that the Iranians had agreed to a nine-point, not a seven-point, plan. He led Poindexter to believe that the agreement provided for:

1. They pay $3.6M[illion] next week.
2. We deliver 500 TOWs (no Hawk parts) 9 days after payment.
3. Copp & Sam [Secord and Hakim] help prepare a plan for approaching the Kuwaitis to guarantee no more terrorism against the Amir and by which the Amir will use a religious occasion to release some of the Da'wa. They will take this plan to

the Hizballah as their idea (face saving gesture w[ith] the Hizb[allah]).

4. Two hostages (if possible, but no less than one) released w[ith]in four days of TOW delivery. If only one hostage released, whole process stops and we meet again.
5. Repeat funding and Delivery cycle as in steps 1 & 2 above.
6. We send Tech[nical] support for Hawks, update on intel[ligence] and secure comm[unications] team to Tehran and provide location/availability of artillery items noted on the original list provided by [the Relative] in Washington mtg [meeting].
7. Iran does utmost to secure release of remaining hostages.

These terms clearly differed from those negotiated by Hakim. In the latter, nothing was said about an Iranian payment of $3.6 million a week later, only that Iran would pay Hakim for 500 TOWs. A U.S. delivery of 500 TOWs nine days afterward was substituted for a delivery of 500 TOWs plus Hawk spare parts and a gift of medicines. Hakim's obligation to produce a plan for the release of the Da'wa prisoners in Kuwait was transformed into a more detailed plan, first advanced as a hypothetical suggestion by North in Frankfurt without getting any particular Iranian reaction. Whatever the trimmings, this was still a sequential arms-for-hostages deal, in which North had so little confidence that he put in a provision for starting it all over again if it failed. By this time, the Lebanese captors had taken four American hostages, of whom North was willing to settle for one definitely and at best two. In fact, North told Poindexter that Secord and Hakim had been advised that the Lebanese group holding Reed and Cicippio "is not responsive to Iran," in which case an arms-for-hostages deal for them through Iran was not even feasible.

North devoted the rest of his report to Poindexter on the Frankfurt meeting to urging him to accept the alleged agreement. North pretended that the only changes from his original seven-point proposal were the sequential nature of the arms-hostage exchange and the omission of getting back Buckley's body and interrogation transcript. North also emphasized that he was not alone in advocating the so-called Iranian plan. Both Secord and Hakim, he said, wanted "to let them stew in Tehran for a few more days" and then accept the plan. Casey and Cave were said to be convinced that "this is best/fastest way to get two more out—probably w[ithin] next 14 days." Twetten was cited as thinking that no time was to be lost, because "the situation in Leb[anon] is getting much worse and that we may be getting close to the end of the line for any further movement."

North himself ended with these words:

BOTTOM LINE: Recommend that we wait for their call on Tuesday, if their position is same as above or better, we sh[oul]d push them to include Buckley remains and transcript and then get on with it. Pl[ea]s[e] advise.[57]

North later testified that he had sought and had received approval of the nine points from Poindexter, though he had not told him that Hakim, not he, had negotiated them.[58] In the end, North admitted that he may have been "most injudicious," but he maintained that Hakim's financial interest in a successful agreement offered an even greater chance for ultimate success.[59]

North had most trouble defending the provision about the Da'wa prisoners. He first did so on the ground that the commitment had been made by Hakim, not by the United States, as if the Iranians had not been given reason to believe that Hakim was negotiating on behalf of the United States.*[60] North also contended that he had advocated the release of the Da'wa prisoners because "it is a simple fact of reality that there will come a time when those 17 will be released."[61] It was not clear why Hakim's commitment and North's acceptance of it were justified by an alleged eventual release of the Da'wa prisoners that might be years away, if ever.

Poindexter also defended the Da'wa agreement by disassociating Secord, whom Poindexter identified with it, from the United States. As Poindexter understood it, "General Secord was to come up with a plan which he could give the Iranians that the Iranians could execute, not that the U.S. Government would do it or not even that General Secord would actually do anything." Yet Poindexter agreed that he had understood that "General Secord was acting in this venture at the request of the United States, namely the NSC."[62] The idea seemed to be to make the Iranians believe they were getting a serious commitment from an authorized representative of the United States but in reality to make the commitment an inconsequential, purely personal one by Hakim or Secord.

Poindexter was asked what President Reagan knew about the nine points. First, Poindexter made a general statement: "I always briefed the President on the results of the discussions, and discussed the possibilities for next steps and got his approval for the major next steps that we took at various times." Later, Poindexter was more definite—that when North came back "and we got to the nine points, I discussed those with the President, and he approved the ones that applied to the U.S. Government." The exception was the point about the Da'wa prisoners, which Poindexter claimed had been a "private arrangement" by Secord and Hakim. In fact, Poindexter considered the nine points to be "operative" until his departure from the White House at the end of November 1986.[63]

Whatever may have been the irregular origin of the nine points, they

---

* North later admitted that Hakim had been "left as the only U.S. negotiator for the agreement that was ultimately agreed upon by the Iranians and the United States" (100-7, Part II, p. 6).

had been accepted—with one exception—by President Reagan, Poindexter, and North. Poindexter also added "Bill Casey, Bill Casey's people at the Agency" among those who had gone along with the nine points.[64] In the end, Hakim had not done so badly.

At this very time, the question of exchanging three U.S. hostages for the seventeen Da'wa prisoners in Kuwait came up as a result of an article in *Newsweek* magazine entitled "America's Forgotten Hostages?" Despite the commitment by Hakim, whom the Iranians had considered an official U.S. representative, to provide a plan for the release of all seventeen Da'wa prisoners, a White House "press guidance" on October 14, 1986, seemed to repudiate any such effort:

> The question is not whether we would seek the release of 3 or 17 prisoners. We will not negotiate the exchange of innocent Americans for the release from prison of tried and convicted murderers held in a third country. Nor will we pressure other nations to do so. To make such concessions would jeopardize the safety of other American citizens and would only encourage more terrorism.[65]

It may well be that this "press guidance" was written and approved by officials who had never heard of the nine points. The "compartmentation" characteristic of this operation presented a constant risk of conflicting approaches.

4

In October 1986, the Iran operation began to approach a climax. North had been given another license—the nine points—to negotiate a new arms-for-hostages deal. Other forces, however, began to work against him.

The first break in the North-Poindexter-Casey front threatened to come from the CIA. Whatever misgivings there may have been, no one in the CIA or NSC staff had previously challenged the validity of the operation. Apparently the first one to do so, however tentatively, was Charles E. Allen, the CIA's national intelligence officer for counterterrorism. He had joined the CIA in 1958 immediately after graduating from college and had spent most of a professional career of almost thirty years in the Agency. He had worked closely with North since 1981, soon after North had come onto the NSC staff.

Allen had been temporarily injected into the Iran affair by North at an early stage in September 1985, when North had asked him to work up an intelligence study of two Iranians, one of whom was Manucher Ghorbanifar.[66] Allen's role was marginal until, in January 1986, he was asked by Director Casey to meet with Ghorbanifar and find out all he knew about terrorism.[67] Thereafter, Allen had served as Casey's watchdog in the Iran-hostage operation, while recognizing that the CIA's role was one of operational support for North.

When Allen had met with Ghorbanifar for five hours on January 13, the latter had given him his standard "sales pitch," as Allen later called it.[68] Ghorbanifar said that he merely wanted to find support to change the extremist, hard-line Iranian regime. He was willing to help with freeing the American hostages, thwarting Iranian, Libyan, and Syrian terrorism, and overthrowing the Libyan leader, Muammar al-Qaddafi. He had convinced Iranian Prime Minister Moussavi and Oil Minister Aqazadeh to trust the United States, with Israel acting as an intermediary. In fact, they owed him money, and one high Iranian official had been photographed "in compromising situations with Western women." They had been ready to accept U.S. assistance, military advice, and an unofficial U.S. presence in Tehran, but had been held back by the cheating "thing"—the wrong missiles at four times the proper price—the previous November. Yet Ghorbanifar had made the release of the hostages seem simple if only a satisfactory U.S.-Iran agreement could be reached. Prime Minister Moussavi had only to issue an order for the hostages to be freed. But he could also have them killed if there was no agreement. Last but not least, Ghorbanifar had stated that he and "his organization" should be handsomely rewarded with millions of U.S. dollars in return for warning of and assisting in the prevention of terrorist attacks, especially on Gulf state leaders. The figure of $100 million was apparently mentioned, to be split in various ways.

Allen was not unimpressed with Ghorbanifar. He regarded him as "a highly energetic, excitable individual who possesses an extraordinarily strong ego that must be carefully fed." He gave Ghorbanifar credit for apparently having influence over or business arrangements with a substantial number of individuals in the Middle East, Europe, and Iran itself. According to Allen, the CIA had "hard evidence" that Ghorbanifar was close to the prime minister, the oil minister, and other senior officials in Iran. Allen recommended that more meetings should be held with Ghorbanifar to determine "all aspects of the plot."[69]

More than anyone else in the CIA, Allen had been in a position to know what North and Ghorbanifar had been up to. Allen had spent so much time talking with and reporting on Ghorbanifar that Clair George, the CIA's deputy director for operations, had said to Allen that he was essentially Ghorbanifar's "case officer."[70] Nir and Ledeen were others whom Allen dealt with, and for a time Nir was cut off from North and could get in touch only with Allen. If anyone outside of North's inner circle had reason to know what was going on, it was Allen.

Thus Allen had about six months of intimate involvement and observation of North's operation before it began to trouble him. Allen says that he first felt that something was "amiss" in late August 1986 as a

result of the imbroglio with the microfiches and the security problem
resulting from the effort to shuck off Ghorbanifar, who was demanding
to be paid. At that time, he had first confided his doubts to Deputy
Director of Intelligence Richard Kerr, as a result of which Kerr had said
"it's not a matter of whether it's going to be exposed but when." Allen
says he had replied that "it's going to be extremely messy if there is
something amiss about the operation."[71] His suspicions had been aroused
mainly by North's insistence on misleading the Iranians by fabricating a
new and higher price list.[72] Allen said that the prominent roles of Secord
and Hakim had also begun to bother him.[73] Everyone—Allen included
Ghorbanifar, Nir, Secord, and Hakim—seemed to be charging such
exorbitant prices that he came to suspect just what North was most anxious
to hide. "I began to think," Allen said, "that perhaps the additional
charges were being made of the Iranian middle man and financiers to
cover costs of supporting the contras in Central America."[74] Allen says
that he had talked to Cave, who was also worried, about something being
amiss "and maybe something was happening in respect to the contras."[75]

By making this connection, Allen was treading on the most dangerous
ground in North's dual operations. He says that he came to North on
September 9 and "pointedly said you've opened up a second channel.
You've shut down the first channel. And you've got creditors out there
yelling for $10 million, $11 million. What are we going to do about it?"
Allen added:

And he said something, well, maybe we'll have to take it out of
the reserve. That was a devastating statement to me.[76]

Yet Allen had not asked North what "reserve" he had had in mind.
Allen later said that he had thought it might have come from the Israelis.[77]
By not asking further questions, Allen missed an opportunity to learn
about the Secord-Hakim secret accounts in Geneva, basically controlled
by North.

On October 1, however, Allen acted more decisively. He went to see
Robert M. Gates, McMahon's successor as the CIA's deputy director, to
bring him up to date on the First and Second Channels. Allen related:

I went over the original channel and my whole concern of the
operational security as an intelligence officer. I went through all
the reasons why this thing seemed to be going off the rails, that we
were reaching some very serious decision points, that the first channel had not been satisfied, and that millions of dollars were owed
to creditors.

I said that this was going to be quite a disaster. I said there is a
pricing impasse that has occurred and it's been going on—and he,

I think, had some general awareness of this, not any detailed awareness—and that I feared that this issue would blow up.

And also at the end of the conversation I said I can't prove it,
but based just on the indicators I've come [to] sort of an analytical
judgment that money was perhaps being diverted to the contras,
that the pricing impasse has occurred because the United States,
believe it or not, was actually overcharging the middlemen in these
transactions.

Allen continued with Gates's reaction:

And I remember he was very startled at this. He started to laugh
because it sounded absurd, but then he became very serious and
said, well, that would be a very serious thing. Operationally, you
can't commingle two operations. You can't commingle this operation with our duties in Central America, that this was very serious,
that in the past he had admired Colonel North because of his work
in crisis management and things of this nature, but that this was
going too far, and asked that I see the Director.[78]

Gates remembered that Allen had come to him with two main concerns, the security problem and the contra diversion, the latter at the
very end of the conversation. By the time Gates testified, the second was
stressed more than the first. Gates recalled:

He wanted to bring to my attention intelligence information that
he had received or been looking at that led him to believe that the
operational security of the Iranian initiative was in jeopardy and,
finally, to express his concern over a development that he or—he
wanted to inform me of his speculation, looking at the intelligence,
that there might have been a diversion of money from the Iranian
affair to Central America.

He acknowledged that he didn't have any evidence of such a
diversion and no indication that there was any involvement by a
U.S. person or persons in the activity or in what he was thinking
about. It was just that between the overcharging that he saw in the
intelligence materials and the cheating that he perceived was going
on and the fact that there were—and I should have said earlier U.S.
Government persons—and the fact that some of the players in the
Iranian affair were also active in support of the contras, he was
concerned that some of that money might be going.[79]

Gates claimed that he had known "the basic outlines of what was
happening in terms of the arms," but little about the intermediaries, such

as Secord. After Gates had urged Allen to tell what he knew or suspected to Casey, the three of them met on October 7.

One of the critical dates in this story was October 7, 1986. Two things that happened on that day were potentially explosive.

5

The first thing that happened on October 7 was that Roy M. Furmark—the American business associate of Adnan Khashoggi—came to see William Casey.

Furmark had been getting damaging inside information on the Iran arms deals from Khashoggi and Ghorbanifar. Back in June, Khashoggi had told him that he had given Ghorbanifar $15 million as "bridge financing" for the arms—to pay the Americans until Iran paid Ghorbanifar—and had not received any of it back from Ghorbanifar. Khashoggi said he was worried and asked Furmark to "stay on top with Ghorbanifar" to find out what was happening.[80] In July and August, Furmark understood that Ghorbanifar had paid Khashoggi with three checks for $1 million, $11 million, and $5 million for a total of $17 million. Of this sum, $10 million was supposed to go to two Canadians and $6 million to someone else who had lent Khashoggi the money to give to Ghorbanifar. Khashoggi had apparently paid off the $6 million but not the $10 million. Ghorbanifar was in deep trouble, according to Furmark, because he had given Khashoggi worthless checks.[81] Furmark's financial testimony is a tangle of figures, which do not always fit together, except that they showed something was dreadfully wrong with Khashoggi's and Ghorbanifar's finances.[82]

When Furmark saw Ghorbanifar in July and August, the latter was cracking under the strain. Furmark recalled:

> I believe that it was during this period of time that he went—I'm told to Tehran, then to Damascus, then to Beirut to accelerate or to assist in getting the release of Father Jenco because he knew unless a hostage was out, Khashoggi would get no more money, no more shipment and Khashoggi would be out his money. He was taking medication, high blood pressure, pains—he was in terrible, terrible shape with the pressure because here, you know, Khashoggi, who he had developed a relationship with, was out $15 million.[83]

At some time in this period, Ghorbanifar is said to have been hospitalized in London.[84] Meanwhile, Ghorbanifar gave Furmark his version of why he was in such grave trouble—the overpricing of 300 to 600 percent on the arms to Iran, the telltale microfiches, 63 Hawk parts that were defective with a value of $3 million, 299 parts never delivered with a value of $7.1 million, and, above all, that he was being cut out. Furmark added, as if it were an afterthought: "He made the comment, you know, some of the funds may have gone to the contras."[85]

Thus by October the diversion had come up twice—once from Allen to Gates and again from Ghorbanifar to Furmark. The latter was more dangerous, because it meant that Ghorbanifar, who had—according to North—helped to hatch the idea of the diversion in the first place, now had a power of blackmail over the entire operation.

Khashoggi was so worried that he asked Furmark to see Casey to straighten out the mess: "You got to complete the contract so Ghorbanifar can be paid by Iran so Khashoggi can get his money, and that is the basis of [my] going to see Casey."[86]

Furmark had known Casey through a mutual friend, John Shaheen, Furmark's former employer and Casey's old comrade-in-arms from the OSS days and a client of Casey's law firm. Furmark said that he had seen Casey last at Shaheen's funeral in November 1985 and apparently had no trouble getting to see him.

The meeting with Casey lasted about half an hour. Furmark's version is:

> I said I was there at the request of Mr. Adnan Khashoggi and I said that he had been doing the bridge financing for Ghorbanifar in the transaction involving Iran, and that Mr. Ghorbanifar was now out of the picture. I explained to him the bridge financing mechanism and that Mr. Khashoggi can only be paid if the Americans deliver the rest of the goods, and then Iran will pay Mr. Ghorbanifar into his account and then Khashoggi will be paid.

Furmark continued in a more alarming vein:

> I told him that it [the Canadians] was in Khashoggi's mind. Khashoggi had financed it through Canadians, which is what I was told, and I told him that Ghorbanifar was thinking of talking to some members of the intelligence committee. I mentioned two names. I mentioned Senator Moynihan and Senator Leahy.

If Furmark can be believed, Casey did not give anything away:

> I had mentioned that the money was paid into Lake Resources, and he said he never heard of that account. He said I don't think it is one of our accounts. He said this is not my operation. Sounds like it is an Israeli operation. Then I told him that it was being handled by North, and he said, well, I will look into it, and then he got on the phone. He was going to call Poindexter and have him come over and Poindexter was not there.

As Furmark was leaving, Casey asked him to "see one of my guys and give them all the details of everything that you know about it, which I said I would do."[87] As for the operation itself, Casey obviously knew better than to attribute it solely to the Israelis.

We have Casey's memorandum of his meeting with Furmark. It provides some additional details and shows that Casey was apparently most worried about the Canadian involvement:

> 1. A New York man whom I haven't seen in some years came in to tell me that he is currently working for Adnan Khashoggi and is involved in transactions involving Iran.
>
> 2. Khashoggi apparently got some Canadian investors to put $15 million into a company called Lake Resources which was to acquire goods for shipment to Iran. The Canadians are said to have put up their money as a loan which was repayable in 30 days. As of now they have been waiting five months for their money and are very close to doing something to recover money put up since May 15 without any collateral or signatures. Credit Suisse in Geneva is in some way involved in this. Khashoggi put the group of Canadians together but feels their panic about their money is such that he will not be able to control it for long. He believes that members of the Canadian group have been talking to [Senators] Leahy, Cranston and Moynihan. They are claiming that the latest shipment was $10 million short because 63 pieces were defective and 299 were missing.
>
> 3. The final message was that the only way to handle this matter is to supply the rest of the equipment or agree on a refund of X number of dollars or repay $10 million.[88]

Furmark later said that he had told Casey that the loan from the Canadians was long overdue, not that it was repayable in thirty days, and not that it was without any collateral. Furmark also claimed that he had said that Ghorbanifar "was talking about talking" to the three senators, not that the Canadians were talking to them, and that the Canadians had put in $10 million, not $15 million.[89]

But Casey was now forewarned. Furmark should have been enough to set alarm bells ringing.

6

If Furmark was not enough, Allen should have been more than enough.

After Furmark had left on October 7, Allen and Gates came to see Casey. According to Allen, his purpose had been to inform him of the operational security aspects of this initiative and the fact that this program was spinning out of control and to tell him also of the potential—just sheer speculation at that point; we had no evidence—that money might have been diverted to the contras in Central America.

Allen said that Gates had chimed in, "saying yes, Charlie had raised this issue with him and that this was an issue of real concern if there was any truth in it."

Casey did not give anything away even to his closest associates:

> He seemed very surprised. He said he had just had a call from Mr. Furmark. Mr. Furmark had come down and had talked to him about some of the problems relating to the initiative. And he said yes, there's a real security issue involved here, and he asked me. At that stage I said all this troubles me greatly, and he directed that I prepare a memorandum that would lay out the concerns and he said that he had talked to Admiral Poindexter after Mr. Furmark. . . .
>
> He asked me—he just mentioned Mr. Furmark was an old friend at that stage. He was a man with whom he had done business ten or so years ago, that he had not seen Mr. Furmark in five or six years, and that he thought Mr. Furmark was a very straightforward, reliable man. That's what he said, sir.[*90]

Casey informed them that he had told Poindexter on the phone that "there was a real problem in the repayment of the creditors and that Adnan Khashoggi was a creditor, and that he had borrowed money from some Canadians and this was a very serious issue." Casey said two other striking things. One was something about "his admiration for Colonel North as a man that gets things done, but that this was going too far, if this was true." The other was that he had told Poindexter "you've got to get the White House counsel involved, and Admiral Poindexter said I don't know that I can trust the White House counsel."[91]

This hostile reference to the White House counsel, Peter Wallison, was later borne out by the way he was treated. One thing Casey did not tell Allen and Gates was that Furmark had already spoken to him about the possible diversion.[92]

On October 9, Nir called Allen. Nir's news was ominous.

---

[*] Another version by Allen reads: "I also raised the issue of diversion to the contras, and Mr. Casey at that stage said Mr. Furmark has just talked to me, and he didn't talk about the contras, but he talked about the problems of the Canadian investors, and that they are threatening to take law suits to try to take some action" (TB, p. B-168).

The purpose is to just say the situation is very bad relating to Mr. Ghorbanifar, the financing—his finances, repayment of creditors— and a warning, in essence, a very serious warning that Mr. Ghorbanifar is a man who is not easily reckoned with, that he will take his revenge, that he will not stand in awe of the United States, that he believed he had been hurt and that his whole financial status, his legal status, was in question and that something had to be done. It was a rather serious call.[93]

The combination of Furmark, Allen, and Nir on October 7 and 9 was fair warning that the operation was "spinning out of control" and needed immediate, drastic action to get back "on track." Yet nothing of the sort happened.

Still on October 9, Casey and Gates had lunch with North to be debriefed on the latter's meeting in Frankfurt.[94] The meeting provided an opportunity to ask North about the allegations made by Furmark and Allen. Now, again, the contra affair intersected with the Iran affair. Eugene Hasenfus had been shot down in northern Nicaragua four days earlier and had publicly declared that he had been working for the CIA. As a result, the discussion in Casey's office touched on both affairs.

According to Gates, North told them about his meetings with the Iranians, and Casey talked about Furmark's allegations about the unhappy investors and Allen's problem of operational security. North betrayed no sign of disquiet. "He didn't fall over backward in his chair and say that's the most horrible thing I've ever heard." The matter of the diversion of Iran money to the contras was never raised. As for the Hasenfus incident, North assured them that no CIA assets, directly or indirectly, were in any way implicated.

North also made a mysterious reference to "Swiss bank accounts." Neither Casey nor Gates picked it up, but Gates later went back to Casey's office and said: "You know, he [North] made some strange reference or whatever to Swiss bank accounts and the contras. Is there anything there that we should be worried about or that we should be concerned about?" Casey, it seemed, had not even paid attention, had looked at Gates quizzically, and had waved off North's unguarded remark. Gates saw no reason to pursue the matter.[95]

The impression left by Gates's account is that Casey and North were remarkably unperturbed at this meeting. North made his usual disclaimers, and no one tried to get anything more out of him.

Yet something may have gone on between Casey and North privately, because North later said that Casey had told him in early October, soon after Furmark's visit and the Hasenfus shoot-down, "that things ought to be 'cleaned up,' and I started cleaning things up." If so, Casey had been holding out on his deputy, Gates.

On October 7, Allen had said to Casey: "I think I should put all my troubles down in a memorandum," but he put it off for several days and did not present it until October 14.[96] This memorandum, sent to Casey and Gates, made the "troubles" even more pressing, because they were now down on paper and could not be treated as lightly as oral statements. The main points in this lengthy, seven-page paper were:

> Ghorbanifar and his creditors, including Adnan Khashoggi, appear determined to recoup their "losses," even at the risk of exposing US covert arms shipments in exchange for release of our hostages.
>
> We have a festering sore for which no treatment has been prescribed. . . .
>
> Ghorbanifar claims to have secreted, for "insurance purposes," documentation of events which have transpired so far.
>
> Given this, the major elements of this initiative are likely to be exposed soon unless remedial action is taken. There is no indication that the White House has a plan to prevent the exposure or a plan to deal with the potential exposure. . . .
>
> Ghorbanifar is depressed and claims his financial situation has been damaged. On several occasions, he has said he would not sit idly by and permit himself to be made the "fall guy" in this matter. He claims to have given written accounts of all that has transpired to several persons in America and Europe. He has directed these individuals to make this material available to the press in the event that "something bad" befalls him. . . .
>
> We face a disaster of major proportions in our efforts with Iran despite the apparent promise of the Hakim-[deleted] channel. Too many know too much, and exposure, at a minimum, would damage the new channel badly, perhaps fatally. . . .
>
> [Ghorbanifar would reveal that] the Government of the United States, along with the Government of Israel, acquired a substantial profit from these transactions, some of which profit was redistributed to other projects of the US and of Israel.

Allen made some recommendations for action, "because the risk of exposure is growing daily":

> (A) *Establish a Senior-Level Planning Cell at the White House* to focus on the potential for Rapprochement [sic] with Iran, the appropriate channels to be used, and the separation of the tactical hostage issue from the long-term strategic objective.
>
> This group could consist of two or three experts and should be

headed by someone with the stature of a Henry Kissinger, a Hal Saunders, a Don Rumsfeld, or a Dick Helms.*

(B) *Devise Press Guidance in the Event of an Exposure.* . . .

(C) *Effect an Orderly, Damage-Limiting Shutdown of the Ghorbanifar-[deleted] Channel.* . . .[97]

Allen considered this memorandum so explosive that he gave it to Gates instead of to Casey on October 15. Allen explained:

I took it, the original, to Mr. Gates' office, Eyes Only, to his secretary on the morning of the 15th and I said I have a very exceedingly sensitive memorandum. I said I didn't want to give it directly to Mr. Casey because I wasn't certain what he would do with it. I wanted Mr. Gates to look at it carefully first and decide what to do with it.

I said Mr. Casey might go down and just hand it to someone at the White House straight away, and I said there's a lot of potentially explosive material in this memorandum, and I kept calling. And then I found out later, on the 16th, I was called by Mr. Casey and Mr. Gates and they said that not only had they read the memorandum on the 15th, that Gates had taken the original in, and Mr. Casey and Mr. Gates had called Admiral Poindexter immediately after reading it and set up a meeting.

They took it down and not only let Admiral Poindexter read it, but they gave it to him. And I said, oh, my God. If I'm wrong in this, Colonel North will never speak to me again. And he says, well, we don't think it's that kind of memorandum to find fault. We think it was a good memorandum.

They said Admiral Poindexter read it carefully, asked who wrote it. They told him that I wrote it and Admiral Poindexter said he would study it. And that was on the morning of the 16th, I guess.[98]

Allen's memorandum *was* exceedingly sensitive and potentially explosive. It was not as explosive as it might have been, because Allen had alluded only in a very general and rather cryptic way to the possible diversion of Iranian funds to the Nicaraguan contras, whereas he had apparently been far more explicit in his talk with Casey on October 7. Apart from this reticence, however, Allen's memorandum could hardly have been more ominous in its implications.

Yet it did not seem to be so ominous to Poindexter when he met with

---

* Henry Kissinger was the former national security adviser and secretary of state; Harold H. (Hal) Saunders was a former assistant secretary of state for the Near East and South Asia; Donald Rumsfeld was a former secretary of defense; and Richard Helms was a former deputy director and director of the CIA.

Casey and Gates on October 15. According to Gates, Poindexter read Allen's memorandum impassively. Casey and Poindexter paid little attention to Allen's suggestion to appoint a panel of "wise men" to look into the Iran operation. Curiously, Gates says that Casey talked about making the entire affair public, and it was possibly on this occasion that Casey suggested getting the White House counsel to review the affair. Poindexter did not take kindly to the idea, and it went no further.

Gates, however, had asked Casey whether he could brief the CIA general counsel, David Doherty, on the entire operation, including everything he had heard from Allen, in order to make sure that "everything was proper, that there were no problems." Casey agreed, whereupon Doherty recommended that the matter should be reviewed by White House Counsel Wallison. This recommendation was not carried out, because Poindexter opposed it, but later Gates again asked Doherty to review the case himself. Gates was told that "he did not believe there were any concerns from a legal or propriety standpoint for CIA."[99]

The week of October 7–15 presents some tantalizing questions about the course of the impending crisis of the Iran and contra operations. Almost nothing was made of this period in the congressional hearings, for one reason because the principal witnesses to the events of that week, Charles Allen and Robert M. Gates, were not asked to testify publicly. Their roles were not known until their private depositions were published months afterward. Poindexter and North, who could have shed some light on this week, were never questioned about it. Casey died without having given anything away. The voluminous Iran-Contra Report of the joint congressional committees ignored this period altogether.

Yet enough had come out in the inner circles of the CIA in those seven days so that the crisis might well have taken a different turn. North and Poindexter had been questioned superficially but had never been pressed for answers to the hard questions. It was enough for Gates that Allen's memorandum had not specifically implicated someone in the U.S. government in the diversion to excuse not raising the question at all.[100] Allen had previously spoken to Gates about a possible diversion in a way that had clearly implicated U.S. government personnel, and even his memorandum had implicated the "White House" in the entire operation.[101] As Gates recalled the episode, Casey acted as if he knew nothing about the diversion, even though, if we can believe North, Casey had been enthusiastic about it and had approved it.[102] According to Gates, Casey had risked blowing the whole thing wide open by making the entire affair public and by asking the White House counsel to review it. According to North, Casey had already told him to hide the evidence by cleaning up his files.

The case of William Casey largely depends on who is to be believed. What is not in doubt is that Casey had enough reason by the first half of October 1986 to institute a full investigation of the revelations by

Furmark, Allen, and Nir—and he did not do so. He was either playacting or already so weakened by illness that he was incapable of facing "a disaster of major proportions."

7

What Casey did was to tell Allen to talk to Furmark, as if Casey did not know enough already.

Allen met with Furmark on October 16. Allen learned that Furmark had known far more about some details of the Ghorbanifar-Khashoggi operation from its inception than Allen or any other American, including North and Secord. Furmark had allegedly been present, with Ghorbanifar and Khashoggi, at the birth of the scheme in the summer of 1985 to get the United States to trade military equipment for the American hostages as a way of reestablishing relations between Washington and Tehran and, incidentally, of opening up a potentially lucrative market for the intermediaries. Allen again heard how Khashoggi owed $10 million to two Canadians, who he now was told had a reputation for "dealing roughly with those who did not meet their obligations." The Canadians had allegedly set a deadline of about October 15 to get some payment on the principal from Khashoggi, or they intended to go to Senators Leahy, Moynihan, and Cranston with the story of the "back-channel deal with Iran and how they have been swindled." Ghorbanifar, with whom Furmark had talked in London for two days the week before, was in a "devastated" condition and did not know how to pull himself together financially. Furmark advised sending more arms to Iran in order to enable Ghorbanifar to borrow more money and possibly achieve the release of additional hostages.

Allen sent Casey another nervous report. He found Furmark's detailed knowledge of Ghorbanifar's affairs "deeply troubling." He predicted that exposure "will almost certainly have a crippling effect on the new channel"—and "the risk of exposure is growing daily." Allen repeated his proposal for the formation of an advisory group to consider how "to cope with this burgeoning problem. If this is not done immediately, I predict an exposure of this activity in the near future." Allen's proposal of an advisory group was clearly a counsel of desperation, as if the mental resources of the government had been totally exhausted and a deus ex machina was required.[103]

Casey knew Furmark well enough for the two of them to fly together to New York on October 16. According to Furmark, they talked about Ghorbanifar's financial woes, Furmark's idea that they could be relieved by enabling Ghorbanifar to get another $5 million from Iran in return for a partial shipment of Hawk parts, their families, and the like. Casey seems to have said little more than that Furmark should "just sit tight," that he was "working on the problem," and "just give me some time."[104]

When Allen briefed Casey on October 22 about his encounter with Furmark, the CIA director told him that Furmark was "trustworthy," thereby making Furmark's dire warnings all the more ominous.[105] On that day, moreover, Furmark gave Allen and Cave even more startling information.

This time the three met at the Hotel Roosevelt in New York. After repeating much of what he had already told them, Furmark said something that Allen noted on a hotel pad: "*Ghorba*—believed $15 m[illion] went to Nicaragua." Furmark added that a "leak would not be good, esp[ecially] for things 'south of the border.' "[106]

Heretofore, Allen had merely suspected that a diversion had occurred. Now for the first time his suspicion seemed to be confirmed. According to Cave, the two of them had been suspicious for some time about the exorbitant prices charged to Iran for the weapons, but Allen had talked openly to him about the possibility of a diversion only after Furmark's remarks on October 22. "And, Furmark pretty much laid out the whole thing," Cave recalled, "in that Ghorbanifar had told him the reason for the high price to him, 15 million dollars was, that was charged to him of 15 million dollars [sic] because the rest of the profits from it were being diverted to the contras."[107]

On October 22, North was still totally befuddled about what the Khashoggi-Furmark-Ghorbanifar problem was. He confided to his notebook:

Adam [Nir] to call Khashoggi
    Find out who is owed what
Very dirty operation
Merchant [Ghorbanifar] says he is personally owed $2M[illion] in
    addition to $10M[illion] for Khashoggi consortium . . .
Best way to recoup funds to pay off Furmark et al is to overcharge
    on subsequent deliveries . . .
Next shipment will have to be higher ($10K [$10,000] each) or we
    cannot do[108]

These comments indicate that North and Nir had been taken in completely by Khashoggi, Ghorbanifar, and Furmark. North and Nir were prepared to overcharge the Iranians for the next shipment of weapons in order to pay Ghorbanifar's putative debts to Khashoggi. Yet North and Nir had no way of finding out how legitimate those debts were or even what they were. They could think of nothing better than to ask Khashoggi, as if he could be trusted to tell them the unvarnished truth.

On October 23, Allen and Cave briefed Casey about what they had heard from Furmark. Casey, according to Allen, was "deeply disturbed." Casey phoned Poindexter, apparently to tell him what had transpired.

Casey also asked Allen and Cave to put Furmark's information in a memorandum, which Casey intended to send to Poindexter.[109]

This memorandum brought Poindexter up to date on Furmark's disclosures—the origins of the Khashoggi-Ghorbanifar plot in 1985, the complex trail of money leading to the two Canadians and their pressure on Khashoggi, Furmark's "solution" to let Ghorbanifar handle the shipment of the remaining Hawk parts.[110]

But the memorandum said nothing about the suspected diversion, though Allen later thought that it had done so.[111] For some reason, this memorandum was never sent, but it was Allen's impression that Casey "had given a lot of warning to Admiral Poindexter that this operation was spinning out of control."[112] Inasmuch as Poindexter had admittedly approved the diversion months earlier, he did not need to get Furmark's confirmation of Allen's suspicion about the diversion.

By the third week of October, more than a month before it was publicly announced by Attorney General Meese, the diversion of Iranian funds to the Nicaraguan contras was no longer a secret limited to North, McFarlane, Secord, and Poindexter. In the CIA, Casey, Allen, and Cave knew about it. North's chief aide, Earl, knew about it.[113] Ghorbanifar, Khashoggi, and Furmark knew about it. Ghorbanifar was allegedly threatening to go to three U.S. senators with the whole story. Yet there is no indication that any of the Americans did anything to forestall the eventual political disaster. The attitude seems to have been that of Casey's "just sit tight" and "give me some time." Instead, North was still hell-bent on another arms-for-hostages deal with his favorite Second Channel.

A POSTSCRIPT

Thus far, the reader has been led to believe that there were two angry Canadians who had lent Adnan Khashoggi $10 million and who threatened to blow the Iran operation wide open if they did not get their money back. Furmark told this story to Allen and Cave, and they told it to Casey. It has been related here in the same way in order to reconstruct the events as they occurred at the time.

But, as it turned out, there was no truth in the tale of the two Canadians.

In December 1986, after the public exposure of the diversion, Furmark was called to testify before the House Intelligence Committee. To prepare for his testimony, he asked Khashoggi about the Canadians and was told that the money had actually come from a group of Saudi Arabians.[114] Khashoggi later went into more detail in an interview with Jeff Gerth of *The New York Times*. Gerth reported:

Mr. Khashoggi said he masterminded a deliberate deception of Mr. Casey last fall, when Mr. Casey was still head of the Central

Intelligence Agency, by inventing a group of angry Canadian investors who were supposedly threatening to disclose the Administration's secret arms sales to Iran unless they were immediately
reimbursed for a $10 million contribution to a $15 million arms
sale to Iran last May.[115]

The Canadians were Donald Fraser and Ernest Miller. They were real
enough, but their roles in Khashoggi's scheme had been invented. Fraser
later testified that he had first met Khashoggi as late as March 1986. He
had become the president of a company controlled by Khashoggi, who
asked him to reorganize it. Fraser said that he had put $1,760,000 of his
own money into it but had resigned two years later when the company
had gone bankrupt.[116] Miller did not testify but had been associated with
Khashoggi for many years.

The $10 million, Khashoggi said, had actually come from a Saudi
business associate. Information provided by Khashoggi indicated that the
principal source of funds for the Iran arms sales had been Saudi Arabian.
In addition to the $32 million which the Saudis contributed to the contras,
Ghorbanifar was said to have asked Khashoggi in 1986 "to raise $100
million for the contras from the Saudi royal family so that he and Mr.
Khashoggi could gain 'influence in Washington' "—a proposal which
Khashoggi did not accept.

Records made available by Khashoggi, including a transfer by Khashoggi of $25 million to the Secord-Hakim Lake Resources account in
the Crédit Suisse bank in Geneva in 1986, seemed to confirm his role
as banker for the Iran arms deals—or at least as go-between for the real
bankers in Saudi Arabia. Khashoggi was apparently so worried about
Ghorbanifar's vulnerability as a result of the latter's unpaid debts that he
had taken out a $22 million short-term life insurance policy on Ghor-
banifar in May 1986. North knew about this insurance policy; in July
1986, he had used it to put pressure on Reagan and Poindexter to approve
one of his arms-for-hostages schemes: "Ghorbanifar will be killed by his
creditors (they are beneficiaries for a $22M life insurance policy)" if the
deal did not go through.[117]

The deception practiced by Khashoggi about his mythical Canadian
creditors did not reflect well on CIA Director Casey's acumen in this
final phase of his life. He seems to have been easily taken in by Furmark's
alarmist story and, in fact, to have made it a key factor in the unraveling.
Khashoggi himself showed no contrition for having misled the Americans.
"During the interview," Gerth reported, "Mr. Khashoggi seemed to revel
in the games he had played with American officials, portraying the complicated series of financial transactions and occasional misstatements to
Americans as good financial sport."

21

Battle Royal

North's new hope for the long-awaited understanding with Iran rested on the nine-point agreement reached by Hakim and Samii in Frankfurt on October 7. It had been approved by Poindexter and, according to Poindexter, by President Reagan, except for the point about the Da'wa prisoners. With this official endorsement, North was ready to negotiate again.

According to an official Israeli source, North, Secord, and Nir met in Geneva on October 22 to decide on how to manage the next arms shipment to Iran. They are said to have agreed that the 500 TOWs sent to Iran would come out of the 508 sent to Israel in May that had been rejected by the Israeli Defense Forces as "inadequate." To make up for them, North committed the United States to supplying Israel with 500 presumably adequate missiles.[1]

This agreement again showed what risks North and Secord were willing to take in their dealings with Iran. The Iranians had long complained to Secord that they had been getting overage, inferior TOWs that had misfired and, as Secord put it, "went ballistic and didn't steer correctly."[2] Yet North apparently agreed to send Iran missiles that Israel considered defective and did not want. Secord testified that he had not participated in the decision to switch the missiles.[3]

On October 28, a flight crew retained by Secord flew the 500 TOWs to Iran aboard a camouflaged Israeli plane.[4] Iran paid $3.6 million for them. Secord and Hakim turned over to the CIA just over $2 million from their Swiss account for the TOWs. With their expenses of about $220,000, the surplus in favor of Secord and Hakim came to approximately $1.3 million.[5] There had now been three such transactions—the first of 1,000 TOWs, the second of Hawk spare parts, and the third of 500 TOWs. The combined surplus for all three, according to Secord, amounted to $14 million.[6]

2

An American recording device was surreptitiously introduced at a meeting with the two main Iranians of the Second Channel—Bahramani and Samii—in Mainz, West Germany, on October 29–30, 1986. The Americans at the meeting were North, Secord, Cave, and Hakim. It was held to arrange for the expected release of two hostages in exchange for the 500 TOWs and to implement the rest of the nine points. Apart from the intrinsic interest in what was said and done at Mainz, the tapes provide another rare opportunity to eavesdrop on these negotiations as if we were present.

The meeting began with startling news from the Iranians, though the Americans did not immediately realize how damaging it was. Bahramani announced that on October 15 radical university students in Tehran had distributed five million leaflets exposing the trip of McFarlane's group to Tehran the previous May, including a picture of McFarlane. The repercussions in Iran had almost prevented the two Iranians from coming to the meeting.[7] The leaflets were allegedly inspired by Mehdi and Hadi Hashemi, two of the Ayatollah Montazeri's supporters, and Mehdi Hashemi had already been arrested on orders of the Ayatollah Khomeini.[8]

Nevertheless, the Americans were assured that the Iranians had "brought it under control."[9] North consoled himself by saying: "If it was blown, it was only blown inside," and not in the United States.[10] At another point, referring to the Iranian request for American technicians, North revealed how sensitive he was to public exposure: "We want to make sure that we can do it right. And that it's not going to cost anything to put these people [technicians] over there—it won't cost you anything, but because of the risk of that becoming public, we can't do that while these other guys [hostages] are still being held."[11]

A similar discussion took place among the Americans:

North: We've got to get this S.O.B. working. That's what we've got to do. And it's going to be all over the freakin world. What we've got to do is figure out how we're going to handle the next, literally, few days. At some point along the line, we're going to be forced into acknowledging that we're holding private discussions with the Iranians. . . .

Cave: (few words missing) to get those guys to release the damn hostages so that we can put the best light on this.

Secord: Well, if they do that, it would make it easier on us.

North: Well, that's what I'm aiming for.[12]

At Mainz, the Americans were forced for the first time to face the risk of public exposure of the U.S.-Iran deals. They went ahead to make the ultimate deal, as if the nine-point agreement could still be implemented if only both sides were sufficiently determined to see it through. By assuming, however, that the deals with Iran could not be justified publicly so long as all the hostages were not freed, they made the United States hostage to Lebanese and Iranian internal political factionalism.

As a result, the meeting in Mainz continued to be preoccupied with arms and hostages. The Americans came with the expectation that they were going to get two hostages out promptly in return for the 500 TOWs.[13] The Iranians unexpectedly wanted American technicians to make their old Phoenix missiles operable. While the Iranians wanted to talk about Phoenixes, Secord burst out in exasperation: "But we're still not talking about the god-damned hostage thing . . . I mean we need to get to this. We need to get this off the table." To which North added: "That is important."[14]

Secord spoke as if he knew what President Reagan had in mind: "I think the President will authorize us to do some technical work—we've always talked about it, if we get our three people back. That's why I said, You give me the three people tomorrow, and I'll bet you he'll say okay go get some technicians next week."[15] Secord could be even more expansive: "Tell him that if he just goes out tomorrow or the next day and grabs those three guys out of Lebanon, we'll go back in and rebuild his goddamn air force. I built it once and I'll go back in and build it again."[16] It seemed as if the Americans were willing to promise almost anything to get the hostages back.

By this time, the two sides were exchanging political confidences. Bahramani wanted to know who was supporting the Iran initiative in the U.S. government. He had heard only two names, President Reagan and National Security Adviser Poindexter, and wondered whether there were any others. North answered: "On the for side you would have Reagan, Regan, Poindexter, Casey, and over here [against] you would put Shultz and Weinberger. And after that, nobody else counts. But right now, nobody in our Congress even knows about it. And we're not going to tell them until we get the hostages out."[17]

Bahramani was equally free with inside information on the internal Iranian political lineup. He was most enlightening about what had happened between the Iranian factions before McFarlane's visit to Tehran in May. He explained that there were three groups—a radical faction headed by the Ayatollah Hussein Ali Montazeri; a right-wing faction whose leader was not named; and a third, middle-of-the-road group led by Speaker Rafsanjani. These three groups, he maintained, had the same objectives but differed in their approaches or tactics. When the issue had been raised, before May 1986, of establishing relations with the United States, Bahramani related, Rafsanjani had favored it, "but for his own politics he decided to get all the groups involved and give them a role to play." Rafsanjani's idea of having all the groups participate in this venture was not new—"it dated back a long time ago," and he was still sticking to it. Rafsanjani's policy was "a double-edged sword" with positive and negative points—"the positive point being that if it would be a failure and all parties are involved so there would not be an internal war, and the negative part is that because different views and opinions are under the same roof, it's very difficult to manage." According to Bahramani, Montazeri had lost ground within the Iranian regime and had been forced to withdraw from public activity.[18]

This explanation of internal Iranian politics undercut the main premise that had motivated the Americans ever since they had undertaken to reach an understanding with the new rulers of Iran. The Americans had been coached for over a year by Ghorbanifar that they were dealing through him with Iranian "moderates," who had been seeking either to overthrow the Khomeini regime or to reform it from within. It now appeared that all the Iranian factions had known what was going on, and that the American connection had had little or nothing to do with changing the character of the existing regime.

For this reason, the risk of exposure from the Iranian side if any of the three groups should become disaffected had long hung over the U.S.-Iran negotiations. It had never been faced, and no provisions had been made for dealing with it. According to Cave, it was not in North's nature to consider risk.[19]

In line with Rafsanjani's strategy to implicate all the Iranian groups, Bahramani revealed that a four-man committee had been formed in Tehran to oversee Iranian relations with the United States. These four included two from Rafsanjani's following and one each from the other two.[20]

At Mainz, North betrayed an anxiety that time was running out. "My problem," he told the Iranians, "is that my boss, the President who wrote in that Bible for you, and Poindexter who is my boss, are losing patience and I am under great pressure, as are these gentlemen, to show that this connection that we have made is going somewhere."[21] North's patience was also wearing thin. "I mean," he complained, "if we're really sincere about this whole friggin thing, what we ought to be doing is, they ought to be exercising every possible amount of leverage they've got to get those people out, and we agree that as soon as they're out, we can do all kinds of good things. . . . You guys don't trust us, and we don't trust you, and so we end up doing it a little bit at a time, and it takes forever."[22]

North also tried to impress the Iranians with fictional exploits. When Samii said that an Arab country had agreed to put pressure on Iraq, North exclaimed: "That's us doing that." North also claimed that the United States had stopped arms from a Western country from going to Iraq.[23] One of North's private jokes dealt with the Da'wa prisoners in Kuwait:

North: I have already met with the Kuwaiti minister, secretly.

(Hakim interprets)

North: In my spare time between blowing up Nicaragua (laughs).[24]

Ghorbanifar was still on everyone's mind. An Iranian put in a good word for him on the ground that he "can do, unofficially, things that we cannot do officially" and was believed to have "a lot of influence with Americans." North denied that Ghorbanifar had any such influence, dismissed his power as "purely negative," and warned that "Ghorbanifar believes he has not been paid the full amount by Iran and he is threatening to make public the earlier transactions." When Secord volunteered the opinion that Ghorbanifar "should be paid something right away," North retorted: "Well, quite frankly, I don't give a shit if he gets paid. What I'm more interested in is that the people to whom he owes money get paid." These "people," North still thought, were the Canadians.[25] An additional count against Ghorbanifar was the disclosure by the Iranians that Ghorbanifar and Montazeri had been friends for fifteen years and that Ghorbanifar had told Montazeri all that went on.[26]

In fact, the only real question for the Americans in Mainz, as before, was how many hostages were going to be released, and how soon. North made plain that without the freedom of the hostages nothing could be accomplished. He told the Iranians: "Look, let me tell you something [about] the problem—just so we all understand it—is if a visible effort is made by the United States Government when there's a long list of hostages being held in Lebanon, this President is going to get stoned."[27]

Bahramani had pacified the Americans by making them believe that two of the three American hostages were sure to be freed in the next few days.*[28] Yet, on November 2, 1986, only one hostage, David P. Jacobsen, director of the American University Hospital in Beirut, in captivity since May 28, 1985, was released in Beirut. Jacobsen was the third and last of the American hostages to be freed in exchange for American weapons.

This transaction was typical of the arms-for-hostages deals. For all the brave talk about a "strategic dialogue," an arms-for-hostages deal was all that North was capable of making. From time to time, he tried to inject his larger vision of future U.S.-Iran relations into the discussion. North once told the Iranians that the aim "is to get beyond the hostages and get on with a formal relationship."[29] North cited what McFarlane had tried to tell them at Tehran: "Think big. Think beyond the hostages. Think economic aid. Think of all kinds of ways in which we can help

---

* Three hostages were usually mentioned in Mainz, but North once called attention to the fact that there were as many as six hostages and named them: Thomas Sutherland, acting dean of agriculture, American University in Beirut; David P. Jacobsen, director, American University Hospital in Beirut; Terry A. Anderson, chief Middle East correspondent, Associated Press; Joseph J. Cicippio, acting comptroller, American University in Beirut; Frank H. Reed, director, Lebanese International School; and Edward A. Tracy, writer (A-1, pp. 1635–36).

you, not just Phoenix missiles, that's nothing. Think big, and that's the important thing to do. But we can't think big when we've got that [hostage problem] staring at us."[30]

But the Iranians were not interested in "thinking big." They wanted to think about weapons, the fate of Iraq's Saddam Hussein, and the release of the Da'wa prisoners in Kuwait. On these points the Americans could not satisfy them. The all-important American hostage issue was for them a nuisance into which they were forever reluctantly being drawn. As Cave put it, "there were no real concrete proposals from the Iranian side on a strategic and political relationship."[31] Whenever this kind of relationship came up, the Americans virtually talked to themselves.

Yet the Iranians could not avoid doing something periodically about the hostages, and on these occasions they showed that they had some influence with the Lebanese captors by obtaining the release of a hostage, but they persisted in doling out the hostages one by one, despite promising more, thereby always having more to dole out. In a quintessential Iranian move after Jacobsen's release, Samii tempted Hakim with the offer of getting another hostage out as soon as possible in exchange for another 500 TOWs.[32]

When North was still sure of getting two hostages out, he sent word to Poindexter about how to manage their reception for the greater glory of President Reagan, toward whom he was always extremely solicitous. "Our effort," he advised, "is to have RR [Ronald Reagan] make the announcement before CNN [television] knows it has happened, but after the AMCITS [American citizens] are in USG [U.S. government] hands, so that RR is seen to have influenced the action and Syrians are not."[33]

One of North's lighter experiences in Mainz was the offer to him by an Iranian of an $8,000 rug. It was to be presented to him as a person "who cared deeply about reopening a relationship with his country." North declined the gift as something he could not accept and was instead given a handful of pistachio nuts, which he felt it was permissible to eat.[34]

On the whole, however, the Mainz meeting seemed to stretch North's nerves almost to the breaking point. He once burst out: "I want to get back to the states. I've got so much goddamn work."[35] In a prophetic vein, he warned: "I'm telling you, we're so close to having done the right thing—you and I and [deleted] and the men in this room, and yet we're going to foul it up. I can see it coming."[36]

To Poindexter, North had sent an equally gloomy message from Mainz: "This is the damndest operation I have ever seen. Pl[ea]s[e] let me go on to other things. W[oul]d very much like to give RR [Ronald Reagan] two hostages that he can take credit for and stop worrying about these other things."[37]

3

The explosive potential of the exposure of the U.S.-Iran arms-for-hostages deals in the Iranian student leaflets took some time to sink in.

Soon after the student leaflets of October 15, a small newspaper in Baalbek, Lebanon, published a similar story mentioning McFarlane by name. This obscure publication was followed by a fuller, though not altogether accurate, version of McFarlane's mission in a Lebanese weekly, *Al-Shiraa*, on November 3, 1986. It had apparently been chosen by friends of Mehdi Hashemi, a supporter of Montazeri, to make public the arrest of Hashemi and many of his followers, because the Iranian press was controlled by Rafsanjani. *Al-Shiraa*'s exposé was presented in the guise of impartially giving the views of both sides on the reasons for Hashemi's arrest, in the course of which the story of McFarlane's mission was attributed to Hashemi's followers. The account was not strictly accurate; it placed McFarlane's visit to Tehran in September 1986 rather than in May and garbled other details of the visit. Nevertheless it succeeded in making known that there had been a secret deal between the United States and Iran by which the United States had provided weapons to Iran in exchange for an Iranian promise to stop supporting "liberation movements in the world."[38]

This revelation was calculated to embarrass both the United States and Iran—the United States because it was officially committed to an international ban on sales of arms to both sides in the Iran-Iraq war, and Iran because it had been officially denouncing the United States as the "Great Satan" with which it was irrevocably at war. Yet both sides responded to the challenge in different ways.

In Iran, the story forced Rafsanjani to come out into the open. On November 4, 1986, he made a speech in the Iranian parliament in which he acknowledged that an American delegation had visited Tehran. After having received a letter from Japanese Prime Minister Nakasone, who had evidently been used by the United States as an intermediary, Rafsanjani said that he had replied: "I told him that if we were sure that America was sincere, then we would take steps to help. Our suspicion was that the Americans were engaged in deceit." McFarlane, Rafsanjani claimed, had come to Tehran uninvited and had been detained in the hotel for five days. "Their immediate aim," Rafsanjani said, "was to turn us into interceders in Lebanon, and their distant goal was to create amicable relations and the golden visions that they had in mind! They begged, pleaded and sent messages requesting that one of our country's responsible officials receive them." Rafsanjani spoke as if there had been no negotiations in Tehran but still held out a vague offer of doing something for the hostages: "If your governments prove to us in practice that they are not fighting against us, if they prove in practice that they do not engage in treason against us, if they prove in practice that they do not confiscate our assets through bullying tactics . . . then the Islamic Republic in a humane gesture is prepared to announce its views to its friends in Lebanon."[39]

Prime Minister Moussavi, however, took a harder line. He declared that the major aim of the secret American visit to Tehran had been to resume relations with the Islamic Republic. "Iran has friendly relations with many countries," he said, "but negotiations with the United States in the light of its crimes against the Islamic Revolution will never take place."[40]

In the United States, one reaction, for the benefit of Poindexter, came from Howard Teicher, now the senior director for political-military affairs on the NSC staff. Teicher interpreted the *Al-Shiraa* story as coming from "pro-Syrian Lebanese newspapers" and as one of "the clearest possible signals we could receive that the succession struggle is underway and U.S.-Iranian relations are bound to play an important role in the struggle." Teicher's assessment showed that the Americans had only a dim idea of where the story was coming from and where it might lead. He hastened to admit that "we may never know the exact reason" for it, but advised that "we must not let this opportunity to assess the consequences in Iran of these revelations from slipping through our fingers." He urged Poindexter "to discuss our options with Shultz and Casey" in order that "as a minimum, we need to determine how best, other than parts, etc., to signal the Iranians in a productive manner."[41] Teicher seemed to think that the revelations gave the United States another opportunity to get on with reaching an agreement with Iran.

Chief of Staff Donald Regan says that he had had a strong difference of opinion with Poindexter. According to Regan, he had told staff members: "The cover is blown here. We have got to go public with it, we have got to tell the Congress, we have got to tell the American public exactly what went on so they are aware of it." Poindexter was inflexibly opposed to this course of action. Regan says that Poindexter argued that North was about to go to London—Regan should have said Geneva—and might get two more hostages out. "And why blow that chance. We got to keep the lid on this, we got to deny it, we're endangering their lives."[42] President Reagan agreed with Poindexter. In an unusually "adamant" tone, Regan recalls, the president said, "in no way would we discuss publicly any of the methods we used to gain the release of the hostages or comment on whether Bud McFarlane had gone to Tehran or not."[43]

Later, Poindexter gave a briefing to members of the House Permanent Select Committee on Intelligence, the record of which amounted to his version of "the leak that blew the cover of the U.S. secret dealings with Iran":

Montazeri may have revealed some of Rafsanjani's contacts with the United States. To defend themselves, Rafsanjani then publicly talked of the McFarlane mission in a speech that was laced with factual errors. For example, Rafsanjani claimed McFarlane's visit occurred in September when it actually was in May. Such deliberate falsehoods are being viewed as sending the U.S. a signal that this was a defensive measure on the part of Rafsanjani to a domestic audience. Subsequently, Rafsanjani's [deleted] told the U.S. government of the desire to keep the channel open to the United States.*[44]

In effect, Poindexter took the reaction in Iran to the *Al-Shiraa* story to be a positive sign, calling for no change in American policy.

Casey, according to North, had reached the conclusion that the game was up, but in a different way from Regan. After North had returned from Beirut, where he had gone to collect Jacobsen, Casey had told North: "Look, this revelation that is either occurring or about to occur is the end." And Casey had advised him: "You ought to go out and get a lawyer."

After the disclosure of the McFarlane mission in the press, North had received a telephone call from Nir expressing concern about the public position of the United States. When North was asked whether Nir had advised him that President Reagan should flatly deny that McFarlane's trip had ever occurred, North replied: "That sounds correct."[45]

In the end, the policy adopted by the Americans was one of "stonewalling" or letting nothing out. The only one who claims to have thought differently is Regan, and he was easily brushed aside. The best characterization of the policy was given by North's aide, Lieutenant Colonel Robert Earl: "The posture that was adopted by the Administration, by those in the box that were familiar with it, was to treat this [disclosure in the press] similarly, that no comment where possible, what I call a very carefully crafted artful truth, where possible or necessary or, if there is no other way, outright denial—in other words, cover story to protect the box and not to divulge what was in the box."[46]

As if nothing had really changed, North, Cave, Secord, and Hakim went off to still another meeting with the usual Iranians in Geneva on November 8–10, 1986. Some time was spent on the *Al-Shiraa* revelations. The Iranians seemed to want to put the blame for it on anybody

---

* Another memorandum on the meeting, signed by Mike O'Neill, states: "The U.S. side is encouraged by the fact that contacts with [Iranians] continue after publicity about the covert arms sales to Iran and that Rafsanjani, in his speech about McFarlane's trip, deliberately misstates some details so as to permit the U.S. to deny the story. Rafsanjani, it is believed, also gave information to the Iranian ambassador in the U.N. who later made remarks to the press the U.S. considered positive under the circumstances" (Memorandum for the Record, November 28, 1986, 100-8, p. 781). The misstatements had originally appeared in the *Al-Shiraa* story.

but themselves. An Iranian first claimed that the paper was under Syrian control and then tried to implicate the CIA. Cave maintained that the information available to the United States pointed to the Lebanese Hizballah and Mehdi Hashemi. No one was the wiser after this exchange.

The inevitable Ghorbanifar problem was gone over once again, without any real resolution. Samii told Cave that the Iranian intelligence people "had taken a hard look" at the Ghorbanifar-Khashoggi-Israeli connection and had decided that Ghorbanifar was an Israeli agent. Nevertheless, the Iranians had decided to buy some more weapons from him to keep him quiet. It was true that they owed him $10 million, but he allegedly owed them 1,000 TOWs.

A long discussion of four or five hours dealt with the intractable issue of the Da'wa prisoners in Kuwait. The Iranians took the position that no senior Iranian government official could go to Kuwait unless the release of the Da'was was agreed to in advance. The Americans pleaded that they had done as much as they could and now it was up to Iran to send a delegation to Kuwait, with an American assurance that it would be "warmly received." The main thing that came out was the Iranian admission that the fate of the remaining American hostages was bound up with the release of all or some of the Da'was and not only with more arms for Iran.

The meeting ended with a fervid Iranian appeal for "getting rid" of Iraq's Saddam Hussein, without which the Iran-Iraq war could not end.[47] It was a fitting conclusion to a futile, fruitless rendezvous between Iranians and Americans on the eve of the final crisis of America's secret Iran adventure. The main significance of the Geneva meeting is the evidence that North and the others still had no intimation of the crack-up that was about to occur at home.

At about this time, Nir gave North the latest news on Ghorbanifar's financial woes. Ghorbanifar claimed that he had paid $12,000 for each missile and had sold them for $13,200 each, of which $500 went to Michael Ledeen and $700 to himself—an allegation that Ledeen later hotly denied but which did not seem to weaken his faith in Ghorbanifar.[48] To show how desperate he was, Ghorbanifar reported that he had received a threat from Iran: "You owe us $7.5 million (which is 5K × 1500 TOWs) which must be paid within 1 w[ee]k or your family in Iran is not safe." Ghorbanifar's message was: "Americans will have to get me out of this."

Above all, North might better have paid more attention to a warning that he received in the same conversation with Nir and which he recorded as: "Gorba says that we (USG) is [sic] spending Iranian $ in Nicaragua."[49] This note is curious, because it suggests that Nir—who is supposed to have put the idea of diverting Iranian money to the Nicaraguan contras in North's head at the beginning of the year—passed on this information from Ghorbanifar as if it were news.

4

The decisive threat to the Reagan administration's Iran initiative did not come from Ghorbanifar, Khashoggi, or the mythical Canadian financiers. It came from where it was least expected—from within the U.S. government itself.

The weakest link in the administration's handling of the Iran initiative was the Department of State. It had been kept out of the covert operation, but it had remained in charge of the overt policy vis-à-vis Iran. The world—and most Americans—looked to the State Department for statements of American policy. As the covert and the overt approaches drew further and further apart, the authorized, official spokesmen of American foreign policy were faced with a crisis of confidence.

For years, the State Department had been charged with carrying out Operation Staunch, on behalf of which it had been hectoring and importuning foreign countries to prevent the sale of arms to Iran on the ground that it was a "terrorist state." Congress was repeatedly told that this was official American policy. For example, on July 9, 1986, in reply to Senator David L. Boren, the assistant secretary for legislative and intergovernmental affairs, J. Edward Fox, had stated the policy unequivocally: "We do not oppose all trade with Iran; what we oppose is the sale of arms by any country to Iran."[50] The State Department had a special official of ambassadorial rank detailed to tracking down countries that might be selling arms to Iran and putting pressure on them to stop.[51] On October 1, 1986, Secretary of State Shultz told the Gulf Cooperation Council at the United Nations: "We have intensified our efforts to discourage our friends from selling arms to Iran with significant, but not complete success." This policy, repeated endlessly in public for the benefit of both Americans and foreigners, now haunted Secretary Shultz.

Shultz was, in principle and as he thought, second only to the president in the conduct of American foreign relations.[52] In practice, he knew only as much about the relations with Iran and Nicaragua as National Security Adviser Poindexter cared to tell him or as he himself cared to know.

Shultz repeatedly defended himself on the ground that he had been "deliberately deceived" by Poindexter and his staff.[53] Shultz insisted that he had had no reason to fight any harder for his point of view, because he had been given to understand throughout 1986 that the deals with Iran had "fizzled" and had been dropped.[54] He had not been informed beforehand of McFarlane's mission to Tehran in May 1986.[55] He had never heard of Albert Hakim and had heard only vaguely of Richard Secord.[56] He had had such an unfriendly relationship with the CIA and the rest of the "intelligence community" that he had unsuccessfully tried to resign in August 1986.[57] He had not known about the nine-point agreement and was appalled by it: "Our guys, to the extent that the staff people who were doing this, they got taken to the cleaners. You look at the structure of this deal. It's pathetic that anybody would agree to anything like that. It's so lopsided. It's crazy."[58]

Poindexter had consistently cut Shultz and others out of the Iran affair. Just before leaving for Tehran in May 1986, North had suggested to Poindexter a meeting with Shultz, Weinberger, and Casey. Poindexter had brusquely replied: "I don't want a meeting with RR [Ronald Reagan], Shultz, and Weinberger."[59] In June 1986, Poindexter told North: "To my knowledge Shultz knows nothing about the prior financing" of the contras by Saudi Arabia and Taiwan. Poindexter added: "I think it should stay that way."[60]

On one occasion, however, Shultz had given Poindexter a pretext for telling him only as much as Poindexter wanted to tell him. According to Poindexter, Shultz had informed him that "he didn't particularly want to know the details. He said just, in effect, tell me what I need to know."[61] Shultz's version of the same conversation was: "What I did say to Admiral Poindexter was that I wanted to be informed of the things I needed to know to do my job as Secretary of State. But he didn't need to keep me posted on the details, the operational details of what he was doing."[62] Representative Michael DeWine taunted Shultz with having "walked off the field when the score was against you. You took yourself out of the game."[63] Shultz disagreed, but he had apparently given Poindexter an opening to do what Poindexter wanted to do anyway—to cut the secretary of state out of the Iran affair. At any rate, Shultz did not seem very zealous about asserting himself in this foreign affair.

This background helps to explain why the reanimation of George Shultz was so unexpected. He had spoken his mind forthrightly at the beginning of the year and, whether from ignorance or prudence, had largely withdrawn as an active participant between January and November 1986. Suddenly, the secretary of state came out fighting.

5

Shultz hesitantly reentered the Iran arena as a result of the worldwide repercussions of the *Al-Shiraa* revelations. On the following day, November 4, he was on a plane bound for a conference in Vienna. He held his usual in-flight press conference, which was so trying that he found it necessary to send a worried message to Washington: "Please have following text delivered by hand directly to Adm Poindexter from the Secretary":

> The big story the press is after is to establish that the U.S. violated its own policy by cutting a big secret arms deal with Iran in order to get our hostages released. In accordance with the agreed guidance,

I totally refused to engage with their questions, saying that they will have to direct all their questions to the White House. But they are likely to file a story of some sort speculating on some sort of White House deal with the terrorists.

Shultz was shaken by this line of questioning and immediately realized that it was not likely to go away:

I have been racking my brains all day to figure out a way to help turn this situation in the best possible direction. I have not come up with a satisfactory answer. At this point the story is building and there are so many aspects to it—political, legal, diplomatic, and in policy terms—that leaks and revelations could keep it going for a long time in a bigger and bigger way.

The best that he was able to offer, Shultz said, was "to give the key facts to the public." He proposed a way that showed that he himself did not know what the key facts were:

We could make clear that this was a special, one-time operation based on humanitarian grounds and decided by the President within his constitutional responsibility to act in the service of the national interest—and that our policies toward terrorism and toward the Iran/Iraq war stand. There will be many loose ends to try to tie up for a long time to come, but it seems to me that this is the right way to get all this behind us as rapidly as possible and to be able to continue building on the impressive achievements which the President's anti-terrorist policies have made possible.[64]

This message indicated that Shultz still thought that the McFarlane mission leaked by *Al-Shiraa* had been a "special, one-time operation" and that the whole story could be put behind the administration by taking refuge in the usual ritual expressions of presidential responsibilities.

Poindexter answered the next day in the same way that he had treated a similar suggestion by Chief of Staff Regan. Poindexter was "convinced that we must remain absolutely close-mouthed" and still believed that the relations with Iran, and particularly with Speaker Rafsanjani, could go on. He had talked with Vice President Bush, Secretary of Defense Weinberger, and CIA Director Casey, and they had agreed with him. He appended an "Iran Press Guidance," which forbade any official comment on McFarlane's mission or on arms to Iran.[65]

Shultz at first saw nothing wrong in this "Press Guidance." On second thought, as he put it, it "set my alarm bells ringing hard." In reply to the question "Does the U.S. still have an arms embargo against Iran in the Iran-Iraq war?" the answer had been given as: "As long as Iran advocates the use of terrorism, the U.S. arms embargo will continue."[66] As events unfolded, Shultz soon realized that the answer revealed a reluctance to say "flat out 'no more arms sales' " and made him suspect a willingness to get around a continued prohibition on the ground that Iran was no longer advocating the use of terrorism. Shultz came to regard it as more deception—"the kind of tricky and misleading statement that looks great on the surface, but then you start looking at it more carefully and you saw it is going in a different direction entirely."[67]

As for months past, Poindexter was now the commanding figure in the White House in the making and implementation of Iran policy. He had much greater access than Shultz to President Reagan. Poindexter briefed the president every day, whereas the secretary of state saw him "sparingly," though whenever he so chose.[68] The exchange between Shultz and Poindexter on November 4–5, 1986, made it clear that the question of what to do about the *Al-Shiraa* revelations was becoming a classic struggle between the secretary of state and the national security adviser. Poindexter was following in the footsteps of Henry Kissinger and Zbigniew Brzezinski in a contest with a secretary of state who had not yet shown whether he was willing to be a William Rogers or a Cyrus Vance—or, for that matter, an Alexander Haig faced with a William Clark.

6

It was with increasing suspicion and disquiet that Shultz came to a top-level meeting at the White House on November 10, 1986. It was the beginning of the final crisis of the Iran affair, which came to a climax fifteen days later.

Present were President Reagan, Vice President Bush, Secretary of State Shultz, Secretary of Defense Weinberger, CIA Director Casey, Attorney General Meese, Chief of Staff Regan, National Security Adviser Poindexter, and Alton G. Keel, Jr., the deputy national security adviser. We have full notes of the meeting by Regan and Keel and memoranda by Weinberger and Meese.[69] The peculiar significance of this meeting for the next stage of the affair repays the effort to piece together what took place.

President Reagan first declared that the purpose of the meeting was to decide on what kind of public statement to make. He asserted that "we have not dealt directly with terrorists, no bargaining, no ransom."*[70] This statement was the president's leitmotif, several times repeated.

Next, Poindexter made a report on the course of U.S.-Iran relations

---

* Weinberger's memorandum reads: "The President said we did not do any trading with the enemy for our hostages" (100-10, p. 578).

in the past two years. It was the first such account ever given even to this group. He told of the January 17, 1986, Finding, which most had never before seen or heard of. Most startling, especially to Shultz, was his version of the weapons sold to Iran. Poindexter put the entire onus on Israel, which, he said, had sent the first 500 TOWs without U.S. permission, but the president had later agreed to replenish them. Poindexter also repeated the apocryphal tale about the chance discovery of the Israeli arms shipments, because someone had "stumbled on this [by] tracking down its shipments to Iran" from a European warehouse.[71] In all, Poindexter said, Israel had sold 1,000—later changed to 2,000—TOW missiles and 240 Hawk spare parts to Iran, for which Iran had paid Israel, and Israel had paid the United States.[72]

At this, Meese interjected: "We didn't sell; Israel sold."[73] No one tried to tell him that the transaction had been somewhat more complicated.

Poindexter then gave a most optimistic account of the present state of relations with Iran. The United States had made "solid contact" with Speaker Rafsanjani. He was described as the leader of the middle-of-the-road faction "interested in some relationship with U.S." or even a "strategic relationship."[74] Rafsanjani had deliberately made "factually incorrect" statements about McFarlane's visit to Tehran because he wished "to keep contact."[75] The Iranians were "happy with our no comment" policy.[76]

On the domestic political side, Poindexter said that he had talked to ten or more members of Congress, and only Senator Robert C. Byrd of West Virginia, the Democratic majority leader, "has problems." In any case, Poindexter gave assurances that we "can continue to get hostages out."[77]

Poindexter's recital was a farrago of truths, half-truths, and untruths, of which the last were the most prominent. Israel had not sold the first TOWs to Iran "without permission"; the Americans had not "stumbled" on the Israeli shipments in a warehouse; the United States, not Israel, had sold the other TOWs and Hawk spare parts to Iran. Poindexter's version of the Rafsanjani connection was equally tendentious; it was designed to give the impression that all was going well and nothing needed to be changed.

As in the previous January, both Weinberger and Shultz showed that they were unhappy with the policy. Weinberger says that he had intervened after the president had first spoken: "I pointed out we must bear in mind we have given the Israelis and the Iranians the opportunity to blackmail us by reporting selectively bits and pieces of the total story. I also pointed out that Congress could—and probably would—hold legislative hearings." When Weinberger made the same point a second time, Reagan replied that "we need to point out any discussion endangers our source in Iran and our plan, because we do want to get additional hostages released."[78]

Weinberger relates that he also confronted Poindexter with the re-minder "that he always told me that there would be no more weapons sent to Iran, after the first 500 TOWs, until *after all* of the hostages were returned, but unfortunately we did send a second 500 because it 'seemed the only way to get the hostages out,' according to Poindexter."[79] This response seemed to admit that there had been arms-for-hostages deals. Poindexter, according to Keel, replied to Weinberger that he "always came back [to the] President, he always agreed to go ahead."[80]

Shultz was also troublesome. Like Weinberger, he indicated that the last 500 TOWs and the January 17 Finding were news to him. In Keel's abbreviated notation, Shultz asked: "How did last 500 come about? Who arranged?"* When Meese tried to make a distinction between trading directly with those who held the hostages and doing it through Iran, Shultz again spoke up skeptically—he believed that "ransom" had been paid and cautioned against saying "something that's technically correct but not exactly representative of what we've done."[81]

Shultz made a disparaging reference to Israel which we have in two versions. According to Regan's notes: "[Shultz] thinks Israel suckered us into this so we can't complain of their sale."[82] Weinberger's memorandum uses a slightly different expression: "He said he felt the Israelis sucked us up into their operation so we could not object to their sales to Iran."[83]

Shultz's view of Israel's role seemed to reflect Poindexter's misinfor-mation about Israel's sole responsibility for the arms sales to Iran. Later, questioned about his various statements on Israel, Shultz would only say that the interests of the United States and Israel were not always exactly the same and that the United States could not blame Israel for whatever the United States decided to do.†

Shultz repeatedly tangled with Reagan and Meese. One three-way exchange was recorded by Regan as follows:

Shultz: Be careful of linkage between hostage and defense equipment.

Meese: We have not dealt directly with terrorists.

President: Terrorists have not profited. We let Iranians by supplying [them] and they influenced. No benefits to terrorists. We [are] work-

---

* Poindexter appeared to respond: "Casey's guy; my guy, in October." It is not clear who "Casey's guy" was; "my guy" was probably North.
† In the course of Shultz's congressional testimony in July 1987, Senator James A. McClure cited a series of statements by Shultz on Israel. One of them went back to what Shultz had told the Tower Board about Amiram Nir's effort to "revive" the connection with Iran in January 1986: "I felt that one of the things Israel wanted was to get itself into a position where its arms sales to Iran could not be criticized by us because we were conducting this Operation Staunch and we were trying to persuade everybody not to sell arms. That is what all that is about" (100-9, pp. 182–83; TR, p. B-58).

King Fahd ibn Abdul-Aziz of Saudi Arabia—greeted by Vice President George Bush and Secretary of State George Shultz during a visit to Washington in February 1986, when Fahd informed President Reagan that he was making a contribution of $24 million to the contras

Prince Bandar bin Sultan—the Saudi ambassador to the United States, who transmitted the news to National Security Adviser McFarlane of Saudi Arabia's first contribution of $8 million to the contras

Ali Akbar Hashemi Rafsanjani— speaker of the Iranian parliament, with the Ayatollah Ruhollah Khomeini peering down on him

Secretary of State George Shultz joins hands with the contra triumvirate—Adolfo Calero, Enrique Bermúdez, and Alfredo César

Eugene Hasenfus—shot down during a resupply operation for the contras, as he was captured in the Nicaraguan jungle by Sandinista soldiers

David Kimche—the director general of the Israeli Foreign Ministry, who was the first responsible Israeli negotiator in 1985

Amiram Nir—adviser to the Israeli Prime Minister on counterterrorism, who replaced Kimche in 1986 and worked most closely with Oliver North; he later died in a mysterious plane accident in Mexico

Adolph (Al) Schwimmer
(at left)—
the other unofficial Israeli
representative, shown
meeting with former
Iranian General Razvani

Yaacov Nimrodi—shown
with Adnan Khashoggi
in the latter's villa in
Marbella, Spain; one of
the two unofficial Israeli
intermediaries until
the unfortunate mishap
of the "horror story"

Stanley Sporkin—CIA general counsel, who drafted the Findings which grew out of the ill-fated "horror story"

Abraham Sofaer—the State Department's legal adviser, whose suspicions of an official cover-up helped to bring about the public revelation of the "diversion" by Attorney General Meese

Adolfo Calero (center) and Alfonso Robelo (right)—with President Reagan, as Calero shows his determination to fight on

National Security Adviser Poindexter—during his testimony at the congressional hearings

ing with moderates, hoping in future to be able to influence Iran after Khomeini dies.

Shultz: It is ransom. But we have made more good contacts in Iran than he was aware of. But [we] must not gild lily. Some undesirable effects of these actions. We are paying a high price. Afraid of technically correct statements that are not fully descriptive—could get us into trouble.[84]

One of the most revealing exchanges took place on whether there should be a statement at all. In Regan's notes, it went as follows:

President: We must say something but not much.

Poindexter: If we go with this we end our Iranian contacts.

Regan: Must get statement out now, we are being attacked, and we are being hurt. Losing credibility.

President: Must say something because I'm being held out to dry. Have not dealt with terrorists, don't know who they are. This is long range Iranian policy. No further speculation or answers so as not to endanger hostages. We won't pay any money or give anything to terrorists.

Poindexter: Say less about what we are doing, more about what we are not doing.

Weinberger: Be careful of Raf[sanjani] + Israel + blackmail. What we say will be repudiated.

Shultz: We are saying only what we did and know has happened.

Bush: [reference to a case in New York] Israel may try to squeeze us.

Shultz: Finding was not known to me from Jan to Nov—amazing. . . . Asked question about what if they ask for more than what they have received.

Poindexter: Can't tie hands that way.

Regan: Should answer Geo's question later in week.

Shultz: No debriefing—what to say

President: Support Pres' policy but say nothing else due to danger to hostage*

Shultz: Support Iran long range policy of contact—Know [mistake for no] support for weapons for hostages

---

* Reagan, according to Keel's notes, twice said: "We don't talk TOWs, don't talk specifics" and "avoid specifics, declare consistent with our policy can't engage in speculation" (B-14, p. 1021).

President: Side with mil[itary] superiority will win. We want to have things even. This helps Iran which was weaker.[85]

Other aspects of the meeting can be reconstructed from Keel's notes. As if to anticipate trouble within the administration itself, Meese stressed the need to "get away from idea people were bypassed, division within U.S. government." Toward the end, Shultz asked inconveniently: "Do we trade any more arms for hostages?" to which he received no answer. Instead, the president said that he would "appreciate people saying you support policy." Meese immediately put in that he agreed, while Shultz seemed to temporize by saying: "I support you, Mr. President, but [I] am concerned about policy." As if he sensed that Shultz was holding back, the president felt it necessary to respond that he had always viewed his policy as that of "giving muscle" to those in Iran who could help the hostages. Poindexter's last words were that he hoped those present would say that they had been "aware of [the Iran] project" and had been "consulted." Finally, Meese suggested that this pretense of unanimity should be put in the public statement.[86]

The meeting of November 10 was a turning point, though none of those present were yet aware of it. No open break in the ranks occurred, though Weinberger and Shultz again betrayed their uneasiness. Yet the next stage of the crisis immediately followed and emerged from it.

What comes out most sharply from the exchanges is the dominant role of President Reagan. He spoke more often and more authoritatively than anyone else. Poindexter was the source of his information but he had overridden Poindexter on the advisability of issuing a statement. A simple litany seemed to have been imprinted on the president's mind: his Iran policy had nothing to do with terrorists, no ransom, no arms for hostages. He completely exonerated Iran, because it had enabled the United States to deal indirectly with the Lebanese hostage takers, as if he had been made to believe that there was no connection between Iran and the Lebanese.

Meese had come forward as the president's most loyal henchman. He had rushed in to back Poindexter's allegation that Israel, not the United States, had sold the arms to Iran. As if he already knew just what had happened, he had repeated whatever the president had chosen to believe. Regan cited Meese as having said: "Each of these [transactions] is a set of complex incidents, not related—no ransom, no money to Hizballah— trying to help moderates in Iran who also tried to help us."[87] Of the proposed statement, he had asserted: "We are saying only what we did and know has happened."[88] He had also tried to get those present to pretend that all of them had been consulted and that nothing had divided them. Meese had taken on the role of the president's obsequious mouthpiece, despite his later admission that he had known nothing about the Iran events between January and November 10, 1986.[89]

Casey's contribution had been minor. According to Regan, he had intervened on only two subjects. When Weinberger had questioned Rafsanjani's reliability and had complained that "his statements blew us out of [the] water in one way," Casey had retorted that "all of [our] people are convinced these are best to work with—but don't go all out to rely on Raf[sanjani]—we are feeling him out." Casey had also encouraged the issuing of a public statement by saying that "we have a good public position if we put it out in a simple way" and had brought a draft of it with him. It had stressed the long-range relationship with Iran as a reason for the contacts and had deemphasized the hostage motive.[90] Keel's notes make Casey even less important in the course of the discussion.*

Vice President Bush seems to have spoken up only once. His main concern was: "Israel may try to squeeze us."†[91]

In the end, the most important outcome of the meeting was its effect on Shultz. It seems to have crystallized in him the realization that he had been left out of major decisions for almost a year. The disclosure of more sales of TOWs and Hawk spare parts, after he had been given to believe that the sales were over, had apparently hit him particularly hard. His suspicions had also been aroused by the difference between President Reagan's assertion that Iran was weaker than Iraq and therefore deserved to be helped and the intelligence information Shultz was receiving that Iran was the stronger of the two. Against a united front of Reagan, Bush, Meese, Casey, and Poindexter, Shultz had not made a frontal attack on the Iran policy and had contented himself with making disconcerting remarks.

The meeting, however, had another disturbing aftermath. Meese and Poindexter went over Casey's proposed statement, much of which was cut out, because North told them that two and perhaps five of the remaining hostages might be freed as a result of his meeting in Geneva. Poindexter obtained the approval of Reagan, Weinberger, Meese, and Casey but could not reach Shultz, because he had gone off to Guatemala for an Organization of American States meeting.[92] Shultz received the text by cable on his plane and was surprised to read that there had been "unanimous support for the President's decisions" by the president's senior advisers.[93] Such a statement might well have passed unremarked in ordinary times, but these times were no longer ordinary.

Shultz described how he had objected to "this seemingly innocent press guidance":

> . . . he [Poindexter] said this had been cleared by everybody who was at the meeting and they were coming to me and I said I won't

* Keel's notes have Meese asking who were holding the hostages, with both Poindexter and Casey answering "Lebanon." Later Casey joined with Meese and Reagan to say "No Q & A's" [Questions and Answers] (B-14, pp. 1019, 1022).
† Keel's notes attribute only this to Bush: "What about Israelae [sic] case [?]" (B-14, p. 1022).

clear it and it has to be changed, and he said that's very unfortunate. But they did change it. I wasn't altogether comfortable with the way it was changed, but anyway it was changed.[94]

The change was from "unanimous support for the president's decisions" to "unanimous support for the President."[95] In that one word was hidden the gap that was opening up between the president and his secretary of state.

7

Meanwhile, pressure was building up within the administration to find a way to hold back what was fast becoming a major political crisis. The American media were shocked by the revelation that the administration had been saying one thing publicly and doing the opposite clandestinely. Poindexter's statement of November 10 had failed of its purpose to say as little as possible and had even aroused suspicions that the truth about the Iran connection was too discreditable to be revealed.

By November 12, the political damage seemed to be so great that the ultraconservative White House director of communications, Patrick J. Buchanan, sent a near-panicky message to Chief of Staff Regan:

> This may be redundant, but you ought to know that we face a grave communications problem over this Iranian/Hostage Issue. The *appearance* of things is that we have negotiated with a terrorist regime more detested by the American people than the Soviet Union, that we have paid in spare parts and military equipment for our hostages, that we violated our policy and traduced our principles, that we are now stonewalling. Not since I came here has there appeared such an issue which could do such deep and permanent damage to the President's standing. I realize this is all being held extremely tight, for obviously good reasons, but we have already witnessed some jubilant assaults upon Ronald Reagan's reputation for principle— from his enemies—and some bitter assaults from some of his friends. (We got them on the weekend shows.) We are fortunate Congress is out.

Buchanan's advice was to make the "earliest and fullest disclosure of what we did, what we attempted, why, etc. The story will not die, until some much fuller explanation—giving our arguments—is provided."[96] Regan told Buchanan that he agreed with him and had advocated the same course for a week.[97]

On November 12, too, Shultz had apparently made up his mind to persuade the president to take the Iran policy away from Poindexter and turn it over to the State Department as well as to end all arms sales to Iran. Shultz is said to have asked Regan to help convince the president to take both decisions.[98]

By this time, the media were in full cry after the Iran story, which had begun to take on the appearance of a Watergate type of cover-up. With little hard information coming from the administration, leaks, rumors, and speculation filled the press and the air. In the government bureaucracy itself, officials were said to be so appalled by the disclosures that they were thinking of resigning. North's aide Lieutenant Commander Craig P. Coy heard from Assistant Secretary of Defense Armitage that "some Pentagon folks might quit over this."[99] Armitage was also the bringer of unhappy tidings about what was being said in the bureaucracy about the State Department. Earl described a conversation with him on November 10:

> *Earl:* Well, he characterized the State Department as being shameless in this episode, whereas—
>
> *Question:* Shameless in that it was running from it?
>
> *Earl:* It was being disloyal, that it was leaking information, that it was just not supporting the President in coming to grips with this problem, whereas DoD [Secretary of Defense Weinberger] showed, he characterized them as coming across more as stupid but loyal, and that the sharks were out for Admiral Poindexter and the entire NSC structure, not just at Colonel North, but it was payback time for getting at the NSC as an organization from the various bureaucracies.[100]

To restrain this open warfare among departments, an effort was made on November 10 to enlarge the circle of those dealing with the growing crisis in order to make a more persuasive case for a united administration. Two "compartments" or groups were set up, one for policy, dealing with the strategic relationship with Iran, and the other for operations, dealing with the hostages and the Second Channel. The State Department wanted to get into the second as well as the first compartment, but the NSC staff firmly kept it out.[101]

By the morning of November 12, the president was convinced that he was obliged to make a public statement, in which he intended to insist that there had been no ransom and nothing illegal, but that he could not divulge everything in order not to endanger the participants.[102] The clamor for an official explanation was so great that a precipitous decision was made for the president to make a television speech on November 13.

This decision opened the way for the next stage of the Iran affair—a twelve-day domestic political crisis. As long as the operation was truly covert, the public did not worry about it and Congress was fobbed off with denials and deceptions. At best, a more open phase of the operation would have been tricky in view of the decision to tell something, but not much. It was made all the more difficult, however, because the admin-istration was totally unprepared for it. No thought had been given to the evil day when it might be necessary to reveal what had transpired between the United States, Israel, and Iran. The old policy of "no comment" was no longer feasible, and a new, less rigid policy had to be devised under duress and in a headlong hurry.

To complicate matters, a bitter quarrel was blowing up between former National Security Adviser McFarlane and Chief of Staff Regan. Mc-Farlane heard that Regan was already giving news magazines a "White House version" of events that blamed McFarlane for the original Israeli shipment of arms to Iran in 1985 and claimed that the president had approved it only after the fact. On November 7, an enraged McFarlane sent off a protest to Poindexter, which began:

> Having been out of town for two days and maintaining the no comment line, I returned today to find that Don Regan has back-grounded the weeklies and laid the entire problem at my feet, my idea, my management, a strict arms for hostages deal, no larger agenda in mind, etc. I was told this not by a journalist but by my closest friend who had been getting calls all day to the effect that "Bud is being hung out to dry by Don Regan." I still have not commented to anyone.
>
> But I must tell you that if this is true, I will be quite mad. This will be the second lie Don Regan has sowed against my character and I won't stand for it.

Whereupon McFarlane gave Poindexter a brief review of "just what the truth is." It emphasized that he had agreed to replace the Israeli TOWs only after checking with the president and that McFarlane had repeatedly opposed arms deals. McFarlane concluded by threatening a libel suit against Regan.[103] In reply, Poindexter doubted that Regan had done what McFarlane had been told and reiterated his view that "right now would be an absolutely stupid time for the administration to say anything."[104] McFarlane had blamed Regan, but Poindexter in the No-vember 10 meeting, only three days after he had received McFarlane's complaint, had told the group, which included President Reagan and Regan, that the United States had been informed by Israel "after the fact" (in Regan's notes) or "without permission" (in Keel's notes). It would seem that this was the "White House version," which Poindexter and Regan were putting out.[105] McFarlane was not able to take them on from within the government, but he was in a position to add to its disarray.

On November 13, President Reagan was set to read a speech, which, as usual, was written for him. Typically, a draft was first put together and then sent to the speech writers for polishing. In this case, the entire process was given no more than about twenty-four hours. It was started on November 12, the draft had to go to the speech writers by 5 a.m. on November 13, and be delivered by the president at 8:01 p.m. the same day.[106] The preparation of the draft was entrusted to an NSC staff group headed by North that included his two aides, Lieutenant Colonel Earl and Lieutenant Commander Coy, and Howard Teicher, with some assistance from McFarlane.[107] North had no reason to feel threatened; he was still given assignments which put him in a key position to influence events.

Before the president made his speech, Poindexter for the first time gave background briefings on the Iran affair—two for the benefit of congressional leaders, the third to reporters. The congressional briefings were short and general; Poindexter said nothing about the contras and emphasized that the arms sent to Iran had been very limited.[108] According to Regan, who was present, the two senators, Republican Robert Dole and Democrat Robert Byrd, and the two representatives, Republican Dick Cheney and Democrat James Wright, were obviously "skeptical—you could see it in their faces, hear it in their voices."[109]

The reporters were equally skeptical. They pressed Poindexter about the arms shipments in 1985, about which the media had become increasingly suspicious. A question forced Poindexter into a corner and brought from him a reply that showed how the administration had opened itself to outright falsification by adopting the new policy of justifying itself publicly:

> *Question:* —a few things on the shipments, just to clarify this. Any shipments that were made prior to January of 1986 you're saying the U.S. had no role in, either condoning, winking, encouraging, or anything of that nature? Is that correct.
>
> *Poindexter:* That's correct.[110]

It was not correct. The unfortunate shipment of November 1985 had been carried out with the cooperation of American officials, from North and McFarlane to CIA and State Department personnel in Washington and Lisbon. Poindexter was never very good at reinventing the past.

8

In his television speech of November 13, President Reagan tried to tell just enough to allay any doubts about his Iran policy and not enough to reveal anything that might be embarrassing.

Most of the speech was made up of generalities: a dialogue with Iran to end the Iran-Iraq war, to safeguard Iran from the Soviet Union, and to free the hostages. When he went into some of the details, however, he came dangerously close to distorting them.

> The charge has been made that the United States has shipped weapons to Iran as ransom payment for the release of American hostages in Lebanon, that the United States undercut its allies and secretly violated American policy against trafficking with terrorists. Those charges are utterly false. . . .
> These modest deliveries, taken together, could easily fit into a single cargo plane. . . .
> It's been widely reported, for example, that the Congress, as well as top executive branch officials, were circumvented. . . . all appropriate Cabinet officers were fully consulted. . . .
> We did not—repeat—did not trade weapons or anything else for hostages nor will we.[111]

The charges that arms payments had been made for the freed hostages—whether they should be called "ransom" or not—were not false. The deliveries could not have fitted easily into a single cargo plane. Top executive branch officials had opposed the arms-for-hostages deals and had been circumvented. Weapons had been traded for hostages, at least indirectly, through Iran.

In effect, the speech had been conceived to justify all that had gone before and serve notice that nothing was going to change. Those who had been responsible for the speech had made it in the president's image and had incorporated into it his favorite preconceptions and misconceptions. As a result, the speech did little or nothing to deflect the growing pressure on the administration to make a full disclosure of the entire Iran affair. A poll in the *Los Angeles Times* showed that only 14 percent believed the President's statement that he had not been trading arms for hostages. White House polls came out with the same result. The president is said to have been "shaken."[112] Soon after the speech, McFarlane sent an ominous message to Poindexter: "I lived through Watergate John. Well-meaning people who were in on the early planning of the communications strategy, didn't intend to lie but ultimately came around to do it."[113]

Above all, the speech failed to convince Secretary of State Shultz. He met with President Reagan on November 14, the day after, and made an effort, as he put it, "to change this around." Shultz says that "I didn't want to become [sic] in one of Admiral Poindexter's compartments, I wanted to get this out where I could see it for myself and get it managed right." He was most disappointed in the failure of the speech to say "flat out, no more arms sales."[114]

In effect, Shultz was heading toward an open challenge to Poindexter's control of Iran policy. In preparation for this counteroffensive, the State Department had prepared a statement of what the policy should and should not be, which Shultz gave to Chief of Staff Regan on November 15. Much of it was aimed against using arms sales to get a better relationship with Iran or to free the hostages, but it ended with a warning that the worst was still to come, even after the president's speech: "There is a real danger of spinning a web of misleading if not incorrect statements that won't stand up to press and Congressional investigation. If there is not full and swift disclosure—to the public and to the intelligence committees, as appropriate—this affair is going to go on and on in an agonizing and terribly corrosive way."[115]

Shultz was rebuffed. Regan told him that the White House was not in a position to accept it.[116] The sides were drawn, and Shultz was getting nowhere.

Twenty-four hours later, Shultz was put in an even more awkward position. He had been asked to appear on the television program *Face the Nation* on November 16 and had been reluctant to accept. His problem was, as he realized, that he could not claim to support President Reagan and admit that he did not support the president's policy of arms sales to Iran. But Regan prevailed on him to go on as an administration spokesman, with predictably disastrous results. The program opened with a replay of two recent statements by senators from both parties:

Senator Carl Levin (D.—Mich.): How in the name of heaven we could be saying one thing so clearly in public, we could be certifying one thing so clearly to the Congress, and doing something so totally different in fact.

Senator Barry Goldwater (R.—Arizona): I think President Reagan has gotten his butt in a crack on this Iran thing.

Senator Goldwater, sometimes known as "Mr. Republican," was an especially damaging critic. Secretary Shultz's partner in the program, the House majority leader, James Wright, was less disrespectful but made it clear that he already knew a great deal that had not been publicly divulged. He charged that "laws have been broken" and revealed that a presidential Finding of January 17, 1986, had instructed the CIA to withhold information from Congress. He evoked the memory of the Watergate scandal and President Nixon's handling of it.

When Secretary Shultz's turn came, the moderator, Lesley Stahl, insisted on concentrating on the arms deals. Shultz seemed to want to absolve himself by explaining that "my own information about the operational aspects of what was going on was fragmentary at best." She reminded him that he had assured the moderate Arab states at the UN only six weeks earlier that the United States was not selling arms to Iran. Finally, Shultz was faced with just the line of questioning that he feared the most:

> *Stahl:* Will there be any more arms shipments to Iran, either directly by our government or through any third parties?
>
> *Shultz:* It's certainly against our policy.
>
> *Stahl:* That's not an answer.
>
> *Shultz:* And I think the signal has been given.
>
> *Stahl:* Well, sir, it was against our policy before and we went ahead and did it. You seem to be saying there will be.
>
> *Shultz:* We gave a signal and the signal was given, and, as far as I'm concerned, I don't see any need for further signals.
>
> *Stahl:* Well, then, why don't you answer the question directly? I'll ask it again. Will there be any more arms shipments to Iran, either directly by the United States or through any third parties?
>
> *Shultz:* Under the circumstances of Iran's war with Iraq, its pursuit of terrorism, its association with those holding our hostages, I would certainly say, as far as I'm concerned, no.

Then came the climactic question and answer:

> *Stahl:* Do you have the authority to speak for the entire administration?
>
> *Shultz:* No.[117]

The program ended on this note. It was a shattering experience for Shultz. "It was a sad day for me, very sad," Shultz said in retrospect. "But it was the truth."[118] By telling the truth, he had revealed what Reagan and Poindexter had taken pains to conceal—that the president's senior advisers were not united behind him and that his most senior adviser in the field of foreign policy had been ignorant of and opposed to an essential element of that policy. Shultz had attempted to resign several times previously for much lesser reasons; he was now confronted with the alternative of resigning once again.

As Shultz has described his position at this time, he had become a pariah within the administration: "Now this was a very traumatic period for me because everybody was saying I'm disloyal to the President, I'm not speaking up for the policy, and I'm battling away here, and I could see people were calling for me to resign if I can't be loyal to the President, even including some of my friends and people who had held high office

and should know that maybe there's more involved than they're seeing.
. . . it was a battle royal."[119]

One of those who went beyond asking Shultz to resign was Casey,
who tried to get him fired. Casey wrote to President Reagan advising him
to get a "new pitcher" in the State Department and to replace him with
former ambassador to the UN Jeane Kirkpatrick.[120]

Shultz was not the only one who exposed himself on television on
November 16. Poindexter submitted to questioning on a rival program,
Meet the Press, but was in no danger of suffering the same embarrassment,
because he came through as a true-blue defender of the president's policy,
for which he had been largely responsible. Poindexter had some difficulty
explaining that the arms embargo against Iran was still in force, despite
the arms sales to Iran. Like the president earlier, he pretended that all
the arms could fit into a single cargo plane. He talked as if the arms sales
had nothing to do with the hostages and were merely intended to demonstrate that the Iranians were dealing with the U.S. government. The
arms, he said, were supplied to the "moderate elements," not to overthrow
the Khomeini regime but to change its policies. Poindexter came through
this trial by television as no novice in the arts of evasion and
concealment.[121]

A "battle royal" had been engaged by November 16, but how it would
come out was still uncertain. As Reagan's speech of November 13 and
Poindexter's television interview of November 16 showed, the administration was still determined to justify its past actions and continue to do
business with the Second Channel.

The battle could still go either way.

22

Cover-up

By November 16, the crisis of the Iran policy had moved out of the government into the domain of public opinion. Despite the best efforts of President Reagan and National Security Adviser Poindexter, a miasma of doubt and incredulity continued to hang over the Iran affair. In the opinion of James Reston, the senior political commentator of *The New York Times*, "there is now a crisis of confidence in the Government."[1] When Poindexter was interviewed, the moderator, Marvin Kalb, had confronted him with the state of political opinion in the capital: "It is the broad consensus here in Washington that this new Iranian connection has damaged America's credibility among moderate Arab states and West European allies, and, in addition, raised questions about the administration's competence in the handling of recent foreign policy problems, including a disinformation campaign against Libya that backfired, a summit in Iceland that produced confusion and damaged chances of an arms control agreement, and now Iran."

After that day, he might also have said: and now Secretary of State Shultz. In that climate of opinion, Shultz's implicit admission that he did not approve of the president's policy and, therefore, that the administration was not as united as it pretended to be was inflammatory. It was clear after Shultz's "No" that there was much more to the Iran story than Reagan and Poindexter had let out and that what Shultz knew had caused him to make a painful confession.

In a way, Poindexter had been right. He had fought against divulging anything about the Iran policy and had been overruled. Shultz and Regan had advocated full disclosure. The president's decision had gone in favor of neither one nor the other but something in between. Reagan had come to feel that he had to make a public statement, but one that concealed more than it revealed and raised more questions than it answered. Going public but saying little only made matters worse.

Shultz had put himself in such an exposed position that the question immediately arose whether he could remain in office. In his television appearance, he had been asked whether he had ever considered resigning and had answered: "Oh, I talked to the President; I serve at his pleasure, and anything that I have to say on that subject I'd just say to him."[2] This reply had been taken as an implicit affirmation that he had talked to the president about resigning. President Reagan had watched Shultz's television interview, and the next step seemed up to the president.

The stakes were so high that Reagan acted almost immediately. In a "photo opportunity" at the White House with a visiting dignitary on the same day, November 17, he was asked whether he planned to fire Shultz and had answered: "I'm not firing anybody." Asked whether he was going to ship any more arms to Iran, Reagan answered: "We have absolutely no plan to do any such thing."[3]

Larry Speakes, the White House press secretary, was prepared for the same question. "The President does want Secretary Shultz," Speakes was instructed by the president to say, "to remain on the job and has no reason to believe it will be otherwise." Speakes was also asked about the apparent discrepancy between the president's and the secretary's positions on arms shipments to Iran and replied: "The President's policy is no further shipments. The Secretary's policy is no further shipments. So where's the difference?"[4]

But the difference would not go away. Despite Reagan's statements that he had absolutely no plans to send arms to Iran, *The New York Times* reported that "it was far from clear that this would put to rest widespread speculation in Washington that Mr. Shultz's days in the Reagan administration may be numbered."[5]

That Shultz was the one to stand his ground and put President Reagan's Iran policy in jeopardy was not to be expected from Shultz's past behavior. He had expressed himself clearly in opposition, but that had been almost a year ago and in a confidential setting. In this area, Shultz had not been the administration's chief foreign-policy adviser and spokesman for so long that the sudden stubborn assertion of his prerogatives came without warning.

Though it was not the last word, Reagan's reaction to Shultz's interview was the first sign that the president's iron front was cracking. As Reagan began to retreat, Shultz pushed ahead.

2

Once aroused, Shultz began to mobilize his department for the still undecided battle royal. He was not the only one in the department in a mood for confrontation. Back in July 1986, Under Secretary of State Michael Armacost had advised Shultz that "as this [Iran] story surfaces, we are going to sow more and more confusion among our friends, who will recall our frequent lectures on no deals for hostages and no arms for Iran."[6] In fact, the State Department was regarded as a hotbed of hostility to the Iran policy, and most of the news leaks—with good reason—were attributed to it.

Shultz's offensive began to roll on November 18. He told Armacost and Charles Hill, the department's executive assistant, that the State Department had to have access to all the facts concerning the Iran initiative.[7] It was late in the day for the State Department to want to get all the facts, but the order was intended to prepare Shultz to question the "facts" in the president's mind.

Meanwhile, Reagan changed his mind about refusing to hold a question-and-answer press conference. The speech of November 13 had admittedly failed of its purpose and another presidential effort was deemed necessary, but this time one much riskier than a speech. The news conference was scheduled for the next day, November 19, and another round of hectic preparations got under way.

Reagan was not the only one who prepared for this ordeal. Shultz's staff also prepared him to prepare the president. With their increased knowledge of the U.S.-Iran connection, Shultz's aides detailed what to say to the president. They wanted Shultz to rule out any more arms to Iran, to regard Iran as a terrorist state, to shift control of U.S.-Iran relations from Poindexter to Shultz, and to hold out against freeing the hostages by giving in to terrorist demands.[8]

A new and unexpectedly formidable figure now entered the penultimate phase of the Iran crisis. He was Abraham D. Sofaer, the State Department legal adviser. He had had a distinguished legal career as a federal prosecutor, law professor at Columbia University, federal judge in the Southern District of New York, and legal adviser at the State Department since 1985. Until now, Sofaer had known nothing of the Iran initiative.

On November 18, Sofaer was summoned to a conference called by the White House counsel, Peter Wallison. Among those present were David Doherty, the CIA general counsel; Paul Thompson, the NSC staff counsel; and Assistant Attorney General Charles J. Cooper. According to Sofaer, Wallison called the meeting to get information on the Iran initiative in order to be able to give the president advice for his coming press conference. When Wallison called on Thompson, who knew more than anyone else at the meeting about what had been going on, Thompson replied that the congressional intelligence staffs were going to be briefed that day and that Poindexter had instructed him not to give out any information to anyone who did not need to know. Sofaer gathered that Doherty and Cooper already knew a great deal and that this implied that he and Wallison did not need to know. Sofaer would not submit to such discrimination without protest. The matter could be handled in that way, Sofaer said, but in that case he and Wallison could not be asked for legal opinions or support for the policy, which would become the sole responsibility of Attorney General Meese.

Nevertheless, enough was brought up at the meeting to suggest what the legal concerns were going to be. Sofaer heard for the first time that there had been a Finding on January 17, 1986, and pre-January shipments of arms. As Sofaer put it, the discrepancy would "obviously raise a very serious legal question. The Finding was in January, what happened before the Finding?" Thompson had said nothing about the November 1985 shipment of arms to Iran, which would have made the case even more serious, but enough had come out to give Sofaer the impression that something of questionable legality had taken place.

Sofaer came out of the meeting with two reasons for disquietude. One was the legal problem of the pre-January 1986 arms deals. The other was the exclusion of Wallison and himself from knowledge of the Iran affair when other legal advisers were included, while at the same time Sofaer and Wallison were expected to give legal advice to the secretary of state and the president. After the meeting, Sofaer told Wallison that their exclusion was "extremely serious." Sofaer later recalled why: "That we had not been briefed. And that they were going to say things to Hill staffers that they weren't telling us—shocking. And that it was particularly serious from his point of view because he [Wallison] was the President's counsel and that he should act accordingly." Sofaer says that Wallison agreed with him and went to talk to Thompson.[9]

As a result of this meeting, Poindexter invited Armacost and Sofaer to meet with him and Thompson later that day. Poindexter gave them a more detailed account of the dealings with Israel and Iran and for the first time showed them the January 17, 1986, Finding. Sofaer left feeling that he still had not been told the whole story.[10]

By this time, Shultz was fired up for the last, decisive rounds of the battle royal. The first took place on November 19 before the president's scheduled press conference. According to the State Department record, Shultz spoke to him with brutal candor. "We have been deceived and lied to," Shultz said. "And you have to watch out about saying no arms for hostages." Shultz revealed that McFarlane had once told him that a planeload of arms would go to Iran if hostages were released. The president said that he knew of it, but told Shultz that he was "telling me things I don't know." Shultz replied: "Mr. President, if I'm telling you something you don't know—I don't know very much—so something is wrong here." After it was over, Shultz called Chief of Staff Regan and expressed concern about the president's press conference that same evening, because the president had been misled on the facts. *11

A few hours later, President Reagan faced a large roomful of reporters bent on getting all the facts.

3

The press conference of November 19 was the most disastrous in President Reagan's presidency.

Unlike the television speech six days earlier, the president now made some admissions and concessions. He admitted that "several top officials" had opposed the sale of any weapons to Iran. The exchange of arms for hostages was a "mistaken perception," but he had decided to eliminate it by directing that "no further sales of arms of any kind be sent to Iran." He had the legal right to defer reporting to Congress, but was going to have the proper congressional committees briefed in the coming week.

These admissions did not appease most of the reporters, who were unforgiving in their belief that he had long been holding out on them. Reagan was again led into pleading that the arms sent to Iran "could be put in one cargo plane, and there would be plenty of room left over." Inasmuch as the media already knew that at least 1,000 TOWs had been sent, and that so many TOWs could not possibly get into one cargo plane with plenty of room left over, this version did not help Reagan's cause. The president also described the TOW as a "shoulder-mounted weapon" and was instructed by a reporter that it was a "ground-to-ground weapon." TOWs were, in fact, too heavy to be used from the shoulder and were fired from tripods, vehicles, or helicopters.

The president also seemed to have changed his mind about the Iranians with whom the Americans had been dealing. On November 13, he had implied that the U.S. government had been dealing with the Iranian government by saying that the United States had made "overtures" to the government of Iran.[12] On November 19, however, he said that the United States had been dealing with a "particular group" of individuals who needed arms to prove that they were dealing with the head of the U.S. government, though the United States was not dealing with the head of the Iranian government. The discrepancy did not go unnoticed.

The most serious blunder on November 19 was made twice. It first took the form of "We did not condone and do not condone the shipment of arms from other countries," and a second time as "We, as I say, have

---

* In his congressional testimony, Shultz said that the president had told him: "You are telling me things that I don't know, that are news to me." Shultz recalled saying: " 'Well, Mr. President, I don't know very much, but if I am telling you things that are news to you, then you are not being given the kind of flow of information that you deserve to be given,' or something like that" (100-9, p. 44).

had nothing to do with other countries or their shipment of arms or doing what they're doing."

Unfortunately, Chief of Staff Regan had already disclosed that the United States had condoned an Israeli shipment of arms to Iran in September 1985. When Regan's statement was pointed out to him, the president pleaded that he had not heard Regan say it and intended to ask him about it.

The president's faux pas in denying the U.S. role in the shipment of arms to Iran from other countries was so flagrant that aides rushed to their offices and issued a correction within the hour. It admitted that "there was a third country involved in our secret project with Iran," but still insisted that "all the shipments of token amounts of defensive arms and parts that I have authorized or condoned taken in total could be placed aboard a single cargo aircraft."[13]

The questioning of the president was so hostile that he would have had to put forward an exceptionally strong case to turn the tide of media opinion in his favor. Instead, he was described as "grim and testy," unsure of his answers, and no more forthcoming than he had been on November 13. It appeared that only an admission that the Iran policy had been a mistake might have enabled the president to put the issue to rest. One questioner gave the president a chance to back down gracefully, but he would have none of it:

> *Question:* I just wanted to ask you what would be wrong at this stage of the game, since everything seems to have gone wrong that could possibly go wrong, like the Murphy Law, the Reagan Law, the O'Leary Law, this week—what would be wrong in saying that a mistake was made on a very high-risk gamble so that you can get on with the next two years?
>
> *President:* I don't think a mistake was made. It was a high-risk gamble, and it was a gamble that, as I've said, I believe the circumstances warranted. And I don't see that it has been a fiasco or a great failure of any kind. We still have those contacts. We still have made some ground. We got our hostages back—three of them. And so I think that what we did was right, and we're going to continue on this path.*[14]

This defiance of a media and a public opinion largely convinced that his policy had failed and should never have been tried ensured that the crisis of confidence in the government would have to run its course. President Reagan's worst enemy in this crisis was himself, because his evident lack of mastery of the facts deprived him of the public's willingness to take his word on trust and give him credit for knowing what he was

---

* The questioner was Jeremiah O'Leary of *The Washington Times.*

doing or what was done in his name. His press conference on November 19 was another high-risk gamble—and it failed.

4

After this press conference, Secretary Shultz and his staff were more than ever convinced that the president had lost his way and needed very different advice and advisers to find it again.

Shultz wasted no time calling the president after the press conference. According to Shultz, he told Reagan that it was personally a very courageous thing to have held it, but that he felt many of his statements had been false or misleading. "If you would like," Shultz recalled saying, "I would welcome a chance to come around and go through it with you, and I will go through these points and tell you what I think is wrong with them and why." Reagan replied: "Well, I welcome seeing you."

In preparation for his next meeting with Reagan, Shultz's staff had worked up "talking points" for him. In effect, they provided Shultz with the factual ammunition for an all-out, full-scale assault on the version of events with which Reagan and Poindexter were identified. Shultz was also given a proposed alternative policy that was a root-and-branch repudiation of the old one. By following it, Shultz would have talked the president into coming out against sending any more arms to Iran. But that was not all; the president was also told that his Iran policy had been wrongheaded in virtually every other respect—that Iran supported terrorism; that the United States had been dealing with "unscrupulous and untrustworthy" Iranians; that Iran was "without any qualification" the "main banker, patron, arms supplier, and adviser" of the Lebanese Hizballah; that arms had been traded for hostages; and that there were serious questions whether the president had the right to defer for so long reporting to Congress.[15] These "talking points" for Shultz were the result of pent-up opposition in the State Department, which for too long had had no outlet.

With Regan present, Shultz presented some version of these points to the president. It must have been a racking encounter, because Shultz later described it as "a long, tough discussion, not the kind of discussion I ever thought I would have with the President of the United States." Shultz seems to have wanted mainly to get across the idea that Reagan had been a victim of wrong information and advice:

> The President—he didn't disagree with me. He corroborated things like the November 25 [1985] things, very open, strong discussion, but he had in his mind that what he authorized and what he expected to have carried out was an effort to get an opening of

a different kind to Iran and the arms and the hostages were ancillary to that. That was not his objective.

And that—and I am sure that is what the President felt. He wasn't just saying that. That was his idea, and I kept trying to say, "Well, I recognize that, Mr. President, and that is a good objective, but that isn't the way it worked," at least insofar as I can see.

So we—and then there were other things that were said that I was very concerned about. He was being given information that suggested that Iran was no longer practicing terrorism. That was wrong. And I don't know, various other things, but the gist of it was that there were things that he had been given as information from the people who were briefing him and providing him with the information and the press conference preparatory sessions that were not, in my view, correct.

And I don't think that the people doing that were serving the President. In fact, I know they weren't serving the President, and I was trying to get that point across in as strong a way as I could with not just sort of listing the arguments, but saying, "You have got to look at the facts."[16]

Regan recalled that Shultz had warned the president that CIA Director Casey and Under Secretary of State Armacost were expected to testify before the House Intelligence Committee the next day, November 21, and were going to disagree publicly on past dealings with Iran.[17] A wide-open, unprecedented split in the government appeared to be imminent.

According to Reagan, the meeting with Shultz and Regan was arranged after Regan had told him Shultz wanted to deliver an ultimatum—fire Poindexter or I quit. At the meeting, Shultz is said to have blamed Poindexter for having misled Reagan and to have urged Poindexter's dismissal. Shultz did not threaten to quit, but Reagan's diary for that day reads: "I fear he [Shultz] may be getting ready to say, 'either someone else is fired or I quit.' " At this late date, Reagan would have us believe, he wondered for the first time whether he had not known all about the dealings with Iran.[18]

Shultz seemed to assume that President Reagan had been an innocent bystander in the Iran initiative and had been a victim of Poindexter's misinformation. Shultz also took the line that he agreed with the president's objective but parted company with the way it had been carried out. In this way, Shultz was able to criticize and absolve the president at the same time and to come out as a defender of the president's best interests.

One way or another, by November 20 President Reagan was clearly losing control of his administration and was faced with a State Department determined at all costs to reverse his Iran policy.

5

While Shultz was blaming Poindexter for misinforming the president, Poindexter was trying to put together an official version of what had happened between the United States and Iran. This effort took the form of a "chronology," which Poindexter intended to use once the Iran project came under scrutiny.

Poindexter had ordered the preparation of a chronological narrative soon after the appearance of the *Al-Shiraa* story. As usual, he put North in charge, telling him only to leave out all mention of the diversion of Iran funds to the Nicaraguan contras.[19]

The production of this chronology is of special interest because it confronted North and others with an awkward dilemma—if they told the truth, they risked admitting to unlawful acts, and if they told untruths, they might not be able to sustain them if they were looked into, especially by congressional committees. The chronology, therefore, was a test of how confident they were of the lawfulness or permissibility of what they had been doing. If they tampered with the truth, they risked revealing just when and where they had overstepped the very thin line within or beyond which they had been operating.

North, with the help of a few others, wrote and rewrote the chronology at least a dozen times between about November 5 and November 20.[20] Records had been poorly kept. North himself did not know much about the early phase of the U.S.-Israel-Iran connection in 1985 and had to resort to McFarlane to fill in gaps. Above all, North tried to hide or distort some aspects of the story, as a result of which he repeatedly found himself in trouble.

One of the most troublesome subjects for North was the November 1985 "horror story." As North later explained, his version was largely false "because we were at that point in time making an effort to dissociate ourselves with the earlier Israeli shipments."[21] In a chronology of November 17, he made it appear that the Israelis had been solely responsible for providing Iran with Hawk missiles in November 1985 and that the United States had disapproved of the Israeli action.[22] This version was drastically altered in the last chronology of November 20, in which a number of new falsehoods were added.

As North now told the story, he had specifically told the Israelis that no U.S. carrier could be used, but that the name of a CIA proprietary had been made known to the Israelis, who had chartered it for what they told the Americans were "oil-drilling parts." When the Americans had belatedly discovered that the proprietary aircraft had been used to deliver the Hawk missiles instead of oil-drilling parts, the incident had "raised serious U.S. concerns that these deliveries were jeopardizing our objective of arranging a direct meeting with high-level Iranian officials."[23]

North later admitted that this version was false but put all the blame on McFarlane, who, he said, had provided it to him. * North related that he had shown it to Secord, who had burst out: "That's not true. I'm not going to help any more in this. I'm leaving."[24]

Secord's recollection was slightly different. He said that he had read one of the earlier versions in which the arms sent to Iran by Israel in August 1985 had been approved "at the highest level" of the U.S. government, by which he understood the president. But when he came back and read the later version, Secord had found that it had the president withholding his approval. At this, according to Secord, he had told North that the latter "is not my understanding of the facts," whereupon North had replied that McFarlane "had drafted that section himself." Secord's response had been: "Fine, thank you very much, I will get out of you guys' hair and I left."[25] Secord seems to have been the only one unwilling to take part in fictionalizing the chronology.

North was right about McFarlane's role. On November 18, McFarlane had sent additions to the chronology which had failed to say that the president had approved the Israeli shipments of arms to Iran in August 1985.[26] McFarlane later admitted that he had participated in an "exercise" to "gild the President's motives" and that he had concealed the fact that the U.S. government had approved of the Israeli shipments.[27] McFarlane was apparently influenced by a "climate in which there was an obvious effort to, as I said, distance and to blur the President's role in the initial authorization, in both timing and substance."[28] McFarlane later acknowledged that it had been "misleading, at least, and wrong, at worst, for me to overly gild the President's motives for his decisions in this, to portray them as mostly directed toward political outcomes," instead of toward the return of the hostages.[29]

North also had some trouble fitting the CIA into the story. According to North, the CIA had given him a version which made it appear that it had had little to do with the Iran operation and that the NSC staff was largely or wholly responsible for it.[30] North was disturbed, because it implied that he and the NSC staff had acted on their own and had to accept full responsibility for everything.

The issue came to a head at a meeting in Poindexter's office on the afternoon of November 20, 1986, at which Poindexter, Casey, Meese, Gates, Thompson, Cooper, and North were present.[31] The matter was

---

* At his trial, North went so far as to say that he had been telling the truth but that McFarlane had told him "we shouldn't acknowledge it [the November 1985 shipment] and my acquiescing in it because I did realize the one key point for me was the fact that the hostages would indeed be jeopardized by a public revelation about that, that the hostages were at risk because the Iranians were outraged about that November shipment which he had arranged" (NT, pp. 7597, 7600–1). Yet the Iranians had long gotten over the November 1985 shipment and had continued to negotiate. In any case, the chronology was not then a public document, and the information in it was intended for top officials of the U.S. government.

urgent, because Casey was scheduled to testify before the Senate and House Intelligence Committees the following day.

This meeting later played a prominent part in Poindexter's trial in 1990. Once again the missile shipment in November 1985 arose to haunt those in the group who had known about it. The issue came up in a peculiar form. The CIA had produced a single page, headed "CIA Airline Involvement." One sentence read: "We in CIA did not find out that our airline had hauled Hawk missiles into Iran until mid-January when we were told by the Iranians."[32] North was offended by the first three words because they implied that others in the U.S. government outside the CIA, and specifically the NSC staff, might have known about the shipment. The document had previously referred to the NSC as the agency which had requested the shipment and had made the CIA no more than an innocent bystander, merely lending its assistance to get an airline for the weapons transfer. North wanted the first three words changed to "No one in the U.S.G[overnment]" and had his way without objection.[33]

North's change in the wording was even more extreme than the original. It made him, Poindexter, Casey, and everyone else in the know ignorant of what had happened in November 1985. Yet Poindexter, Casey, and Thompson, who knew better, remained silent throughout and permitted North's version to be written into the document. As North later put it: "That was a false statement when it arrived. It was still a false statement when I changed it, and to my knowledge, at the time, everybody in the room knew it." Questioned more closely, North said that he had "assumed" everyone in the room knew it but could be sure that only Casey, Poindexter, Thompson, and he himself had known that it was false.[34] In fact, Meese, Cooper, and Gates had had no reason to know all that had happened in November 1985, and the belated realization that they had been deceived contributed to the shock with which they soon learned that they could not trust what they had heard.

The participants received other fictitious information. According to Meese, "we were told at that meeting that these were, to the best of the knowledge of people in the U.S. Government, these were oil-drilling parts, and we were also told that the only involvement of the U.S. Government was to suggest an airline, and that the CIA would notify the airline that they should take this shipment." Meese said that North had appeared to be "the most knowledgeable person about what had taken place." If so, North was the source of the oil-drilling story or at least had not contradicted it.[35]

In the end, North said, he and Casey went back to Casey's office and "fixed that testimony" simply by deleting all mention of the Hawks.[36] North's account of the meeting stressed that he did not want the NSC staff to be held entirely responsible for the action. According to North, he had insisted: "Look, you got to stop calling this a NSC activity, the NSC is not a government unto itself, despite of what some of you may believe—the NSC is an organ of the U.S. Government—and would you therefore get closure, let's take out NSC and CIA and put the U.S. Government everywhere we can in the document."[37] The incident was symptomatic of the way the chronology and Casey's testimony were patched together—to tell the story in such a way that the telltale facts would be concealed or misrepresented. It was also increasingly clear that the greatest difficulty was being encountered in putting together a plausible account of the November 1985 shipment of arms to Iran, the "horror story," without revealing that the NSC staff, the CIA, and even the State Department had been implicated before there had been a Finding allegedly making it legitimate. For this reason, Poindexter said little at the meeting; he had already realized that, as he put it, "the big question in my mind at that point was the question of whether or not the President had approved the Hawk shipments before they had taken place or not, and I didn't know the answer to that question and I didn't want to discuss in such a group that issue until I was on much firmer ground."[38]

Gates had other sidelights on the meeting. He said that North had tried to persuade the CIA drafters of Casey's testimony that the Israelis or someone else had called to set up the proprietary flight in November 1985. Gates told the meeting that CIA officers were prepared to testify under oath that North had been the one who had called or had arranged for the proprietary flight. It was decided to adopt Gates's version. Gates also related that the first draft of Casey's testimony had been prepared by the CIA's Operations Directorate with North's assistance. North had tried to include a sentence that no one in the U.S. government had known what was on the airplane, but Casey himself had removed that sentence. At the meeting, North had attempted to reinsert the same sentence, but Casey had not used it.[39]

From all that we have been told about this meeting on November 20, it was most significant as a last-ditch effort by North to concoct an official version that contained false or misleading statements at key points. At issue were the arms shipments of 1985 that had not been covered by the Finding of January 17, 1986. It is hard to say what would have happened if the truth had come out and the administration had been forced to admit that it had done something in violation of the law, but it is safe to say that the heavens would not have fallen. Even an admission of error might have been forgiven in the interest of freeing the hostages. So much of the story had already appeared in the media that little would have come as a surprise.

The reason the chronology and the testimony were so meaningful is that they led directly to the next and final stage of the crisis of confidence. The details were less important than what they came to symbolize—an administration that had done something that it was hiding from or falsifying to Congress and the public. Both Casey and Poindexter were scheduled to report to the Senate and House Intelligence Committees on the morning of November 21, and whatever they said was bound to be closely examined and skeptically received. The very task of constructing the chronology had brought the secret life of the Iran operation to the attention of many who had never before been permitted to look into it. Poindexter later admitted that "I was aware that the chronologies were inaccurate."[40] He claimed that he did not know what was accurate, but that did not stop him from telling the committees what he knew was inaccurate.

6

Something else happened on November 20 of even greater immediate consequence. The final collapse of the Poindexter-North front began that evening.

It will be recalled that Abraham Sofaer, the State Department legal adviser, had come out of the meeting on November 18 with the other counsel—Doherty of the CIA, Wallison of the White House, and Thompson of the NSC staff—disturbed by two things that he had just learned. They were the arms shipments to Iran in 1985 before the Finding of January 17, 1986, and the exclusion of Wallison and himself from all previous aspects of the Iran affair.

On the morning of November 20, Secretary of State Shultz told Sofaer that he wanted him and Under Secretary of State Armacost to be briefed by the executive assistant, Charles Hill, about all that was known in the department about the arms sales to Iran.[41] From Hill, Sofaer learned more that was new to him, especially that former National Security Adviser McFarlane had called Shultz back in November 1985 and had told him that 100 Hawks were being sent to Iran in exchange for hostages and that Shultz had been opposed to the deal.[42] Hill read from notes which seemed to come from a recording of the 1985 McFarlane-Shultz conversation.[43]

In this way, Sofaer learned about the November 1985 arms deal. As Hill was proceeding with the briefing, a CIA official, David Gries, the director of congressional relations, arrived with a copy of Casey's proposed testimony before the congressional intelligence committees the next day, for which Sofaer had asked. This draft aroused Sofaer's suspicions that something questionable was going on. He tried without success to question Gries about a statement that "the CIA and the NSC did not know that these were weapons rather than oil-drilling bits."[44] Prices charged for the TOW missiles struck him as too low. The CIA, it was said, had agreed to assist Israel in shipping oil-drilling bits by finding an airline, but only this one time. "This made me skeptical," Sofaer recalled, "because I didn't see any reason why they would be reluctant to help Israel get the name of an airline if all they were doing was shipping oil drilling bits. So that story did not hang together." Sofaer also saw the name of Southern Air Transport in the proposed testimony and associated it with the Hasenfus incident the month before. "And to me," he explained, "it was a red flag indicating a possible connection to Central America."[45]

At this, Sofaer went to see Hill and told him there seemed to be serious questions about the November and possibly August–September 1985 arms shipments. Attorney General Meese might have approved of the January 17, 1986, Finding without knowing of the previous activities. In any case, Casey's projected testimony appeared to contain a misstatement about oil-drilling bits.

Sofaer asked for permission to call Meese to tell him about his misgivings. "With great apprehension," Sofaer said, Hill agreed. Early that afternoon—still November 20—Sofaer called Deputy Attorney General Arnold Burns and told him about his suspicions. Burns called back to say that he had conveyed the information to Meese, who had assured him that he knew "of certain facts that explained all these matters and that laid to rest all the problems I might perceive." Burns did not know what the facts were but said that he found Meese's assurance "mysterious."

Sofaer was not satisfied. "I was not speculating in my mind as to what had happened," he recalled, "but obviously one of the possibilities I had in mind was that people in the NSC [staff] or others, Casey included, had convinced the Attorney General of a story that I might find unconvincing." Sofaer was asked: "So you feared that there may be a cover-up in progress?" Sofaer answered: "I was very afraid."

As a result, Sofaer decided to call White House Counsel Wallison. Sofaer went on: "I told him everything that I had learned up to that point. I told him that he was the President's lawyer, that I felt an obligation to tell him these facts. That I had reviewed the CIA testimony. That I felt that it included a false story about oil drilling equipment, and that he should look into it."

Wallison, according to Sofaer, was "shocked." Wallison had been totally shut out and knew nothing. Assistant Attorney General Cooper and NSC staff counsel Thompson were just then in Wallison's office.[46] Wallison gave the phone to Cooper, to whom Sofaer repeated what he had told Wallison. The oil-drilling story, Sofaer said, was untenable in the light of the Shultz-McFarlane conversation in November 1985, when McFarlane had told Shultz about the arms-for-hostages deal. Cooper advised Sofaer that Casey's testimony had been changed to say that no one in the U.S. government had known that the November shipment was made up of Hawks rather than oil-drilling equipment.

The questioning of Sofaer on this incident continued:

Sofaer: And that generally the whole thing smelled to me like the kind of thing you see in a trial—and I've presided over hundreds— in a narcotics case, for example, where they refer to the drugs as "shirts" or something like that. You always have some kind of phrase that you use to describe what you're selling when you don't want to talk about it directly.

Question: And here it was oil drilling equipment?

Sofaer: Right, oil drilling bits.

Question: But what you heard from Cooper on his end was that, if anything, from the time you had seen the draft of Director Casey's statement until the time of this conversation, in between which you had conveyed a message to the Justice Department, the draft had gotten worse?

Sofaer: That's true.

Question: And now the draft had gone out to say that nobody in the United States Government knew anything other than the oil drilling story?

Sofaer: That's what Cooper told me.

Sofaer told Cooper that "he should follow up and make sure the Attorney General was not being sold a bill of goods." Cooper agreed. Sometime later, Wallison informed Sofaer of what North had said at the meeting in Poindexter's office earlier that afternoon.

Sofaer: He said that, according to North, all North did was to give the Israelis the name of a proprietary airline. They, then, made the arrangements to use the airline. That he, North, denies that he knew it was HAWK missiles or arms. He says he understood it was drill bits.

Then Wallison said to me the President keeps getting deeper into this because people are operating in his name.

Question: Who did you understand Wallison to be referring to when he said people are operating in his name?

Sofaer: People were operating in his name. I understood it to be Poindexter, North and others were taking actions, had taken actions without the President's approval.

Sofaer and Cooper talked again that evening about North's denial that he had made an urgent call to the CIA in November 1985 to get the proprietary airline to transport the missiles to Iran. Sofaer called it "nonsense" and argued that "it couldn't be correct, that we had a contemporaneous note of McFarlane's call [to Shultz]." According to Sofaer, Cooper "expressed shock in a way that would not be polite in a public record." Sofaer says that he told Cooper "both Armacost and I were extremely concerned that people were not telling the full truth and we were scared—I was scared that the President would be in trouble if the testimony was not changed and if people were not forced to tell the truth about all this." If the testimony was not changed, Sofaer declared, he would be forced to resign from the government. Cooper is said to have responded that he would leave with Sofaer.

"Let me say," Sofaer explained, "that I was more concerned about cover-up than I was about anything else. I believed that Cooper and I and a number of other people had a duty to insure that no cover-up occurred." Sofaer added: "I was not assuming that anything that had been done was illegal. What I knew was that a cover-up was illegal and whatever you might be able to say about the legality of something you did, there is no way you could claim that a cover-up was legal."

By the evening of November 20, Poindexter had also realized that Casey could not be permitted to go on with his prepared text. He called Casey to tell him that he was "uneasy with the section on the Hawks" and that it would be better to tell the congressional committees that there had been a shipment in November 1985 but that they did not have all the facts and were looking into them.[47] Later, Poindexter explained that he, too, had been worried the White House might be accused of a cover-up and had made some mistakes in handling the issue in November 1986 for that reason.[48]

Just before midnight on November 20, Cooper called Sofaer to say that he had reached Attorney General Meese and had told him all about Sofaer's difficulties with Casey's proposed testimony. Meese, then in West Point, was scheduled to go to Harvard the next day. Meese was so concerned about Casey's testimony the next day that he told Cooper to get in touch with CIA General Counsel Doherty immediately and, if necessary, to go out to the CIA early enough the next morning to head Casey off.[49] Cooper informed Sofaer that the oil-drilling story and the claim that no one in the U.S. government had known about the Hawk shipment had been removed from Casey's testimony.

Sofaer was satisfied. He congratulated Cooper, and the crisis of November 20 was over for him.[50]

Without this episode, the climactic events of the next five days cannot be fully understood. They could not be fully understood until Sofaer's deposition was printed and made available in 1988, after the intense interest in the Iran affair had subsided. By then, little attention was paid to it.

The catalyst in the administration's desperate efforts in the next few days to avoid a charge of cover-up was Secretary Shultz's recollection of a telephone call from former National Security Adviser McFarlane on November 18, 1985, telling him of an impending arms-for-hostages deal. Shultz's executive assistant, Hill, had made a contemporaneous note of the Shultz-McFarlane conversation and had located it a year later. Without the somewhat fortuitous year-old telephone call and Shultz's memory of it, the handling of the entire matter might have taken a different turn. This one piece of information enabled Sofaer to see through the false-hoods that had been smuggled into the North-produced chronology and Casey's proposed testimony. If Sofaer had not been so determined to expose the suspected cover-up, there is no reason to believe that it might not have succeeded—at least for a time.

7

Casey's role during these days is something of a puzzle. He was far from being the commanding figure who masterminded the abortive cover-up or manipulated North and others to do his bidding.

By November 16, three days after the president's unsuccessful speech and three days before his disastrous press conference, the crisis of confidence in the government was clearly apparent. Yet Casey chose that day to go down to Central America for a week. He already knew that he would be testifying before the congressional intelligence committees. While North was floundering about trying to put together a chronology of events and intervening in the preparation of Casey's own testimony, Casey was not there to give him any advice or direct any of the activity.

Before leaving, Casey sent a memorandum to Deputy Director Gates in which he asked for materials on which to base his testimony. Among other things, he wanted evidence that there were Iranians who had acted in good faith and asked to be brought up to date on what was happening in Tehran and Lebanon.[51] As early as November 17, Gates telephoned Casey to come back sooner than planned.[52] By November 19, Gates had a group working on Casey's testimony, only to be told by Doherty, who had been present at the conference called by Wallison the day before, that the facts were getting to be so shaky that the testimony might have to be postponed; but Gates thought this would be impossible.[53]

On November 19, a special assistant who had worked on the testimony, Norman Gardner, flew down to Central America to deliver the papers to Casey, including North's chronology. Gardner left Washington so hastily that he did not have a passport or visa with him. Casey decided to work on the material on the plane going back to Washington that night. Gardner described how Casey worked:

> After he reviewed these documents, then I gave him our best draft of the testimony that we had done, that we had worked on at headquarters. He didn't say anything. But he got out a—there is like a rack of papers and pencils and tablets and stuff, and he got out a legal pad, a yellow legal pad, and he put it down there.

He set our testimony aside and he started writing it himself. I mean, he didn't—I mean, he didn't say, I think this is garbage that you wrote. He just started—I knew he didn't like the testimony because he started drafting his own.

The trouble was that Casey could not read his own handwriting. He decided to dictate into his recorder but could not find it in his briefcase. "So he said, well, I bet it is in my suitcase. So the two of us got up, and there is a door in the back of the box which leads to the back of the airplane." They found the suitcase with about ten others stacked on top of it, whereupon the entire pile started to fall down. After all this, there was still no recorder.

He said, no, it isn't that one. It is probably that one.

We finally find the suitcase. There are no lights back there, just the lights coming out from the box [a compartment for Casey]. We get this suitcase and bring it back into the compartment. It is one of these things that zips on the top. He opens it up and feels around the sides, and he can't find this recorder.

So he takes all these beautiful suits, clothes, and dumps them on the floor.

I say, you know, Sophie [Casey's wife] is really going to be irritated if you do that with all these suits.

He said, she will never know. But it wasn't there.

Finally, they found that the security guard had the recorder. Casey dictated into it for the next five or six hours, until the plane arrived in Washington in the early morning hours of November 20.[54]

It was another hectic day. At 4 p.m., about fifteen people came together to work on the testimony with Casey. "I think," said Gates, "that the kindest word to describe that meeting was 'pandemonium.' "

And Mr. Casey basically ran the meeting, going through, making changes in the testimony, updating and changing things we weren't sure of. People were passing comments and conversations, and Casey was tearing off pages and it was just mass confusion. During the course of that there were a lot of questions.[55]

Just why Casey behaved this way in the preparation of his testimony is not clear from what we have been told by his associates. He seemed to depend on them to come up with the facts and then to decide on what he could safely say. He was not the Casey who had supposedly manipulated North to do his bidding and who should have known more than anyone else. In these tense and critical days, Casey was more a subordinate figure than a ringleader. Casey suffered a cerebral seizure almost a month later, and he may have been too ill to take hold at this time. In any case, Poindexter and North were still out in front, with Casey doing little to help them just when they needed help the most.

Until it was too late, Casey and Poindexter did not seem to realize that their affair with Iran was coming to an end. On November 21, they went through the motions of reporting to the congressional intelligence committees with prefabricated evasions and studied falsehoods. Casey alluded to "oil-drilling parts" that he said "we" had not learned were missiles until January 1986. He made McFarlane's mission to Tehran in May 1986 seem successful.[56] When Casey was asked whether he thought it was a good idea for the NSC staff to carry out operations, he replied that he did not think it was a good idea, as if he had had nothing to do with it. Representative Bernard J. Dwyer of New Jersey wanted to know about the NSC staff's activities in providing weapons for the contras, whereupon Casey said that he had kept away from the details because he was barred from doing anything. Apparently Casey was let off easily and was asked no embarrassing questions.[57]

Poindexter was equally devious. Poindexter made President Reagan totally oblivious of the Israeli arms shipments in August–September 1985; Reagan had merely been "upset" about them and the way they had obtained the release of the Reverend Weir. Poindexter told exactly the same false story as Casey about the November 1985 transaction. Poindexter was particularly optimistic about the Second Channel and what it might still produce.[58]

In effect, the two officials in possession of more secrets than anyone else in the U.S. government appeared strangely ignorant or unsure of what had gone on in the dealings with Iran. Yet they were dealt with gently and neither had reason to believe that they were close to a smash-up of all they had worked for.

8

When Assistant Attorney General Cooper in Washington called Attorney General Meese in West Point at about 10:30 p.m. on November 20, the crisis of confidence in the government had been building for two weeks. After the call, instead of going on to Harvard the next day, Meese decided to come right back to Washington.

The reason for Meese's haste was Cooper's alarming report about the rebellious state of mind in the State Department. As Meese later put it with great restraint, "there was a good deal more knowledge within the U.S. Government about the fact of Hawks being shipped in November

1985 that was known then than anything we had been led to believe earlier that afternoon" at the meeting in Poindexter's office. *59 According to Cooper, Meese "fully agreed that he should return, that this was a matter the potential of which was dramatic." Cooper told Meese they could not possibly let Casey testify the next day with erroneous information.[60]

Meese had also ordered Cooper to get in touch with Poindexter and Casey immediately to advise them to revise their stories to the congressional committees the next day. Cooper reached Poindexter, who said that he had awakened Casey from sleep but that Casey was so groggy it was unclear whether he had understood.[61]

These frantic telephone calls suggest the charged atmosphere that prevailed in Meese's immediate circle on the night of November 20. Yet all that was in question so far were some details about the year-old "horror story." Was the shipment to Iran made up of oil-drilling equipment or Hawk missiles? Did anyone in the U.S. government at the time know that a CIA proprietary had hauled Hawk missiles to Iran?

It would seem that something more must have been at stake to provoke Sofaer and Cooper to threaten to resign and to cause Meese to rush back to Washington. These details were part of a covert operation that was still only dimly understood by all but a few officials. The imminent entrance of the congressional committees into the affair ensured that it was about to become a wide-open political battleground. The very extent of the leakage to the media revealed that the administration was fatally divided and warring within itself. A policy of publicly denouncing Iran as a terrorist state and barring it from all access to weapons, together with an official repudiation of all arms-for-hostages or any other kinds of ransom deals, could not be quickly or easily reconciled with secret, back-door deals with Iran of arms for hostages or anything else.

In Congress, the media, and the general public there was already a predisposition in such circumstances to suspect a "cover-up," a word that had come to represent all that was evil and corrupt in American government. Indirectly, former President Richard Nixon was responsible for the predicament in which the Reagan administration now found itself.

---

* Meese could not remember whether Cooper had told him about Sofaer's threatened resignation but, in the circumstances, it is highly unlikely that Cooper would have neglected to mention it, inasmuch as Cooper himself had—according to Sofaer—agreed to resign with him if nothing was done to change the official account of the November 1985 transaction.

23

Panic

A daunting problem faced Attorney General Meese as he traveled from West Point to Washington.

The Reagan administration had tried about everything to overcome the crisis of confidence without success. It had steadily retreated in the face of almost universal disbelief and denunciation. President Reagan did not want to go through a question-and-answer press conference—and had submitted to one. On November 10—the day the House Intelligence Committee had asked Poindexter and Casey to testify[1]—Chief of Staff Regan had threatened to invoke executive privilege if Congress tried to look into the secret contacts with Iran[2]—and both Casey and Poindexter were made available to the Senate and House Intelligence Committees on November 21. As a result of the elections early that same month, both houses of Congress—and their intelligence committees—were controlled by opposition Democrats. Poindexter had held out for a policy of explaining nothing—and even he had gone on television to explain. The opposition to the Iran policy by the two senior cabinet members, Secretary of State Shultz and Secretary of Defense Weinberger, was out in the open. The leakage in the media had become torrential. Virtually everything had come out—the missiles and spare parts to Iran, Israel's role, McFarlane's mission to Tehran in May 1986, North, Ghorbanifar, Ledeen. Throughout the world, the duplicity of preaching one policy and doing the opposite had made the United States an object of scorn.

Even the pillars of the Republican Party could not uphold the Iran policy. Senator Barry Goldwater called it "a dreadful mistake, probably one of the major mistakes the United States had ever made in foreign policy." The best thing Senator Robert Dole could think of saying was that the policy was "well motivated" but "a little inept."[3]

But all this had not been enough to send Meese into action. Cooper's telephone call to West Point had apparently tipped the balance, because it threatened a revolt within the cabinet. Meese, moreover, had been given the impression at the meeting in Poindexter's office on November 20, 1986, that the November 1985 shipment had been made up of nothing more than oil-drilling parts and that the U.S. government had had no more to do with it than the CIA's recommendation of an airline.[4] The one break by Shultz in this cover story—that the cargo had been weapons, not oil-drilling parts—apparently served to make Meese realize that the ground under the whole administration case was shaking and could collapse at any time. If he had been deceived, he no longer knew whom or what to believe.

When Meese returned to Washington on the morning of November 21, he first held a staff meeting, at which Cooper and others brought him up to date on the latest developments.[5] What he heard could not have been reassuring, because he immediately arranged to see President Reagan at 11:30 a.m.

Meese met with the president in the presence of Regan and Poindexter. According to Meese, he told the president that there was so much confusion about the whole Iran affair that it was necessary for someone "to develop a coherent overview of all the facts." Meese himself volunteered to do the job, to which the president readily agreed. He asked Meese to get it done by November 24, only three days away, in order to have the report ready for a meeting of the top-level National Security Planning Group. Regan and Poindexter went along.[6]

In this way, four days—Friday, November 21, to Monday, November 24—held the final fate of the Iran affair and those most prominent in it. The interval was hardly enough to get to the bottom of such murky, secretive, largely undocumented events, about which McFarlane knew most for 1985 and Poindexter and North for 1986. None of them had been outstanding for their willingness to tell the unvarnished truth. *

By noon on Friday, Meese had brought together a small team to start working on his "overview." It consisted of William Bradford Reynolds, the assistant attorney general for the civil rights division, John N. Richardson, Jr., Meese's chief of staff, and Assistant Attorney General Cooper. They drew up a list of names for interviewing and investigating, including Vice President Bush, McFarlane, North, Casey, and others. At 3 p.m., Meese telephoned Poindexter to say that he wanted to have access to every document, telephone log, or anything else that might be helpful.[7]

All this time, there was still one main subject in Meese's mind—the Hawk shipment of November 1985. Peculiarly, it was pursued as if everything about the Iran affair hinged on the failure of Poindexter, Casey,

---

* Though Regan prefers to forget about his zealous efforts to defend the Iran policy publicly in his book and in his testimony, he did his part in loyally trying to fend off criticism. In a television interview on November 14, he said: "We have never authorized, never allowed, never condoned large shipments by anyone, by Far Easterners, Mideasterners, Europeans, Israelis or anyone else" (New York Times, November 15, 1986). All this virtuous protestation depended on what Regan understood by the word "large," which he did not define.

and North to tell the truth about it. In effect, Meese's "fact-finding" mission was largely focused on this one fact because it implied a violation of the law requiring a presidential Finding for such actions. Meese had been given so little time that a narrow inquiry was all he could cope with. None of this might have happened were it not for one little "if"— if Shultz had not remembered that McFarlane the year before had told Shultz in a telephone call to Geneva about an arms deal with Iran.

2

Another extraordinary, unforeseeable event occurred on Friday, November 21.

After Meese had telephoned Poindexter that his aides were coming over to examine the files on the Iran affair, with special attention to the Finding of January 17, 1986, Poindexter turned the task over to his counsel, Paul Thompson. According to Thompson, Poindexter told him to be cooperative and handed him an accordion file, which Poindexter said was all he had. Thompson put the file in his safe without looking through it.

Sometime later, Thompson attended another meeting in Poindexter's office. Thompson heard Poindexter say: "There is yet another document" or "There is some memo that we still haven't come up with that I know has to be somewhere." Thompson thought it might be in the accordion file he had been given earlier and went to get it. As others talked, Thompson opened the file, took out documents, glanced at them briefly, and handed one after another to Poindexter. Thompson related what happened next:

> He [Poindexter] was sitting off to my left, and he would just kind of look at them and drop them or leave them on his lap. One document we came to he ripped up, not as a major action, but merely as he came to it. He ripped it up saying, "This is no longer necessary." Or, "this has no future." That document turns out to have been the Finding of the fall of 1985.[8]

It was the Finding of December 5, 1985, the first of the three Findings. Thompson gave his reaction to Poindexter's action:

> It was kind of like what is this. Where have you had this, Admiral? Here we have been desperately looking for documents, for the last several weeks. And he kind of winked and said well, these are just things I have had elsewhere, home or in my briefcase or something. We were basically managing the case at that time and the paperwork and suddenly he produces an accordion file with papers in it on the

21st of November. I think I said, "They'll have fun with this," meaning Meese's people, or, "They will be pleased there's some additional paperwork in this case."[9]

Unfortunately for Poindexter, a CIA copy of the December 5, 1985, Finding was later found. Poindexter subsequently explained that he had destroyed his copy because he considered it to be "a CYFA effort on the part of the CIA to protect their particular small involvement with the project up to that time."[10] His main reason, however, was that he had recognized that the Finding, if made public, would prove to be "politically embarrassing," because it had given President Reagan's approval to what was clearly an arms-for-hostages deal.[11] Poindexter also argued that he had been hurried by the CIA into putting through a Finding that was not fully staffed, that it did not represent his or the president's full thinking on the Iran policy, and that he had regarded all three Findings as one. Yet he had torn up the Finding so impulsively that all these factors were unlikely to have crossed his mind in the instant. The immediate problem at hand was much more specific and less complicated.

For the issue on November 21, 1986, was precisely whether weapons had been sent in November 1985. Even Attorney General Meese, only the day before, had been given to understand that oil-drilling parts, not weapons, had been sent to Iran. The raison d'être of the December 5, 1985, Finding had expressly been to legitimate an arms shipment retroactively, for which reason it was so explicit. Whether or not the other factors mentioned by Poindexter weighed in his decision to tear up this Finding, the fact remained that it was mute evidence against his claim that he had not heard about an arms shipment until January 1986. Poindexter blamed his memory for his blunder, but it seemed strange that he had still held on to it after days of effort by North, with some assistance by McFarlane, both of whom knew that weapons had been sent, to establish the facts surrounding the much-abused November 1985 "horror story"—now made all the more horrible by its ghostly reappearance a year later.

In any case, Poindexter's action in destroying the December 5, 1985, Finding took on a later significance because it seemed to fit into the kind of cover-up that Sofaer had begun to suspect.

3

Meese interviewed McFarlane first on November 21. Cooper was present, and we have his notes. Of greatest interest to Meese and Cooper was McFarlane's memory of the November 1985 transaction. Cooper's notes read:

At summit in Geneva learned that Isr[ael] had shipped oil equipment. Rabine [sic] called from N.Y. & said they have problem w[ith] shipment to Iran. M[cFarlane] asked N[orth] to assist. N rept'd back that Isr. hit snag in customs in [Portugal—deleted], & that it may take a call to Prime Min[ister]—a couple of days later he [McFarlane] talked with [Portuguese] Prime Minister—M. said it was an important project & would appreciate his assistance. M. remembers no mention in all this of arms.

M. didn't know this involved procuring a plane; doesn't remember chat w[ith] G.S. [George Shultz], but probably had one.[12]

McFarlane also claimed that he had been "made aware of the arms angle" during his preparations to go to Tehran in May 1986. On the plane, McFarlane said, North had told him the "*nitty-gritty* of arms transfers" and McFarlane had "expressed dismay."[13] Meese's later version of McFarlane's statement on November 21 also stressed McFarlane's alleged ignorance of what had been going on the year before. McFarlane, according to Meese, had been told that oil-drilling equipment was being sent to Iran and that he had not learned that the spare parts were for Hawk missiles until months later.[14] In effect, McFarlane, like North, was still sticking at this late date to the cover story about oil-drilling equipment. After the interview, Meese and McFarlane talked together. According to Meese, McFarlane "wanted me to know that the President was generally in favor of pursuing the Israelis' ideas all along." Meese says that he told McFarlane: "Well, Bud, just be sure that whatever you do you tell the truth. Don't try to shade this one way or the other, thinking you are helping the President, because the best thing to do is just get the whole truth out. It might even be helpful to the President, not hurtful, if he is generally supported [sic] this from the start"—or words to that effect.[15]

After leaving Meese, McFarlane sent a message to Poindexter in which he reported: "The only blind spot on my part concerned a shipment in November 1985 which still doesn't ring a bell with me." McFarlane continued:

But it appears that the matter of not notifying about the Israeli transfers can be covered if the President made a "mental finding" before the transfers took place. Well on that score we ought to be ok because he was all for letting the Israelis do anything they wanted at the very first briefing in the hospital. Ed [Meese] seemed relieved at that.[16]

Judging from Cooper's notes, McFarlane had not had such a "blind spot" concerning the November 1985 shipment; he had spoken definitely of "oil equipment" and could remember nothing about arms. Meese later denied that he had used or would have used the phrase "mental finding."[17] That Meese felt it necessary to urge McFarlane to tell nothing but the truth suggests that Meese had reason to believe he might not always tell it. In fact, Meese thought at the time that McFarlane had "certainly shade[d] his testimony because he had some idea that this was protecting the President."[18]

McFarlane did not contradict this version of his meeting with Meese. McFarlane was unable to recall just what he had said but thought that "I told him that it was ambiguous, that there had been reports of Israel believing that oil drilling equipment was perhaps more effective, but that ultimately I learned . . ." But whether he had told Meese that he knew they were Hawk parts, McFarlane again could not remember. He did remember, however, that he had said "the President had been supportive of this from the very first and was foursquare behind it"—the effort to free the hostages. Why, McFarlane was asked, had he not told Meese about the "diversion"? Because Meese had not asked him about it: "Perhaps it was something that I should have told him."[19] Cooper's notes of the meeting indicate that Meese had trouble getting McFarlane to talk about anything but oil-drilling equipment even at this late date.

Next, Meese saw Shultz the following morning, November 22. Cooper again took notes. This time Shultz gave Meese an account of how he had learned from McFarlane in November 1985 that arms were going to Iran. Cooper's notes read:

Nov.—Hawk episode

[*Shultz*]: during Geneva summit—after 2d day's meeting ([Nov] 18)—M[cFarlane] came to G.S. [George Shultz] hotel & said that a complex deal was under way—shipment of arms (may have said Hawks) would go to Ir[an] on assumption that hostages would be released.

Hill: M said plane would go from Isr[ael] to [Lisbon—deleted], if hostages released it would go to Iran, if not, back to Isr (we would be advised through [deleted] hostages released).

Shultz: G.S. said very bad idea, didn't think it would work. —G.S. was consulted, not for approval. G.S. thought it didn't happen, w[ith] no hostages released.

G.S. told around Thanksgiving that it hadn't worked out, & whole thing shut down—& G.S. heaved sigh of relief. . . .

G.S. rep[or]t'd Geneva conversation to C. Hill & he made notes.[20]

Shultz talked about other aspects of the Iran affair, but this portion most directly concerned the point at issue with McFarlane—oil-drilling equipment or Hawk missiles in November 1985. Meese tended to think that Shultz's memory was the more trustworthy because of the note taken by Hill.[21]

We are still in Saturday, November 22, and the facts about the November 1985 shipment and the subsequent Findings were as yet the most troubling issues facing Meese.

4

After leaving Shultz, Meese went back to his office at the Justice Department and met with his team of attorneys. At this time he sent Reynolds and Richardson to the Old Executive Office Building, an adjunct of the White House, to see what they could find out from documents in North's office.

At about 10:30 a.m., Thompson received a telephone call from Cooper that Reynolds and Richardson were coming over and could he get them into the building. They arrived a half hour later, and Thompson escorted them to North's office on the third floor. Earl, but not North, was there to let them in. Thompson soon left, and they proceeded to go through files that Earl had set out on a table.[22]

What they were looking for has been described by Richardson: "It was clear to me that what had happened in '85 was unclear and who had known about it or endorsed it was unclear. That was the principal area at that point that we were interested in, because of the legal significance of what had happened." Richardson elaborated: "I knew when I went over there that our interest was '85, and trying to determine if the U.S. Government role in the shipments, whether they were authorized, acquiesced in, or otherwise known about, and so I had that clear understanding."[23]

It was not an exhaustive search. Reynolds and Richardson were dependent on whatever files Earl put before them and had no way of knowing what was missing. They did not actually look at North's own file cabinets. They found it difficult to take notes and merely pulled individual documents for later copying. Richardson began to take notes on a legal-sized pad, but he explained: "I took several pages and gave up that because the volume of documents was greater than would allow me to take detailed notes. So I stopped that and I just kept reading through documents."[24] They worked so quickly that they hardly had time to do more than glance at most pages. When Reynolds was asked questions about the "awful lot of documents" that he had seen, he was hazy about describing most of them.[25]

Suddenly, Reynolds looked at one document in two parts that startled him. One part was headed: *"Release of American Hostages in Beirut,"* the other: *"Terms of Reference U.S.-Iran Dialogue."* The first occupied five pages, the second three. Reynolds gathered from the context that they had been drawn up between April 3 and 7, 1986. They represented an effort to sum up the main stages of U.S.-Iran relations from June 1985 to the date of composition. Oddly, Reynolds came across three versions of this document, but one was different from the others.

Only one copy had this section:

—The residual funds from this transaction are allocated as follows:

—$2 million will be used to purchase replacement TOWs for the original 508 sold by Israel to Iran for the release of Benjamin Weir. This is the only way that we have found to meet our commitment to replenish these stocks.

—$12 million will be used to purchase critically needed supplies for the Nicaraguan Democratic Resistance Forces. This material is essential to cover shortages in resistance inventories resulting from their current offensives and Sandinista counter-attacks and to "bridge" the period between now and when Congressionally-approved lethal assistance (beyond the $25 million in "defensive" arms) can be delivered.[26]

The latter paragraph confirmed two things. One was that the release of the Reverend Weir had been purchased with the 508 TOWs sold by Israel to Iran in August–September 1985. But of far greater import to Reynolds was the implication that funds from the Iran affair had been used for or "diverted" to the contra affair. This document was forever after known as the "diversion memo." There was no name signed to it, but it could only have been written by Oliver North for the benefit of his superior, National Security Adviser Poindexter. As usual in these memoranda, this one ended with the words:

That the President approve the structure depicted above under "Current Situation" and the Terms of Reference at Tab A.

Approve_____   Disapprove_____

There was no indication that the president had approved or disapproved or even that he had seen this memorandum.

When Reynolds spotted the telltale paragraph, he uttered "holy cow or something to that effect"—or "it may have been a little more graphic."[27] Reynolds says that Richardson heard him and looked up. Richardson has a somewhat fuller account of the historic moment:

He either kicked me under the table or something and we were sitting across from each other about the same distance you and I are now, just a foot or two, and he passed it over, directed me to at [sic] the top paragraph and had an expression of this was a surprising entry. So I read it and I gave a similar look back and I think I probably said something like that didn't happen or something along those lines, that's hard to believe that had happened and passed it back to him and then that was it, we did not discuss it at the time and I don't think Earl noticed anything particular about it. *[28]

Reynolds put it back in the folder to be copied with the stack of other documents. He explained that he did not want to call attention to this particular document and "it seemed to me that the more discreet way to handle it was not to flag the fact that we had found something of this nature."[29] Just as they were leaving for lunch, North arrived and they exchanged a few words with him. Richardson recalled:

He [North] had said, Where are you fellows going? And we introduced ourselves, and Brad, I think at that point, said—we told him we were going to lunch and Brad said, by the way, we have just had 1986 documents. We would like to see the 1985 ones, and Colonel North seemed surprised.
He said, well, you should have them all. I will make sure you have them when you get back. I will get them out, something like that.[30]

What Reynolds and Richardson did not know was that Earl could not have shown them the complete files on the Iran affair. North had begun shredding documents weeks earlier. He says that he began shredding them in earnest in early October after a discussion with Casey following the capture of Hasenfus and more after Casey's discussion with Furmark.[31] The files that Reynolds and Richardson were shown were those from which North had been removing and shredding documents for several days past and had lined up on the table.[32] He had shredded so thoroughly that he was sure nothing on the so-called residual funds or diversion remained and had assured Poindexter: "Don't worry. It is all taken care of."†[33] North boasted that he had even shredded documents while the two lawyers were sitting in his office. "And I was working at my desk on other things, literally cleaning up files on lots of things," he recalled. "And when I would finish with a handful of documents, I'd walk up, walk past them, out the door—you know where the shredder was—turn the corner, turn on the shredder and drop them in."[34] North later said that he had shredded "dozen and dozens of memoranda relating to the

---

* In his testimony at the North trial, Richardson said that Reynolds "sort of gave me a nudge under the table and handed me a document that was folded open and pointed to a paragraph . . . I said something under my breath, like, Geez, can't be or something like that. And Brad [Reynolds] shrugged and put it back into what he was working on and we continued" (NT, pp. 6047–48).
† At Poindexter's trial, North told a somewhat different story: "I found another one and assured him [Poindexter] that all of the others were destroyed and that one was on its way the same way, I guess, or words to that effect" (PT, p. 1220). North added that he had in fact destroyed it (p. 1223).

residuals and the application to the Contras, among other things," including several copies of the diversion memo.[35]

North did not deny that he had shredded on November 21 for the very reason that he had learned that Justice Department lawyers were coming the next day to examine his files.

Question: So you shredded some documents because the Attorney General's people were coming in over the weekend?

North: I do not preclude that as part of what was shredded. I do not preclude that as being a possibility, not at all.[36]

He also did not deny that one of his motives was political:

Question: Do you deny, Colonel, that one of the reasons that you were shredding documents that Saturday was to avoid the political embarrassment of having these documents be seen by the Attorney General's staff?

North: I do not deny that.[37]

North was not the only shredder. His aide Earl also began to shred documents on November 21 after he learned that the Justice Department representatives were coming over. When they went to work in North's room, Earl told them nothing about the destruction of the very documents they wanted to see.*[38] While Reynolds and Richardson went to lunch, North collected another stack of documents and took them to a shredder in the White House Situation Room because the shredder in North's office had broken down.[39] In effect, Reynolds and Richardson saw only those documents that North wanted them to see or that North had unintentionally failed to prevent them from seeing.

It was, therefore, pure chance that enabled Reynolds to hit on the one paragraph that North had been most determined to conceal. One wonders what might have happened if North had successfully destroyed the telltale document and had obliged the two lawyers to come back without their revelation.

5

After North's arrival, Reynolds and Richardson walked over to the Old Ebbitt Grill, not far from the White House, to meet with Meese and Cooper for lunch. The two did not reveal their secret immediately and

---

* In his deposition, Earl denied that any documents had been "altered" on November 21 (B-9, p. 632). His memory seemed to be remarkably improved at North's trial.

waited dutifully for Meese to talk about his own interviews. Only after some time had elapsed did Reynolds tell about their discovery.

We have different versions of the reaction. Reynolds related that Meese "said something to the effect, 'Holy Toledo!' It was probably a little harsher than that. And Chuck [Cooper] reacted similarly."[40] Under questioning by Meese, Reynolds was unable to tell from the document in question whether the transfer of funds from the Iran to the contra operation had actually occurred. He thought that it would be necessary to ask North about it in order to find out whether it was more than an "aspiration."[41]

Richardson's account of the scene is somewhat more vivid. They first talked about a number of things they had found, when Reynolds bethought himself to say, "Oh, we found another document which seems to indicate that funds might have gone from this transaction to the contras." Meese "expressed great surprise. He visibly said something like, oh, a curse word, and sort of squinted his eyes and that sort of thing, and we said something like we haven't found—Brad [Reynolds] indicated we haven't found anything else to indicate that happened, and Meese said, be sure you bring a copy of that out when you come, and we said, we are marking things to copy, and I think that was it on that front." Only about five minutes was spent on the subject.[42] Cooper was also surprised and said "something like you are kidding."[43]

It appears that the first report of the diversion did not result in any great outburst of alarm. "Well," Reynolds later recalled, "there was a recognition it was politically significant, and that probably understates the assessment. And there was certainly a recognition stated that in fact we would need to explore with everybody involved up to and including the President regarding this matter and who had knowledge, if indeed it took place, and where the direction came from."[44] Meese indicated that the lack of actuality in what seemed to be no more than a plan had made him reserve judgment.[45] Cooper says that Meese showed some surprise, but Cooper himself did not immediately appreciate its legal significance.[46]

The diversion as a political bombshell was yet to come.

After lunch, Meese and Cooper interviewed former CIA General Counsel Stanley Sporkin, who had been largely responsible for drafting the first, December 5, 1985, Finding. They mainly learned that he had known at that time that the Finding had been intended to cover arms shipments, not oil-drilling equipment.[47] By now, Meese could have had little doubt that the oil-equipment story would not stand up and that Poindexter, North, and McFarlane could not be trusted on this point.

Meanwhile, Reynolds and Richardson returned to North's office and resumed their examination of the files put before them. "I think Brad said," Richardson recalled, "Mr. Meese would like us to make copies of some of the documents. Colonel North said, that's fine, and he and

Colonel Earl volunteered to make the copies of documents we had already marked. And we said, thank you. And they made some copies."[48]

North sat at his desk reading a newspaper, commenting on the accuracy or inaccuracy of the accounts of his activity. He spoke to the Israeli Amiram Nir on the phone and told them that Nir was perturbed by the news stories. Richardson understood that Nir said "things like your government, everyone in your government and my government is overreacting or panicking or something like that." North and Richardson left the room to make a pot of coffee, talked about how bad marine coffee was, and North said his was not much better. At one point, North came over to them and said: "All right shoot, let me know I'm ready to take your questions or I guess you are ready to ask them, something like that." But they were not ready and explained that they were just supposed to go through the documents; the attorney general would ask questions tomorrow.

According to Richardson, the three also talked about the Iran policy debate that had blown up. North commented angrily on Secretary of State Shultz's "hypocrisy" and public criticism of the president's Iran initiative.

Through it all, North seemed carefree. Richardson recalled: "He was very friendly and outgoing and—I mean he gave the appearance of being relaxed. But he said something like well, I'm not worried, in six weeks I'll be commanding a Marine battalion of infantry troops, or something to that effect, that I won't be—he knew he would not be long for this job, something to that effect." The three left at about 7 p.m. and walked to their cars. North and Reynolds talked about their daughters' mutual interest in riding horses and the strain it put on their parents.

Richardson and Reynolds returned on Sunday, November 23, and worked until noon, without completing their examination of all the files. They asked to have all of them left in place until they could come back, but they did not return.[49]

This fact-finding inquiry was peculiar in several respects. It was originally limited to the Iran affair. The two fact-finders did not even ask for any documents on the contras. North had every reason to be friendly and relaxed because he, in fact, controlled what they saw, even if his control turned out to be imperfect. Later, they did not seem to have learned anything worth recounting, except for a single paragraph about the still unresolved diversion. Curiously, they had found something, but it was not what they had been sent to find.

Meese's personal fact-finding took other directions for the rest of Saturday, November 22. At 3:40 p.m., he received a call from North, whom he had been trying to reach. Meese wanted to set up an interview for the next morning, but North begged off until 2 p.m. because he wanted to go to church with his family. At 3:46 p.m. that Saturday, Casey called

Meese. Casey said that he had something he wanted to talk about and asked Meese to drop by his house that evening.[50]

Meese's conversation with Casey was different from those he had held with McFarlane, Shultz, and Sporkin. In each of these cases, he had had Cooper along to take notes. This time he went to see Casey alone, and we know only what Meese has told about this meeting. If Meese expected anyone to know most about U.S. covert operations, it would have been the director of the CIA. Yet it was Casey who called Meese, not the other way around, and Meese came to listen, not to ask questions. Meese later called it "just a casual visit."[51]

Meese claimed that he had intended to interview Casey at a later date but that he never got around to it because "the finding of the so-called diversion short-circuited that because I wanted to find out whether there was any truth to it, which is what we did on Sunday, and then to talk to the President about it, which is what we did on Monday."[52] It is difficult to follow this reasoning. Meese had learned about the so-called diversion only a few hours before he went to see Casey. He could not tell what he would get out of North the next day, and any leads from Casey would presumably have been most helpful. Besides, there was much more than the diversion Casey could have told him about. Why talking to North on Sunday and the president on Monday should have short-circuited an interview in depth with Casey does not appear to be obvious.

According to Meese, Casey wanted to tell him about the visit by Furmark at which the threat from Ghorbanifar and Ghorbanifar's alleged Canadian financiers "to go public" had been made. Furmark's visit to Casey had occurred as long ago as October 7, 1986. Meese now learned that Furmark "had said that people were, in effect, trying to extort money from the U.S. Government," but for six weeks Casey had not seen fit to tell the attorney general about an extortion plot.

Yet some time was apparently spent on the diversion scheme. Since no notes were taken, we are totally dependent on Meese's memory, which in this case is peculiarly unsatisfactory because his answers to questions varied. Meese could not even be sure that Casey had said anything about Furmark's allusion to a diversion scheme or that he had learned about it later.* Asked whether he had brought up the subject, Meese said no. He gave as his reason that he "felt it was not appropriate to discuss this with anyone, even as good a friend as Mr. Casey, until after I found out what it was all about."[53] This seems strange, since one way to find out what it was all about was to ask someone like Casey.

---

* "In the course of that conversation, he [Casey] said that they might even claim that the money that should have gone to them was used for other—I am not sure whether he told me this in so many words, but I later learned in other documents that Mr. Furmark had described it as going for United States and Israeli projects other than what was involved in the Iranian transfer" (Meese, 100-9, p. 237).

But Casey did say something of particular interest about the diversion. "He told me," Meese said, "that he had talked to Admiral Poindexter about this—I believe it was at that time that he told me this—and that Admiral Poindexter had told him that nothing wrong had been done and that there was nothing to this."[54] In that case, the national security adviser had deceived the CIA director, because Poindexter admittedly knew that there was something to the diversion of funds for other purposes. And Casey, according to North, had known of the diversion and had called it "the ultimate irony, the ultimate covert operation kind of thing and was very enthusiastic about it."[55]

Thus ended Meese's fact-finding review on Saturday, November 22. All that remained was the rendezvous with North the next day.

6

Oliver North's day of reckoning came at 2:13 p.m. on Sunday, November 23, 1986. With him in the attorney general's office were Meese, Cooper, Reynolds, and Richardson. Richardson acted as note taker, and we have twenty-seven pages of his notes. North's final hours in the Iran and contra affairs can be reconstructed with unusual completeness.

North still did not know what awaited him. So far as he could tell, Meese was merely trying to put together the whole complex and confused story of the Iran initiative. Meese opened gently. Richardson's notes read:

> 2:13 p.m. A.G. [Attorney General]: Want to get all facts from everyone involved. Flesh out diff[erent] recollections. Talk to RR [Ronald Reagan], John P[oindexter]. Worst thing can happen is if someone try to conceal something to protect selves, RR, put good spin on it. Want nothing anyone can call a cover up. What happened early on? How does Ledeen fit in?

At this early stage of the questions, Meese was already thinking politically. "We wanted to be sure that no one, and I was thinking then of political opponents, could call this a cover-up of any sort," he explained.[56] Under questioning by Meese, North went through the various stages of the Iran initiative, beginning with Ledeen's initial role. They spent much time on the November 1985 arms shipment and the subsequent Finding designed to legitimate it. North said that Israeli Defense Minister Rabin had told him it was made up of oil-related equipment and that he had not learned it was Hawk missiles until Secord had arrived in Tel Aviv a few days later.[57]

This was not the story that North later told. He testified that in "the discussions I had with Israeli officials we agreed that the story line would be that they were shipping oil-drilling equipment, and so when I contacted the CIA in November of 1985 and asked them to provide the name of an air carrier that was discreet in Europe, I told them it was oil-drilling equipment. I lied to the CIA because that was the convention that we had worked out with the Israelis, that no one else was to know."[58]

At his trial, North gave another version of the attitude toward the Israelis:

> The only people in the world they [radical elements in Iran] may have hated more than us were the Israelis and we did not throughout this whole activity want to be seen as associated with the Israelis in any way of this, particularly the 1985 Hawk shipment which had outraged the Iranians.[59]

North also described how the Americans had tried to put all the blame for the 1985 shipment on the Israelis:

> There had been a cover story since February of 1986 when we started to get the Hawk missiles back out of Iran. We told the Iranians because they were so upset with that Israeli shipment that we had nothing to do with it because we wanted to assure them that we were the good guys and even though the Israelis and we had worked on it together we told with the agreement of the Israelis that the Americans didn't have anything to do with that shipment and that had been a consistent story ever since the meetings in February with the First Channel and we carried that through with the Second Channel.*[60]

After about an hour mainly devoted to the 1985 episode, Meese suddenly changed the subject. He showed North the "diversion memo," as Richardson noted:

> *Show memo:* Is it something you prepared? W[ith] terms of reference dated Apr 1986—
> On 13 Sep[tember], with endorsement of US gov't, Israelis transfer 508 TOWs—
> —[North] don't know who did it; think M[cFarlane]—based on gen[era]l understanding from RR [Ronald Reagan]—
> A.G.: Some have concern protect RR but we need to know facts.[61]

From this, we may gather that Meese was not satisfied with North's reply. In any case, Meese quickly changed the subject back to the arms

---

* At Poindexter's trial, North said that he "took steps . . . to perpetuate the cover story which we had for a year on that [the November 1985 shipment] . . . We for 11 months or thereabouts had said that a cover story—we didn't have anything to do [with it], blame the Israelis with the agreement of the Israeli government for that shipment" (PT, pp. 1176–77).

deal with Iran. Richardson thought that Meese had made a "tactical determination" to ask North about the earlier portions of the memo before confronting him with the details of the diversion.[62] According to Cooper, Meese "handed him this memo and asked an innocuous entirely unnoteworthy question or two before he asked him about the contra diversion."[63]

North's earlier answers, however, were not unnoteworthy. Richardson's notes state:

> N[orth] *believes* RR [Ronald Reagan] authorized it himself b/c [because] M[cFarlane] wouldn't go off on own—*think* M K[imche] understanding.
> N[orth] went to talk to RR re: strategic relation & w/RR [with RR] it always came back to hostages—.
> Drawn to linkage.
> Terrible mistake to say RR wanted the strategic relationship—b/c RR wanted the hostages[64]

North later claimed that he had participated in at least three briefing sessions with the president, but always in the presence of others. On these occasions, North appears to have been brought in to report on the contras rather than on the strategic relation with Iran. There is no evidence or reason to believe that he "went to talk to RR."[65]

Meese now went back to the diversion memo and handed it to North. As Cooper recalled the scene, North's self-possessed manner did not change when he was handed the memo, because he did not immediately recognize its significance. Only when Meese mentioned the paragraph on the diversion of funds to the contras did his demeanor change from one of calm to one of "great surprise."[66] According to Richardson, North first asked whether the memo was in his files and was "visibly surprised." Meese asked him "if this took place. He said yes."[67] North himself said that Meese had asked him point-blank: "Did this happen?" and he had first answered that it had not. "He then asked me if anything like that had ever happened, or words to that effect, and I told him it had."

In his testimony at the North trial, Richardson said: "Well, Mr. Meese asked—he basically asked two lines of questions. The first concerned whether the President had been informed about the plan or had authorized it. And as I recall Colonel North said that it had not been discussed with the President with Colonel North present. He didn't think that he had authorized it. Mr. Meese asked about the transactions, I think his first question was how much money had gone to the Nicaraguan resistance. Colonel North said he didn't know. And then Mr. Meese asked about U.S. government involvement and Colonel North said our involvement was none . . . The CIA, NSC, none. And he later said no other U.S. official was involved. McFarlane and Poindexter were knowledgeable. And he was asked—Mr. Meese asked who else knew about it and he said the only three who could know were McFarlane, Poindexter and himself."⁶⁸

Reynolds recalled that North had asked whether there was a "cover memo," designating its recipients, with the diversion document and was told there was not. If there had been a "cover memo," it would have indicated whether the document had gone to the president and he would have known about it.⁶⁹

Later, North melodramatically described the diversion as "the secret within the secret" and "the deepest, darkest secret of the whole activity."⁷⁰ If it was such a deep, dark secret and could not be told even to the president of the United States, North must have recognized inwardly that there was something indefensible about it.

Richardson's notes convey only the essential information elicited by Meese without the drama:

AG [Attorney General]: Same memo, appears to be written between 4–7 April—
Mention of use of $—
Transferred ?—
[*North*]: Yes, b/c [because] used it f[or] Hawk parts—
    16 May $ deposited—to Israeli acc[ount]

Use of $—
    —$2.—million for Israeli replacem[en]t.
$12 M[illion] residual funds for Nicaraguan
    resistance.

    cost: [$]6.5 [million] parts
            2.5 replac[ement] TOWs Isr[ael]
           ——
           9.00 total, so 3 M[illion] of
    residual funds

    Don't know how much was moved to *Nicaraguans*—

Israeli decides $ to Resistance.
Our involv[e]m[en]t—none—CIA, NSC none.

AG: how[?]

[*North*] *Nir*: Israelis, in Jan 86, approach[ed] w[ith] 2 ways to help—
    Arrange to take residuals from these transactions & to Nic[aragua].
AG: disc[ussed] w[ith]—
[*North*]—not w[ith] N[orth].⁷¹

These notes indicate that the contras received only $3 million of the $12 million that came to Secord and Hakim. North seemed bent on putting the responsibility for the diversion on the Israelis; he insisted that they had come up with the idea and had decided how much money to give the contras. Another reference to Israel in Richardson's notes reads:

> An Israeli idea—wanted to be helpful.
> Guess money got to them from this [profits from arms
>   deal]. Contras knew $ came & apprec[iated].
>
> Israeli offer [to] Calero [to] open 3 acc[oun]ts in
>   Switz[erland].[72]
> N[orth] gave $ to Israelis—
> $ to acc[oun]ts.
> CIA no knowledge—[73]

These notes were clarified by Reynolds, Cooper, and Meese. "As he [North] explained it to us," Reynolds recalled, "it was the Israelis who had received the profit and had asked—had indicated they wanted to send that profit to the contras and North's involvement had been, as he explained it to us, simply to give them account numbers and Swiss bank accounts where they could take the money and deposit it in those accounts which would then be drawn out by the contras."[74] When North was asked whose idea it was to divert the funds to the contras, he had answered, according to Cooper, "Nir. Nir of the Israeli Government."[75] Meese agreed that North had said "it was the Israelis who decided how much money went to the Nicaraguans of the Iranian arms sales." North had told them that "this was an Israeli idea because they wanted to be helpful." When the Israelis had made the offer, North had "contacted a Mr. Calero and suggested he open three accounts in Switzerland and Colonel North indicated he then gave those numbers of those accounts to the Israelis and the Israelis then deposited the excess funds from the transactions to those accounts."[76]

Richardson's version at North's trial makes it appear that North concocted a wholly fictitious story in reply to a question by Meese about how the diversion plan had evolved:

> He [North] said it had been an Israeli proposal that had come up in January of 1986 in a meeting when a Mr. Nir was here in the United States and that the Israelis had discussed several ways to be helpful and that the discussion had involved use of a diversion of U.S. government funds but that Colonel North had rejected that because that was not within the law at the time. Then he said the Israelis had discussed use of Israeli money. I think aid money. And that Colonel North had said that could not be done and then

Colonel North said that the Israelis had suggested just have the Iranians pay.[77]

Altogether suppressed was the bathroom incident with Ghorbanifar, which would have put a different light on the origin of the idea. In addition, North said that the Israelis had given him the fallacious figure, which he had put in the memorandum, of $12 million for the diversion.[78]

Of all of North's fictions, foisting the entire responsibility for the diversion on the Israelis was one of the most unconscionable. He was, after all, telling a blatant falsehood to the attorney general of the United States on a fact-finding mission assigned by the president, not to some dubious Iranians. Judging from Richardson's and Reynold's accounts, North gave the impression that the Israelis had virtually masterminded and executed the diversion all by themselves. There had long been a provisional plan to use Israel as a scapegoat if the operation misfired, but North seems to have held on to it even in these final hours.

In his congressional testimony eight months later, North admitted that he had known the money for the contras had come from accounts controlled by Secord, not the Israelis. To explain how he had come to mislead Meese, he entangled himself in a maze of contradictions:

> I did not have on that day [of the interview with Meese] as good a feel or as good an understanding of the actual financial transactions that I came to have in the days thereafter, and—first of all, it is important that you understand that we believed, at least I was led to believe that our intelligence services saw Mr. Ghorbanifar as an Israeli agent. He is an Iranian, at least that is where he was born and lived, but that he was viewed by—certainly Director Casey and other members of the intelligence community as an agent of the Israeli intelligence services.
>
> And so, my assumption was that if an Israeli agent was giving money to an account in this case, an account which included the Nicaraguan Resistance, that there would be an Israeli connection to that.
>
> I may well have been wrong, because in the subsequent days— in fact, later that day or perhaps the day afterwards—it was described to me differently. That no, the moneys came directly from other places and went in there and a whole host of other people to include Mr. Khashoggi and others were mentioned.
>
> I did not know that at the time I was talking to the Attorney General.
>
> Question: But you knew that the residue—the residuals as you have called them, went into the custody of Mr. Secord and his Swiss bank accounts, didn't you?

North: And I did know that they did go to the support of the Nicaraguan Resistance, and those other activities I have described at the time I talked to him and that is what I tried to express.

Question: No. That was not quite my question. My question was you knew that the residuals had gone into accounts controlled by General Secord, not accounts controlled by the Contras?

North: That is correct.[79]

In this interrogation, North first said that Ghorbanifar had given the money to the contra account, and only after being pressed to stop ducking and weaving was he forced to admit that the money had come from accounts controlled by Secord, not by the contras. He claimed that he had known later that same day or at most the day afterward that he had told Meese a fictitious story but did nothing to make Meese aware of it before Meese told the same fictitious story at a press conference on television two days later. *

This was not the only evidence of North's curious forgetfulness. When Meese asked him who else had known about the diversion, North named McFarlane, Poindexter, and himself in the United States.[80] North seems to have deliberately excluded Casey, whom he named in his congressional testimony. Earl also knew about the diversion, and he recalled that North had mentioned to him that North had told Casey about it.[81] In effect, Meese obtained from North confirmation of the diversion but in the form of a largely fictionalized account that drew Meese's attention mainly to the Israelis and away from Ghorbanifar as North's inspiration, to Secord for the actual operation, and to Casey as someone in the know. The interview with North was actually no more than a starting point in any serious fact-finding about the diversion. It was full of loose ends and false leads. Yet for Meese, it was the be-all and end-all of his inquiry.

At one point, North offered some advice to Meese:

If this doesn't come out, only other is Nov. Hawks deal[.] Think someone ought to step up and say this was authorized in Nov.[82]

Meese agreed that the first sentence was a suggestion by North that the diversion of funds should not come out publicly. Meese interpreted the second sentence as a demand by North that the president's authorization of the November deal should be openly acknowledged.[83]

After almost two hours of interrogation, Meese left for a previous

---

* At the Poindexter trial, however, North again put all the responsibility for the money transfers on the Israelis: "The Israelis were the only ones that took the money from Iran, put it into various accounts, and moved the money financially from one place to another. We then paid the Department of Defense, through the CIA, and then the missiles were shipped" (PT, p. 1100). In fact, the Iranians refused to deal with the Israelis directly and the Iranian money went into the Secord-Hakim account, sometimes through Ghorbanifar.

appointment, and the other three carried on for the better part of two more hours. Much of the discussion now turned to the November 1985 arms shipment, which North explained with greater candor than before. He said that he had guessed it was made up of arms, not oil equipment, but that he had told the CIA it was oil equipment. Asked who knew about the 508 Hawk missiles deal, North named McFarlane, Reagan, Thompson, Poindexter, Regan, and Bush.[84]

After North had left, Cooper, Reynolds, and Richardson remarked on the change in North's composure as soon as the diversion issue had been raised.[85] Richardson recalled that they were mainly concerned about getting confirmation of the diversion, despite North's confession, as well as needing to find out who else had known about it and who had authorized it. Both Cooper and Richardson said that they had wondered what the legal ramifications might be.[86] Once the diversion was revealed, according to Richardson, they thought that it was much more significant than the original November 1985 episode.[87]

North's reaction to his treatment at the interview seems to have been that something had been put over on him. He talked to Thompson the next morning about Meese's questionable "tactics" in confronting him unexpectedly with the diversion paragraph. As Thompson recalled North's grievance, "they spent most of the time talking about all aspects of the Iranian initiative and so forth and then at the very end Meese pulled out that April memo that you referred to earlier and said, 'What about this?' And North said, 'Oh geez, I didn't realize you had that' or 'I don't know where that came from,' or something like that."[88] Actually, Meese pulled out the April memo after about an hour and not at the very end of the interview, but otherwise the conversation with Thompson suggests that North was unhappy at the way Meese had sprung the memo on him. Earl gave a different version of North's reaction to the diversion memo. Earl said North had told him that he had asked Meese, "Did it count?" and whether it could be used against him since he had not been warned of his rights.[89] This also suggests that North had quickly realized the jeopardy in which Meese's unexpected production of the incriminating memo had put him.

After the interview with Meese, North telephoned Poindexter to tell him "when the issue had come up about using the arms money to Iran for the purpose of supporting the Resistance, that I had told the truth about it; that this was the secret within the secret and was undoubtedly going to be an even bigger problem than we had before." North also called Nir in Israel and "a couple of other people in the system" to tell them that he would be leaving.[90]

On Sunday night after the interview, North went back to his office and shredded some more until 4 o'clock the next morning.[91] By this time he was in no doubt that his days on the NSC staff were numbered.

7

The fate of Poindexter and North was settled on Monday, November 24, 1986. Yet it was not clear until North's trial in 1989 why such drastic action was taken so hastily.

On Saturday, November 22, Meese first learned about the diversion memorandum. On November 23, he confirmed that the diversion had been carried out. He knew no more than North told him. What North told him was riddled with half-truths and untruths. Cooper, Reynolds, and Richardson agreed that more work was necessary to get more information about the diversion. They were unsure about its legal ramifications.

According to Meese, once he learned about the diversion, the focus of his inquiry "changed entirely," and it was what he decided would be presented to the American people.[92] This abrupt change of course took place in no more than twenty-four hours. The diversion alarmed him, mainly because he thought that it had not been authorized by the president.[93] At that time, Meese saw no criminal aspect in anything he had learned. Meese says that he asked Cooper to look into possible criminal offenses on Monday, November 24, "because at that time there did not appear to be any apparent." Cooper came up with some ideas the next day, after the decisions on Poindexter and North had been made, but nothing definite was arrived at. Late Tuesday afternoon, November 25, however, Meese asked William Weld of the Justice Department's Criminal Division to cooperate with Cooper to determine "whether there was any possible basis for a criminal investigation."[94] But these belated legal qualms had little or nothing to do with the frantic decisions on Monday.

In a sense, the discovery of the diversion was providential. The diversion was, after all, only a single episode in two lengthy, tangled, covert operations. It resulted from North's position at the center of both of them and was a way of getting around Congress's power of appropriations. Poindexter argued that the diversion money "was very similar to the third country and private support for the contras."[95] But the other third countries had given money of their own volition, whereas Iran was not asked for permission to use arms-sales profits for the benefit of the contras.

Poindexter also had some reason to believe that he knew President Reagan's mind after working closely with him for five and a half years, the last three very closely. "So, although I was convinced that we could properly do it," he said, "and that the President would approve if asked, I made a very deliberate decision not to ask the President so that I could insulate him from the decision and provide some future deniability for the President if it ever leaked out."[96] After all, the president had gratefully accepted money from the Saudis in the same secret way that North had used the Iran money. "I was aware," Poindexter said, "that the President was aware of third country support, that the President was aware of private support, and the way Colonel North described this to me at the time, it was obvious to me that this fell in exactly the same category that these funds could either be characterized as private funds because of the way that we had—that Director Casey and I had agreed to carry out the Finding." For Poindexter, the diversion was "a matter of implementation of the President's policy with regard to support of the contras."[97]

But there was a difference, which Poindexter said he recognized, between the Iran money and other third-country money. The difference as he saw it was purely political: "Now, I was not so naive as to believe that it was not a politically volatile issue, it clearly was, because of the divisions that existed within the Congress on the issue of support for the contras, and it was clear that there would be a lot of people that would disagree, that would make accusations that indeed have been made."[98] To Poindexter, it was the controversial nature of this implementation of the president's policy that led Poindexter to make the decision alone "so that he would be protected."[99] Poindexter's destruction of the December 5, 1985, Finding was in the same category as the diversion; it had to be covered up because it was "politically embarrassing."[100]

If we can trust North, Casey's reasoning had been similar. North says that Casey recognized the risk entailed in going through with the diversion. But it was a "very political risk" that "could indeed be dangerous or not dangerous so much as politically damaging."[101]

Politics were the reason Poindexter and Casey had wanted to cover up the diversion. Politics were the reason Meese now wanted to uncover it.

8

At North's trial on March 28, 1989, Attorney General Meese for the first time revealed what had been in his mind during his interview with North on November 23, 1986, and what had driven him to take action afterward.

At the beginning of the interview, Meese had told North that "the worst thing that could happen is if someone tried to conceal anything to protect themselves or the President or to put a good spin on it." Meese now explained why he had said it: "We wanted to be sure that no one, and I was thinking of political opponents, could call this a cover-up of any sort."[102]

Brendan V. Sullivan, Jr., North's lawyer, asked Meese why he had focused on whether North had actually carried out the diversion. Meese was exceptionally candid, as he had not been at the congressional hearings:

Sullivan: It is also fair to say, based on your testimony, Mr. Meese, that when you went into the meeting on November 23rd on a Sunday, you were basically focusing at that time on the fact that your associates in the Justice Department had found a document in Colonel North's office which reflected that residuals from the arms sales had been used by the Freedom Fighters, or possibly had been, correct?

Meese: That's correct.

Sullivan: And you sensed immediately, when you heard that, that that could create an enormous political problem because it merged or married together two separate problems that the Administration had; one, the support of the Freedom Fighters which was hotly contested, and two, the sale of arms to Iran which had been by order of the Finding kept from Congress, correct?

Meese: Yes. I was concerned that two major policy issues within the Administration at that time would be merged together and that this would—could complicate the ability of the President in both of the issues.

Sullivan: In fact, your assessment at the time was that unless something was done, a strong response, that the merging of those two factors could very well cause the possible toppling of the President himself, correct?

Meese: Yes.

Sullivan: And there was discussion, in fact, that on the days November 23rd and 24th that unless the Administration, unless you and the President himself, put out to the public the facts of the use of residuals for the Freedom Fighters, unless you got it out the door first, it could possibly lead to impeachment by the Congress, correct?

Meese: Yes. That was a concern, that political opponents might try that kind of tactic.

Judge Gesell: And you discussed that with the President. He is asking you.

Meese: I believe I discussed it with the President. I certainly discussed it with others in high ranking positions such as the Chief of Staff.

Judge Gesell: Well, he is asking you whether you discussed it with the President.

Meese: I don't know whether the actual word "impeachment" was referred to, but I certainly discussed the tremendous consequences for the President personally and for the Administration.

Sullivan: And, in fact, the people that worked with you on this inquiry, Mr. Reynolds particularly, and Mr. Cooper, were strongly advising that you release this information about the use of residuals in order to prevent that kind of aggressive action from the Congress of trying to impeach the President, correct?

Meese: Yes, sir. We were all of the same mind on that subject.[103]

From this, it is clear that a kind of panic had gripped Meese and his closest associates as a result of the interview with North. They were haunted by former President Nixon's debacle as a result of his attempted cover-up in the Watergate case and were determined at all costs to avoid a repetition. Nixon had been forced to resign, but impeachment now seemed to threaten President Reagan unless he did what Nixon had not done—come out publicly with the information at hand. Yet nothing more appeared to be at stake here than the merging of the Iran and Nicaragua operations. It was certainly an operational monstrosity of the most serious kind, as even North admitted, though he claimed to have had no alternative. Still, such a furor over an operational blunder needs explanation.

Cooper had previously hinted at a reason other than Congress why the information had to be made public without delay:

> Well, we recognized the sensitivity of this information, the fact that it was information that had to be made public by the President and nobody else, that if the *Washington Post* made this fact public prior to the time that the President did, it would be very calamitous, because no one would believe that we had discovered this along the lines that we had and that it was something that, you know, we fully intended to make public.
>
> The point was can we verify and touch the bases that we need to touch between now and the time that we make this public before some other leak or some other reporter or something gets wind of this.
>
> We didn't have a sense that there was, you know, a *Post* reporter or anything else breathing down the neck of this information, but we did fully discuss and recognize that it may well be no more than a week away.[104]

Richardson had also alluded to the political race to get the information about the diversion out first.

Question: It [diversion] was explosive from a political point of view, wasn't it?

Richardson: Absolutely.

Question: And if the President didn't get this out he was in deep trouble with the Congress of the United States, right?

Richardson: Yes, sir, if someone else got it out first.[105]

It was with this panicky sense that time was running out on them that President Reagan's closest advisers decided that he could not wait to divulge the diversion scheme. It was a strange ending to a fact-finding inquiry which had started out to learn what had happened in the arms deal of November 1985. The original inquiry was now abandoned in favor of finding a single link in the arms-for-hostages chain of events, and one that had little to do with the main purpose of the arms deals.

24

The Bitter End

Attorney General Meese was given only seventy-two hours to get to the bottom of what had been wrong with the Iran project. He concentrated on the period before the January 1986 Finding and particularly on the arms deal of November 1985. He completely neglected the Nicaraguan affair, which he had not been asked to look into. Yet he sprang into action on the morning of November 24, 1986, because he had unexpectedly hit on an aspect of the Iran and contra affairs that had little to do with his interest in the first and had much to do with the second. The diversion cut across both, but in a way that he hardly had time to figure out. He merely knew that the two operations had been temporarily "merged"—a procedure that was undoubtedly improper from the viewpoint of good covert methodology but was not understood to be illegal.

Nevertheless, once the diversion was discovered, it swept everything else aside and made Meese feel that President Reagan could even be impeached if it was not made public by the president himself before the political opposition could find out and beat him to it. Whatever else was wrong with Reagan's Iran policy no longer mattered.

Monday, November 24, was a busy day for Meese. At 7:20 a.m., he held a meeting with his aides and directed Assistant Attorney General Cooper to see whether any criminal or other statutes might apply to the case. At 9:55 a.m., Meese called William Weld, assistant attorney general, Criminal Division, to say that he had purposely decided not to involve Weld's division. Weld says that he cautioned Meese that "if you try to carry too much water here that some may spill on you."[1]

At 10 a.m., Meese met with McFarlane to make sure that the former national security adviser had known of the diversion. According to Meese, McFarlane said that North had told him about it "more or less in passing" on the way back from Tehran in May 1986 and that he had been given to understand that it had been authorized. Meese learned little more, because he spent little time with McFarlane.

At 11:02 a.m., Meese called Chief of Staff Regan and met with him before the two went to see President Reagan. According to Regan, Meese briefly told him about the diversion of funds and the necessity to see the president without delay. When Regan was asked what his reaction to the news had been, he used one word: "Horror." If we can believe Regan, the very word "diversion" was enough to horrify him.*[2]

Meese and Regan went off to horrify President Reagan but, to their frustration, he had a previous appointment with Zulu Chief Mangosuthu Gatsha Buthelezi of South Africa. As a result, Meese could only get in a few words with him. Meese says that he managed to tell him that, as a result of an interview with North, he had found evidence of a diversion of funds from Iran money to the contras. The president was "quite surprised" and indicated he had known nothing about it.[3] Regan's version is that Meese told the president he had bad news and may have said something about a possible diversion of funds. Meese also said: "I have a few things to button up, then I want to get back to you and tell the full story." They agreed to meet at the scheduled meeting of the top-level National Security Planning Group, which had set the deadline for Meese's report in the first place.[4]

At 2 p.m., Meese attended the NSPG meeting with President Reagan, Vice President Bush, Secretary of State Shultz, Secretary of Defense Weinberger, CIA Director Casey, Chief of Staff Regan, National Security Adviser Poindexter, and CIA consultant George Cave. This meeting, which brought together all the main officials of the administration, seems to have been peculiarly uninformative. Instead of sharing his great secret with these most responsible advisers, Meese decided to say nothing about the diversion, allegedly because he had not yet discussed it fully with the president. The November 1985 Hawk shipment came in for discussion, but apparently without eliciting answers to Regan's questions: Who authorized it? Who knew about it? Was President Reagan told about it? Poindexter put the responsibility wholly on the departed McFarlane, who, he said, had handled it by himself, and no document had been found. Shultz observed that he had known about the situation and had opposed it.[5] Strangely, according to Meese's notes and from what he could recall, President Reagan did not respond to Regan's question whether he had been told about it.[6] Shultz had a hard time remembering what went on at this meeting.[7] In effect, Meese permitted the meeting to proceed without telling the participants that the November 1985 problem no longer took precedence and that everything now hinged on the diversionary aspect of the Iran-contra operations.

* In his deposition, Regan was even more dramatic: "Horror, horror, sheer horror" (B-22, p. 656). In his book, *For the Record*, Regan gave this account of his horror:

"Meese told me that he had to see the President at once: his investigation had discovered, in his words, 'things the President didn't know'—including a possible diversion of funds from the Iran arms sale.

"A diversion of funds? The phrase made my blood run cold; I had had thirty-five years' experience in handling other people's money, and I knew what lay ahead for the President and the country.

"'Ah,—!' I said. 'Damn it all! Well, we'd better go see the President'" (pp. 38–39).

At about 4 p.m., Meese met with Cooper and Reynolds, who told him about a strange interlude with Thomas C. Green, a Washington lawyer. Green had called Reynolds in the morning to say that he had important information that could not wait. Green had been put up to it by Secord, his client, who was worried that too much would come out too quickly.[8] At 2:20 p.m., Reynolds and Cooper met with Green, whom Secord had hurriedly briefed shortly before sending him off. From Green, Cooper and Reynolds heard a Secord-inspired running account of the Iran operation—Hawks, Israelis, the January 1986 Finding, Ghorbanifar, Hakim, and all the rest.

Green even seemed to know about the diversion or at least gave them a garbled version of it. According to Reynolds, Green informed them that the Iranians had been told to make a contribution to the contras in return for access to American supplies and that the Iranians had been " 'conned' into contributing to the contras."[9] Cooper recalled that "Mr. Green presented an understanding of the contra diversion that was at odds with the one that we had received from Colonel North, and he opened his discussion of that element of it by saying that Colonel North is the ultimate Marine, and he wants to step forward and take the spears in his own chest."[10]

In the end, Green revealed that his real purpose was to prevent the Iran operation from being made public. He gave them a number of familiar reasons—Iran would kill American hostages as well as Iranians with whom the Americans had dealt, the American effort to reach out to Iranian "moderates" would go "up in smoke," and publicity about how the Iranians had been "conned" would "*expose* the situation."[11] The reasons came from Secord but might just as well have come from North.

When Cooper and Reynolds told Meese about their session with Green, it seemed more likely to have the effect of bringing about an early public disclosure than to delay it.[12] If an outsider like Green knew so much—and Meese was fearful above all that someone would get to the media or Congress before he could—there was no time to lose.

At 4:15 p.m., Meese met with Poindexter for only five to ten minutes, alone and without taking notes, as was now his habit. By this time, Meese was really interested in only one question: Did Poindexter know of the diversion? According to Meese, Poindexter replied: "Ollie has given me enough hints about this so that I generally knew, but I did nothing to follow up or stop it"—or words to that effect. Meese also asked whether Poindexter had told anyone else or did anyone in the White House know. When Poindexter answered: "No," Meese departed.[13]

Poindexter's version of the meeting is somewhat fuller. He recalled that Meese had started off by saying: "I assume you are aware of the memo that we found in Ollie's files." When Poindexter said: "Yes," Meese asked: "Were you aware of this?" Poindexter replied only that he "was generally aware of the transfer of funds or the plan to transfer funds."

But Poindexter also told Meese that he was prepared to resign and trusted Meese to tell him when it was best to go. On this point, an exchange took place at the congressional hearings:

> *Liman:* Can you tell us why you didn't tell him that Colonel North was acting pursuant to your authority?
>
> *Poindexter:* I wanted—in continuing the plan that I had always had of providing deniability to the President, I did not want to provide that detailed information at the time, because I wanted the President and his staff to be able to say they didn't know anything about it.[14]

Three things stand out in Poindexter's responses. He, too, believed that the diversion was such an enormity that it required his immediate resignation. Clearly, there was something about the diversion that violated the norms of acceptable conduct as nothing else did, but just what was never explained. Yet he was willing, at that late date, even after North had admitted the reality of the diversion, to keep the whole truth from the attorney general in order to protect everyone but himself.

After Poindexter, Meese had only to tell President Reagan the bad news.

2

At 4:22 p.m., still Monday, November 24, Meese and Regan held their delayed meeting with President Reagan.

For a crisis so explosive that it could threaten the president with impeachment, Meese's account of the meeting is remarkably short and uneventful. Meese said:

> I then related in more detail to the President, and also added what I had just learned from Admiral Poindexter about his knowledge and participation. There was a discussion then in the President's office between Don Regan and the President and myself about the next steps to take.
>
> I indicated that I probably ought to do some additional checking or at least there were other people that I wanted to talk with. One of them—just to touch all the bases—with the Vice President.
>
> And also there was a discussion of—I know distinctly there was a discussion: should John Poindexter be relieved of his duties?
>
> And the President said he would like to think about it overnight as to what steps should be taken, and we agreed to meet again in the morning, I believe, at 9 o'clock.
>
> Let me say there was one other thing. The President said at that

time, again, reiterated what he had said to me on a previous occasion, that was that we want to be sure that we get this out as soon as possible or words to that effect.[15]

One gets the impression from this that there was no great discussion or analysis of what the diversion meant or violated. There could not have been any deliberation in depth, because the meeting among the three of them lasted only sixteen minutes.[16] It was apparently taken for granted that only the diversion was now relevant to the fact-finding task that the president had given Meese and, in fact, that the original task of inquiring into the Iran operation as a whole, with special attention to the pre-Finding period, was no longer of any importance or even interest.

Regan gave a somewhat more detailed and melodramatic version of this critical meeting. He says Meese related that the Iranians had apparently paid $30 million for the equipment sold to them; the U.S. government had received only $12 million; nobody seemed to know where the other $18 million had gone and what had been done with it. But Lieutenant Colonel Oliver North had admitted diverting some of these funds to the Nicaraguan contras.[17] The president had greeted Meese's report with "deep distress, deep distress."*[18] Regan had no doubt of the president's sincerity: "You know, the question has been asked, I've seen it in the paper time and time again: did the President know? Let me put it this way. This guy I know was an actor, and he was nominated at one time for an Academy Award, but I would give him an Academy Award if he knew anything about this when you watched his reaction to express complete surprise at this news on Monday the 24th. He couldn't have known it."[19]

Regan's emphatic disclaimer reflected the increasing obsession with the question: "What did Reagan know about the diversion?" as if that were all there was for him to know. It had the political virtue of blanketing another question: "What did he know about everything else?"

Regan also revealed that the discussion had touched on another obsessive question: "Where was the money?"

> Well, the President wanted to know, well, did any Americans get their hands on that money? Was there anything of that nature? And the answer was no, the money had gone directly from Iran bank account to Israeli to Swiss bank account to contras, and no U.S. person had been involved—in the handling of money.[20]

In effect, Meese gave Reagan the same fraudulent story that North had given him. The money did not go from an Israeli to a Swiss bank account to the contras. It had gone from Iran to the Secord-Hakim Swiss

---

* In his deposition, Regan was more theatrical: "Horror again, and thinking back on it, it is hard to—it is like a person was punched in the stomach. I mean, the air goes out of him, crestfallen. You know, a slumping in the chair kind of thing" (B-22, p. 664). In *For the Record*, Regan gave this version: "The President, in person, is a ruddy man, with bright red cheeks. He blanched when he heard Meese's words. The color drained from his face, leaving his skin pasty white" (p. 38).

bank account to the contras. Americans had certainly gotten their hands on the money, and U.S. persons had been very much involved in handling it. Reagan and Regan were then in no position to know what was imaginary about the North-Meese account because Meese told them only what North had told him and had not bothered to check on North's story. If Meese had gone to Secord, who he already knew was deeply implicated in the entire Iran affair, he could have learned that North's concoction about the Israelis and the contras was humbug.

All agreed that their information, such as it was, should be made public by the president as quickly as possible, but Regan, from past experience, did not have confidence that Reagan could successfully face an inquisitive press. Regan says that he went along with a preliminary presidential announcement but told Meese: "Probably, Ed, that should be followed by your taking the questions, rather than the President, because you will know the details and the President certainly won't be able to answer press inquiries." They decided to "keep the thing quiet overnight, and then break the news in the morning."[21]

Reagan's version of this meeting comes from his diary. If it had been known at the time, it would have saved the press the trouble of looking for a "smoking gun":

> After the meeting in the Situation Room, Ed M. and Don R. told me of a smoking gun. On one of the arms shipments the Iranians had paid Israel a higher purchase price than we were getting. The Israelis put the difference in a secret bank account. Then our Col. North (N.S.C.) gave the money to the "Contras." . . . North didn't tell me about this. Worst of all, John P. found out about it and didn't tell me. This may call for resignations.[22]

Thus the smoking gun was partially blamed on Israel in line with North's spurious story to Meese. In Reagan's mind, Poindexter was clearly the chief villain and had to go, as Shultz had previously demanded.

After Meese had left, Regan says that he gave the president more forceful advice. The chief of staff, who had been left out when Meese had taken charge, now made up for lost time. He was particularly anxious to get rid of Poindexter: "I think John Poindexter has got to go. We just can't have a guy like that around here if he didn't follow up on this."*[23]

---

* In *For the Record*, Regan puts most of the discussion about Poindexter in Meese's presence and adds some further details: "What does John Poindexter say about this? the President asked." Meese replied that Poindexter had said he "knew something about North's activities, but he hadn't wanted to investigate too deeply for fear of what might turn up." In his testimony, Regan cited Meese as having quoted Poindexter: "I should have been supervising North better, and I didn't. I didn't look into this" (p. 30)—not quite the same thing.

Regan's book continues: "The President looked at Ed Meese in disbelief. Meese left. . . . 'This is a bitter blow, Mr. President,' I [Regan] said. He [Reagan] shook his head in bewilderment. He was pale and unsmiling. What went on in their minds? he asked. Do you understand it, Don? I [Regan] did not know how to answer his question" (p. 39).

The president, Regan says, did not comment, which Regan took to mean that he could proceed with Poindexter's dismissal.[24] Nothing was said about North, who had done what Poindexter had not followed up on. Regan also suggested that it would be necessary to appoint an independent commission to investigate the whole affair, because "nobody would believe it if just Ed Meese looked into this." Regan explained his preference for a commission instead of an independent counsel on the ground that the latter would have taken too much time—"that from a public relations point of view simply couldn't be condoned."[*][25]

Thus Reagan, Regan, and Meese made the final decisions in no more than a few minutes. According to Regan, "a lot of our discussion was how to make it public," not what to make public.[26] Yet there had been a meeting only the day before of the top-level NSPG, at which the vice president, the secretaries of state and defense, and other notables were present, presumably called together to offer the president their best advice. They had not even been told what Meese had in mind for the president to decide, let alone asked for advice.

Donald Regan had not had much to do with the Iran affair until Monday, November 24. Once drawn in, however, he seemed determined to make the most of it. In the next twenty-four hours, President Reagan seems to have lost his nerve and permitted Meese and Regan to take charge of the cleanup operation. On November 13, Reagan had made a television speech, and on November 19 he had held a press conference to show that he could manage the uproar over the Iran affair. Now he virtually stepped aside and let Meese and Regan take over the management of the worst crisis of his presidency.

3

One of the striking things about these last few weeks is the very minor role played by CIA Director Casey.

Casey as the mastermind of the Iran-contra affairs may well be the creation of Oliver North. In his public testimony at the congressional hearings in the summer of 1987, North portrayed a Casey who was his mentor, manipulator, and evil genius. North's most sensational revelation was Casey's alleged intention to create an overseas "off-the-shelf," "self-financing," "independent of appropriated monies," "stand-alone," "full-service covert operation."[27] That North said so did not make it true, any

---

* In *For the Record*, Regan says that Meese declared that an independent counsel might have to be appointed instead of a nonpartisan commission. Yet, according to Regan, the president, "as usual listening more than he talked, accepted all these recommendations and told Meese and me to get to work on them" (p. 39). How Reagan could have accepted two different recommendations is not explained. In his deposition, Regan said that during their meeting Meese and Reagan had favored a commission (B-22, p. 667).

more than that other things said by North were necessarily true. Yet this purported plan by Casey has been widely accepted, even by Senators William S. Cohen and George J. Mitchell in their otherwise informative book on the Iran-contra congressional hearings. They plead in favor of the congressional concessions made to North on the ground that his testimony was crucial, "if only because he disclosed the existence of the so-called off-the-shelf covert capability that is so inimicable [sic] to our concept of democracy."[28]

Unfortunately, the private depositions taken by the congressional committees' lawyers were published long after the public hearings. They passed largely unnoticed by the media, and their thousands of pages did not invite interest elsewhere. One of the most important depositions was given by John N. McMahon, Casey's deputy director until his resignation in March 1986. McMahon had spent over thirty-four years in the CIA. He was made deputy director in 1982 and had thus worked more closely with Casey than anyone else in the Agency. His office adjoined Casey's; the door between them was always open; he was privy to all that went on, as deputies are supposed to be. He was an honorable man who had demanded the presidential Finding as soon as he had found out, in Casey's absence, that CIA officials had engaged in unlawful cooperation with North in the ill-fated transport of arms from Israel to Iran in November 1985.

McMahon gave the "off-the-shelf capability" a quite different interpretation. He said that Casey wanted to build an intelligence capacity outside the established CIA mechanism "but all part of the Central Intelligence Agency, nothing on the shelf or as described by Colonel North." McMahon maintained that Casey's idea was to be funded by congressionally appropriated funds, not North's unappropriated funds, and in compliance with U.S. laws requiring presidential Findings and notification to Congress, not North's outlaw version of it. The following exchange took place:

> *Counsel:* As I stated before, I don't believe we have any corroborative evidence of Colonel North's testimony on this particular point, and what he did relate were conversations that he had and discussions he had with the Director apparently one to one in this area.
>
> *McMahon:* Casey never related that or even gave a hint to me that anything like that was fermenting in his mind.*[29]

McMahon was not the only one mystified by North's off-the-shelf story. Robert M. Gates, McMahon's successor as Casey's deputy director,

---

* I tried to get more information from Mr. McMahon about the intelligence capacity outside the CIA mechanism but part of the CIA. He declined to give me any more information on the ground that it was classified.

was asked whether Casey had ever said anything to him about the scheme. Gates replied: "No. He never suggested anything that would have even suggested that he was thinking of such a thing." To Gates's knowledge, no such entity was ever discussed by anyone at the Agency. Gates said that he would have resigned if the off-the-shelf project had been pursued and, anyway, he thought it was "fundamentally unnecessary."[30]

The least that can be said about the depositions of McMahon and Gates is that they must be taken into account in any consideration of North's off-the-shelf story. North asks us to believe that Casey had confided to him alone a palpably unlawful, unconstitutional scheme that could not have been put into effect by Casey and North alone and would have had to draw in others in the Agency as high up as McMahon or Gates. We have evidence that Casey inspired or supported some of North's activities, but nothing of a piece with this intrigue.

Casey probably knew of North's reputation for make-believe. McFarlane said that he had had "four or five years experience of reading things [by North] which I knew to be not compatible with the realities of things." Asked whether North was "a bit of a dramatist, prone to hyperbole at times . . . even a romanticist perhaps on certain occasions with respect to facts and the way he would brief people on subjects," McFarlane agreed that that was the case.[31] The CIA's Clarridge described one side of North as "sort of boyish and boastful, and it would be in character for him to say I won't be here tomorrow, I will be down South, and then for him to say, yes, it was a quick trip and I flew all night and I came back and I haven't slept for 48 hours, always complaining about how busy he was and how terribly overworked."[32] The CIA's Clair George was asked: "Did Ollie ever tell you things that weren't true?" George replied: "Yes—for instance, his endless conversations with the President, and other such minor details." Question: "Did he frequently exaggerate?" George: "Sure, he did."[33] This testimony coincides with what Constantine C. Menges says that he told Elliott Abrams: "I urge you, never take *any* important action based solely on what Ollie tells you."[34]

Casey may have been guilty of all sorts of shady practices, and, in fact, in his autobiography Reagan makes one of his few derogatory remarks at Casey's expense—that Casey had apparently deceived him.[35] But this off-the-shelf plot is inherently implausible; it was featherbrained, and no one ever accused Casey of that particular imperfection. Whatever we may think of Casey, the issue here is one of fact, not Casey's character or general record. In fact, the only such off-the-shelf scheme of which we can be certain was concocted and carried out by North and Secord; it was already a reality by the time North attributed it to Casey as a plan for the future. North's Casey conveniently advocated what North was doing.

The Casey that we encounter in the Iran-contra record is much more cagey and cautious. He traveled so much that he was not present in Washington either at the time of the November 1985 mix-up or in the days just before the November 1986 climax. He handled both the Nicaraguan and Iran affairs by hiding the CIA behind the NSC staff in what was a quasi-constitutional maneuver of dubious legitimacy. In the inner councils, he seems to have supported whatever he thought President Reagan wanted to be supported rather than coming out with his own ideas and pushing them on the president. He saw the president far less often than Poindexter and even less often than Shultz. Casey, in fact, usually reported to the president through Poindexter and met privately with the president infrequently.[36] In the critical weeks of November 1986, Casey played almost no role at all and does not seem even to have been in touch with the president. It is difficult to square Casey's known behavior with the mythology that has romanticized him as the larger-than-life mastermind.*

Moreover, it is hard to explain why someone as allegedly sharp and hardheaded as Casey should have had so much confidence in someone as amateurish as North in the ways of covert operations. If Casey was willing to let North carry almost the entire burden of both the Iran and contra affairs, Casey's judgment is open to question.†

In any event, Casey did not get into the activities of November 24 until Regan, at Casey's request, stopped over to see him for a short time that evening. Peculiarly, according to Regan, Casey wanted to talk to him about his congressional testimony on Iran—a strange desire inasmuch as Casey had testified three days earlier. Regan says that he reported to Casey what Meese had told him and the president a few hours earlier, without Casey asking any questions. When he was asked about Casey's reaction, Regan replied: "Well, you don't get much facial reaction, or didn't get much facial reaction from Bill Casey. You wouldn't know

---

* In his book romanticizing Casey, Bob Woodward tells of a peculiar incident at a reception in Washington in March 1986. Casey is said to have known for more than a year that Woodward was writing a book on him and the CIA. They had talked together many times. Yet Casey mistook Woodward for Arthur Ochs Sulzberger, publisher of *The New York Times*. One wonders what was happening to Casey for him to make such a blunder (*Veil*, pp. 455–56).

† Casey's contact with North has been greatly exaggerated. Joseph E. Persico claims: "North's detailed logs show fairly frequent contact between the Marine and Casey, averaging perhaps a phone call or a visit a week" (*Casey*, p. 433). I have tested this statement for the key year of 1986. North's notebooks or "logs" show only three or possibly four phone calls, only one meeting, and three other unspecified references to Casey in the entire period. The calls were far apart—January 14, February 19, and June 10. If the notebooks are supposed to show how close North was to Casey, they demonstrate just the opposite. In fact, North found it necessary to explain why there was so very little in his notebooks about meetings with Casey; North said that Casey did not "like to have people taking notes with him" (NT, p. 7172).

Persico says that he was given exclusive access to over three hundred thousand pages of Casey's personal papers by Mrs. Sophia Casey. Yet I found very little apparent use of such files in Persico's treatment of the Iran and contra affairs. By deliberately failing to give any references to these files, Persico made it impossible to determine what he got out of those three hundred thousand pages.

exactly how he was taking this news. It did seem to surprise him, because originally he asked, he said, 'Where are we? Why can't we get this thing straight? Why can't we get a story out?' "*37

Instead, after hearing about Meese's discovery, Casey urged Regan to consider the possible consequences of making the scandal public—no more funds to the contras, Central America poisoned by the Sandinistas, Arab outrage over the Israeli role, Iranian wrath at having been overcharged for the missiles.38 After Regan asked him: "How can we sit on this stuff for any longer?" Casey said: "Well, I guess you got to do it," but "I hope you realize, you know, this is going to cause quite a few upsets and is going to be a major story." Regan replied: "I know it, Bill, but that is the only thing we can do," and cut the visit short.39

From what we are told by Regan, Casey had known nothing of Meese's earthshaking revelation. No one had bothered to tell Casey about it, though it was now about forty-eight hours old. Regan did not treat Casey as if he were a major influence and needed to be mollified.

It can be said with some confidence that Casey was not the driving force in the Iran-contra affairs, at least not in 1986, and that the closer we get to the climax, the less he had to do with it. Poindexter did not take his orders from Casey, no matter what Casey told North, about which, in any case, North is the only witness. Poindexter, not Casey, was North's superior, and the responsibility for what North did was Poindexter's, not Casey's.

4

By the end of November 24, all the main characters in this drama knew that it was coming to an end. Reagan, Meese, and Regan were set to make their public announcement the next day. Poindexter and North exchanged farewell messages. Yet even these two did not yet realize how close they were to disgrace and the ruination of their careers.

Poindexter's last words to North read:

Thanks, Ollie. I have talked to Ed [Meese] twice today on this and he is still trying to figure out what to do. I have told him I am prepared to resign. I told him I would take the cue from him. He is one of the few beside the President that I can trust. If we don't leave, what would you think about going to the CIA and being a special assistant to Bill [Casey]? That would get you to the opera-

---

* In his deposition, Regan explained Casey's reaction: "You have to know Director Casey to be aware of what I am saying here. The man's face never reflects anything. I won't say he had a poker face, but he certainly didn't show surprise at that point, didn't utter any expletives, didn't leap out of his chair or any of those things." *Question:* "Did he mumble anything?" *Regan:* "He always mumbled" (B-22, p. 676).

tional world officially. Don't say anything to Bill yet. I just want to get your reaction.[40]

North replied:

There is the old line about you can't fire me, I quit—but I do want to make it official, so that you know I sincerely meant what I said to you over the course of these last several difficult weeks: I am prepared to depart at the time you and the President decide it to be in the best interest of the Presidency and the country. I am honored to have served the President, you, and your predecessors these 5½ years. I only regret that I could not have done so better. My prayer is that the President is not further damaged by what has transpired and that the hostages will not be harmed as a consequence of what we now do. Finally, I remain convinced that what we tried to accomplish was worth the risk. We nearly succeeded. Hopefully, when the political fratricide is finished, there will be others, in a moment of calm reflection who will agree. Warmest regards, Semper Fidelis.[41]

North was proud of his role to the last. His thoughts at this moment were less for himself than for the president, the hostages, and the enterprise which he could not bring himself to understand had merely succeeded in making some arms-for-hostages deals that could only be followed by more arms-for-hostages deals. He clearly did not expect that the president, to whom he was blindly devoted, would agree to make him a prime scapegoat for the political disaster. Poindexter did not think that North's service was over; in Poindexter's mind, a move to the CIA would have enabled North to do officially what North had been doing "unofficially."

Yet North had long seen himself cast in the role of scapegoat. Poindexter recalled that "periodically Ollie would indicate that he was 'willing to take the rap,' and I always told him when he said that that was a ridiculous position and that he had no need to say that."[42] North himself said that he had spoken in this vein: "I had made it clear to Mr. McFarlane, I made it clear to Mr. Casey, and I made it very clear to Admiral Poindexter that I recognized that there would come a time when you may have to have a political—I emphasize the word 'political'—fall guy or scapegoat or whatever."[43] North also said that he had told his courier to the contras, Robert Owen, and perhaps others, that "I would be the person who would be dismissed or reassigned or fired or blamed or fingered or whatever one wants to use as a description that I was willing to serve in that capacity."[44] After Hasenfus's capture in early October 1986, North related that he had recognized he would be leaving the NSC staff, "because that was the purpose of my departure, to offer the scapegoat, if you will."[45] On November 21, the day North had learned Meese's men were coming to examine his files, Robert Earl, his aide, remembered North saying: " 'It's time for North to be the scapegoat, Ollie has been designated the scapegoat,' or something like that."[46] In the same month, Casey and North had had a conversation which turned on who was going to be sacrificed. North related that Casey had agreed with his assessment "that the time had come for someone to stand up and take the hit or the fall." North thought he had said, "Well, when that happens, it will be me," but Casey did not think that North was senior enough and had suggested it might be Poindexter.[47]

North's bravado took the form of playing both hero and victim, or the hero as victim. Yet he would not have had such a sense of impending downfall if he had not known that he too was walking a very thin line between the permissible and the impermissible. It was a line, however, that was not well marked out. Speaking about whether anything wrong had been done, Earl once said that "I had not been clear in my own mind where I may have crossed the line."[48] North conceived of himself as part of a small, embattled company of the elect, surrounded by at best dupes and at worst traitors. He saw a continuity between his service in Vietnam and his work on the NSC staff, in both of which he could be sent on suicide missions. Still, he did not fully realize how high was the price he would be asked to pay.

North was not the only one who knew that his fate was sealed on that foreboding November 24. Chief of Staff Donald Regan also heard the voice of doom.

That evening, Regan received a telephone call from the president's wife, Nancy, who had been told by her husband about Meese's discoveries. According to Regan, she asked many questions, made many suggestions, and gave him an unmistakable message: "Heads would roll."[49] Regan says that he sensed his "was one of the heads that would have to roll." Asked what gave him that impression, Regan replied: "Well, when people talk about a thorough housecleaning starting at the top, one gets the impression that one may be considered."[50]

Mrs. Reagan later revealed that she had tried to get Regan fired for months past. She had never forgiven him for his *mot juste* about his "shovel brigade."* When her husband had learned about the diversion, she related, he came into their bedroom looking pale and absolutely crushed, saying: "Honey, I've got some bad news. Ed Meese just came in and told me that money from the sale of arms to Iran went to the contras." Mrs. Reagan was not one to take bad news quietly. As was her wont, she went to the telephone: "If Ronnie was incredulous, I was furious. Later that evening I called Don Regan to let him know how

---

* After Reagan's inept performance at the summit meeting in Reykjavík, Iceland, Regan had said: "Some of us are like a shovel brigade that follow a parade down Main Street cleaning up" (*New York Times*, November 16, 1986).

upset I was. I felt very strongly that Ronnie had been badly served, and I wanted Don to know. Maybe this was unfair of me, but to some extent I blamed him for what had happened. He was the chief of staff, and if he didn't know, I thought, he should have. A good chief of staff has sources everywhere. He should practically be able to smell what's going on."[51] Mrs. Reagan does not tell us what she thought a good president should know and smell, especially since her husband was the one, not Regan, to whom Poindexter reported daily.

Curiously, Mrs. Reagan has no complaint about Casey, who if North can be believed knew all, or should have known, if anyone was in a position to know, and should have been able practically to smell what was going on. Mrs. Reagan seems to forgive Casey on the ground that he had been suffering lapses of memory and making bad decisions as a result of his lymphomatous brain cancer.[52] This may account for Casey's inability to assert himself in the final phase of the affair. It does not account for the failure of those who worked with him to realize that he was no longer fit for the job and to do something about it.

5

The bitter end came on Tuesday, November 25, 1986.

For Meese, the day started with a telephone call from Casey as he was leaving his house at about 6:30 in the morning. Regan had called him the night before, Casey said, and had told him about the diversion of funds. Casey wanted to talk about it and asked Meese to drop by his house, which Meese agreed to do.

Meese did not drive to Casey's house alone. His young aide, John Richardson, lived near Meese and sometimes rode in with him. This was one of those times, but Richardson—who had taken voluminous notes during the interview with North two days earlier—stayed outside in the car and did not go in with Meese.[53] As a result, Meese spoke with Casey for the second time in three days without anyone taking notes.

Meese talked with Casey for twenty minutes, but we know very little about what they said.[54] Meese has related no more than that Casey indicated he had been surprised by what Regan had told him and that Casey had advised Meese that "we have got to get this out as soon as possible." Meese did not ask whether Casey had known about the diversion, or apparently about anything else.[55] Thus Casey was never really questioned during Meese's fact-finding inquiry, though Meese had at least two chances to do so. Yet Casey had had at least two major informants, Allen and Cave, reporting to him in the last few months of the Iran affair and had allegedly had something in the nature of a father-and-son relationship with North.

Later that day, however, Casey sent Meese a letter and two memoranda—"as promised this morning"—about his seven-week-old meeting with Roy Furmark, as if Casey could not get it out of his mind.[56]

After leaving Casey, Meese called Poindexter on the car phone just as the latter was driving through the southwest gate of the White House and told Poindexter that he wanted to see him in Meese's office. At 7:30 a.m., Poindexter met with Meese and was told that "the time had come that I should submit my letter of resignation." Poindexter answered: "Fine, I was prepared to do that," as Poindexter had told him the day before. Meese charitably indicated a sense of regret. Meese also remarked that "he did not feel at that point that Colonel North had done anything illegal," and they talked about North being transferred to the Defense Department.[57]

Shortly afterward, Regan came to see Poindexter with the same message. The scene, as Regan described it, was not that of a man about to be executed:

> He was sitting at the end of his conference table having breakfast from a tray, and I went in and in my normal fashion said, you know, "What is going on, John?" You know, "What the heck happened here?"
>
> And he was very careful, deliberate. John is a deliberate man. He adjusted his glasses, he dabbed at his mouth with his napkin, put it down. He said, "Well, I guess I should have looked into it more, but I didn't."
>
> He said, "I knew that Ollie was up to something, but," he said, "I didn't know what." And he said, "I just didn't look into it."
>
> I said to him, "Why not? What the hell? You are a vice admiral. What is going on?"
>
> And he said, well, I suppose this will get me in trouble now with one of my old neighbors from my old neighborhood back in Cambridge, MA, but he said, "Well, that damned Tip O'Neill [Democratic Speaker of the House Thomas P. O'Neill, Jr.]."
>
> He said, "The way he is jerking the contras around, I was just so disgusted," he said, "I didn't want to know what he was doing."[58]

At this Regan says that he administered the coup de grace: "Well, John, I can tell you when you come in at 9:30, you better have your resignation with you." Poindexter replied: "I have been thinking of that. I will."*[59] Regan evidently did not know that Meese had gotten in first

---

* In his deposition, Regan said that his words were: "Well, John, I can tell you when you come in at 9:30, you better have your resignation with you" (B-22, p. 671). In *For the Record*, the words change to: "I'm sorry, John, but I think you'd better have your resignation ready when you come in to see the President at nine-thirty" (p. 42). Regan gives the time of this meeting as 7:40 a.m., which is probably too early (ibid., p. 41). Poindexter says it probably took place between 8 a.m. and 8:30 a.m. (B-20, p. 1237).

with the same message and that Poindexter had been prepared for the second blow.

After Regan left, Poindexter thinks that he called North and told him he was going to resign but that North would be transferred back to the Defense Department. North gave Poindexter the impression that he wanted to go to the National Defense University for a year's sabbatical.[60] At this point, Poindexter thought of himself as the only one who was going to pay for the exposure of the diversion.

At 9:30 a.m., Poindexter went to his usual meeting with the president but not as usual to brief him. In addition to Reagan, Vice President Bush, Regan, and Meese were there. Poindexter described how he ended his career as national security adviser:

> I came in and told him that I was certain that the Attorney General had told him about his conversation with Colonel North on Sunday and the memo that they had found, and I told the President that I was aware of the transfer of funds to the contras and that I thought it was best that I resign to give him as much latitude as possible. And he said that he regretted it and said something to the effect that it was in the tradition of a captain accepting responsibility.
>
> And I stood up to leave, shook hands with everybody. Everybody said nice words. And I left the office. I was only there about five minutes.[*][61]

Poindexter never heard from President Reagan again.

Reagan, Regan, and Meese agreed that North should simply go back to the Marine Corps.[62] They differentiated between North and Poindexter; North was merely a marine temporarily detailed to the NSC staff whereas Poindexter held two commissions: as an admiral of the navy and as assistant to the president, the latter an appointed post.[63] Poindexter's resignation made it easy to deal with him, and what to do about North

---

* In his public testimony at the congressional hearings, Poindexter gave his statement as follows: "Mr. President, I assume that you are aware of the paper that Ed Meese has found that reveals a plan to transfer funds to the contras. I was generally aware of that plan, and I would like to submit my resignation to give you the necessary latitude to do whatever you need to do." Poindexter added: "And the President responded and said that he had great regret and that this was in the tradition of a Naval officer accepting responsibility" (100-8, p. 121).

Regan's version is: "He came in and immediately started the discussion by saying—he told the President he was sorry for what had happened and again repeated that he probably should have looked into it more, but didn't. And he was submitting his resignation. Well, it was a very sorrowful moment, a very hushed moment. The Attorney General was there, as I recall. And the President nodded and said, 'I understand.' He said, 'This is a shame that it has happened this way, that a man with your great naval record,' and so on, 'has come to this end,' but he said, 'That is it,' and there was sort of an awkward silence" (100-10, p. 34).

As usual, Regan tells the story differently in *For the Record*, where he has contradictory versions on successive pages. On p. 42, Poindexter says: "I'm sorry it's come to this, Mr. President," and the President replies: "So am I, John." On p. 43: "The President said nothing in reply to the words that he heard that morning in the Oval Office" (pp. 42–43).

did not seem to be a problem. Before leaving, Poindexter made sure to delete 5,012 messages from his recording machine.[64]

After these preliminaries, the time had come to go through the formalities of briefing the rest of the National Security Council and congressional leaders. Everything was moving fast now—NSC at 10:15 a.m., congressional leaders at 11, press conference at noon. We have detailed notes by Richardson of the congressional meeting, which was a dress rehearsal for the press conference. President Reagan, Attorney General Meese, Chief of Staff Regan, CIA Director Casey, Secretary of State Shultz, Secretary of Defense Weinberger, Senators Byrd, Dole, and Warner, and Representatives Wright and Michel attended.[65] The main interest is in what the inner political circle said among themselves.

President Reagan opened with a few words about having received new information the day before; he then called on Meese to make a fuller report. Meese told how the Iranians had been overcharged for weapons, as a result of which a surplus went to the contras. In effect, Meese told North's trumped-up story, but blamed North far more than Poindexter. Richardson's abbreviated notes read:

Dole: Transferred by Israeli gov't

Meese: Yes . . .

Wright: Done w[ith] knowl[edge] & approval [of] someone in US?

Meese: Yes

Wright: Who?

Meese: North

Wright: Resigned?

Meese: Yes

Wright: Poin[dexter] not know?

Meese: Knew $ going to contras, didn't know details, didn't look into it. He was hopeful contras w[ou]ld get $

Poindexter, not North, had resigned. Later, President Reagan had a good word for Poindexter: "Oversight has been by Nat[ional] Sec[urity] Adv[iser]—& has served this country well." Senator Byrd wanted to know whether Poindexter's resignation had been asked for; President Reagan said that Poindexter had "volunteered it—in Navy tradit[ion]—even though no partic[ipant]." When Senator Byrd asked how Poindexter had explained how "this having gone on 10 mo[nth]s," Meese said that Poindexter only "knew gen[era]lly." Speaker Wright was curious: Was Poindexter "vaguely aware?" "Yes," said the president. Wright asked whether the CIA knew. "No, I didn't," said Casey.

Israel, as North had told Meese, was made largely responsible for the transaction with Iran. Dole asked: Had the money "been transferred by the Israeli Government?" Meese replied: "Yes." Meese was also asked who had persuaded Israel "to inject itself." Meese answered that he was not sure, but understood that Israel had "volunteered." Wright thought that it "strain[s] credulity that Israelis thought it up on own," whereupon Meese said: "No q[uestion]—our people—North or other set it up." No mention was made of Secord's role; instead, President Reagan referred to "[an]other country as wholesaler—w[ith] profit." The main impression left by the official version was that Israel had profited from the arms deals with Iran and had voluntarily passed on some of the profit to the contras.

At a late stage of the meeting, President Reagan seemed to sum up by saying that "w/o [without] condoning, it wasn't contrary to *policy*." He spoke of the problem with "human lives at stake." He defended the policy of keeping the information from Congress as a case of telling only those with a "need to know" and in order "to control damage." In general, those present could not have left with a very clear idea of what had happened, except that Israel had been the transmission belt to the contras, that North had played the main role, and that Poindexter had been vaguely guilty of inattention.[66]

Apparently before Reagan and Meese went before a more demanding audience, North received a call from Poindexter. In his notebook, North put down these words:

Call from JMP
    VP call Peres
    Discovered contra connection
    W[oul]d be best if Israel w[oul]d accept that they were aware
        that some funds were diverted
    Albert [Hakim] contact [unclear]
    Put it off on Gorbanifar
    Ought to be reassigned to USMC [U.S. Marine Corps][67]

From this, one gathers that they were still considering how best to ride out the approaching storm. Vice President Bush was apparently chosen to tell Israeli Prime Minister Peres that Israel should take some responsibility for the diversion of funds, Ghorbanifar was set up to take the most blame, and North was comforted with the thought that he was merely going to return to the Marine Corps.

6

At noon, Tuesday, November 25, 1986, Ronald Reagan gave the most disagreeable performance of his career. After his fiasco on November 19, he could not be trusted—or could not trust himself—to go on the stage and face a disbelieving, tumultuous press conference alone. He agreed that it was best for his role to be drastically cut and for him to say only a few words before introducing Meese for the main event.

The lines written for Reagan made him say that he had not been "fully informed" on the nature of "one of the activities" undertaken in connection with the Iran initiative. This activity raised "serious questions," but only as a matter of "propriety." Poindexter had asked to be relieved as national security adviser, although he was not "directly involved." A reference to North was much more abrupt: "Lieutenant Colonel Oliver North has been relieved of his duties on the National Security Council staff." The president still believed that the "policy goals toward Iran were well founded," but their implementation was "seriously flawed" in only "one aspect." He was initiating steps to assure that all future foreign and national security initiatives "will proceed only in accordance with my authorization." Finally: "And now, I'm going to ask Attorney General Meese to brief you."[68]

This statement was carefully framed to draw attention to a single aspect of the Iran initiative and only in one respect—that it had not been authorized by the president. Questionable "propriety" was its only flaw, Poindexter was its hapless victim, and North was ruthlessly cast off. The president himself was wholly blameless, because he "had not been fully informed."

Meese undertook to explain how the diversion had come to pass. Unfortunately, he knew only as much as North had chosen to tell him—or rather, he did not know that North had chosen to tell him a farrago of falsehoods about Israel. Meese held forth:

> What is involved is that in the course of the arms transfers, which involved the United States providing arms to Israel and Israel in turn transferring the arms—in effect, selling the arms to representatives of Iran. Certain monies which were received in the transaction between representatives of Israel and representatives of Iran were taken and made available to the forces in Central America which are opposing the Sandinista government there.
>
> In essence, the way in which the transactions occurred was that a certain amount of money was negotiated by representatives outside the United States with Iran for arms. This amount of money was then transferred to representatives as best we know that can be described as representatives of Israel.

Meese did little more than elaborate on this imaginary scenario. He was asked how it had come to his attention. Instead of answering that it had come through North's diversion memo and his interview with North, Meese first pretended that he had learned about it "in the course of a number of intercepts, and other materials," which had been "pursued

with the individuals involved." Later, Meese came closer to reality by
referring to the discovery of "one particular document," which had led
to a discussion with "one of the participants."

Who had known of the diversion? The only one who knew "precisely"
was Lieutenant Colonel North and, Meese said, he "has requested to
return to the Marine Corps and that has been accomplished." Poindexter
had known "something of this nature was occurring, but he did not look
into it further."

But did Poindexter approve? Meese denied that Poindexter had approved of the diversion and let him off gently as having known "generally
that something of this nature was happening. He did not know the details." Later, Meese feigned that Poindexter had requested reassignment
to the navy "of his own volition."

By this time, it occurred to one questioner that Meese's only subject
had been the diversion, whereas "the central questions that have been
asked for the last three or four weeks [are] about the propriety of shipment
to—arms to Iran, about the U.S. arms embargo at the time." Meese
sidestepped this line of inquiry by saying that "we have heard nothing
new that hasn't been testified to essentially on the Hill"—as if Casey had
given the congressional intelligence committees a full and truthful account in his testimony on November 21.

Was North guilty of a crime and would he be prosecuted? In view of
North's interest in Meese's answer, it is worth citing in full:

> We are presently looking into the legal aspects of it as to whether
> there's any criminality involved. We're also looking precisely at his
> involvement and what he did, so that the conclusions as to whether
> there's any criminal acts involved is still under inquiry by us.

Later, Meese again said that it was necessary to look at the question
whether North "committed any violation of law at the time he did that."

But Meese could not shake off more questions about the diversion.
How had the funds been used? Meese said that he only knew that funds
had been deposited in a Swiss bank account, and no one in the U.S.
government had known "anything about what happened to them." In
fact, he again put the onus on Israel:

> Bank accounts were established, as best we know, by represen-
> tatives of the forces in Central America. And this information was
> provided to representatives of the Israeli government and the funds—
> or representatives of Israel, I should say—and then these funds were
> put into the accounts. So far as we know at this stage, no American
> person actually handled any of the funds that went to the forces in
> Central America.

In response to another question, Meese gave as his understanding that the United States had been paid only $12 million for the arms but that Israel had sold them for $10 million to $30 million more, thereby making the huge profit which allegedly enabled it to give funds to the contras. Meese also asserted that Israel had shipped weapons to Iran in 1985 without U.S. authorization.

One suspicion was expressed that the discovery of the diversion was itself a diversion: "What's to prevent an increasingly cynical public from thinking that you went looking for a scapegoat and you came up with this whopper, but it doesn't have a lot to do with the original controversy?" Meese replied that the "facts" were being laid out "just as rapidly as we've gotten them," without saying anything more about the "original controversy," about which almost nothing was said in the entire press conference.

Meese was evasive about whether there was anything wrong about the diversion. He took the position that the United States had no control over the diverted funds, because "it was never the property of United States officials." He also did not know "that anybody's money was misappropriated." Whose money, then, was it? Meese was asked. He would assume, he said, that it probably belonged to "the party that had sold the weapons to the Iranians." According to Meese's previous answers, that "party" was Israel, not Secord and Hakim, whom he never mentioned.

Meese also had some difficulty with questions about responsibility. He completely absolved everyone in the higher ranks: "I don't think anyone can be responsible if someone on the lower echelons of government, does something that we don't feel—or that—objectively viewed is not correct." As if Poindexter were not a top administration official, Meese said: "There's no question whatsoever or no implication that anything that was done was administration policy or directed by top administration officials."

But why didn't the president know? someone asked. Because, Meese answered testily, "somebody didn't tell him, that's why." The people who were involved, he went on, "didn't tell anybody, including the President. So, it's common understanding why the President wouldn't know, because no one in the chain of command was informed."

The press conference came to an end with a question about whether Hasenfus's unlucky mission over Nicaragua had been funded with any of the diverted funds. Meese blandly said that "we have no information about how those funds were used once they were ultimately received."[69]

Meese gave disingenuous replies at least twice. He fibbed that Poindexter had chosen to resign "of his own volition" and denied that Poindexter had approved the diversion, though later at the congressional hearings Meese said that Poindexter had told him he had "condoned or allowed" the diversion to go forward.[70] Meese also falsely stated that North had requested his own return to the Marine Corps and that it had already been accomplished. The closest North had come to making such a request was in the private communication to Poindexter of November 24, in which he had said that he was "prepared to depart at the time you and the President decide it to be in the best interest of the Presidency and the country"—hardly the same as having asked to return to the Marine Corps.*[71] At North's last meeting with Meese on November 23, North had said nothing about returning to the Marine Corps, and he had not seen Meese or Regan afterward.

In fact, it was Regan's idea to get rid of North without ceremony. At the meeting of the National Security Council at 10:15 a.m. on November 25, Regan says he told Secretary Weinberger that he thought "North should be detailed back to the Marine Corps," and Weinberger subsequently told the congressional leaders that North was being returned to the Corps.[72] Regan was also responsible for inserting the passage about North's dismissal from the NSC staff in President Reagan's opening remarks at the press conference.[73]

At this stage, Poindexter and North were treated differently. Poindexter was let off gently, but no account was taken of North's sensibilities.

7

In the end, Meese left two main impressions. Both made the strange case of the diversion even stranger than it had been in reality.

One was his account of Israel's role. He attributed the diverted funds to Israel's profit on its arms sales to Iran and the transfer of money to the contras to Israel's presumed desire to help the United States. In that case, the Israeli contribution was very similar to other "third country" gifts to the contras, such as those of Saudi Arabia and Taiwan. Meese himself could not see anything wrong with it, because the money had been Israel's and nothing had been misappropriated. Since, so far as he knew, no American had handled any of the funds, it remained a mystery why North should have had any responsibility for a purely Israeli philanthropic gesture made in the interests of U.S. policy. Yet North was going to be investigated to see whether he had committed any criminal acts in connection with a diversion conducted solely between Israel and the contras.

Ironically, Meese owed the entire fabrication of the Israeli connection to North.† If Meese had not been seized with a panicky fear of Reagan's possible impeachment, he would almost certainly have acted less hastily

---

* North testified that he had told Poindexter on November 21 "that I thought I would have to leave right away" and that he had said, several times before, "that it was important to defuse the controversy, that I would be relieved, that and I would be transferred" (100-7, Part I, p. 148). This premonitory talk by North in private circumstances was hardly the same as a request by North to return to the Marine Corps.

† At the congressional hearings in July 1987, Meese stated that he had merely repeated what North had told him on November 23, 1986 (100-9, pp. 258–59).

and have sought out other witnesses to the actual transfer of funds. The main reason for the haste, as Meese later put it, was the concern that "there would be no hint that anyone was trying to cover up the facts."[74] Even Meese's chief aide, Assistant Attorney General Cooper, was surprised by the speed with which Meese decided to go public.[75]

The one who knew most about these facts was North's chief accomplice, Richard Secord. He admittedly gave "oral direction" to Albert Hakim about the use of the Swiss bank account of Lake Resources, the account into which the Iran money was deposited. It was from this account that the money had flowed to the contras. According to Secord, North made requests to him; Secord made the decisions in line with North's requests; and Hakim executed them.[76] The mystery of Meese's presentation was why Poindexter and North should have been penalized if Israel had decided to part with some of its own money for the benefit of the contras.

Soon after the Meese-North story about Israel's responsibility for the diversion was known in Israel, Meese received a telephone call from Israeli Prime Minister Peres. As Meese later related, Peres told him that "the money had been paid directly by the Iranians, not by Israelis, to the account of an American company in Switzerland. The Israelis were only told the amount, they didn't know the end user."[77] In effect, Meese learned within about two hours that the Israelis had not sent funds to the contras; the money had gone into the Secord-Hakim Swiss account and from there to the contras.

Nir also called North to say that their work had come to the "worst possible end" and that Meese's version could be "easily proven wrong." Meese's story about the transfer of money by Israel had been "invented," and Israel had not served as such a "conduit." Nir was appalled by Meese's public performance, knowing, as he did, that much of it was not accurate.[78]

No correction was made to the fictitious story of Israel's role that North had foisted on Meese and Meese had foisted on everyone else.

The second impression left by Meese is that everyone but North and perhaps Poindexter was absolved from responsibility for the still nebulous impropriety of the diversion. If President Reagan knew nothing about it, his defense went, he was totally without fault. Since no one had told him anything, he could not be held accountable. Even Poindexter escaped censure on the ground that "he did not know the details." Meese went so far as to say that "no one in the chain of command was informed," though Poindexter was certainly in the chain of command and above him there was only the president. Regan pleaded that Poindexter did not report to him. Ignorance was innocence.

Yet this line of defense raised an even more awkward question. How could a single lieutenant colonel on the NSC staff successfully manipulate an entire area of U.S. foreign policy as he saw fit without anyone in the enormous bureaucracy of American government knowing or doing anything about it? What did this extraordinary anomaly tell about the existing structure of the government and the unacceptable risks of covert operations?

Only one question at the press conference made any reference to such considerations: "Mr. Meese, how high did this go? In other words, do you believe, and are we being asked to believe, that a Lieutenant Colonel took this initiative and had these funds transferred, and that only Admiral Poindexter knew about it? How high did it go?"

Meese replied that "it did not go any higher than that." Throughout the press conference, he was primarily concerned with shielding the higher-ups from any connection with the transfer of funds, rather than with explaining what there was in the system that made it possible for them to have no connection with it. Meese's strategy was not unsuccessful. Despite the contradictions and obscurities of his account, he managed to keep it on such a superficial level that no one was much the wiser after he had finished, except for learning that some strange aberration had mysteriously occurred.

8

The one person in the entire government at whom an accusing finger seemed to be pointed watched the press conference on television in his office with increasing disbelief and anger. With him was his secretary, Fawn Hall. She says that as she was sitting at her desk before the conference began, North told her that the president had fired him. She could not believe it and said: "Ollie, come on." He assured her: "No, I'm serious." She was so overwrought by the news that she began to cry.[79]

When North heard Meese say that the United States had not been involved in the arms transfers to Iran in 1985, North was later asked what conclusion he had drawn. "Well," said North, "it was not only contrary to my knowledge and my participation, it was contrary to what I had said the very day before, or on Sunday. It was contrary to what I believed the President had authorized. It was contrary to what I believed all of the other people I had worked with up the chain in the cabinet knew to be the truth."[80]

But what had outraged North most of all was Meese's repeated implication that North might have been guilty of criminal wrongdoing and that he was being investigated for possible violations of the law. "What was your reaction to that?" North was asked. "I was shocked," he replied. "It was—I guess probably one of the most shocking things I had ever heard. That, coupled with what had gone on before, made me wonder whether I had actually talked to the Attorney General the day before."[81]

North explained that he had been ready to play the scapegoat, but he had understood that it was to be a political, not a criminal, role. "Well," North said, "I had, as my note to Admiral Poindexter of the day before indicated, I had long been aware that if there was a political blow-up over this whole issue of either one, support for the contras or the Iranian initiative, that someone would have to go; someone would have to be the political scapegoat." But "it had never entered my mind that this could be contemplated as criminal behavior."[82]

On another occasion, North said that "I had made it clear to Mr. McFarlane, I made it clear to Mr. Casey, and I made it very clear to Admiral Poindexter that I recognized that there would come a time when you may have to have a political—I emphasize the word 'political'—fall guy or scapegoat or whatever. I never in my wildest dreams or nightmares envisioned that we would end up with criminal charges. It was beyond my wildest comprehension right up until the 25th."[83]

Just as North was listening to the press conference with growing agitation, Thomas Green, Secord's lawyer, who had tried to prevent the public exposure of the Iran affair, came into his office. Green asked whether North had anyone to "protect" him, whereupon North asked Green to represent him. North gathered up a number of documents and his notebooks, put them in his briefcase, and walked out with Green. The two went to a hotel to meet Secord, because the latter's own office was besieged by the press.

While North was at the hotel, he received a telephone call from President Reagan. North later described the call:

> The Presidential operator was on the telephone and said, "The President would like to talk to you."
>
> The President came on the line and he said, I want to thank you for all your work. I am sorry that it happened the way it did. He said, you are an American hero.
>
> He asked me to understand that it was—he just hadn't known or didn't know, words to that effect. I thanked him for the phone call and told him that I was sorry that this had created so much difficulty for him, for the country.[*][84]

---

* North's version at his trial is the fullest and most circumstantial of the various accounts. North himself told about the call more briefly in his testimony at the congressional hearing: "The President of the United States saw fit to call me later the same day and in the course of that call, which was also intensely personal, he told me words to the effect 'I just didn't know.' . . . I simply expressed my thanks for having been able to serve him for 5½ years and my regrets that my service had brought forth a political fire storm and difficulties when all I sought to do was to help, and that what I may have done was to hurt him" (100-7, Part I, p. 246).

North's aide Lieutenant Colonel Robert Earl said that North had told him the president had said in a phone call that "he, the President, recognized or that it was important that he, the President, not know—words to that effect" (B-9, p. 895).

North's other aide, Lieutenant Commander Craig P. Coy, vaguely remembered having heard of "the President calling Ollie, saying that he was sorry that he had to let him go . . . And Ollie said he was sorry it had to end this way and didn't mean for it to end this way, didn't think it would end this way" (B-7, pp. 1093–94).

North's secretary, Fawn Hall, said that North had told her the president had telephoned him and had called him "an American hero" (100-5, p. 502).

Reagan took the initiative to call North to thank him for his work and to salute him as an American hero just hours after he had permitted North to be threatened with criminal proceedings. That he had actually called North an "American hero" is altogether likely, because Reagan talked to Hugh Sidey of *Time* magazine the very next day and told him what he thought of North: "He is a national hero."[85] In his autobiography, Reagan says that he called North merely "to wish him well."[86] Even so, it was a peculiar thing for a president to do when he had just heard his attorney general imply that North may have been guilty of criminal malfeasance.

One does not know what to make of this duality. It is as if Reagan did not know what Meese was going to say about North at the press conference and wanted to dissociate himself from Meese. Or was Reagan trying to tell North that he really sympathized with what North had done—after all, to benefit Reagan's favorite cause—but that it was better for North to suffer for it than himself? Whatever the reason, Reagan was able to have it both ways by permitting North to be made a potential criminal in public and hailing him as an American hero in private.

North's attitude toward Reagan was equally curious. In his congressional testimony, North told of having asked Poindexter pointedly whether Reagan had known of the diversion, and Poindexter had answered "no." When North was asked why he had not tried to find out why Poindexter had not discussed it with the president, North answered:

First of all, I am not in the habit of questioning my superiors. If he deemed it not to be necessary to ask the President, I saluted smartly and charged up the hill. That's what lieutenant colonels are supposed to do. I have no problem with that.

I don't believe that what we did even under those circumstances is wrong or illegal. I told you I thought it was a good idea to begin with. I still think it was a good idea, counsel.

Then came this exchange:

Liman: And have you wondered why, if it was a good idea, that the President of the United States dismissed you because of it?

North: Let me just make one thing very clear, counsel. This lieutenant colonel is not going to challenge a decision of the Commander in Chief for whom I still work, and I am proud to work for that Commander in Chief, and if the Commander in Chief tells this lieutenant colonel to go stand in the corner and sit on his head, I will do so. And if the Commander in Chief decides to dismiss me from the NSC staff, this lieutenant colonel will proudly salute and say, "thank you for the opportunity to have served," and go, and I am not going to criticize his decision no matter how he relieves me, sir.[87]

Yet North drew the line at the threat of criminal charges, which his commander in chief did nothing to prevent. After all his brave talk about being willing to play the scapegoat, this type of scapegoating was too much for him. When he was told, in effect, to stand in a corner and sit on his head, he refused. He seems to have had in mind a willingness to be blamed for the diversion and to be removed from the NSC staff for it, so that he would have been made into what he wanted to be—a *political* scapegoat. Since he could not bring himself to admit that he had done anything wrong, he was prepared to be a political martyr in a holy cause. He could not accept criminal scapegoating, apparently because it lessened his self-esteem and gave him a sense of having been betrayed.

Yet he did not seem to see anything contradictory in swearing undying fealty to a commander in chief who would not defend him against what he saw as an outrageous accusation of criminal wrongdoing. His commander in chief in turn did not seem to see anything contradictory in letting an American hero be pilloried.

9

Another significant incident took place soon after the press conference.

After North's conversation with the president, one more telephone call demanded his attention. It came from Fawn Hall, who tried to tell him in a whisper that he needed to come right back to his office. She did not want to be heard, because North's office was just then being sealed by Brenda Reger, an NSC staff member in charge of documentation. As she and an assistant were putting documents into boxes, North's secretary suddenly realized that she had not finished filing documents that North, on November 21, had asked her to alter and substitute for the originals. North had handwritten these alterations to conceal evidence of his activities going back to 1985, but a weekend had intervened and she had not had time to complete the filing job. North had never asked her to change such documents before.[88]

As she told the story, she panicked at the realization that some of these documents—in both altered and original forms—were still piled on her desk. She called North at the hotel to tell him that the office was being sealed before she had had a chance to finish substituting the altered documents. She spoke so softly that she was not sure he understood, but in any case she asked him to come back immediately, and he answered, "No, you know, there is really no need."

Nevertheless, North and Green started back to the office as Fawn Hall was desperately hiding documents, including those about McFarlane's mission to Tehran in May 1986, inside her boots and belt in the back of her clothing. "Out of panic," she related, "I ran into Colonel Earl's office," and he gallantly offered to put the documents in his jacket. "No," she recalled saying to him, "you shouldn't have to do this. I will do it." She turned to him and asked if he could see anything unusual in her back. "No," he said, and they started to walk downstairs. *

Just then, North and Green walked in. Again she asked, this time of North, whether he saw anything in her back, and he also said: "No." As they left the office, Brenda Reger was inspecting the briefcases that North and others carried, but Fawn Hall walked by undisturbed. In the corridor, she indicated that she wanted to give North the documents, but he turned to her and said: "No, just wait until we get outside." When they got in Green's car, she pulled the documents out from her boots and back. Green asked her what she would say if she was asked about the shredding. "We shred every day," she answered. "Good," he told her.[89] And they went home. Later, she reflected on her action: "It was a very stupid thing that I did that day."[90]

But all the shredding, alterations, and surreptitious removals of documents did North little good. So many hundreds of incriminating documents and memoranda were left or recovered that it was possible to reconstruct the course of the Iran and contra affairs in extraordinary detail. Even the diversion, "the deepest, darkest secret of the whole activity," as he called it, came to light.[91] Like many other things North did, this effort to hide the traces of his activity was marked as much by ineptitude as by anything else.

North gave as a reason for his shredding that he could not be certain that a replacement on the NSC staff "shares your same values or necessarily shares the same perspective that you have on a number of things."[92] This explanation was an expression of the quasi-conspiratorial and junta-like sense which North and those closest to him had of themselves. They were privileged because they had values and perspectives which set them apart from almost all others in the government. They played by their own rules and were not accountable to everyone else's government. The last-minute destruction and alteration of documents suggest both an ultimate attempt at cover-up and an implicit recognition that they had crossed a very thin line into the impermissible.

---

* Earl's version of the same scene goes: "She came into my office, had some documents, asked if I would take them out. I took them, and I think I folded them and put them in my suit coat, which was hanging up on the wall, and she left. Sometime after she came back and said that she couldn't have me do that or she didn't want me to do that, she asked for them back, so I handed them back to her or went over to my suit coat, took them out, handed them to her, and she proceeded to conceal them on her person" (B-9, p. 650).

10

After the press conference on November 25, 1986, the Iran and contra affairs were effectively finished. It only remained to clean up the traces. A show of purification was urgent because some of those close to Reagan expected him to be one of the prime victims of the scandal. Michael Deaver, of the early Reaganite "troika," who was still close to the president and his wife, urged him to get a criminal lawyer to defend himself. Deaver reasoned that Poindexter and North might try to absolve themselves by putting all the blame on Reagan.[93] In fact, at North's trial, his lawyer, Brendan Sullivan, put up just such a defense on North's behalf. But Reagan got off without much trouble, for one reason because no one wanted another Nixon.

On November 26, President Reagan appointed a Special Review Board to conduct a comprehensive study of the procedures and future role of the National Security Council staff. The board was made up of former Senator John Tower, former Secretary of State Edmund Muskie, and former National Security Adviser Brent Scowcroft.[94]

On the same day, Attorney General Meese instructed William Weld, assistant attorney general for the Criminal Division, to undertake a criminal investigation focusing on the diversion of funds from Iranian arms sales to the contras.[95]

On December 2, President Reagan called for the appointment of an independent counsel to investigate the arms sales to Iran and the diversion of profits to the contras. On December 19, a three-judge panel named Lawrence E. Walsh, a former district court judge, diplomat, and deputy attorney general, as independent counsel. As Meese later admitted, one motive for these measures was political. "The actions were taken," he explained, "because they were the appropriate actions under any circumstances but one of the concerns was to prevent this situation from being used by policy opponents of the President, yes."[96]

On December 4, plans were announced by the House of Representatives for a fifteen-member select committee to investigate covert arms transactions with Iran and by the Senate for an eleven-member select committee on secret military assistance to Iran and the Nicaraguan Opposition.

By this time, all the branches of government had been mobilized to show that the Iran-contra affairs were going to be thoroughly investigated and possible legal violations punished. All the shovel brigades had been called out. It only remained to see what kind of cleanup they were going to accomplish.

With the elimination of North and Secord, the machinery they had set up to support the contras collapsed. The official pro-contra policy remained but lacked the backing it had earlier received.

The Iran affair was more difficult to close. After the press conference, unfinished business with Iran remained. The State Department, which had taken over responsibility for Iran policy, agreed to another meeting with the Iranian Second Channel in Frankfurt, West Germany, on December 13, 1986, and added one more to an already long list of inept muddles.

The Americans chosen to meet with the Iranians were Charles Dunbar, a Farsi-speaking State Department officer, and George Cave, the Farsi-speaking expert previously used by the CIA. They had never met before. Dunbar knew little about the past dealings with Iran, and Cave, who knew a great deal, was never asked to brief him. Meanwhile, the coming meeting with the Iranians turned into an "internal battle" between Casey and Shultz.[97]

According to Shultz, the issue between them turned on the instructions to Dunbar and Cave for the meeting. Shultz wanted the two Americans to discuss "intelligence" only and not "policy" with the Iranians. Shultz recalled that he was determined "to get the Agency separated from policy" and that "Director Casey was concerned that he stay in the policy loop, and I was concerned that he get out of the policy loop." Shultz says little more than that he and Casey fought over the word "policy" in the instructions for no other reason than to decide whether Casey was in "the loop."

What also irked Shultz was that Under Secretary of State Armacost and Casey had apparently agreed on December 12 on "ground rules" limiting the Iranian channel to intelligence only. Casey was said to have double-crossed Shultz by getting Chief of Staff Regan to go to President Reagan and have "policy" put back into the instructions to Dunbar and Cave.[98]

We have a different story from Cave. He and Dunbar received the original "ground rules" only on the morning of December 12, the day before they were to leave for Frankfurt. Cave immediately went to the CIA's national intelligence officer, Charles Allen, to whom he complained that the instructions were too limited and were "just going to click everything off," as he later put it. They went to Casey, who told them to write a memo, which Casey gave to Chief of Staff Regan, who gave it to President Reagan, who agreed to a change in the instructions.[99]

Shultz's anger was wholly spent in denouncing Casey for his "deceptive way," without mentioning the awkward fact that President Reagan had made the final decision in Casey's favor and was presumably swayed by the Cave-Allen memo. Cave, on the other hand, understood that Shultz was concerned about barring more arms shipments to Iran and maintained that both the original and the revised instructions said the same thing about arms shipments.[100] Shultz later agreed that "the talking points continued to say no arms sales," so that there seems to have been no substance to the argument over "policy."*

The final instructions to Dunbar and Cave ordered them to tell the Iranians that "the mutual strategic interests of our nations remain unchanged despite recent revelations." The same channel "will continue to be used for both policy and intelligence discussions." The State Department, however, was to be the only source of "authoritative policy messages." Then came the main policy message: "There will be no further transfers of American military equipment to your government while Iran refuses to negotiate an end to Iran-Iraq war and while Iran continues to support terrorism and subversion."[101]

For all this backbiting in Washington, the real trouble in Frankfurt was apparently something else.

We have Dunbar's report of the meeting. The Iranian spokesman tried to be "ingratiating" but had little new to say. He still demanded the removal of the Iraqi strongman, Saddam Hussein, and asked for 1,500 TOW missiles and 100 launchers from the United States. Iran, he said, was willing to do something about the U.S. hostages in Lebanon but was not sure of being able to succeed and would not try to force their release.

As Cave had feared, Dunbar's reply quickly brought the meeting to a standstill. Dunbar merely recited his instructions "with no embellishment." The Iranian was "polite but obviously nonplussed." He confronted Dunbar with the nine-point agreement which Hakim had negotiated in early October and which provided for a staggered delivery of more U.S. arms. When the Iranian realized what he was up against, he commented that they had "returned to zero." Dunbar was at a disadvantage because he had not been told about the nine-point agreement. Only after the meeting was over did Cave give Dunbar an extended lesson in the background of the dealings with the Iranians, including the nine-point agreement—or "sort of briefing him trying to bring him up to snuff," as Cave put it.[102] Later, Secretary Shultz was amazed that the Iranian should have brought up the nine-point agreement: "Nobody had informed me of this so-called nine-point agenda."[103]

Cave had one more unlucky encounter with the Iranian. Dunbar left Frankfurt early, but Cave stopped over to see his grandchildren in Europe. When he returned to Frankfurt on Sunday, December 14, he heard from the Iranian late that night that word had come from Tehran that the Iranian wanted passed on to Dunbar. As Cave later told the story, he saw the Iranian briefly the next morning in Dunbar's absence, took down the message, and sent it off to Washington.[104] Little did Cave realize

---

* "The question of what was involved in Director Casey's reinsertion of the word 'policy' into the talking points, as I understand it, is the source of misunderstanding. Those talking points continued to say no arms sales. That is what was read out. That is why it basically didn't make much difference as far as the Iranian end of it was concerned" (Shultz, 100-9, p. 67).

that this event was going to go down in the history of the Iran affair as an unauthorized meeting with the Iranian and stir up bad blood between the secretary of state and the secretary of defense.

Shultz reported to President Reagan on December 14. According to the official State Department version, Shultz told him about Dunbar's discovery of a "previous agreement re release of Da'wa prisoners" in Kuwait—obviously a distortion of point 3 of the nine-point agreement, which had merely provided for a plan to be presented by Hakim for their release—and considerably less than a U.S. "agreement" to get their release. "The President was stunned," Shultz said, "and he was furious . . . he reacted like he had been kicked in the belly."[105] The president was stunned because the "agreement" had allegedly been kept from him, but the larger question, never discussed, was how a president could be misled so flagrantly and for so long without the secretaries of state and defense, who had their own intelligence organizations, knowing or doing anything about it.

On December 15, 1986, William J. Casey suffered a "minor cerebral seizure." He died on May 6, 1987.

The Shultz-Casey falling-out was not the only "internal battle" brought on by the Frankfurt meeting. On December 19, six days after the meeting, Secretary of Defense Weinberger learned about it, not from the State Department or anyone in the U.S. government but from a foreign intelligence agency. Weinberger, who had for months failed to protest his exclusion from Iran policy, now reared up in righteous anger against the failure to consult him about the latest dealings with Iranians. What he had been bottling up for months came out in his memorandum to the White House through Poindexter's acting successor as national security adviser, Alton G. Keel, Jr. It read in part:

> I must point out as strongly as I can that any attempt to conduct major activities in the security field with the deliberate exclusion of those who have some responsibility for security cannot succeed in anything but adding to the troubles we already have. I would very much have appreciated an opportunity to present to the President arguments as to why we should *not* continue dealing with these channels in Iran. Their total unreliability and inability to produce anything except public accusations against the United States makes the entire procedure not only fruitless, but particularly dangerous in view of today's Iranian problems.
>
> I think the President was entitled to have the advice of all of his security advisors, and I must strongly object that the continuation of this practice of secrecy and attempts to exclude various advisors whose advice it is apparently feared may not support the agenda of the State Department, in this case, or some other agenda in other

cases, can only get us in more and more difficulty, and serves the President very badly.[106]

Weinberger went on to demand a meeting of the top-level National Security Planning Group to discuss whether there should be a presidential decision on whether to meet or discuss anything with Iranians—as if a presidential decision had not been responsible for the recent meeting and discussion with Iranians. Weinberger also complained that he had only recently learned that former National Security Adviser McFarlane had offered sensitive intelligence information to the Iranians—an offering for which Poindexter, North, and Secord had actually been responsible, not McFarlane.

Weinberger's belated indignation was aimed at the State Department, which he took to be the villain in the plot to exclude him from Iran affairs. He also sent off a "Dear George" letter to Shultz enclosing his memorandum to the White House and complaining about the State Department's public statements.[107]

Shultz called Weinberger the same day. "I told him," Shultz wrote in a memorandum for his files, "his assumptions were wrong, that I was glad to let him know what is going on and if he wanted to know the facts he ought to cease firing off intemperate memos about the State Department and instead pick up the phone and call me. Cap [Weinberger] said he would do that."

Shultz's explanation to Weinberger of what had happened was not altogether disingenuous. He blamed Cave for having maintained contact with the Iranians—as if Cave alone could have decided to maintain contact with them. The State Department, Shultz went on, saw the meeting as an opportunity to tell the Iranians no more arms and no more policy discussions—"we were there to listen"—an oblique way of admitting that the State Department had agreed to the meeting. But Casey, he said, had made an "end run" around him to the president, who had decided in favor of both policy and intelligence. When Shultz found out about this, he had gone back to the president and regained State Department control of all the various channels. The president, however, "said he wanted to pursue contacts with the Iranians but no more arms would go to them." The decisions, then, had been made by President Reagan, not Casey.

Shultz next gave a murky, truncated version of what had happened in Frankfurt: "When the meeting took place, our representative Dunbar found out that the Iranians didn't have the word that this channel had changed, were operating on promises of arms and trying to negotiate with us on the basis of a nine point agenda which they claimed had been agreed upon."[108] If the Iranians did not have the word, it was hardly their fault, and if they tried to negotiate on the basis of a nine-point agenda, it was because it had been agreed upon at least as high up as

Poindexter, or, as Poindexter insists, President Reagan.* Getting the initial instructions to Dunbar and Cave only twenty-four hours before the meeting, changing the instructions after they had reached Frankfurt, and sending Dunbar out without a detailed knowledge of past dealings with the Iranians were more to the point in this instance than Casey's allegedly nefarious influence.

Weinberger had also heard something about Cave's second meeting with the Iranian in Frankfurt to get his message from Tehran. The secretary of defense thought it important enough to use it for one more charge that "United States 'negotiators' were still meeting with the same Iranians" after he had assumed that "we were finished with that entire Iranian episode." Whereupon the secretary of state explained laboriously to the secretary of defense: "After Dunbar left Frankfurt, Cave met with his Iranian contact the next day for the second time. The CIA contends this meeting took place at Iranian request. We did not authorize this second meeting and we were not informed in advance it was to take place."[109] Cave was the last scapegoat.

Finally, Shultz told Weinberger, the CIA had decided on January 20, 1987, to close down the "Cave channel."[110] Petty as all this may seem, it is symptomatic of what the Iran affair did to the government of the United States.

---

* "Is it your best recollection that you obtained the approval of the President of the United States [for the nine-point plan]? *Poindexter:* Yes, it is" (Poindexter, 100-8, p. 68).

25

People With Their Own Agenda

The questions that arise most forcefully from a study of the Iran and contra affairs are: How could a handful of little-known officials take virtually complete control of American foreign policy in areas of major concern? How could they operate in total disregard of Congress, outside the purview of the two departments most concerned, State and Defense, and indeed of almost the entire structure of the government?

Part of the answer lies in the very nature of covert operations. When the NSC staff took over the Iran and contra affairs from the CIA, it practiced the same rules of covert activities, but with even greater powers of concealment. The national security adviser, unlike the director of the CIA, did not have to be confirmed by Congress and did not have to testify before congressional intelligence committees. The execution of both affairs was concentrated in one man, Oliver North, responsible only to one man, National Security Adviser McFarlane or Poindexter. By using outside accomplices, such as Secord and Hakim, who did not have to report to any official agency, North's operations were largely impervious to the normal reach of government. North's methods resembled those of a private rather than a public way of doing business, since Secord and Hakim were beholden only to him. As Secretary Weinberger observed: "I think any of these things that attempt to run private operations of this nature become private governments, is totally wrong and I would be totally opposed to it."[1]

The accepted rules of covert operations were made to order for North's purposes. Compartmentation, deniability, secrecy, as we have seen, were the watchwords of these operations.

The CIA's National Intelligence Officer Charles Allen noted that "this was the most compartmented effort under way in the U.S. Government at that time."[2] Those not in the compartment made it their business not to know. Alan Fiers, chief of the CIA's Central American Task Force, candidly admitted that "we remained in the status of willful ignorance" about the flight on which Eugene Hasenfus had crashed.[3]

This self-contained system was made all the more hermetic by Poindexter, who was obsessive about secrecy. He was asked: "Admiral, did you also want to keep what your plans and operations were relating to the contras secret from people in the NSC and in the White House?" He replied: "Yes, I did."[4] Poindexter did not want to discuss North's pro-contra activities even with Casey, because the CIA chief had to testify before congressional committees.[5]

According to Secretary Weinberger, however, Poindexter was encouraged in this mania for compartmentation by President Reagan. "It was a very small narrow circle of people who needed to know," Weinberger explained about the transfer of arms to Iran, "and it was deliberately kept small because of the considerations the President continually emphasized that it was necessary to make sure that very few people knew about it." Weinberger himself thought that "you can carry compartmentalization too far, and I think that it probably was in this case without any question."[6]

In order to keep others in the government from knowing what was going on, putting information and instructions in writing was forbidden— as much as possible. "I was often cautioning Colonel North about putting things in writing about his operational activities, especially with regard to the support for the Contras," Poindexter declared.[*7] The CIA's head of station in Lisbon testified that cables were missing "because of the nature of the channel used. It is outside and is designed to be outside the records-keeping system."[8] At some point in 1985, North said, a decision was made not to put documents "in the system."[9] According to Susan Crawford, the Army's general counsel, the Army's handling of the weapons that it delivered to the CIA for transfer to Iran "was highly sensitive. There was to be no paperwork on the activity."[10]

Thousands of relevant documents survived mainly because they were unexpectedly rescued from the machines that sent and received messages. North shredded hundreds of documents, but even he did not get them all. "I assured Admiral Poindexter, incorrectly, it turns out," he ruefully testified, "that all of the documents that pertained to the residual funds being used to support the Nicaraguan Resistance had already been destroyed."[11]

Above all, covert operations prized "deniability" or, as it was often termed, "plausible deniability." Since such operations were inherently dangerous politically or otherwise, it was not enough to carry them out; ideally, they were set up in such a way that they could be disavowed if they miscarried.

The idea is probably as old as the existence of rulers and no doubt will

---

* Poindexter also said: "In fact, my operating assumption was that there wasn't anything in writing on it, because I told Colonel North repeatedly not to put anything in writing on the transfer of funds to the contras and not to talk to anybody about it" (B-20, p. 1176).

be with us for as long as there are governments. But it clearly sought to enable the U.S. government to disclaim responsibility with respect to other governments, not to keep the entire U.S. government in such ignorance of what was done in its name by subordinate officials that responsible government officials would not even know what to deny.

Yet this was the reason Poindexter gave for why he had not told President Reagan about the diversion scheme:

> Now, the reason that—frankly, as Colonel North has testified, I thought it was a neat idea, too, and I'm sure the President would have enjoyed knowing about it. But, on the other hand, because it would be controversial—and I must say that I don't believe that I estimated how controversial it would be accurately—but I knew very well that it would be controversial, and I wanted the President to have some deniability so that he would be protected, and at the same time we would be able to carry out his policy and provide the opposition to the Sandinista Government.[12]

Poindexter's motivation, then, was largely political; he sought to protect the president from domestic "controversy," not foreign enemies.

North used "plausible deniability" as a justification for employing Secord in his operations: "We were trying to provide a plausibly deniable link directly back to the U.S. Government; and it was accepted that he could provide that kind of deniability. The effort was made, in other words, that the hand of the Government of the United States was not showing in this action."[13]

In the planning for McFarlane's mission to Tehran in May 1986, one of the reasons for cooperating with Israel in the effort was that "Israelis provide some degree of plausible deniability," according to Lieutenant Colonel Earl, who heard it said at a planning meeting. Earl was asked about his understanding of the term:

> *Question:* Was plausible deniability a term that you associated with anyone in particular?
>
> *Earl:* It's a term of art that I'm very familiar with from my days at the CIA. It's a general mode of operation in establishing covert operations.
>
> *Question:* It's a CIA term, though, isn't it?
>
> *Earl:* Oh, definitely. If you set up a cover, if you have a covert operation, unless everything you do will be seen by no one, then what's the difference of doing nothing, then? You have to do something that somebody can see. You have to have an explanation for what you're doing that does not give away that which you are attempting to keep secret.[14]

Mere denial, then, may not be enough. Plausibility must be built into the denial in order to make it successful. The assumption is that the government is doing something which it cannot afford to do openly or admit afterward. By their very nature covert operations make it possible to put the good name or best interests of the country in such jeopardy that the only way to escape from the cost of failure or exposure is the ability to deny that they ever happened or to put the blame on someone else.

The least of the measures that can be taken in a democratic system to control the danger of playing with such fire is that the highest political authority should be responsible for permitting such operations and for maintaining control over them. Unauthorized and uncontrolled covert operations put the covert operators in a position to jeopardize the entire government, or even to take its place. Such covert operations become indistinguishable from government by junta or cabal.

It was precisely to prevent such a takeover that the institution of Findings, signed by the president and conveyed to Congress "in a timely fashion," was introduced in 1974. Representative Louis Stokes addressed North directly on the issue:

> Colonel, you have on several occasions made reference to the term "plausible deniability," with reference to covert operations. I really do not want anyone to think that the concept as you describe it has any real validity today. In fact, yesterday afternoon, you used the term in these hearings "plausible deniability." We did away with this concept that you referred to after the Church and the Pike committee investigations in the mid-1970s. That is why we have a statute that requires Findings. That is why we require that authority from the President be in writing. That is why we require that professionals conduct covert operations. That is why Congress is informed. There is no plausible denial as far as the President is concerned.
>
> The establishment of permanent intelligence committees— oversight committees in the Congress means there is no plausible denial to Congress. What we seek to do in covert operations is to mask the role of the United States from other countries, not from our own government. [15]

As this short lesson on the concept of plausible deniability suggests, the very meaning of the term was perverted. If it were applied to the U.S. government, and especially to the president and Congress, it would make those responsible for the operation accountable to no one, for no one else would know about it. Since accountability is a basic principle of the American political system, deniability cannot be applied to the highest elected American officials in the executive branch and Congress without nullifying accountability. This perversion of deniability, therefore, strikes at the very foundation of the American constitutional order. That some higher authority should and must know without undue delay is fundamental to the American system.

Yet "plausible deniability" was not enough for National Security Adviser Poindexter. He advocated and carried out a policy of "absolute deniability." This exchange took place between Senator Sam Nunn and Poindexter:

Nunn: Everybody I have talked to in the intelligence community and around town where that term has been used tells me that the definition of that term is that when you set up plausible deniability for someone, the President or someone else, what that means is that they know the facts in question, but they can deny the knowledge and that the denial is believable.

Now would you tell us whether that is your definition or whether you have some other definition in mind?

Poindexter: First of all, Senator, I believe if you go back and look at my testimony on May 2nd, when this issue first came up, I used the term deniability, that I wanted to provide the President deniability and insulate him from the decision.

Since that testimony, the terminology has been raised in these hearings of plausible deniability and I have gone along with that definition.

Since this is not any sort of printed doctrine or dogma, it simply is a concept, I think it is open to interpretation; and my interpretation of it is simply and very straightforwardly the ability of the President to deny knowing anything about it and be very truthful in that process. He didn't know anything about it.

Nunn: That is what I would call absolute deniability. If you don't know, it is not only plausible, it just didn't happen. Is that what you mean then?

Poindexter: Absolute deniability would be a more accurate description.

Nunn: Because that word has been used quite a bit during these hearings.

Poindexter: It has been. And again because it is not something that is codified, it is the same thing with covert action and special activities. We use covert action when most of the time we are talking about special activities. But because deniability, plausible deniability or absolute deniability are not defined in statute any place, it is obviously open to interpretation.

Nunn: Well, you are not—let's just make the record clear. You are not using plausible deniability as it has commonly been used and I define it?

Poindexter: As discussed in the morning newspaper, I believe, I am not using plausible deniability in that way or the way that you defined it.[16]

This revealing dialogue made clear what Poindexter's deniability entailed. By making it absolute, he allowed himself to engage in activities which he did not even report to the president, let alone to Congress. Yet there was a statute on the books that mandated Findings, defined how covert activities were to be approved by the president, and determined when they were to be reported to congressional authorities. Poindexter could not "insulate" the president without assuming the powers of the presidency. By making deniability "absolute," he gave himself—on such occasions—absolute power.

For all the contempt of North and those like him for professional diplomats and the traditional bureaucracy, it is hard to see how professionals could have done worse. At least the much-despised bureaucrats would have had to account to others at various stages and might have been made to change course or cut their losses. North and Poindexter spoke of "compartmentation" of covert operations as if it were the supreme virtue. In fact, the exaggerated secrecy of compartmentation protected them from criticism and supervision, with the result that they were beholden only to themselves and blundered from one miscalculation to another. If there are two words that best describe the conduct of Poindexter and North, they are *incompetence* and *gullibility*. The story of these deals with the Iranians is one of obstinate ineptitude.

The combination of compartmentation, deniability, and secrecy made it possible for a few of the self-elect to become, as Secretary Weinberger put it, "people with their own agenda."[17] This phrase starkly expresses what was most significant about the Iran-contra affairs—the takeover of governmental policies by a few strategically placed insiders infatuated with their own sense of superiority and incorruptibility.

2

Who were the "people with their own agenda" and what was their interrelationship?

North was the "action officer," the workhorse. He did not make the basic agenda; he carried it out. Yet he played such a large role in these affairs because he was no ordinary junior officer. He was zealous to the point of fanaticism. No one on the NSC staff and probably in the entire government worked as long and as hard as he did. His superiors did not hesitate to load him with responsibilities that would long since have burned out anyone else. He was, in fact, the victim as well as the beneficiary of poor administration on the part of both national security advisers. In 1985, North managed with a single secretary.[18] In 1986, he had two aides, Earl and Coy, and two secretaries. Unlike everyone else on the NSC staff, North reported directly to Poindexter and could do virtually anything he pleased so long as Poindexter approved or did not hold him back.

The relationship between Poindexter and North is one of the main reasons why North was able to pursue an agenda with a bare minimum of awareness on the part of the massive bureaucracy. The evidence is that North rarely went off on his own. On the contrary, he kept Poindexter meticulously informed, and his unceasing flow of memos to Poindexter is one reason why so many have survived. For one thing, Poindexter had so much to do that he was content to spend little time on North. It is exhausting to read about how Poindexter spent his day:

> I would usually get up around between 5:30 and 6:00, get to the office by 7:00. My first meeting was with the office directors of the NSC staff at 7:30. At 8:00, the Chief of Staff had a daily operations meeting that I attended. At 9:30, I met with the President, usually it lasted about a ½ hour, and then at 10:00, my day began, depending on the particular schedule.
>
> Often I would spend several additional hours a day with the President in meetings that he attended on issues in my area of responsibility, national security.
>
> *Leon* [counsel]: Were you supposed to take the lead in many of those meetings?
>
> *Poindexter:* Yes, I was, in the NSC and NSPG meetings and briefings for the President on various subjects.
>
> And I would work until usually somewhere around 9:00 p.m. in the office, and leave, go home, have dinner, then work until about midnight, go to bed and get up the next morning.
>
> *Leon:* Seven days a week?
>
> *Poindexter:* Six days a week. I went to church sometimes on Sunday morning—not as often as my wife would have liked.
>
> *Leon:* You had five boys to attend to as well?
>
> *Poindexter:* That is correct. I did paperwork then on Sunday afternoon or Sunday evening.

Then came a question about Poindexter and North:

Leon: How much of your time did you spend supervising and over-seeing Colonel North? Or should I say, could you have spent?

Poindexter: In terms of the total number of hours that I worked, it would be a relatively small percentage.[19]

Poindexter's daily routine was so strenuous that something had to give—and he chose to favor other demands on his time rather than supervise North closely. Poindexter had more than enough to do staying close to President Reagan, preparing him to make decisions and getting him through innumerable meetings. "Colonel North was given a very broad charter to carry out a mission," Poindexter explained, "and I did not micromanage him."[20] For the most part, North was a free agent who did pretty much as he pleased, so long as he sent Poindexter a memo about it. There are very few memos extant in which Poindexter tells North what to do or say—and North did not abide by one of the most important.*

President Reagan was not the only one whom Poindexter "insulated." North was another. Only Poindexter stood between North and the rest of the American government. These two, otherwise so different—one frenetic, the other phlegmatic—determined the fate of American foreign policy in two key areas, Iran and Nicaragua. Without a Poindexter, there would not have been a North.

Yet both were enmeshed in circumstances not of their own making. Once it was decided to give these covert operations to the NSC staff, the national security adviser was faced with a task for which his staff was not prepared. The NSC staff had no experience or structure for such extended covert operations. It took over the work of the CIA without the CIA's resources. The next-best thing to do was to call on the services of a marine who was most available and willing to take on whatever he was called on to do. North happened to be a marine who flung himself into un-familiar political territory as if he were engaged in a military operation or crusade. The "can do" marine could never admit that he was not capable of doing anything and everything. Meanwhile, the rest of the NSC staff went on doing what it had always done, such as collecting information and writing papers for higher-ups, sealed off from North's little band.

The NSC staff had never before had such a predominance of military personnel, especially at the top. McFarlane had been a marine officer. North was a marine officer on active service temporarily detailed to the NSC staff. Poindexter was a naval officer still on active service. North's

---

* Poindexter's instructions to North in April 1986 permitting him to go to a meeting with the Iranians in Frankfurt on condition that no arms were to be delivered unless *all* the hostages were released (100-8, p. 555). North proceeded to advocate sequential deals whereby arms were exchanged for a single hostage—and Poindexter went along.

two aides were military officers. By McFarlane's time, one-third of his staff consisted of "career military," a third were from the CIA or the State Department, and a third from the outside.[21] When Poindexter gave North an assignment, it was one military officer telling another what to do.

The extraordinary military presence on the NSC staff brought an extraneous element to the contra affair. North was not merely fighting one war; symbolically, he was also fighting another one. McFarlane, who knew from personal experience the psychological scars which that war had left on its veterans, talked about North's political outlook:

> He is quite cynical about government. Ollie is a man that is a veteran of an experience in Vietnam, of which I was very conscious, and I think not uncommon to the experience of many people— that is a situation that anyone who exposes himself to the loss of life, his own, has to deal, and that is, is it worth it? . . .
>
> Now, in the wake of his service there, having to cope with the vivid reminders of how worth it it was and how tragic a loss of life of Vietnamese—tens of thousands occurred from it—I believe that he committed himself to assuring that he would never be party to such a thing again if he could prevent it.
>
> And I think for him, when it became a matter of association with the contra movement, that it was again a circumstance where we had made a commitment to people, that he could see we were just about to break, and that the bottom line consequence of that would be the death of a lot of people, contras, and that he couldn't be party to that.

McFarlane said that his own views were somewhat different:

> In my own case, I shared some of those feelings, that it seemed to me that if at the end of the day your country has the opportunity in the United States to do one or two things, that you should choose those things which you can do, which you can get support for, and go ahead and lend U.S. influence to them, and however much I and others might regret not being able to help deserving people, that it is more of a service to them never to get started with it than to falsely lead them on.[22]

The influence of the Vietnam War on the American military over a decade later was also stressed by Secretary Weinberger:

> I don't think it is generally understood how deeply scared [seared?] the American military was by Vietnam. We should never, ever consider entering any kind of conflict unless it's important enough

for us to win, and then entering it with the resources that are required to win, and if we do anything other than that, we are, I think, betraying the men and women we ask to serve and perhaps to die for the rest of us.

And that was a perception that was not only that the politicians at that time were responsible, but that the press were not in any sense favorable to the United States. And without in any sense passing judgment on whether this was correct or not, this is a feeling which a very large number of people have, and it has led me to conclude that we should be cautious about intervention but that we should not hesitate to do so if the cause is important enough for us to require intervention, but then if it is, to intervene in a way that guarantees, to the extent you can in war, that we will prevail.

But there is that feeling, and that's why I have studiously refrained from trying to pass judgment on anybody else except with respect to particular actions that involve this whole transaction, not their past records or their character, most of whom I think I admire and most of whom I think, as you said, are honorable, decent people.

They had a different agenda. They had a different set of ideas, but then a lot of people have a different set of ideas than I do.[23]

Weinberger indicated how far the people with a different agenda were willing to go to put it across. One of their ways, he said, "was to keep away from the President views that they suspected, quite correctly most of the time, differ with theirs."[24] Those people, Weinberger charged, had made "a deliberate attempt to prevent information" contrary to their own from reaching the President and had, in fact, fed him intelligence which Weinberger believed to be unsound and tendentious.[25] Weinberger's view was very much like that of Secretary Shultz, who believed that President Reagan "was not given the right information" by people who "were trying to use his undoubted skills as a communicator to have him give a speech and give a press conference and say these things and, in doing so, he would bail them out."[26] In effect, both secretaries thought that the people with a different agenda had succeeded in winning the president to their cause by deceiving and encircling him. If so, they make Reagan into a political puppet without the will or intelligence to see through this systematic deception.

These were people who felt that, having once been betrayed by their government, they were licensed to prevent what they believed to be another threatened betrayal, even if in a different conflict in which the United States was not directly engaged. North virtually accused Congress of betrayal: "The Congress of the United States left soldiers in the field unsupported and vulnerable to their Communist enemies."[27] He linked Vietnam with Nicaragua:

It is my belief that what I saw in Vietnam, where I saw the Army of South Vietnam and I saw the Vietnamese Marines, one of whom was my roommate as I went through basic school at Quantico, and who gave their lives for their country, the parallel is to see that in the campesinos, the young men and women of the Nicaraguan Resistance, is extraordinarily profound.[28]

North was relatively mild. One of his main supporters was Patrick J. Buchanan, the director of communications in the Reagan administration. In defense of North, he charged that "the liberal wing of the Democratic Party has made itself the silent partner—the indispensable ally—of revolutionary communism in the Third World."[29]

Lurking in the background of these affairs, then, was the ghost of McCarthyism in search of a scapegoat for a foreign setback. The injection of domestic pro- or anti-Communism into these matters envenomed rational disagreement by openly or implicitly hinting at treason and betrayal. Pushed to the extreme, it is a formula for latent civil war. Even in the existing American political climate, which is far from civil war, it may be well to remember that other democratic countries have been vulnerable to such destructive agitation.

It was one thing for North and others like him to use the accepted processes of democratic government to shape American policy; it was another thing to do it surreptitiously by virtue of finding themselves in key but obscure positions in a government agency that had not been intended to replace most of the executive branch and Congress. By chance, North had the motivation, the opportunity, and the rules of covert operations to enable him to put his personal stamp on the Iran and contra affairs. Such a role for a lieutenant colonel on temporary loan to the White House was something new in the annals of American government.

3

In the entire government, as we have seen, there was no one between North and Poindexter and no one between Poindexter and President Reagan. On these pinpoints stood the entire structure of government in the Iran and contra affairs. In national security affairs, Poindexter reported only to the president, took his instructions only from the president, and represented the president in his dealings with the rest of the government. Among the members of this triangle of North, Poindexter, and Reagan, we know more about the first two than about the third.

But we know enough about Reagan to come to some firm conclusions. We need not assume that he acted on all questions in the same way. He may have been, as some who worked with him in other connections have related, uninformed, uninterested, and unteachable. This cannot be said of his participation in the Iran and contra affairs, however. He was constantly informed about them and obsessively interested in them, though it is questionable how much he managed to understand about them.

When the storm over these affairs broke, President Reagan behaved as if he could get off scot-free if only he could deny that he had known anything about them. His chief defense was a vacant memory. In the interview he gave only one day after Attorney General Meese's press conference of November 25, 1986, President Reagan said: "My only criticism is that I wasn't told everything."[30]

Even if Poindexter did not tell the president about the diversion, there was much more to the Iran and contra affairs than that. When Reagan complained that he had not been told "everything," it hardly meant that he had been told nothing. Poindexter, after all, admitted withholding from the president only one thing—the diversion. About everything else, Poindexter had plenty of time and opportunity to tell him at his daily briefings. Poindexter well knew that Reagan was obsessively interested in the fate of the hostages and the war of the contras. We have it on the authority of then Vice President Bush: "Though he [Reagan] didn't dwell on the subject publicly, it became an overriding issue inside the White House."[31] Reagan himself has made known: "Almost every morning at my national security briefings, I began by asking the same question: 'Any progress on getting the hostages out of Lebanon?' "[32] It may well be that Reagan knew little and cared less about fiscal matters, but he felt deeply, even passionately, about the Iran and contra affairs.

Some time passed before Reagan was willing to admit that anything had been amiss. In a speech on March 4, 1987, he tried simultaneously to accept responsibility for and to plead ignorance of any wrongdoing:

First let me say I take full responsibility for my own actions and for those of my own administration. As angry as I may be about activities undertaken without my knowledge, I am still accountable for those activities. As disappointed as I may be in some who served me, I am still the one who must answer to the American people for this behavior. And as personally distasteful as I find secret bank accounts and diverted funds—well, as the Navy would say, this happened on my watch. . . .

A few months ago, I told the American people I did not trade arms for hostages. My heart and my best intentions still tell me that's true, but the facts and evidence tell me it is not. What began as a strategic opening to Iran deteriorated, in its implementation, into trading arms for hostages.[33]

It was a strange explanation. In effect, Reagan assumed responsibility for irresponsibility. The Constitution expressly makes it incumbent upon the president to "take Care that the Laws be faithfully executed."[34] In this statement, Reagan admitted that he had not taken care. Activities by his closest personal foreign-policy aide, the national security adviser, had been carried out ostensibly without his knowledge; he had let the falsehood that arms had not been traded for hostages stand without correction for months. His "heart and . . . best intentions" still told him to believe in the falsehood, but he had been belatedly and reluctantly made to realize by "the facts and evidence" that he had been wrong. These facts and this evidence had been presented by the Tower Board about a week earlier and had forced him to make his nonconfessional confession. For Reagan did not confess to anything he had done or decided; he merely confessed not to have known what others around him had done. Yet, on this occasion, he at least admitted that at long last he had come to know about "secret bank accounts and diverted funds."

Having said that he was "angry" about activities "undertaken without my knowledge" and "disappointed . . . in some who served me," which could only have meant in the first place Poindexter, Reagan was curiously forgiving of what would seem to have been a serious dereliction of duty. In an interview on April 28, 1987, he expressed confidence in Poindexter as "an honorable man" who "was being, in some way, protective of me." He again admitted that "the whole thing just began to deteriorate into a hostage sale thing" as the Iranians demanded more and more arms, but that he "wasn't aware of that."

As time passed, he wavered between assuming more personal responsibility and falling back on his ignorance. He blurted out to a group of newspaper editors on May 15, 1987: "As a matter of fact, I was very definitely involved in the decisions about support to the freedom fighters. It was my idea to begin with." In a televised performance on August 12, 1987, he finally admitted that his preoccupation with the hostages "intrude[d] into areas where it didn't belong." The main point the president seemed determined to make was that "in capital letters, I did not know about the diversion of funds."

At Poindexter's trial, Reagan finally assumed full responsibility for the Iran-contra affairs, referring to both of them in the singular. "It was a covert action," he said, "that was taken at my behest."[35] Despite this, he claimed that he did not know what the details were:

> When I authorized and approved the sale of arms to moderate elements in Iran, I implicitly authorized the acts that were necessary to accomplish these sales. Because I did not discuss the details of the transactions during that time, I do not recall ever authorizing any operational role by either Secord or Hakim in the Iranian

initiative. I do not believe I ever was asked to authorize or approve this covert action in such detail.[36]

This is probably as close as we can get to Reagan's own view of his role. He was responsible for the policy. How much he was told—or could remember—of the details in carrying it out is another question.

But the most astounding statement made by Reagan about the diversion came during Poindexter's trial. He stated that "to this day, I don't have any information or knowledge that . . . there was a diversion . . . I, to this day, do not recall ever hearing that there was a diversion."[37] He said that he did not even know that the report of the Tower Board in February 1987 had referred to the diversion. As if he had never read the report, he said that he was now hearing about its reference to the diversion for the first time.[38] When he was asked whether "this [was] the first time in this courtroom that you came to realize in fact that a diversion had actually occurred," Reagan answered: "Yes."[39]

How are we to explain this extraordinary aberration? Had the Reagan of 1990 deteriorated so much in about three years that he could remember nothing about the diversion—which he had admittedly known about at least since March 4, 1987, or even earlier, November 25, 1986, when Meese had publicly talked about it in the famous press conference?

Finally, one of Reagan's protestations at the Poindexter trial was peculiarly double-edged, though he did not seem to realize it. He repeated again and again that he had always instructed Poindexter and others to stay "within the law." Reagan felt it necessary to say: "I emphasized that at every time."[40] It seems odd that a president should have to say that he had told the leading officials of his administration that they should remember to stay "within the law," as if he could not take it for granted that they would do so as a matter of course.

The main question is whether President Reagan made the critical decisions, not whether he approved of every detail. Of his responsibility for the critical decisions, there can be no doubt. The most fateful one was the Finding of January 17, 1986; from it the entire sequence of events for the rest of the year flowed. At that time, he did not make the decision to go ahead with the Iran initiative hastily or absentmindedly. He made it after weeks of indecision and against the opposition of his two senior cabinet secretaries. Weinberger could not remember another time when President Reagan had rejected a view on which both secretaries had agreed.[41] At all the top-level meetings of which we have a record, he spoke more often than anyone else and clearly steered the discussions. Even in the darkening days of November 1986, he stepped out as the main protagonist in defense of his policy, in the television speech on November 13 and the press conference on November 19. It was only at the fatal press conference on November 25 that he had lost his self-confidence and had handed the responsibility over to Attorney General Meese.

Both Secretaries Shultz and Weinberger in their various ways acknowledged that President Reagan had led the country into the Iran affair. They exculpated him only to the extent that he had allegedly been deceived and misled by others—the "people with their own agenda"—into doing what he did. The choice seemed to be whether to portray President Reagan as a false leader or as an innocent dupe—and they chose the latter as the lesser evil. Yet they described Reagan as a stubborn man once he had made up his mind about something that touched him deeply. Secretary Shultz said: "He is decisive, he steps up to things, and when he decides, he stays with it. And sometimes you wish he wouldn't, but anyway, he does."[42] Secretary Weinberger's experiences had taught him that the president "has his own judgements and his own ideas, and he's going to listen to advice and he's going to listen to recommendations, but he's not always going to follow them." When Weinberger was asked who had made the best argument for selling arms to Iran, he answered: "Perhaps the President."[43]

Poindexter, who dealt with him in this period more than anyone else, said that President Reagan was "not a man for great detail." Poindexter was also asked whether Reagan was a "decisive person." His answer was: "On some issues, he is. If he is confident and has a strong feeling about something, he can be very decisive." Poindexter briefed him, as might be expected, "primarily in the policy area and it was a judgment call every day as to exactly what level of detail I had to get into." On North's level, Poindexter said, "I briefed the President on most all aspects of all the projects that Colonel North was involved with."[44] Yet the president told the Tower Board on January 26, 1987, "that he did not know that the NSC staff was engaged in helping the contras."[45] Since the president also admitted that it was his idea to help the contras, one wonders who in the government he thought was helping them. It would seem that President Reagan was clearly reluctant to blame Poindexter and North for anything but the diversion, because he knew that, except possibly for that, they had been carrying out his wishes.*

---

* Fred Barnes of *The New Republic* subsequently gave a revealing account of the president's memory during an interview on October 2, 1987. The president, Barnes reported, recognized a photograph of himself taken for a movie in 1937, immediately named the movie, *Sergeant Murphy*, gave a detailed version of the plot, and even remembered having been tricked into riding an unruly horse one afternoon after the filming had been done. But he had difficulty remembering the Iran affair, and what he did remember suggested that he had been pretending contrition in his televised performance on August 12, 1987. Whereas he had then confessed that "the sale of arms got tangled up with the hostages," he now insisted that "it was not trading arms for hostages." As for Poindexter and North, he was most forgiving because "they must have felt that somehow they were protecting me" (*The New Republic*, October 26, 1987).

4

Vice President Bush's role presents a different kind of problem.

The American vice presidency is not an "operational" office that demands active participation in the implementation of policy. Yet Bush brought trouble on himself by denying too much about what he knew, if not about what he did.

The two questions that must be asked about Bush are: What did he know? And what did he do? Bush's role can be understood only by considering these questions separately.

In his campaign autobiography published in 1987 to advance his candidacy for the presidency, Bush gave this account of how much he knew about "the affair":

> My first real chance to see the picture as a whole didn't come until December 1986, when Dave Durenberger, then chairman of the Senate Intelligence Committee, briefed me on his committee's preliminary investigation of the affair.
>
> What Dave had to say left me with the feeling, expressed to my chief of staff, Craig Fuller, that I'd been deliberately excluded from key meetings involving details of the Iran operation. . . .
>
> Not one meeting of the National Security Council was ever held to consider all phases of the operation—not only its possible benefits, but the problems and pitfalls it might face. . . .
>
> In retrospect there were signals along the way that gave fair warning that the Iran initiative was headed for trouble. As it turned out, George Shultz and Cap Weinberger had serious doubts, too. If I'd known that and asked the President to call a meeting of the NSC, he might have seen the project in a different light, as a gamble doomed to fail.[46]

At the time this book was written, the congressional hearings had not yet taken place and much of the documentary material had not been released. As a result of the voluminous material now available, we know that Bush could not have failed to know a great deal about the problems and pitfalls, because he was usually present, as Poindexter testified, at the latter's morning briefings of President Reagan.[47] Indeed, Republican Senator William S. Cohen and Democratic Senator George J. Mitchell devote an entire chapter of their book, *Men of Zeal*, to the exposure of Bush's spurious innocence. They show that Bush was present at the top-level meeting in January 1986 at which Shultz and Weinberger forcefully expressed their opposition. They refer to the meeting in Jerusalem in July 1986 at which Bush and Fuller were briefed by Amiram Nir at considerable length and in intimate detail about the background and status of

the dealings with Iran. Bush later protested that he had not fully understood what the Israeli representative had told him, though Fuller seems
to have understood it without difficulty. Anyone who reads Fuller's account cannot fail to see that even less than a full understanding must
have been enlightening. When asked by Dan Rather about "arms for
hostages" in a television interview, Bush for once did not quibble:

> I went along with it—because you know why, Dan . . . when I
> saw Mr. Buckley, when I heard about Mr. Buckley being tortured
> to death, later admitted as a CIA Chief. So if I erred, I erred on
> the side of trying to get those hostages out of there.[48]

In the end, there was little difference between Bush's support of "arms
for hostages" and Reagan's. Bush later urged future presidents "never try
to strike a bargain with terrorists."[49] He evidently became aware of this
rule or decided to abide by it only after he had made up his mind to
become a future president.

Bush's responsibility for the Iran-contra policies went at least as far as
his support for them. As vice president, he was not called on to originate
policies or see them through. Vice presidents have rarely if ever opposed
presidential policies, and certainly not if they want sitting presidents to
support them for the succession.

Bush and his subordinates also chose to deny any implication in the
contra affair. According to Donald P. Gregg, Bush's national security
adviser, El Salvador was considered a proper area for Bush's activity but
Nicaragua was not. This strange discrimination also raised some awkward
questions about what Bush knew.

Oliver North's activities were not unknown to Bush. North had first
come to Bush's attention in 1983 when he arranged the vice president's
trip to El Salvador, on which both North and Gregg had gone along.
Bush had been sent to pass on the message that the Salvadoran "death
squads" were endangering U.S. aid to El Salvador.[50] In the next two
years, Bush had followed North's activities sufficiently to send him a
Thanksgiving message on November 27, 1985, which read in part: "Your
dedication and tireless work with the hostage thing and with Central
America really gives me cause for great pride in you and *Thanks*."[51]

North was also implicated in a mysterious tangle of circumstances that
linked Bush, Gregg, and Felix Rodriguez, alias "Max Gomez."

Rodriguez had been known to Bush from the time the latter had been
director of the CIA in 1976. That year, on retirement from the CIA after
fifteen years' service, Rodriguez had received the CIA's Intelligence Star
for Valor during Bush's incumbency.

What Bush knew about Rodriguez came mainly from Gregg. Rodriguez
and Gregg had worked together in Vietnam, where Gregg had been a
CIA regional station chief and Rodriguez a "contract employee."[52] As

Vietnam veterans, their personal ties were unusually staunch; Gregg considered Rodriguez to be "one of the really extraordinary human beings I know."[53] On January 22, 1985, Gregg arranged for Rodriguez to meet the vice president and inform him of his desire to work in El Salvador against the insurgency there.[54] Bush met with Rodriguez on two other occasions.

Ten years later, Bush and Rodriguez had had their picture taken together in the vice president's office—a picture which Bush inscribed with the words: "To Felix Rodriguez—with high esteem and admiration— George Bush." A Christmas greeting from Bush to Rodriguez, dated December 23, 1988, on the vice president's stationery, referring to Rodriguez's congressional testimony, reads in part: "You have told the truth faithfully—and have won a lot of respect in the process. . . . With admiration and respect."[55]

The relationship between Rodriguez and North came to a different end.

Back on September 20, 1985, Rodriguez had received a letter from North requesting him to use his influence with two Salvadoran generals, the minister of defense, General Vides Casanova, and the Air Force commander, General Juan Rafael Bustillo. North wanted Rodriguez to get them to permit the servicing of the Secord operation's aircraft at the Ilopango military air base in El Salvador for flights into Honduras.[56] Rodriguez subsequently acted as North's liaison agent in El Salvador.

Almost a year later, North and Rodriguez had a falling-out. On August 5 or 6, 1986, North called Gregg to denounce Rodriguez for having allegedly misappropriated an airplane belonging to Secord's "Enterprise."[57] Meanwhile, Rodriguez had been openly criticizing Secord and his chief associates on the ground that they were managing the operation incompetently and were guilty of profiteering. Two or three days after North's call to Gregg, on August 8, 1986, Rodriguez came to see Gregg in Washington and gave him a full bill of particulars against North, Secord, and the rest. The most explosive charges were that North was using the "Ed Wilson group" in Secord's entourage and that Secord's men were taking unconscionable rake-offs, such as $20,000 which Secord's purchasing agent, Richard Gadd, had allegedly "ripped off" the contras on the sale of a piece of communications gear. Far from having stolen the plane, Rodriguez explained, he had had it repaired in Miami, and it was ready to go back filled with medicines.[58]

The chief interest in this imbroglio is how Gregg handled it on behalf of Vice President Bush. Gregg says that he trusted Rodriguez and was so impressed by him that he called a meeting on August 12, 1986, at which he assembled representatives of the CIA, State Department, and NSC staff, including North's chief aide, Lieutenant Colonel Earl, to tell them of Rodriguez's charges.[59]

Yet Gregg insisted that he had told Bush nothing about the charges, though they were serious enough to prompt him to call together a high-level interdepartmental group to learn about them. When Gregg was asked why he had not done so, he replied that he did not think they were "really Vice Presidential."[60] Gregg was asked why matters in El Salvador were Vice President Bush's concern but not matters in Nicaragua. Gregg could not answer this question and tried to evade it by talking about North.[61]

What emerges most strikingly from this story is the similar way in which the two national security advisers behaved. Poindexter protected President Reagan by allegedly not telling him about the diversion, and Gregg protected Vice President Bush by allegedly not telling him about Rodriguez's revelations. Poindexter gave President Reagan the alibi of "I didn't know," and Gregg gave Vice President Bush the variant of "I didn't tell him."

Unlike Poindexter, Gregg did not suffer for his similar service to Bush. When Vice President Bush became President Bush, Gregg was sent to South Korea as U.S. ambassador.

In his campaign autobiography of 1987, Bush explained the way he had made his Iran-contra decisions: "It was a fine line . . ."[62]

5

There remains the question: How could a handful of subordinate officials take virtual control of U.S. foreign policy in two critical areas and impose their will on the enormous American bureaucracy?

As we have seen, North could have accomplished little alone. It was necessary for him to call on other agencies and departments of the government in order to carry out his projects. He was able, when necessary, to call upon personnel in the CIA, Defense Department, State Department, Drug Enforcement Administration, and elsewhere for assistance. To get arms for Iran, North had to get the CIA to request them from the secretary of defense, who ordered the Army to release them to the CIA, from where they went to Secord's operation. As Casey himself made it known, the CIA had conveniently put itself in a "support mode" to Poindexter.[63]

These "people with their own agenda" manned the center of a tentacular operation that was located in the White House. The secret of their power was that they could get things done by acting in the president's name. How this worked again leads us back to President Reagan.

"I suffer the bureaucrat's disease," confessed the CIA's Clair George, "that when people call me and say, I am calling from the White House for the National Security Council on behalf of the national security adviser, I am inclined to 'snap to.' "[64] When the CIA's Clarridge was asked why he obeyed North without consulting his superiors, despite a

CIA regulation that all requests from the White House had to be cleared with the director, he replied lamely: "Ollie North calls up and says that he needs some urgent assistance," as if a call from Ollie North in the White House were enough to countermand a formal rule. Assistant Secretary of Defense Armitage explained with some disgruntlement: "Look, we've already seen, I think it's become painfully clear to most of your bosses and painfully clear, embarrassingly clear to the rest of us, that the National Security Council, when a staff officer asks, whether it's Ollie or anybody, generally you respond."[65]

Ambassadors also snapped to. When Tambs was appointed ambassador to Costa Rica in 1985, North instructed him to open a "southern front" for the contras and to get permission from the Costa Rican government for the construction of an airstrip to supply them. Tambs never checked with anyone in the State Department about whether he should obey North's instructions.[66] In 1986, John H. Kelly, the U.S. ambassador in Lebanon, received a call from North to expect the release of American hostages. It was followed by a message from Poindexter telling Kelly to communicate only with Poindexter and not with anyone in the State Department. When Kelly reported to the State Department that David P. Jacobsen had been released, he received a stern rebuke from one of North's aides that he had violated Poindexter's instructions. Kelly was later reprimanded by Secretary Shultz for having bypassed the State Department.[67]

Secretary of Defense Weinberger was asked about an order from Poindexter to a defense intelligence agency to take the secretary off the list for distribution of intelligence. Weinberger commented: "You know there is a certain mystique that goes with somebody receiving a call from the White House that says to do such and such and there has been a tendency to accept that, but I am confident that it will never happen again."[68] The question of a "White House mystique" came up again in connection with a request in November 1984 by North to General Paul F. Gorman, head of the Southern Command, for information about the location and status of Nicaraguan Sandinista helicopters. This exchange followed:

> *Representative Edward P. Boland:* Let me ask, given the disparity of their rank, between general and lieutenant colonel, would you attribute General Gorman's compliance with North's request to that "White House mystique" that you mentioned last Friday?
>
> *Weinberger:* Well, if there was, indeed, compliance with it, yes. There are a number of people who feel that when the White House calls, that everything has to be done, but in accordance with that call.[69]

In effect, North's secret weapon was that he could pick up the phone and call from the White House. The accessories to North's activities were so many and various that they brought on an indignant outburst, addressed to North, from Representative Jack Brooks of Texas:

> The Defense Department helped, provided DEA [Drug Enforcement Administration] agents, held off the FBI. The Department of State helped. The ambassadors were used to facilitate the movement of weapons, construction of clandestine air strips.
>
> And despite what Assistant Secretary Abrams said about not knowing nothing about nothing—he had to be authorized to tell the truth, you recall—it was very clear that you testified that he didn't have to ask. He already knew everything you were doing in Central America. The CIA helped. You testified, you talked to Director Casey several times a week; worked closely with him. The CIA bought the missiles from the DoD [Department of Defense], sold them to Iran. The CIA operatives assisted in setting up and running the air supply into Nicaragua.
>
> And, of course, you were not the only one at the National Security Council involved. You testified that everything you did, all the machinations, the operations, the phone calls, the traveling, was supported by your superiors, Mr. McFarlane, Admiral Poindexter. Your secretary, Ms. Hall, even testified that your travel was authorized by someone higher than you. And you've testified repeatedly that you thought you even had the help of the President of the United States.

Representative Brooks saw a "government within a government" in this network:

> Most of these activities could have been carried out by these same people in the normal course of their duties. They would have had to comply with certain accountability provisions, like written Findings as provided by the President's own National Security Decision Directive 159. Reporting to the House and Senate Select Committees on Intelligence as required by the Intelligence Oversight Act; reporting to the Foreign Affairs Committee as required by the Foreign Military Sales Act. And I guess they would have had to deposit the proceeds in the U.S. Treasury since those missiles were paid for with the taxpayers' money.
>
> Now instead, this elaborate scheme to carry out these activities was worked out by the government within a government and it's a rather interesting variation of now you see it, now you don't. The U.S. government was acting as a party when needed and it was a private citizen when it came to reporting to Congress or counting the profits.[70]

The fact remains, however, that these virtuous preachments by senators and representatives came too late to do any good. The committees of Congress had been easily bamboozled by McFarlane and Poindexter in 1985 and 1986, when real congressional oversight might have done some good. In the hearings in 1989, not a word of self-criticism was uttered by members of the two congressional committees. No effort was made to examine how and why a mockery had been made of the oversight function of Congress.

This alleged "government within a government" was a junta-like cabal. This cabal did not have the resources of a separate government and had to manipulate the real government in order to accomplish its ends. Yet the cabal was the victim of its own limitations. Its leadership was very narrowly based in the White House. Its main support came largely from an improvised, shadowy underworld. Its very tenebrous, conspiratorial nature turned against it as soon as it was exposed to the light of day. It was unable to show itself openly to rally timely support in Congress. It had to contend with opposition at the top of the State and Defense Departments. Its greatest asset, the president whose policies it served, was given the alibi of "plausible deniability," which he used to abandon his own faithful henchmen to their fates.

Of all those who crossed very thin lines, the most oblivious seemed to be the president of the United States.

26

Unfinished Business

The unfinished business of the Iran-contra affairs will not go away. The Iran-contra affairs amounted to more than good plans gone wrong or even bad plans gone wildly wrong. They were symptomatic of a far deeper disorder in the American body politic. They were made possible by an interpretation of the Constitution which Poindexter and North thought gave them a license to carry on their secret operations in the name of the president, in defiance of the law and without the knowledge of any other branch of the government. We have barely begun to face the issue which this constitutional perversion presents, with the result that some Iran-contra variant could, sooner or later, recur.

One would not ordinarily think of Poindexter and North as authorities on the power of the presidency in foreign policy. Yet, to justify their actions, they held forth on just this constitutional issue. Somehow the highly dubious theory of a presidential monopoly of foreign policy had filtered down to them and given them a license to act as if they could substitute themselves for the entire government. In effect, they reflected a school of thought that calls into question the constitutional foundations of this country.

On May 2, 1986, Poindexter sent a revealing message to his deputy, Don Fortier, about a conversation with President Reagan. Poindexter said that he and the president had discussed an aid bill for the contras which was not going through Congress fast enough to please him. Reagan had started the conversation with "I am really serious." He then said: "If we can't move the contra package before June 9, I want to figure out a way to take action unilaterally to provide assistance." After telling about some discussion on how to accomplish this end, Poindexter observed: "But the fact remains that the President is ready to confront the

Congress on the Constitutional question of who controls foreign policy."*1

Poindexter brought up another critical question bearing on who controls foreign policy. Of all the powers given to Congress by the Constitution, none is more fundamental than congressional control of appropriations.2 Without it, Congress would be deprived of any effective share in the governance of the United States. Yet Poindexter took it upon himself to declare that the constitutional authority of Congress to appropriate moneys should not be used "to restrict what the President can do in foreign policy."3 In effect, he wanted congressional control of appropriations to stop at foreign policy, thereby depriving Congress of any fully effective means of influencing it.

North also posed as an authority on the president's constitutional powers. At one point in the congressional hearings, he said:

I deeply believe that the President of the United States is also an elected official of this land, and by the Constitution, as I understand it, he is the person charged with *making* and carrying out the foreign policy of this country [italics added].4

It was this assumption of a president almighty in foreign policy that underlay the Poindexter-North belief that they could do anything they pleased in the Iran-contra affairs so long as they had the president's implicit or explicit approval.

Poindexter and Fortier were sometimes more extreme than North. The difference once came up in connection with soliciting money from "third countries." In November 1985, Fortier wrote to McFarlane: "Ollie believes we need to flag the possible option of a Finding permitting us to seek third country support. John [Poindexter] and I are both uneasy about raising this."5 They were uneasy because it was still understood that a Finding had to be communicated to Congress, which might not be in favor of the idea. "I didn't want to resurface the issue on the Hill and get an answer that we didn't want to hear," Poindexter explained.

Another issue was whether funds were appropriated solely by Congress. In this case, Poindexter admitted, "you probably have to have, as we do have, a very detailed accounting system to make sure the money is all spent for its intended purpose." But there was an escape hatch. If *unappropriated* money were used, Poindexter held, no accounting would

---

* According to this message, President Reagan was influenced by reading a book edited by Benjamin Netanyahu, then the permanent representative of Israel to the United Nations, "and he was taken with the examples of Presidential actions in the past without Congressional approval." The book was *Terrorism: How the West Can Win* (Farrar, Straus and Giroux, 1986). The selection which impressed President Reagan so much was made up of six pages on "Constitutional Power and the Defense of Free Government" by Professor Walter Berns. It dealt wholly with "The Case of Abraham Lincoln," who took unilateral actions early in the Civil War. Reagan apparently mistook himself for Lincoln and the covert operation against Nicaragua for the Civil War.

be necessary. In the case of Secord's operation, Poindexter said, "we are talking about private funds, third-country funds that really are outside of the purview of the U.S. government."[6]

North also claimed to know the constitutional difference between appropriated and unappropriated funds. He maintained: "We lived within the constraints of Boland, which limited the use of appropriated funds."[7] When unappropriated funds were used, he thought, there was no need to abide by the Boland Amendment, prohibiting support of the contras.

If this rationale had occurred only to Poindexter and North, it might be dismissed as an amateurish aberration. Two years later, however, the very same argument was put forward by Senator Jesse Helms, the ranking Republican on the Foreign Relations Committee, against the most important bill as yet offered as a consequence of the Iran-contra affairs. The issue will not die, as will become clear when we come to the fate of the bill presented by Senator Daniel Patrick Moynihan in July 1989.

The question of the appropriations power of Congress over foreign policy is only a special case of other, more far-reaching questions:

Is the president a free agent with complete power over American foreign policy? Do the other branches of government, especially Congress, have any part to play in it? Does the Constitution draw a fundamental distinction between the conduct of foreign and domestic affairs? Do we have an authoritarian president in foreign but a democratic president in domestic policy?

The way these questions were answered influenced the way the Iran-contra affairs unfolded. The premise of a presidential monopoly in foreign policy emboldened Reagan, Poindexter, and North to play fast and loose with constitutional constraints. In its ultimate significance, nothing was more important in these affairs than how the power of the president in foreign policy was understood—and nothing was more neglected. The Iran-contra affairs were not an aberration; they were brought on by a long process of presidential aggrandizement, congressional fecklessness, and judicial connivance. If anything is to be gained from this costly experience, it should be the belated realization that this process has put the Constitution in danger.

2

But in what sense?

There is little agreement on what the Constitution says on foreign policy. For one reason, the Constitution itself says comparatively little about it. Article I, Section 8, mainly gives Congress the power to provide for the common defense and to declare war. Article II, Section 2, empowers the president to make treaties with the advice and consent of the Senate, provided two-thirds of the senators present concur; to appoint ambassadors with the advice and consent of the Senate; and to be the commander in chief of the armed forces. That is not very much on which to base a complete constitutional doctrine. These few hints were hardly enough to guide the nation even in its infancy.

The framers of the Constitution, moreover, were not models of consistency. They frequently said different things or said one thing and did another. Alexander Hamilton, traditionally considered the early exponent of a strong presidency, gave expression to the classical rejection of an all-powerful presidency in foreign affairs:

> The history of human conduct does not warrant that exalted opinion of human virtue which would make it wise in a nation to commit interests of so delicate and momentous a kind as those which concern its intercourse with the rest of the world to the sole disposal of a magistrate, created and circumstanced, as would be a president of the United States.[8]

Later, however, Hamilton wanted to give the presidency virtually unlimited power, except where the Constitution contained specific exceptions and qualifications, which were few. Thomas Jefferson appealed to James Madison "to cut him to pieces," which Madison tried to do in the great debate between Pacificus (Hamilton) and Helvidius (Madison). A critical issue was whether the executive as well as the legislature had the "right" to judge whether to make war or not—a test of how far the executive could go in its control of foreign policy. Madison argued heatedly:

> In no part of the constitution is more wisdom to be found, than in the clause which confides the question of war or peace in the legislature, and not to the executive department . . . War is in fact the true nurse of executive aggrandizement . . . The strongest passions and most dangerous weaknesses of the human breast; ambition, avarice, vanity, the honorable or venial love of fame, are all in conspiracy against the desire and duty of peace.
>
> Hence it has grown into an axiom that the executive is the department of power most distinguished by its propensity to war; hence it is the practice of all states, in proportion as they are free, to disarm this propensity of its influence.[9]

A few years later, Madison wrote to Jefferson:

> The management of foreign relations appears to be the most susceptible of abuse of all the trusts committed to a Government, because they can be concealed or disclosed, or disclosed in such parts and at such times as will best suit particular views; and because

the body of the people are less capable of judging, and are more under the influence of prejudices, on that branch of their affairs, than of any other. Perhaps it is a universal truth that the loss of liberty at home is to be charged to provisions against danger, real or pretended, from abroad.[10]

Yet President Jefferson and his secretary of state, James Madison, stretched the powers of the presidency beyond anything they had previously envisioned in order to obtain the Louisiana Territory in 1803. Previously "strict constructionists" of the Constitution, they waived their principles for what Jefferson said was a "higher obligation."[11] Since the Constitution did not provide for the acquisition of territory, which would have required a constitutional amendment, Jefferson admitted that it was "an act beyond the Constitution."[12] The congressional defenders of President Reagan's handling of the Iran-contra affairs did not fail to note such historical precedents and inconsistencies.[13]

As a result, what the Constitution actually says is little guide to what it has been made to say or what has been done whatever it may say. The Constitution clearly does *not* charge the president with "making" foreign policy. But presidents have effectively made foreign policy. The Constitution does not make a distinction in principle between foreign and domestic policy; it charges Congress with making and the president with executing both. But this "separation of powers" has been honored in the breach. In foreign affairs, the Constitution limits the president the most in his ability to declare war. Yet it has done little to prevent presidents from making war so long as they do it without declaring it or pretend that they are waging something else. If Congress does not choose to be faithful to the Constitution and make itself responsible for declaring war, presidents can do almost anything they please.

3

Historically, the argument for making foreign policy the sole business of the president largely depends on sources other than the Constitution. One of the most influential and misrepresented of the grounds is associated with the term "sole organ." It figures prominently in almost all arguments for presidential ascendancy in foreign policy.

Rarely have two words taken on such enormous significance, despite a highly questionable lineage.

In a "Pacificus" article, Hamilton contended that the "Executive Department" was "the *organ* of intercourse between the Nation and foreign Nations."[14] This phrase has been distorted to say that the president "is the 'sole organ' of the government in foreign affairs."[15] The "sole organ" phrase actually turned up for the first time in a speech by John Marshall in the House of Representatives in 1799.

The occasion was President John Adams's extradition of an alleged British fugitive, Jonathan Robbins. Adams was challenged in Congress on the ground that Congress had not given the president statutory authority for his action. Marshall, the congressman, not yet the famous chief justice, upheld Adams's prerogative to act on his own, because Congress had not yet legislated on such a matter. In the course of his argument, Marshall said: "The President is the sole organ of the nation in its external relations, and its sole representative with foreign nations." He also said: "Congress unquestionably may prescribe the mode, and Congress may devolve on others the whole execution of the contract; but, till this be done, it seems the duty of the Executive department to execute the contract by any means it possesses." This hardly suggests that Marshall had meant to deprive Congress of any voice in foreign policy. The "sole organ" allusion, in context, was, as Professor Edward S. Corwin put it, "simply the President's role as *instrument of communication* with other governments."[16]

Not until 1936 was this term used to give the president exclusive power over foreign policy. It came up in an opinion by Justice George Sutherland of the U.S. Supreme Court in the celebrated case of *U.S.* v. *Curtiss-Wright*. The issue itself was hardly one in which it was appropriate to make a sweeping judgment on the whole range of foreign affairs. The historical context is again important. A joint resolution of Congress had authorized President Franklin D. Roosevelt to prohibit arms sales to Paraguay and Bolivia, then at war. Curtiss-Wright and other companies were indicted for violating the embargo. They came up with the defense that Congress had failed to set adequate standards for the authority delegated to the president. Curiously, given the subsequent history of Sutherland's opinion, the policy had been set by Congress; the president was simply executing it. The case concerned the validity of a law, not the relations between the president and Congress. There was no question of any challenge by Congress to the president's authority; the challenge to both the president and Congress came from private parties.

Justice Sutherland sustained President Roosevelt's action on the ground that limitations on congressional delegation of power to the president in domestic matters did not carry over to foreign affairs. But instead of limiting himself to the point at issue, he went on to engage in a flight of general constitutional theory, regarded as dicta (personal views not necessary to the decision of the particular case), that has reverberated through succeeding decades. It was another case of tearing words from their historical context and applying them to all manner of circumstances.

Citing Marshall's speech of 137 years earlier, Sutherland went on:

The broad statement that the federal government can exercise no powers except those specifically enumerated in the Constitution, and such implied powers—as are necessary and proper to carry into effect the enumerated powers, is categorically true only in respect to our internal affairs . . .

Not only, as we have shown, is the federal power over external affairs in origin and essential character different from that over internal affairs, but participation in the exercise of power is significantly limited. In this vast external realm with its important, complicated, delicate and manifold problems, the President alone has the power to speak or listen as a representative of the nation . . .

It is important to bear in mind that we are here dealing with an authority vested in the President by an exertion of legislative power, but with such an authority plus the very delicate, plenary and exclusive power of the President as "the sole organ of the federal government in the field of international relations"—a power which does not require as a basis for its exercise an act of Congress, but which, of course, like every other governmental power, must be exercised in subordination to the applicable provisions of the Constitution.

This decision has been cited so often by government attorneys bent on defending the president's exclusive power in foreign affairs that it has come to be known as the *"Curtiss-Wright*, so I'm right, cite."* In fact, more has been read into Sutherland's opinion than was actually there. The only monopoly specifically noted is the president's power "to speak or listen as a representative of the nation"—a hoary prerogative never contested since the early years of the Republic. And if the president's power "must be exercised in subordination to the applicable provisions of the Constitution," the president is still empowered only so far as the Constitution permits.

But equally significant was Sutherland's apparent separation of external from internal affairs. He created a bifurcated presidency by splitting the Constitution in two and having it say one thing for internal affairs and another for external affairs. He actually limited the external side, given solely to the presidency, to speaking and listening as the national representative, but this inconvenient qualification has been forgotten or ignored in the interest of making the president all-powerful in foreign policy as a whole. The external-internal bifurcation lived on.[17]

Curiously, *Curtiss-Wright* came up in Oliver North's testimony at the congressional hearings. It even provoked an exchange between North and Senator George J. Mitchell:

* Harold Hongju Koh, *The National Security Constitution: Sharing Power After the Iran-Contra Affair* (Yale University Press, 1990), p. 94.

North: That was again debated in the 1930s in the *U.S.* v. *Curtiss-Wright Export Corporation*, and the Supreme Court held again that it was within the purview of the President of the United States to conduct secret activities and to conduct secret negotiations to further the foreign policy goals of the United States.

Mitchell: If I may just say, Colonel, the *Curtiss-Wright* case said no such thing. It involved public matters that were the subject of a law and a prosecution—you said this isn't the appropriate form [forum?] to be debating constitutional law, and I agree with you.[18]

North was fuzzy about what *Curtiss-Wright* had actually been about; it had concerned arms sales in Latin America, not secret activities or secret negotiations. But it was significant that he should have mentioned the case at all, probably because he had heard about it in reference to the president's presumed powers in foreign policy.

Another Supreme Court decision has been famous for the opposite reason. In 1952, during the Korean War, President Truman ordered the seizure of the steel industry, which was threatened with a nationwide strike, though there was no statute authorizing such action. The case of *Youngstown Sheet & Tube Co.* v. *Sawyer* went to the Supreme Court, where the vote was six to three against the seizure.

The majority opinion by Justice Hugo Black upheld the classical constitutional principle that presidents could only execute laws made by Congress and that President Truman had violated this hallowed rule. The Court's opinion stated unequivocally:

> In the framework of our Constitution, the President's power to see that the laws are faithfully executed refutes the idea that he is to be a lawmaker. The Constitution limits his functions in the lawmaking process to the recommending of laws he thinks wise and the vetoing of laws he thinks bad. And the Constitution is neither silent nor equivocal about who shall make laws which the President is to execute. The first section of the first article says that "All legislative Powers herein granted shall be vested in the Congress of the United States."

A concurring opinion by Justice Felix Frankfurter held that the fundamental doctrine of the "separation of powers" made President Truman's action unacceptable. But it was Justice Robert Jackson's concurring opinion that attracted most subsequent attention and seemed to offer the best way out of the excessive presidential permissiveness of *Curtiss-Wright*.

Instead of formally deciding what was constitutional and what was not, Jackson took a practical, relativist approach that there were degrees of presidential authority. They were:

1. When the President acts pursuant to an express or implied authorization of Congress, his authority is at its maximum, for it includes all that he possesses in his own right plus all Congress can delegate. . . .

2. When the President acts in absence of either a congressional grant or denial of authority, he can only rely upon his own independent powers, but there is a zone of twilight in which he and Congress may have concurrent authority, or in which its distribution is uncertain. . . .

3. When the President takes measures incompatible with the express or implied will of Congress, his power is at its lowest ebb, for then he can rely only upon his own constitutional powers minus any constitutional powers of Congress over the matter. Courts can sustain exclusive presidential control in such a case only by disabling the Congress from acting upon the subject.[19]

This Solomonic judgment seems to distinguish between minimum and maximum presidential authority. Yet Jackson had to decide one way or the other on the president's action in *Youngstown*, which was a minimum case, and the way he decided implied that the minimum was not enough to stand constitutional scrutiny. Those who deny that the president has a constitutional monopoly in foreign affairs, therefore, have seen *Youngstown* as the answer to *Curtiss-Wright* and as the judicial vindication of "Congress's role in the foreign-policy decision-making process."[20] Jackson made the president and Congress share in foreign policy, in varying degrees, depending on how they worked together. For him, "sole organ" was clearly no warrant for sole power. Who is right or wrong in this dispute is likely to go on being argued as long as we have a foreign policy, because it is as much a struggle for power and policy between the branches of government, whenever they disagree, as it is about constitutional interpretation.

A great constitutional scholar, Edward S. Corwin, was asked where the Constitution vested authority to determine the course of American foreign policy. "Many persons are inclined to answer offhand 'in the President,' " he replied, "but they would be hard put to it, if challenged, to point out any definite statement to this effect in the Constitution itself." What the Constitution actually says, he maintained, "is an invitation to struggle for the privilege of directing American foreign policy."[21] Yet it is doubtful whether the Constitution actually says even this much. It has invited a struggle more by what it does not say than by what it does say. But Corwin was on to something deeper—the "struggle."

This struggle began in the infancy of the Republic and still goes on. It is in form a constitutional struggle, yet a democracy which conceives of itself as the rule of law, not of men, can ill afford to take such a struggle lightly.

4

Another aspect of the struggle may be shown as it has gone back and forth in this century.

Theodore Roosevelt was the kind of president who chose to act with undisguised contempt for Congress. "I took the [Panama] Canal Zone and let Congress debate," he boasted in 1911, "and while the debate goes on the canal does too."[22] But he was followed in office by William Howard Taft, who went back to the more traditional view. "The President," Taft said in 1915, "can exercise no power which cannot be fairly and reasonably traced to some specific grant of power or justly implied and included within such express grant as proper and necessary to its exercise. Such specific grant must be either in the Federal Constitution or in an act of Congress passed in pursuance thereof. There is no undefined residuum of power which he can exercise because it seems to him to be in the public interest."[23] Taft knew something about the Constitution; he soon became chief justice of the Supreme Court.

Then came Woodrow Wilson, who advocated what amounted to a free hand for the president in foreign affairs. "The initiative in foreign affairs, which the President possesses without any restriction whatever," he said in 1907, "is virtually the power to control them absolutely."[24] He repeatedly acted imperiously, as in the dispatch of an American expeditionary force to Siberia in 1919, with virtually no congressional consultation. Whereupon the Senate took revenge by refusing to approve the Treaty of Versailles and thus permit the United States to join his great hope, the League of Nations. A long period of "isolationism" followed, requiring little presidential initiative.

The issue did not become acute again until President Franklin D. Roosevelt was faced with Britain's military collapse in 1940. He handled the "destroyers deal"—trading fifty U.S. destroyers for the lease of some British naval bases—very much the way Jefferson had dealt with the Louisiana Purchase. Roosevelt, too, knew that his action was constitutionally dubious but decided to go ahead anyway without congressional approval. "Although the transaction was directly violative of at least two statutes and represented an exercise by the President of a power that by the Constitution is specifically assigned to Congress," Professor Corwin pointed out, "it was defended by Attorney General, later Justice, Jackson as resting on the power of the President as Commander-in-Chief to 'dispose' the armed forces of the United States, which was ingeniously, if not quite ingenuously, construed as the power to *dispose of* them."[25] No wonder, then, that Jackson's opinion in *Youngstown* twelve years later came as something of a surprise. Corwin could not restrain his disquiet. He called the destroyers deal "an endorsement of unrestrained autocracy in the field of our foreign relations."[26]

The Rooseveltian precedent presents the problem of presidential latitude at its most problematic. Roosevelt at least did not have any illusions about what he was doing. He knew he was stretching the prerogatives of a president to their utmost limit but felt justified in doing so by the extreme menace of a Nazi victory over the whole of Europe and its consequences for the United States. The first question that must be asked in the circumstances of a Franklin D. Roosevelt or Abraham Lincoln is: How serious, even desperate, is the situation? Very few situations can compare with theirs.

Roosevelt privately consulted with the Republican and Democratic leaderships, who supported him in his action but asked him not to submit the deal to Congress, because they were worried about its divisiveness and the possibility of defeat. Here again, the Rooseveltian precedent hardly justifies the extreme claim that presidents have an inherent power to do anything they please in foreign policy. Whatever one may think about the destroyers deal, it was clearly an exceptional act in an exceptional situation—and Roosevelt thought of it as such. Yet exceptions are dangerous unless they are handled with care. This one has not been handled with care.

Nevertheless, Roosevelt acted far more carefully when it came time to declare war. In 1941, he sent Congress the Lend-Lease Bill, which was hotly debated for two months and then passed both houses decisively. After the Japanese attack on Pearl Harbor, Congress declared war. It was, in fact, the last time a U.S. president permitted Congress to declare war before engaging U.S. armed forces in major hostilities. President Harry Truman set the precedent in 1950 by deciding on his own to send U.S. forces into combat in the Korean War without a declaration by Congress. Every president since then has done the same thing.

After World War II, the greater the power of the United States in the world, the greater have become the pretensions of the presidents to monopoly over that power. "The postwar Presidents," Arthur M. Schlesinger, Jr., noted, "though Eisenhower and Kennedy markedly less than Truman, Johnson, and Nixon, almost came to see the sharing of power with Congress in foreign policy as a derogation of the Presidency."[27]

By 1950, a leading student of American government and politics, Robert A. Dahl of Yale University, boldly attacked the contradiction between constitutional principles and political realities. He recognized that "Congressional prerogatives stipulated by constitutional theory and practice stand directly athwart presidential supremacy in foreign affairs." He was not sure of the outcome. "Is it not possible," he asked, "that in foreign policy the executive can take the substance of power and leave Congress the shadow?" If the former won out, he foresaw that we might reach the point "where the Chief Executive is a kind of constitutional dictator in foreign policy." Dahl did not rule out the possibility that such a dictatorship might come about and wrote his book in an effort to avoid it. Yet he could hardly have foreseen how far we have gone toward accepting "a kind of constitutional dictator in foreign policy."[28]

This specter has returned as the Supreme Court, especially in the Reagan years, has increasingly reflected the influence of Justice Sutherland's one-sided *Curtiss-Wright* opinion in favor of presidential preeminence over Justice Jackson's more cooperative *Youngstown* view. One constitutional scholar, Professor Harold Koh, has noted:

> In short, far from maintaining a rough balance in the congressional-executive tug-of-war, the Court's decisions on the merits of foreign-affairs claims have encouraged a steady flow of policy-making power from Congress to the executive. Through unjustifiably deferential techniques of statutory construction, since Vietnam the courts have read *Curtiss-Wright* and its progeny virtually to supplant the constitutional vision of *Youngstown*. As a result, in the years leading up to the Iran-contra affair, the courts became the president's accomplices in an extraordinary process of statutory inversion. It is hardly surprising, then, that Oliver North should have cited *Curtiss-Wright* to Congress as the legal basis justifying all of his action during the Iran-contra affair.[29]

Oliver North was not the only one to cite *Curtiss-Wright*. In fact, this fifty-year-old opinion, so dubious in its rationale and application, has been blown up into the main legal basis on which to defend the Reagan administration's handling of the Iran-contra affairs. Representative Henry J. Hyde of Illinois also cited *Curtiss-Wright* to suggest that Congress through the Boland Amendment could not "bind and gag the Executive department in the conduct of foreign policy in Nicaragua."[30]

But a more serious, official effort was made by Charles J. Cooper, head of the Office of Legal Counsel of the Justice Department. Soon after the exposure of the Iran-contra affairs, Cooper produced a memorandum for Attorney General Meese which sought to justify President Reagan's action in withholding notification to Congress of his dealings with Iran. In order to inflate presidential power to the maximum and reduce the congressional component to a minimum, Cooper cited *Curtiss-Wright* no fewer than seven times. It was, he claimed, the "leading case," in which the Supreme Court had allegedly recognized the president's "far-reaching discretion to act on his own authority in managing the external relations of the country."[31]

Cooper, who had been brought into the diversion-induced crisis at the last minute by Meese, had been out of law school for only four years when he had obtained a job at the Justice Department. Four years later, he was made the chief legal authority in the department, although he admitted that he had not even known what a Finding was before the first week of November 1986.[32] The president as "sole organ," which had originally referred to communications with foreign nations, was now inflated to mean "managing the external relations of the country" on the president's "own authority."

The use of expansive circumlocutions has been the main technique for magnifying the president's power in foreign policy. There is no telling where words like "managing" begin or end, with the result that the president's power becomes indefinitely extensible. When an effort is made to set any limit on his power, the presidential reaction is predictably hostile and uncompromising.

Such an effort was made as a direct result of the Iran-contra affairs. It was the only piece of serious legislation offered as a consequence of the affairs. Its fate is revelatory.

5

In July 1989, Senator Daniel Patrick Moynihan introduced a bill to forestall one of the means used by the Reagan administration to evade the Boland Amendment. The bill sought to prohibit "soliciting or diverting funds to carry out activities for which the United States assistance is prohibited." A Boland Amendment had prohibited U.S. assistance to the contras; the Reagan administration had solicited and obtained foreign or third-country funds to assist the contras. Moynihan's bill made such an evasion of Congress's express intention a felony. It was debated in the Senate on July 17–18, 1989.

The debate was held in the face of a threat by President Bush to veto the bill if it ever passed. Meanwhile, the State Department sent a representative, Sally Cummins, from the Office of the Legal Adviser, to appear on May 18, 1989, before the Senate Foreign Relations Committee. Later, letters were sent by Assistant Attorney General Carol T. Crawford of the Office of Legislative Affairs and Under Secretary of State Lawrence S. Eagleburger, both dated July 17, 1989.

These three efforts to head off the bill charged that it violated the president's prerogative in foreign affairs. They made this claim in different but similar ways:

Cummins: . . . it is certainly an intrusion on the President's ability under the Constitution to carry out his responsibilities and obligation to conduct foreign policy.

Crawford: In particular, it has long been recognized that the President, both personally and through his subordinates in the executive branch, determines and articulates the Nation's foreign policy. *See* statement of John Marshall . . . ; *Curtiss-Wright* . . .

Eagleburger: . . . an impermissible intrusion on the President's constitutional prerogatives . . . this proposed amendment would seriously impair the President's ability to carry out his Constitutional responsibility to conduct relations with foreign governments . . . [33]

We have here the terms "conduct" and "determines" as the key to the president's role in foreign policy. Neither word is in the Constitution. Neither word appears in Marshall's 1799 speech or in Justice Sutherland's 1936 dicta. They are part of the linguistic game of smuggling in verbal switches in order to give the president far more power in foreign affairs than the Constitution conceivably provides for. "Conduct" has been taken to mean something as limited as "communicate" or "negotiate" and also something as extreme as "make" or "determine." Crawford's letter used "determine" in two different senses within the space of three paragraphs. She first made it apply to "form and manner" and then to "foreign policy"—the former relating to style, the latter to substance. Whatever the language, the purpose has remained the same—to deprive Congress of any share in the shaping of foreign policy. [34]

But most revealing of all was the debate between Senator Moynihan, sponsor of the bill, and Senator Helms, its chief opponent. In a strange way, the latter's contribution did more than anything else to illuminate what was really at stake.

Moynihan agreed that it was up to the president "to conduct the foreign policy of the United States." But the problem is how to construe "conduct." He pointed out that Article I, Section 8, of the Constitution gave Congress powers "singularly associated with foreign policy, with defense policy." It then provided for Congress "to make all laws" necessary and proper to execute the foregoing powers. Congress's law, in the instance of the Boland Amendment, had been flagrantly flouted by the presidential expedient of soliciting and distributing foreign funds. The issue was nothing less than whether the United States was a government of laws:

> It is the essence of a government of laws, a constitutional government, that congressional mandates must be obeyed. . . . That is what a system of laws is about. It is in that spirit that we offer a direct, simple amendment that says what Congress prohibits may not be countermanded. [35]

Helms's argument was ingenious as well as ingenuous. He did not take refuge in double-talk about what John Marshall had said in 1799 or Justice Sutherland in 1936. In essence, his view was not altogether different from the traditional one; he diverged from it in a peculiarly shifty way. He agreed that the president could not pursue a policy which Congress had countermanded by withholding appropriations for it. But he gave the president a way out:

Congress has the power to withhold the appropriations necessary to provide the means to execute a policy if it disagrees with that policy. But please observe carefully, Mr. President, that Congress has only the power of the purse, period.

Congress has no constitutional power to prohibit, let alone criminalize, a foreign policy which any President wishes to pursue. If the policy can be implemented without the expenditure of funds, Congress can have no effect on the outcome in any manner under the Constitution of the United States. [36]

Here was the nub of the matter: "if the policy can be implemented without the expenditure of funds." But what if the policy can only be implemented *with* the expenditure of funds—but *not* the funds of the United States? In the case in point, the funds for the contras came from private sources and third countries explicitly or implicitly solicited by the president and his agents.

The implication is that the president can make and implement his own foreign policy without or against the will of Congress so long as he uses nonappropriated money, even from foreign countries. Yet these private and third-country funds were not made available to President Reagan as if he were a private individual, for his own ends; they were given to the president of the United States on behalf of a national, not an individual, purpose. The president met with and thanked donors in the White House. They had been persuaded to contribute by a lieutenant colonel of the U.S. Marine Corps with an office in the White House, who spoke to them as a representative of the president.

The question arises: Is the president exempted from a constitutional imperative and the principle of accountability by the device of obtaining private or third-country money? Since this is precisely what President Reagan did in the case of Saudi Arabia and Taiwan, these nations substituted for Congress in the making and carrying out of American foreign policy. They broke the constitutional umbilical cord between the president and Congress and made the president "a kind of constitutional dictator in foreign policy"—if one accepts Senator Helms's interpretation of the Constitution.

A study by Professor Kate Stith, "Congress' Power of the Purse," published before the presentation of Moynihan's bill, clearly sets forth the impermissibility of using nonappropriated funds to thwart the will of Congress:

If the Executive could avoid limitations imposed by Congress in appropriations legislation—by independently financing its activities with private funds, transferring funds among appropriations accounts, or selling government assets and services—this would vitiate the foundational constitutional decision to empower Congress to determine what accounts shall be undertaken in the name of the United States

Federal agencies may not resort to nonappropriation financing *because their activities are authorized only to the extent of their appropriations.* Accordingly, without legislative permission, a federal agency may not resort to private funds to supplement its appropriations because it has no authority to engage in the additional activity on which it would spend the private funds.[37]

Yet Helms immeasurably clarified the issue by being half right. He agreed that the president cannot act alone if he needs funds which only Congress can appropriate. That he should be able to act alone so long as he has private or third-country funds is a reductio ad absurdum of the argument. It puts wealthy donors or foreign countries in a position to conduct, determine, or make American foreign policy—whichever term would best fit the occasion—by providing funds to, or withholding them from, the president. This is "sharing" power, but with a foreign country, not with the American Congress.

Moynihan's amendment passed both the Senate and the House of Representatives. It was vetoed by President Bush on November 21, 1989, on the ground that it was "an unacceptable risk that it will chill the conduct of our Nation's foreign affairs." The veto presented the risk that the third-country shenanigans of the Reagan administration, in which Bush had played such a prominent part, could be repeated.

The Constitution—pushed and pulled, twisted and battered so much over the decades—has shown an amazing resilience and vitality through two centuries of social and economic change. Styles in constitutional interpretation have alternated before, and there is always hope that the latest is not the last. Not every dispute over a clause in the Constitution is equally ominous. Yet the doctrine of the bifurcated presidency does not present an ordinary danger. It strikes at the very heart of the Constitution as we have known it—a constitution that is not authoritarian in foreign policy and democratic in domestic policy, that gives the president and Congress a share in both, and that provides checks and balances for both.

The question is no longer whether the president has some special prerogatives in foreign policy by virtue of his unique status as the elected representative of all the people. It is whether he alone can "make," "manage," or "conduct" foreign policy. The idea that the president and his agents can do anything they please in foreign policy brought on the Iran-contra affairs. This idea percolated down simplistically to Poindexter and North and made them feel that they were empowered to act with impunity in their president's name.

Not every dispute over the Constitution endangers it. This one, however, is qualitatively different. An authoritarian, autocratic presidency in "the management of foreign relations" is still a clear and present danger, "most susceptible of abuse of all the trusts committed to a Government." And whatever one may think of the constitutional issue, there remains the question: Do we want that kind of presidency?

6

It is not enough to recognize that each branch of the American government has a share in shaping foreign as well as domestic policy. Each branch can participate only if it is willing to make a serious effort to uphold its share of responsibility. Such an effort was not made in the Iran-contra affairs, with the result that the president and his proxies were able to go their own way for so long.

Indeed there was little to admire in the behavior of the highest American leaders. With few exceptions, the safeguards in the system failed to operate, and when some alarms did go off, it was almost too late.

President Reagan clearly set the main policy but refused to take responsibility for it. When the storm broke, he behaved as if he could get off scot-free by denying that he had known what had been going on. In the case of the diversion of funds from the Iran arms sales to the Nicaraguan contras, he chose to defend himself on the ground that he had not taken care, as if ignorance made him innocent.

Reagan was not unsuccessful in this ploy. The Tower Report is at its worst in its verdict on what was wrong with President Reagan's handling of these affairs. The emphasis is put on his "management style" instead of on his political decisions. Most blame is put on Chief of Staff Regan, who is said to bear "primary responsibility for the chaos that descended upon the White House when such disclosure did occur." In fact, the disclosure was primarily handled by Attorney General Meese, and Regan, whatever his shortcomings, was not responsible for National Security Advisers McFarlane and Poindexter.[38] Reagan's "management style" undoubtedly left much to be desired, but in these affairs it was distinctly secondary to the basic direction of his policy.

Congress was an easy, almost willing, victim of the administration's machinations. After passing the critical Boland Amendment in 1984, the intelligence committees barely paid attention to their responsibility for "oversight" over the way it was carried out. The press, not the committees, succeeded in getting wind of North's activities and in forcing the committees to go through the motions of asking for information. The efforts made in 1985 to get information from McFarlane and in 1986 from Poindexter were derisory. Both national security advisers easily misled the committees, which made no effort to follow up on the bald assurances given them.

The Majority in the congressional committees' Final Report on the

Iran-contra affairs virtuously upheld the constitutional role of checks and balances in which both Congress and the executive branch "are given specific foreign policy powers." But it had nothing to say about how Congress had gone about fulfilling its share of these powers. In its twenty-seven recommendations, none suggested that Congress had done anything worth criticizing, and they mainly called for strengthening the oversight capabilities of the intelligence committees by "the acquisition of an audit staff."[39]

The authors of the Minority report spent most of their critical faculties with respect to Congress on "the need to patch leaks," admittedly as common in the executive branch as in the legislative branch. None of its recommendations had anything to do with the way Congress had failed to live up to its responsibilities in 1985 and 1986.[40]

The cases of Secretary of State Shultz and Secretary of Defense Weinberger were more complicated. When the arms deals with Iran were first considered, they left no doubt that they were strenuously opposed to them. Shultz was at first dubious about getting third-country money for the contras and even cited then Chief of Staff James Baker to the effect that it was an "impeachable offense." But once President Reagan decided in favor of the arms deals, they folded their tents and stole away. By telling Poindexter that he did not want to know about the "operational details" of the Iran affair, Shultz seemed deliberately to have chosen to stay out of the line of fire. Shultz also lent himself to seriocomic "tin-cup diplomacy" to relieve the Sultan of Brunei of some of his money for the benefit of the contras. Yet a new Shultz, breathing fire, did in November 1986 what he had failed to do for months past—he refused to be a party to the falsification of the November 1985 "horror story" and virtually forced President Reagan to face the unpleasant facts. Weinberger had grimly suppressed his wrath at the dealings with Iran and then, after the damage had been done, had let it out—at Shultz. The chapter in his memoirs dealing with "Iran and the Hostages" is a travesty of the actual course of events.

In effect, by cutting out Shultz and Weinberger after January 1986 and thus signaling to them that he did not want to hear any more of their opposition, Reagan gutted the National Security Council until he called it together in the very last days of his political crisis. He depended wholly on its misnamed staff under Poindexter, and in fact on the latter alone. The Council had been intended to give the president the benefit of a structured system of advice from his two senior cabinet members, the heads of departments with ample, far-flung resources. The only other statutory member was the vice president, who, in this case, did little more than echo his master's voice.

Almost throughout the Iran-contra affairs, President Reagan made policy without Congress or the National Security Council. Few presidents have been as little prepared as he was to be his own secretary of state.

Yet reelection to a second term in 1984 and the adulation of true believers seem to have instilled in him mild delusions of grandeur that made him determined to hear only what he wanted to hear and do only what he wanted to do.

In a parliamentary system, Shultz and Weinberger would almost certainly have been obliged to resign if they had opposed a major policy which they saw was leading the country to costly failure and public derision. In the preceding Carter administration, Secretary of State Cyrus Vance had resigned in protest against the ill-fated mission to rescue the hostages taken in the American embassy in Tehran. This precedent was not followed by Shultz and Weinberger, with the result that they permitted months to go by without doing much of anything to prevent or even protest against what they knew to be wrong. Weinberger merely sulked in self-imposed silence. Shultz at least woke up in the last days of November 1986 and, pressed by his legal adviser, Abraham Sofaer, to take a stand, compelled President Reagan and Attorney General Meese to face the issue. If more officials had behaved as resolutely and honorably earlier, the country could have been spared the trauma of the Iran-contra affairs.

The constitutional division of labor in the shaping of foreign policy does not make for quick and easy decisions or actions. Friction is built into the system, and the more disagreement there is, the more friction. Justice Louis D. Brandeis best expressed the great tradition in 1926:

> The doctrine of the separation of powers was adopted by the Convention of 1787, not to promote efficiency but to preclude the exercise of arbitrary power. The purpose was, not to avoid friction, but, by means of the inevitable friction incident to the distribution of the governmental powers among three departments, to save the people from autocracy.[41]

There can be no other way if we are to be true to what we have long professed to believe in. The best in our history is based on the premise that the dangers of arbitrary power are vastly greater than the disadvantages of shared power. If we give up this premise, we must become a very different country, with a very different constitutional foundation.

The Iran-contra affairs showed where arbitrary power can lead us. They were made possible by a breakdown in the American system of government. The most important thing that we can learn from them is what broke down and why. If the lesson is not learned, we can expect similar trouble every time a president takes some critical action in foreign policy on his own and overreaches himself. The bifurcated presidency has not been put behind us, nor is there any reason to believe that the three branches of government have risen to their responsibilities. Until they do, the Iran-contra affairs will be unfinished business.

Who's Who

Abrams, Elliott: Assistant Secretary of State for Inter-American Affairs

Allen, Charles E.: CIA National Intelligence Officer for Counterterrorism

Allen, Richard V.: National Security Adviser, 1981

Arias Sánchez, Oscar: President of Costa Rica, 1986

Armacost, Michael H.: Under Secretary of State for Political Affairs

Armitage, Richard L.: Assistant Secretary of Defense for International Security Affairs

Artiano, Martin L.: Partner of David C. Fischer; associated with Channell

Bahramani, Ali Hashemi: the "Second Channel," also known as "the Relative" or nephew of Speaker Rafsanjani

Baker, James A., III: White House Chief of Staff, 1981–85

Bandar, bin Sultan: Prince, Saudi Arabia; Ambassador to the United States

Barnes, Michael: Representative; Chairman of House Subcommittee on Western Hemisphere Affairs, 1985

Ben-Jousef, Avraham: Israeli purchasing agent in New York, 1985

Bermúdez, Enrique: Military leader of contras

Boland, Edward P.: Democratic Representative from Massachusetts

Buchanan, Patrick J.: White House Director of Communications

Buckley, William A.: CIA Station Chief in Lebanon; taken hostage in Beirut in March 1984; died in captivity June 1985

Bush, George: Vice President of the United States, 1981–88

Calero, Adolfo: A leader of the Nicaraguan Democratic Force (FDN)

Calero, Mario: Brother of Adolfo; in charge of NHAO warehouse in New Orleans

Cannistraro, Vincent: NSC staff, 1984–86

Casey, William J.: Director of Central Intelligence Agency, 1981–87; died May 6, 1987

Castillo, Tomás: Alias of Joseph F. Fernandez

Cave, George: Retired CIA officer; consultant to CIA, 1986; Farsi-speaking participant in negotiations with Iranians

Channell, Carl R. (Spitz): Fund-raiser for contras; founder of National Endowment for the Preservation of Liberty and other organizations

Chardy, Alfonso: Reporter of *Miami Herald*

Clark, William P.: National Security Adviser, 1982

Clarridge, Dewey R. (Duane): Chief of CIA Latin American Division, 1981–84; Chief of European Division, 1984–86

Clines, Thomas G.: Former CIA official, associate of Richard V. Secord

Conrad, Daniel L.: Associate of Carl R. Channell

Cooper, Charles J.: Assistant Attorney General, Office of Legal Counsel

Cooper, William J.: Pilot of resupply plane shot down over northern Nicaragua on October 5, 1986

Coors, Joseph: Contributor to Channell's fund-raising for contras

Coy, Craig P.: Lieutenant Commander, U.S. Coast Guard; aide of Oliver North

Crowe, William J., Jr.: Admiral; Chairman of Joint Chiefs of Staff

Cruz, Arturo, Sr.: Contra leader

deGraffenreid, Kenneth: NSC staff, Senior Director of Intelligence Programs

Duemling, Robert W.: Head of Nicaraguan Humanitarian Assistance Office (NHAO)

Dutton, Robert C.: Colonel (ret.), U.S. Air Force; associate of Richard Secord and Oliver North in contra affair

Earl, Robert: Lieutenant Colonel, U.S. Marine Corps; aide of Oliver North

Fahd ibn Abdul-Aziz: King, Saudi Arabia

Fernandez, Joseph F. (José): CIA Station Chief in Costa Rica (alias "Tomás Castillo")

Fiers, Alan: CIA Chief of Central American Task Force

Fischer, David C.: Former Special Assistant to President Reagan; associated with Channell; partner of Artiano

Fortier, Donald R.: Deputy National Security Adviser, 1985–86

Fraser, Donald: One of two Canadians falsely alleged to have threatened Adnan Khashoggi if he did not repay a mythical loan of $10 million

Fuller, Graham L.: CIA National Intelligence Officer for Near East and South Asia

Furmark, Roy M.: Associate of Adnan Khashoggi

Gadd, Richard B.: Lieutenant Colonel (ret.), U.S. Air Force; associated with Secord in contra affair

Garwood, Ellen: Contributor to Channell's National Endowment for the Preservation of Liberty

Gates, Robert M.: CIA Deputy Director, 1986

George, Clair: CIA Deputy Director of Operations

Ghorbanifar, Manucher: Iranian émigré; middleman in Iran-Israel-U.S. deals

Goldwater, Barry: Senator; Chairman of Senate Committee on Intelligence, 1984

Gomez, Francis D. (Frank): Associated with Richard R. Miller in International Business Communications

Gomez, Max: Alias of Felix Rodriguez

Gorman, Paul F.: General; head of U.S. Army's Southern Command

Green, Thomas C.: Attorney for Richard Secord; temporarily represented Oliver North in November 1986

Gregg, Donald P.: Vice President Bush's National Security Adviser

Hakim, Albert: Naturalized U.S. citizen of Iranian birth; business partner of Richard Secord

Hall, Fawn: Secretary of Oliver North

Hamilton, Lee H.: Representative; Chairman of House Intelligence Committee

Hasenfus, Eugene: Shot down over Nicaragua on October 5, 1986

Hashemi, Cyrus: Naturalized U.S. citizen of Iranian extraction; charged with exporting weapons to Iran; tried to make deal with John Shaheen

Hashemi, General Manucher: Former head of counterespionage Department VII of SAVAK, Shah's secret police

Haskell, William Charles (alias "Robert Olmstead"): Sent to Costa Rica by Oliver North to acquire land

Hill, Charles: Executive Assistant to Secretary of State Shultz

Hunt, Nelson Bunker: Contributor to Channell's fund-raising

Hussein, Saddam: Ruler of Iraq

Jacobsen, David P.: Director of the American University Hospital in Beirut; American hostage in Lebanon, released November 2, 1986

Jenco, Lawrence: Catholic priest, American hostage in Lebanon; released July 26, 1986

Juchniewicz, Edward S.: CIA Associate Deputy Director of Operations

Kangarlou, Mohsen: Iranian representative

Karoubi, Hassan: Known as "First Iranian" to negotiate in Iran affair

Keel, Alton G., Jr.: Deputy National Security Adviser, 1986

Kelly, John H.: U.S. Ambassador to Lebanon, 1986

Kemp, Geoffrey: NSC staff, Senior Director for Near East and South Asian Affairs, 1984

Khamenei, Ali: President of Iran

Khashoggi, Adnan: Saudi Arabian entrepreneur; associated with Manucher Ghorbanifar in arms-for-hostages deals

Khomeini, Ruhollah: Ayatollah, head of Iranian movement that overthrew Shah in February 1979

Kimche, David: Director General of Israeli Foreign Ministry, 1985–86

Kirkpatrick, Jeane J.: U.S. Ambassador to the United Nations

Koch, Noel C.: Deputy Assistant Secretary of Defense for International Security Affairs

Ledeen, Michael A.: Consultant to National Security Adviser McFarlane, 1985; first intermediary with Israelis, May 1985

Masoudi, Ibrahim al- (False Saudi Arabian Prince Ebrohim bin Aboul-Aziz bin Saud al-Masoudi); probably an Iranian, Mousalreza Ebrahim Zadeh

McFarlane, Robert C.: Deputy National Security Adviser, 1982–83; National Security Adviser, October 1983–December 1985

McMahon, John N.: CIA Deputy Director, 1982–86

Meese, Edwin, III: White House Counselor, 1984; Attorney General, 1985–86

Menges, Constantine C.: CIA National Intelligence Officer for Latin America, 1981–83; same assignment, NSC staff, 1983–85

Miller, Ernest: One of two Canadians falsely alleged to have lent $10 million to Adnan Khashoggi (see Donald Fraser)

Miller, Johnathan: Worked in Office of Public Diplomacy (LPD) under Otto J. Reich until August 1985; NSC staff until May 1986; Deputy Assistant to the President for Management, resigned in May 1987

Miller, Richard R.: President of International Business Communications (IBC); associate of Francis D. Gomez; worked with Carl R. Channell

Moellering, John: Lieutenant General, Special Assistant to Admiral William J. Crowe, Jr.

Monge, Luis Alberto: President of Costa Rica, 1985

Montazeri, Ayatollah Hussein Ali: Iranian rival of Speaker of the Majlis Rafsanjani

Moussavi, Mir Hussein: Prime Minister of Iran

Moynihan, Daniel Patrick: Senator; Vice Chairman of Senate Committee on Intelligence, 1984

Murphy, Richard W.: Assistant Secretary of State for the Near East and South Asia

Najafabadi, Ali Hossein or Hadi: Higher Iranian official who met with American delegation in Tehran, May 25–28, 1986

Najavi, Ali: Alleged name of Iranian who met with American delegation in Tehran, May 25, 1986

Negroponte, John: U.S. Ambassador to Honduras, 1985

Newington, Barbara: Contributor to Channell's fund-raising for contras

Nidal, Abu (Sabry al-Banna): Palestinian terrorist; head of Al Fatah Revolutionary Council

Nimrodi, Yaacov: Israeli middleman

Nir, Amiram: Adviser to Israeli Prime Minister Shimon Peres on counterterrorism

North, Oliver L.: Lieutenant Colonel, U.S. Marine Corps; Assistant Deputy Director for Political-Military Affairs, NSC staff

O'Boyle, William B.: Contributor to Channell's fund-raising for contras

Owen, Robert W.: Aide of Oliver North ("Courier")

Pastora, Edén: Dissident contra leader

Peres, Shimon: Israeli Prime Minister, 1984–86

Perot, H. Ross: Texas tycoon who tried to ransom American hostages

Platt, Nicholas: Executive Secretary of State Department

Poindexter, John M.: Vice Admiral, U.S. Navy; Deputy National Security Adviser, 1983–85; National Security Adviser, 1986

Qaddafi, Muammar al-: Libyan dictator

Quintero, Rafael: Cuban-American; former CIA agent; associate of Secord and Clines in contra affair

Rabin, Yitzhak: Israeli Minister of Defense, 1984–86

Rafsanjani, Ali Akbar Hashemi: Speaker of Majlis (Iranian Parliament)

Raymond, Walter, Jr.: Head of Central American Public Diplomacy Task Force

Razmara: Associate of Theodore G. Shackley

Reagan, Ronald: President of the United States, 1981–88

Regan, Donald T.: Chief of Staff, 1985–86

Reich, Otto J.: Director of Office of Public Diplomacy for Latin America and the Caribbean (LPD)

Reynolds, William Bradford: Assistant Attorney General, Civil Rights Division

Richardson, John N., Jr.: Chief of Staff to Attorney General Meese

Robelo, Alfonso: Contra leader

Robinette, Glenn A.: Former CIA employee hired to arrange for construction of security fence around North's home

Rodriguez, Felix: Former CIA employee recruited for resupply operation (alias "Max Gomez")

Rowland, Rowland W. (Tiny): Head of British Lonrho group of companies

Samii, Ali: Iranian representative (also known as "the Monster" and "the Engine")

Sawyer, Wallace (Buzz): Copilot of resupply plane shot down over northern Nicaragua, October 5, 1986

Schwimmer, Adolph (Al): Israeli middleman

Sciaroni, Bretton G.: Only professional member of President's Intelligence Oversight Board

Secord, Richard V.: Major General, U.S. Air Force (ret.); North's chief associate in the contra affair; partner of Albert Hakim

Shackley, Theodore G.: CIA Associate Director of Operations, 1976–79; retired to head "risk management" firm, Research Associates, Inc.

Shahabadi, Dr.: Head of Iranian purchasing office in Hamburg, West Germany

Shaheen, John: Friend of William Casey; reports offer in 1984 of Cyrus Hashemi to gain release of American hostages in Lebanon in return for U.S. arms

Shultz, George: Secretary of State, 1982–88

Sigur, Gaston J., Jr.: NSC consultant for East Asian and Pacific Affairs, 1985; Assistant Secretary of State for East Asian and Pacific Affairs, 1986

Singlaub, John K.: Major General, U.S. Army (ret.); solicited funds for contras

Sofaer, Abraham: Legal Adviser, State Department

Sporkin, Stanley: CIA General Counsel

Steele, James J.: Colonel, U.S. Army; commander of U.S. Military Group (MilGroup) in El Salvador

Suazo, Roberto: President of Honduras, 1985

Sultan of Brunei (Haji Hassanal Bolkiah Mu'izzaddin Waddaulah)

Tabatabai, Sadegh: Iranian businessman in London, used by Albert Hakim to arrange for "Second Channel"

Tambs, Lewis A.: U.S. Ambassador to Costa Rica

Teicher, Howard J.: Former Senior Director of Political-Military Affairs, NSC staff

Thompson, Paul B.: Counsel, NSC staff

Twetten, Tom: Chief of CIA Near East Division

Walker, David: British provider of mercenaries

Watson, Samuel J., III: Deputy Assistant for National Security Affairs to Vice President Bush

Weinberger, Caspar: Secretary of Defense, 1981–88

Weir, Reverend Benjamin: U.S. hostage in Lebanon, released September 15, 1985

Wilson, Edwin P.: Former CIA official who supplied explosives to Libya

Zucker, Willard: Hakim's attorney in Switzerland

Chronology

1979

January 16. Shah Mohammed Reza Pahlavi leaves Iran, ending his 37-year rule.

February 1. Ayatollah Ruhollah Khomeini returns after an exile of 15 years and takes power.

July 17. In Nicaragua, the dictatorship of Anastasio Somoza collapses. A Sandinista National Liberation Front takes power a few days later.

November 4. U.S. embassy in Tehran stormed by Iranian extremists and 52 U.S. hostages held for 14 months.

1980

April 7. President Jimmy Carter bans trade with Iran.

April 25. A U.S. rescue mission to free American hostages fails.

September 22. Iraq attacks Iran.

1981

January 20. Ronald Reagan inaugurated as president of the United States.

January 20. American hostages in Iran freed.

February. Reagan administration suspends all aid to Nicaragua.

August 4. Oliver L. North joins National Security Council staff for three-year period.

1982

June 8. President Reagan proposes Project Democracy in speech before British Parliament.

December 1. First Boland Amendment, attached to omnibus appropriations bill for fiscal year 1983, signed, to go into effect from December 21, 1983, to December 8, 1984.

1983

March–April. State Department launches Operation Staunch to prevent arms from other countries to Iran.

May 4. President Reagan announces "covert aid" for Nicaraguan contras.

October 17. Robert C. McFarlane appointed national security adviser.

October. North accompanies Kissinger Commission to Central America.

December 8. Second Boland Amendment signed into law, in effect from December 12, 1984, to September 30, 1985.

1984

President Reagan tells National Security Adviser McFarlane to keep the contras together "body and soul" (exact date unstated).

January 13. Geoffrey Kemp, NSC staff's senior director for Near East and South Asian

Affairs, proposes reevaluation of U.S. policy toward Iran with program of covert activities to help Iranian exiles.

Spring. North becomes "point man" with Nicaraguan contras.

Summer. Former Air Force Major General Richard V. Secord joins North to aid contras.

July. Robert W. Owen attaches himself to North as "courier" and "secret agent."

August 31. National Security Adviser McFarlane requests formal interagency analysis of U.S. policy on Iran; completed in October; implies "relative American powerlessness."

October. North ordered to attend Naval War College but obtains one-year extension.

November 20. Shackley and Razmara meet with General Manucher Hashemi in Hamburg, West Germany, and are introduced to Manucher Ghorbanifar, Dr. Shahabadi, and Hassan Karoubi.

December 11. Shackley informed State Department not interested in Ghorbanifar's overtures.

1985

April. Khashoggi and Furmark meet with Ghorbanifar in Hamburg (according to Khashoggi).

Early spring. Ghorbanifar and Cyrus Hashemi meet with Israelis Adolph Schwimmer and Yaacov Nimrodi in London, Geneva, and Israel (Israeli Historical Chronology).

May 2. Ghorbanifar writes report for Israeli intelligence agency, Mossad, on Iranian political affairs (according to Raviv and Melman).

May 4 or 5. Michael A. Ledeen meets with Israeli Prime Minister Peres to get information on Iran; soon reports to McFarlane.

May 17. Graham Fuller, CIA national intelligence officer for Near East and South Asia, submits memorandum, "Toward a Policy on Iran," to CIA Director Casey advocating arms to Iran through "friendly states."

June 11. Donald Fortier and Howard Teicher present "provocative" proposal to encourage Western allies to provide "selected military equipment" to Iran.

June 23. North learns that Iran has discovered false microfiche prices.

July 3. David Kimche informs McFarlane on Israeli contacts with alleged Iranian officials. Ledeen soon meets with Schwimmer.

July 8. Hassan Karoubi, alleged leader of Iranian "moderates," meets with Khashoggi, Ghorbanifar, Kimche, Schwimmer, and Nimrodi in Geneva.

July 10. Schwimmer meets with Ledeen to pass on Ghorbanifar's proposal that Israel sell TOW missiles to Iran.

July 13. President Reagan enters hospital for abdominal surgery.

July 16. McFarlane visits president in hospital and gets approval for Israel to negotiate an arms-for-hostages deal.

July (end). Ledeen meets with Ghorbanifar in Tel Aviv in presence of Kimche, Schwimmer, and Nimrodi; Ghorbanifar proposes an arms-for-hostages deal.

August 2. Kimche meets with McFarlane in Washington; asks for U.S. approval of Israeli sale of U.S.-made arms to Iran in exchange for hostages.

August 3 or 4. More U.S. arms flown to Iran.

August 6. Meeting in White House of President Reagan and principal advisers. Secretary of State Shultz and Secretary of Defense Weinberger strongly oppose sale of arms to Iran. No decision reached.

August 20. First delivery of 96 TOW missiles by Israel to Iran.

September 15. Second delivery of 408 TOW missiles by Israel to Iran.

September 15. Reverend Benjamin Weir released.

October 7. Ledeen meets with Hassan Karoubi, Ghorbanifar, Kimche, Schwimmer, and Nimrodi in Geneva.

October 7. Italian cruise ship *Achille Lauro* seized by Palestinian hijackers.

October 17. President Reagan meets with Carl R. Channell and his contributors.

November 18–25. The "horror story"—the miscarriage of the attempt to deliver Israeli missiles to Iran.

November 19–21. First summit meeting of President Reagan with new Soviet General Secretary Gorbachev in Geneva.

November 25. Ledeen dismissed from Iran affair.

December 5. President Reagan signs Finding No. 1.

December 7. Meeting of National Security Council, at which Secretary of State Shultz and Secretary of Defense Weinberger express strong opposition to arms deals with Iran.

December 8. McFarlane's disastrous meeting with Ghorbanifar in London.

December 10. McFarlane reports to President Reagan on unsuccessful meeting in London.

December. Amiram Nir replaces Kimche, Schwimmer, and Nimrodi as Israeli representative in Iran affair.

1986

January 2. Nir presents plan to Poindexter for Israeli sale of 1,000 TOW missiles in exchange for all U.S. hostages.

January 6. President Reagan inadvertently signs Finding No. 2.

January 7. Another meeting of National Security Council, at which Shultz and Weinberger again oppose arms deals with Iran, but President Reagan indicates he favors them.

January 11. Ghorbanifar fails another polygraph test.

January 17. President Reagan signs Finding No. 3.

January 18. Poindexter orders Secretary Weinberger to release 4,000 TOW missiles for sale to Iran.

January 18. Secord is designated "cutout" or "third party" to make arms deals with Iran.

January 18. North's name appears in *Miami Herald* in report by Alfonso Chardy.

January 22. Ghorbanifar allegedly suggests "diversion" of Iranian funds to Nicaraguan contras to North in London bathroom.

February 17. 500 TOWs delivered from Israel to Iran.

February 25. North, Nir, Secord, and Hakim meet with Ghorbanifar and Iranian representatives, Mohsen Kangarlou and Ali Samii, in Frankfurt.

March 7. North, Cave, and Twetten meet with Ghorbanifar and Nir in Paris. Ghorbanifar presents Iranian request for Hawk spare parts.

March 9–30. Telephone conversations between Ghorbanifar and Allen.

March 26. John McMahon resigns as deputy director of CIA.

April 3. Ghorbanifar meets with North and Cave in Washington.

April 3–7. North's "diversion memorandum."

April 16. Poindexter instructs North to go ahead with preparations for meeting in Tehran on condition that all hostages are freed.

April 22. Ghorbanifar arrested in Switzerland in "sting" operation, soon released.

April 30. North again named by Alfonso Chardy in *Miami Herald*.

April. Ghorbanifar, Khashoggi, and Nir meet with "Tiny" Rowland of Lonrho Group in London ostensibly to sell grain, spare parts, and weapons to Iran with Rowland's participation.

May 6. North, Nir, Cave, and Ghorbanifar meet in London, make arrangements for meeting in Tehran.

May 25. American delegation, headed by McFarlane, plus Nir, arrive in Tehran.

May 28. American delegation leaves Tehran.

June 2. Plane makes emergency landing at Santa Elena airstrip in Costa Rica, stuck in mud.

June 8. Article in *Miami Herald* by Alfonso Chardy headed "Despite Ban, U.S. Helping Contras."

June 11. Associated Press picks up above article, story appears in *Washington Post*.

June 22. North again appears in article by Alfonso Chardy in *Miami Herald*.

June 24. Representative Ronald Coleman of Texas introduces a Resolution of Inquiry seeking information about North.

June 25. Representative Dante B. Fascell, chairman of House Committee on Foreign Affairs, requests comments on Coleman Resolution from President Reagan.

June 25. CBS program *West 57th* reveals private aid network directed from White House to aid contras.

July 1. Representative Lee H. Hamilton, chairman of House Permanent Select Committee on Intelligence, requests information on pro-contra activities of Oliver North and others.

July 14. Another CBS program on aid to contras.

July 15. An article in *Washington Times*, entitled "Going After North," brings an offer by North to Poindexter to retire from NSC staff.

July 21. National Security Adviser Poindexter replies to Representatives Fascell and Hamilton with misrepresentations and evasions.

July 26. Reverend Lawrence Jenco, hostage, released.

July 27. North, Cave, Nir, and Ghorbanifar meet in Frankfurt.

July 29. Israeli Amiram Nir briefs Vice President Bush in Jerusalem.

August 4. Iran receives more Hawk spare parts.

August 6. North meets with members of House Intelligence Committee; successfully deceives them.

August 8. North, Nir, and Ghorbanifar meet in London, discuss another sequential arms-for-hostages deal.

August 8. Assistant Secretary of State Elliott Abrams solicits $10 million contribution from Brunei foreign minister in London.

August 20. Nir tells North that Iranians are complaining about missing and malfunctioning Hawk spare parts received on August 4.

August 25. Secord and Hakim meet in Brussels for the first time with Ali Hashemi Bahramani, the "Second Channel."

Summer. Khashoggi, Ghorbanifar, and Karoubi meet in Hamburg with three Israelis—David Kimche, Adolph Schwimmer, and Yaacov Nimrodi (according to Khashoggi).

September 9. Another American hostage, Frank H. Reed, director of the Lebanese International School, kidnapped in Beirut.

September 10. Costa Rican security forces close down Santa Elena airstrip.

September 12. Joseph J. Cicippio, acting comptroller of the American University in Beirut, taken hostage.

September 19. Bahramani, the "Second Channel," comes to Washington to meet with North, Secord, and Cave.

October 1. Charles E. Allen, CIA national intelligence officer for counterterrorism, expresses concern to Robert M. Gates, CIA deputy director, about "pricing" of weapons to Iran.

October 5. Sandinista forces shoot down resupply plane belonging to Secord's organization.

October 6. North, Secord, Cave, and Hakim meet with Bahramani and Samii in Frankfurt; North presents seven-point plan.

October 6. Eugene Hasenfus of downed plane captured by Nicaraguan forces.

October 7. Hakim and Iranians in Frankfurt agree on nine-point plan.

October 7. Roy M. Furmark informs CIA Director Casey of Ghorbanifar's financial troubles and intimates knowledge of the "diversion."

October 15. University students in Tehran distribute leaflets exposing McFarlane's unsuccessful mission to Iran in May.

October 16. Furmark tells Allen story of two Canadians to whom Khashoggi allegedly owed $10 million. (Khashoggi subsequently reveals that he had invented story of the Canadians to put pressure on United States.)

October 22. Furmark talks to Allen and Cave about "diversion."

October 22. North, Secord, and Nir meet in Geneva to decide on next arms shipment to Iran.

October 28. 500 TOW missiles delivered to Iran.

October 29–30. North, Secord, Cave, and Hakim meet with Bahramani and Samii in Mainz.

November 2. American hostage, David Jacobsen, director of American University Hospital in Beirut, released.

November 3. Lebanese weekly Al-Shiraa publishes partially accurate exposé of U.S.-Iran dealings, including McFarlane's mission in May 1986.

November 4. Speaker Rafsanjani gives Iranian Parliament (Majlis) a partial, tendentious account of previous U.S.-Iran dealings.

November 8–10. North, Secord, Cave, and Hakim meet with Bahramani and Samii in Geneva.

November 10. President Reagan, Secretary of State Shultz, Secretary of Defense Weinberger, and other principals meet to discuss repercussions of Al-Shiraa revelations.

November 13. President Reagan makes television speech which unsuccessfully tries to explain dealings with Iran.

November 13. National Security Adviser Poindexter for the first time briefs congressional leaders.

November 14. Secretary of State Shultz makes first attempt to change President Reagan's Iran policy.

November 16. Secretary Shultz makes embarrassing appearance on Face the Nation television program.

November 18. Legal meeting called by White House counsel Peter Wallison, which first alarms Abraham D. Sofaer, State Department legal adviser.

November 19. Secretary Shultz privately tells President Reagan he has been misinformed.

November 19. President Reagan holds disastrous press conference.

November 20. Discussion in Poindexter's office on "chronology," implying systematic deception about November 1985 "horror story."

November 20. State Department legal adviser Sofaer suspects a "cover-up."

November 21. Attorney General Meese is commissioned "to develop a coherent overview of all the facts."

November 21. Poindexter destroys copy of Finding No. 1.

November 22. Attorney General Meese's aides, William Bradford Reynolds and John N. Richardson, Jr., discover "diversion memo" in Oliver North's office.

November 23. Meese interviews North, who confirms that "diversion" was in fact carried out.

November 24. Meese briefly informs Reagan of the diversion of funds from the Iran arms sales to the Nicaraguan contras.

November 25. Poindexter offers resignation. National Security Council and congressional leaders briefed.

November 25. Press conference at which Meese gives a distorted version of the "diversion" and threatens North with possible criminal charges.

November 26. President Reagan appoints Special Review Board (Tower Board) to conduct study of NSC staff.

December 4. Senate and House of Representatives announce plans for investigation of and hearings on covert arms transactions with Iran and secret military assistance to contras.

December 13. Charles Dunbar of State Department and George Cave of CIA meet with Iranians in Frankfurt for last time.

December 19. Lawrence E. Walsh named as independent counsel to investigate arms sales to Iran and diversion of profits to contras.

Bibliography

Anderson, Martin, *Revolution* (Harcourt Brace Jovanovich, 1988).

Armstrong, Scott, Malcolm Byrne, and Tom Blanton, *Secret Military Assistance to Iran and the Contras: A Chronology of Events and Individuals* (National Security Archive, 1987).

Bartholomew, James, *The Richest Man in the World: The Sultan of Brunei* (Viking, 1989).

Bradlee, Ben, Jr., *Guts and Glory: The Rise and Fall of Oliver North* (Donald I. Fine, 1988).

Bush, George (with Victor Gold), *Looking Forward* (Doubleday, 1987; Bantam Books, 1988).

Chalfont, Lord, *By God's Will: A Portrait of the Sultan of Brunei* (Weidenfeld and Nicolson, 1989).

Congressional Quarterly, *The Iran-Contra Puzzle* (1987).

Cruz, Arturo, Jr., *Memoirs of a Counter-Revolutionary* (Doubleday, 1989).

Deaver, Michael K. (with Mickey Herskowitz), *Behind the Scenes* (Morrow, 1987).

Gutman, Roy, *Banana Diplomacy* (Simon and Schuster, 1988).

Haig, Alexander M., Jr., *Caveat: Realism, Reagan, and Foreign Policy* (Macmillan, 1984).

Kessler, Ronald, *Khashoggi: The Rise and Fall of the World's Richest Man* (Bantam Books, 1986).

Leary, William M., ed., *The Central Intelligence Agency: History and Documents* (University of Alabama Press, 1984).

Ledeen, Michael A., *Perilous Statecraft* (Scribner's, 1988).

Livingstone, Neil C., and Terrell E. Arnold, eds., *Beyond the Iran-Contra Crisis* (Lexington Books, 1988).

Martin, David C., and John Walcott, *Best Laid Plans* (Harper & Row, 1988).

Mayer, Jane, and Doyle McManus, *Landslide* (Houghton Mifflin, 1988).

McNeil, Frank, *War and Peace in Central America* (Scribner's, 1988).

Menges, Constantine C., *Inside the National Security Council* (Simon and Schuster, 1988).

Persico, Joseph E., *Casey: From the OSS to the CIA* (Viking, 1990).

Raviv, Dan, and Yossi Melman, *Every Spy a Prince* (Houghton Mifflin, 1990).

Reagan, Nancy (with William Novak), *My Turn* (Random House, 1989).

Reagan, Ronald, *An American Life* (Simon and Schuster, 1990).

Regan, Donald T., *For the Record* (Harcourt Brace Jovanovich, 1988).

Rodriguez, Felix I., and John Weisman, *Shadow Warrior* (Simon and Schuster, 1989).

Segev, Samuel, *The Iranian Triangle* (Free Press, 1988).

Speakes, Larry (with Robert Pack), *Speaking Out* (Scribner's, 1988).

Taheri, Amir, *Nest of Spies* (Pantheon, 1988).

Tanter, Raymond, *Who's at the Helm? Lessons of Lebanon* (Westview Press, 1990).

Treverton, Gregory F., *Covert Action* (Basic Books, 1987).

Weinberger, Caspar, *Fighting for Peace* (Warner Books, 1990).

Woodward, Bob, *Veil: The Secret Wars of the CIA 1981–1987* (Simon and Schuster, 1987).

Wright, Robin, *In the Name of God* (Simon and Schuster, 1989).

Key to Sources

Testimony at Joint Hearings before the House Select Committee to Investigate Covert Arms Transactions with Iran and the Senate Select Committee on Secret Military Assistance to Iran and the Nicaraguan Opposition, 1987.

The 12 volumes of this series are numbered in small print from 100-1 to 100-11; one volume contains two parts.

Appendix B of the Report of the Congressional Committees Investigating the Iran-Contra Affair contains depositions.

The 27 volumes in this series contain private testimony, the most important of which for this work are:

Notes

1. Contexts

1. Carnes Lord, *The Presidency and the Management of National Security* (Free Press, 1988), pp. 26–27.
2. B-14, pp. 367–68, for the letterhead of North's letters.
3. George Bush (with Victor Gold), *Looking Forward* (Doubleday, 1987; Bantam Books, 1988), pp. 240–41.
4. McGeorge Bundy, "The National Security Council in the 1960's," in Senator Henry M. Jackson, ed., *The National Security Council: Jackson Subcommittee Papers on Policy-Making at the Presidential Level* (Praeger, 1965), p. 278.
5. John P. Roche, "Taming the NSC," *National Review*, March 27, 1987, p. 42.
6. McFarlane, NT, p. 3923.
7. PT, p. 1281. After Poindexter was replaced by Frank Carlucci in December 1986, it was reported that the NSC staff numbered 186. About a third of the staff was made up of secretaries and support personnel; another third of technicians working at computers and advanced communication equipment; and 59 "professionals," mainly from the military and CIA, State Department personnel on temporary leave, and a few academicians, with about 15 of this group in top levels (James Bamford, *The New York Times Magazine*, January 18, 1987).
8. William M. Leary, ed., *The Central Intelligence Agency: History and Documents* (University of Alabama Press, 1984), pp. 5, 128–33.
9. National Security Council Directive 5412/2, December 28, 1955, ibid., pp. 146–49.
10. *Washington Post*, December 22, 1963.
11. Robert H. Farrell, ed., *Off the Record: The Private Papers of Harry S. Truman* (Harper & Row, 1980), p. 408.
12. Cited by Leary, *The Central Intelligence Agency*, p. 66.
13. Arthur M. Schlesinger, Jr., *A Thousand Days* (Houghton Mifflin, 1985), pp. 150, 407, 420–21, 435.
14. Theodore C. Sorensen, *Kennedy* (Harper & Row, 1965), pp. 263, 270.
15. Dean Rusk, as told to Richard Rusk, *As I Saw It* (Norton, 1990), pp. 197, 222, 520–21.
16. Henry Kissinger, *White House Years* (Little, Brown, 1979), p. 728. All the evidence of the dealings by Nixon and Kissinger comes from this book.
17. Zbigniew Brzezinski, *Power and Principle* (Farrar, Straus and Giroux, 1983), pp. 37, 65–66, 72.
18. Alexander M. Haig, Jr., *Caveat: Realism, Reagan, and Foreign Policy* (Macmillan, 1984), pp. 12, 53, 84, 306–7, 339, 341, 356.
19. Leary, *The Central Intelligence Agency*, p. 175.
20. FR delicately alludes to the Argentine role: "Initial support for the Nicaraguan resistance came from another country, which organized and supplied paramilitary forces in early 1981" (p. 29).
21. Roy Gutman, *Banana Diplomacy* (Simon and Schuster, 1988), says that the Argentines maintained their presence in Honduras through 1984 (p. 107).
22. Ibid., pp. 115–17. A similar but shorter version appears in Bob Woodward, *Veil: The Secret Wars of the CIA 1981–1987* (Simon and Schuster, 1987), pp. 225–26.
23. *Public Papers of the Presidents of the United States: Ronald Reagan*, 1983, Vol. 1, pp. 539, 541.
24. Ibid., pp. 603–4.
25. FR, pp. 34–35.

26. Gregg testimony at hearing of Senate Committee on Foreign Relations, May 12, 1989, cited by Daniel Patrick Moynihan, *On the Law of Nations* (Harvard University Press, 1990), pp. 135–37.
27. The entire letter, with the exception of one word, was put into the *Congressional Record* of March 3, 1988, p. S 1865, by Senator Moynihan.
28. FR, pp. 5–6.
29. *Congressional Record*, March 3, 1988, p. S 1864.
30. Oliver L. North and Constantine Menges to Robert C. McFarlane, March 2, 1984, Part III, pp. 726–27.
31. *Congressional Record*, October 10, 1984, p. 31576.
32. Hamilton, PT, pp. 2234–36.
33. Ibid., p. 2156.

2. Body and Soul

1. *Public Papers of the Presidents of the United States: Ronald Reagan*, 1983, Vol. 1, p. 642.
2. Ibid., April 27, 1983, p. 605. Reagan made a similar statement in his press conference of May 4, 1983 (p. 638).
3. McFarlane, 100-2, pp. 11–12.
4. Thomas L. Friedman, *From Beirut to Jerusalem* (Farrar, Straus & Giroux, 1989), p. 200.
5. Raymond Tanter, *Who's at the Helm? Lessons of Lebanon* (Westview Press, 1990), p. 87. Tanter was a member of the NSC staff in 1981–82.
6. Daniel Patrick Moynihan, *On the Law of Nations* (Harvard University Press, 1990), p. 141.
7. Michael K. Deaver, *Behind the Scenes* (Morrow, 1989), pp. 129–30.
8. Robert C. McFarlane, with Richard Saunders and Thomas C. Shull, "The National Security Council: Organization for Policy Making," *The Presidency and National Security Policy*, ed. by R. Gordon Hoxie (Center for the Study of the Presidency, 1984), pp. 265–66.
9. McFarlane, 100-2, p. 270.
10. Ibid., p. 116.
11. North, 100-7, Part I, p. 189.
12. North, NT, p. 7647.
13. Schweitzer, B-24, p. 351.
14. Tanter, *Who's at the Helm?*, p. 123.
15. General Paul X. Kelly, NT, pp. 6272–74.
16. Ibid., pp. 6276, 6284.
17. Secord, 100-1, p. 48.
18. North, NT, p. 7584.
19. Ibid., p. 6947.
20. McFarlane, NT, pp. 2946, 4352.
21. McFarlane, 100-7, Part II, p. 225.
22. Ibid., p. 208.
23. North, 100-7, Part I, p. 268.
24. Ibid., p. 205; 100-7, Part II, pp. 85, 185.
25. McFarlane, 100-2, p. 206. On Boland specifically, see McFarlane, NT, p. 4550.
26. McFarlane, NT, p. 4154.
27. McFarlane, 100-2, p. 6.
28. North, 100-7, Part II, p. 85.
29. North, 100-7, Part I, p. 205.
30. McFarlane, 100-2, p. 5.
31. Ibid., pp. 40, 158.
32. North, 100-7, Part II, p. 82.
33. North, 100-7, Part I, pp. 75, 88.
34. Cannistraro, NT, pp. 6405, 6409–10. Cannistraro mentioned that he was present at this

meeting (p. 6448). Cannistraro first put the meeting in early 1984, then in late spring, possibly as late as June 1984 (p. 6448).

35. Ibid., p. 6451.
36. Ibid., pp. 6406–7.
37. Ibid., p. 6409.
38. North, NT, pp. 6781–82.
39. North, 100-7, Part I, p. 75.
40. Secord, 100-1, pp. 46–47.
41. Ibid., p. 55.
42. Ibid., p. 48.
43. North, 107-1, Part I, p. 167.
44. Hakim, 100-5, pp. 195–97.
45. Lake Resources received $9,999,850 in February 1986 and $15 million in May 1986; Hyde Park received $3,599,933.07 on October 28, 1986 (Zucker, NT, pp. 5211–31). Just how these sums fitted into the Iran-contra operations was not explained.
46. North, 100-7, Part I, p. 119.
47. Quintero, NT, pp. 2882–85, 2945–50.
48. Ibid., pp. 2885, 2943–44; PT, p. 2005.
49. Secord, 100-1, pp. 50, 303.
50. Ibid., p. 303.
51. Ibid., pp. 51–52.
52. Ibid., p. 53.
53. Owen, 100-2, pp. 361–62. Adolfo Calero testified that he had never heard of the North-Secord decision in the summer of 1985 (Calero, 100-3, pp. 16–17); elsewhere Calero implied that North had decided to make Secord the procurement manager for the FDN (Calero, B-3, p. 108).
54. Owen, 100-2, pp. 423–24.
55. Secord, 100-1, pp. 51–53.
56. North, NT, p. 7181.
57. Gadd, B-11, p. 197.
58. Secord, 100-1, p. 54; Gadd, B-11, pp. 198–201.
59. North, NT, p. 6817.
60. North, 100-7, Part I, p. 207.
61. Gorman, B-12, p. 910.
62. North to McFarlane, November 7, 1984, 100-2, pp. 463–65.
63. Ibid., p. 166.
64. North to McFarlane, December 4, 1984, ibid., p. 470.
65. 100-7, Part II, pp. 86–87.
66. Ibid., p. 159.
67. Owen, B-20, p. 656.
68. Dutton, 100-3, pp. 201–4.
69. Ibid., p. 212.
70. North to McFarlane, February 6, 1985, 100-2, pp. 471–72.
71. TR, p. C-4.
72. McFarlane, 100-2, pp. 31–32.
73. North, 100-7, Part II, pp. 118–19.
74. North, 100-7, Part I, p. 207.
75. Owen, pp. 325–26; Owen, B-20, p. 791.
76. Owen, B-20, pp. 647–48, 743–44.
77. Adolfo Calero told a somewhat different story—that he had never intended to hire Gray & Co. but that Owen had left Gray and had come to him "and said, you know, he could help us out and we did use him as a sort of—he knew a lot of Congressional people" (Calero, B-3, p. 163).

78. Owen, B-20, pp. 650–53, 657–58, 750. Owen told this story more than once, not always in the same way.
79. Owen, 100-2, pp. 776–77.
80. Owen to North, April 1, 1985, ibid., pp. 799–805.
81. Ibid., pp. 816, 818, and others.
82. Ibid., p. 332.
83. Ibid., pp. 780–82.
84. North, 100-7, Part I, pp. 173–74, 179, 206.
85. Owen, B-20, pp. 671–72.
86. Owen, 100-2, p. 385.
87. Ibid., pp. 432–33.
88. Ibid., p. 74.
89. "NHAO was about to be formed, and the thought was that it would be best to have me become legitimate and therefore possibly go to work for NHAO" (Owen, B-20, p. 681).
90. Owen, NT, p. 2264.
91. Duemling, B-9, pp. 62–63, 100. Owen says that Duemling "didn't see that there would be a place for me" (Owen, B-20, p. 696).
92. Duemling, B-9, pp. 64–65.
93. Calero-Cruz-Robelo to Duemling, October 3, 1985, 100-2, pp. 828–30.
94. Duemling, B-9, pp. 48–50.
95. Ibid., pp. 68–71.
96. Owen, 100-2, pp. 831–38.
97. Duemling, B-9, p. 73.
98. Owen, B-20, p. 785.
99. Owen, B-20, pp. 751–52. Gadd said that Secord and North had told him to meet with Owen, who suggested that Gadd should contact Mario Calero, after which Gadd obtained the contract from the NHAO. North had also accompanied Gadd to see Duemling before the NHAO made its commitment to Gadd (Gadd, B-11, pp. 216–17).
100. Duemling, B-9, pp. 16, 20, 51–58.
101. TC to BG, March 17, 1986, 100-2, pp. 820–24.
102. Ibid., p. 828.
103. Owen, NT, p. 2307.
104. Owen, B-20, p. 692.

3. Big Money

1. *Public Papers of the Presidents: Ronald Reagan*, 1982, Vol. 1, pp. 745–48.
2. Casey to Clark, December 21, 1982, cited by Robert Parry and Peter Kornbluh, *Foreign Policy*, Fall 1988, p. 10.
3. Walter Raymond, Jr., B-22, pp. 12–15. This term was used as early as March 1983 (ibid., p. 433).
4. Ibid., p. 23.
5. Thompson to Casey, January 25, 1983, B-22, p. 425.
6. Gutman, *Banana Diplomacy*, p. 139.
7. Otto J. Reich, B-22, p. 723.
8. Francis D. Gomez, B-12, p. 462.
9. FR, p. 87.
10. Richard R. Miller, B-19, pp. 569–82.
11. Otto Reich to Pat Kennedy, September 24, 1985, B-19, p. 795.
12. Miller, B-19, p. 462; FR, p. 87, says $441,084.
13. B-19, p. 796.
14. Johnathan Miller (sometimes spelled Jonathan), B-18, pp. 618–23.
15. Ibid., p. 837.
16. *Public Papers of the Presidents: Ronald Reagan*, 1983, Vol. 1, pp. 683–89.

17. Casey to McFarlane, March 27, 1984, 100-2, p. 456.
18. Memorandum for the Record, July 16, 1984, ibid., p. 460.
19. Carl R. Channell, B-4, pp. 3–24.
20. Ibid., pp. 34–66.
21. Channell, NT, pp. 6833–34.
22. North, NT, p. 7255.
23. Channell, B-4, p. 42.
24. Fraser, B-10, pp. 832–40.
25. Ibid., pp. 824–26, 860–62.
26. The invitation is reproduced in B-4, p. 475.
27. Fraser, B-10, p. 834.
28. The letter is reproduced in B-4, p. 699.
29. Fraser, B-10, pp. 852–53, 857, 881.
30. Bradlee, *Guts and Glory*, p. 223.
31. Channell, NT, p. 3352.
32. FR, p. 87.
33. Conrad, NT, p. 3719.
34. Ibid., pp. 3668–3756.
35. Channell, B-4, pp. 44–45.
36. Ibid., p. 49.
37. Ibid., p. 53.
38. Ibid., p. 54.
39. Ibid., pp. 54, 56.
40. Ibid., p. 58.
41. Richard R. Miller, B-19, p. 67.
42. Channell, B-4, p. 89.
43. Ibid., p. 91.
44. Ibid., pp. 93–95.
45. Ibid., pp. 101–6.
46. *New York Times*, September 1, 1983.
47. Newington, B-20, pp. 363–72.
48. Calero to Newington, July 11, 1985, B-20, p. 469.
49. Newington, B-20, pp. 463–65.
50. Ibid., pp. 375–83.
51. Channell, B-4, p. 155.
52. Ibid., p. 161.
53. Artiano, B-2, pp. 406–88.
54. Fischer to Regan, January 5, 1986. This document does not seem to have been printed. The copy in my possession is marked N 22737.
55. Fielding to Ryan (Deputy Assistant to the President), January 21, 1986, Part III, p. 909; Channell, B-4, p. 379 (Kuykendall).
56. North to Poindexter, January 28, 1986, Part III, p. 940.
57. Channell, NT, pp. 3478–79.
58. Ibid., p. 3480.
59. Ibid., pp. 3504–6.
60. Newington, B-20, pp. 396–98, 407–8.
61. North to Newington, January 24, 1986, B-20, p. 468.
62. Ibid., pp. 417–18.
63. Ibid., p. 410.
64. Ibid., pp. 433–34.
65. North, NT, p. 7200.
66. Ellen C. Garwood, 100-3, pp. 110–13; B-11, pp. 773–77.
67. Garwood, B-11, p. 782.
68. Ibid., pp. 842–43.

69. Garwood, 100-3, p. 137.
70. Channell said that he had merely mentioned "a substantial amount of money" and denied that he had named the sum of $300,000 to O'Boyle (Channell, B-4, pp. 143–44).
71. O'Boyle, 100-3, p. 140.
72. Ibid., p. 150.
73. Coors, 100-3, pp. 126–29.
74. Nelson Bunker Hunt, B-14, pp. 394, 414.
75. Channell, NT, p. 3423.
76. Channell, B-4, pp. 680–81.
77. FR, p. 98.
78. Channell, B-4, p. 683.
79. FR, p. 98.
80. North to Channell, August 15, 1985, B-4, p. 491.
81. North to Dr. Mary Adamkiewicz, January 24, 1986, B-4, p. 545.
82. North to Frank Darlington, December 17, 1985, B-19, p. 760.
83. B-19, pp. 760–62; Part III, pp. 910–39.
84. B-19, p. 783.
85. Bruce H. Hooper to Jane E. McLaughlin, May 27, 1986, B-4, p. 582. Jane E. McLaughlin was employed by the NEPL.
86. Reagan to Newington, October 10, 1985, B-20, p. 467.
87. B-19, pp. 78, 262.
88. B-4, p. 218.
89. North to Poindexter, May 16, 1986, Part III, pp. 30–31.
90. B-19, p. 27.
91. B-21, pp. 1032–33.
92. B-19, pp. 179–80.
93. Ibid., p. 73.
94. Ibid., p. 183.
95. Miller, NT, pp. 3776–77.
96. Ibid., p. 3884.
97. Ibid., p. 191.
98. Ibid., pp. 39, 224–26.
99. Ibid., pp. 554–55.
100. Ibid., pp. 273–86.

4. Third Countries

1. FR, p. 54, note 119.
2. McFarlane, 100-2, pp. 14–15.
3. Casey to McFarlane, March 27, 1984, 100-2, pp. 456–57. This copy deletes Israel and "perhaps" (see FR, p. 38). More of Casey's message appears in the course of McFarlane's testimony at the North trial, where Israel is identified (pp. 4615–17).
4. Teicher, B-26, pp. 778–80; McFarlane, NT, p. 4619.
5. McFarlane to Teicher, April 20, 1984, 100-2, pp. 458–59.
6. Shultz to Reagan, September 6, 1983, 100-9, p. 467.
7. Shultz, 100-9, pp. 13–14; McFarlane, 100-2, pp. 15–16.
8. Clarridge cable to South Africa, May 11, 1984, B-17, p. 328.
9. B-17, p. 329.
10. The material on this incident comes from the testimony of Dewey R. Clarridge, 100-11, pp. 25–34, and the deposition of Clarridge, B-5, pp. 631–33. In his deposition, Clarridge denied all knowledge of any dealings with South Africa; in his later testimony, he was more forthcoming as a result of the documentation shown him. More may be learned from the deposition of John N. McMahon, B-17, pp. 42–50, with the documentation at pp. 316–32. The subject is briefly discussed in FR, p. 38. More reliance should be placed on the documentation,

though it is not completely self-explanatory, than on the testimony of Clarridge and McMahon, which was not fully satisfactory.

11. Shultz to Reagan, May 25, 1983, 100-9, pp. 454–59.
12. Reagan to Shultz, 1983 (no date on document), B-9, pp. 462–64.
13. The reference to "differences on negotiating" is to the so-called Contadora process with Mexico, Colombia, Venezuela, and Panama.
14. Reagan deposition, PT, p. 63. This deposition was given in California and its pages were numbered separately.
15. McFarlane, NT, p. 3945.
16. Baker deposition, Senate Select Committee, June 22, 1987.
17. FR, pp. 40, 55 (note 155).
18. This document does not appear to have been printed. The document in question is addressed to the General Counsel from the Office of General Counsel, August 23, 1984, OGC-84-51747.
19. This document also does not seem to have been printed. It is addressed to the Deputy Director of Central Intelligence from Stanley Sporkin, General Counsel, and dated December 27, 1984. The office number is not legible.
20. Shultz, 100-9, p. 17.
21. McMahon, B-17, p. 54.
22. McFarlane, NT, p. 3935.
23. McFarlane, 100-2, p. 131.
24. McFarlane gave the date as June 1984 (McFarlane, 100-2, p. 202).
25. McFarlane, 100-2, p. 86. The figure of $8 million comes from North to McFarlane, April 11, 1985, ibid., p. 520.
26. McFarlane, NT, p. 3983.
27. Ibid., p. 3933.
28. McFarlane, 100-2, pp. 16–18.
29. Ibid., pp. 22–23.
30. The sum of $2 million a month is mentioned on p. 23 of McFarlane, 100-2, and a lump sum of $25 million "in two or three deliveries" on p. 29.
31. McFarlane, NT, p. 4022.
32. Reagan deposition, PT, p. 75.
33. Ibid., pp. 85, 87.
34. McFarlane, 100-2, p. 24. (Also see p. 36: McFarlane "did not want to impose certain knowledge on the Secretary of State.")
35. Ibid., pp. 24–25.
36. McFarlane later said that Reagan, Poindexter, North, Weinberger, and the chairman of the Joint Chiefs of Staff knew of the Saudi money, but not Casey or anyone in Congress (McFarlane, NT, pp. 3936–37).
37. John W. Nields (Chief Counsel, House Select Committee), 100-2, p. 85.
38. McFarlane, 100-2, p. 25.
39. McFarlane to Max L. Friedersdorf, March 12, 1985 (copy released at PT).
40. North to McFarlane, April 11, 1985, 100-2, pp. 520–22.
41. McFarlane, 100-2, p. 35.
42. John N. McMahon, Memorandum for the Record, March 22, 1985, 100-2, p. 518.
43. McFarlane, 100-2, p. 25.
44. These two sentences apparently do not appear in the printed document; they come from Senators William S. Cohen and George J. Mitchell, Men of Zeal (Viking, 1988), p. 94.
45. Owen, 100-2, p. 782. This document is incorrectly listed in this volume as "Letter, undated, from North to Owen" (p. v). The letter makes clear that Owen was merely the courier to Calero (p. 780).
46. North to McFarlane, December 4, 1984, 100-3, p. 484.
47. Owen, 100-2, pp. 351–52; North, 100-7, Part I, p. 80.
48. Gaston J. Sigur, B-25, pp. 487–90; Sigur, 100-2, pp. 286–93.

49. Sigur, B-25, pp. 499–500.
50. Sciaroni, 100-5, pp. 392, 406, 408, 421–22, 435, 447–48, 451–52; B-24, pp. 918–25; North, 100-7, p. 171.
51. Singlaub, NT, pp. 2790, 2841.
52. Singlaub, 100-3, pp. 69–71.
53. Ibid., pp. 938–39.
54. Ibid., p. 75; Singlaub, B-25, p. 915.
55. North, 100-7, Part I, p. 79.
56. Calero, 100-3, p. 14. North's notebook for October 17, 1984, records a call from Singlaub about buying 160 T-54s from the Soviet Union.
57. Singlaub, 100-3, p. 181.
58. Calero, 100-3, pp. 35–36.
59. Singlaub, 100-3, p. 179. Singlaub gave extravagantly larger figures to the press. *The Washington Post* of February 26, 1987, quoted him as saying that he had raised $10 million in humanitarian and other aid. Singlaub admitted this and other statements but attributed it to Calero and tried to make it appear that he had been referring to "in-kind" contributions (Singlaub, B-25, pp. 937–38).
60. North to McFarlane, December 4, 1984, 100-3, p. 485.
61. 100-3, p. 469 (date unclear).
62. Singlaub, 100-3, p. 174.
63. Ibid., p. 953.
64. McFarlane to Lee Hamilton, February 8, 1987, 100-2, p. 677. This letter was sent to the chairman of the House Permanent Select Committee on Intelligence because McFarlane had previously testified that he had known nothing of this episode.
65. To Director, FBI, attention Financial Crimes Unit, Criminal Investigative Division, July 1985, 100-2, pp. 681–85.
66. The name is given in Chronology of Events, Appendix C, p. 28.
67. Miller, B-19, pp. 211–13, 371–72, 382–412, 431–33.
68. Calero, 100-3, p. 15.
69. North, NT, pp. 6842–50, 7137–44, 7163–69.
70. NT, p. 6823.

5. Arms and the Man

1. Secord, 100-1, pp. 57–61.
2. Ibid., pp. 61–62.
3. North, 100-7, Part I, p. 207.
4. Ibid., p. 153.
5. Ibid., pp. 154–56; Exhibit OLN-88, Part III, p. 464 (signed by "Goode," an alias of North).
6. Gadd, NT, p. 3047.
7. Gadd, B-11, p. 213.
8. Gadd, NT, p. 3171.
9. Dutton, 100-3, pp. 201–5.
10. Dutton, NT, p. 3275.
11. Dutton, B-11, p. 202.
12. Ibid., p. 209.
13. Ibid., pp. 224, 230. Dutton also said that he reported back to North after each trip to Central America and saw North at first about three times a week, daily in September 1986 (NT, p. 3307).
14. B-9, p. 531.
15. Dutton, 100-3, p. 216.
16. Ibid., p. 217.
17. Quintero, NT, pp. 2996, 2968–3005.
18. Ibid., p. 2938.

19. Ibid., pp. 2938, 2988, 3006.
20. B-26, p. 452.
21. Dutton, NT, pp. 3322–23.
22. Secord, 100-1, p. 65.
23. Dutton, 100-3, p. 208.
24. Tambs, 100-3, p. 367.
25. Ibid., p. 371.
26. Castillo is the name used in the printed records.
27. Quintero, PT, p. 2050.
28. "Tomás Castillo," B-3, p. 297.
29. Tambs, 100-3, p. 375. North claimed that Casey had authorized him to bring Castillo into the "resupply network" (North, 100-7, Part II, p. 177).
30. Tambs, 100-3, pp. 424–25.
31. Francis J. McNeil, *War and Peace in Central America* (Scribner's, 1988), pp. 235–36.
32. Paragraphs 66 and 67 in the "admitted facts" submitted in the trial of Oliver North, United States District Court for the District of Columbia, April 19, 1989.
33. *Washington Post*, April 15, 1989.
34. Tambs, 100-3, p. 381.
35. North, NT, pp. 6940.
36. Owen, B-20, pp. 679–81; Castillo, B-3, p. 14.
37. Haskell, NT, pp. 6559–90.
38. Exhibit 14, 100-1, p. 549. Hakim was authorized to represent the Udall Research Corporation at the Crédit Suisse bank in Geneva (p. 547).
39. Secord to Earl, 100-1, Exhibit 3, p. 430.
40. Secord, 100-1, pp. 75, 221. McNeil says that the airstrip was apparently leased to Udall, with an option to buy (p. 240).
41. Quintero, PT, p. 2036.
42. Castillo, 100-4, p. 16.
43. Secord, 100-1, p. 62.
44. Goode (North) to Secord, March 3, 1986, Castillo, 100-4, Exhibit TC-6, p. 115; Secord, 100-1, p. 67.
45. Castillo, 100-4, p. 18.
46. Dutton, B: 9, Exhibit 4, June 16, 1986, p. 527; p. 487 (for explanation).
47. Dutton, 100-3, p. 231.
48. Ibid., pp. 202, 207, 209.
49. Castillo, 100-4, pp. 23–24.
50. Tambs said that the new Arias administration wanted the agreement "rephrased or renegotiated" (Tambs, 100-3, p. 377).
51. Castillo, B-3, p. 275.
52. Singlaub, B-25, p. 1054; Singlaub, 100-3, p. 92.
53. Abrams, 100-5, p. 29.
54. Ibid., p. 27.
55. Tambs to Fiers, Abrams, and North, March 27, 1986, Tambs, 100-3, Exhibit LAT-1, p. 595.
56. Castillo, B-3, p. 405.
57. Singlaub, B-25, pp. 1057–58.
58. Tambs to Fiers, Abrams, and North, March 27, 1986, 100-3, Exhibit LAT-1, pp. 595–96.
59. Ibid.
60. Singlaub, 100-3, p. 93. The "token amount of military equipment" by the UNO to Pastora's group is spelled out in Melton to Abrams, May 8, 1986, Abrams, 100-5, Exhibit EA-2, p. 585.
61. Castillo (Fernandez), B-3, pp. 404–5.
62. C/CATF (Alan Fiers), B-3, p. 1232.
63. Abrams to Tambs, March 29, 1986, Tambs, 100-3, Exhibit LAT-2, p. 597. Abrams's impression that Fernandez had associated himself with the Singlaub-Pastora agreement apparently

came about as a result of the dispatch of Tambs's original report through the CIA rather than the State Department channel (100-3, p. 388).

64. Abrams to Tambs, March 29, 1986, Tambs, 100-3, Exhibit LAT-2, pp. 597–99.
65. Tambs to Abrams, March 31, 1986, ibid., Exhibit LAT-3, pp. 601–3.
66. Shultz to Tambs, April 1986, ibid., Exhibit LAT-4, pp. 605–6.
67. Singlaub, 100-3, p. 93.
68. Abrams, 100-5, p. 28. The understanding is implied in Melton to Abrams, May 8, 1986, ibid., Exhibit EA-2, p. 585.
69. Ibid., p. 29.
70. Melton to William G. Walker, May 10, 1986, ibid., Exhibit EA-3, p. 587.
71. Melton to Abrams, May 12, 1986, ibid., Exhibit EA-4, p. 588.
72. Melton to Abrams, May 15, 1986, ibid., Exhibit EA-6, p. 590.
73. In a handwritten note to a May 8, 1986, message from Melton about the token amount of military equipment to Pastora, Abrams had written: "R.M. [Richard Melton]—Seems to me so little to Pastora that it will keep him on board without screwing [chief of CIA Central American Task Force] up" (100-5, Exhibit EA-2, p. 28). The blacked-out name was paraphrased by Abrams (p. 28). Fiers (C/CATF) openly expressed his hostility to Pastora in his deposition (B-3, pp. 1115–16).
74. C/CATF (Fiers), B-3, p. 1232.
75. *United States of America* v. *Oliver L. North*, in the United States District Court for the District of Columbia, "admitted facts," p. 2.
76. North, NT, p. 6828.
77. Examples of these Guatemalan end-user certificates appear in McFarlane, 100-2, pp. 499–507 (in Spanish). They are explained in North to McFarlane, March 5, 1985, ibid., Exhibit No. 35, p. 494.
78. North, NT, p. 6885.
79. Secord, 100-1, p. 61.
80. Admitted Fact No. 44, p. 12.
81. Admitted Fact No. 50, p. 16.
82. Admitted Fact No. 51, pp. 16–17.
83. Admitted Fact No. 54, p. 18. The text appears in McFarlane, NT, pp. 4519–20.
84. North to McFarlane, "Central America Trip Notebook for your Visits to Guatemala, El Salvador, Panama, Costa Rica and Honduras," January 15, 1985, read into the record of the North trial by Sullivan, pp. 4680–81.
85. Admitted Fact No. 57, p. 19.
86. Admitted Fact No. 58, p. 19.
87. North, NT, pp. 6643–44.
88. Ibid., pp. 6831–32.
89. Cited in McFarlane, NT, p. 4543.
90. Admitted Facts Nos. 62–64, pp. 25–26.
91. McFarlane, NT, pp. 4554–55.
92. Quintero, NT, pp. 2917, 2921. Montero's men worked with two or three U.S. technical advisers (pp. 2919–20).
93. Admitted Fact No. 91, p. 32.
94. Admitted Fact No. 95, p. 34.
95. Admitted Fact No. 97, pp. 34–35.
96. Admitted Fact No. 99, p. 35.
97. North, NT, pp. 6826–27.
98. Small to McFarlane, May 31, 1985, Part III, p. 751.
99. North to Poindexter, June 3, 1985, ibid., p. 750.
100. NN, August 6, 1985.
101. Ibid., August 8, 1985.
102. Ibid.
103. Ibid., August 9, 1985.

104. Bradlee, *Guts and Glory*, pp. 282–83.
105. *New York Times*, August 17, 1985.
106. Constantine C. Menges, *Inside the National Security Council* (Simon and Schuster, 1988), p. 280.
107. Jacqueline Tillman, B-26, pp. 1192–93, 1201.
108. Menges, *Inside the National Security Council*, p. 194.
109. Cannistraro, NT, pp. 6485, 6493–94, 6496.
110. Ibid., p. 6507.
111. Barnes to McFarlane, August 16, 1985, McFarlane, 100-2, Exhibit 40A, pp. 546–47.
112. Hamilton to McFarlane, August 20, 1985, ibid., Exhibit 41, p. 559.
113. McFarlane, 100-2, p. 119.
114. McFarlane to Hamilton, September 5, 1985, 100-2, Exhibit 41A, pp. 550–63.
115. McFarlane to Barnes, 100-2, Exhibit 40B, pp. 548–50.
116. McFarlane to Hamilton, October 7, 1985, 100-2, Exhibit 41C, pp. 573–80, esp. p. 576.
117. Durenberger and Leahy to McFarlane, October 1, 1985, 100-2, Exhibit 41D, pp. 581–82; McFarlane to Durenberger and Leahy, October 7, 1985, 100-2, Exhibit 41E, pp. 583–86.
118. Charles Mohr, *New York Times*, October 24, 1985.
119. McFarlane, NT, pp. 4810–11.
120. Poindexter, 100-8, Exhibit 7A, p. 426.
121. Ibid., pp. 82–83.
122. Ibid.
123. North, 100-7, Part I, p. 171.
124. North, NT, p. 6871.
125. Ibid., p. 6872.
126. McFarlane, 100-2, p. 77.
127. North to McFarlane, August 10, 1985, cited in NT, p. 4047.
128. McFarlane, 100-2, p. 123.
129. Ibid., pp. 115–16.
130. Ibid., p. 7.
131. Hamilton, PT, pp. 2100–10.

6. Middlemen

1. *New York Times*, July 1, 1985.
2. TR, p. B-2.
3. Howard Teicher, B-26, p. 661; TR, p. B-2.
4. TR, p. B-2.
5. Ibid., pp. B-2, 3.
6. The biography is Ronald Kessler, *Khashoggi: The Rise and Fall of the World's Richest Man* (Bantam Press, 1986; reprinted Corgi Books, 1987; references are to the latter). The novels are *The Pirate* by Harold Robbins (1974) and *Bakchich* by Michel Clerc (Paris, 1977).
7. Serge Chauvel-Leroux, *Figaro* (Paris), June 9, 1976.
8. *Figaro*, July 19, 1976; *The Observer* (London), March 14, 1976; Kessler, *Khashoggi*, pp. 52–55, 108.
9. *L'Expansion* (Paris), November 5, 1981.
10. Anthony Sampson, *The Observer*, March 14, 1976.
11. *Le Quotidien* (Paris), January 22, 1987.
12. Emanuel A. Floor (who worked for Khashoggi), B-10, p. 485.
13. *Time*, January 19, 1987, p. 30.
14. *Fortune*, September 16, 1985, p. 108.
15. Floor, B-10, p. 547. *The Independent* (London), April 22, 1989, also noted Khashoggi's desire to be known as a "merchant statesman."
16. Interview with Khashoggi, *El País* (Madrid), March 16, 1987.
17. McFarlane, 100-2, p. 244. McFarlane said that he had received Khashoggi's first paper in 1982.

18. McFarlane to Teicher, April 20, 1984, 100-2, p. 458.

19. TOW was an acronym for tube-launched, optically tracked, wire-guided missiles.

20. "American Hostages in Lebanon," November 22, 1984, A-1, p. 955.

21. Theodore G. Shackley, B-25, pp. 142–43.

22. George Cave, B-3, p. 862.

23. "American Hostages in Lebanon," A-1, p. 956.

24. This account of the meeting in Hamburg is based on "American Hostages in Lebanon," A-1, pp. 955–59; Shackley, B-25, pp. 141–50; TR, p. B-3; FR, p. 164.

25. TR, p. B-3.

26. "Allen Interview with Ghorbanifar, January 13, 1986," Memorandum for the Record, January 29, 1986, B-1, p. 992. George Cave testified that he had met Ghorbanifar in 1980 and had recommended terminating an "operational relationship" with him probably in September 1981. Cave said that much of Ghorbanifar's information did not "check out" and that he made exorbitant financial demands (Cave, B-3, pp. 570–71).

27. Report on Ghorbanifar's polygraph, January 13, 1986, B-1, p. 985.

28. "Fabricator Notice—Manuchehr (Gorbanifar)," July 25, 1984, A-1, pp. 935–37. Also see p. 934 for one-page summary.

29. This report was made in support of subjecting Ghorbanifar to a polygraph test (A-1, pp. 942–43).

30. FR, p. 164; TR, p. B-3.

31. Interview with Michel Clerc, Figaro-Magazine, April 17, 1987, pp. 24–26. Khashoggi told a similar story in an interview with Jesús Cacho, El País, March 16, 1987, p. 2.

32. Furmark, B-11, pp. 36–37.

33. Kessler, Khashoggi, p. 342.

34. New York Times, February 1, 1987.

35. Samuel Segev, The Iranian Triangle (Free Press, 1988), pp. 12, 319n.

36. Figaro-Magazine, April 17, 1987. Khashoggi mentioned Mehdi Karoubi, brother of Hassan Karoubi. The two Karoubis were evidently confused by Khashoggi. Mehdi was then Speaker of the Majlis, the Iranian Parliament, and Hassan was almost certainly the one who attended the meeting in Hamburg and elsewhere.

37. Segev, The Iranian Triangle, pp. 2–3.

38. Dan Raviv and Yossi Melman, Every Spy a Prince (Houghton Mifflin, 1990), p. 259.

39. Ledeen says that Schwimmer was Peres's "closest personal friend" (Perilous Statecraft [Scribner's, 1988], p. 108). Raviv and Melman say that both Nimrodi and Schwimmer were friends of Ariel Sharon, on the other end of the Israeli political spectrum from Peres, but that Schwimmer was made a "special adviser to Peres" (Every Spy a Prince, pp. 259, 327).

40. Raviv and Melman, Every Spy a Prince, pp. 260–63. Segev tells a similar story somewhat differently: Two former Iranian generals in exile, accompanied by Nimrodi, came to see Sharon in September 1982 with a plan for Israel to help overthrow the Khomeini regime by making the Sudan the military base for the operation. Nimrodi and Schwimmer brought Khashoggi into the plot, whereupon Khashoggi obtained the "tacit support" of King Fahd to help finance it. The Iranians claimed that CIA Director Casey had given them the "go-ahead." The plan was aborted in Israel owing to internal opposition and Sharon's forced resignation in February 1983 as a result of the Sabra and Shatila massacres in Lebanon (pp. 6–11).

41. Thomas L. Friedman, interview with Nimrodi, New York Times, February 1, 1987.

42. Segev, The Iranian Triangle, pp. 14–17. Segev says that the source of this version is one of the Israeli participants, either Nimrodi or Schwimmer.

43. Ibid., pp. 138–39.

44. Raviv and Melman, Every Spy a Prince, pp. 331–32.

45. Ibid., pp. 334–35. This report is confusingly mentioned by Segev, who says that it was sent on May 2, 1985, by Khashoggi to McFarlane (The Iranian Triangle, pp. 134–35). It appears that Khashoggi did include—or made use of—Ghorbanifar's report of that date in Khashoggi's own memorandum to McFarlane later that month.

46. Ledeen, Perilous Statecraft, pp. 108–11.

47. FR, pp. 163–64; see p. 171, notes 18–19.
48. Furmark, B-11, p. 66.
49. Ibid., p. 53.
50. *Figaro-Magazine*, April 17, 1987, p. 26.
51. Casey to Chief, Near East Division, DO, June 17, 1985, B-2, pp. 660–61.
52. Robin Wright, *In the Name of God* (Simon and Schuster, 1989), p. 118.
53. Chief/NE, B-5, pp. 856–58.
54. Murphy to Armacost, June 24, 1985, B-2, pp. 662–63.
55. Memorandum for the Record, A-1, p. 1003.
56. Ibid., p. 1006.
57. Ibid., p. 1004.

7. Catalysts

1. Ledeen, *Perilous Statecraft*, p. ix; Ledeen, B-15, pp. 944–46.
2. Ledeen, B-15, p. 964.
3. Ibid., pp. 950–52.
4. NN, March 21, 1985.
5. Teicher, B-26, pp. 676, 804. In his own deposition, Ledeen said that it was his impression "that Teicher thought it was a good idea" (B-15, p. 957).
6. Fortier to McFarlane, March 9, 1985, A-1, p. 964.
7. Ledeen, B-15, p. 956. Ledeen does not give McFarlane's instructions in *Perilous Statecraft* and merely says that the trip was made to "raise the Iranian question" with Peres (p. 102).
8. TR gives the dates as May 4 or 5, 1985 (p. B-5). FR has May 3, 1985 (p. 164). *Perilous Statecraft* mentions the first week of May (p. 102). Ledeen's deposition seems to be contradictory; he says that he met with Peres on May 4, 5, and 6, but that he also saw Peres only once at a single meeting (B-15, pp. 957–58).
9. *Perilous Statecraft*, pp. 102–3. Ledeen gave two versions of this first visit, in his deposition and in his book. They do not always coincide but the differences are generally minor.
10. Israeli Historical Chronology, cited in FR, p. 165.
11. Raviv and Melman, *Every Spy a Prince*, pp. 332–34. Segev, who has a similar version, says that Ghorbanifar first came to Israel on April 9, 1985, and paid two more visits that same month. Peres gave the responsibility for this deal, which amounted to $33 million, to Nimrodi personally, cutting out Mossad. The Iranian turnabout "caused Nimrodi much agony and great financial loss." Ghorbanifar tried to tempt the Israelis to get U.S. approval for the sale of TOWs by injecting the possible release of the CIA's prisoner, Buckley, into the deal (pp. 23–25, 134).
12. McFarlane later revealed that Rabin had reported the contact with Ledeen to Ambassador Lewis (McFarlane to Shultz, July 3, 1985, 100-9, pp. 505–6).
13. Shultz to McFarlane, June 5, 1985, 100-9, pp. 494–95.
14. McFarlane to Shultz, June 7, 1985, 100-9, p. 498.
15. McFarlane, 100-2, pp. 42–43.
16. Raviv and Melman, *Every Spy a Prince*, pp. 336–37.
17. McFarlane to Shultz, July 13, 1985, 100-9, pp. 505–10. The message is not dated in the printed document but toward the end mentions that President Reagan was being operated on; the operation took place on July 13, 1985.
18. McFarlane, 100-2, p. 175.
19. For McFarlane's accreditation of Ledeen to Kimche as the "proper channel," see *Perilous Statecraft*, p. 119. In his message of July 13 to Shultz, McFarlane stated that he had "received a private emissary" from Israel (Shultz, 100-9, p. 505). In his testimony, however, McFarlane mentioned Schwimmer's visit on or about July 13 only as having been reported to him by Ledeen (McFarlane, 100-2, p. 45). It may well be that McFarlane was informed by Ledeen of Schwimmer's report but made it seem in his message to Shultz that it had come directly to him. In any case, McFarlane gave Shultz a garbled account, such as that a proposal had

been made by an Iranian official endorsed by the government of Israel. Whatever Ghorbanifar may have had in mind, it had come first by way of Ghorbanifar to Schwimmer, then from Schwimmer to Ledeen, and finally from Ledeen to McFarlane.

20. McFarlane, 100-2, p. 43.
21. Ibid., p. 175.
22. Ledeen, B-15, pp. 968–69.
23. Ibid., pp. 971–72.
24. Ledeen, *Perilous Statecraft*, pp. 118–19.
25. McFarlane, 100-2, p. 171.
26. Kemp to McFarlane, January 13, 1984, TR, p. B-2.
27. TR describes the analysis as relating to "American relations with Iran after Khomeini" (TR, p. B-2). Teicher said that it dealt with "what the U.S. might do to have some influence in a post-Khomeini Iran" (Teicher, B-26, p. 661).
28. TR, p. B-2.
29. Ibid., pp. B-2, 3.
30. Teicher, B-26, pp. 665–66.
31. TR, pp. B-6, 7.
32. Ibid., pp. B-7, 8.
33. "U.S. Policy Toward Iran," with memorandum from McFarlane to Shultz and Weinberger, June 18, 1985, 100-10, pp. 512–18.
34. Shultz to McFarlane, June 29, 1985, 100-9, pp. 499–501.
35. Teicher, B-26, p. 671.
36. Weinberger, 100-10, pp. 510–11.
37. Weinberger to McFarlane, July 16, 1985, 100-10, pp. 519–22.
38. Casey to McFarlane, July 18, 1985, TR, p. B-10.
39. Ibid., p. B-10.
40. The number of pages was given to Michel Clerc by Khashoggi in *Figaro-Magazine*, April 17, 1987, p. 26. Segev, *The Iranian Triangle*, has 47 pages (p. 153).
41. Segev, *The Iranian Triangle*, pp. 153–55.
42. Khashoggi to McFarlane, July 1, 1985, B-11, p. 190.
43. Segev, *The Iranian Triangle*, pp. 162–63.
44. Ibid., pp. 156–61. The transcript of the tape recording is on pp. 157–60.
45. Ibid., p. 160.
46. McFarlane, 100-2, p. 244.
47. Cave, B-3, pp. 864–65.

8. The First Deal

1. Regan, B-22, pp. 573–75; Donald T. Regan, *For the Record* (Harcourt Brace Jovanovich, 1988), pp. 6, 11. In his public testimony at the Iran-contra hearings, Regan said: "What McFarlane was trying to do was to find or get permission from the President to initiate such discussions in order to have authority to continue or rather to undertake in accordance with what the Israelis had suggested some openings to these Iranian persons who at that point were unknown factors" (Regan, 100-10, p. 10).
2. McFarlane, 100-2, p. 46.
3. TR, pp. B-15, 16.
4. McFarlane to Poindexter, November 21, 1986, 100-8, p. 689.
5. McFarlane, NT, p. 4761.
6. TR, p. B-16.
7. Ibid., p. B-15.
8. Reagan deposition, U.S. Court of California, February 17, 1990, p. 226.
9. Reagan, *An American Life* (Simon and Schuster, 1990), pp. 504–5.
10. Ibid., pp. 506–7.
11. Ledeen, B-15, p. 969.

12. Ibid., pp. 973–75; *Perilous Statecraft*, p. 121.

13. This version is from Ledeen, B-15, pp. 979–86. The later version in *Perilous Statecraft* is much less detailed (p. 122).

14. McFarlane, 100-2, p. 48.

15. Ibid., p. 48.

16. TR, p. B-19.

17. Ibid., p. B-19.

18. McFarlane, NT, p. 4762.

19. Israeli Historical Chronology, from FR, p. 167.

20. McFarlane, 100-2, p. 172. McFarlane also said that Kimche had talked to him of 10 TOWs (p. 174).

21. FR, p. 167.

22. TR, p. B-20.

23. McFarlane, 100-2, p. 49.

24. TR, pp. B-22, 23; 100-9, p. 27. McFarlane later said that he had "never felt for the past 10 years that there is such a thing as deniability" and that he could not recall advocating the idea at the meeting (100-2, p. 49).

25. Shultz, 100-9, p. 27.

26. Weinberger, 100-10, p. 135.

27. TR, p. B-22.

28. Regan, B-22, p. 578.

29. Shultz, 100-9, p. 27. Shultz's statement to the Tower Board did not go so far; Shultz merely said that "I do not recall the President having decided at that meeting to approve the Iranian offer." Shultz thought that the August 6, 1985, meeting had merely been "one of my regular meetings with the President" (TR, pp. B-22, 23).

30. Weinberger, 100-10, p. 135; TR, p. B-22.

31. Regan, 100-10, p. 13.

32. Regan, B-22, p. 578.

33. TR, p. B-22.

34. McFarlane, 100-2, p. 47. McFarlane also believed that the president had said in August that "he was willing to take the heat of making a decision to try to save the hostages" (p. 59).

35. Regan, *For the Record*, p. 268.

36. Furmark, B-11, pp. 73–76.

37. FR, p. 168 and p. 172, note 88. In his interview with Michel Clerc, Khashoggi confirmed that he had first invested $1 million for 100 missiles and was paid back by Ghorbanifar (*Figaro-Magazine*, April 17, 1987, p. 26).

38. Segev, *The Iranian Triangle*, p. 165.

39. FR, p. 168.

40. Ibid. The dates here seem to be confused. Ghorbanifar is said to have made this statement on August 19, 1985, after his return to Israel, and to have left with the first planeload on August 20.

41. McFarlane, 100-2, p. 50.

42. Israeli Historical Chronology, in FR, p. 169 and p. 172, note 108.

43. The number 100 is usually used for the first installment, as by Ledeen (B-15, p. 994). The number 96 was not introduced until it appeared in FR, p. 168.

44. Ledeen, B-15, pp. 994–96.

45. Israeli Historical Chronology, from FR, p. 168.

46. Ledeen, *Perilous Statecraft*, p. 134.

47. The total is sometimes given as 508 owing to the assumption that 100, not 96, were delivered on August 20, 1985.

48. TR, p. B-26.

49. McFarlane, 100-2, p. 50. Ledeen, as usual, makes the Weir release a triumph for Ghorbanifar: "With the release of Weir, our basic questions had apparently been answered, and it seemed the president had made a good decision to approve the reciprocal test. Ghorbanifar was indeed

a legitimate channel to the highest levels of the Khomeini regime, the Iranians could indeed determine the destiny of the hostages, and there was at least some interest on the Iranian side in an improved relationship" (*Perilous Statecraft*, pp. 136–37).

50. FR, p. 172, note 110, has the following comment about these financial transactions: "The Tower Report's analysis of this transaction differs from that provided by the Israelis. According to Tower, Ghorbanifar initiated the transaction with a $4 million check to Khashoggi. Khashoggi transferred $4 million to the Israeli account on September 14. The Iranians transferred $5 million to Ghorbanifar's Swiss account on September 18. Ghorbanifar then notified Khashoggi to negotiate the $4 million check. Ghorbanifar paid later an additional $250,000 to the Israeli account for 'additional TOW missiles.' Tower at B-176, 177."

51. Segev, *The Iranian Triangle*, p. 175.

9. Horror Story

1. McFarlane, NT, p. 3917.
2. NN, September 17, 1985.
3. Ibid., October 5, 1985.
4. North, NT, p. 5828.
5. North to McFarlane, October 8, 1985, NT, Defense Exhibit 62.
6. TR says that North, Nimrodi, Schwimmer, and Ghorbanifar met on October 8, 1985 (p. B-29). Ledeen questions this statement, allegedly based on North's calendar, and says that North was too busy to meet with them. Ledeen, however, asserts that he introduced Schwimmer to North in connection with this meeting (B-15, pp. 1012–13). In his book, Ledeen says that North met separately with Schwimmer and Ghorbanifar, but mistakenly gives the date of his meeting with the others as October 3, 1985 (*Perilous Statecraft*, p. 137).
7. Ledeen, B-15, p. 1014; *Perilous Statecraft*, p. 137.
8. Ibid.
9. Ledeen, B-15, p. 1015; *Perilous Statecraft*, pp. 137–38.
10. Ledeen, B-15, p. 1016.
11. Ibid., pp. 1019–20.
12. Ibid.
13. TR, p. B-30.
14. Ledeen, B-15, pp. 1021–22.
15. Ibid., p. 1037. This is not mentioned in Ledeen's book.
16. Ibid., pp. 1219–20.
17. Ledeen, *Perilous Statecraft*, p. 142.
18. Segev, *The Iranian Triangle*, p. 183.
19. Ibid., pp. 183–84.
20. NN, October 30, 1985.
21. Ibid.
22. Ledeen, B-15, pp. 1024–27.
23. Ledeen, *Perilous Statecraft*, p. 143.
24. Ibid., p. 150; FR, p. 175.
25. North, 100-7, Part I, p. 223.
26. NN, November 14, 1985.
27. These questions were deleted in the copies of North's notebook but appear in FR, p. 176. Segev says that the covert operation was designed to rescue the hostages in Lebanon by force (*The Iranian Triangle*, p. 195).
28. McFarlane's words, as given in a "Memorandum for the Record" by McMahon, dated November 15, 1985, appear in FR, p. 176. This memorandum has been deleted from the printed documents (B-17, p. 369, for deletion). FR then goes on: "McMahon said McFarlane provided this information casually as the meeting was breaking up. Casey related this information to McMahon on his drive back to Langley" (attributed to McMahon deposition). But in his deposition, McMahon testified that Casey had told him McFarlane had merely said "the

Israelis either had or proposed to ship arms to Israel—arms to Iran—and that was the extent of it" (McMahon, B-17, p. 92).

29. McFarlane, 100-2, pp. 51–52. The Israeli Historical Chronology states that Rabin also asked whether the United States was still committed to replenishing the 504 TOW missiles sent by Israel to Iran in August–September 1985. McFarlane is said to have replied that he was aware of the difficulties and intended to send North to Israel within two weeks to find a technical means to carry out the replacement (FR, p. 176; also see note 17, p. 189).

30. NN, November 15, 1985.

31. Ibid., November 19, 1985. North also put down: "$220K/230K each for Hawks."

32. Regan, 100-10, p. 12.

33. TR, p. B-31.

34. McFarlane, 100-2, p. 100.

35. McFarlane, B-16, pp. 629–30.

36. NN, November 17, 1985. It could be that Rabin told North to call McFarlane, because North merely noted "told to call RCM."

37. Ibid.

38. The presence of Nimrodi, Ghorbanifar, and Kangarlou in Geneva appears in both Segev (p. 199) and Raviv and Melman (p. 324). The information clearly comes from Nimrodi.

39. NN, November 18, 1985.

40. North, 100-7, Part I, p. 53.

41. McFarlane, NT, p. 4240. At the congressional hearings, McFarlane testified that he had received a telephone call from Rabin, who had said that "he had a problem that had come up in the transfer of certain items" and "was there anyone in the United States that might be able to help him?" McFarlane called Poindexter and North about Rabin's problem and said to them: ". . . please take steps to see if you can be of help" (100-2, pp. 52–53).

42. North, NT, p. 5971.

43. Ibid., pp. 6971–72.

44. Ibid., p. 6977.

45. Ibid., p. 7600.

46. Secord, 100-1, p. 415.

47. McFarlane, 100-2, p. 54.

48. In his deposition, Secord gave the date as November 18 (B-24, p. 1103). In his testimony, he said it might have been November 18 or 19 (100-1, p. 79). In view of the letter from North, November 19 seems right. He is also mentioned in North's notebook on that date.

49. Secord, 100-1, p. 80.

50. Ibid., pp. 80–81; Secord, B-24, p. 1102.

51. North to Poindexter, November 20, 1985, 100-2, pp. 587–88. A readable text of this document may be found in TR, pp. B-31, 32.

52. These notes all come from NN, November 21, 1985. A few of them may have related to November 22, 1985, but were marked by North as of November 21, and I have put them in November 21 for this reason.

53. Deputy Chief of Mission, B-8, p. 280.

54. Ibid., p. 271. The CIA chief of station says that the counselor had replied that "he knew nothing that would justify the mission" (B-4, p. 1159).

55. CIA Chief of Station, B-4, p. 1160.

56. Affidavit of Robert B. Oakley, Part III, pp. 1324–25.

57. Ibid., p. 1324. The words "in Portugal" are deleted in this volume but appear in FR, p. 181. This is the same story told by North, in a somewhat different form, in his message to Poindexter of December 5, 1985 (100-8, p. 476).

58. FR, p. 181, says that "North falsely told Oakley" this story.

59. Shultz, TR, January 22, 1987, cited in FR, p. 181.

60. Shultz, 100-9, p. 29.

61. CIA Air Branch Chief, B-4, p. 810.

62. CIA Chief of Station (Lisbon), B-4, pp. 1151–52.

63. C/Eur to CIA Station (Lisbon), Part III, p. 312.
64. This is the version of the CIA chief of station (B-4, p. 1161). The chargé merely says that he did not talk with the foreign minister on November 22, 1985 (B-8, p. 275).
65. McFarlane, 100-2, p. 53.
66. The CIA chief of station was informed that the foreign minister had agreed to the clearance (B-4, p. 1164), but it was later denied by the foreign minister to the chargé (B-8, p. 276); also see p. 286 for difference of opinion about McFarlane's telephone call.
67. U.S. chargé, B-8, p. 292.
68. North to Poindexter, November 22, 1985, Part III, p. 262.
69. Ibid., p. 263.
70. According to Secord, Schwimmer also had a new idea—to charter a smaller plane to stop at Cyprus and then go on to Iran. But Schwimmer could not get insurance for this plane and gave it up (100-1, p. 82).
71. CIA Chief of Station, B-4, p. 1165.
72. Ibid., pp. 1163–64.
73. Deputy Chief of Mission, B-8, pp. 276, 287.
74. Ibid., p. 278.
75. Ibid., p. 296.
76. CIA Air Branch Chief, B-4, p. 809.
77. Airline Proprietary Project Officer, B-1, pp. 18–19; CIA Air Branch Chief, B-4, p. 799.
78. Airline Proprietary Project Officer (CIA proprietary controller), B-1, p. 33; Chronological Report, Exhibit 3, ibid., p. 164.
79. The decision in Washington appears in the deposition of the CIA Air Branch Chief, B-4, p. 847. Ledeen mistakenly says that only the second plane came from the CIA proprietary (*Perilous Statecraft*, p. 157). It is only one of the many inaccuracies in his account, which is apparently based on Israeli sources. Ledeen has North undertaking in the first half of November 1985 to commission "a jumbo jet that would carry the eighty Hawks from Israel to Iran" (p. 151). North did not get into the act until November 17 and then only because Rabin had appealed to McFarlane for help and McFarlane had turned the problem over to North.
80. Airline Proprietary Project Officer, B-1, p. 38.
81. FR, p. 184.
82. The adventures of this flight are mainly based on the deposition and final report of the Airline Proprietary Project Officer (B-1, pp. 33–43, 164–69).
83. Ibid., p. 169.
84. Segev, *The Iranian Triangle*, p. 205.
85. Raviv and Melman, *Every Spy a Prince*, pp. 325, 330.
86. Ledeen, B-15, p. 1217; *Perilous Statecraft*, p. 161.
87. Secord, 100-1, p. 84.
88. FR, p. 192, note 201.
89. Ibid., p. 187.
90. All these figures come from FR, p. 187, where they are largely based on the Israeli Historical Chronology.
91. FR, p. 192, note 215.
92. Ledeen, *Perilous Statecraft*, p. 162.
93. Poindexter, B-20, pp. 1356–57.
94. Ledeen, *Perilous Statecraft*, p. 162.
95. Secord, B-24, pp. 1104–6.
96. North, 100-7, Part I, p. 54.
97. Secord, B-24, p. 1106.
98. North, 100-7, Part I, p. 56.
99. Ibid.
100. Israeli Historical Chronology, cited in FR, p. 187 and p. 192, note 196.
101. North sometimes misdated his notes, in this case as "26 Oct" instead of "26 Nov." It is printed with other notes with those of November 26 in Part III, p. 374. The context shows that it

could not have been written on October 26 and must have been written on November 26. FR, p. 193, gives the date incorrectly as November 27, 1986 (p. 193).

102. FR says that the meeting took place in late November 1985 (p. 193). Secord said that the approximate date was the first week of December 1985 (Secord, 100-1, p. 90). North's notebook for December 1, 1985, states that Secord "proceeded to Paris mtg" and met with Ghorbanifar.

103. NN, December 1, 1985.

104. Secord, 100-1, p. 90.

10. Finding No. 1

1. North, 100-7, Part I, p. 88.
2. Clarridge, B-5, p. 520.
3. Edward S. Juchniewicz, B-14, pp. 617–18.
4. Ibid., pp. 625–26.
5. Ibid., p. 626.
6. McMahon, Memorandum for the Record, September 23, 1985, in B-17, p. 367; it is discussed on pp. 84–88.
7. McMahon, B-17, p. 92.
8. Ibid., p. 93.
9. McMahon said that he thought this cable had been sent by McFarlane or Poindexter (ibid., p. 96). "Portuguese government" is deleted in the printed version.
10. Ibid., pp. 97, 297.
11. Juchniewicz, B-14, p. 630.
12. McMahon, B-17, p. 97.
13. Ibid., p. 232.
14. Memorandum for the Record, December 7, 1985, B-12, p. 166.
15. Juchniewicz was almost certainly wrong about the date; it was Monday, November 25, not—as Juchniewicz said—Saturday, November 23.
16. Juchniewicz, B-14, pp. 627–29.
17. George, B-12, p. 79.
18. Ibid., p. 82.
19. Ibid., p. 89.
20. Part III, p. 366.
21. George, B-12, p. 89.
22. McMahon, B-17, p. 228.
23. Ibid., pp. 228–31.
24. NSDD 159, January 18, 1985, reads:

    Approval Procedures for Intelligence

    1. *Presidential Findings.* The President shall approve all covert action Findings in writing. Under Section 662 of the Foreign Assistance Act of 1961, as amended, all covert actions undertaken by the Central Intelligence Agency must be authorized by a Presidential Finding that each such operation is important to US national security. E.O. [Executive Order] 12333 and this Directive establish that covert actions (intelligence "special activities") undertaken by components other than CIA also require a Presidential Finding. Each covert action is also considered a significant anticipated intelligence activity under Section 501 of the National Security Act and is subject to certain Congressional reporting procedures. The Congressional reporting procedures for significant intelligence activities apply to all agencies of the intelligence community. Finding shall remain valid until formally cancelled.

    2. In accordance with Executive Order 12333, the Central Intelligence Agency shall conduct covert actions unless the President specifically designates another agency of the government. When the provision of substantial support by one government component to another is essential to the conduct of a covert action, indication of the extent and nature of that support shall be included as part of the Finding or Memorandum

of Notification. However, the provision of routine support in the form of personnel, funds, equipment, supplies, transportation, training, logistics, and facilities by Government components other than CIA to support a covert action shall not in itself be considered a separate covert action by the supplying agency [100-8, p. 864].

25. McMahon, B-17, p. 290.
26. Ibid., pp. 246–47.
27. Poindexter, 100-8, p. 182.
28. Clarridge, B-5, p. 539.
29. Ibid., p. 851.
30. Earl, B-9, pp. 576, 761.
31. CIA Air Branch Chief, B-4, p. 818.
32. Clarridge, B-5, p. 863.
33. George, B-12, p. 92.
34. Juchniewicz, B-14, p. 630.
35. McMahon, B-17, pp. 147–48.
36. Ibid., p. 78.
37. Ibid., pp. 165–66.
38. Ibid., p. 233.
39. Ibid., p. 245.
40. George, B-12, p. 145.
41. McMahon, B-17, p. 165.
42. Poindexter, 100-8, p. 18.
43. NN; see Part III, pp. 332–68.
44. North to Poindexter, November 20, 1985, Part III, pp. 257–58.
45. North to Poindexter, Part III, p. 1059, where the date is given as November 22, 1985 (p. ix). The date is unclear, but November 21, 1985, is given in TR, p. B-3, and appears to be more accurate.
46. North to Poindexter, November 22, 1985, Part III, pp. 262–63.
47. NN, November 21, 1985; see Part III, p. 254.
48. Juchniewicz, B-14, p. 631.
49. McMahon, B-17, pp. 295–96.
50. Sporkin, 100-6, p. 120.
51. Part III, p. 267.
52. Sporkin, 100-6, p. 123. At the Poindexter trial, Sporkin said that "I used something that is not ordinarily used, and indeed I think there is a precedent—but it might have been one or two times" (PT, p. 1699). No precedent was ever cited.
53. Poindexter, 100-8, p. 249.
54. Ibid., p. 273.
55. Sporkin, 100-6, p. 124.
56. Sporkin, PT, p. 1699.
57. Meese, B-18, pp. 19, 33–34.
58. North to Poindexter, December 4, 1985, Part III, p. 268. This message is incorrectly dated as December 5, 1985 (p. iv). A more readable copy may be found in TR, where it is correctly dated as December 4, 1985 (p. B-34).
59. Sporkin, NT, p. 6373.
60. Casey to Poindexter, November 26, 1985, Part III, p. 266.
61. Poindexter, 100-8, pp. 118, 188, 300.
62. Ibid., pp. 22, 190.
63. Ibid., pp. 124, 464.
64. Ibid., p. 23.
65. Ibid., p. 395.
66. Ibid., p. 30.
67. Ibid., p. 344.

11. *Finding No.* 2

1. Poindexter, 100-8, pp. 181, 353.
2. Ibid., p. 13.
3. Ibid., p. 1070.
4. Ibid., p. 1155.
5. Regan, *For the Record*, p. 325.
6. Michael K. Deaver, *Behind the Scenes* (Morrow, 1987), p. 259. Bob Woodward says that Deaver told Mrs. Reagan that he had doubts about Poindexter; Deaver "thought military men were not good as national-security advisers." Deaver is also said to have called Secretary Shultz, who told Deaver that he thought Poindexter would be "good" and that anyway it was too late to stop the appointment (*Veil*, p. 427).
7. Poindexter, 100-8, pp. 165–66.
8. Ibid., p. 166.
9. Ibid., p. 168.
10. Ibid., pp. 53, 101, 362, 372.
11. Ibid., pp. 162, 372.
12. Ibid., p. 61.
13. Ibid.
14. Ibid., pp. 95, 335.
15. North, 100-7, Part II, p. 88.
16. North, 100-7, Part I, pp. 39, 233.
17. Ibid., pp. 245–46.
18. Ibid., pp. 286, 384.
19. Poindexter, 100-8, pp. 17, 118.
20. Ibid., pp. 26, 205.
21. Ibid., p. 199.
22. Ibid., pp. 166, 229.
23. Ibid., p. 341.
24. Ibid., pp. 468–71. A more readable transcription, minus the first paragraph, appears in TR, pp. B-34–36.
25. Poindexter, 100-8, pp. 476–79. This statement is unsigned but follows the message of December 4 very closely, in some places almost word for word.
26. McFarlane, 100-7, Part II, p. 55. McFarlane's other version is that he had told the president in California that it "is for us to avoid dealing through intermediaries and to talk to Iranians directly, and he agreed with that. And he said convene the NSC—the Secretary of State and Defense—and let's talk it over when we get back" (TR, p. B-44). Poindexter thought that he had "encouraged" the meeting (Poindexter, B-20, p. 1116).
27. Armitage, B-2, pp. 11–16.
28. Shultz, 100-9, p. 7. Shultz said that Poindexter had told him on December 5 that "the operation was at a decision point, and that he had set up a meeting for Saturday, December 7." Poindexter also said that there would be "[n]o calendar to show it." Shultz replied "that the operation should be stopped; that I had been informed that Iran was playing a big role in Lebanon which even Syria could not influence. I told him: 'We are signalling to Iran that they can kidnap people for profit' " (TR, p. B-40).
29. Shultz, 100-9, pp. 30–31.
30. Israeli Historical Chronology, cited by FR, p. 197.
31. North, 100-7, Part I, pp. 298–99.
32. McFarlane, 100-7, Part II, p. 223. There are similar versions by McMahon (B-17, p. 126) and Poindexter (B-20, p. 1119) on what McFarlane said about Israeli policy and motives.
33. Shultz, 100-9, pp. 31, 523.
34. Ibid., p. 31.
35. Weinberger, 100-10, pp. 139–40.

36. TR, p. B-45.
37. Regan, 100-10, p. 14.
38. Ibid., pp. 46–47.
39. McMahon, B-17, p. 126.
40. Poindexter, 100-8, p. 25; McMahon, B-17, p. 127.
41. McFarlane, 100-2, p. 56.
42. Poindexter, B-20, p. 1117.
43. Weinberger, 100-10, pp. 140–41.
44. Shultz, 100-9, pp. 31–32.
45. Ibid., p. 32. FR assumes that this remark about "visiting hours" was made by Weinberger, as seems most likely (p. 198).
46. Regan, 100-10, p. 14.
47. TR, p. B-45.
48. McFarlane, 100-2, p. 59.
49. Ibid.
50. McMahon, B-17, p. 127; TR, p. B-45.
51. Reagan, An American Life, pp. 510–13.
52. Poindexter, 100-8, pp. 26, 326.
53. Secord, 100-1, p. 91. Secord says that an Israeli representative of the Ministry of Defense was also there (p. 92).
54. TR, p. B-45.
55. Ibid., pp. B-46, 47.
56. McFarlane, 100-2, pp. 57, 103.
57. TR, pp. B-47, 48. This quotation from Ghorbanifar comes from an interview with him in Paris by two aides of the Tower Board and represents how he spoke.
58. Secord, 100-1, p. 92.
59. Ibid., p. 93.
60. McFarlane, 100-2, p. 180.
61. North, 100-7, Part I, pp. 283–84.
62. Poindexter, 100-8, pp. 473–75.
63. This attendance is in FR, pp. 199-200. Based on interviews with McFarlane, TR has Vice President Bush and John McMahon there, the latter in the absence of Casey, and then has McFarlane referring to the presence of Casey and Secretary of Defense Weinberger, who could not remember being there. It also mistakenly gives the date as December 11, 1985 (TR, p. B-50).
64. TR, pp. B-50, 51.
65. George, 100-11, p. 890. Poindexter also said the same thing about McFarlane's view of Ghorbanifar (100-8, p. 337).
66. TR, p. B-51.
67. McFarlane, 100-2, p. 59.
68. Casey to McMahon, December 10, 1985, 100-11, p. 890.
69. TR, p. B-52.
70. Poindexter, 100-8, p. 127.
71. North, 100-7, Part I, p. 286.
72. McFarlane to North, November 26, 1985, in TR, p. B-33, note 23.
73. Raviv and Melman, Every Spy a Prince, p. 336. Ledeen claims to know that Kimche, Schwimmer, and Nimrodi were all "regarded critically by Mossad" and that "in the corridors of the Mossad, Nir's name was a source of mirth and their derision was not confined inside the community" (Perilous Statecraft, pp. 116, 168). Both Ledeen and Segev say that Nir was boycotted by the Mossad (Segev, The Iranian Triangle, p. 220).
74. Sporkin, 100-6, p. 188.
75. Ibid., p. 189.
76. Ibid., p. 128.

77. Ibid., p. 131.
78. Ibid., pp. 132–33.
79. Ibid., pp. 135–45.
80. 100-8, p. 487.
81. Sporkin, PT, p. 1704.
82. Poindexter, 100-8, p. 30.
83. Ibid.
84. "Memorandum for the President," 100-8, p. 484.
85. North to Poindexter, "Memorandum for the President," 100-8, p. 483.
86. Ibid.
87. FR, p. 201.
88. This plan in the event of a leak appears in 100-8, p. 482. It seems that the Israelis were asked in a message attributed to President Reagan if they could live with a "no comment" response to the exposure of the operation. North believed that this response had been put forward by the Israelis and that both sides had agreed on a "no comment" plan (100-7, Part I, p. 289).
89. Poindexter, 100-8, pp. 480–82. Poindexter's notes also mention 4,500 replacements, the additional 500 to be replacements for the Israeli shipment in September 1985. Poindexter says that he wrote these notes on the plane coming back with the president from California, not during or immediately after the meeting with Nir (ibid., p. 30).
90. Poindexter said he thought Nir had indicated that the Israelis planned to go ahead on their own "whether we were going to go forward with the initiative" (100-8, p. 388).
91. North, 100-7, Part I, p. 288.
92. The exchange between Powell and North appears in North's message to Poindexter, January 15, 1986. This portion of the message was removed from the text given in Part III, p. 300, but it is contained in a copy in my possession.

12. Finding No. 3

1. Poindexter, 100-8, p. 30.
2. Smith to Casey, October 5, 1981, 100-9, p. 1240.
3. Meese, 100-9, pp. 206–7.
4. Weinberger, 100-10, p. 143.
5. Shultz, 100-9, p. 33.
6. Regan attributed his reversal to Poindexter's presentation of a new plan, which Regan was barely able to describe: "As I recall, on January 7th he [Poindexter] did go into some detail as to what the new plan would be and that there would be a new cast of characters and that we would—I think he forecast—that we would be going inside Iran to make contacts within the country itself" (100-10, p. 47).
7. TR, p. B-62.
8. Ibid., pp. B-63–64.
9. Reagan, An American Life, pp. 516–17.
10. FR, pp. 203–4; NN, Part III, pp. 388–95.
11. Noel C. Koch, B-15, p. 31.
12. Ibid., p. 36.
13. Rudd and Gaffney testified at length about their participation in the replenishment problem (B-11). There is a summary of their roles in FR, p. 204.
14. Koch, B-15, pp. 21–22.
15. Ibid., pp. 26–27.
16. Ibid., p. 51.
17. Koch says Powell suggested going to Weinberger (ibid., p. 53). Powell thought that Koch or both of them had decided to see Weinberger. Powell did not remember what Weinberger had said (Powell, B-21, pp. 287–89).
18. Koch, B-15, pp. 55–57.

19. Memorandum, January 6, 1986, Part III, pp. 289–92. This memorandum was written by Betty Ann Smith, a lawyer in the office of the CIA general counsel (George Clarke, B-5, p. 386). Clarke, the associate general counsel, was her superior.

20. George W. Clarke to Sporkin, January 7, 1986, B-5, pp. 482–83. The same document in Part III, pp. 293–94, deletes Clarke's name—an example of finding in one volume what is concealed in another.

21. Memorandum, January 13, 1986, Part III, p. 295. This memorandum is unsigned, but FR says that it was sent to Casey (p. 206), probably by Poindexter.

22. NN, January 13, 1986.

23. Ibid., January 15, 1986.

24. Ibid., January 13, 1986.

25. Ibid., January 14, 1986.

26. Ibid.

27. Ibid.

28. Ibid.

29. North to Poindexter, January 15, 1986, Part III, pp. 299–300.

30. Ibid., January 15, 1986, p. 401. This note seems to read: "25% to other apples," which FR gives as "Iranians" (p. 207).

31. FR, p. 207.

32. North to Poindexter, January 15, 1986, Part III, p. 302.

33. Ibid., pp. 302–3.

34. Ibid., p. 303.

35. Clarke, B-5, pp. 420–21.

36. Clarke, Memorandum for the Record, January 15, 1986, B-5, pp. 489–90.

37. Sporkin to Casey, "Talking Points," January 15, 1986, 100-6, pp. 456–59.

38. Clarke, B-5, p. 382.

39. Sporkin, 100-6, p. 179.

40. Clarke, B-5, pp. 433–34. Sporkin left the CIA on February 7, 1986, not, as Clarke vaguely recalled, a month earlier (100-6, p. 155).

41. Poindexter, 100-8, p. 31.

42. The two Findings may be found side by side in Part III, pp. 1070–71.

43. Sporkin, 100-6, p. 155.

44. The two memoranda can be compared in 100-6, pp. 447–49 (January 6, 1986) and pp. 465–67 (January 17, 1986).

45. 100-6, p. 467.

46. TR, p. III-12.

47. Press conference of November 19, 1986, 100-9, p. 1316.

48. Reagan deposition, PT, p. 261.

49. Shultz, 100-9, pp. 147–48.

50. Weinberger, 100-10, pp. 136–37, 185–88.

51. Caspar Weinberger, *Fighting for Peace* (Warner Books, 1990), p. 376.

52. Ibid., pp. 145–46.

53. Ibid., p. 145.

54. Ibid., pp. 353–85, esp. pp. 360–65, 383–84.

55. Shultz, 100-9, p. 59.

56. Ibid.

57. Interview with Shultz, *New York Times*, December 18, 1988.

58. Shultz, 100-9, p. 59.

59. Ronald Reagan, *An American Life*, pp. 477, 523–4.

60. The clearest acknowledgment by Poindexter of the NSC staff's "operational role"—which he shortened to NSC—came in his testimony before the Senate Select Committee on Secret Military Assistance to Iran and the Nicaraguan Opposition, August 6, 1987, p. 7 (not printed; typewritten copy in my possession).

61. Those present at this meeting vary with the telling. TR names Sporkin, George, C/NE (his

name has not been divulged), Poindexter, North, and Secord (p. B-70). FR names Sporkin, George, Poindexter, North, Secord, and the deputy chief of the Near East Division (DC/NE), but not the C/NE (p. 213). Secord said that Sporkin brought one or two members of his staff, and that the NSC staff counsel, Commander Paul Thompson, was also present (100-1, p. 97). The C/NE testified that he was present but not Secord (B-5, pp. 896–902).

62. C/NE, B-5, pp. 899–900.
63. DC/NE, cited in FR, p. 213.
64. Secord, 100-1, pp. 96–99.
65. Ibid., p. 101.
66. Ibid., p. 326.

13. Ghorbanifar

1. North, 100-7, Part I, pp. 64, 109.
2. Ibid., pp. 220–21.
3. The circumstances are related in a memorandum of October 7, 1985, by Charles E. Allen, in B-1, pp. 934–35.
4. Allen, B-1, p. 362. Allen says neither he nor McMahon knew who "Ascari" was, but no effort was made to check because it was considered a "White House directed activity" (pp. 365–66).
5. Ledeen, B-15, p. 1203.
6. Ibid., p. 369.
7. Ledeen, B-15, pp. 1198–1203. Ledeen's book has the wrong date for this meeting (pp. 137–38).
8. Ledeen, *Perilous Statecraft*, pp. 201–2.
9. That Ledeen first told the story to Clarridge and Allen on December 4 is shown in Allen's Memorandum for the Record, December 18, 1985 (B-1, p. 966).
10. Ledeen, *Perilous Statecraft*, p. 201.
11. Allen, B-1, p. 464. FR has improved on this statement by making it: "a good fellow who is a lot of fun" (p. 200).
12. Allen, B-1, p. 967.
13. Memorandum, "The Iranian Political Scene," December 6, 1985, B-1, pp. 970–72.
14. Ledeen, *Perilous Statecraft*, pp. 202–3.
15. Allen, B-1, pp. 476, 508.
16. CIA Chief, Near East, to Casey, B-1, p. 976.
17. B-1, pp. 978–79.
18. Ledeen, *Perilous Statecraft*, pp. 203–4.
19. B-1, pp. 982, 985.
20. Ledeen writes that North told him, when he was informed of Ghorbanifar's coming polygraph, that "there is no way they will let him pass that test. Once the CIA has taken a position on a man, they don't ever admit that they were wrong" (*Perilous Statecraft*, p. 203).
21. NN, January 14, 1986. North's notes for January 22 and February 18, 1986, contain similar plans, evidently refinements of the previous one.
22. North's notes for January 14, 1986, about a meeting with Secord indicate that they discussed an option of making Secord an "Israeli agent."
23. George, B-12, p. 99.
24. Ibid., p. 101.
25. Ibid., pp. 101, 105–6.
26. Clarridge, B-5, pp. 874, 889.
27. Charles E. Allen, Memorandum for the Record, January 29, 1986, B-1, pp. 992–1000. Allen was also questioned about a phrase in his report about "thwarting terrorist acts" (p. 999), which lent itself to the conjecture that Ghorbanifar might have suggested using Iran profits to support the Nicaraguan contras. Allen denied that he had thought of it that way (pp. 561–68).

28. Allen to Carroll L. Hauver, CIA Inspector General, February 13, 1987, A-1, p. 1157. Allen said that Ghorbanifar's statement appeared in the notes he had taken at the time.

29. Allen's handwritten notes, ibid., p. 1159.

30. B-1, pp. 555–60.

31. Ibid., p. 575.

32. B-12, p. 111.

33. B-1, p. 977.

34. North, 100-7, Part I, p. 56.

35. Israeli Historical Chronology, cited in FR, p. 197.

36. North, 100-7, Part I, p. 108.

37. The exact date and place are uncertain, because North wavered between London and Frankfurt. He first said that it might have taken place in London, which would put it on January 22, 1986, or in Frankfurt, which would make it February 25, 1986. Later North alternated between London and Frankfurt, mentioning January in one sentence and Frankfurt in another (North, 100-7, Part I, pp. 108–9). FR assumes that North meant London and ignores his reference to Frankfurt (p. 216). Other circumstances make London more probable, the most important being Poindexter's recollection that North had mentioned the diversion to him for the first time after North had come back from London (Poindexter, 100-8, pp. 35–36).

38. North, 100-7, Part I, p. 109.

39. A transcript of this tape appears in A-1, pp. 1166–67. I have given it the way it appears there. The version in FR, p. 216, changes some of the wording and punctuation for reasons not clear to me. The deleted passage after "free of charge" is said to read "[First Iranian official] visit," which would be a reference to Karoubi.

40. North, PT, p. 1091. North also said: "In fact, the original idea came from Mr. Nir and Mr. Ghorbanifar" (p. 1394).

41. Ibid., pp. 1385–86.

42. Ibid., p. 1094.

43. PT, pp. 1101, 1106.

44. Ibid., p. 1103.

45. North, 100-7, Part II, p. 167.

46. North, 100-7, Part I, p. 109.

47. Poindexter, 100-8, p. 185.

48. Ibid., pp. 35–36.

49. Ibid., p. 36.

50. Ibid., p. 40.

51. Ibid., pp. 250–51.

52. Ibid., p. 37.

53. Ibid., p. 20.

54. Ibid., p. 120.

55. FR, pp. 214–15.

56. North, 100-7, Part I, p. 110.

57. NN, January 21, 1986. There is a fully detailed plan in the entry for January 22, 1986.

58. North, 100-7, Part I, p. 168.

59. North, 100-7, Part II, pp. 166, 168.

60. Secord, 100-1, pp. 103–4.

61. North to Poindexter, January 24, 1986, Part III, pp. 1074–80.

62. B-1, Exhibit 32, pp. 1023–31, esp. p. 1029.

63. Memorandum for the Record, February 18, 1986, B-1, pp. 1032–35.

64. McMahon to Casey, January 25, 1986, A-1, pp. 1183–84.

65. Ibid., p. 1184.

66. Secord's message was transmitted by North to Poindexter, February 18, 1986, Part III, p. 1081. In the printed version, the words "if intelligence is good" have been deleted. They appear in FR, p. 218.

67. Ibid., p. 1081.
68. Secord, 100-1, p. 107.
69. Ibid., p. 108.
70. North to McFarlane, February 27, 1986, A-1, p. 1179.
71. C/NE, B-5, p. 923.
72. NN, February 19, 1986.
73. C/NE, B-5, pp. 933–34.
74. "Conversation with G on 23 February," B-1, pp. 1051–52.
75. Secord, 100-1, p. 107.
76. North to McFarlane, February 27, 1986, Part III, p. 1084.
77. NN, February 21, 1986.
78. Hakim, B-13, pp. 591–92. Hakim gave another, similar version of his disguise in 100-5, p. 224.
79. Hakim, B-13, p. 599. According to Hakim, Secord gave the name incorrectly as Ebraham Ebrahim (Secord, 100-1, p. 107).
80. Hakim, B-13, p. 598.
81. Ibid., p. 593.
82. C/NE, B-5, pp. 936–37. Hakim also refers to the "Volkswagens" (Hakim, B-13, pp. 597–98).
83. C/NE, B-5, p. 936.
84. Ibid., p. 938.
85. Hakim, B-13, pp. 598–601; Hakim, 100-5, p. 286.
86. Secord, 100-1, p. 109.
87. Ibid., pp. 108–9.
88. North to McFarlane, February 27, 1986, A-1, p. 1179.
89. McFarlane to North, February 27, 1986, ibid., p. 1178.
90. North to McFarlane, February 27, 1986, ibid., pp. 1179–80.
91. McFarlane to North, February 27, 1986, ibid., pp. 1180–81.

14. The Diversion

1. North to McFarlane, February 27, 1986, A-1, p. 1179.
2. NN, March 2, 1986.
3. Cave, B-3, pp. 569–81.
4. C/NE, B-5, p. 223. George claimed that he was personally responsible for bringing in Cave (B-12, p. 120).
5. Cave, B-3, pp. 580, 582.
6. Cave memorandum, March 7, 1986, B-3, pp. 1007–8.
7. C/NE, B-5, p. 948.
8. NN, March 7, 1986.
9. C/NE, B-5, p. 947. Here the number of wanted parts is given as 240 or 260. Cave gave the number as 940 line items (B-3, p. 592).
10. Cave memorandum, B-3, p. 1007.
11. Ibid., p. 1008. "Other operations" is deleted in the printed memorandum but restored in FR, p. 223.
12. North to McFarlane, March 10, 1986, A-1, p. 1190.
13. McFarlane to North, March 10, 1986, ibid., p. 1192.
14. North to McFarlane, March 11, 1986, ibid., p. 1193.
15. Cave, B-3, p. 590.
16. Allen, Memorandum for the Record, March 11, 1986, B-1, p. 1068. The dates of the conversation and memorandum are not the same.
17. Ibid., p. 1067.
18. Ibid., March 18, 1986, p. 1066.

19. Ibid., March 21, 1986, pp. 1064–65. Nir is always referred to as "Adam" and Ghorbanifar as "Subject."
20. Ibid., March 24, 1986, p. 1063.
21. Ibid., March 28, 1986, p. 1061.
22. Ibid., p. 1060.
23. Ibid., March 31, 1986, p. 1059.
24. Ibid., April 2, 1986, p. 1058.
25. Ibid., p. 1057.
26. Ibid., p. 1058. There is another version of these two telephone calls by Cave, who translated them, apparently from a recording. Cave said "that it was an attempt to go—that is apart from the Ghorbanifar channel to try to convince—through another channel to convince the Iranians that we were sincere and would do what we said we would do by Ghorbanifar" (B-3, p. 645).
27. Cave, B-3, p. 575.
28. Ibid., pp. 584–86.
29. Ibid., p. 591.
30. Ibid., p. 600.
31. Secord, 100-1, p. 105.
32. Cave, B-3, pp. 604–9; Cave memorandum, A-1, pp. 1198–99.
33. NN, March 7, 1986.
34. C/NE, B-5, pp. 945–46. In his biography of Casey, Joseph E. Persico says that over ten thousand letters demanding McMahon's resignation were "generated" to the White House by "super-patriot organizations like Free the Eagle and the Federation of American Afghan Action" (Joseph E. Persico, *Casey* [Viking, 1990], p. 495).
35. The memorandum itself is not dated. FR places it at "about April 4, 1986" (p. 225). The memorandum notes that the final meeting with Ghorbanifar in Washington had lasted "nearly all night on April 3–4," so it must have been written after Ghorbanifar's departure. It was accompanied by another statement, "Terms of Reference: U.S.-Iran Dialogue," which is dated April 4, 1986. The likelihood is that the "diversion memorandum" was also written on April 4, 1986, or shortly afterward.
36. North to Poindexter, "Release of American Hostages in Beirut," A-1, pp. 1201–5.
37. North to McFarlane, April 7, 1986, ibid., p. 1206.
38. North, 100-7, Part I, p. 11.
39. Poindexter, 100-8, pp. 43, 45.
40. Ibid., pp. 517–50. Chief Counsel Liman mentioned four copies (North, 100-7, Part I, p. 302).
41. North, 100-7, Part I, p. 241.
42. 100-8, pp. 522–24.
43. C/NE, B-5, p. 916.
44. North to McFarlane, April 7, 1986, A-1, p. 1206.
45. NN, April 3, 1986. The date here is deceptive, because there is a 4 at top of page.
46. Ibid., April 7, 1986.
47. Cave, B-3, p. 601. Howard Teicher also "strongly recommended" against Nir's participation (B-26, p. 707).
48. North, 100-7, Part I, p. 229.
49. McFarlane, 100-2, p. 253.
50. Cave, B-3, pp. 605–6.
51. Ibid., p. 606.
52. Secord, 100-1, p. 112.
53. Allen, Memorandum for the Record, May 5, 1986, A-1, p. 1217.
54. Ghorbanifar interview, TR, p. B-120.
55. Poindexter, 100-8, p. 178.
56. Allen, Memorandum for the Record, April 16, 1986, A-1, pp. 1208–9.
57. A-1, p. 1211. The name of Kangarlou as the Second Iranian Official appears in FR, p. 227, but not in the exhibit, on p. 1211.

58. Poindexter to McFarlane, April 22, 1986, A-1, p. 1212. Kangarlou's name has been omitted here but appears in FR as the "Second Iranian Official," p. 227. The Frankfurt meeting mentioned by Poindexter never took place; he may have meant the meeting in London, without Kangarlou, on May 6.
59. McFarlane to Poindexter, April 22, 1986, A-1, p. 1213.
60. Copp [Secord] to North, April 21, 1986, ibid., p. 1214. Kangarlou's name has again been omitted but may be identified in FR, p. 227.
61. NN, April 22, 1986.
62. Ibid., April 24, 1986.
63. Allen, Memorandum for Deputy Director of Operations, May 5, 1986, A-1, p. 1218. FR fails to underline "only" (p. 228).
64. Shultz, 100-9, p. 8.
65. Cave said that Rowland was asked for $15 million to finance the deal (B-3, p. 937).
66. Price, B-21, pp. 348–49.
67. Misspelled "Fraser" in Price, B-21, p. 348; the correct spelling is in the Price memorandum, 100-8, p. 561.
68. Price, memorandum of conversation, May 3, 1986, 100-8, p. 561.
69. Poindexter to North, May 3, 1986, 100-8, p. 558.
70. North to Poindexter, May 5, 1986, ibid., p. 559.
71. Ibid., pp. 559–60.
72. Shultz, 100-9, pp. 9–10.
73. Allen, Memorandum for the Record, March 24, 1986, B-1, p. 1063.
74. Ibid., p. 1061.
75. Allen, B-1, p. 659; *The Iran-Contra Puzzle* (Congressional Quarterly, 1987), pp. A8, A21, A36–37, D32. It was thought, according to Cave, that Ghorbanifar and Khashoggi had been trying to raise $50 million. Cave also said that Hashemi had "ratted" on Ghorbanifar, as a result of which Ghorbanifar had been arrested and had probably lost a lot of money (B-3, pp. 634, 937).
76. Poindexter to North, May 5, 1986, 100-9, p. 537.
77. Cave, B-3, p. 638.
78. NN, May 6, 1986, A-1, pp. 1219–20.
79. Cave, B-3, pp. 906–7.
80. Allen to Casey, October 14, 1986, ibid., p. 1050.
81. Ibid., pp. 627–29. This arrangement is said to have been confirmed by Nir (Israeli Historical Chronology, cited in FR, p. 230).
82. NN, May 7, 1986.
83. Memorandum for the Record, May 9, 1986, A-1, pp. 1222–24.
84. Ibid., p. 1225.
85. North to Poindexter, May 17, 1986, Part III, p. 1154.
86. Poindexter to North, May 19, 1986, ibid., p. 764. Reagan was not mentioned in North's previous message; FR, p. 231, mistakenly adds the president to the other three.
87. Cave, B-3, p. 645.
88. A-1, p. 1228.
89. Ibid., p. 1251.
90. Poindexter to North, May 19–20, 1986, Part III, pp. 764, 767.
91. North to Poindexter, May 20, 1986, ibid., pp. 765–66.
92. Cave, B-3, pp. 624–25.
93. See the names in A-1, p. 1261.
94. Cave, B-3, p. 839.
95. Ibid., p. 741.
96. Ibid., p. 839.
97. McDaniel, PT, pp. 2848–49.
98. TR, p. B-96.

15. Tehran

1. McFarlane, 100-2, p. 253.
2. Cave, B-3, p. 834.
3. Robin Wright, *In the Name of God* (Simon and Schuster, 1989), p. 145. This information is said to be based on interviews in 1988 with members of the McFarlane delegation and interviews in Tehran, June–July 1989.
4. The spokesman is said to have called himself "Ali Najavi" and is described as a deputy to Prime Minister Moussavi, but the name is said to be false (Mayer and McManus, *Landslide*, p. 232). Cave mentioned the third as an intelligence officer (A-1, p. 1261). Since "Ali Samii" has also been identified as an intelligence officer, Cave may be referring to him. FR says that "Samii"—otherwise known as "the Monster" or "the Engine"—participated in the Tehran negotiations (p. 254).
5. Cave, A-1, p. 1302.
6. Teicher, Memorandum of Conversation, May 25, 1986, A-1, pp. 1256–57; McFarlane to Poindexter, May 27, 1986, ibid., p. 1269; NN, May 25, 1986. Some details vary in different versions. Cave's memorandum says that the group waited for two hours (A-1, p. 1261). McFarlane put the wait at "over an hour" (McFarlane to Poindexter, May 27, 1986, ibid., p. 1269).
7. Cave memorandum, ibid., p. 1261.
8. Teicher memorandum, ibid., p. 1258. The identity of the Iranian is given as the "Second Iranian"—who was Kangarlou—in FR, p. 238.
9. Teicher memorandum, ibid., p. 1259. Cave's memorandum says that Ghorbanifar had already told them at the airfield that an Iranian representative had been sent to Lebanon to secure the release of the hostages (p. 1261). North's notebook says that the Iranian said at the first meeting: "We will send necessary delegation to cause release" and linked it with a complaint about the Americans having brought "very few items you promised."
10. Teicher memorandum, ibid., p. 1260.
11. Cave memorandum, ibid., p. 1261; Cave, B-3, pp. 838–39.
12. McFarlane to Poindexter, May 27, 1986, A-1, p. 1269.
13. Cave memorandum, ibid., p. 1262.
14. NN, May 26, 1986.
15. Teicher memorandum, A-1, p. 1272.
16. Ibid., pp. 1272–74.
17. Segev says that the Iranian team meeting with McFarlane was made up of: Mohammed Ali Hadi Najafabadi, chairman of the Majlis Foreign Affairs Committee; Ali Mohammed Bisharati, senior deputy to the foreign minister; Hossein Sheikh El-Islam Zadeh, deputy foreign minister; and Mohammed Lavassani, head of the political department of the Foreign Ministry (*The Iranian Triangle*, p. 273). This list is almost certainly unreliable; it does not include Kangarlou, who was undoubtedly one of those who met with the Americans; except for Najafabadi, it is untrustworthy. Robin Wright refers to Hadi Najafabadi, deputy chairman of the Majlis Foreign Affairs Committee (*In the Name of God*, p. 144). Najafabadi appears in Mayer and McManus, *Landslide*, pp. 235–43, 244. Najafabadi is given as Naja Fabadi by Ben Bradlee, Jr. (*Guts and Glory*, p. 379). McFarlane described him as "you might say, in the outer office of the speaker there" (McFarlane, 100-2, p. 252). Cave says he was the "most senior official" we met (B-3, p. 833).
18. Teicher memorandum, A-1, pp. 1275–80.
19. McFarlane to Poindexter, May 27, 1986, ibid., p. 1270.
20. Cave memorandum, ibid., p. 1262.
21. McFarlane to Poindexter, May 27, 1986, ibid., pp. 1252–54.
22. McFarlane to Poindexter, May 26, 1986, ibid., p. 1269. The words "Tatar became" are deleted; they are included in TR, p. B-101.
23. McFarlane to Poindexter, A-1, p. 1289.
24. Teicher memorandum, May 27, 1986, ibid., pp. 1286–87. NN, May 27, 1986, implies that

the Iranians were playing for time: "We are waiting for results. We must see how we can do. We will have news tomorrow. If all are serious, it will work. We will do the job w/o [without] waiting for other supplies."

25. McFarlane's message to Poindexter says "Ghorbanifar and [deleted]" (A-1, p. 1289). The other was probably Kangarlou.
26. NN, May 27, 1986.
27. North, 100-7, Part I, p. 229.
28. Cave, B-3, p. 652.
29. McFarlane to Poindexter, May 27, 1986, A-1, pp. 1288–90.
30. Teicher memorandum, May 27, 1986, ibid., pp. 1291–93.
31. For the text of this agreement, ibid., pp. 1294–95.
32. Cave said that the Iranians made clear shortly after the Americans arrived that they could only get two hostages and were negotiating for two (B-3, p. 775).
33. Ibid., p. 820.
34. McFarlane, 100-2, pp. 64, 112, 250.
35. North, 100-7, Part I, p. 230.
36. McFarlane, 100-2, p. 250.
37. Teicher's memorandum, May 28, 1986, A-1, p. 1304.
38. Ibid., pp. 1297–98.
39. Cave memorandum, ibid., p. 1302. Teicher put the departure at 8:55 a.m. (ibid., p. 1304).
40. Teicher memorandum, May 28, 1986, ibid., p. 1304. Cave says that an Iranian on the morning of May 28 asked "if we would accept two [hostages] being released immediately and two more after the [arms] delivery." He was told that the Americans were leaving the hotel after breakfast (Cave memorandum, ibid., p. 1302).
41. North, 100-7, Part I, p. 230.
42. Ibid., p. 229.
43. TR, pp. B-120–21.
44. Secord, 100-1, pp. 116–18.
45. Ibid., p. 115.
46. Cave, B-3, p. 849.
47. NT, p. 4245.
48. Memorandum of Conversation, prepared by Howard Teicher, May 29, 1986. It is marked N 15387. This document has apparently not been published; a copy is in my possession. Those present are listed as: the president, the vice president, Donald Regan, John Poindexter, Robert McFarlane, Oliver North, Howard Teicher, and Rod McDaniel. The meeting began at the regular 9:30 a.m. time for the president's briefing by the national security adviser; it ended at 9:40 a.m., having lasted only ten minutes. North recorded the meeting in his notebook with the statement: "No further meetings until hostages come out."
49. TR, p. B-127.

16. Narrow Escapes

1. A-1, p. 370.
2. Dutton, 100-3, pp. 211, 228; Dutton, NT, p. 3297.
3. North to Poindexter, May 16, 1986, Part III, p. 30.
4. 100-8, p. 588.
5. This article was incorrectly dated in FR as having been published on "1/18/85" (p. 135, note 65).
6. Karna Small to North, date unclear but probably in week before June 25, 1986, A-1, p. 919.
7. A-1 contains 71 pages on Terrell (808–79); his story is briefly told in FR, pp. 112–13.
8. North to Karna Small, June 27, 1986, A-1, p. 920.
9. North's statement to the FBI, A-1, p. 855.
10. North to Poindexter, July 15, 1986, Part III, p. 1179.
11. Poindexter to North, July 15, 1986, TR, p. B-126.

12. Poindexter, 100-8, p. 253.
13. FR, p. 138.
14. General Paul X. Kelly, NT, pp. 6270–77.
15. North to McFarlane, February 27, 1986, 100-2, p. 615.
16. McFarlane to North, March 11, 1986, ibid., p. 616.
17. North to Poindexter, May 6, 1986, Part III, p. 1150.
18. North, 100-7, Part I, p. 130.
19. Robinette, B-23, p. 629.
20. Ibid., pp. 686–87.
21. Ibid., pp. 647, 656, 705.
22. Ibid., pp. 660–73.
23. North, 100-7, Part I, p. 132.
24. William S. Cohen and George J. Mitchell, *Men of Zeal* (Viking, 1988), p. 163.
25. Secord, 100-1, pp. 45, 73.
26. Ibid., p. 45. Secord informed North that he was asking for a fixed price of $1.2 million for six months and that the operating costs would probably come to $50,000 monthly (TR, p. C-13).
27. Cannistraro to Poindexter, May 14, 1986, Part III, p. 760.
28. TR, p. C-13.
29. One message from North to Poindexter on this subject was deleted in 100-8, p. 629, but it is given in FR, p. 75.
30. FR, p. 75.
31. Poindexter to North, May 15, 1986, 100-8, p. 570.
32. Poindexter, 100-8, p. 60.
33. Ibid., p. 61.
34. Ibid.
35. North to Poindexter, May 16, 1986, ibid., pp. 582–83.
36. Note from Poindexter, recipient and date unclear, ibid., p. 571.
37. Poindexter to North, June 1986, ibid., pp. 584–85.
38. North to Poindexter, probably June 16, 1986, ibid., p. 589.
39. NT, p. 6955.
40. North to Poindexter, June 10, 1986, 100-8, p. 588.
41. McFarlane to Poindexter, June 11, 1986, 100-2, p. 624. The Marine Corps "survey" refers to a disability review.
42. PT, pp. 2846–47.
43. North to Poindexter, September 17, 1986, Part III, pp. 1217–18.
44. Thomas Latimer (staff director of the House Intelligence Committee), NT, p. 4994.
45. Poindexter, 100-8, p. 83.
46. Part III, pp. 546–48; FR, p. 139, has the wrong date.
47. Part III, p. 550.
48. Poindexter to Hamilton, July 21, 1986, ibid., p. 551.
49. Poindexter, 100-8, p. 96.
50. Ibid.
51. Ibid., p. 89.
52. Ibid., p. 53.
53. Reagan deposition, PT, pp. 147–48.
54. The denial of military advice appears in the report of the meeting to Poindexter by Robert Pearson, NSC staff counsel, who was present (August 6, 1986, Part III, p. 555).
55. NT, pp. 1701, 1961–62.
56. Ibid., pp. 4978, 4984, 4979.
57. Memo to the Files by Steven K. Berry, associate counsel, Part III, pp. 553–54.
58. Poindexter to North, August 11, 1986, ibid., p. 555.
59. North, 100-7, Part I, pp. 179–80.
60. NT, p. 7601.

61. Tambs said that the new Arias administration wanted the agreement "rephrased or renegotiated" (100-3, p. 377).
62. Ibid., p. 382.
63. Ibid., pp. 383, 407.
64. Ibid., p. 391.
65. 100-4, p. 32.
66. Secord, 100-1, p. 74; Copp [Secord] to North, June 12, 1986, ibid., p. 427.
67. Secord, 100-1, p. 75; Earl to Secord, August 13, 1986, ibid., p. 430.
68. Secord to Earl, August 13, 1986, ibid., p. 430.
69. Secord, 100-1, pp. 75–76.
70. NN, cited in FR, p. 142.
71. North to Poindexter, September 6, 1986, 100-3, p. 609. Fiers's name is deleted in this document but given in TR as "CIA CATF" (p. C-13).
72. Poindexter to North, September 7, 1986, FR, p. 143.
73. Tambs, 100-3, pp. 383–84.
74. Abrams, 100-5, pp. 24–25.
75. North, 100-7, Part II, p. 89.
76. Poindexter, 100-8, pp. 252–53.
77. Shultz, 100-9, p. 108.
78. C/CATF (Fiers), 100-11, p. 135.
79. Ibid., p. 171.
80. Secord, 100-1, p. 435.
81. North to Poindexter, September 26, 1986, A-1, p. 567.
82. *New York Times*, September 29, 1986.
83. Poindexter to North, September 25, 1986, A-1, p. 567.
84. North to Poindexter, September 26, 1986, ibid., p. 567.
85. North to Poindexter, September 30, 1986, Part III, p. 561; "Press Guidance Re Airstrip in Costa Rica," September 30, 1986, ibid., p. 563.

17. The Unraveling

1. North, 100-7, Part I, p. 253.
2. D-4, p. 815.
3. Rodriguez, B-23, pp. 803–4.
4. Gregg, B-12, pp. 1059–66, 1135–37.
5. "Summary of Contacts with Felix Rodriguez," B-12, p. 1133.
6. Hasenfus, B-14, pp. 67–69.
7. Ibid., pp. 95, 175.
8. Ibid., pp. 138–39.
9. "Tomás Castillo" (Fernandez), 100-4, p. 24. Almost two months earlier, on August 18, 1986, Colonel James Steele, the commander of the U.S. military forces in El Salvador, had warned North (through Earl) that daytime drops "increases the possibility of being shot down by Sam-7 or intercepted by TD-33 . . . recommend it be rescheduled as a night mission" (Dutton, 100-3, p. 509). The message shows how deeply implicated Steele himself was in the North-Secord operation.
10. Dutton, NT, pp. 3305–6.
11. Ibid., p. 3306.
12. Ibid., p. 527. For Watson's original notes, see Part III, p. 479, with an incorrect name for Hasenfus.
13. North, 100-7, Part I, p. 182.
14. Ibid., pp. 158, 182.
15. NT, p. 7088.
16. Ibid., p. 7560.
17. *Washington Post*, October 8, 1986, p. A-1.

18. Abrams, 100-5, p. 65.
19. Ibid.
20. *New York Times*, October 9, 1986.
21. *Washington Post*, October 8, 1986.
22. Cannistraro to Poindexter, October 8, 1986, Part III, p. 570.
23. *New York Times*, October 14, 1986. The contra statement was evidently arranged by North on October 9, when this entry appears in North's notebook: "Call C/CATF [Fiers], Cruz, Calero [about] press release. The A/C [aircraft] was providing humanitarian supplies to UNO fighters."
24. Text of Evans and Novak show (CNN), October 11, 1986, in 100-5, pp. 628–41.
25. Ibid., pp. 637, 641.
26. Ibid., p. 65.
27. Ibid., pp. 66–67.
28. TR, p. C-13.
29. 100-5, pp. 67–68.
30. 100-5, p. 647.
31. TR, p. C-14.
32. 100-11, pp. 216, 669.
33. Ibid., p. 217.
34. Ibid., p. 220.
35. Ibid., p. 218. The story of the three airplanes appears in B-3, pp. 1199–1202.
36. Ibid., p. 1205.
37. Ibid., pp. 121–22.
38. Ibid., p. 147.
39. Ibid., p. 162.
40. Ibid., p. 169.
41. Ibid., p. 1209.
42. North, 100-7, Part I, p. 137.
43. North, NT, p. 7029.
44. North, 100-7, Part I, pp. 19–20.
45. Ibid., p. 137.
46. Ibid., pp. 136–37.
47. Ibid., p. 137; 100-7, Part II, p. 110.
48. 100-7, Part I, p. 254.
49. Poindexter, B-20, pp. 1183–85; Poindexter, 100-8, pp. 106-7. Poindexter told this story twice in the same way. Yet deGraffenreid said that he could not recall the incident (B-8, p. 1029).
50. North, 100-7, Part I, pp. 147–48.
51. "Tomás Castillo" (Fernandez), B-3, pp. 358, 489.
52. 100-9, p. 540.
53. North to Poindexter, June 10, 1986, 100-9, p. 553.
54. Poindexter to North, June 10, 1986, ibid., pp. 552–53.
55. 100-5, p. 668.
56. Ibid., pp. 668–71.
57. Ibid., p. 42.
58. James Bartholomew, *The Richest Man in the World: The Sultan of Brunei* (Viking, 1989), p. 16. A sycophantic biography has been written by Lord Chalfont, *By God's Will: A Portrait of the Sultan of Brunei* (Weidenfeld and Nicolson, 1989).
59. Sigur, B-25, p. 536.
60. Abrams, 100-5, pp. 596–610.
61. Ibid., p. 676.
62. Ibid., p. 47.
63. Ibid., pp. 47–48.
64. Ibid., p. 48.
65. Ibid., p. 191.

66. Ibid., p. 595, for a reproduction.
67. Ibid., p. 49.
68. Ibid., p. 614.
69. Ibid., pp. 50–51, 677–79.
70. Ibid., pp. 611–12.
71. Ibid., pp. 659, 662.
72. Ibid., pp. 693–94.
73. Ibid., pp. 700–2.
74. Ibid., pp. 707–8.
75. Ibid., p. 746.
76. Shultz, 100-9, p. 94.
77. Abrams, 100-5, p. 191.

18. End Run

1. McDaniel log, May 28, 1986, cited in TR, p. B-127.
2. Poindexter to North, May 31, 1986, ibid., p. B-128.
3. North to Poindexter, June 3, 1986, ibid., p. B-128.
4. McDaniel log; Poindexter to Casey, June 19, 1986, ibid., p. B-128.
5. North to McFarlane, June 7, 1985, 100-2, pp. 537–42.
6. Poindexter to the President (prepared by North), June 10, 1986, Part III, pp. 1159–60.
7. FR, p. 245; p. 264, note 2.
8. Cave, B-3, p. 661.
9. Ibid., p. 662. Allen, Cave's superior, said that Cave made this telephone call at "the direction, detailed direction, of Colonel North" (Allen, B-1, p. 673).
10. Cave, B-3, p. 658.
11. "Dubai" was used as a code name for Tehran in this and other conversations (see also B-3, p. 1015).
12. Cave memorandum on meeting of June 13, 1986, A-1, p. 1312. Cave's code name is "O'neil" in this memorandum; Kangarlou's name is deleted, but FR, p. 245, refers to him as the "Second Iranian." The date is given erroneously as "6/23/86" in FR, p. 264, note 3.
13. This conversation was transcribed, B-3, p. 1018.
14. Cave memorandum, B-3, p. 1015.
15. Cave, B-3, p. 664.
16. NN, June 23, 1986.
17. Transcript of Cave-Kangarlou telephone conversation, June 30, 1986, A-1, pp. 1315–20. There is a Cave memorandum on the same conversation in B-3, p. 1016.
18. Ibid., p. 1321.
19. Allen, B-1, pp. 671, 677.
20. A-1, p. 1320 (bottom). In another message, Ghorbanifar said that the increase was 60 percent (p. 1151).
21. Allen, B-1, pp. 672–73.
22. Ibid., p. 673.
23. Ibid., pp. 664, 667.
24. Gates memorandum, June 8, 1976, B-1, p. 1069 (for Gates, see p. 668).
25. Israeli Historical Chronology, cited by FR, p. 246.
26. NN, July 2, 1986. Nir's alias in this and other places was "Adam."
27. Allen, B-1, pp. 683–84.
28. Ibid., p. 610.
29. TR, p. B-131, note 73, names Cave as the one who obtained this letter; FR, p. 246, says that North received a copy of the purported letter. Conceivably, North may have received it from Cave. In TR, the date is first given as July 8, 1986 (p. B-131), but it is said that Ghorbanifar had signed it on July 9, 1986 (p. B-135)—a discrepancy for which there is no explanation.
30. TR, pp. B-132–135.

31. North to Poindexter, July 10, 1986, TR, p. B-136.
32. North to Poindexter, July 17, 1986, ibid., p. B-137. The country of this foreign official may have been Syria, which is mentioned in a similar context on p. B-139.
33. North to Poindexter, July 10 and 17, 1986, TR, pp. B-136–38. This message was evidently passed on to the Iranian foreign minister (B-138).
34. North to Poindexter, no date but probably July 26, 1986, Part III, p. 1189.
35. Israeli Historical Chronology, cited by FR, p. 246 and p. 264, note 16.
36. TR, p. B-138.
37. North to Poindexter, probably July 26, 1986, Part III, p. 1189.
38. North to Poindexter, July 29, 1986, Part III, p. 1182. This deal also appears in NN, July 27, 1986, with a seventh step: "Last hostage & last HP [HIPAR radar]."
39. North to Poindexter, July 29, 1986, Part III, pp. 1181–83.
40. McFarlane to Poindexter, July 26, 1986, TR, p. B-139. The reference to Syria is unclear. Poindexter and North told McFarlane two different versions about Syria's alleged role. Poindexter thought that the Syrians had entered into the Jenco release at the last minute (Poindexter to McFarlane, July 26, 1986, TR, p. B-139). North said that the Jenco release "is the direct result of your mission and neither the Syrians nor the non-existent Casey trip had anything to do with it" (North to McFarlane, July 26, 1986, ibid., p. B-139, note 81). This divergence suggests that neither of them really knew what the Syrians had done. The reference to the "non-existent Casey trip" is also unexplained.
41. Poindexter to McFarlane, July 26, 1986, TR, p. B-139. This version is what is published here. "The Tehran contact" was almost certainly Kangarlou, with whom Cave had been having conversations.
42. This reference to additional Israeli arms to Iran is not further explained.
43. The name of Kangarlou has been deleted in the documents and, therefore, has been put in brackets. On July 27, North's notebook contains the line: "Call to Australian: Thank you!" Secord referred to Kangarlou as "the Australian," as in TR, p. B-147, where he is identified as an "official in the Prime Minister's office"—the usual designation for Kangarlou.
44. Casey to Poindexter, July 26, 1986, Part III, pp. 1197–99.
45. Armacost to Shultz, July 2, 1986, 100-9, p. 554.
46. These notes cover two and a half pages; the decipherment is sometimes difficult. The lines given here are almost entirely clear but the context is not.
47. North/Cave, June 27, 1986, Part III, p. 1186.
48. Report of member of Hostage Location Task Force, July 30, 1986, based on information from the CIA's Charles Allen, TR, p. B-144.
49. August 3 is based on the Historical Chronology, 11/20/86, Part III, p. 142; August 4 on the Israeli Historical Chronology, cited by FR, p. 247 and p. 264, note 24. TR chooses August 3 (p. B-147).
50. This seems to be the sense of the testimony by Craig L. Fuller, Bush's chief of staff, who accompanied Bush to the meeting with Nir (Fuller, B-10, p. 925). In his notes on the meeting, Fuller says that "Nir began by indicating that Peres had asked him to brief the VP" (TR, p. B-145).
51. Craig Fuller's notes, "The Vice President's Meeting with Mr. Nir," King David Hotel, Jerusalem, July 29, 1986, TR, pp. B-145–47. The words in brackets are Fuller's; the rest are Nir's.
52. This section is entirely based on the deposition of Admiral William J. Crowe, Jr., B-8, pp. 122–91.

19. The Second Channel

1. Cave said that he had received the microfiches sometime in July 1986 (B-3, p. 672). The Israeli Historical Chronology, cited by FR, says the Israelis received them on August 6, 1986 (p. 248 and p. 264, note 50).
2. B-3, pp. 670–71.

3. Allen, B-1, pp. 774–77. Part of p. 777 is deleted; the information in FR, p. 248, seems to be based on it. There is also an allusion to North's idea "of printing up to date microfiches that had the prices higher" in Cave, B-3, p. 807.

4. Allen, B-1, p. 676. The story relating to the price was "that these [spare parts] were one-time manufactured years ago and very costly to manufacture, and we had to get some of them out of current stocks" (p. 671).

5. Cave, B-3, p. 673.

6. North, 100-7, Part I, p. 327.

7. Secord, 100-1, pp. 235–36.

8. Cave, B-3, pp. 669, 722.

9. NN, A-1, p. 1329.

10. FR, p. 248, attributes this portion of North's notebook to Q 2314, only part of which appears in A-1, p. 1329.

11. The sum of $15 million is mentioned by House of Representatives Chief Counsel John W. Nields, Jr., with Secord's assent (100-1, p. 118).

12. NN, August 8, 1986.

13. Ibid.

14. Ibid., August 20, 1986; also see North to Poindexter, September 2, 1986, in TR, B-150.

15. Allen, B-1, pp. 689–90, 1097–1100. Ghorbanifar told TR that Khashoggi had lent him $10 million on February 6, 1986, at 15–20 percent interest; Khashoggi had deposited the money in the Lake Resources Swiss account on February 7, 1986 (TR, p. B-74). Ghorbanifar deposited $3.7 million in a CIA account to pay for 1,000 TOW missiles (ibid.).

16. FR, p. 248. Ghorbanifar needed only $5 million to avoid ruin in June 1986 (TR, B-131). Hakim was also told by Iranians that they owed $10 million to Ghorbanifar (Hakim, B-13, pp. 860–61).

17. TR, p. B-87.

18. NN, August 27, 1986.

19. Ibid., September 3, 1986.

20. Ibid., September 4, 1986.

21. Ibid., September 30, 1986.

22. North to McFarlane, February 27, 1986, Part III, p. 1085.

23. Cave, B-3, p. 584.

24. McMahon to Casey, January 25, 1986, B-17, p. 379.

25. Secord, 100-1, p. 207. FR says: "Shortly after the Tehran breakdown, Poindexter authorized North to seek a new opening to Iran for continued negotiations—a 'Second Channel' " (p. 249). Hakim also gave Secord credit for the opening of a Second Channel (Hakim, B-13, p. 418). Hakim said that North knew all about his efforts to find a Second Channel (Hakim, 100-5, p. 241).

26. Hakim, 100-5, pp. 382, 429.

27. Hakim, B-13, p. 735. Tabatabai was named in TR, p. B-148, note 86, where it is said that Tabatabai met with Cave in London on July 25, 1986. "Number One" is used in Hakim, B-13, p. 735; "First Contact" is used in FR, p. 249.

28. North to Poindexter, July 21, 1986, TR, p. B-138. Segev says Tabatabai was Khomeini's son-in-law and that he was associated with Mehdi Bahramani, Rafsanjani's eldest son, and Khomeini's son, Ahmed (The Iranian Triangle, p. 253). Segev's information seems to be dubious.

29. TR, pp. B-138–39.

30. Hakim, B-13, p. 737.

31. Ibid., p. 829.

32. Ibid., p. 841.

33. Ibid., pp. 673–75.

34. Ibid., p. 308.

35. TR says that North met with Tabatabai, possibly with Senator Helms, on June 27, 1986 (p. B-128, note 80).

36. Hakim, B-13, pp. 826–27.

37. Cave's notes, July 10, 1986, B-3, p. 1021.

38. Cave's notes, July 11, 1986, B-3, p. 1022. Tabatabai's name is here deleted.

39. Cave, B-3, p. 851. Cave described Tabatabai's sources in a memorandum, July 10, 1986 (p. 1021). FR, p. 249, says that the "Second Contact" had direct connections to the Iranian government.

40. NN, August 19, 1986.

41. North, 100-7, Part II, p. 7; FR, p. 249.

42. Hakim, B-13, p. 832.

43. Ibid., pp. 424–31, 673–75, 831–32; Hakim, 100-5, p. 309.

44. Secord to North, August 26, 1986, original in B-13, p. 967; typed version in A-1, pp. 1349–50.

45. Cave, B-3, p. 856.

46. North to Poindexter, "Next Steps with Iran," September 2, 1986, Part III, p. 1207.

47. Poindexter to North, date unclear but probably about September 3, 1986, Part III, p. 1202.

48. North to Poindexter, "Next Steps with Iran," September 2, 1986, Part III, p. 1207. The five alternatives were mentioned earlier but deleted (p. 1206).

49. This sentence is deleted in the printed version. It appears, however, in the copy made available at the North trial (in my possession). The deletion in the printed version shows how inconsistent and capricious the practice of "redaction" was. The originally deleted sentence about the CIA cannot be justified on any grounds of "security." Moreover, a line, "Go/No Go on sequential deliveries," in North's notebook on September 4, 1986, is not deleted (A-1, p. 1351).

50. North to McFarlane, September 3, 1986, Part III, p. 1203.

51. "Next Steps with Iran," Part III, p. 1207.

52. North to Poindexter, September 8, 1986, "Next Steps with Iran," Part III, p. 1211.

53. TR, p. B-153, note 90.

54. Allen to Casey, September 10, 1986, B-3, p. 1031.

55. McDaniel log, TR, p. B-152. Rodney McDaniel was the NSC executive secretary.

56. The reference to the $4 million had arisen, according to Cave, during meetings immediately before Bahramani's arrival on how to get Ghorbanifar out "and still preserve the secrecy of the operation." The Iranians told Cave that they had first paid Ghorbanifar $4 million for the spare parts, to which they had later added $8 million in cash. It had then been agreed that "all their accounts were square." Nir subsequently told Cave that Ghorbanifar had received an additional $6 million for a total of $18 million. It also seems that Ghorbanifar paid his creditors only $6.1 million out of the $18 million, leaving him in debt for almost $12 million, though $10 million was later taken to be his problem. Just why it was thought that $4 million would be enough to quiet him is not clear, but Cave says it was viewed as a "bribe" (B-3, p. 932).

57. Allen to Casey, September 10, 1986, B-3, p. 1031.

58. Allen, B-1, pp. 802–3.

59. North to Poindexter, September 9, 1986, TR, p. B-153.

60. FR, p. 251.

61. TR, p. B-153.

62. North to Poindexter, September 9, 1986, TR, pp. B-153–55.

63. FR, based partially on the Israeli Historical Chronology, states: "At the meeting, among other things, Poindexter told Nir that the United States would continue seeking the release of the hostages in Lebanon; that the United States developed the Second Channel; that the Second Channel was connected with Speaker Rafsanjani; and that the President had approved proceeding with a meeting with the Rafsanjani representative" (p. 251).

64. An expurgated version appears in North to Poindexter, September 15, 1986, Part III, p. 1215. I have included portions in the copy made available at the North trial and which also appear in TR, p. B-156.

65. 100-8, pp. 629–30.

66. Secord, 100-1, p. 99.

67. North to Poindexter, September 17, 1986, TR, p. B-156.

68. Poindexter to North, September 17, 1986, ibid.

69. North to Poindexter, September 17, 1986, ibid., pp. B-156, 157.

70. Secord to Goode [North], September 17, 1986, ibid., p. B-157.

71. Secord's staff assistant at Stanford Technology, Shirley A. Napier, recalled three Iranians at a meeting which she attended at this time. Two, in their early forties, were called "Chang Iz" and "Darvish"; she did not know the name of the third, who was in his mid- to late twenties (Napier, B-20, pp. 274–76). The first has been identified as Changiz Farnajad, an Iranian businessman in London, and the second as Kamal Darvish, an Iranian procurement officer in the United Kingdom (NT, defendant's Exhibit 100, p. 4).

72. We have three versions of these meetings. The longest is in A-1, pp. 1374–91. Another is in Part III, pp. 1224–26. A preliminary report is in North to Poindexter, September 22, 1986, A-1, pp. 1412–13. I have made a brief synthesis of all three.

73. North to Poindexter, September 22, 1986, TR, pp. B-158, 159.

74. A-1, p. 1377; Part III, p. 1224.

75. A-1, p. 1413.

76. Ibid., pp. 1381, 1383.

77. NN, September 20, 1986.

78. A-1, p. 1413.

79. Ibid., pp. 1382, 1388, 1413; Part III, pp. 1229–30.

80. A-1, pp. 1379–84.

81. NN, September 19, 1986.

82. A-1, p. 1379.

83. Ibid., pp. 1377, 1380.

84. North to Poindexter, October 2, 1986, ibid., p. 1415.

85. Ibid., p. 1385; Cave, B-3, p. 927.

86. A-1, p. 1385.

87. Hakim, 100-5, p. 244. There is another version of the same story in Hakim, B-13, p. 628.

88. This Iranian had been present at the Brussels meeting with Secord and Hakim on August 25, 1986, when Secord had described him as a former Iranian naval officer and alleged London businessman, who was "definitely an important agent for Rafsanjani g[rou]p and possibly Savama" (Copp [Secord] to North, August 26, 1986, TR, p. B-149). This part of the message was deleted in A-1, p. 1349. He seems to be the same as the "Second Contact" in FR, where he is described as an Iranian businessman with direct connections to the Iranian government (p. 249).

89. Hakim, 100-5, pp. 244–45.

90. North to Poindexter, September 24, 1986, Part III, p. 1222.

91. North to Poindexter, September 22, 1986, FR, p. 253. This portion of the message does not appear in A-1, p. 1411. The Russo-Japanese War broke out in 1904 but ended in 1905.

92. North to Poindexter, September 22, 1986, TR, p. B-158.

93. North to Poindexter, September 24, 1986, Part III, p. 1222.

94. North to Poindexter, September 17, 1986, 100-9, p. 558.

95. TR, p. B-159.

96. North to Poindexter, September 22, 1986, TR, p. B-158; North to Poindexter, October 2, 1986, A-1, p. 1414. Kangarlou's name is not mentioned; he is identified as "the official in the Prime Minister's office."

97. NN, September 24, 1986.

98. Ibid., October 1, 1986.

20. Out of Control

1. North to Poindexter, October 2, 1986, A-1, p. 1414.

2. Ibid., p. 1415.

3. Ibid., p. 1416.

4. Ibid., p. 1419. The deleted portions are given in TR, p. B-163.

5. North to Poindexter, October 2, 1986, A-1, p. 1416. The deletions are indicated in TR, p. B-162.
6. *"Instructions to Copp [Secord] for Meeting with Nir,"* Saturday, October 4, 1986, Tel Aviv, Israel, A-1, pp. 1422–25.
7. Secord's handwritten notes of the meeting mention the letter (B-13, p. 947). But the contents of the letter come from the Israeli Historical Chronology, cited in FR, p. 253.
8. B-13, p. 947.
9. Poindexter to McFarlane, October 3, 1986, A-1, p. 1427.
10. McFarlane to Poindexter, October 4, 1986, ibid., p. 1428.
11. FR, p. 254.
12. The name "Ali Samii" is handwritten into the printed translation of Hakim's nine points in 100-8, pp. 635–36. It is also given as "Samii" in the translation of Hakim's nine points by the Congressional Research Service. The name "Samaii" is mentioned in Woodward's *Veil*, p. 496, and "Samai'i" in Ledeen's *Perilous Statecraft*, p. 241. The spelling "Samii" will be used here, because that is how it is spelled in the printed record by an ostensibly knowledgeable source. He is referred to as "the Monster" in TR and as "the Engine" in FR.
13. A-1, p. 1475.
14. Hakim, 100-5, pp. 248, 282.
15. There seems to be a mistake in the covering memorandum for the tapes to Charles Allen. It refers to a meeting in Frankfurt on October 29–30, 1986, which should be October 8–10. There was no meeting in Frankfurt on October 29–30, 1986, but there was one in Mainz on October 29, 1986 (A-1, p. 1442). North's notebook for October 6–8, 1986, contains his record of the Frankfurt meeting.
16. Only a portion of the tape seems to have been transcribed and printed, and some of the latter parts are partially illegible. Fortunately, many of North's interventions are legible.
17. Probably should be Fao.
18. A-1, p. 1454.
19. Ibid., p. 1474.
20. Ibid., p. 1476.
21. Ibid., p. 1481. This statement is incorrectly attributed to North in FR, p. 254.
22. Ibid., p. 1481.
23. Ibid., p. 1477. The Iranian speaker is identified as "the Engine" in FR, p. 254.
24. A-1, p. 1531.
25. Ibid., p. 1479.
26. Ibid., pp. 1480, 1484.
27. Ibid., p. 1500.
28. Ibid., p. 1497.
29. Ibid., p. 1500.
30. Ibid., p. 1497.
31. Ibid., p. 1480.
32. Ibid., p. 1518.
33. 100-5, pp. 1070–71. The list is in North's handwriting.
34. North, 100-7, Part I, p. 334.
35. A-1, pp. 1530–31.
36. Ibid., p. 1529.
37. This version is presented in FR as the Iranian's "own list" (p. 256). It is based on the transcript of Hakim's interpretations and clearly does not represent the actual language used by the Iranian author. It seems to be a mixture of the Iranian original and Hakim's explanations. It is probably close enough—or as close as we can get from the existing material—to show what the Iranians wanted.
38. A-1, pp. 1534–35.
39. Ibid., pp. 1537–38.
40. Ibid., p. 1533.
41. Ibid., p. 1532.

42. The passage in the president's handwriting appears in ibid., p. 1421.

43. This statement appears on p. C 408 of the documentary collection, but does not appear to have been printed; a short but similar version appears in FR, p. 255.

44. North, 100-7, Part I, pp. 233, 332.

45. NN, October 7, 1986.

46. A-1, p. 1538.

47. Hakim, 100-5, p. 247.

48. Ibid., p. 719.

49. 100-5, p. 1072 (in Secord's handwriting).

50. Ibid., p. 380.

51. Secord, 100-1, pp. 210–11.

52. This is Hakim's translation as given in 100-8, pp. 635–36. The name of "Ali" has been written into point 5 and of "Samii" in an addendum to point 9. A different translation appears in A-1, p. 1540. Another translation by the Library of Congress appears in FR, p. 257.

53. Ibid., pp. 720–21.

54. Ibid., pp. 631–32.

55. Ibid., p. 295.

56. North, 100-7, Part I, p. 233.

57. North to Poindexter, October 10, 1986, A-1, p. 1541 (where last two sentences are missing). The entire text, but with point 3 missing, appears in TR, pp. B-166, 167.

58. North, 100-7, Part I, pp. 335–36.

59. North, 100-7, Part II, p. 7.

60. North, 100-7, Part I, pp. 335–36.

61. North, 100-7, Part II, p. 126.

62. Poindexter, 100-8, p. 68.

63. Ibid., pp. 68–69, 377. Poindexter also said that Secord and Hakim were not authorized to reach any agreement, because "all their meetings and discussions were what we call ad referendum" and had to be referred back to Washington (p. 339). But since he considered the nine points to have been "operative," they must have been approved in Washington.

64. Ibid., p. 235.

65. "Press Guidance," October 14, 1986, A-1, p. 1563.

66. Allen memorandum, October 7, 1985, B-1, pp. 934–36.

67. Allen, B-1, p. 547.

68. Ibid., p. 561.

69. Memorandum for the Record, January 29, 1986, B-1, pp. 992–1000.

70. Allen, B-1, p. 628.

71. Ibid., pp. 679, 779–80.

72. Ibid., pp. 677, 773.

73. Ibid., p. 775.

74. Ibid., pp. 677–78.

75. Ibid., p. 782.

76. Ibid., p. 678.

77. Ibid., pp. 803–4.

78. Ibid., pp. 823–24. Allen's other testimony is similar: ". . . And I added at the end of my conversation, I said, and this first channel that has been shut down by the NSC is a running sore. The creditors are demanding payment and I said this is going to be exposed if something isn't done. I said perhaps the money has been diverted to the contras, and I said I can't prove it. Gates was deeply disturbed by that and asked me to brief the Director" (TR, p. B-168).

79. Gates, B-11, p. 969.

80. Furmark, B-11, pp. 108–9.

81. Ibid., p. 119.

82. Ibid., pp. 110–12.

83. Ibid., pp. 113–14.

84. Ibid., p. 119.

85. Ibid., p. 115.

86. Ibid., p. 118.

87. Ibid., pp. 123–24.

88. DCI (Casey) to CNE (Twetten), October 8, 1986, B-1, p. 1168.

89. Furmark, B-11, pp. 125–26.

90. Allen, B-1, pp. 827–29.

91. Ibid., pp. 830–31. In other testimony, Allen put this statement by Casey to Poindexter about Wallison, but without Poindexter's reply, as occurring on October 15, 1986 (TR, B-169). Gates told the same story as Allen about Casey, Poindexter, and Wallison but put it on November 6, 1986 (Gates, B-11, p. 997).

92. Allen, B-1, p. 831.

93. Ibid., p. 832. Allen's handwritten notes on the call are on pp. 1169–70.

94. Gates, Memorandum for the Record, October 10, 1986, B-11, p. 1057. The meeting is incorrectly dated October 10, 1986, in B-1, p. 835.

95. Gates, B-11, pp. 993–96.

96. TR, p. B-168.

97. Allen to DCI (Casey) and DDCI (Gates), October 14, 1986, B-1, pp. 1171–78. A somewhat clearer copy appears in B-11, pp. 1049–56.

98. Allen, B-1, pp. 836–37.

99. Gates, B-11, pp. 981–82.

100. Ibid., p. 995.

101. Allen memorandum of October 14, 1986, B-1, p. 1173.

102. North, 100-7, Part I, p. 243.

103. Allen to Casey, October 17, 1986, B-1, pp. 1180–82. The handwritten notes on which this report is based appear on pp. 1184–90.

104. Furmark, B-11, pp. 134–36.

105. Allen notes, October 22, 1986, B-1, pp. 841, 1183.

106. Allen, B-1, pp. 1196, 1209.

107. Cave, B-3, pp. 936–37.

108. NN, October 22, 1986.

109. Allen, TR, p. B-169.

110. Casey to Poindexter, October 23, 1986, B-1, pp. 1212–14. The date is given by Allen in TR, p. B-169.

111. Allen also said that "it laid out starkly that there would be allegations, that Ghorbanifar had made allegations of diversion of funds to the contras" (TR, B-169). The memorandum did nothing of the kind.

112. Allen, TR, pp. B-169, 170.

113. Earl, B-9, pp. 760, 886–88.

114. Furmark, B-11, pp. 174–75.

115. Jeff Gerth, "Saudi Businessman in Iran Affair Tells of 'Playing Games' with U.S. Aides," New York Times, March 10, 1987.

116. Fraser, B-10, pp. 718–27.

117. North to Poindexter, July 29, 1986, Part III, p. 1182.

21. Battle Royal

1. Israeli Historical Chronology, cited by FR, p. 259. The relationship between the North-Nir conversation on October 22 and the meeting between them in Geneva on the same date is unclear. The conversation recorded in North's notebook may conceivably have taken place in Geneva or just prior to Geneva; the latter seems most likely but cannot be established from the notebook, one page of which is unmistakably dated "22 Oct."

2. Secord, 100-1, p. 311.

3. Ibid., p. 313.

4. Israeli Historical Chronology, cited by FR, p. 259. The date is given as "approximately October 30th" in Secord, 100-1, p. 124.
5. Secord, 100-1, pp. 123–24.
6. Ibid., p. 124.
7. Transcript of Mainz meeting, October 29, 1986, A-1, pp. 1585, 1595, 1633. The transcripts of the tapes have been most carelessly assembled in this volume; they are given out of order, as if the editors had taken no trouble putting them together. I have also relied on the version of the contents in FR, p. 259. The date and leaflets derive from Cave, B-3, p. 712. Cave's dates, however, may be suspect; he also said that, according to Bahramani, the information in the leaflets had been published in a little-known newspaper in Baalbek in the Bekaa Valley in Lebanon on October 26 or 27, although it was published in this paper, Al-Shiraa, on November 3, 1986.
8. Segev, The Iranian Triangle, pp. 284–85. The arrest is mentioned in A-1, p. 1589.
9. A-1, p. 1595.
10. Ibid., p. 1585. This comment is incorrectly attributed to Secord in FR, p. 259.
11. A-1, p. 1614.
12. Ibid., p. 1588.
13. Ibid., pp. 1589, 1594, 1635, for references to two hostages.
14. Ibid., p. 1635.
15. Ibid., pp. 1604–5.
16. Ibid., p. 1612.
17. Ibid., p. 1592.
18. Ibid., pp. 1574–78, 1588.
19. Cave, B-3, p. 742.
20. The information on this committee is confusing. Cave reported to Casey that it had been formed in Tehran "to oversee their relations with the United States" (Allen [Cave] to Casey, November 3, 1986, B-3, p. 1075, see note 27). FR interprets this reference to mean Iranian representation on the "joint commission" and gives the appointees as follows: ". . . the Engine [Samii], a participant in meetings held under the auspices of both channels; the Adviser [Kangarlou?], who negotiated with McFarlane in Tehran; a member of the Iranian Parliament, the Majlis; and the Second Iranian, the primary Iranian official in the First Channel and the man who the Relative [Bahramani] had said was responsible for Reed's kidnapping" (p. 261).
21. A-1, p. 1596.
22. Ibid., p. 1605.
23. Ibid., p. 1596.
24. Ibid., p. 1609.
25. Ibid., pp. 1575–78.
26. Allen to Casey, November 3, 1986, B-3, pp. 1072–74. According to Allen, this memorandum was actually prepared by Cave (B-1, p. 850). The memorandum itself is Cave's report on the Mainz meeting, which he and not Allen attended, but is carelessly attributed to the "Frankfurt Meetings," probably because Mainz is just southwest of Frankfurt and the airport for Mainz is nearer to Frankfurt.
27. A-1, p. 1609.
28. Earl to Poindexter (from North), October 29, 1986, A-1, p. 1747; see TR for "Relative" (p. B-171).
29. A-1, p. 1605.
30. Ibid., p. 1612.
31. Cave, B-3, p. 690.
32. Secord to North, undated but internal evidence indicates after Jacobsen's release, A-1, p. 1748.
33. Earl to Poindexter (for North), October 29, 1986, A-1, p. 1747.
34. North, 100-7, Part II, p. 134.
35. A-1, p. 1641.

36. Ibid., p. 1607.
37. North to Poindexter, through Earl, October 29, 1986, TR, p. B-172.
38. Foreign Broadcast Intelligence Service, November 6, 1986, pp. 11–13, cited in D-5, pp. 24–26.
39. Foreign Broadcast Information Service, November 5, 1986, cited in D-5, pp. 34–35.
40. Ibid.
41. Teicher to Poindexter, November 4, 1986, A-1, pp. 1749–50; TR, pp. B-171–72.
42. Regan, 100-10, p. 21.
43. Regan, *For the Record*, p. 26.
44. "HPSCI Meeting with National Security Adviser Admiral Poindexter, November 21, 1986—White House Situation Floor," 100-8, p. 787.
45. Ibid., p. 231.
46. Earl, B-9, p. 979.
47. Cave's notes on the Geneva meeting, A-1, pp. 1762–65.
48. This is the second time that North mentioned Ledeen in connection with the sale of TOWs. On February 27, 1986, North jotted down, in connection with the delivery to Iran of 1,000 TOWs: "Gorba got 13,200/missile. Gets $260/missile. Gives $50/missile to Ledeen" (TR, p. B-78). North said that the information had been provided to him by "two foreigners." As to its accuracy, North would only say: "I do not know if he did [make money on it]. And I do not know if he didn't" (100-7, Part I, p. 228). Ledeen has indignantly denied this allegation. According to Ledeen, North said to him in the autumn of 1986 that "some people in the Pentagon think you made money from the TOW sales." Ledeen told him that "it was nonsense, and would be delighted to sue anyone who said it publicly" (*Perilous Statecraft*, p. 188). At that time, Ledeen did not know of North's note of November 9, 1986, about an even larger alleged payoff to Ledeen, ostensibly originating with Ghorbanifar via Nir (these pages were not released until 1990). The later story would seem to be even more evident nonsense than the earlier one, for one reason that Ledeen was not in a position to perform any service for the money. It would seem to be the old story that anyone who had Ghorbanifar for a friend did not need an enemy.
49. NN, November 9, 1986.
50. Fox to Boren, July 9, 1986, 100-9, p. 555.
51. Shultz, 100-9, pp. 70–71.
52. Ibid., p. 3.
53. Ibid., pp. 134, 170.
54. Ibid., pp. 11, 58, 109, 133, 170.
55. Ibid., p. 4.
56. Ibid., p. 49.
57. Ibid., p. 102.
58. Ibid., p. 72.
59. Poindexter to North, May 19, 1986, 100-9, p. 544.
60. Poindexter to North, June 10, 1986, ibid., p. 552.
61. Poindexter, 100-8, p. 71.
62. Shultz, 100-9, p. 6.
63. Ibid., p. 181.
64. Shultz to Poindexter, November 4, 1986, 100-9, pp. 563–64.
65. Poindexter to Shultz, November 5, 1986, ibid., pp. 565–67.
66. Shultz, 100-9, pp. 38, 568.
67. Ibid., p. 38.
68. Ibid., p. 103.
69. Keel's notes are in B-14, pp. 1015–23. They are hard to decipher, but Keel himself interpreted many of them (ibid., pp. 974–1010). Regan's notes are in 100-10, pp. 755–69. Weinberger's memorandum is in 100-10, pp. 578–80. Meese's memorandum is missing in D-5, pp. 59–60. The fullest and clearest notes are Regan's; the least informative is Meese's memorandum.
70. 100-10, p. 755.

71. Ibid., pp. 22, 755. Keel's notes also mention the "warehouse" (B-14, p. 1015).

72. 100-10, pp. 756–57. Keel reports the 1,000 TOWs and 240 spare parts without stating who had paid whom (B-14, p. 1016).

73. Keel, B-14, pp. 980–81, and notes, p. 1016.

74. Regan's notes have "some relationship" (100-10, p. 758); Keel's notes have "strategic relationship" (B-14, p. 1017).

75. Regan's notes have "factually incorrect" (100-10, p. 759); Keel's notes have "purposely had inaccuracies" (B-14, p. 1017).

76. Regan, 100-10, pp. 758–59.

77. Regan, 100-10, p. 760; Keel also named Byrd (B-14, p. 1018).

78. Weinberger, 100-10, pp. 578–79.

79. Ibid., p. 579.

80. Keel, B-14, p. 1018.

81. Ibid., p. 1019.

82. Regan, 100-10, p. 764.

83. Weinberger, 100-10, pp. 579–80.

84. Regan, 100-10, p. 762.

85. Ibid., pp. 764–67.

86. Keel, B-14, pp. 1022–23.

87. Regan, 100-10, p. 764.

88. Ibid., p. 766.

89. Meese, 100-9, p. 196.

90. Regan, 100-10, p. 763.

91. Ibid., p. 766.

92. Ibid., p. 769.

93. Shultz, 100-9, p. 569.

94. Ibid., pp. 41–42.

95. Ibid., p. 570.

96. Buchanan to Regan, November 12, 1986, 100-10, p. 394.

97. Regan to Buchanan, November 12, 1986, ibid., p. 395.

98. Shultz's appeal for help to Regan on November 12, 1986, was put to Shultz by Senate counsel Mark A. Belnick without getting any objection from Shultz (100-9, p. 42).

99. This is how Armitage's message was described by North's other aide, Lieutenant Colonel Earl (B-9, p. 996).

100. Ibid., p. 1022.

101. Ibid., pp. 1023–26.

102. Keel's notes of daily briefing at which Poindexter, Regan, and Keel were present, November 12, 1986 (100-10, pp. 397–98).

103. McFarlane to Poindexter, November 7, 1986, 100-2, p. 627. McFarlane later corrected some of the timing in the memorandum (ibid., p. 78). He discussed the circumstances briefly in TR, p. D-4.

104. Poindexter to McFarlane, November 7, 1986, 100-2, p. 629. Regan gave his side of the controversy in For the Record, pp. 80–84, where Regan does not quite deny McFarlane's charge that he had been the source of the early stories in the news weeklies.

105. In his testimony, Regan made Poindexter responsible for having described the Israeli action "to the rest of us and saying the same thing [as Regan said]" (100-10, p. 45).

106. Coy, B-7, p. 1034.

107. Keel, B-14, pp. 888–89; Coy, B-7, pp. 1034–36. McFarlane's proposed addition to the speech appears in 100-2, pp. 632–34. Some of it was used in the speech.

108. Poindexter, 100-8, pp. 244–45, 312–13.

109. Regan, For the Record, p. 31.

110. TR, p. D-12.

111. The speech appears in 100-8, pp. 641–43.

112. Regan, For the Record, p. 32.

113. McFarlane to Poindexter, November 15, 1986, 100-2, p. 637.
114. Shultz, 100-9, p. 42.
115. The State Department statement of November 15, 1986, is mentioned in 100-9, p. 47. The statement itself appears to be in ibid., pp. 580–82.
116. Ibid., p. 42.
117. The entire text of the program appears in ibid., pp. 587–99.
118. Ibid., p. 43.
119. Ibid., pp. 40–41.
120. Ibid., p. 107.
121. The text of the Poindexter interview appears in 100-8, pp. 645–50.

22. Cover-up

1. *New York Times*, November 19, 1986.
2. Shultz, 100-9, p. 597.
3. *New York Times*, November 18, 1986; Larry Speakes, *Speaking Out* (Scribner's, 1988), p. 292.
4. *New York Times*, November 18, 1986.
5. Bernard Gwertzman, ibid.
6. Armacost to Shultz, July 2, 1986, 100-9, p. 554.
7. Shultz, 100-9, p. 451.
8. Ibid., pp. 603–4.
9. Sofaer, B-26, pp. 235–47.
10. Sofaer memorandum, 100-9, pp. 248–55, 600–2 (also see B-26, p. 249).
11. This version appears in Shultz, 100-9, p. 451.
12. 100-8, p. 643.
13. 100-9, p. 1324.
14. Ibid., p. 1323.
15. Ibid., pp. 603–10.
16. Ibid., p. 45.
17. Regan, B-22, p. 643.
18. Reagan, *An American Life*, p. 529.
19. Poindexter, 100-8, p. 108; North, 100-7, Part I, p. 27.
20. TR names November 5 as the starting date (p. D-1). North said that his "first effort" came about November 7 (North, 100-7, Part I, p. 27).
21. North, 100-7, Part I, p. 29.
22. Maximum Version, "U.S./Iranian Contacts and the American Hostages," November 17, 1986, Part III, p. 97. This account was repeated in the next "Maximum Version" of November 18, 1986 (ibid., p. 116).
23. "Historical Chronology," a change of title from the previous "Maximum Version," Part III, p. 135.
24. North, 100-7, Part I, p. 31.
25. Secord, 100-1, pp. 126–28.
26. McFarlane to Poindexter, November 18, 1986, TR, pp. D-5–7, which contain all three sections of McFarlane's addition. The first section only appears in Part III, pp. 127–29. At no point in these additions does McFarlane say that President Reagan had approved in any way the Israeli shipments in 1985, though McFarlane later testified that Reagan had indirectly approved of them by agreeing to replace the Israeli weapons. The language in the paragraph beginning "Mr. McFarlane elevated this proposition" in McFarlane's addition is almost the same as that in the relevant portion in the chronology of November 20, 1986 (TR, p. D-6, and Part III, p. 134).

Nevertheless, the Majority Report errs in trying to make McFarlane as responsible as North for preparing "a false chronology" (FR, p. 285). McFarlane's additions were made on November 18, 1986, and he had nothing more to do with the chronology, not as the Majority Report has it, on November 19 and 20 or November 20 and 21 ("in the two days following the press conference [of November 19]").

27. McFarlane, 100-2, pp. 78–79, 91.

28. TR, p. D-8.

29. Ibid., p. D-5.

30. North, 100-7, Part I, p. 38.

31. These names are given by Cooper (B-7, p. 87). Thompson was omitted in Poindexter, 100-8, p. 109. Meese recalled Thompson (100-9, p. 217).

32. Part III, p. 213.

33. The change was written in by Meese (100-9, pp. 218–19).

34. NT, pp. 7632–33.

35. Meese, 100-9, pp. 218–19.

36. North, 100-7, Part I, p. 38.

37. Ibid., p. 40.

38. Poindexter, 100-8, p. 112.

39. Gates, B-11, pp. 1010–15. There is additional, less conclusive testimony by Paul Thompson, the NSC staff counsel, on this point (B-26, pp. 1004–8).

40. Poindexter, 100-8, p. 108.

41. Sofaer, B-26, p. 258. The date is incorrectly given as November 19, 1986, in 100-9, p. 451.

42. A State Department chronology dated the McFarlane-Shultz call as November 18, 1985 (100-9, p. 445). Shultz repeated the same story in his testimony at the congressional hearings, with the addition that he had told Hill on November 23, 1985, that he thought the deal had collapsed (ibid., pp. 28–29). The State Department chronology says that Shultz told Hill: "It's over" (ibid., p. 446).

43. Sofaer, B-26, pp. 259–60.

44. I have not been able to find these exact words in either the text of Casey's testimony or the page insert, "CIA Airline Involvement," the latter discussed in the meeting in Poindexter's office on November 18, 1986. The published testimony refers to "spare parts for the oil fields" (100-8, p. 673), and the insert says that "no one in the USG [instead of "We in CIA did not find out"] found out that our airline had hauled Hawk missiles into Iran until mid-January [1986] when we were told by the Iranians" (ibid., p. 671). Sofaer was quoting from memory or had seen a different version, though the sense is similar.

45. Sofaer, B-26, pp. 260–62.

46. Thompson mentions Sofaer's call while Thompson was meeting with Cooper and Wallison (B-26, p. 1010).

47. Poindexter, 100-8, p. 113. Thompson seems to have alerted Poindexter on the night of November 20 that "the testimony was not going to be acceptable the way the CIA was depicting the November shipment" (B-26, p. 918).

48. Poindexter, 100-8, p. 121.

49. Meese, 100-9, p. 222.

50. This section is based on Sofaer, B-26, pp. 258–76.

51. Casey to Gates, November 16, 1986, B-11, p. 1058.

52. Gates, B-11, p. 1000.

53. Ibid., p. 1008.

54. Gardner, NT, pp. 6624–29.

55. Gates, B-11, p. 1018.

56. There are two versions of Casey's testimony in B-7, on pp. 572–92 and a somewhat different one on pp. 698–707.

57. PT, pp. 2319–21.

58. A memorandum by Eric Newsom of Poindexter's briefing of two members and two aides of the Senate Intelligence Committee appears in Poindexter, 100-8, pp. 683–88, and there is another memorandum by Mike O'Neil of Poindexter's briefing of members of the House Intelligence Committee (ibid., pp. 778–81).

59. Meese, 100-9, p. 222.

60. Cooper, 100-6, p. 112.
61. Ibid., p. 114.

23. Panic

1. Hamilton, NT, pp. 1706–7.
2. *New York Times*, November 11, 1986.
3. Ibid., November 14 and 15, 1986.
4. Meese, 100-9, p. 219.
5. Cooper had meanwhile seen Casey on the morning of November 21 before the meeting called by Meese, and Casey seems to have been strangely passive in response to Cooper's effort to dissuade him from saying anything that might conflict with Shultz's memory of the November 1985 episode (B-7, pp. 115–20).
6. Meese, 100-9, pp. 224–25. In his book, *For the Record*, Regan takes credit for having suggested to the president that Meese should be asked to verify all the facts in Casey's testimony and complete his inquiry by November 24 (p. 37). Meese says that Regan expressed agreement with his—Meese's—proposal, but that Regan probably asked him to get the task done by 2 p.m. on Monday, November 24, for an NSPG meeting (100-9, p. 225). Regan, however, has this episode on November 20, the day before, in the presence of Shultz and Poindexter, whereas Meese has Regan and Poindexter present. Meese's version appears to be more likely.
7. Meese, 100-9, pp. 224–27.
8. Thompson, B-26, pp. 1065–67.
9. Ibid., p. 1068.
10. Poindexter, 100-8, p. 118.
11. Ibid., p. 135.
12. 100-9, p. 1377.
13. Ibid., pp. 1378–79.
14. Meese, NT, p. 5855.
15. Meese, 100-9, pp. 230–31.
16. McFarlane to Poindexter, November 22, 1986, ibid., p. 1381.
17. Meese, 100-9, p. 231.
18. Ibid., p. 341.
19. McFarlane, 100-2, p. 71.
20. Cooper's notes, 11/22/86, Meese, Shultz, Hill, Cooper present, 100-9, pp. 611–12.
21. Meese, 100-9, p. 233.
22. Thompson, B-26, p. 1075; Reynolds, B-22, pp. 1105–6; Richardson, B-23, p. 272.
23. Richardson, B-23, pp. 259–61. In his testimony at the North trial, Richardson said that Reynolds had told Earl: "We would just like to see the files on the Iran arms transactions" (NT, p. 8043).
24. Richardson, NT, p. 6045.
25. Reynolds, B-22, p. 1128.
26. Part III, pp. 1–8, esp. p. 5.
27. Reynolds, B-22, p. 1129.
28. Richardson, B-23, pp. 284–85.
29. Reynolds, B-22, p. 1132.
30. Richardson, NT, p. 6049.
31. North, 100-7, Part I, pp. 15, 19.
32. Ibid., p. 22.
33. Ibid., pp. 22–23.
34. Ibid., p. 257. Reynolds said he was not aware of anyone using the shredding machine in his presence (B-22, p. 1152).
35. North, 100-7, Part I, p. 254.
36. Ibid., p. 23.

37. Ibid., p. 259.
38. Earl, NT, pp. 5620, 5625.
39. Ibid., p. 5625.
40. Cooper later said that the actual words were "Oh, shit" (B-7, p. 160).
41. Reynolds, B-22, pp. 1142–43.
42. Richardson, B-23, pp. 293–94, 297.
43. Richardson, NT, p. 6050.
44. Reynolds, B-22, p. 1144.
45. Meese, 100-9, pp. 235–36; NT, pp. 5720–21.
46. Cooper, B-7, p. 159.
47. Ibid., pp. 166, 610–12.
48. Richardson, NT, p. 6051.
49. Reynolds, B-22, 1149–72; Richardson, B-23, pp. 302–4; Richardson, NT, pp. 6053–54.
50. Meese, 100-9, pp. 236–37.
51. Ibid., p. 183.
52. Ibid., pp. 117–18.
53. Ibid., p. 238.
54. Ibid., p. 240.
55. North, 100-7, Part I, p. 142.
56. Meese, NT, p. 5725.
57. 100-9, pp. 1400–2. At the North trial, Meese testified that North "indicated initially he had been told it was oil drilling parts and that through Mr. Secord he had learned that actually it was Hawk missiles" (NT, p. 5860).
58. North, 100-7, Part I, p. 39.
59. North, NT, p. 7085.
60. Ibid., pp. 7033–34.
61. Richardson notes, 100-9, p. 1411.
62. Richardson, B-23, p. 31.
63. Cooper, B-7, p. 199.
64. Richardson notes, 100-9, p. 1412.
65. North, 100-7, Part I, p. 310.
66. Cooper, B-7, p. 199.
67. Richardson, B-23, pp. 320–21.
68. NT, pp. 6070–71.
69. Reynolds, B-22, pp. 1185–86.
70. North, NT, p. 7669; 100-7, Part I, p. 146.
71. Richardson notes, 100-9, pp. 1413–14.
72. Richardson interpreted this to mean that North had told Calero to open three accounts, whereupon North gave the account numbers to Nir, who put money in the accounts (B-23, p. 330).
73. Richardson notes, 100-9, p. 1415. North referred to the Israelis a third time (p. 1414). Cooper understood that North had said it was Amiram Nir's idea to divert the funds to the contras (B-7, p. 200). In his testimony at the North trial, Richardson said that Meese asked North who knew how much money went to the contras. "He [North] said that the Israelis knew" (NT, p. 6071).
74. Reynolds, B-22, pp. 1186–87. Richardson's version is similar: "As I recall, again without looking at the notes, that he said he called Calero, told him to open up three accounts, got three account numbers, and he gave the account numbers to Nir who put money in the accounts" (B-23, p. 330).
75. Cooper, B-7, p. 200.
76. Meese, NT, pp. 5728–29.
77. Richardson, NT, pp. 6071–72. Also see pp. 6111–13 for more of the same.
78. Richardson, 100-9, p. 1416.

79. North, 100-7, Part I, p. 145.
80. Richardson's notes, 100-9, p. 1415. Later North also named Secord but never Earl or Ghorbanifar (Richardson, NT, pp. 7947–48).
81. Earl, B-9, p. 886.
82. Richardson's notes, 100-9, p. 1418.
83. Meese, ibid., p. 414.
84. Richardson's notes, 100-9, pp. 1422–23, 1425.
85. Cooper, B-7, p. 201.
86. Richardson, B-23, pp. 328–29; Cooper, B-7, p. 201.
87. Richardson, B-23, p. 338.
88. Thompson, B-26, pp. 930–31.
89. Earl, B-9, pp. 645, 1069.
90. North, NT, p. 7669.
91. Ibid., p. 5630.
92. Meese, 100-9, p. 403.
93. Ibid., p. 406.
94. Meese, B-18, pp. 155–56.
95. Poindexter, 100-8, p. 252.
96. Ibid., p. 37.
97. Ibid., p. 36.
98. Ibid., p. 37.
99. Ibid., p. 40.
100. Ibid., p. 135.
101. North, 100-7, Part I, p. 142.
102. NT, p. 5725.
103. Ibid., pp. 5749–51.
104. Cooper, B-7, p. 202.
105. Richardson, NT, p. 6082.

24. The Bitter End

1. Weld, B-27, pp. 602–3. Weld thought the call had come at 10 or 10:30 a.m.; Meese's home and work logs say 9:55 (C, p. 124).
2. Regan, 100-10, p. 29.
3. Meese, 100-9, p. 251.
4. Regan, 100-10, p. 29.
5. The discussion on the Hawk shipment is based on Meese's notes, 100-9, pp. 1429–30.
6. 100-9, p. 253.
7. Ibid., p. 46.
8. Secord, 100-1, pp. 134–35.
9. Reynolds notes, B-22, pp. 1287–90. The allusion to the exchange of American supplies for a contribution to the contras occurs on p. 1289. It appears to refer to the offer of such an exchange if Iran stopped sending weapons to the Sandinistas. The reference to the Iranians having been "conned" appears separately on p. 1290. Cooper's notes make one apparent allusion to the diversion: "No U.S. $ involved here—only Iranians making contribution" (Cooper, 100-6, p. 599).
10. Cooper, 100-6, pp. 280–81.
11. Reynolds notes, B-22, p. 1290.
12. The "Chronology of Events" gives 2:05 p.m. as the time of the Cooper-Reynolds meeting with Green and the report to Meese (C, p. 126). Cooper's chronology gives the time of the meeting with Green as 2:20 p.m. to 3:45 p.m. (100-6, p. 512). Meese met with Reagan and Regan at 4:30 p.m.
13. Meese, 100-9, p. 254.
14. Poindexter, 100-8, p. 119.

15. 100-9, p. 255. In his testimony at the North trial, Meese said that he met with Reagan to decide whether Poindexter should resign that afternoon or that night. At this, Reagan had said that he wanted to think about it overnight and for Meese to come back on the morning of November 25, 1986 (NT, p. 5759).
16. The time is noted in Regan, *For the Record*, p. 39.
17. Ibid., p. 38.
18. Regan, 100-10, p. 29.
19. Ibid., pp. 29–30.
20. B-22, p. 664.
21. Ibid., p. 666.
22. Reagan, *An American Life*, p. 530.
23. Regan, 100-10, p. 30.
24. Ibid., p. 31.
25. Regan, 100-10, pp. 30–31; Regan, B-22, p. 667.
26. Regan, B-22, p. 669.
27. North, 100-7, Part I, pp. 124, 317–18; 100-7, Part II, pp. 8, 12, 52.
28. Senators William S. Cohen and George J. Mitchell, *Men of Zeal* (Viking, 1988), p. 307.
29. McMahon, B-17, pp. 178, 182, 270.
30. Gates, B-11, pp. 964–67.
31. McFarlane, 100-2, p. 144.
32. Clarridge, B-5, p. 923.
33. George, B-12, p. 149.
34. Menges, *Inside the National Security Council*, p. 280.
35. Reagan, *An American Life*, p. 486.
36. Poindexter, 100-8, pp. 170, 348.
37. Regan, 100-10, p. 31.
38. Regan, *For the Record*, p. 40.
39. Regan, 100-10, p. 32; *For the Record*, p. 40.
40. Poindexter to North, November 24, 1986, Part III, p. 1366.
41. North to Poindexter, November 24, 1986, ibid., p. 1366. The versions in 100-8, p. 179, and in D-5, pp. 779–80, slightly depart from the original text.
42. Poindexter, B-20, p. 1238.
43. North, 100-7, Part I, p. 148.
44. Ibid., p. 236.
45. Ibid., p. 16. At Poindexter's trial, North said he knew he was leaving after the plane with Hasenfus was shot down (PT, p. 1216).
46. Earl, B-9, p. 624.
47. North, 100-7, Part I, pp. 249–50; 100-7, Part II, p. 42.
48. NT, pp. 5641–42.
49. Regan, *For the Record*, p. 40.
50. Regan, B-22, pp. 680–81. Mrs. Reagan's name is deleted in the deposition.
51. Nancy Reagan, *My Turn*, pp. 62, 314, 317–18.
52. Ibid., pp. 322–23.
53. Richardson, B-23, p. 343.
54. Richardson kept a log of November 25, 1986, in which he noted that Meese met with Casey from 6:40 a.m. to 7:00 a.m. (100-9, p. 1434; B-23, p. 429).
55. Meese, 100-9, p. 256.
56. Ibid., pp. 1477–87.
57. Poindexter, 100-8, p. 120; B-20, p. 1236. Richardson's chronology of November 25, 1986, has the Poindexter-Meese meeting from 7:30 a.m. to 7:40 a.m. (100-9, p. 1434).
58. Regan, 100-10, p. 33. In *For the Record* (pp. 41–42) and in his deposition (B-22, p. 671), Regan changed some of the details but told essentially the same story.
59. Regan, 100-10, p. 34.
60. Poindexter, B-20, p. 1237.

61. Ibid., pp. 1235–36.
62. Meese, 100-9, p. 256. In his testimony at the North trial, Meese said that they had decided on Poindexter's resignation and on North's reassignment to the Marines (NT, pp. 5761–62).
63. Poindexter, 100-8, p. 164.
64. Kelly Williams testimony, PT, p. 1765.
65. These are the names identifiable in Richardson's notes. Regan's "Plan of Action" includes Representative Robert H. Michel among those to be invited, but he does not seem to be mentioned in Richardson's notes.
66. Richardson notes, November 25, 1986, 100-9, pp. 1436–55.
67. NN, November 25, 1986.
68. *Weekly Compilation of Presidential Documents*, December 1, 1986, pp. 1604–5, reproduced in 100-9, pp. 1432–33. Reagan's introductory statement was drafted by Charles J. Cooper, Peter Wallison, and Dennis Thomas (Cooper, 100-6, p. 268).
69. The transcript of Meese's press conference from *Washington Post*, November 26, 1986, appears in 100-9, pp. 1456–74.
70. Meese, 100-9, p. 257.
71. North to Poindexter, November 24, 1986, Part III, p. 1366.
72. Regan, 100-10, p. 34.
73. Regan, B-22, p. 672.
74. Meese, 100-9, p. 260.
75. Cooper, 100-6, p. 303.
76. Secord, 100-1, pp. 42–44, 131.
77. Meese, 100-9, p. 262.
78. NN, November 25, 1986.
79. Hall, 100-5, p. 501.
80. NT, p. 7106.
81. Ibid., p. 7104.
82. Ibid., p. 7108.
83. North, 100-7, Part I, p. 148.
84. NT, p. 7111.
85. *Time*, December 8, 1986. The interview by telephone occurred on November 26, 1986.
86. Reagan, *An American Life*, p. 486.
87. North, 100-7, Part I, pp. 245–46.
88. Hall, 100-5, pp. 484–97.
89. Ibid., pp. 502–6. She told much the same story at the North trial.
90. NT, p. 5359.
91. North, 100-7, Part I, p. 146.
92. Ibid., p. 261.
93. Reagan, *An American Life*, p. 534. Deaver does not mention this advice in his own memoirs, *Behind the Scenes*.
94. The text is in 100-9, p. 1433.
95. Weld, July 16, 1987, 100-9, pp. 1620–22.
96. Meese, NT, p. 5764.
97. Shultz, 100-9, p. 67.
98. Ibid., pp. 47, 453.
99. Cave, B-3, pp. 989–90.
100. Ibid., p. 993. Cave read from both versions, which were virtually identical.
101. Cave/Dunbar talking points, 100-9, pp. 630–31.
102. Charles Dunbar, Memorandum for the Record, December 14, 1986, 100-9, pp. 632–39; Cave, B-3, p. 996.
103. Shultz, 100-9, p. 49.
104. Cave, B-3, p. 996.
105. Shultz, 100-9, pp. 49, 62, 453.
106. Weinberger to Keel, December 22, 1986, 100-9, pp. 643–44.

107. Weinberger to Shultz, December 23, 1986, ibid., p. 642.
108. Memorandum for the Files, ibid., pp. 645–46.
109. Ibid., p. 645.
110. Ibid., p. 646.

25. People With Their Own Agenda

1. Weinberger, 100-10, p. 254.
2. Allen, B-1, p. 469.
3. C/CATF (Fiers), B-3, pp. 1205, 1207.
4. Poindexter, 100-8, pp. 61, 76.
5. Poindexter, B-20, pp. 1166–67.
6. Weinberger, 100-10, pp. 161, 163, 197.
7. Poindexter, 100-8, p. 48.
8. CIA Chief (Lisbon), B-4, p. 1177.
9. North, 100-7, Part I, p. 88.
10. Susan Crawford, B-8, p. 15.
11. North, 100-7, Part I, p. 22.
12. Poindexter, 100-8, p. 40.
13. North, 100-7, Part I, p. 216.
14. Earl, B-9, pp. 732–33.
15. Stokes, 100-7, Part II, p. 157.
16. Poindexter, 100-8, pp. 343–44.
17. Weinberger, 100-10, p. 186.
18. North said that his staff in 1985 was limited to himself and a secretary (North, 100-7, Part I, p. 272).
19. Poindexter, 100-8, pp. 165–66.
20. Ibid., p. 229.
21. McFarlane, 100-2, p. 265.
22. Ibid., p. 146.
23. Weinberger, 100-10, p. 195. The word "scared" appears as "seared" in the original transcript.
24. Ibid., p. 187.
25. Ibid., pp. 178, 246.
26. Shultz, 100-9, p. 40.
27. North, 100-7, Part I, p. 191.
28. Ibid., p. 193.
29. *Newsweek*, July 13, 1987.
30. *Time*, December 8, 1986 (the interview occurred on November 26, 1986).
31. George Bush, *Looking Forward* (Doubleday, 1987; Bantam Books, 1988), p. 239.
32. Reagan, *An American Life*, p. 492.
33. *Weekly Compilation of Presidential Documents*, March 9, 1987, p. 220.
34. Article II, Section 3.
35. Reagan deposition, PT, p. 9.
36. This statement is from the interrogatory of Reagan in advance of his deposition at the trial itself and is cited in PT, p. 275. Yet Reagan gave a seemingly contradictory answer in his deposition. After he was asked by Richard W. Beckler, Poindexter's counsel: "Did you authorize or approve the payment of any proceed from any sale of United States arms to Iran to Secord, Hakim, North, or any entity?" Reagan replied: "I imagine so, yes. I would assume so" (p. 276).
37. Ibid., pp. 156, 240.
38. Ibid.
39. Ibid., p. 289.
40. Ibid., p. 53.
41. Weinberger, 100-10, p. 244.

42. Shultz, 100-9, p. 63.
43. Weinberger, 100-10, p. 247.
44. Poindexter, 100-8, pp. 42, 66, 89, 289.
45. TR, p. III-24.
46. Bush, *Looking Forward*, pp. 238, 241–42. Bush also said: "If I'd sat there and heard [Shultz and Weinberger] express opposition strongly, maybe I would have had a stronger view" (*New York Times*, January 29, 1988).
47. Poindexter, B-20, p. 1468.
48. William S. Cohen and George J. Mitchell, *Men of Zeal* (Viking, 1988), pp. 264–72.
49. Bush, *Looking Forward*, p. 242.
50. Gregg, B-12, p. 1056.
51. Bush to North, November 27, 1985, B-12, p. 1143.
52. Felix I. Rodriguez and John Weisman, *Shadow Warrior* (Simon and Schuster, 1989), p. 193.
53. Gregg, B-12, p. 1053.
54. Ibid., pp. 1053, 1131 (official chronology).
55. The picture and letter appear in Rodriguez's book *Shadow Warrior*.
56. The letter is reproduced in *Shadow Warrior*.
57. Gregg, B-12, pp. 1057–58.
58. Ibid., pp. 1059–64, 1135–37 (copy of Gregg's contemporary notes).
59. Ibid., p. 1132.
60. Ibid., pp. 1076–77.
61. Ibid., pp. 1087–88. Gregg first gave as an excuse that he had not known North was involved, until he was reminded that his notes of the August 8, 1986, meeting had Rodriguez telling him that North was "using Ed Wilson group for supplies" (p. 1088).

    A somewhat similar question attracted more congressional attention than it was worth. When Rodriguez came to see Vice President Bush on May 1, 1986, the purpose of the meeting was stated as "To brief the Vice President on the status of the war in El Salvador and resupply of the Contras" (ibid., pp. 1140–42). Gregg insisted that contra resupply had never been discussed; he could not account for the fact that the head of the vice president's scheduling office had written those words in the briefing memorandum and Gregg's own secretary had countersigned his initials (ibid., pp. 1099, 1140). Rodriguez says that he discussed contra resupply with a member of Bush's staff but not with Bush himself (B-23, p. 777).
62. *Looking Forward*, p. 239. The entire sentence reads: "It was a fine line, but consistent with what those inside the administration knew of the President's concern about the hostages."
63. Interview with Casey, *Time*, December 22, 1986, p. 31.
64. George, 100-11, p. 199.
65. Armitage, B-2, p. 205.
66. Tambs, 100-3, pp. 367, 371.
67. Kelly, B-14, pp. 1164, 1168, 1181, 1188–89.
68. Weinberger, 100-10, p. 188.
69. Ibid., p. 239. Weinberger said that he had issued very strict instructions that any such calls or requests had to be referred to his office or that of the deputy secretary of defense.
70. North, 100-7, Part II, pp. 120–21.

26. Unfinished Business

1. Poindexter to Fortier, May 2, 1986, 100-8, p. 568.
2. "No Money shall be drawn from the Treasury, but in Consequence of Appropriations made by Law" (Article I, Section 9, clause 7).
3. Poindexter, 100-8, p. 372.
4. North, 100-7, Part I, p. 181.
5. Fortier to McFarlane, November 22, 1985, 100-8, p. 418.
6. Ibid., p. 358.

7. North, 100-7, Part I, p. 338.

8. *The Federalist*, ed. by Jacob E. Cooke (Wesleyan University Press, 1961), pp. 505–6.

9. Philip B. Kurland and Ralph Lerner, eds., *The Founders' Constitution* (University of Chicago Press, 1987), Vol. 4, p. 65 (Hamilton), pp. 76–77 (Madison).

10. Madison to Jefferson, May 13, 1798, *Letters and Other Writings of James Madison* (Lippincott, 1865), Vol. 2, p. 141.

11. *The Writings of Thomas Jefferson* (Putnam, 1903), Vol. 9, p. 279.

12. Jefferson to John Breckinridge, August 12, 1803, ibid., Vol. 10, p. 411.

13. FR, p. 465.

14. Harold C. Syrett et al., eds., *The Papers of Alexander Hamilton* (Columbia University Press, 1969), Vol. 15, p. 38 (italics in original).

15. In FR, p. 470, note 1, and p. 473, the Minority cites Hamilton's language incorrectly as "sole organ" instead of *"organ."* It also interprets Hamilton's context incorrectly by making it relate to foreign affairs in general. Hamilton was concerned specifically with treaties as a mode of "intercourse between the Nation and foreign Nations."

16. Edward S. Corwin, *The President: Office and Powers 1787–1957* (New York University Press, 4th rev. ed., 1957), pp. 177–78 (italics in original).

17. See the excellent letter on *Curtiss-Wright* by H. C. Merillat, former director of the American Society of International Law, in *The New York Review of Books*, July 19, 1990, p. 53.

18. North, 100-7, Part II, p. 38. This discussion had begun with Senator Mitchell's questioning of North's contention "that the President could authorize and conduct covert actions with unappropriated funds" and then had wandered off to whom, in that event, the president would be accountable (p. 37).

19. This is the version used by the Minority in FR, p. 471. It leaves out the words "zone of" in the second point.

20. Harold Hongju Koh, *The National Security Constitution: Sharing Power After the Iran-Contra Affair* (Yale University Press, 1990), p. 94.

21. Corwin, *The President*, p. 171.

22. Walter LaFeber, *The Panama Canal* (Oxford, 1978), p. 61.

23. William Howard Taft, *Our Chief Magistrate and His Power* (Columbia University Press, 1916), pp. 139–40.

24. Woodrow Wilson, *Constitutional Government in the United States* (Columbia University Press, 1908), p. 77.

25. Corwin, *The President*, p. 238.

26. Cited by Arthur M. Schlesinger, Jr., *The Imperial Presidency* (Houghton Mifflin, 1973), p. 108.

27. Ibid., p. 206.

28. Robert A. Dahl, *Congress and Foreign Policy* (Harcourt, Brace, 1950), pp. 107–8, 118, 264.

29. Koh, *The National Security Constitution*, p. 146.

30. FR, p. 419. Hyde made this statement during the testimony of Bretton G. Sciaroni.

31. Charles J. Cooper, Memorandum for the Attorney General, December 17, 1986, 100-9, pp. 1546–72, esp. p. 1552. Cooper saw fit to mention *Youngstown* only twice, once merely in connection with whether the Court's statements in *Curtiss-Wright* were dicta, which hardly touches the significance of *Youngstown*, and once to make the point that "Congress has not always accepted the most far-reaching assertions of presidential authority," as if Justice Jackson had spoken for Congress (notes, pp. 1552, 1555).

32. Cooper, B-7, pp. 8, 14.

33. *Congressional Record*, 101st Congress, 1st Session, July 17, 1989, pp. S 8031–35.

34. Senator Moynihan entered into the *Congressional Record* of July 17, 1989, two masterly analyses of the constitutional record by Raymond J. Celada and Johnny H. Killian of the Congressional Research Service, in rebuttal to Carol T. Crawford and Lawrence S. Eagleburger.

35. *Congressional Record*, July 17, 1989, p. S 8028.

36. *Congressional Record*, ibid., p. S 8033.
37. Kate Stith, "Congress' Power of the Purse," *Yale Law Journal*, June 1988, p. 1356 (italics in original).
38. TR, pp. IV-10, 11.
39. FR, p. 426.
40. Ibid., pp. 575, 583–85.
41. Ervin H. Pollack, ed., *The Brandeis Reader* (Oceana Publications, 1956), p. 134.

Index